CAMBRIDGE LIBRARY COLLECTION

Books of enduring scholarly value

Technology

The focus of this series is engineering, broadly construed. It covers technological innovation from a range of periods and cultures, but centres on the technological achievements of the industrial era in the West, particularly in the nineteenth century, as understood by their contemporaries. Infrastructure is one major focus, covering the building of railways and canals, bridges and tunnels, land drainage, the laying of submarine cables, and the construction of docks and lighthouses. Other key topics include developments in industrial and manufacturing fields such as mining technology, the production of iron and steel, the use of steam power, and chemical processes such as photography and textile dyes.

The Midland Railway: Its Rise and Progress

Frederick Smeeton Williams (1829–86) was a Congregational minister and pioneering railway historian. His first major transport work, *Our Iron Roads* (1852), enjoyed significant popularity, reaching its seventh edition by 1888. This, his second such effort, first published in 1876, is a lively history of the incorporation and development of one of Britain's first major railway companies following the earliest large-scale railway amalgamation of the Victorian age. Including 123 illustrations and 7 maps, this book is valuable for its contemporary description of the building of the Settle and Carlisle line, a notoriously difficult and expensive route to construct, with costs reaching £3.8 million by the time of its opening in 1875. Williams's spirited style lends colour to his portrayal of the Midland Railway's beginnings, its increasing competitiveness and the everyday concern of railway operations, making this an engaging resource for historians of transport, business and engineering.

Cambridge University Press has long been a pioneer in the reissuing of out-of-print titles from its own backlist, producing digital reprints of books that are still sought after by scholars and students but could not be reprinted economically using traditional technology. The Cambridge Library Collection extends this activity to a wider range of books which are still of importance to researchers and professionals, either for the source material they contain, or as landmarks in the history of their academic discipline.

Drawing from the world-renowned collections in the Cambridge University Library and other partner libraries, and guided by the advice of experts in each subject area, Cambridge University Press is using state-of-the-art scanning machines in its own Printing House to capture the content of each book selected for inclusion. The files are processed to give a consistently clear, crisp image, and the books finished to the high quality standard for which the Press is recognised around the world. The latest print-on-demand technology ensures that the books will remain available indefinitely, and that orders for single or multiple copies can quickly be supplied.

The Cambridge Library Collection brings back to life books of enduring scholarly value (including out-of-copyright works originally issued by other publishers) across a wide range of disciplines in the humanities and social sciences and in science and technology.

The Midland Railway: Its Rise and Progress

A Narrative of Modern Enterprise

Frederick S. Williams

Cambridge University Press

CAMBRIDGE UNIVERSITY PRESS

Cambridge, New York, Melbourne, Madrid, Cape Town,
Singapore, São Paolo, Delhi, Mexico City

Published in the United States of America by Cambridge University Press, New York

www.cambridge.org
Information on this title: www.cambridge.org/9781108050364

This edition first published 1876
This digitally printed version 2012

ISBN 978-1-108-05036-4 Paperback

The original edition of this book contains a number of colour plates, which have been reproduced in black and white. Colour versions of these images can be found online at www.cambridge.org/9781108050364

THE MIDLAND RAILWAY:

ITS RISE AND PROGRESS.

A Narrative of Modern Enterprise.

THE

MIDLAND RAILWAY:

ITS RISE AND PROGRESS.

A Narrative of Modern Enterprise.

BY

FREDERICK S. WILLIAMS,

Author of "Our Iron Roads."

"Let the country make the railroads and the railroads will make the country."
EDWARD PEASE.

LONDON:
STRAHAN & CO., PATERNOSTER ROW.

BUTLER & TANNER,
THE SELWOOD PRINTING WORKS,
FROME, AND LONDON.

TO

EDWARD SHIPLEY ELLIS, ESQ.,

AND TO THE BOARD

OF WHICH HE IS THE CHAIRMAN;

AND TO

JAMES ALLPORT, ESQ.,

AND TO THE EXECUTIVE

OF WHICH HE IS THE CHIEF;

WHO, BY PROBITY, SAGACITY, AND ENTERPRISE,

HAVE CONFERRED

UNTOLD BENEFITS

UPON

THE MIDLANDS OF ENGLAND,

THIS VOLUME IS DEDICATED BY

THEIRS, OBLIGED AND FAITHFULLY,

The Author.

PREFACE.

MR. CHARLES DICKENS was accustomed to account for his fondness for books by the fact, that when he was a child a pile of ponderous and learned folios used, at dinner time, to be placed on the chair on which he was seated; and it was thus that he contracted his early literary tastes. And if the Author were asked why *he* should write the present volume, he is prepared to assign reasons equally philosophical and profound. He has ascertained that both the Midland Railway and himself were born about the same time and near the same place; and doubtless there thus arose, even in their tender years, certain occult but powerful affinities, which strengthened with advancing time,—affinities which the advances of biological science will before long satisfactorily account for! And if, unhappily, such an explanation should not, in the judgment of some, justify what they may deem an irrelevant predilection, the Author can only add, to borrow the humour of another,—*Hic non meus* SERMO.

The last forty years have witnessed a mighty and beneficent revolution in the midlands of England. A few men of enterprise have led others on to a work which has revived trade, created new industries, enriched at once the landlord and the peasant, the manufacturer and the merchant, and promoted the happiness and well-being of the nation. And in this service the Midland Railway has been especially concerned.

How all this came to pass the Author has now to tell. How the Midland Railway originated at a village inn in the necessities of a few coal-owners; how it has gradually spread its paths of iron, north and south and east and west, through half the counties of England, till they stretch from the Severn to the Humber, the Wash to the Mersey, and the Thames to the Solway Firth; how a property has been created that has cost £50,000,000 of money, and that brings in a revenue of £5,000,000 a year; and how there lies before it a limitless future of usefulness,—these are facts which, in the judgment of the Author, are worthy of record. Yet it so happens that the men who have been most deeply engaged in this work have been so busy with their work that they seem never to have thought of explaining why or how they did it; and so the Author has been led to try, before it is too late, to weave together, from the fragmentary records of the dead and from the fading recollections of the living, a narrative of modern enterprise which has been honourable to those engaged in it, and has been wide spread and beneficent in its results. Accordingly the first part of this book is *historical.*

The second portion of the work is *descriptive* of the Midland Railway—of its engineering works, and of the country through which the line passes. The roads which Roman hands have made and Roman legions have trodden; the ancient manor houses of Wingfield, Haddon, and Rowsley; the abbeys of St. Albans, Leicester, Newstead, Kirkstall, Beauchief, and Evesham; the castles of Someries, Skipton, Sandal, Berkeley, Tamworth, Hay, Clifford, Codnor, Ashby, Nottingham, Leicester, Lincoln, and Newark; the battlefields of Bosworth, St. Albans, Wakefield, Tewkesbury, and Evesham,—these, and a thousand spots besides on the route of the Midland line, ought to be familiar to every Englishman.

The third part is *administrative.* It endeavours to indicate the machinery—comprehensive, intricate, and exact—by which a great system of railway is kept in motion by day and by night, in summer and in winter.

The Author begs to tender his grateful acknowledgments to the numerous officers of the Company, and other gentlemen, who have rendered him cordial and valuable aid in his work—aid to which the following pages bear testimony. To the Chairman, to Mr. Allport, and also to his able Chief Secretary, Mr. Robert Speight, he is under special obligation for the kind and courteous assistance they have frequently rendered him. It is right, however, to state that he is solely responsible for any statements of opinion or fact which this volume contains.

He will only add the expression of his hope that the reader may find as much pleasure in following the thread of this remarkable narrative as the Author has had in unravelling it for himself.

CONTENTS.

LIST OF ILLUSTRATIONS.

FROM DRAWINGS BY T. SULMAN, E. M. WIMPERIS, THE AUTHOR, ETC., ENGRAVED UNDER THE SUPERINTENDENCE OF T. SULMAN.

LIST OF MAPS.

CHAPTER I.

A village inn.—The Erewash* Valley.—The coal owners of the Erewash.—Navigable highways.—The river Soar.—An accident.—The Charnwood Forest Canal.—A new competitor.—Mr. John Ellis.—"Old George."—The Leicester and Swannington Railway.—Cheap coals at Leicester.—Conferences of the Canal Committees.—The Midland Counties Railway projected.—Earliest subscribers.—Meeting at Leicester.—Mr. Jessop's report.—Identity of the earliest scheme with that eventually carried out.—Mr. George Rennie's report.—Mr. Vignoles appointed engineer.—Excellence of the route.—Trent Bridge.—Proposals of Northampton people and others.—Financial arrangements of the Midland Counties Company.—Evidence submitted to Parliament concerning the trade and trading facilities of the Midland counties.—Private Bill legislation of the time.—Objections to Railways.—Opposition to the Erewash Valley Railway project.—The North Midland.—"A slip 'twixt the cup and the lip."—First general meeting of Midland Counties shareholders.—Progress of the works.—A curious incident.—Opening of the Nottingham and Derby portion.—Opening of the whole line.—Prospects of the undertaking.—Threatened competition.—The Birmingham and Derby.—Mr. Hutchinson's protest.—Fierce contest.—Disappointment.—Reduction of expenditure.—After war, peace.—Amalgamation proposed and effected.

A LITTLE group of plain practical men were, on the morning of the 16th of August, 1832, sitting round the parlour table of a village inn in Nottinghamshire. They were coal-masters—deep in mines, in counsel, and in pocket. Once a week they were wont to meet at "The Sun," at Eastwood, to ponder their dark

* The initial letter represents the source of the Erewash, at Kirkby, in Nottinghamshire.

B

designs; and, when business was over, they solaced themselves with the best fare the landlord could provide, and with wine from their private cellar, for the safe custody of which mine host levied a toll of half a crown for every cork he drew. From that hill-top could be seen the valley of the river Erewash, with its rich meadows and doddered willows by the water-courses, its grey uplands and scanty timber: that valley then, as now, one of the great highways of England, beneath which, centuries before, the lead-miners of Derbyshire had come to delve for coal, and where many a deep shaft had since been driven, and whence many a working ran.

Five miles to the north of Eastwood, a tramway, worked by horses, had for twelve years or more wound its devious way among the hills, carrying coals and cotton

PINXTON WHARF.

from the Pinxton wharf of the Cromford Canal up to Mansfield, and bringing back stone, lime, and corn to the canal. And many a deeply-laden barge floated from thence down the broad coal valley of the Erewash, past the hills and pits of Eastwood, across the Trent, up the Soar, and on to Leicester and the south, bearing comfort to many a hearth, and bringing back gold in return.

The coal-owners of the Erewash were a very prosperous race, and they won their prosperity by an accident. From time immemorial the coals that any district yielded had usually been consumed within that district; for pack-horses and mules could not bear so heavy a commodity very far from home. Thus the pits of Nottinghamshire had supplied Nottinghamshire, and those of Leicestershire, Leicestershire. But when the last century was drawing to a close, and inland navigation was spreading its watery highways far and wide through the land, canals were projected down the Erewash Valley to the Trent, and it was proposed to make the Soar navigable on to Leicester, so that the products of Nottinghamshire and Derbyshire might be conveyed, not only into the town of Nottingham, but on to the Leicestershire markets and the south. The Leicestershire coal-owners were alarmed. They saw how, if these plans were carried out, it would soon be cheaper to bring coals by canal from the northward, than by road from the pits in their own county, and that their trade would be ruined. Resistance was organized. Nor was it stayed until the projectors of the Soar navigation undertook to make, not only their canal from the Trent to Leicester, but also a branch canal from Loughborough, across Charnwood Forest, to the Leicestershire pits at Coleorton and Moira. Thus, it was thought, equal facilities would be secured for each competitor: there would henceforth be water-carriage for both counties and from both coal-fields.

Events, however, issued otherwise. In the year 1798, the Loughborough Canal and the extension to Coleorton were made. But in the succeeding winter a very deep snow-fall was followed by a rapid and disastrous thaw, and the embankments of both the reservoir and the canal were broken down, and much property was destroyed. The works were never restored; and, in 1838, an Act was obtained to authorize the abandonment of the line and the sale of the land. And "The Charnwood Forest Canal" may still be traced among the wooded hills and dales of Leicestershire: anon a dry ditch, tangled over with briers and underwood, and then carried across massive bridges and along lofty embankments, the sides of which have been planted with saplings and burrowed by rabbits; here it has been levelled down by the plough-

THE CHARNWOOD FOREST CANAL.

share and is fruitful with grain, and there it is overshadowed by trees half a century old.

Meanwhile the Loughborough Canal prospered; and well it might. "There was only one Soar to be had," as the Midland Chairman remarked to us the other day. "It had easily been turned into a canal; it obtained the monopoly, and kept it." The shares, on which £140 had been paid, rose to £4500 each, and were considered to be as safe as consols. And so matters continued for more than thirty years.

But at length the monopoly even of canals began to be threatened. A new competitor was coming into the field. The Stockton and Darlington Railway had been completed, the Liverpool and Manchester line was in course of construction, and the idea was spreading that railways were likely to succeed. Two or three enterprising men in Leicester shared these impressions, and they conferred on the subject with Mr. John Ellis, their townsman. He replied that he had no practical acquaintance with the making or working of railways; but he did not discourage the project. At that time he was associated with some other gentlemen in the reclamation of a part of Chat Moss,—that vast morass over which George Stephenson was then carrying the Liverpool and Manchester Railway; and Mr. Ellis promised that he would ask the advice of his friend Stephenson. Accordingly, a week or two afterwards, Mr. Ellis went from Chat Moss in search of the great engineer, and found him very busy, and, we must add, very "cross," in Rainhill Cutting. "Old George," as he was familiarly called, refused to discuss the matter. Mr. Ellis for a while forebore with his friend's infirmity, and at length induced him to go to a village inn hard by, that they might have a beefsteak together for dinner. Here good humour soon returned; Mr. Ellis explained his plans, and George Stephenson undertook to go over to Leicester and see the country. He did so; and his report as to the practicability of a railway being carried through it was favourable. He was then requested to undertake the office of engineer. This he declined. "He had," he said, "thirty-one miles of railway to make, and that was enough for any man at a time." But, being asked if he could recommend any one for this service, he mentioned the name of his son Robert, who had recently returned from South America, and the father added that he would himself be responsible that the work should be well done. The matter was so arranged; and when, not long afterwards, a difficulty arose in obtaining the requisite capital for the new undertaking,—in consequence of many of the well-to-do Leicester people being already interested in canals,—

George Stephenson further showed his practical interest in the work. "Give me a sheet of paper," he said to his friend Ellis, "and I will raise the money for you in Liverpool." In a short time a complete list of subscribers was returned.

The Leicester and Swannington line was commenced about the latter end of the year 1830; and one spring morning in 1832 Mr. Ellis said to his son, then a lad of fifteen, "Edward, thou shalt go down with me, and see the new engine get up its steam." The machinery had been conveyed by water from Stephenson's factory at Newcastle-on-Tyne to the West Bridge Wharf at Leicester; it had been put together in a little shed built for its accommodation; it was named "The Comet;" and it was the first locomotive that ever ran south of Manchester.

On the 17th of July, 1832, amid great rejoicings, and the roar of cannon that had been cast for the occasion, the new line was opened—a line which brought the long neglected coalfields of Leicestershire almost to the doors of the growing population and thriving industries of the county town.

These events could not but exercise a decisive influence on the position and prospects of the Nottinghamshire and Derbyshire coal trade; and when the coalmasters met at the "Sun Inn" on the 16th of August, 1832, a shadow rested on their faces. The dry ditch in Charnwood Forest could no longer shut Leicestershire coal out of the Leicestershire market; the Swannington line had been five weeks at work; George Stephenson had opened his new pits at Snibston, and was delivering coal at Leicester at less than ten shillings a ton; and the people of Leicester would soon be saving £40,000 a year in fuel—enough to pay all the parochial and government taxes of the town. The Nottinghamshire coal trade had, of course, immediately suffered; and it was obvious that, unless the cost of carriage southward could be reduced, the coal masters of Eastwood and of all that country side would be excluded from their chief markets, and the mining population would be thrown out of employment.

Conferences had already been held with the committees of the Erewash, the Soar, and the Leicester canals; and the latter had admitted that they were "very desirous to endeavour to agree on such a reduction of tonnage on coals as would enable the Derbyshire and Nottinghamshire coals to be sold in the Leicester market in fair competition with the coals brought by the Leicester and Swannington Railway." It was indispensable, however, that a reduction of 3*s*. 6*d* on every ton of coals delivered at Leicester should be obtained: the only question was whether the coal-owners or the canal proprietors were to make the sacrifice. "After a consultation of two hours" the canal committees offered to lower their rates 1*s*. 6*d*.; but they insisted that the coal-owners should consent to reduce their prices 2*s*. a ton. "To this proposition the coal-masters did not see right to agree;" and they contended that each of the three canals ought to lower their rates a shilling, and the coal-owners would reduce their coals a shilling; a reduction, they astutely suggested, "which would have the effect of not merely enabling the Derbyshire coals to compete on equal terms with the Bagworth and other coals brought by the railway, but would have a great effect in deterring persons from investing capital in sinking to other and better beds of coal." In answer to this proposal, the canal committees gave in their ultimatum—that they would each allow a drawback of sixpence a ton "on such coals only as should be delivered at Leicester at 10*s*. a ton." This "extraordinary proposal" — as the coal-owners pronounced it—was "at once rejected," and the meeting broke up.

Such were the reports that were presented when the coal-masters met on the memorable 16th of August, 1832. After anxious deliberation upon all the facts before them, they proceeded to enter on their minutes the declaration, that "*there remains no other plan for their adoption than to attempt to lay a railway from these collieries to the town of Leicester.*" A committee of seven gentlemen was appointed to give effect to this decision by taking "such steps as they may deem expedient." Such was the origin of the Midland Counties Railway; and the "Sun Inn," at Eastwood, was thus the birthplace of the earliest of those lines which afterwards became united into what is now known as the Midland Railway.

BIRTHPLACE OF THE MIDLAND RAILWAY.

Further consideration served only to strengthen the resolution at which the coal-masters had arrived.

Eleven days afterwards—August 27th—at the neighbouring town of Alfreton, it was decided that the public should be invited to co-operate for a continuation of the Mansfield and Pinxton line from Pinxton to Leicester; and on the 4th of October, at a special meeting at the "Sun Inn" at Eastwood, it was unanimously decided, that a "railway be forthwith formed from Pinxton to Leicester, as essential to the interests of the coal-trade of this district." Words were succeeded by deeds, and the following gentlemen put down their names and promises of subscriptions for the accomplishment of the object contemplated:

Messrs. Barber and Walker	£10,000
Mr. E. M. Mundy	5,000
Mr. John Wright	5,000
Mr. Francis Wright	5,000
Mr. James Oakes	2,500
Mr. Brittain	1,500
Messrs. Coupland and Goodwin	1,500
Messrs. Haslam	1,500
	£32,000

It was also directed that steps should be taken for giving the requisite notices preliminary to an appeal to Parliament in the ensuing session. It was subsequently announced that the Duke of Portland, Mr. Morewood, and Mr. Coke had each subscribed £5000; and deputations were appointed to endeavour to secure the cooperation of the Dukes of Newcastle and Richmond, of Lord Middleton, and Sir F. Freeling. It is significantly added in the Eastwood minutes that "a report on the subject of carriage by locomotive power was laid before the meeting:" no decision having then been arrived at on that essential matter.

A meeting also was held in Leicester, October 4th, 1832,

of subscribers to the projected line; Mr. Mundy occupying the chair. "The construction of a railway from Leicester to Swannington," said the local journal, "and the speculations in progress for bringing the coal of the contiguous district into the Leicester market, having threatened the collieries of Derbyshire and Nottinghamshire with the loss of that portion of their trade which they have hitherto enjoyed along the navigation of the Soar, amounting to a quantity perhaps not less than 160,000 tons annually," an effort had been made to induce the canal proprietors so to lower their charges that "the trade, or at least a portion of it," might be retained in its "antient channells." These attempts, however, had failed, and the coal proprietors had adopted the only alternative left to them, of proposing the construction of a railway to Leicester; in which, on account of the benefits it would confer on the town, and also as a profitable investment of capital, the co-operation of the public was invited.

It was added, that, "in the approaching session of Parliament, the legislative sanction is confidently anticipated for the formation of a railway from London to Birmingham," which, "on the completion of the Midland Counties Railway, would admit of a grand central communication being effected from London to Mansfield."

In February, 1833, Mr. Jessop, the engineer, reported to his friends at Eastwood that there had been "no possibility of bringing a bill into Parliament" during that session; but that they "had met with much encouragement in London to prosecute the measure before the next session." It has, indeed, been suggested that, at this period the original project of the Eastwood coal-masters was abandoned; and that the scheme eventually carried out was entirely new. "The former company," said Mr. J. Fox Bell, the secretary of the Midland Counties Railway, "now wound up its affairs and died."

"The first line failed," he added, "because it stopped at Leicester, and did not go on to join the London and Birmingham line of railway." But though, as Bishop Butler shows, it is sometimes difficult to apply the doctrine of personal identity, and though, for forensic reasons, it may have been convenient to separate in thought the original Pinxton and Leicester project from the Pinxton and Rugby line, yet it is unquestionable that the promoters of the former undertaking were the promoters and directors of the second; that the route selected (with the exception of the extension from Leicester to Rugby) was the same; that the subscribers of capital were the same; that the solicitors were the same; that the interests involved and the objects kept in view were the same; and that nothing was done to disconnect in the public mind the scheme of the beginning of 1833 from that of the end of the same year. Moreover, we can find no trace in the minute-books of the Eastwood coal-masters of any indication of any break in their course of action: on the contrary, the continuity of the whole is plainly implied. In August, Mr. Jessop reports, in the same breath, the increase of the Swannington coal trade, the decrease of their own, the necessity for a reduction of price, and the result of a meeting just held at Leicester in the interests of the intended railway; and before the year had closed, the Eastwood coal-masters expressly requested those of their number who had "subscribed for shares in the Midland Counties Railway," to enter their names in the subscription list, and "to pay their deposit money."

Meanwhile, Mr. George Rennie, the civil engineer, was requested by the Provisional Committee to examine the line which Mr. Jessop had proposed, to report upon its eligibility, and to point out any improvements that could be effected. Accordingly, Mr. Rennie accompanied Mr.

Jessop over the route, and minutely compared the plans and sections of the projected line with the natural features of the country. He at length reported that the district through which it was intended to carry the railway included "portions of the valleys of the rivers Soar, Derwent, Erewash, and Trent. These valleys converge together from almost opposite points of the compass, resembling in figure a bent cross." Three of them fall from three to five feet in a mile, and the Erewash descends twelve feet in a mile. "Their width," he continued, "is sufficient to allow a line of railway to be carried in nearly a straight direction. In selecting a line, therefore, little else seemed to have been required than to preserve the natural inclination and direction of the country; but as, practically, there were obstacles to be overcome, it was found not only necessary to raise the surface of the line above the heights of the floods, but to regulate the levels by the existing bridges and roads. This Mr. Jessop has done very judiciously, and the line, though sufficiently elevated, still follows the natural inclination of the country. From the direct course of the valleys, the length of the line in the distance of thirty-four miles between Leicester and Pinxton is only two and a half miles more than a straight line from point to point. In like manner the line from Derby to Nottingham is only one mile longer than a straight line." The line from Leicester to Rugby, though passing through a more varied and irregular country, could be made without "any difficulty which could not be overcome at a comparatively moderate cost."

Mr. Rennie concluded by saying that, "taking all these circumstances into consideration, its locality in an extensive and populous manufacturing and mining district, and the very important communications it would effect from its central position," he was of opinion that the project was one that "presented advantages which seldom occurred in similar undertakings."

In November, 1833, the parliamentary notices for the Midland Counties Railway were deposited, and the usual documents were lodged with the clerks of the peace of the counties through which the line was to run; and shortly afterwards it was publicly announced that the projected line was "intended to connect the towns of Leicester, Nottingham, and Derby, with each other, and with London: a junction for this latter object being designed with the London and Birmingham Railway near Rugby. A branch would also extend to the Derbyshire and Nottinghamshire collieries, and to the termination of the Mansfield Railway at Pinxton." It was added that, "from a very careful estimate of the sources and amount of income on this railway, it appears that a clear annual return of twenty per cent. might be expected from the capital invested." The works north of Leicester might, it was thought, be completed within two years from the passing of the Act, and the portion between Leicester and Rugby would be ready by the time the London and Birmingham line was opened.

But these encouraging anticipations were not realized. Though, by the March following (1834), application had been made for shares to the amount of more than £125,000, this was insufficient to justify an appeal to Parliament in the ensuing session. Accordingly, the notices previously given were repeated, the plans were again deposited, and several thousand additional prospectuses were issued; but the enterprise itself remained for another year in abeyance.

The delay thus occasioned was not without advantages. Opportunities were secured for reconsidering some of the contemplated arrangements, and in the summer of 1835 it was suggested by certain of the

Lancashire shareholders that the entire route should be re-surveyed, in order "to find out the very best line to join the London and Birmingham Railway; combining as much as possible the communication to the west with the best line to London;" and it was proposed that Mr. Charles B. Vignoles, now the President of the Institution of Civil Engineers, should be employed in this service. That gentleman had acquired much experience as an engineer in the construction of the Kingstown and Dublin, and other public roads; he had laid out several railways, and he was favourably known in the north when engaged under George Stephenson on the Liverpool and Manchester line. Accordingly in August, 1835, Mr. Babington, the chairman of the projected Midland Counties Railway, requested Mr. Vignoles to meet him in Liverpool to arrange the terms on which his professional services might be secured; in the following month Mr. Vignoles became the responsible engineer of the line; the appointment was officially confirmed about the close of the year; and he undertook, as he expressed it, to prepare the line for Parliament "as though no other engineer had been engaged on it."

Mr. Vignoles had not been long at work before he found that the estimates previously made would not, in his judgment, be sufficient for the proper completion of the undertaking; and in the following January (1836) his official report confirmed this opinion. He accordingly recommended that, at some additional cost, a tunnel, which it had been intended to make between Rugby and Leicester, should be avoided, and that other material improvements should be effected; and eventually it was decided that the capital previously estimated at £600,000 should be increased to £800,000.

The line as thus planned was excellent. The quantity of materials required for embankments and cuttings balanced each other. There was a uniform gradient falling from Leicester to the Trent of only 1 in 1000, which was practically equal to a level. There was no curve of less than a mile radius. The bridge over the Trent was provided for at an estimated expense of £9000. The line from Derby to Nottingham also was pronounced to be on a "remarkably favourable" gradient. There were no tunnels on the whole system except the archway near Leicester, and a short tunnel under Redhill, near the Trent. Embankments of sufficient but not serious

BRIDGE OVER THE TRENT.*

elevation would raise the line above the flats and the floods of Loughborough meadows, and of the valley of the Trent.

In the month of November of the same year, an

* The entrance to Red Hill tunnel, and also the junction of the river Soar with the Trent, are seen on the right.

important change was suggested in the policy of the promoters of the new line. The people of Northampton had begun to repent of the opposition they had previously given to the London and Birmingham Railway—an opposition which had driven that line four miles to the west of their town, and had compelled the construction at enormous cost of the Kilsby tunnel; and some influential residents now addressed a letter to the committee of the new undertaking inquiring whether it was "yet open for consideration" to alter the course of the projected Midland Counties line so as to pass through Northampton instead of to Rugby, "if a certain number of shares were subscribed for in some degree to meet the additional expense incurred." It was intimated that by crossing Northamptonshire a large trade, especially in cattle, would be secured to the railway, and that it was "altogether a better route for traffic than the one now selected."

The reply was unequivocal. It had been "decided," said Mr. Bell, for the Midland Counties Railway to join the London and Birmingham Railway at Rugby; the plans and other documents as required by Parliament had been prepared, and they would be deposited on the following Monday, "the last day allowed for that purpose."

But the advocates of the Northampton extension were not silenced by this rebuff; and when, in the following February, 1836, a town's meeting was held at Leicester to support the Midland Counties project, a deputation from Northampton came upon the field. In fact, three opponents, in three different interests, appeared. One person moved a resolution condemning the line altogether. But he was soon disposed of, for "only *one finger* was held up for his motion." Others advocated a change in the route: that it should be carried to the west of Leicester instead of to the east, that it should have a junction, with the Swannington line, and then proceed northward through Wanlip and Quorndon. But this alteration was objectionable to the friends of the Midland Counties line for several reasons. The western route would have had inferior levels; it would have entered the outskirts of the worst part of the town; it would have been a mile from the market-place, and from the principal inns and warehouses; it would in its course have interfered somewhat needlessly with private residences; its cost would have been considerably greater because its embankments would have required 300,000 cubic yards, and its cuttings 500,000 cubic yards more material, and its masonry would have been much heavier than on the eastern route, besides leaving a deficiency of earth with which to make the embankment that must be carried across the Loughborough meadows. In addition to all this, there was the fact that a junction with the Swannington line would have enabled the Leicestershire coal to compete with that from Nottinghamshire and Derbyshire wherever the Midland Counties line ran: and this was to its projectors a sufficient objection to the proposed change of route; though it was an argument which they, rather than the public, might be expected to appreciate. On this subject the Leicester meeting appears to have been agreed: only one hand was held up for the amendment.

On the third point—the Northampton route—its advocates were allowed to say their say. But one fact outweighed all their arguments. It was, that the Leicester traders were anxious for an outlet not only to London and the south, but also to Birmingham and the west of England, and this the Northampton route would not have supplied. Though the proposed Northampton line would have been more than twice as long as the extension to Rugby—and would have cost, according to the estimate of Mr. Vignoles, £500,000 additional—it would, on a journey through Northampton to London, have been only four miles shorter than through Rugby; while the distance from Leicester to Birmingham by way of Northampton and Blisworth would have been so circuitous as in the opinion of Leicester men to have been practically valueless. In fact the feeling of the meeting was so decided that the amendment was withdrawn without being put to the vote. "The proposal," said some who were present, "was scouted by the meeting."

After five hours' discussion the meeting drew to a close, the last speakers being interrupted by cries of "Question! question! Dinner! dinner!" And eventually, as a local chronicler records, the "worthy ratepayers" of Leicester hurried home to their "beef over-roasted and puddings overdone."

The financial arrangements of the Midland Counties Railway project, were, when laid before Parliament, satisfactory. The proposed capital was £1,000,000, with borrowing powers for a third more; it being estimated, however, that the works could be completed for £800,000. Of this amount £786,500 had been subscribed in shares of £100, on each of which a deposit had been paid of £2, and a call of £5. It is worthy of notice that the directors,—who included the names of T. E. Dicey, Matthew Babington, William Jessop, E. M. Mundy, and J. Oakes,—held more than £95,000 of shares; and also that among the earliest supporters of railway enterprise were the then Prime Minister, Viscount Melbourne, "Downing Street," whose name is on the shareholders' list for £5,000; John Cheetham of Staley Bridge, £10,000; and Thomas Houldsworth, Manchester, £15,000; while among those who were considered to have had a local interest in the line were—

	£
John Ellis, Beaumont Leys, Farmer	500
William Evans Hutchinson, Leicester, Druggist . .	1,000
Thomas Edward Dicey, Claybrooke Hall	2,000
Joseph Cripps, Leicester, Draper	2,000
George Walker, for Barber, Walker & Co., Eastwood	10,000

To aid in obtaining so large an amount of support, Mr. Bell, the Secretary, had visited several of the towns in the midland counties, and also in the north of England; and partly as a result of these efforts, Manchester had subscribed no less than £356,200; Yorkshire had contributed £7,000; Bath, £500; and Cheltenham, £1000. Ireland also had taken £1,800 of capital; South America, £2,000, and the West Indies, £2,000. On returning from this circuit Mr. Bell announced that the subscription list was full. The shares, too, were at a premium.

"Should you consider,"—ingenuously suggested one of the counsel for the bill, when it was before Parliament,—"Should you consider it any objection to a scheme of this kind, that it has commanded the favour and support of the whole world?"

With equal naïveté the witness replied, "Certainly not."

It is due to these early friends of the Midland Counties Railway to add that "the railway mania" had not at this period begun to make the projection of new lines a fashion and a passion in the land.

The benefits that were likely to be conferred by the contemplated railway, will, perhaps, be better understood, if we ascertain, from the evidence formally submitted to Parliament, the nature of the trade and of the trading facilities at that time possessed by the midland counties of England. Nottingham, Derby, and Leicester were then, as now, important centres of industry, receiving and distributing large quantities both of the raw material and of the products of their manufacturing skill, and holding constant communication with the metropolis, with Birmingham, with the West of England, and with each other.

But the only modes of conveyance at that time were three: the canal, the fly waggon, and the coach; and the charges made were proportionate to the speed. Wool, for instance, required two days to travel the fifteen miles between Leicester and Market Harborough, and the expense was sixpence a hundredweight, the distance being it was said "so short, and the traffic so unimportant that they are obliged to charge an extra price." Only three coaches ran daily each way from Leicester to Nottingham, in addition to those that passed to and from more distant points, and on which little reliance could be placed by local travellers. Similarly many of the "fly waggons" were long stagers, and were of secondary benefit to the intermediate towns. Meanwhile the charge for haberdashery, from London to Leicester, was £2 15*s.* a ton by canal, 5*s.* a hundredweight by waggon, and a penny a pound by coach.

Such means of communication and such prices could not but cripple a growing trade. Thus Mr. James Rawson, of Leicester, stated that he employed from 1,000 to 1,400 people in the staple trade of that town—the manufacture of worsted and of stockings; that it was indispensable to obtain the wools of the West of England, "because the wool grown in Leicestershire would not supply a twentieth part of the quantity required;" yet that the canal communication between Leicester and Birmingham was double the distance of a direct route; and the land carriage cost 30*s.* a ton.

The respective conveyances, too, were often unable to carry the quantity of goods offered. Thus, a woolstapler stated that he frequently had from 200 to 500 bags of wool lying at Bristol which could not be brought forward by land, and he had to divide the bulk and send it by different routes; that which went by road occupied from seven to ten days in the transit, and that by water from three weeks to a month. Further west, the difficulties increased, so that goods for instance from Plymouth, had to come by sea to London, and were in consequence not unfrequently a great length of time on the voyage and the land journey, and often arrived in a wet and damaged condition.

Similar difficulties were experienced in the Nottingham lace trade. Many of the largest manufacturers of lace lived in Devon and Somerset, and they sent the products of their industry to Nottingham for sale, the costliest fabrics having to run all the risks by land or water.

Leicester had also intimate business relations with the north. That town was a sort of depôt for the wool trade of the adjoining counties, and to it Yorkshire dealers resorted. Their purchases had then to be conveyed northward, from whence machinery was brought in return. Yet the route by water from Leicester was first *viâ* Nottingham to Gainsborough, and thence to Leeds and the West Riding generally, the voyage occupying from twenty-four days to a month.

Complaints of inadequate facilities came also from Derby and Macclesfield. "Our heavy goods," said a witness, "must go through two or three different channels by water—the Trent, the Soar, and the Leicester Navigation, so that they cost nearly £1 a ton average from Derby to Leicester;" while the expense of carriage of Mansfield stone, though it is of a remarkably fine quality, was such as "to amount almost to a prohibition" of trade.

Such were some of the data laid before the Committee of the House of Commons, when, with Mr.

Gisborne as chairman, it sat for some seventeen days to consider the claim of the Midland Counties Bill on the sanction of Parliament Meanwhile the original projectors of the undertaking had vigilantly regarded the great interests of their trade; for, in the minute-book of the Eastwood coal-masters, it is recorded that on February 4th, 1836, Mr. Tallents had engaged "to watch the progress of the Midland Counties Railway Bill in Parliament, with a view of protecting the mineral property and rights of coal-owners and lessees, and to attend generally to their interests;" and on the 26th of the following April, "Messrs. Mundy and Potter reported to the meeting that they had succeeded in their mission to London, and had procured insertion in the Midland Counties Railway Bill of every necessary clause for protecting and securing the rights of the owners of mineral property." And "the thanks of the meeting were given to those gentlemen."

But the difficulties with which the friends of the Midland Counties Company had to contend, did not cease when the Bill entered Parliament. Railway enterprises at that time were novelties, not only to the counties, but to the legislature. Several important towns had resisted the intrusion of railways; and many a member of either House regarded himself as bound by the most sacred obligations of patriotism to protect his innocent urban constituents against such wild innovations, and to defend the farmers against having their crops burned up and their cattle frightened to death by whistling engines and rushing and roaring trains. Instead, too, of railway bills being, as they were subsequently, relegated to the scrutiny of small but impartial bodies of members, the committees were then open to the members of the boroughs and counties, and of adjoining counties through or near which the projected line was to be carried, and members sometimes attended solely for the purpose of voting on the preamble, or on a particular clause, and in some instances, we are assured, "the whip applied was tremendous."

The Midland Counties Bill survived the ordeal of the House of Commons, only, however, to encounter more searching hostility in "another place." The Erewash Valley projectors of the undertaking had, to their sorrow, to learn that for great coal-masters, as well as for common mortals, there is many a slip 'twixt the cup and the lip. Powerful foes were in the field. The Midland Counties line had been originated with the avowed intention of breaking up canal monopoly, and the local canal interests were not unready for any reprisal. The North Midland Company had been formed to construct a line from Derby to Leeds, and had lent their influential patronage to a projected extension from Derby and Birmingham, by means of which an additional and independent outlet could be obtained to the west and the south; and the North Midland regarded the Erewash Valley portion of the Midland Counties line with special jealousy, because it *pointed north*, and therefore looked suggestive of competition and aggression. The Midland Counties Company, too, had spoken of extending their Erewash line up the valley, over the ridge near Clay Cross, and on to Chesterfield; and it was very doubtful whether Parliament, which at that time was scrupulous in its cession of railway powers, would sanction the construction of two parallel lines, one through the Erewash Valley towards Chesterfield, and the other from Derby to Chesterfield; in which case the North Midland Company might be required to effect its junction with the Erewash Extension of the Midland Counties near Clay Cross; to lose some twenty miles of line, of rates, and of profits; and to abandon its intended direct connection with Derby, with Birmingham, and the West. These were, to the North Midland, serious considerations. It has been suggested that George Stephenson was also influenced by a desire that the products of his projected coal-works at Clay Cross should find their way direct to Derby and the West, rather than through the Erewash Valley; but at this period Clay Cross was not in contemplation. Yet when he found opponents arise to advocate a plan which, on other accounts, he regarded as undesirable, he exclaimed, in his native Doric, "This warn't do."

But in addition to powerful opponents who had to be resisted, the Midland Counties Company had entered into an alliance with powerful friends whose judgment must be deferred to. It is true that the necessities of the Erewash Valley coal-masters had given birth to the Midland Counties Company; but the original subscribers to that undertaking had had, as we have seen, to call in the substantial assistance of moneyed men of the North, whose only anxiety was to secure a great through route to the South, and who cared little for the solicitude of a few coal-owners in a remote Nottinghamshire valley. When, therefore, "the Liverpool party," as it was called, saw that, by the double pressure of the North Midland Company and of the canal interests, there was danger of the Midland Counties Bill being rejected; when the alternative was, "Shall the Erewash Extension be sacrificed, or the bill be lost?"—it was replied that the little coal line might be made at any time, or be made independently; and so it was abandoned. And thus it came to pass that the Midland Counties Bill became law, *minus* the portion that was most dear to the hearts of the original projectors of the Company; *minus* that very part which they had fondly hoped would have restored their languishing fortunes by opening a cheap and expeditious route from their pits to Leicester and the South. "Oakes and Jessop," as Mr. Vignoles remarked to us the other day, "were disgusted and angry; but they could not help themselves. Their line and themselves were left out in the cold."

The first general annual meeting of the Midland Counties Railway was held at Loughborough, June 30, 1837, a little more than a month after the first sod of the Derby and Nottingham line was turned. Mr. Thomas Edward Dicey occupied the chair. The directors "could not refrain from observing at the outset," that "the result of their exertions had been such as to afford them a sure and well-founded cause of congratulation to the shareholders," concerning the position and prospects of the Company. Action, it was stated, must now be taken to give effect to the parliamentary powers that had been obtained; and this was done. The necessary arrangements for commencing the line were soon afterwards made by Mr. Vignoles, assisted on the Leicester and Trent portion by Mr. Woodhouse, the resident engineer; and on the Nottingham and Derby line by Mr. William Mackenzie, who had been the confidential assistant of Telford; and so successfully were their labours prosecuted, that, by the close of 1837, nearly all the contracts were let, and some of the works were in full operation. The contract for the Leicester and Rugby portion was confided to Mr. Mackintosh, who had been only a few years previously a ganger or sub-contractor in Scotland, but who was now "supposed to be worth £1,000,000 of money."

Early in the year 1838, important negotiations arose between the boards of the Midland Counties and of the North Midland for a future interchange of traffic. The Midland Counties contended that their route, by

Rugby, to the South, was nine miles shorter than that which the projected Birmingham and Derby line could offer; and they hoped that they should be able to secure almost a monopoly of the through traffic between the great towns of Yorkshire and the metropolis. Eventually an agreement was made for seven years, and was unanimously ratified at a meeting of the Midland Counties proprietors, at Loughborough, in the following March (1838). On that occasion a favourable report of the financial prospects of the Company was presented, and Captain Huish, who had been residing at Nottingham, stated that, whereas the directors had estimated that the probable traffic on the line would yield rather more than £99,000 a year, his calculation was £104,000. "I am inclined to believe," he added, "that the most sanguine expectations of the proprietors can scarcely fail to be realised."

In the following month (April, 1838) the whole line was under contract. Between Nottingham and Derby 1000 men were directed to press on with the work, because that portion of the line was the easiest to complete, and because it would bring an immediate return for the capital expended. In the course of the spring, nearly 3500 men and 328 horses were in full employment on various parts of the Midland Counties line.

In carrying on these works, a curious incident occurred at Spondon, three miles from Derby. The railway had here to be conducted between the river Derwent and the Nottingham Canal, over a space so narrow that a diversion of the canal was necessary. But this could not be effected without temporarily suspending the navigation, for which a penalty was demanded of £2 *an hour*. In the month of August, the contractor was preparing to undertake the work, and, of course, to pay the price, when suddenly the canal itself had to be stopped in order that some indispensable repairs might be made. Mr. Mackenzie immediately mustered his men from various points of the railway, and while the repairs of the canal were being effected, he succeeded in effecting his diversion of the line,—to the great diversion of the neighbourhood, who came to watch the relays of 200 or 300 men, fed most bountifully, and labouring most energetically to complete, within the given time, the novel task.

At the second annual meeting of the Midland Counties Railway, held at Loughborough, in June, 1838, Mr. T. E. Dicey, the chairman, stated that at that time 4000 men were employed on the works; and that the agreement with the North Midland for the exchange of traffic had been ratified. He mentioned that as many stone sleepers and rails, and as much rolling stock, had been contracted for as would be required for the Derby and Nottingham portion of the new line; the Nottingham station had been let; agreements had been made with the directors of the North Midland and Birmingham and Derby Companies for the erection of contiguous stations at Derby; and a station to be jointly used by the London and Birmingham and the Midland Counties, was to be proved at Rugby. It was also intended that a branch should be formed to connect the main line with the granite quarries of Mount Sorrel.

The engineer expressed his belief that the permanent way between Nottingham and Derby would be better than any hitherto made. Some fourteen miles of it were to be laid on blocks of Derbyshire millstone grit, each of them containing five cubic feet, and the bearings being five feet in length; the rest were to be on transverse larch sleepers, kyanized, and three feet nine inches apart. All the rails were to be seventy-seven pounds to the yard, which was heavier than any previously employed. The ends of the rails were to be secured in "joint chairs," each weighing twenty-eight pounds. Nearly 550,000 cubic yards of earthwork was to be made; the deepest cutting was to be thirty feet; the highest embankment, twenty feet; and one, approaching Nottingham, would be three miles in length.

The cofferdam for the deepest pier of the bridge over the Trent was in course of construction, and as the bottom of the river was found to consist of strong red marl, it would furnish an excellent foundation for the masonry. A short tunnel, through the adjoining ridge, called Red Hill, had been commenced; and at several parts of the line, where the works were heavy, gangs of men were employed both day and night. The cutting at Leir Hill, between Leicester and Rugby, was the most serious earthwork on the line; and here, to facilitate his operations, the contractor had erected a steam engine, and had made an inclined plane from the cutting to an embankment where the material was to be deposited, the plane descending in the direction of the embankment, at an angle just sufficient to enable the wagons to run down with their burdens to the plane of their destination. The empties were drawn back by an engine. The building of the Avon Viaduct, consisting of eleven arches of fifty feet span had been commenced, and, despite unusual delays, arising from the severity of the weather in the early part of the year, would, it was anticipated, be completed by the winter. And "it is somewhat remarkable," said Mr. Woodhouse, the engineer, "that in many contracts to the amount of nearly £500,000, they should have been let within less than £5000 of the estimates."

About two years after the first sod of the Midland Counties line was turned, on Thursday, the 30th of May, 1839, the opening of the Railway took place. The occasion was celebrated with honour. The day was bright. The bells of St. Mary's Church, Nottingham, pealed merrily.

Thousands of people took their places on the eminences of the Park, on the tops of houses, or on the route of the line, to see the first train pass; and even opposition coaches came into being under the inspiration of the event. Special privileges were provided for five hundred favoured guests. Each of them received a ticket of admission, emblazoned with gold, bearing the arms of the Company; and each passenger found a card affixed over a seat specially reserved in the train for his accommodation. "The busy hum of the assembly, the threading and bustling of railway-guards and policemen in their new uniforms, the several elegantly painted carriages, with the Company's arms richly emblazoned on the panels," each carriage mounted with a Union Jack or an ensign: and we have "a scene" which the modesty of a local chronicler compelled him to "confess his inability adequately to do justice to." At length the passengers were seated; and then "amid the slamming of carriage-doors, the blowing of horns, and the roar of the steam," the signal was given to start, and "at no drawling pace either." At every station along the line, and on the roads that crossed it, were crowds of spectators, some of whom had climbed to dangerous eminences in their love of science or of curiosity.

At Derby also, a wondering and cordial welcome was afforded. Here the train stayed an hour, and then returned to Nottingham, accomplishing the journey in forty-two minutes. And here, according to British usage, a sumptuous entertainment had been provided, to which all parties endeavoured to do justice; and then, once more, the train returned to Derby, running the distance in thirty-one minutes, part of it at the rate of forty miles an hour. The festivities of this occasion were considered, we presume, to have lent a sort of anticipated lustre to the whole undertaking; for when, in the following summer, the remainder of the Midland Counties line was opened, the Directors merely made a private excursion over it the day before.

The benefit conferred by the railway on both the travelling and trading classes were, however, none the less real. "For some time," remarked a Leicester journal, "we certainly had our doubts relative to the success of this great and expensive undertaking, but from daily increasing experience, we have no doubt of its paying the shareholders, judging as we do from the increase of passengers and merchandise, together with a large concern shortly to be opened in the traffic of coal." A number of wharfs had already been built and let, and a large warehouse for corn was about to be erected; while at Loughborough, Syston, Wigston, Crow Mill, Ullesthorpe, and Rugby, wharfs were being made near

NOTTINGHAM (OLD) STATION.

to the various stations for the purpose of selling coal, and which would be found of great convenience to the farmers, many of whom had to send their teams to Leicester. Meanwhile the shares advanced from 77 to 80.

Thus, one of the earliest, and, as it proved, one of the most important lines of railways in the country, was completed. Its cost fell within the amount of capital authorized by the Act; and the line was, as the Directors remarked, "one of the lowest per mile of any similar work of the same extent." But it soon began to be suggested that it would not "be matter of any surprise to those who are conversant with what has occurred" elsewhere, that "additional requirements for the accommodation and safety of the public, as well as for ultimate economy in the working of the railway," would have to be made at an expenditure of additional capital; and before long it was announced that the amount needed would be £150,000.

At the annual meeting in 1841, it was proposed that for the future, though not required by the charter of incorporation, the meetings of proprietors should be held half yearly, instead of annually; and a resolution to that effect having been carried in Feb. (1842), the practice was established, and has since been continued. A copy of the balance-sheet also was now for the first time sent to each proprietor previously to the meeting. That document showed that the gross receipts of the Company were increasing; that there had been a reduction of about twelve per cent. in the working expenses; and that the balance enabled the Directors to declare a dividend at the rate of four per cent. per annum, and to carry forward a surplus of £2000. In a discussion that followed, it was stated that "in a new line like the Midland Counties, the cost of maintenance was sure to be higher than on old lines, from slips and other repairs;" an opinion somewhat at variance with that expressed about the same time by railway authorities elsewhere.

But while the Midland Counties line was thus endeavouring to overcome the unavoidable difficulties, and to earn the reward, of its new position, it had been gradually drifting into the midst of the anxieties and perils of that great enemy to the financial prosperity of all railways—competition. The alliance it had formed with the North Midland for the exclusive interchange of northern and southern traffic, had, from the outset, been regarded by the Birmingham and Derby Company, which had opened its line to Hampton-in-Arden, as a tocsin of war. It was of little avail that the Midland Counties Board uttered a disclaimer against any hostile intention. They alleged, what indeed was correct, that the standing orders of Parliament required a declaration whether any given line would be competitive or not; that the projectors of the Birmingham and Derby had declared that their line was non-competitive, and only a link between East and West. But the Midland Board complained that, no sooner had the Birmingham and Derby obtained their act, than they neglected their communications with Birmingham and the West; that they hastened to complete that portion of their line which—bending southward from Whitacre—brought them at Hampton-in-Arden, ten miles south of Birmingham on the way to London; and that they then commenced a competition with the Midland Counties for the traffic between the North and the Metropolis. This was, in the judgment of the Midland Counties Board, to act "evasively and delusively."

But these arguments and appeals did not avail to check the asperity of controversy and competition. Before long the directors of the Birmingham and Derby began to proclaim that they had special facilities for carrying on the trade to the South; an announcement which was energetically challenged on behalf of the Midland Counties by Mr. W. E. Hutchinson. "Is it not," he said, "absolutely ludicrous for a Company whose line possesses so small a population between its termini as the Birmingham and Derby, to talk of abstracting traffic from its direct channel by a circuitous route of ten or eleven miles, and conveying it 'at a remunerating charge very much less than that which the Midland Counties must make,' and because, forsooth, they have constructed their line 'entirely for other purposes'!"

The conflict, having thus commenced, waxed hotter and hotter, till at length it was conducted by both parties in a manner that showed they were regardless of any loss they suffered so long as greater loss was inflicted upon their opponents. The Midland Counties Directors complained that the Birmingham and Derby Company was attempting "to divert the traffic between London and Derby from the direct line, and to force it along an indirect and circuitous one, possessing no advantages whatever over that of the Midland Counties; but, on the contrary, being about eleven miles farther round. It will suffice to say," they continued, "that the Birmingham and Derby Company, for the purpose of attracting to their line, and withdrawing from the natural and direct channel the London and Derby traffic, have adopted the altogether unprecedented course, of charging in respect of persons travelling between Derby and London only 2*s*. for a first class, and 1*s*. 6*d*. for a second class passenger, for the whole distance of thirty-eight miles from Derby to Hampton;" while "they continue to exact from all other passengers, though in the same carriages and going exactly the same distance, their original fares of 8*s*. each for first class, and 6*s*. for second class passengers. To correct "this singular mode of charging," the Directors stated that they had applied to the Court of Chancery for an injunction; and though this application had been unsuccessful, they believed that "a very different result would attend" an appeal to the Court of Queen's Bench.

Meanwhile the Directors had resolved that their own fares between Derby and London should be "invariably charged at rates not exceeding those charged by the Birmingham and Derby Company." It was believed that very low fares *might* have the counterbalancing advantage of encouraging additional traffic; and "even if the anxiety of the Birmingham and Derby Company to obtain business on any terms should lead them to make still further reductions, and to convey passengers over their line *without any charge whatever*," yet, since the Midland Counties delivered its passengers to the London and Birmingham line at a point somewhat farther south than its competitor, it would have the advantage in the conflict. At one time apprehension was expressed lest the London and Birmingham Company should provide special facilities to Birmingham and Derby passengers for reaching the Metropolis; but a Midland Counties proprietor stated that at a recent meeting of the London and Birmingham Company, he had himself put a question on this subject to the chairman, and that he had received "the distinct avowal of one of the most honourable men in existence that they would preserve a strict neutrality." Ungenerous feeling towards the Birmingham and Derby Company was, by the Midland Counties Board, publicly disclaimed, and it was declared that the existing rivalry was "a scandalous reproach to the railway system, and no less detrimental to the dignity and respectability of the respective Companies, than inimical to their real interests."

At the half-yearly meeting, held August 13th, 1842, the chairman, Mr. T. E. Dicey, stated that the bill for raising the new capital had received the Royal assent; but that it was now for the first time required by Parliament that the authorised amount of shares should be subscribed for before the power to borrow could be allowed to take effect. A dividend was proposed at the rate of three per cent. per annum. A long and, eventually, stormy debate followed. Mr. James Heyworth, whose family held about a twentieth part of the shares of the Company, stated that many of the shareholders were "disappointed, nay, irritated with the position of the Company. They recommended the Directors to make a searching inquiry, and wherever curtailment could be made, consistent with the safe working of the line, he hoped they would carry it out." He suggested that the number of the Directors might be reduced to twelve, with an allowance of £600 a year instead of £1200; and that, if the maintenance of the way were undertaken by contractors, some economy might be effected.

The dissatisfaction thus expressed led to the summoning, in the following November (1842), of a special meeting of the shareholders—"one of the most memorable of railway meetings," as it was characterized at the time. It had been intended to hold it at the Derby station, but for more adequate accommodation it was adjourned to the Athenæum. In a lengthened speech, Mr. Heyworth contended that, without intending the slightest disrespect to the Directors, he thought that the time had come at which a Committee of Investigation should be appointed to examine into "the past, present, and probable future expenditure of the funds of the Company (both on the capital and interest account), also with reference to the rates and freights charged, and proper to be charged," for passengers and goods, and to the general management of the Company's affairs. He hoped that this resolution would not be regarded by the Board as any infringement of their rights. "The sooner," he said, "such a doctrine is repudiated, and the practice abolished, the better. By-and-by, should the doctrine of non-interference be sanctioned, it will lead to this,—that a mercantile man, on going into his count-ing-house, and wishing to inspect his ledger or his cash-book, will be told by some fastidious and upstart clerk, that he had no right to interfere with his department, that the books are his clerk's, and that any investigation of them would show want of confidence."

An animated debate ensued. The Directors opposed the resolution; but to show that they did not cling to office, stated that at the meeting of the Company in the following February, they would "place in the hands of the proprietors the free choice of a new Board, and that they would immediately after make such arrangements as would at once transfer the direction from their own hands into those of the persons chosen by the proprietors." In the course of the discussion, it transpired that the secretary, Mr. Bell, had voluntarily relinquished £200 a year out of his salary of £800, and that other economies had been practised. Eventually, the resolution, appointing a committee, was carried by a majority of about three to one.

Meanwhile, with only one brief interval, the competition with the Birmingham and Derby Company continued. Amalgamation was indeed proposed; but the Birmingham and Derby Company laid down the proviso that the market price of the stock of the two Companies should be taken as the value of the respective properties,—an arrangement that would give £40 to the Birmingham and Derby to each £60 of the Midland Counties. The latter, however, replied, that the then price of stock did not represent the intrinsic worth of the respective properties; and that it would be better that the amount should be determined by a year's independent working of the two lines, at the expiration of which their true value could be ascertained.

These negotiations failed, and at the half-yearly meeting, in August, 1843, the Directors of the Midland

Counties Company stated that "the attempt to divert from the Midland Counties line, by a reduction of fares, the traffic which would naturally flow along it, was still carried on," by the Birmingham and Derby Company, "with unabated activity," even though "at prices which could yield no profit whatever." The Midland Counties Directors announced that they were advised, on eminent legal authority, that the mode of charging practised by the Birmingham and Derby Company was "as illegal as it was unfair and unreasonable." Acting upon these opinions, the Directors had made application to the Court of Queen's Bench for a mandamus to compel the Birmingham and Derby Company to equalize their fares. A rule *nisi* had been obtained, and subsequently a *mandamus* had been "served upon the Birmingham and Derby Company, requiring them to charge all persons equally who travel between Derby and Hampton." The Directors stated that they entertained the most perfect confidence in securing a decision which would render it "impossible for the Birmingham and Derby Company to persevere in their present mode of opposition."

But as with kings and nations, so with railways,—after war comes peace; after rivers of blood or of gold have been wasted, come negotiations, treaties, and alliances. So when the owners of both these two costly and valuable properties had exhausted one another and themselves with protracted conflicts, they began once more to think of rest and union. Amalgamation was again proposed, and wise counsels at last prevailed. But concerning these we shall have hereafter to speak.

Such were the circumstances under which the Midland Counties Railway took its rise, and such were the circumstances which gradually, but irresistibly, brought it to the eve of amalgamation—that amalgamation which led on to the formation of the Midland Railway Company of to-day. We retrace with interest and instruction the good example of "the difficulties, discouragements, and disasters encountered by the enterprising men who, at that date, undertook the arduous duty of constructing, from private capital, these great public works, unaided, even discountenanced, by the legislature and the government; regarded with hostility, and even with hatred, by the owners of the land they were destined so materially to benefit; and considered, even by juries of their own countrymen, as proper objects of unlimited and legitimate plunder. Yet did these brave men carry on their undertaking steadily, and stoutly, and manfully, with sagacity, tact, and courage of no common order, till they accomplished their great work." Such enterprises and such men confer honour and strength on a country, and they enlarge the sources of its wealth and the causes of its material and moral prosperity.

And while to-day we watch the flood which pours its volume of beneficence and wealth through the midland counties of England, is there not an air of romance in the story that tells how we can retrace through upwards of forty years the course of the earliest of the tributary streams, and can discern how it took its rise at a little homely inn in a remote village among the hills of Nottinghamshire?

But we must now go back and see how other events, contemporaneous with some we have narrated, have been running their course.

CHAPTER II.

The yellow post-chaise.—The North Midland Railway.--George Stephenson's preference for the valley route.—Opposition from advocates of a high level line.—Surveying for the line.—Perils of engineers.—The engineer and the baronet.—Mr. Waterton's sanctum.—Amusing interview.—Battles in Parliament.—Opposition by Messrs. Strutt and the Aire and Calder Navigation.—Commencement of the works.—Bird's-eye view of the line.—Ambergate Tunnel.—Bull Bridge.—Opening of the North Midland.—The traffic then and now.—Additional capital required.—Reduction of expenditure.—Generous offer of Mr. Robert Stephenson.—Improved arrangements.—Coal rates then and now.—Disappointment.—Committee of Inquiry.—Proposed amalgamation of North Midland with Midland Counties, and Birmingham and Derby Companies.

On a beautiful morning in the autumn of 1835 (three years after the memorable meeting at The Sun Inn, at Eastwood), a yellow post-chaise might have been seen emerging from the New Inn, at Derby, and taking its way up the Duffield Road into the country. It contained two gentlemen: George Stephenson the engineer, who had come over from his residence at Alton Grange in Leicestershire, and his secretary Mr. Charles Binns. They had started on an enterprise of no common importance—to find the best route for a new line 72 miles in length, from Derby to Leeds. The project was, we believe, one of the fruits of George Stephenson's fertile brain; but the responsibility of carrying out the work had been undertaken chiefly by Leeds and London men. Mr. G. C. Glyn, the banker, Mr. Kirkman Hodgson, Mr. Frederick Huth, the German merchant, Mr. Josiah Lewis, of Derby, and others, were on the first directorate, and in such hands the work was likely to succeed.

It is true that the inside of a post-chaise did not seem the likeliest place for surveying the hills and dales, the roads and rivers, of more than 70 miles of country, and the top of the vehicle might, on some accounts, have been preferred; but it was the only means of conveyance then available for any such purpose. Ever and anon the travellers would alight, and walk for miles, surveying the various routes, examining the landscape from different points of view, recording the result of their observations on the old fashioned county map they carried, and storing away fragments of the stones that indicated the changing geological formations over which they passed. And as the engineer and his secretary journeyed on together, many a problem would "Old George" curiously and laboriously solve, and many an anecdote would he tell of other days,—of the toils of his boyhood, of his tender love of all things living, fostered when, as a little lad, he was wont to take his father's dinner to the engine in the wood, where he lingered and watched birds and beasts and fishes; tales of how he at one time had resolved to emigrate to America; of how he narrowly escaped, as he playfully said, of being made a Methodist; and of how he intended to carry on the vast and varied projects which he had then in hand on the Birmingham and Derby, the York and North Midland, and the Manchester and Leeds Railways.

In determining the route which the North Midland line should follow, George Stephenson had to decide between strongly conflicting claims. From Derby to Leeds is a series of valleys, through which flow the rivers Derwent, Amber, Rother, Don, Dearne, Calder, and Aire, affording a route from south to north, available for the conveyance of the vast mineral traffic which the district would eventually yield. To the west of these valleys, among the great hills of Yorkshire, were the towns of Sheffield, Barnsley, and Wakefield, to approach which by the main line would involve enormous earthworks, bad gradients, and vast expenditure. The engineer made his choice: he preferred minerals to men: he would take the lower or valley route; the towns must be satisfied with branches.

Having thus decided, another problem awaited solution. Should he skirt the ranges of hills which on either hand closed in the valleys along which his line should run, and curve to the left or right according to the ground and the gradients? But such a course would involve this serious inconvenience: that the collieries in the bottom of the valley, and those on the slopes of the opposite range of hills, would have to drag their heavy loads up to the level of the line; whereas by placing the railway itself in the middle of the valley—raised only to the point necessary to avoid the floodings of the rivers, both sides of its course would be equally served, and the branches from the pits on the higher ground would all slope downwards to the line. Such an arrangement would obviously be the best for all mineral purposes, and would also supply a short and level course from south to north. To these opinions George Stephenson inclined, and the more so because he had laid it down as an axiom that no gradient on a mineral line ought to exceed 1 in 330, or 16 feet in a mile. Eventually the North Midland Railway was laid out at that gradient, except for a short distance south of Clay Cross Tunnel, where the gradient is slightly increased. And George Stephenson always, and not unnaturally, regarded the North Midland as one of his favourite lines.

The decision of the engineer, however, was not adopted without a fierce contest both within Parliament and without. Mr. Vignoles avowed his preference for a high level route; and he proposed a line which should serve as a continuation of the Erewash portion of the Midland Counties, through the ridge up to Clay Cross and down to Sheffield. He also had surveys taken northwards to Leeds and southwards to London; for as engineers were at that time the chief promoters of railway extension, it was expected that they should be prepared to justify to Parliament the comprehensiveness and practicability of their proposals. The arguments for and against the high and low levels were submitted to the committee, not on lodged plans for competing schemes, but on the North Midland Bill proper.

The views of Mr. Vignoles were supported by Lord Wharncliffe and by other influential persons interested in Sheffield, some of whom announced their preference for a line to run from Chesterfield direct through Sheffield, and thence over the hills to the north; but the plans proposed involved "excavations and embankments from 90 to 100 feet deep and high," from one end of the route to the other. Some engineers of less adventurous spirit urged that the line should, a few miles north of Chesterfield, bend westward, and, having touched Sheffield, should turn again eastward along the valley of the Don. Mr. Leather, the engineer, was a chief advocate of this scheme; and the war of opinion thus waged, at length induced George Stephenson to reconsider whether some more adequate accommodation could not be provided for Sheffield; and Mr. Frederick Swanwick, "the resident," was instructed to endeavour to find an available route to that town. A local committee also was appointed to promote the same object. But after once more trying the levels by way of Dronfield, it was ascertained that the gradients would be so severe that, according to the power of locomotives in that day, the route would be impracticable. In fact, the tenour of the engineer's report was—that to take the line through Sheffield with gradients equal to those of the valley route would necessitate the formation of 8 or 10 miles of tunnels. Since that decision was pronounced a third of a century has passed away: the impracticable has been achieved, and a direct line runs to-day *viâ* Dronfield, over the high level route, into Sheffield.

In making even the surveys for the new railway many difficulties and some adventures were encountered by the engineers. Thus when Mr. Swanwick was running his levels a few miles south-east of Wakefield, he learned that numerous watchers had been placed across his path, and that other precautions had been adopted, to prevent his intrusion on the estates of Sir William Pilkington. But the inventive genius of the engineer was not unequal to the occasion. Running the risk of being brought before the magistrates, as Mr. Vignoles had been not long before, on a charge of night poaching and trespassing, the engineer gathered together a large staff of assistants, and made his survey while Sir William, his watchers, and all other honest folk were supposed to be safe asleep in bed. It subsequently happened that, in some negotiations that took place in the library of the unsuspecting baronet—who meanwhile had become more propitious to the undertaking—he opened a drawer for a plan of the part of his estate through which he understood the projected line was to pass, "and," he added, "no other survey has ever been made of it." His surprise may be imagined when the representatives of the Company, as blandly as they could, at the same time unrolled their own documents, and showed that they were perfectly familiar with every acre of the district which he had so jealously protected.

On another occasion, when making their surveys in the same neighbourhood, the engineers found their course obstructed by a high wall. Over it Mr. Swanwick at once climbed, in order to ascertain his whereabouts, and he then saw a fine wooded park spreading out before him. This proved to be the sacredly-preserved domains of the celebrated traveller and naturalist, Mr. Charles Waterton, who prided himself that here he could give "a hearty welcome to every bird and beast that chose to avail itself of his hospitality; and by affording them abundant food and a quiet retreat, induce them to frequent a spot where they would feel themselves secure from all enemies;" a spot where the "shyest birds were so well aware of their security that they cared no more for spectators than the London sparrows for passengers." No wonder that instinctively the engineer shrank from the commission of so fragrant an impiety as even to linger there with thoughts of a railway in his breast, and he at once decided to carry his line further to the west.

He was fortunate, as events proved, in this determination; for Mr. Waterton was peculiarly susceptible on the matter of the inviolable sanctity of the home he had provided for himself and his feathered friends, and he had odd and energetic modes of expressing his wrath. Moreover his anger had been especially excited because the Barnsley Canal had dared to wind its way, and to climb up and down by sundry locks, almost at the very gates of Mr. Waterton's park. One day, not very long after Mr. Swanwick had concluded his surveying expeditions, it devolved upon him and upon Mr. Hunt, the solicitor of the projected line, to wait upon Mr. Waterton, in order, if possible, to secure that gentleman's concurrence in the undertaking. On approaching the house by the drawbridge over the moat, the visitors rang the bell; Mr. Waterton himself answered it, and curtly demanded their errand. The solicitor in his gentlest tones intimated its nature. "Come in," said Mr. Waterton. The visitors obeyed; and Mr. Hunt explained the object they had in view. Mr. Waterton answered only with a portentous grunt. "We are anxious," said Mr. Hunt, "to obtain the favour of your assent to the line passing through your property." Mr. Waterton gave another grunt. "What reply may we return?" inquired Mr. Hunt, one of the blandest of men, in his blandest manner. "You may say," exclaimed Mr. Waterton, "that I am most confoundedly opposed." "May I be allowed to record that as your decision?" continued the solicitor. Mr. Waterton once more grunted. "I trust that if you cannot give your assent to the bill you will be neutral?" "Well," replied Mr. Waterton, "I will be neutral on condition that you will faithfully promise me one thing." "Pray, sir, what is it?" "It is that you take care that your railway, when it is established, shall ruin those infernal canals." Mr. Hunt could only in his most winning accents assure the irate naturalist that, while he could perhaps scarcely pledge himself to the entire destruction of the canal property, yet that those whom he represented would, he had no doubt, be delighted to do their best for the attainment of so laudable an end."

"And now," said Mr. Waterton, who had by this time aired his amiability, "come, gentlemen, and see my museum." They did so; and after examining a number of curiosities, which Mr. Waterton had brought from various parts of the world, the little party came to the top floor of the house, and there Mr. Waterton threw open a window, and looked out upon the grounds. "That," he said, "is a safe refuge for all the birds of the air. Everything is secure. No gun is ever fired here. I understand," he added somewhat abruptly, "that a fellow of the name of Swanwick, one of your engineers, once came into my park intending to bring the line this way. As sure as I am alive I would have shot him." "Allow me," gently interposed Mr. Hunt, "to introduce to you my friend Mr. Swanwick." "A good thing you didn't come," added Mr. Waterton, laughing; "I should have shot you!"

The bill and the plans of the North Midland Railway were completed amid the intense excitement involved in the preparation of a vast number of other schemes. George Stephenson and his engineers had several important works on hand; yet everything had to be finished by the date so inexorably defined by Parliament. Early and late they laboured on, till flesh and blood could hardly bear the strain. But within six hours of the time at which the documents must be deposited, an experienced draughtsman might have been seen working upon North Midland plans with the most painstaking love of his task, adding foliage to the trees in the parks, and touches of beauty to his handiwork generally. Suddenly several post-chaises dashed up at the door. The engineer leaped out, snatched up the daintily finished plans, laid them on the ground, remorselessly stitched them together, as quickly as possible corded them up in bundles, and then sent them flying away to Wakefield, Leeds, and other towns at which, before the clock struck twelve, they had all to be delivered.

When the bill came before Parliament, serious difficulties had to be encountered. It had originally been intended that the line should be carried up the valley to the left of Belper, and on through the village of Milford; but the Messrs. Strutt expressed apprehension lest the works should interfere with their supply of water from the river, and they succeeded in driving the line to the east of the town, through a long dismal cutting, where nothing can be seen either of the railway or from it.

The Aire and Calder Navigation, too, was a formidable antagonist to the new undertaking. "That body," said Mr. G. C. Glyn, "was perhaps the most opulent and influential of all that were connected with canals. They might be said to possess almost a monopoly of the traffic of a great part of Yorkshire. They were naturally very unwilling to encounter rivalry; and he did not blame them for it. They had accordingly met the Company with the most inveterate opposition from the very first, both in Parliament and elsewhere."

Eventually, in the House of Commons, the North Midland Company carried its bill; but in the House of Lords the canal interest so far prevailed as to secure the insertion of clauses which would have cramped the energies of the Company, and been seriously injurious to its prosperity. After the bill had passed, the Railway Company endeavoured to come to terms with the canal. But the latter insisted, at the outset of the negotiations, that they should be reimbursed all the expenses they had incurred in resisting the Railway Company in Parliament. "This," said Mr. Glyn, "was like the conduct of the schoolmasters who extracted from the pockets of the pupils the cost of the rod wherewith they themselves were to be flogged. The Directors did not feel themselves at liberty to accede to terms so unjust and so extravagant; and, therefore, the negotiations were for the present in abeyance." They hoped, however, by deviation from the parliamentary line in the neighbourhood of Leeds to overcome all difficulties, and an explanation of the course of action to be taken by the Company would hereafter be given, should the Navigation persist in its "extortionate demands."

In the early part of the following year (Feb. 1837), it was announced that arrangements for the commencement of the North Midland Railway had been made. The Clay Cross Tunnel, and other heavy works, were let. A site had been obtained for the terminus at Derby, which gave easy access to the Birmingham and Derby, and Midland Counties lines and station. Application was about to be made to Parliament for powers to effect some modifications of the line, at Belper, and elsewhere, and to secure increased land for station purposes at Leeds. "The proprietary," said the report of the Directors, with pardonable complacency, "is highly respectable, and affords an undoubted proof of the estimation in which this undertaking is held by the public." The executive engineer's office was established in Chesterfield; and arrangements were completed for the successful prosecution of the work.

In the summer of 1838 a bird's-eye view of the course of the North Midland line would have presented many a scene of interest. Thousands of men were at work; nearly all the contracts were proceeding with energy; and where it was otherwise, "steps had been taken to remove all cause of future complaint." The station at Derby had been marked out; the embankment near it was coming into shape; the Derby and Nottingham turnpike was being lowered; the tunnel at Milford was being made. At Belper Pool, the temporary bridge over the Derwent was finished, and the masonry was proceeding rapidly. At Wingfield, the heavy earthworks, comprising 350,000 cubic yards, were being excavated; and at Clay Cross 400 yards of tunnel had been completed, and six 15-horse whinseys were at work at the six shafts, from the bottom of which men were tunnelling at twelve different faces, besides the ends. To bore through a hill full of wet coal-measures was of course, in effect, to make a vast drain into which enormous volumes of water poured, which had to be pumped away; while at night the huge fires that blazed on the summit of the ridge lit up the rugged outline of the gangs of men, gave a strange and lurid colouring to the spectacle, and helped to make the spot the great wonder of that country side.

In other parts of the line difficulties had to be encountered, difficulties which have since become the commonplaces of the profession, but which then taxed the ingenuity of the engineer. Immediately to the north of what is now the Ambergate Station is a bold eminence, through which a cutting and a tunnel had to be carried. While

AMBERGATE TUNNEL.

making the excavations it was ascertained that the upper half of the hill rested on an inclined bed of wet shale, as slippery as soap. The mass was too lofty and too steep to allow of the removal of the whole; yet the ordinary shape of a tunnel would not afford sufficient strength to resist the enormous pressure. Accordingly it was resolved so to construct an elliptical tunnel of blocks of millstone grit that the flat arch of the ellipse should receive the weight. But the work had not been long completed when it was found that the solid stonework was splintered to such an extent as to endanger the safety of the structure. Fresh means had therefore to be provided: first, by the removal of some of the super-

E

incumbent mass, and by the drainage of the shale bed, that the material should be in part deprived of its unctuous character; and then, by lining most of the tunnel with iron ribs, it became, in fact, a double tunnel, —of milestone and of iron.

About a mile north of this work a perhaps more serious difficulty had to be overcome. Across the path of the future railway lay the Amber River and the Cromford Canal, so near together but at such different levels that the line must pass over the one by an embankment and bridge, and almost at the same moment under the other; and yet the works must be, if possible, so constructed as to avoid stopping the navigation for more than a few hours. As the line where it passes under the canal was itself to be an embankment, the foundations of the piers which were to carry the aqueduct overhead had necessarily to be laid at a considerable depth, and thence they must be raised to a sufficient height to support an iron trough

BULL BRIDGE.

which was to carry the water. This trough was made

the exact shape of the bottom of the canal, was fitted together closely, was then floated to its destination, and was finally sunk on to its resting place without disturbing the navigation, or being thenceforth itself disturbed. At this point, known as Bull Bridge, we have, therefore, a remarkable series of works. At the bottom is a river, and over it there are in succession a bridge, a railway, and an aqueduct; on the top ships are sailing, and underneath trains are running.

Among the heaviest earthworks on the line were the Oakenshaw cutting and embankment, which required the quarrying and tipping of some 600,000 yards of rock. There was also the Normanton cutting, from which 400,000 yards of stuff had to be removed. Yet the whole line, with its 200 bridges and seven tunnels, was completed in about three years, at an outlay of about £1,000,000 a year.

The North Midland line, as thus constructed, has two summit levels. It ascends nearly all the way from Derby, until, at the south end of Clay Cross tunnel, it is 360 feet above the sea. It then falls till it reaches Masborough, where it again begins to rise, and it continues to do so as far as Royston, from whence it slopes downward to Leeds.

The opening of the North Midland Railway, which took place on the 11th of May, 1840, was celebrated in a manner similar to that adopted by the Midland Counties Directors. A train, consisting of thirty-four carriages, containing some 500 passengers, and drawn by two engines, left Leeds at eight o'clock in the morning, was joined near Wakefield by a number of carriages from the York and North Midland line, and arrived at Derby at one o'clock. Here it was welcomed by the cheers of a crowd of spectators; and here, on the station platform, two long lines of tables had been spread with ample provisions, at which the visitors, solaced by music, stood to take their luncheon. After duly celebrating the honours of the occasion they returned home, well satisfied that they had witnessed the commencement of a new era in the history of English locomotion.

Those who are familiar with the North Midland Railway as it is, and who see the enormous traffic that rolls through the busy and growing population that environ it, may have some difficulty in understanding what the district was only thirty years ago. When many of its largest and richest iron fields had been untouched; when the Ambergate lime-works, and the Clay Cross collieries were unknown; when Staveley was only a name; when Sheffield was but half the size it now is; when neither South Yorkshire nor Derbyshire had sent, except by sea, a ton of coals to London; and when the new North Midland quietly ran over sixty miles of almost undisturbed coal-fields,—the line was but a phantom of what it is to-day. Since then, slowly and painfully, often under the pressing needs of its own poverty, yet constantly inviting and rewarding the enterprise of others around, the new Company has had to live on from hand to mouth, and gradually to develop for others the wealth it might some day be permitted humbly to share.

In the early part of 1841 the Directors were able to report that the traffic on their line was increasing. "The quantity of minerals conveyed along this railway," said one of the journals of the time, "is almost outstripping the accommodation at the disposal of the Company; but this inconvenience will easily be remedied. Very considerable additions to the traffic may be expected from the Clay Cross collieries and coke-works, which are on an extensive scale; the latter will, moreover, afford the Company the means of obtaining coke at a much lower cost than heretofore, and so be productive of a material saving in the annual expenditure. Mr. Stephenson's lime-kilns also, at Ambergate, are likely to supply to a great extent the midland counties with an article of great value in agriculture, the lime which is found in those counties being inconsiderable and of inferior quality. The North Midland Railway will also be used for conveying the produce of these kilns as far north as Barnsley."

The increase of accommodation thus required of course involved an increase of capital. A new station was required at Normanton, for the joint use of the North Midland, Manchester and Leeds, and York and North Midland Companies, and additional appliances were needed in the locomotive and carrying departments of the North Midland. To meet this outlay the Directors now proposed that an amount of £300,000 should be raised by shares, and £100,000, if necessary, by the exercise of their borrowing powers. The new shares would be "offered to the present proprietary in equal proportion to the number of shares respectively held by them;" and if they were not all accepted, the remainder would be disposed of to the public for the benefit of the Company. The new shares would be issued at 35 per cent. discount.

Meanwhile strenuous efforts were made to diminish expenditure. It was reported by a committee which was entrusted with this special duty, that a considerable number of the Company's servants—some of whom had been engaged in a work the cost of which would be properly chargeable to capital—might be discharged without detriment to the service; and that some of the salaries had been fixed at too high a scale. The committee therefore proposed that the allowance to the Directors be reduced one half; and that 10 per cent be deducted from the salaries of all officers who had more than £110 per annum, the station-masters alone excepted; and that 5 per cent. be taken from all salaries amounting to less than £110. It was also recommended that certain workpeople at the locomotive department at Derby should be discharged, so as to make a reduction of £3000; that the five superintendents of the Company's police should be dismissed, and the men be placed under the inspector of the line; that sundry other officials should be dispensed with; that the office of architect to the Company, which cost upwards of £1000 a year, should be abolished; that £3343 paid for the engineers' staff should be reduced to the extent of £2000 or thereabouts; that no assistant engineer should be retained on the staff of the executive engineer; and that the wages of porters, police, and "flagmen," should be slightly diminished. These reductions would amount to a total of £13,000. The committee added that they had been guided in the discharge of "a duty neither grateful to their feelings, nor light as to the time, anxiety, and labour expended," by the necessity that had arisen for "a strict observance of economy, so far as it could be secured without impairing either the efficient working of the line, or the convenience or safety of the public."

The spirit in which some who were connected with the Company laboured to improve its position, may be illustrated by a fact that ought to be mentioned. When Mr. Robert Stephenson had retired from the general management of the North Midland, it was considered desirable that he should be retained as superintendent of the locomotive department, at a salary of £1000 a year—a sum which was secured to him by agreement. But when the committee, who proposed the reductions to which we have referred, held their meeting, Mr. Stephenson not only gave valuable suggestions as to the best course that should be pursued, but, to set an example of the economy he wished to be practised, he wrote a letter to the chairman of the Company, requesting that half of a considerable balance due to him might be cancelled, and that £400 a year might be deducted from his salary. These sacrifices were the more to be commended, because Mr. Stephenson had recently incurred losses to the amount of £10,000.

At this meeting, held in August (1841), a motion was introduced, that proprietors should be permitted to travel free to the half-yearly meetings of the Company. The chairman replied, that it was most desirable that these meetings should be largely attended, but that there was no precedent for the course recommended; the matter, however, was one which the proprietors must decide for themselves. In a conversation that followed, some gentlemen suggested objections to the proposal, and requested that the motion might be withdrawn; but Mr. Bradley insisted that it should be put to the vote, not as a matter of personal saving, but because it was likely to effect the end which he had in view—of endeavouring to secure a large attendance at the meetings of the Company; and he was satisfied that the more this was the case, the greater would be the interest, and the better the management of affairs. The motion, however, was rejected by a majority of about 100 to 17.

During this year it was decided that for the future the report and accounts should be circulated a few hours before they were formally submitted to the proprietors. "There were, however," said the chairman, "strong objections to an earlier publication, principally as taking off from the interest of the meetings." In those days it was also the practice for the shareholders to be summoned simply by advertisement; and when it was proposed that each proprietor should have a circular forwarded him, the chairman, Mr. G. C. Glyn, demurred, on the ground that such an arrangement would be "unusual." We advert to these subjects to show how much more satisfactorily these matters are now arranged.

At the spring meeting, in 1842, the Directors were able to report "a continued increase in every branch of the revenue," notwithstanding "the unexampled distress which still pervaded the commercial world." They recommended that £3000 should be set aside from profits to provide for the renewal of locomotive and other stock; but they stated that a larger sum would hereafter be required. The dividend declared was at the rate of 3 per cent. per annum. It was stated that the management of the Company would for the future be carried on at Derby, instead of being conducted also in Leeds and London. Mr. G. C. Glyn now retired from the office of chairman, and was succeeded by Mr. Newton.

At this meeting an important debate took place on the subject of mineral traffic. A memorial had been presented by certain coal-owners and others, asking for a reduction of the rate from three halfpence to a penny a ton a mile, as an experiment for a year, from November, 1841; and this had been acceded to. Mr. Alston, one of the auditors, now expressed grave doubts whether the new rate yielded any profit whatever to the Company. He stated that the quantity carried during the previous six months had increased but little; and he believed that "the whole emolument from this coal traffic was a very bagatelle." Mr. Branker supported this opinion by saying that he had the authority of Mr. Booth, the secretary of the Liverpool and Manchester line, a gentleman of great practical experience, to the effect that unless coal paid twopence a ton a mile, "it was not worth having, and even at that it was very questionable." Of a penny rate Mr. Booth had declared that if "you take the wear and tear into consideration, you have nothing left; in fact, you do not get your own money back again." The chairman replied, that though the Directors had made no contract, they were, he thought, bound in honour to continue the experiment for the year. Thereupon a resolution was proposed, that at the expiration of that period the charge for coals should be increased to three halfpence a ton; but the meeting considered it unadvisable to forestall the future action either of the Board or of the Company; and the motion was withdrawn.

It is interesting, however, to recall these discussions, now that the Midland Company has so large a mineral traffic, and earns a profit at even a greatly reduced rate. They serve also to account for the fact that an important suggestion, offered about this time, was disregarded. It was made by Mr. Swanwick, the engineer, and was to the effect that extensions should be made from the North Midland to the vast coal districts lying to the west of Swinton and Wath; in fact, to the great South Yorkshire fields that have of late years fed the Great Northern system with mineral and profit. Had the advice been followed the destinies of both the Midland Company and the Great Northern would doubtless have been powerfully affected; but the North Midland Directors did not at that period consider the coal traffic of any special value, and did not deem themselves in a financial position sufficiently favourable to justify any large additional expenditure of capital.

The early part of 1842 was a time of disappointment to the shareholders. Complaint was made of extravagant outlay in the erection of unnecessary premises, and in the furnishing of refreshment and waiting rooms, some of which, it was declared, with the hyperbole of disappointed proprietors, were "more like drawing-rooms in palaces, than places of comfortable accommodation;" and chagrin was expressed that, notwithstanding much retrenchment of expenditure, the dividend was at the rate of only two per cent. per annum. The board could only share these regrets, and consent, however reluctantly, to the appointment of a committee of seven shareholders to examine "the position and future management" of the Company.

The report of this committee was presented in the following November (1842). It stated that delay in its presentation had originated from the fact that, though it had been forwarded to the chairman of the Directors two months previously, with a request for its immediate publication, the Board had declined to comply until they had prepared an answer which could be circulated at the same time. A lengthened debate followed, in which it was insisted upon that, as the Committee of Investigation had recommended deductions to the amount of nearly £18,000 a year, and the Directors had since admitted that £11,000 might be saved, the case of the committee was substantially proved, and that the administration of the Board was not deserving of confidence. This view of the matter was generally accepted; but Mr. Newton replied, that his colleagues were unanimously of opinion that the recommendations of the committee could not be carried out with safety to the public. "Then, may I ask," said a shareholder, "the intentions of the Directors?" The chairman answered that he really could not tell; and in the midst of confusion he declared the meeting dissolved, and vacated the chair.

The Directors appear however to have done their best to carry into effect the wishes of the proprietors. Six of the old Directors resigned their seats, and were replaced by the members of the late committee of inquiry; and the new Board endeavoured to accomplish various reductions of expenditure which had been previously proposed. But these efforts were resisted at the outset by the engine-drivers and firemen refusing to consent to any diminution of their numbers. This emergency was promptly met by the substitution of another set of men, who, with some exceptions, proved efficient. One serious accident, however, occurred, which created much public alarm. Further reforms were reported at the autumnal meeting of the year (1843). A reduction of one per cent. on loans falling due also relieved the finances of interest to the amount of £5000 a year. But the independent existence of the Company was now drawing to a close. Proposals were made, and not long afterwards negotiations were opened, for the amalgamation of the North Midland with the Midland Counties and Birmingham and Derby lines.

To the precise nature of these arrangements we shall have hereafter to advert.

CLAY CROSS.

CHAPTER III.

Influence of the Erewash Valley project on the politics of railway enterprise.—Origin of Birmingham and Derby scheme.—Meeting of "the inhabitants of Derby."—Sir Robert Peel's speech at Tamworth.—"Peel's Railway."—Cordial support of the new undertaking.—The Stonebridge branch.—Curious episode.—Abandonment of proposed Stitchford junction with London and Birmingham line.—Commencement of the works.—Course of the line.—Opening of the line to Hampton-in-Arden.—Discouragement.—Committee of investigation.—Completion of direct line to Birmingham.—Competition with Midland Counties Railway.—Proposals for amalgamation with Midland Counties and Northumberland Companies.—Terms proposed.—Objections.—Shareholders' meetings of the several Companies.—Final adjustment of terms.—First meeting of the Midland Railway Company.—Mr. Hudson's speech.—Resolutions for consolidating the three properties.—First General Meeting of Shareholders, July 16th, 1844.—Hopefulness of October Meeting.—Large increase of capital sanctioned.

THE coal-owners of the Valley of the Erewash were destined to exercise a powerful influence on the politics of railway enterprise in the Midland counties of England. It is true that their own peculiar project, which would have brought a line to their pit mouths, was, to their infinite chagrin, placed for years in abeyance; but the very fact that that Pinxton branch was projected, was sufficient, as we have seen, to arouse the jealousy of the North Midland Company, and even led to the construction of yet a third line,—the Birmingham and Derby.

In September, 1835,—the same autumn that Stephenson and his secretary went in the yellow post-chaise on their surveying expedition to Leeds,—"Old George" came over to Birmingham, and took up his quarters at the Hen and Chickens, in order to make arrangements for commencing his new undertaking, by which to connect the centre of the hardware district of England with Derby and the North. Here he found no difficulty in associating with himself a number of influential persons who showed a practical interest in the enterprise. Mr. Henry Smith,—a manufacturer, of high social standing, who might have represented Birmingham in parliament, had he been so disposed, consented to be the first chairman of the Company. Mr. William Beale,—one of the oldest and most respected inhabitants of the town,—whose son Mr. Samuel Beale subsequently became chairman of the Midland Railway Company,—and other gentlemen of similar position became directors, and they constituted, as was lately remarked by one who knew them well, "a first-rate board."

But the circumstances under which the undertaking was first publicly submitted to the consideration of the people of Derby, were more amusing than encouraging. An announcement had been made, in terms of befitting dignity, that a deputation from the promoters of this great enterprise were about to confer with "the inhabitants of Derby," and to seek the support of the said "inhabitants" in carrying it out. The deputation accordingly, at the appointed time, arrived at the hotel, and proceeded to prepare for the duties that lay before them, by dining together. This important part of the programme being concluded, a messenger was despatched to the room, to ascertain in what number "the inhabitants of Derby" had responded to the invitation; and he returned with the intelligence that only three persons were present: three persons, out of a population of many thousands, were all who had thought it worth their while to ascertain on what terms direct railway communication might be obtained with Birmingham and the West of England. The deputation waited half an hour; and then another messenger was despatched, who reported that now twelve people in all had arrived of "the inhabitants of Derby." The folding doors that separated the dining-room and the hall were now withdrawn. The deputation, with all the dignity they could muster, advanced to the platform, and proceeded to unfold their budget to the twelve men of Derby. Fortunately there were some in that audience who were able as well as willing to render efficient assistance in starting so great an enterprise.

At Tamworth a more fitting assembly was convened to express their interest in the project. Sir Robert Peel, one of the members for the borough, spoke in warm approbation of it, and took a comprehensive view of the various similar undertakings then in contemplation. "At the close of the next session," he said, 'we shall probably start them. Besides the lines of railway from London to Liverpool, through Birmingham, there will be a line between Birmingham and Gloucester, effecting a direct communication with the port of Bristol, and, through it, to the West Indies. We shall also find a line connecting Derby with Leeds. Supposing this to be the case, I think, under such circumstances, you cannot entertain a doubt, when you consider the wealth, intelligence, and commercial enterprise of the people of Yorkshire and the North, that they will, by some means or other, effect a communication with Birmingham and its important adjacent districts, as well as the other parts of the kingdom, by an union of these great lines." He then expressed his approval of the route that had been selected; his belief that "on account of the valleys and the natural levels of the country, it will be found that the line could be executed at considerably less expense than any other;" and concluded by saying,—"I most cordially hope this project will succeed; I shall give it my assent as a landed proprietor, and I shall support it in my place in parliament." We need scarcely add that at that time the name of Sir Robert Peel was itself a tower of strength; and so much interest did he manifest in the undertaking, that it was come to be familiarly designated "Peel's Railway."

The project had also substantial support from other quarters. The great landowners—the Marquis of Anglesea, Sir Oswald Mosley, Bart., and others, also gave in their hearty adhesion; and the brewers at Burton-on-Trent, and the towns and the population on the line of road, cordially supported the undertaking. So popular did it become, that as soon as the £100 shares were issued. they rose to 19 premium. "The thing," said one who was connected with it, "took fire like a match."

The Birmingham and Derby line was, as we have seen, originally projected in the interest of the North Midland, and avowedly to connect Derby and the manufacturing districts of Yorkshire with Birmingham and the West. Such an undertaking was of course a serious discouragement to the hopes that had been cherished by the Midland Counties that their connection with the London and Birmingham at Rugby would secure the western trade for themselves; but probably they would have borne their disappointment with tolerable composure had not the other proposed branch line from Whitacre junction to Hampton-in-Arden—the Stonebridge branch, as it was called—of the Birmingham and Derby Company threatened the Midland Counties with direct competition for the traffic with London and the South.

Before any of the three Companies had obtained the sanction of parliament to their projects, a curious episode occurred. The Midland Counties board was urged by the Birmingham and Derby to abandon their Pinxton branch on condition that the Stonebridge branch also was withdrawn. These negotiations were carried so far that they were regarded by the representatives of the Birmingham and Derby Company as concluded; and on the last day on which the advertisements required by parliament could be issued, the Stonebridge branch was omitted from the Birmingham and Derby project. To the chagrin of the latter, however, they found that the Midland Counties Company had retained the Pinxton branch in the announcement of their undertaking. What was to be done? Country newspapers were then published only once a week, and it was now too late to amend the advertisement of the Birmingham and Derby line in all the newspapers of the district through which the railway was to run. Fortunately for themselves—though not for their rivals—the acuteness of the solicitors was sufficient for the emergency. They suggested that another company might yet be projected. Another line might be proposed from Whitacre to Hampton-in-Arden, along the precise route of the proposed Stonebridge branch, and this might be afterwards incorporated with the Birmingham and Derby. Their plan was adopted. Three days afterwards, a Birmingham paper contained an announcement that a new Company was about to be formed to make a line, to be called "The Stonebridge Junction Railway;" and eventually, when the projects were before parliament, this undertaking was united with that from which it had been temporarily severed, and the consolidated body was entitled "The Birmingham and Derby Junction" Railway Company.

Thus did these two little branch lines—the Pinxton and the Stonebridge—vitally affect the position, the policy, and the fate of the three great Companies with which they were connected. Had the Pinxton branch been unattempted, the North Midland would not, at any rate at that period, have thought of urging the formation of the Stonebridge branch, and even of the Birmingham and Derby itself; yet, eventually, as we shall find, it was the Stonebridge branch that enabled the Birmingham and Derby to carry on a fierce and effective competition with the Midland Counties, and finally to insist on terms of amalgamation that otherwise would never have been conceded.

In the original bill it was provided that the new line should join the London and Birmingham Railway at a place three or four miles south of Birmingham, called Stichford. Subsequently it was determined to secure an independent entrance to Birmingham, and powers were accordingly obtained for the line to follow the course of the Valley of the Tame, to a separate terminus at Lawley Street—now the low level goods station of the Midland Company.

In August, 1837, it was announced to the shareholders that the work of constructing the line had been commenced. The land had been taken; the bridges at Derby over the canal, and the Derwent, and the viaduct over the Anker, had been commenced; and the important works at Tamworth had been let to an experienced contractor. Mr. Henry Smith, the chairman, also stated that the Company had endeavoured to obtain an amendment of the Act to authorize them to make a line from Tamworth to Rugby, but that the proposal had encountered such severe opposition that it had been withdrawn. Failing in this, the directors had decided to begin without delay the Hampton branch of their line, by means of which they would be brought near to Rugby and have their course opened to the South; and it was estimated that this part of their works might be completed within twelve months of the opening of the London and Birmingham Railway.

By Midsummer, 1838, the whole of the land required between Derby and Hampton had been purchased, and at a cost in excess of the grant by estimate of only about £10,000. The cuttings and embankments were found to be nearly equal in amount, and only about 55,000 cubic yards to the mile; and most of the excavations being in red marl or gravel, abundance of excellent material was supplied for the formation of the permanent way. Each of the three Companies had bought ground near to Derby for a general station; on this subject all had agreed, and we may add—they agreed on nothing else.

The contractors undertook that the line should be ready to receive the trains as early as the 30th of June, 1839, and it was opened from Derby to Hampton-in-Arden in an unusually early period for so considerable an undertaking. The line of country is however very favourable for a railway. No tunnel was required; the only important embankment is that in the neighbourhood of Tamworth, and the gradients of half the lines are slight, and on the other half are level. The chief works of the

THE ANKER VIADUCT.

engineer were at the Anker viaduct, near Tamworth, formed of eighteen arches at 30 feet span, and one oblique arch of 60 feet span. There was a viaduct of nearly a quarter of a mile in length, which rested on 1000 piles, near Walton.

The period that followed the opening of the line was

however discouraging. Coaches were still running between Birmingham and Derby. Additional capital had also been spent. Only a small dividend was paid, and the hope of future prosperity was dependent on the completion of the North Midland and other lines, which might bring an accession of traffic.

Thus things dragged their slow length along till, at the general meeting held at Birmingham in August, 1841, the chairman stated that, though the receipts had improved, and the prospects of the undertaking were encouraging, he thought that it would be desirable for the shareholders to appoint a committee to investigate the condition of the Company. The suggestion was adopted, and the report was shortly afterwards presented.

This document indicated several methods in which the administration of affairs might be improved; and with regard to the future the committee expressed themselves hopefully. They stated that Mr. Robert Stephenson agreed with them that the local traffic would increase; that the opening of three new stations on the direct line between Whitacre and Birmingham would produce at least £20 a week each additional; that the traffic of Tamworth, Atherstone, Coleshill, and the adjoining districts, when brought by the new route nearer to Birmingham, would be considerably augmented; and that the opening of the direct route to Birmingham would relieve the Company from the toll paid to the London and Birmingham,—an amount equal to one per cent. on the whole capital,—and would provide improved facilities for the transmission of goods and minerals.

Every effort was now made to press forward the completion of the main line into Birmingham. Passenger stations also were established at Castle Bromwich, Water Orton, and Forge Mills (for Coleshill), and it was intended to add one or two more. The traffic, too, increased 16 or 17 per cent. The total expenditure at Christmas, 1841, amounted to rather more than £1,000,000; the cost, including two terminal stations and rolling stock, averaging £24,000 a mile. In the following June, £100,000 additional capital, besides the usual proportion by means of borrowing powers was raised by the allotment of new shares *pro rata* among the shareholders at a heavy discount.

The events that followed the separate history of this company were of little moment. Some economies were made; expectations were raised with regard to the effects of a proposed connection with the Birmingham and Gloucester line so soon as it should be finished, and with other railways to the north, and the discussions with the Midland Counties Company on the subject of the mandamus dragged their slow length along. The contention of the Birmingham and Derby was, that their line was the first opened; that it conveyed passengers from Derby to London for a year before the Midland Counties was able to do so; that it had then carried 200,000 passengers in perfect safety; that previous to the opening of the Midland Counties the directors of the Birmingham and Derby had commenced negotiations for an "equitable division" of the traffic to the south; that the first reduction of fares had been made by the Midland Counties; and that the Birmingham and Derby board had offered to refer the whole question to the arbitration of Mr. George Carr Glyn, the chairman of the London and Birmingham and North Midland railways. "Our line, too," said Mr. Kahrs, "is incapable of being interfered with by new lines, except for its benefit. Not so the others. He had been for some time expecting the announcement of a more direct line between London and York, by way of Peterborough and Lincoln;

and that morning's post brought news that this was already talked of on the Stock Exchange. And what," he asked, "would then be the position of the Midland Counties and North Midland lines?"

At length, however, this controversy drew towards a close; and the directors of the Birmingham and Derby Company announced that with an earnest desire to develop the resources, and to reduce the cost of working the line, they had "approved of a proposition of the directors of the North Midland Railway for an amalgamation of the three lines of railway which centre in Derby, as a measure that would be highly beneficial to them all;" and eventually it was decided that the proprietors should be urged to sanction such an arrangement. The chief feature of it, so far as the Birmingham and Derby Company was affected, was, that its shareholders should receive a smaller dividend on each £100 share than those of the other Companies. To this it was replied that inasmuch as the Birmingham Company and also the Midland Company were suffering from the effects of competition, they ought first to have the opportunity of testing the value of their property when freed from such influences, and that then, and not till then, the relative worth of each could be fairly ascertained.

This opinion was supported by Mr. Dicey, the chairman of the Midland Counties meeting, held September 21st, 1843. The proposal for amalgamation having been moved by Mr. John Ellis and seconded by Mr. William Hannay, the Chairman stated that he had "the misfortune to differ from the plan which had been proposed," on the ground that while the chief, if not the whole, benefit in the economy of expenditure and the increase of receipts would be secured by the cessation of hostilities between the two lines south of Derby, yet the North Midland would secure for itself thousands a year of additional revenue, of which it would not "earn one penny." Mr. Dicey contended that the profits of the two southern lines, freed from competition, ought to be divided between them; and that when the two properties had thus risen to their fair market value, an equitable basis would be supplied on which to form more intimate relations with the North Midland. These objections were, however, after protracted discussion, overruled, and the majority in favour of amalgamation was found to be overwhelming. A joint committee was now arranged—consisting of members from each board—to complete the details of the amalgamation, and to secure the general and final sanction of the several bodies of proprietors. In the course of these negotiations it was determined that Birmingham and Derby shareholders should receive 27*s.* 6*d.* per annum less dividend per £100 share than the proprietors of the other two Companies. These and other terms were approved at meetings of the three Companies held on the 16th and 17th of April, 1844.

The first general meeting of the shareholders of the now consolidated Midland Railway Company was held at Derby, on Tuesday, July 16th, 1844. Mr. Hudson, Chairman of the Board of Directors, presided. He stated that up to the 30th of June the accounts of the three Companies had been kept separate, and that the profits to that period would be divided among the proprietors of those Companies as if no consolidation had taken place. It had been found that the increase of receipts of the three Companies, as compared with those of the corresponding period of the previous year, already amounted to more than £21,000; that the decrease of payments was nearly £9,000; and that the net increase of divisible profits, exclusive of the last balance in hand, was about £33,000. The reduction of expenditure would not, however, be complete until after the expiration of the current quarter, when the salaries of many members of the three staffs would cease. "This reduction," said the directors, "of many useful and valuable officers has been the most painful part of our duty; and it will afford us great pleasure should we be able to assist them in speedily procuring appointments." The last dividends for the half-year of the three separate Companies were as follows:—

	£	s.	d.
North Midland £100 shares	2	2	0
Midland Counties £100 shares	2	2	6
Birmingham and Derby original shares . . .	1	6	6

It will be interesting to note that the total returns for the now united line for the week amounted to a little over £10,000.

We have now reached a memorable period in the history of our subject: the Midland Railway Company, as we understand it, had now been formed.

CHAPTER IV.

Birmingham and Gloucester railway.—The Society of Friends.—Early difficulties of the new project.—The route chosen.—Tramway from Cheltenham and Gloucester.—Progress of works.—The Lickey incline.—Norris's engine.—Opening of part of the line.—Railway tickets adopted.—Carriage of coals.—Committee of inquiry.—A Money bill.—Report of the committee.—Proposed amalgamation with Midland Company.—Bristol and Gloucester.—Coal-pit Heath tramway.—Cheltenham and Great Western union.—Bristol and Gloucester a broad gauge line.—Overtures for a union with the Birmingham and Gloucester.—Opening of the line.—An early break down.—Inconveniences of the break of gauge at Gloucester. —Negociations with Birmingham and Gloucester resumed.—Rival claimants for a western belle.—Terms of the settlement.—Amalgamation with the Midland Railway Company.—Access of Midland Company to New Street Station, Birmingham.—Mr. John Ellis's successful negotiations.

THE line of Midland railway that now connects Birmingham and Bristol is the result of the amalgamation of what were originally four distinct undertakings. It is true that, so far back as 1824, it was proposed that a through line should be made by a single company; that a meeting, "respectably and numerously attended," was held at the White Lion Hotel, Bristol, to carry out the idea; that a large sum of money was subscribed; that a deposit of 40*s*. was ordered to be paid on each share within forty-eight hours; and that, at the end of that time, there was not a defaulter. "Then, why," asked Mr. George Jones, twenty years afterwards, when chairman of the Bristol and Gloucester Company, "why was not the scheme prosecuted? Because," he replied, "the thing was not then well understood. We had not then a Brunel, nor the Stephensons, nor others who might be named. A partial survey of the proposed line was made, and legal and other expenses were incurred, but after some months the intention was abandoned; and, to the credit of the parties concerned, and especially of the solicitors, the deposits were returned with less than half a crown a share deducted for costs."

This scheme for a united through railway having thus fallen into abeyance, the work was left to be undertaken in fragments by various parties, and at different times; but chiefly in two portions—from Birmingham to Gloucester, and from Gloucester to Bristol. To the former of these we have now to advert.

It is here worthy of remark that several of the pioneers of English railway enterprise have been connected with the Society of Friends. The far-sightedness in business matters with which that body is not undeservedly credited, led several of its members at an early period to anticipate that these paths of iron would some day become the highways of inland communication. No sooner was this conviction formed, than action was taken; and while Edward Pease at Darlington, James Cropper at Liverpool, Edward Fry at Bristol, and John Ellis at Leicester were labouring to solve the early practical problems connected with their several railway undertakings, the Sturges—Joseph and Charles—were similarly engaged at Birmingham. As early as 1832, they employed Brunel—then almost a youth—to make a survey for a cheap line between Birmingham and Gloucester. Any further action was, however, suspended; and before long Brunel was taken into the service of the Great Western Company.

The chief difficulty with which the friends of the Birmingham and Gloucester railway had from the outset to contend, was the commonplace one of lack of funds. Canvassing for shareholders went on for years, and the promoters of the undertaking were only too thankful to persuade now one person and now another to become a subscriber. Even when the success of railway enterprise elsewhere gave an impulse to the movement, all the arrangements of the Company, and the very route along which the line was taken, were cramped by considerations of economy. Captain Moorson, the engineer (the brother of the late chairman of the London and North Western Company) was engaged on the modest terms of "no success—no pay." Though the best course for the proposed line would have been through the towns of Stourbridge, and perhaps Dudley, Bromsgrove, Droitwich, Worcester, and Tewkesbury, all these places had to be avoided in order to diminish expense; and in the first instance the direction chosen was such that even Cheltenham should not be touched. The outcry was, however, so energetic, that this part of the arrangement had to be modified: £200,000 additional capital had to be raised, the line was taken more to the east; and, though Worcester was left out, Cheltenham was approached. We may add that the Birmingham and Gloucester was the earliest railway bill that was sanctioned the first time it was submitted to Parliament. One disadvantage of the route finally adopted was that it passed down what is known as the Lickey Incline. To avoid this, Mr. Brunel had proposed that the line should be carried farther to the east, by which he would have secured, what was then deemed indispensable to a heavy traffic, a gradient of 1 in 300. Such a course would, however, have been to give a yet wider berth to the towns and the population, and it was rejected.

In laying out the Birmingham and Gloucester line, the promoters resolved to avail themselves of an old tramway that ran from Cheltenham to Gloucester city and docks. It had cost about £50,000, had been in use for mineral and goods traffic for some 30 years, and had been worked, at first by horses, and subsequently by locomotives built by J. J. Tregelles Price, of Neath Abbey, near Swansea, another "Friend." This tramway was purchased and incorporated with the new undertaking; it was, however, agreed that in the event of a line being brought from Swindon to connect the Great Western Railway with Cheltenham, the two Companies should share in the use and in the cost of the tramway. Meanwhile the hopes of the proprietors were stimulated by the estimate that their profits would amount to "14 per cent. *nearly*."

The first half-yearly report of the Company was presented on February 1st, 1837. Some of the engineering works had been commenced, and shafts had been sunk for an intended tunnel at Moseley; but there had been difficulty at some points in consequence of the exorbitant demand of the landowners. The directors expressed their gratification that the capital of the Company had been "forthcoming with a commendable alacrity, which left no doubt of the whole being obtained at the various periods at which it might be required." But this satisfaction was shortlived; for in the autumn of the same year it was announced, that in consequence of a period of unexampled monetary difficulty, and a reaction in public opinion with regard to such undertakings, there had been an inadequate response to the appeals of the directors. It was, however, hoped that by some improvements that had been made in the arrangements, the works would be pushed vigorously forward; and it was believed that when the line was finished the traffic would be little inferior to that of any railway in the kingdom.

In 1838 the works were rapidly advancing. The contracts for the various descriptions of earthwork, masonry, iron, and fencing, had been divided and let to parties more conversant with each. The geological formation of the country also had been found to be favourable. "The line of junction between the new red sandstone formation and that of the lias runs for several miles parallel to the line of the railway, affording excellent building materials within a few hundred yards of the line, while the railway excavations and embankments are kept within the dry and good materials furnished by the marl and soft sandstone." Nearly 500 acres of land had been required.

TEWKESBURY.

Some time previous to the opening of the line, arrangements were in contemplation for conducting its traffic up and down Lickey Incline by means of locomotives. This was, by both Brunel and George Stephenson, declared to be impracticable. Captain Moorson, however, when in America, had seen engines mount inclines equally steep, and twelve or fourteen of them were accordingly ordered from a builder, one Norris, of Philadelphia, the chief peculiarity of which was that their driving wheels were only 3 feet in diameter. On arriving in this country, and being tested, they did all that was expected from them. Subsequently, Mr. Bury, the well-known engine builder, declared that whatever American engines could do his could do; and he sent one with a five-foot driving wheel for trial. Mr. Bury and Mr. Charles Sturge, of Birmingham, mounted the "Bury" at Bromsgrove, and as it passed through the station, Mr. Sturge humorously called to Gwynn, who had come with the American engines, to join him. "No," he said; "it's no use; you'll soon come back again;" and "back again" they came; for by reason of some conditions which are not easily to be explained, the larger wheels would not "bite" the rails like the smaller ones, and the engine could not mount the incline. The Americans have, however, since been superseded; and the incline is now worked by ordinary engines, aided by a "pilot," with perfect efficiency and success. The last American locomotive was used for some time on the Tewkesbury branch.

On the 24th of June, 1840, the portion of line between Cheltenham and Bromsgrove, 31 miles in length, was opened for passenger traffic. It appears that the directors did not wait for the sanction of the Board of Trade, who were needlessly suspicious of the safety of some of the works. At the ensuing meeting of the shareholders it was stated that the financial results of the enterprise were so far satisfactory that "the cheering inference might be fairly drawn that when the whole line was in operation the traffic would be increased to an amount far exceeding any calculations that had hitherto been made."

Railway tickets, as we now know them, were first adopted on the Birmingham and Gloucester line. Mr. Edmundson, of Manchester, who invented them, consented for a trifling consideration that they should be used by the company, in order that their advantages might be fairly tested and publicly known.

Among the earlier problems of railway administration

was whether coal could be carried to any great distance from the pits at a profit. This question came under the consideration of the Birmingham and Gloucester directors as early as the year 1842, when some coal merchants intimated that they wished to open a trade on the new line. Accordingly "a small quantity was conveyed by way of experiment, at a price which barely reimbursed the cost of conveyance;" but as the result it was reported that "till a return traffic could be found, the coal trade down the line would not be remunerative to the Company."

A special meeting of the proprietors was held on the 18th of January, 1843, at Birmingham, in compliance with a requisition to the directors signed by nearly 1000 shareholders, for the purpose of "considering and determining as to the appointment of a committee of shareholders, *not being directors* of the said Company," who should ascertain the state of the Company financially, materially, and otherwise. Captain Moorson, Chairman of the directors, who presided, said that the number of shares represented by the document fell short of those which were required to make it legal, but that the directors had waived that consideration, and had convened the meeting. He stated that the directors saw no objection to the appointment of a joint committee, consisting of an equal number of shareholders and directors; but that the appointment of a committee from which directors were excluded was to raise the question of confidence. A lengthened discussion followed, in the course of which it was declared that the estimated cost of the line had been largely exceeded, and that there had been many mistakes in its administration. At High Orchard, at Gloucester, for instance, said one of the critics, there is what is called a wet basin, "so ingeniously constructed as to be fed by a stream of water which is fast filling it up with mud, and so admirably situated as to be inaccessible. The presumption would be that this is a receptacle intended for traffic, and that it will be surrounded by sheds and warehouses for the reception of goods; but the only buildings contiguous are six large coke ovens, which are not at work because the coke could be contracted for elsewhere on better terms. The wet basin," continued the speaker, "is a melancholy spectacle; especially when it is considered that at the bottom of its foul waters lie something like £14,000 of our money."

It was also stated at the meeting that the rates required careful reconsideration, that the communication between Spetchley and Worcester was unsatisfactory, and that terms might be made with the Bristol and Gloucester line which would be advantageous to the Company. It was not unnaturally added that, "until the proprietors obtained a dividend they would never cease to be discontented." The Chairman replied to some of these criticisms, and eventually stated that the directors would concede to a proposition of four shareholders on the committee to three directors; and a resolution to that effect was carried unanimously.

At the half-yearly meeting held in the following month, a dividend was recommended of 25*s.* a share. It was understood that the committee of inquiry was slowly proceeding with its work. Another special meeting was convened for the following month, to consider the provisions of a "Money Bill," under which a sum of £250,000 (with the usual permission to borrow one third more) would be raised, the amount being required for making a branch to Worcester, for water connection at Gloucester, for the completion of the works at High Orchard, and for other purposes. Some shareholders, it was said, might counsel delay in obtaining this bill; but, "delay," said the directors, "would oblige the Company to continue borrowing on the inferior security of loan notes, and therefore at a higher rate of interest than would be demanded on the security of mortgage bonds. Delay would leave the High Orchard branch open to a competing company, which would be interested in obstructing the communication of the railway with the water—a connection indispensable, in the opinion of the carriers, to a full development of the goods traffic. Delay would continue the loss and inconvenience arising from the defective communication with Worcester. Delay would bring over again the expenses already incurred, and which always unavoidably attend an application to Parliament. Delay, on the other hand, presents no advantages commensurate with the evils before enumerated." Eventually, by a narrow majority, the money bill was sanctioned.

The committee of inquiry presented their report in the following June. It was of considerable length, and many of the matters with which it dealt have little interest now. Its conclusions may therefore be briefly epitomised. The committee approved of power being taken to raise the £333,333 6*s.* 8*d.* additional capital; they considered the outlay of £14,000 on the High Orchard property to have been injudicious; they had instructed the directors to proceed with a branch line to Worcester, the passenger traffic for which had hitherto been carried by omnibus from Spetchley; and they put on record their regret that in the first design of the railway effort had not been made to secure better accommodation for towns so important as Worcester, Tewkesbury, and Cheltenham. They reported fully on the position and prospects of the traffic; and although they had no hesitation in stating their opinion that on the completion of the Bristol and Gloucester line the passenger traffic would be equal to the parliamentary estimates, yet that meanwhile there was a serious deficiency. As the year (1843) passed on the position of the company did not improve. Expenses were large, trade languished. So doubtful did the prospects of the future appear, that application was made to parliament for powers to "sell or to lease their railway, or parts thereof," to the London and Birmingham, the Grand Junction, the Great Western, or the Bristol and Gloucester Companies. Meanwhile, it was intimated that the Great Western Company would not be unwilling to purchase or lease the whole of the Birmingham and Gloucester line; but on a deputation being appointed to meet a deputation from the Great Western, it was found that the intentions of the latter had been misunderstood.

In 1846 the directors announced that they had made arrangements with the Grand Junction, the Birmingham and Derby, and the Manchester and Birmingham, for the reciprocal interchange of goods "on terms which must promote the mutual interest of the companies so working together." Mr. Robert Stephenson had been directed to survey the ground for a branch to Worcester, and "he had presented a very able and satisfactory report, by which the board were willing to abide." The line between Tewkesbury and Ashchurch was now worked by engine instead of horse-power. No event of special interest marked the brief remainder of the annals of this line as a separate affair. We shall have shortly to see, in another connection, the circumstances under which the Company lost its individuality and became merged in a larger and comprehensive undertaking.

We now turn to the second principal portion of the Birmingham and Bristol line, that which extends from Gloucester to Bristol.

In doing so we must go back to the year 1838, and by a mental effort try to realize the then condition of affairs. A tramway had been made, extending a few miles to the north-east of Bristol to a point now known as the Westerleigh Junction; here it turned away to the left, and threw off several branches, one of which continued to Coalpit Heath. This tramway was called the Coalpit Heath line, and it was proposed that the greater part of it should now be incorporated into the new railway to Gloucester.

Again, at the northern end of the projected line another railway was in contemplation. It was to be called "The Cheltenham and Great Western Union." It was not at that period identified with the Great Western; but it was to be made on the broad gauge, to start from Swindon, to climb up and then to descend the Stroud Valley, to emerge into the open at Stonehouse, and thence to pursue its way to Gloucester and Cheltenham.

The Bristol and Gloucester line being thus flanked on the east and south by the broad gauge, it became committed to broad gauge interests; the line was made as a broad gauge line; and the engineer was that dauntless champion of broad gauge schemes, Brunel himself. In this arrangement there were important advantages: the same railway from Stonehouse to Gloucester could be used by both the new companies; the same station at Gloucester was available for both; a junction could be effected at Bristol with the Bristol and Exeter system; and negotiations were at one time entertained by which the Great Western Company should work the Bristol and Gloucester line. In recognition of these benefits it was arranged that a rent should be paid to the Cheltenham and Great Western Union for the use of the line between Stonehouse and Gloucester of £11,000 a year;

for the portion between Gloucester and Cheltenham, £4000 a year; and for the three stations, £3500 a year; these charges to include the maintenance of the permanent way, parochial and police expenses, and wages. After five years the rent was to be raised £1000. The Bristol and Gloucester Company also agreed to subscribe £50,000 towards the purchase of shares in the capital of a projected extension of the Bristol and Exeter line to Plymouth.

But though the Bristol and Gloucester line was thus originated in broad gauge interests, there were persons of influence who began to recognise the fact that its chief value would be found as part of a through route to Birmingham—a link of connection between the west, the south-west, and the midlands and the north of England. It was with this view that important improvements were effected in the gradients and course of the line within the parliamentary limits of deviation; involving, fortunately, a saving in earthworks to the amount of one-fifth of the original estimate. As early, too, as 1840—four years before the railway was completed—direct negotiations arose between the boards of the Birmingham and Gloucester and Bristol and Gloucester Companies, with a view to a union on equal terms of the two properties; and it was proposed that the portion that belonged to the Cheltenham Company should be obtained by purchase.

The first half-yearly meeting of the Bristol and Gloucester line was held Sept. 29th, 1842, at Bristol. It was reported that the contracts between Westerleigh and Stonehouse were proceeding satisfactorily. The depressed state of the iron trade had enabled the board to supply themselves with rails on favourable terms. Continuous timber bearings were to be used for the support of the rails.

On the 8th of July, 1844, the new line was opened for passenger traffic. A large number of persons assembled at Gloucester to welcome the arrival of the first train; but, unfortunately, it did not approach with the dignity of demeanour befitting so august an occasion. On rounding a rather sharp curve within half-a-mile of its destination, in consequence of a defect in bolting one of the

GLOUCESTER.

sleepers on which the rails rested, the engine went off the rails, and dragged several of the carriages after it. The train was proceeding slowly; the passengers alighted uninjured, and were able to reach the terminus on foot. Here a large party partook of a late breakfast, and speeches were delivered in honour of the occasion.

In the year 1845 the negotiations for a union of the Birmingham and Gloucester and Bristol and Gloucester lines, which had previously been unsuccessful, were resumed. It had been found that the meeting of two independent lines with different gauges had involved serious disadvantages and losses to both companies; and with a view of introducing uniformity of system and of gauge, it was resolved that there ought to be identity of interest. At present, however, it was undetermined whether the broad gauge should be carried through to Birmingham, or the narrow gauge be continued to Bristol: an issue which might appear of secondary moment, but which really involved the question whether

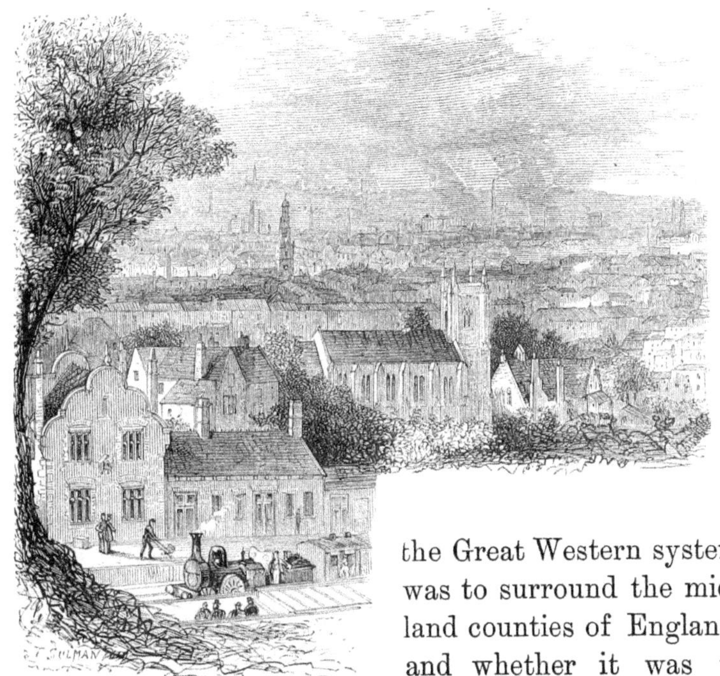

BRISTOL.

the Great Western system was to surround the midland counties of England, and whether it was to perpetuate a conflict of gauge between the north and the west. This was a rivalry, too, in which—though the Midland and the Great Western Companies were the chief competitors—all existing railways were concerned. And thus it came to pass that the two western lines which had been struggling for existence found that they were engaging national attention, the objects of national interest, a prize to be contended for by eager rivals. All this was very flattering to a hitherto unappreciated western belle, who began to feel how pleasant it was to flirt now with one admirer and anon with another, to weigh their respective claims, and eventually to secure for the honour of her alliance a very substantial settlement. The rivalry was close and keen. The endowment offered by the Great Western was in share capital; that of the Midland was in cash—a guaranteed six per cent. dividend. The terms proposed by Mr. Saunders for the Great Western would have been accepted had not Mr. Ellis, on the very same day, submitted his offer on behalf of the Midland, and carried off the palm.

The narrow gauge lookers-on were delighted. The London and North Western Company had been especially anxious to keep the broad gauge in the west; and, with the view of backing up the Midland Company in its conflict, undertook for a time to share in any loss the Midland might incur by its somewhat onerous terms of purchase. The aid thus promised by the London and North Western was subsequently altered, by arrangement, into permission for the Midland to use the New Street Station at Birmingham, which had cost an enormous sum of money, for the nominal rent, besides charges for porters, of £100 a year.

The terms of agreement were sanctioned by the different companies in the usual manner. At the Midland meeting, August 12th, 1845, Mr. Hudson, in commending the lease to the adoption of the shareholders, said: "I take no credit to myself, gentlemen, for having originated this arrangement. My friend, Mr. Ellis, to whom I wish to give all the credit which is so justly his due, suggested to the board this bold course; and I candidly confess that, at first, I shrank from incurring further liabilities on the part of the Midland Company. On looking, however, more closely into the matter, and reflecting on the greater accommodation which by means of this arrangement we could offer to the public, feeling, too, that small and independent companies could not supply such advantages, and having examined carefully the accounts, I concurred most cordially in the views of my excellent colleague, Mr. Ellis, and I am here to-day to take whatever share of the responsibility may attach to me."

On a subsequent occasion, Mr. Ellis remarked that when, by force of circumstances, it had devolved upon him to negotiate the arrangements with the Birmingham and Bristol Company, he had not the opportunities he could have desired of consulting his colleagues; "but having since deliberated on the matter for weeks and months, he was more firmly convinced than ever of the wisdom of the step which had been taken, and which it would have been a dereliction of duty on his part to have neglected."

We may add that at the time these negotiations were concluded, the two western lines were not earning so much as the Midland Company agreed to give for them, and in the first eighteen months there was a deficit of £27,500. Subsequently the accounts of the several lines were not kept separately, and therefore the loss or gain could not be exactly determined; but by a special examination it was ascertained that by the end of 1848 the Western lines had paid their way, or nearly so. From that time to the present the financial advantages of the amalgamation to the Midland Company have been undoubted; to say nothing of the indirect benefits that have been derived from securing an unbroken uniformity of gauge in the midland districts of England.

CHAPTER V.

The Leicester and Swannington Railway.—The Leicestershire coal fields.—Coal below granite.—"Old George's" sagacity.—Metal tickets.—The first steam whistle.—West Bridge station, Leicester.—Amalgamation of Swannington line with Midland.—Proposed Erewash Valley Railway.—Line from Syston to Peterborough—The battle of Saxby Bridge.—"The Railway Mania."—Competition.—A rival line proposed from London to York.—Mr. Hudson's indignation.—"Unusual expedients."—Parliamentary battle.—Proposed line from Matlock to the Midland system.—Remarkable special general meeting.—Countless new projects.—Enthusiasm of the shareholders.—The South Midland and Leicester and Bedford schemes.—Animated meeting at Bedford.—Proposed lease of Leeds and Bradford line.—Protracted debate.

The Leicester and Swannington, as we have already remarked, was the first railway made in the midland counties of England. While it was in course of construction, George Stephenson entered into an arrangement with Mr. Joseph Sanders, the "father" of the Liverpool and Manchester Railway, and Sir Joshua Walmesley, for the purchase of a colliery estate at Snibston, near what is now the Coalville station, and not far from the extinct volcano of Bardon Hill. Here a shaft was sunk, and coal was got. Stephenson, however, arrived at the conclusion that, by going deeper, he should reach a better seam than any heretofore discovered in that district. He set to work accordingly. But suddenly, his sinkers, to their dismay, touched the granite. "Granite," every one said, "was the earliest of all the formations; coal could never be below granite." "You're wrong," replied old George, in homely words and Doric accent, but with the insight of genius, "you're wrong. When Bardon hill was on fire, the pot boiled over, and this granite is only the scum. It is no great thickness. We shall go through it, and find the best coal below." He was right. After proceeding down-

LINES IN AND NEAR LEICESTER.

wards about sixty feet, they pierced the granite; they again entered the coal measures; they passed through a seam which had been turned to cinders by the boiling lava, and they reached the main coal. To these pits the new line was to run: they were to help the railway, and the railway was to be the making of them.

The Leicester and Swannington line, like many others, had troubles in its early days. At one period there was so much trouble in securing from the shareholders its payment of calls that the defaulters were threatened in an original, but, no doubt, effective manner. "I am therefore necessitated to inform you," wrote the secretary, "that unless the sum of £2 is paid on or before the 22nd instant, your name will be furnished to one of the principal and most pressing creditors of the company."

The Swannington line was opened on the 17th of July, 1832; but it may be mentioned, as an illustration of how little was at that time known of the future capabilities of railways, that it had not been intended that this should carry passengers. A carriage, however, was made and placed on the line, and its traffic was so far successful that

after a while it was found that the passenger fares paid one per cent. on the capital. The passenger tickets first used were of metal, of the size and shape indicated in the illustration. If a passenger going from Leicester, for instance, to the then Ashby Road station, "perhaps No. 22" would be issued to him, and the circumstance would be duly recorded by the clerk in a book kept for that purpose, the page of which resembled the "way-bills" of coaching days. When the passenger arrived at his destination, the guard would place the ticket in a leathern pouch he carried at his side, which looked like a modern collecting box, and take them back to be used again.

For six or eight months from the opening of the Leicester and Swannington line it was in the charge of Mr. George Vaughan, who was also manager of the Snibston collieries. Soon after the appointment of his successor, Mr. Ashlen Bagster, a locomotive, while crossing a level road near Thornton, ran against a horse and cart. At that time the drivers and guards of trains were able to give the signal of alarm only by means of a horn; and when Mr. Bagster heard of the misadventure he went over to Alton Grange, and mentioned the circumstances to Stephenson. "Is it not possible," he suggested, "to have a whistle fitted on the engine, which the steam can blow?" "A very good thought," replied Stephenson. "You go to Mr. So-and-So, a musical-instrument maker, and get a model made, and we will have a steam whistle, and put it on the next engine that comes on the line." This was accordingly done. The model was sent to Newcastle; and all future engines that arrived in Leicestershire were thus equipped.

It is interesting to visit the spot, by the broad canal and wharf, where once stood the only railway station in the midland counties of England. What are now the homely waiting room and entrance passage of the booking offices, was then the board-room in which the fifteen railway magnates met to deliberate on the affairs of a line sixteen miles in length—a director to a mile; yet those men were then solving practical problems with astuteness and enterprise which has since enriched the land and benefited the world.

LEICESTER STATION (WEST BRIDGE), 1832.

The Leicester and Swannington line continued its independent existence for some years, when rumours from various quarters of threatened schemes of competition made the Midland board anxious to consolidate their position in the districts they occupied. A Leicester and Tamworth Company endeavoured to obtain possession of the Swannington; but the Midland Company promptly concluded their negotiations, and bought the line. In this transaction the directors of the Swannington were not unwilling to give a preference to the Midland company, which they regarded in the light of a natural ally. The dividend at one time had been about eight per cent.; but, latterly, in order to defray the expense of relaying the line, the shareholders had received only five. The Midland Company guaranteed a dividend of eight per cent. on a capital of £140,000, and consented to take over a debt of £10,000: these terms not being higher than those proposed by other parties.

On coming into possession of the Swannington line, the Midland Company found it necessary to make several important improvements. Near Bardon Hill the line ran up a steep "self-acting incline," along which passengers were required to trudge, whatever might be the inclemency of the weather. Two sets of passenger trains and engines were kept in use, one on the higher and the other on the lower levels, and worked in correspondence with each other. But such an arrangement would no longer suffice, and a deviation of the railway was now ordered to be made, along which locomotives could freely pass. As, too, the old line was only a single line, and passed as such through a tunnel a mile long which could not easily be widened, it was resolved to construct another—a loop or deviation—line, which instead of starting from the West Bridge station, should commence at the Midland main line, about a mile south of the London Road station, and should join the old Swannington at some point north of the tunnel. The old West Bridge line would still be used, but could be relieved of much of its former traffic.

The practical sagacity which had led to the consolidation into one property and under one administration of what had previously been a number of isolated if not rival interests, was now developed into a policy of extension. In 1844, a company was formed for the purpose of constructing the long delayed Erewash Valley line; but in the following February, before the Act could be obtained, the Midland Company agreed to take up the project, the price being a minimum guarantee of six per cent. per annum on a capital not exceeding £145,000 The line, however, was not opened till 1847, and the traffic for some time afterwards was small—a circumstance accounted for by the fact that a canal runs parallel with it for its entire length, and that the canal, unlike the railway, had no outlet to the north. The importance of making it a thoroughfare was however early recognised; and when the amalgamation was effected, Mr. Dicey drew attention to the fact that, by continuing the line northward, a saving of six miles would be effected by trains that avoided the detour by Derby; and a rich mineral district would also be opened up. He further contended that the Midland would thus secure the benefit of a through relief line for their main traffic to and from the north, similar to that enjoyed by the London and North Western by their Trent Valley scheme. The force of Mr. Dicey's remarks would perhaps have been at once allowed; but the minds of the directors were preoccupied by extensions which they deemed essential in order to protect themselves from intended aggressions on their eastern frontier.

One of these projects, immediately contemplated, was for a line to run from Syston, a station about five miles north of Leicester, to the city of Peterborough. It was laid out by George Stephenson,—its winding course being necessary to catch the towns and their tolls, to avoid the uplands and wolds of Leicestershire, and to prevent encroachment on Lord Harborough's park at Stapleford. "I have always held," said Mr. Hudson, in referring to this project, "that a line should bend to the population, and not leave the towns;" and this line had to be bent, in order to satisfy these varied and inexorable conditions, to nearly half a circle, and then to run through the middle of Stamford to Peterborough." It was estimated to cost £700,000, or £15,000 a mile. The towns along its course pronounced in its favour; and their interest in the matter is not surprising, when it is mentioned that during a then recent frost, the price of coals at Stamford had risen to forty shillings a ton, and that there had been a famine of fuel in the neighbourhood. The greatest hostility to the undertaking was, however, shown by the *clientèle* of Lord Harborough; and in one of the attempts made near Saxby to survey the line, a conflict took place, subsequently humorously entitled, "the battle of Saxby Bridge," which led to the incarceration of some of the surveyors in Leicester gaol some weeks as "first-class misdemeanants."

But while the Midland Company board was thus contemplating measures for the consolidation and enlargement of its influence, other minds were equally fertile in devising projects for new railways—some of which might invade the territory which hitherto the Midland Company had regarded as its own. In 1843, twenty-four railway Acts had been passed by Parliament; in 1844, thirty-seven more were added; in 1845, the railway mania reached its height, and in that November no fewer than 1428 railway schemes had been authorised, or were projected—1428 lines, with an estimated capital of more than £700,000,000! But amid the bubbles that came so swiftly to the surface of that strange and, in many respects, disastrous time, there were some solid and honest enterprises, one of which was destined decisively to tell on the fortunes of the Midland Railway. This was the London and York—a line intended to flank the Midland system from south to north, and to "tap" its traffic at almost every vital point.

It is not surprising that such a project was resisted with no common determination. Mr. Hudson poured upon it vials of his hottest indignation, and he declared that if there had been added to the scheme "the humbug of the atmospheric principle, it would have been the most complete thing ever brought before the public." After referring to the heavy earthworks, the gradients, and tunnels of the proposed line, he declared that he had no hesitation in giving a challenge to leave London with twenty carriages by the London and Birmingham and Midland railways, and that he would beat his rival at York; "and more than that, he questioned whether, in foggy weather, they would ever get there at all."

The London and North Western Company united with

the Midland in resisting the proposed undertaking, and the legal battle that was waged proved to be one of the greatest of the kind in the annals of Parliament. Two competitive lines to the London and York—the Direct Northern and the Cambridge and Lincoln—were in the field. No fewer than twenty counsel appeared daily in the committee rooms; and the Commons' Committee sat six days through the quieter part of two sessions of Parliament, the standing orders being suspended to enable them to complete so colossal an investigation. It was even alleged that Mr. Hudson adopted unusual expedients to obstruct the progress of legislation, so that the bill might not pass during that session. Lord Brougham, remarked the *Morning Herald*, "adverted to the manner in which money and time were consumed in the conflicting schemes before Parliament, and said that Mr. Hudson—King Hudson—was working with a twelve-counsel power before the Committee on the London and York line. The object of Mr. Hudson was delay, in order that a report might not be made in the present session, and of course counsel would talk just as long as Mr. Hudson was disposed to spend money. He was, in fact, just as well pleased with a six or eight hours' speech from the counsel opposed to him, as with a speech of six hours from his own counsel. He hoped, however, that the committee would disappoint Mr. Hudson, by reporting during the present session." Lord Faversham said that Mr. Hudson, who was present, and had heard Lord Brougham's speech—cries of "Order"—had authorised him to say that it was incorrect that he had interfered with the committee; whereupon Lord Brougham observed, that "the only sovereign entitled to be present at their debate was Her Majesty The railway potentate had no right to be there."

Mr. Hudson, however, availed himself of another opportunity to deny the charge; and he stated that instead of employing twelve counsel, there were only five who, during the progress of the London and York, attended on his behalf to watch the course of the business. "When the Cambridge and Lincoln came under the consideration of the committee," he said, "our counsel did not attend, because we did not feel ourselves in a position to oppose that Company. We therefore took no part whatever then in the proceedings. Then came on the Direct Northern, in which we were interested, and then our counsel did attend. To say that we were the means of obstructing the business of the committee, was a most unfair and unjust accusation, not only upon you but upon me individually."

Meanwhile the two competitive schemes were merged into the London and York; and, as the proceedings drew to a close, the final decision was awaited with intense interest. The committee room was thronged. Amid breathless silence the chairman announced that the preamble of the bill (with the exception of the proposed Sheffield and Wakefield branches) was proved. Loud applause broke instantly and irresistibly forth, and then the audience rushed helter skelter out of the room to bear near and afar the tidings in which so many, for good or for ill, were deeply concerned.

Mr. Hudson did not fail to avail himself of the earliest opportunity of again expressing his indignation at the injury and injustice that had been done to the interests of the Midland. "I should be unworthy," he exclaimed, "of the position I hold, and of the confidence with which you are pleased to honour me, if I were to shrink from telling you plainly the position in which this Company is placed by the proceedings of the House of Commons, in deciding a question in which we are so deeply interested, without allowing us to adduce one tittle of evidence in the matter." He declared that "the committee had come to a decision on the main question, without knowing anything whatever of the matter submitted to their judgment. (Loud cries of 'Shame, shame.') The committee retired to consider what reason they should give —I will not say what expedient they should devise—to sanction the opposition of the London and York Company to the Doncaster bill; and the reason they alleged was, that it was a competing line with the Wakefield branch of the London and York. How the ingenuity of man, how fruitful soever, could bring forward such an expedient, is to me most marvellous.

"Shut out as we were from all opportunity of being heard, we thought the most dignified course—the course most befitting you and ourselves—would be to retire altogether from the committee, and to take no part in opposition to the clauses of the London and York bill, though I fear the public safety is deeply involved in passing our station at York, and in the interference with our traffic. We felt, however, that before such a committee, we had no chance of being fairly treated, and therefore it was that we requested Mr. Austin, as appearing for the Midland and the York and North Midland Companies, to state that as we could not be heard, we should at once retire from the committee and appeal to the House. (Boisterous applause.) Those who have heard Mr. Austin before parliamentary committees, and know how respectfully he expresses his views, will at once admit that nothing could be said by him unbecoming a gentleman; and yet, no sooner had Mr. Austin opened his mouth, and merely uttered the words, 'we protest,' than the committee rushed from the room, and on their return announced that he could not be heard. (Hisses, and cries of 'Shame.')

"Thus, gentlemen, we have been shut out from a hearing before the committee; but I look to the House for that justice which is the right of the humblest individual,—and certainly not less the right of those who have embarked nearly thirty millions of money in this and other undertakings which are affected—the justice of not having their claims thus summarily disposed of without even the courtesy of a hearing. (Loud applause.) I feel it difficult, as an Englishman, to restrain my feelings when speaking of such proceedings, but I have endeavoured not to exaggerate the facts; and I leave to yourselves to give an opinion thereon. (Renewed applause.) Such a decision cannot possibly stand, and I am satisfied that even those members of the House who are pleased with this triumph—if triumph it may be called—of the London and York, will, when the question is brought before the House, give their vote that at least we shall be heard.

"Had an opportunity been allowed, we should have shown that while the London and York proposed to save by their new line about three quarters of a mile in distance, we should have saved a million and a half of money, and given the public equal, if not greater facilities. Nothing, however, of this kind was permitted. With breathless haste the committee were resolved to pass the preamble of the bill—with breathless haste they are resolved to report upon it; but I hope and believe that our appeal to the House will result in sending back the bill to the committee, so that its opponents may at least bring forward their case. If, after that examination, our schemes are found defective, of course we must submit; but it is one of the most cruel inflictions that could be imposed on the owners of so large a property, that our claims should be rejected unheard. (Hear, hear.) How can the decision of this committee stand if it be true, as rumoured, that it was settled by two individuals, one member of the committee not voting at all, and another voting directly against it!

"Gentlemen, I have little more to say of the London and York scheme. On a previous occasion, some eight or ten months ago, I fully explained my views as to its merits, and that estimate has not only been tacitly admitted by the parties themselves, but has been almost literally borne out by the evidence adduced before the committee. (Hear, hear.) Gentlemen, on the principle that we have not been heard, we take our stand; and it is the anxious wish of my colleagues and myself to fortify our position during the short interval ere the prorogation of Parliament by any means that may be pointed out. I am not an alarmist, nor in the habit of giving way to difficulties; but on the other hand, whilst I would not encourage the notions of the over-sanguine, I believe that this Company is destined to maintain a high position, and that there is nothing either present or in prospect at all tending to interfere with its ultimate and permanent success. (Applause.) I have nothing to add. It may be that I have expressed myself somewhat too strongly—loud cries of 'No, no,' from the entire meeting—but I feel that we have been hardly dealt with —I feel that we have done nothing to forfeit our rights as Englishmen, and I trust that some means may yet be devised of not deciding against us unheard." (Much applause.)

The Chairman resumed his seat amid "a hurricane of applause." The motion having been seconded, was carried unanimously.

At this meeting, July 25th, 1845, it was mentioned that the merchandise and mineral receipts had increased at the rate of more than 27 per cent. on the corresponding half year; and that the directors had arranged for the lease of the Birmingham and Gloucester, and Bristol and Gloucester Railways; of the Leicester and Swannington Railway, and of the Ashby and Oakham Canals. The chairman also proposed that the Midland Company should join certain other companies in subscribing for a piece of plate to be presented to George Stephenson, and for a statue to be erected on the bridge at Newcastle—the quota of the Midland Company to be £2000. Mr. Ellis, the deputy chairman, said that though he was a member of the Society of Friends, he should, "with all his heart," second the motion. One shareholder demurred to the application to any such purpose of the shareholders' money, money he said, that belonged in part to "orphans and widows;" whereupon the chairman declared that if any proprietor objected to the vote "his quota should be calculated, and he (the chairman) would repay the amount out of his own pocket;" a remark, which, we are informed, drew forth "boisterous applause, which lasted for several minutes."

Reference was made at this meeting to a line which had been proposed to connect the Midland system with Matlock, Buxton, and Manchester. Thirty coaches passed along that route every day through the summer months, and the visitors to Chatsworth alone amounted to sixty or seventy thousand a year. The Hon. George Cavendish was one of the earliest supporters of the project, and took in it 520 shares, which, he said, "I do not intend to sell." George Stephenson, too, at a meeting of the new company, stated that though he was about to retire from a profession in which he had spent a long and arduous life, he had come forward to support this line. He recollected well how the York and North Midland had been forsaken notwithstanding his favourable predictions. He had bought shares in it for £1, on which £6 had been paid; and he had had the satisfaction of holding these shares till he made £250 for every £50 he had laid out. The development of this Buxton and Manchester scheme, was naturally watched by the Midland Company with interest; and in order to secure some measure of influence in controlling its destinies the Midland board purchased nearly 10,000 shares, and placed them in trust, and this number was subsequently largely increased. We may add that the London and North Western Company, because they did *not* want a line in this direction, pursued a similar course.

The year 1846 was an important epoch in the history of the Midland Company. At the January meeting, the chairman announced varied projects of extension; and in the following May he stated that the bills had passed the Commons, and had to be submitted for the sanction of the proprietors. It is true that the difficulties that had latterly arisen in the railway world had somewhat abated the ardour of railway enterprise, but the eloquence of the chairman and the ambition of the shareholders gave such enthusiasm to the scene, and reflected so remarkably the temper of the times, that we must dwell somewhat minutely upon it. We may premise that with the proxies that had been sent in, and the shares that were held by proprietors present, there was not less than £6,000,000 of Midland capital represented in the meeting.

The first bill was for a deviation of the Syston and Peterborough line. Its provisions were said to be necessary to meet some objections made by Lord Harborough; and it contained powers for the construction of a small deviation that would improve the communication with Stamford. The chairman admitted that some of the new projects might not be paying lines if they stood alone; but that in hostile hands they would be sources of injury to the Midland Railway, while as parts of a great system they would be remunerative. The resolution was put, and agreed to unanimously.

The next bill was to authorise the construction of an extension of the Leicester and Swannington Railway to Burton-on-Trent, there again to join the Midland. The cost would be £140,000.

The next bill was for making a line from Burton-on-Trent to Nuneaton, with branches, and to authorise the Midland Company to purchase the Ashby-de-la-Zouch Canal, at a total cost of from £70,000 to £80,000. Mr. Franklin objected to proceeding with these schemes on the ground that the shareholders had already incurred sufficient responsibilities. Why not let other parties have a chance as well as themselves. (Hear, and laughter.) But the resolution was agreed to.

The next bill related to the Erewash Valley line, sanctioned last year. It was to authorise the construction of branches to neighbouring coalfields, and also to the town of Chesterfield, and to Clay Cross, in order to shorten the distance between the south and the north. The estimate was £230,000; but the Chairman said that this bill could not be objected to, since the undertakings were likely to prove highly remunerative to the shareholders. Mr. Hudson assured Mr. Franklin that he was by no means desirous of monopolising any districts which if in other hands would be more advantageous to the public. But that objection did not apply to the case before them; for these lines would not remunerate an independent company, though they would pay the Midland. (Hear, hear.) A shareholder here suggested that these lines could not be made for their estimates, for that the price of labour and materials had considerably increased. But the chairman assured the honourable proprietor that he was mistaken. Both materials and labour were as cheap now as they were when he first joined the

Midland, nay, in the case of sleepers which formerly cost 7*s.* each, they now cost only 4*s.* 6*d.* (Hear, hear.) The resolution was then agreed to.

The next bill was for powers to construct a branch from Nottingham to Mansfield, involving an expenditure of £270,000. The line would considerably shorten the distance between these places and the south of England. The resolution was agreed to.

The next bill was to authorise the construction of a line from Clay Cross to join the Nottingham and Lincoln branch, and it also was agreed to.

The next bill was for making a line from Swinton to Lincoln, to connect the West Riding with Gainsborough and Doncaster.

Mr. Franklin: "What is the estimate?"

The Chairman: "£140,000."

Mr. Franklin: "This will never do. Our liabilities are already heavy enough without adding to them."

The Chairman: "I am one of those who think the business of a railway cannot be carried on successfully on a small scale."

Mr. Franklin: "So it seems." (Laughter.)

The resolution was agreed to.

The Chairman said, the next was a little bill to improve their communication with London and Birmingham, and Bristol and Gloucester, and Midland lines at Birmingham. The estimate was £80,000.

Mr. Franklin: "There you go again." (Laughter.)

The Chairman: "Well, the public experience considerable inconvenience from the want of this communication, and could you remove it for a less sum?" (No, no). The bill was approved of.

The Chairman said, the next bill was for connecting the Birmingham and Gloucester line with the docks at Gloucester. Gloucester was a rising port, and the proposed improvements could be accomplished for £150,000. The bill was agreed to.

The Chairman said the next bill was for making a branch from the Birmingham and Gloucester to the rising watering place of Malvern. The line was much wanted, and likely to prove highly remunerative. The estimate for it was £180,000.

Mr. Thompson said there was only one coach running to Malvern.

The Chairman said that was no criterion to go by, and they had an extraordinary proof of this in the Scarborough line. Before that line was made there was only one coach, and it was therefore predicted that a railway would be a ruinous undertaking. What, however, had been the result? The line was already paying 7 per cent. (Cheers.) The bill was approved of.

The Chairman said that the next bill was for power to complete the narrow gauge down to Bristol, which could be accomplished for £100,000, including an extension of eight miles to Stonehouse. A passenger would then be able to travel from Edinburgh to Bristol without change of carriage. (Applause.) The bill was unanimously approved of.

The Chairman said the next bill was for making a communication between Bath and Mangotsfield, and for the shortening of the communication between Gloucester and Bath.

Mr. Franklin. "You will only gain eight minutes by it. How many more irons are you going to put in the fire?"

Mr. Hudson could assure the honourable proprietor that he should be the last man to support a line on the ground of its saving a few minutes' time; but although this line, in point of time, would only save a few minutes, it would afford great local accommodation, and open up to their main line vast coal and mineral fields. The bill was approved of.

The Chairman said that the next bill was for carrying out the agreement for leasing the Bristol and Gloucester, and Birmingham and Gloucester lines. He was perfectly satisfied that in the end they would have no cause to regret their approval of this agreement. The bill was approved of

The Chairman said that the next was the Bedford and Northampton bill. The Huntingdon branch had already passed through the committee of the House of Commons, and the South Midland would be brought on very shortly. They held £600,000 worth of stock in the scheme; but if they thought proper they could dispose of it at a future period. In a similar manner he had induced some York shareholders to subscribe to the North British Railway, and cleared by it something like £25,000. (Cheers.) It was necessary that they should continue to have an interest in this undertaking. (Hear, hear.) It would give them another communication with London, independent of the one by way of Rugby, and enable them to have an entrance into the metropolis by the east as well as the west. (Hear, hear.) The bill was approved of.

The Chairman said, the next bill was for a line to connect the Midland system with Manchester, Buxton, and Matlock, which could be effected at a cost of £270,000. He had no doubt that the line would be found to be as good as any in this part of the country. (Hear, hear.)

Mr. Wellington: "What will the cost per mile be?"

The Chairman said he was not in a position to give a positive answer to that question, but probably it would be about £30,000 per mile. The bill was approved of.

The Chairman said that he had now to call their attention to three bills, prosecuted in conjunction with the London and Birmingham Company. The first was the

Worcester and Weedon, the second the Hampton and Banbury, and the third was the Hampton and Ashchurch. These bills would, in a great measure, do away with the heavy expense attendant on the Lickey incline.

Mr. Williams: "What amount do we subscribe?"

The Chairman: "£600,000."

Mr. Franklin: "There you go again." (Loud laughter).

The Chairman said he had no doubt that if the proprietors were hereafter dissatisfied with this arrangement, the London and Birmingham Company would be glad to relieve them from their liability. (Hear, hear.) The directors themselves felt that all these bills were left in their hands to be dealt with as they should think fit, after a careful and minute review of their objects; and the meeting might depend upon it the best interests of the company was the lever which would guide their minds. (Hear, hear.)

Mr. Ellis said the meeting might take his word for it these bills would prove of considerable service to them. The bill was agreed to.

The Chairman said, the next bill was for making the Trent Valley Midland; but he might state that a negotiation was going on which would no doubt result in the withdrawal of this project. The amount subscribed towards this undertaking was £120,000. The bill was agreed to.

The Chairman said he now came to the last bill on the list which was for making the Manchester and Southampton line. He believed the country through which the line passed would furnish considerable traffic; but, as he said before, he was not there to pledge himself as to the future success of these bills, and he would abstain from going into the merits of the present one. He only asked the proprietary to leave the matter in the hands of the directors, and their interests would not be neglected.

(Hear, hear.) The capital to be subscribed to it was £400,000.

Mr. Franklin said in giving his opposition to the last bill, he wished the directors to understand that he was actuated by no feeling of hostility towards them; but he was induced to dissent from these measures by a sincere conviction that they were incurring too heavy liabilities. (Hear, hear.) They were now rendering themselves liable for between three and four millions of money; and he could not help thinking that they were overshooting their mark. (Laughter.)

The Chairman again told the honourable proprietor that railway business could not be carried on with any chance of success, unless it were upon a large scale. It was true they would require some two or three millions to carry out these projects, but it must be remembered that they had a large surplus capital at their disposal. (Hear, hear.) The bill was agreed to.

The position occupied by Mr. Hudson at this period was remarkable, and we may pause for a moment in our narrative to notice it. "At the beginning of the railway system," said the *Newcastle Chronicle* many years afterwards, "we find him a modest draper, doing a quiet business in the cathedral city of York, with nothing to distinguish him from the rank and file of shopkeepers. Railways became the passion of the hour, and the York draper was bitten by the mania. Mr. Hudson risked all and was successful. Stimulated by success, he played again, again fortune proved propitious. His name became an authority on railway speculation, and the confidence reposed in him was unbounded. For a time the entire railway system of the north of England seemed under his control. What Herculean energy was in the man may be gathered from a couple of days' work, under Mr. Hudson's direction. On the 2nd of May, 1846, the shareholders of the Midland Company gave their approval to 26 bills which were immediately introduced into Parliament. On Monday following, at ten o'clock, the York and North Midland sanctioned six bills, and affirmed various deeds and agreements affecting the Manchester and Leeds, and Hull and Selby Companies. Fifteen minutes later he induced the Newcastle and Darlington Company to approve of seven bills and accompanying agreements; and at half-past ten took his seat as a controlling power at the board of the Newcastle and Berwick. In fine, during these two days, he obtained the approval of forty bills, involving the expenditure of about £10,000,000. For three years matters went bravely on; each succeeding day being a witness of greater wonders than its predecessor." We may add that some of those who were best acquainted with the activities in which Mr. Hudson was at that period engaged, are of opinion that scant justice was done to his work and to the motives by which he was actuated in the performance of it.

An arrangement was made at the commencement of the year 1846, by which the shareholders of the Midland Railway have been allowed to travel without charge to all their meetings on showing their statements of accounts. It is an advantage which ought to be insisted upon by shareholders of all similar undertakings; since it tends to secure larger meetings of the proprietors and a more intelligent interest in the vast properties under their control. The fact that some boards of directors object to this arrangement, and like to keep their constituencies at a distance, should be of itself a sufficient reason for arousing the suspicions of shareholders, and for demanding that they have every facility for understanding the position of their own property.

In the course of the year (1846) satisfactory progress

was made with the numerous undertakings of the Company. The increase of traffic amounted during the first six months to £31,000; and the dividend on the ordinary shares was at the rate of 7 per cent. per annum. The stock of the Company in every department improved; new lines were approaching completion; the Oakham Canal was purchased; the electric telegraph was established over the whole system; and several bills obtained the sanction of Parliament.

Some of the extensions proposed by the Midland Company encountered strenuous resistance. Lines between Clay Cross and Newark, and between Nottingham and Mansfield, were resisted by competitive schemes, brought forward by influential persons locally interested; and eventually it was thought good policy to buy off opposition rather than to incur the risk and cost of a Parliamentary contest. The Boston, Newark, and Sheffield bill was thus withdrawn for a consideration of £50,000 worth of Midland stock at par; and the Nottingham and Mansfield project was similarly silenced by £40,000 stock upon the same terms. The directors stated that they "considered this in every respect a desirable arrangement, as giving to these parties an interest in this Company; and the directors trusted that their action would receive the approval of the meeting."

At about this time the attention of the shareholders was first seriously directed to some new railway schemes that were in contemplation; one of which came eventually to exercise an important influence on the destinies of the Midland Company. This was a proposal for a new line to connect the Midland system with the metropolis. Many complaints had been made that the only access for Midland passengers to London was by the circuitous and uncertain route of Rugby—uncertain because the arrangements for the meeting of trains so frequently broke down.

One gentleman, for instance, declared at a public meeting at Leicester, that he had three times in succession been detained three hours at Rugby; and it was declared that many persons "hated the name of Rugby."

Two new lines were now proposed, by the adoption of either of which it was believed that seventy miles' distance would be saved, delays would be avoided, and lower fares would be secured. One of these projects was named the South Midland, the other the Leicester and Bedford Railway. The latter was intended to remain an independent company, but to form a link of connection between the two great rival companies, joining the London and York line at Hitchen and the Midland at Leicester. Its directors accordingly placed themselves in communication with the London and York board, who "offered," they said, "their most friendly support and cordial assistance." They intended also to place themselves in alliance with the Midland Company; but found that they were "not received with the cordiality they had been led to expect." They stated that they desired a friendly understanding with the Midland Company in order to pass over their line from Leicester; and with the London and York to carry the traffic on to London; that the Leicester and Bedford Company were willing to enter into arrangements with the Midland, so as to give to that company an interest in it equal to that assigned to the London and York; and that they wished to act impartially to both companies.

Of course, such a project and such a policy, which would occupy with a new and entirely independent railway the whole district between the Midland system and the metropolis, was not likely to commend itself to both authorities; and they turned aside from these overtures to encourage the solicitations of other parties who were wishing to run a line in the same direction, and who were at the same time anxious to be brought into entire harmony with the Midland Company. This was the South Midland scheme, with a proposed capital of £2,000,000, to which in the first instance both offered to contribute £600,000; but which eventually they adopted as their own, undertook to carry out, and for which they indemnified the projectors for the expenses they had incurred. Meanwhile the two new rival undertakings appealed to the public for support, and waged dire warfare with each other. As an illustration of the spirit in which this controversy was carried on, we may mention that a meeting of the representatives of the various interests was held at the Swan Inn, at Bedford, September 4th, 1846; and the scene was all the livelier because the precaution of appointing a chairman was neglected. In reply to some animadversions of Mr. Whitbread, Mr. Macaulay, one of the solicitors of the Midland Company, admitted that their intention had been to carry their line at first only as far as Bedford; but he asserted that this was merely in order that they might see what railways south of that town would be granted by the legislature, and that then they would run on by the most direct line to London. "We stated," he said, "over and over again, that we never intended to stop at Bedford, but to go on by the best line sanctioned by Parliament." "I have no hesitation in saying," replied Mr. Whitbread, "that I believe the sole object of Mr. Hudson and his friends in taking up the South Midland scheme, was to floor the Leicester and Bedford, and that they never honestly meant to make a line at all; but were quite content to be floored themselves, so long as the other line was floored also. I believe the Leicester and Bedford to be as honest a line as any before Parliament, and I am anxious to see such a line through Bedford."

"No gentleman has a right," returned Mr. Macaulay, "to misconstrue and distort the motives of another; and the only way I can answer the unwarrantable charge just made is by a flat denial, which I unhesitatingly now give."

A lengthened conversation continued in the same animated strain. Mr. Whitbread declared that the Leicester and Bedford scheme was in existence long before the South Midland, and that the latter was only brought out to floor it; and Mr. Macaulay repeated his denial. One gentleman stated that the engineer admitted before the House of Commons that it was not intended by the South Midland to go to Hitchen; but that, when the bill came before the House of Lords, the policy of its supporters had been changed. "They felt," he said, "that they had a rotten case, and altered their tack." Another gentleman referred to the London and North Western Railway Company's line as the "Bletchley old lady"; and a third declared that it was fit only "to take the charity children to Bedford, and bring them back again." "We want," he said, "a direct line to London; and I implore the Bedford people to see which is the best line, to adopt it, and not to be any more humbugged and sacrificed by a few people who call themselves leading men."

On the following day a meeting was held on behalf of the Leicester and Bedford Company, at the London Tavern. A correspondence was read between Mr. S. Franklin and Mr. Hudson; in which the former proposed that the Midland Company should purchase the Leicester and Bedford Railway at the terms given by them for the South Midland shares, equal to about 30*s*. a share for the Leicester and Bedford. Mr. Hudson, in reply, had suggested the appointment of a committee to confer with him. The meeting was held; but no decision was arrived at. In the following month, however, it was announced that Mr. Hudson, Mr. Whitbread, and Captain Laws (the latter gentlemen representing the London and York Company), had met at Derby, and that they had arranged that the Leicester and Bedford line should be transferred to the Midland Company; that the remainder of the deposits should be handed over to the Midland Company, in return for which the holders should receive 22*s*. worth of Midland stock, for each share; and that the Midland Company should obtain the Act, pay all expenses, and make the line in two years.

In July of this year (1846) a special meeting was held, to consider a proposal to lease the Leeds and Bradford Railway for 999 years, at a rent of 10 per cent. per annum, on £900,000. The line was at that time unfinished; and it was estimated by Mr. Hudson that some £300,000 additional would be required to complete it. The proposal of the Midland Company's board to enter on this lease had already encountered opposition; and the Chairman therefore thought it necessary to defend, at some length, the policy of the board. As he was himself a shareholder of the line which it was proposed to lease, some hints had been thrown out that in this, and also in other negotiations, he had not been insensible to his private interests.

"In the first place," he said, "I must give a broad denial to the assertion that I have purchased or sold a single share since this line came under our consideration. It has been my good or bad fortune to be the purchaser of many railways; and I might frequently have taken advantage of my position and knowledge to go into the market and lay out large sums of money with great benefit to myself; but I here publicly declare that I have never done so, and I call upon any person who can prove anything to the contrary to come forward and do it at once. (Applause.) I have never in one instance purchased a single share till the whole matter was before the public by advertisements, calling a meeting or otherwise; nor have I ever in any way taken advantage of the favourable position I hold over any other proprietor. In the Bristol and Birmingham line I never held a single share, nor do I hold a single share now. I did not hold a single share in the Brandling Junction; nor do I hold shares in the Leicester and Swannington; nor do I hold shares in the Hull and Selby. I did not hold shares till after the purchase in the Great North of England, nor in the Newcastle and Darlington. I never made a single penny by any of these purchases.

"Well, gentlemen, having cleared myself from that imputation. (A voice: You have not.) Well then, gentlemen, I will sit down, and give the honourable proprietor who says I have not, an opportunity of stating anything to the contrary. I am a public man, the property of the public, and I need hardly assure you I have a great desire to maintain that position which entitles me to the public confidence. The amount of responsibility which rests upon me in connection with this Company is so great that I am satisfied if anything can be urged against me derogatory to my character, it would be a most unfortunate thing for the proprietors, for whose interests I have to act."

The Chairman here resumed his seat; but at the request of the meeting he rose again, and proceeded with his address.

"Well, then, we come now to the consideration of the question, whether it is prudent for this Company to lease this railway or not upon the terms proposed. In asking that this Company should lease this line at 10 per cent., I am not proposing anything which is unprecedented.

In the case of one of the Lancashire lines, they have leased a Yorkshire line at 10 per cent.; the Great North of England have leased the Newcastle and Darlington at 10 per cent.; so that I am not introducing to you a line to be leased at an undue rate of interest. Why, just consider: you yourselves this day are receiving as much as 9¼ per cent. on your money. (No, no.) But you are; you have only paid £88 upon your shares." (A voice: You have no right to say that).

The Chairman: "I am stating nothing but facts. The Midland proprietors are receiving 9¼ per cent. on their money, and have still the privilege of participating in future creations.

"For my own part, gentlemen, I am perfectly satisfied that the line will yield a very large income and percentage even upon the price that is now put upon it, and if you will allow me to take it as an individual, I am quite satisfied I should make a large income over and above the sum which you are about to pay for it."

An animated discussion followed. Mr. John Ellis, as "entirely a friend of the Midland Company," urged that "it was essential to the prosperity of the Midland that they should complete this purchase. The line was necessary for their protection, and if it fell into the hands of a company now in existence, which the Chairman would not name, but which was the London and York, where would the Midland Company be then? Away would go half their traffic from London to Glasgow and the north."

Mr. Brancker, of Liverpool, contended that the important proposal now submitted to the meeting had been insufficiently announced; that the shareholders had been taken by surprise; that numbers of those present had not heard a whisper of the intended lease, until they were on the road to, or after they arrived at, the meeting;

that some less burdensome conditions should devolve upon the Midland Company; and that he should therefore move as an amendment that the special meeting be postponed for two months. This amendment was seconded.

Another proprietor wished the meeting to bear in mind that there were but few railways in the country that could pay 10 per cent. at the beginning; but the Chairman replied that there were several such instances, and he cited the Trent Valley as an example. Mr. John Rand, of Bradford, urged that the immediate question before the meeting was, whether the lease was advisable for the Midland Company or not. He did not imagine for a moment that the Leeds and Bradford Company would wait for two months; and he declared that it would be suicidal for the Midland Company to support the amendment. The chairman again stated his views, and unsuccessfully urged Mr. Brancker to withdraw his amendment. Mr. Hudson added that if there were a considerable minority against the lease, he should at once withdraw it. The amendment was then put, and lost by a large majority, only twenty-eight hands being held up in favour of it. The original resolution was then put, and only six hands were held up against it. We may add that it was announced at this meeting that the Sheffield and Rotherham line was now yielding a larger return than the rent; that the wages of the Company's servants had been increased; and that the maintenance of the permanent way south of Derby had been let by public tender at a price which would effect a saving to the Company of nearly £6000 a year.

CHAPTER VI.

Numerous extensions projected.—The zenith.—Opening of the Syston and Peterborough line.—Rumours of Mr. Hudson's resignation.—Death of Mr. George Stephenson.—Abstraction of traffic.—Relations with other companies.—Committee of directors.—Mutterings of a storm.—Mr. Hudson's resignation.—Committee of investigation.—Accountant's report.—Engineer's report.—Proposed reorganization of board.—Mr. Robert Stephenson's report.—Report of committee.—Opposition to the report.—Poor dividend.—Opening of further portion of Great Northern.—Dividend of sixteen shillings for half year.—Access to Worcester obtained.—Arrangement about Leeds and Bradford line.—The Great Exhibition.—Audit committee appointed.—Proposals for getting nearer to London.—Arrangements with "Little" North Western Company.—Commutation of payment to Leeds and Bradford proprietors.—Manchester, Buxton, Matlock, and Midland Junction.—Dispute between Midland and Great Northern.—Heavy floods.—Leicester and Hitchen line proposed.—Proposals of amalgamation of Midland with London and North Western and Great Northern.—Negotiations between the companies.—Special meeting of proprietors.—Union with London and North Western sanctioned.—Select committee of House of Commons report against amalgamation of large companies.—Project abandoned.—A period of rest.—Line from Gloucester to Stonehouse.—Loss of passenger traffic.—Increase of goods.—Resignation of Mr. Ellis.—Appointment and death of Mr. Paget.—Re-appointment of Mr. Ellis.—Continuation of Erewash line to Clay Cross.—Gloucester and Cheltenham tramway.—Seven per cent. dividend.—Extensions.—Purchase of Dursley branch.

THE period from 1847 to 1854 witnessed first the rise, then the culmination, and next, for a time, the decline of the prosperity of the Midland Railway. The confidence that was cherished by the directors and proprietors may be illustrated by the fact that on the 6th of March, 1847, no fewer than thirteen bills were submitted for approval, and that, as the records of the period remark with sufficient succinctness, they were "unanimously sanctioned; after which the Chairman adverted to them in the whole, saying, they had now given their sanction to 251 miles of railway, the estimated expense of which would be £4,680,000,—a large sum; but the directors in consideration of the interests of the shareholders, could not have omitted any of the proposed works."

At the autumnal meeting, Aug. 12th, 1847, great progress was still reported in the affairs of the Company. The dividend, after paying the amount of £47,384 upon the guaranteed 6 per cent. stock and shares of the Birmingham and Bristol, was at the rate of 7 per cent.; and the gross receipts were not much less than £500,000. The stations at Chesterfield, Woodhouse Mill, Clay Cross, Stretton, Belper, and Gloucester, had been enlarged; an extensive wharf at Saltley had been built; and the Westerleigh branch of the Bristol and Birmingham had been made into a locomotive line. A bridge under the main line at Tamworth for the Trent Valley line had been completed; a new passenger station at Nottingham was in course of construction; passenger and engine sheds were being built at Leeds; and the Leicester station was being enlarged. A short branch line to the canal and stone quarries at Little Eaton, near Derby, was about to be commenced; and the electric telegraph was being extended from Birmingham to Gloucester.

Prosperity to the Midland Company was now reaching its zenith. At the eighth half-yearly meeting, held on the 12th of February, 1848, a dividend at the rate of 7 per cent. was again declared. The gross receipts had risen to £586,034. There was activity in all directions. Additional repairing shops were being built at Derby. Accommodation was being furnished for the corn traffic at Lincoln, Leicester, Loughborough, and elsewhere. Gasworks were being erected at Newark, Syston, and Melton. The new Nottingham station was approaching completion, and progress had been made with that at Leeds. The line from Nottingham to Mansfield was proceeding. The Syston and Peterborough was nearly ready. The works on the Leicester and Swannington would shortly be finished; and the extension through Ashby to Burton-on-Trent was being carried forward. And as the last of the old contracts for the maintenance of the way would expire in the following July, it was now resolved to set apart £20,000 annually, to provide for future renewals.

NOTTINGHAM STATION.

A comparison of the rolling stock of the Company at three different but then recent dates will show how rapid had been the development of affairs. Each estimate was taken on the 31st of December.

	1845.	1846.	1847.
Engines and tenders	95	113	164
Carriages	282	366	578
Horse boxes and carriage trucks	95	151	225
Breaks and parcel vans	56	104	167
Waggons	1256	2386	5886

At this meeting the Chairman appeared before his constituents in high spirits. He reminded them that he had previously predicted that the probable revenue for the half-year would be £600,000, and that his anticipations had been fulfilled; he stated that, with regard to the dividend, "every sixpence of interest that could be fairly charged to the revenue account had been so charged;" and he mentioned, as an evidence of the improved power of their engines, that an express had on that morning run to the North, with newspapers containing the budget of the year, at the rate of fifty-four miles an hour, a speed, he added, which he believed had never been exceeded on the narrow gauge.

The earlier half of the year 1848 was not free from difficulty; but the gross receipts surpassed those of the corresponding half-year by upwards of £22,000, and a dividend was earned at the rate of 6 per cent. per annum. The Syston and Peterborough was opened on the 1st of May, the delay having arisen from the inclemency of the weather, and from the inability of some of the contractors to complete their portion of the works: these the Company had to take into their own hands. Meanwhile arrangements had been made for junctions between the Midland system and the Manchester, Sheffield, and Lincolnshire line at Beighton; with the North Staffordshire at Burton-on-Trent; with the South Staffordshire at Alrewas; and with the Oxford, Worcester, and Wolverhampton, at Abbott's Wood and Stoke. Powers were also obtained from Parliament for an extension seven miles in length from Gloucester to Stonehouse, uniting the Birmingham and Gloucester Railway with the Bristol and Gloucester, rendering unnecessary the break of gauge at Gloucester, and securing a continuous narrow gauge from Birmingham to Bristol.

At the August meeting a shareholder inquired if the report was true that Mr. Hudson was about to leave the Midland Railway. The Chairman replied that he could assure the honourable proprietor that he had "no intention whatever of doing so. He would say further, that so long as he had health and strength and enjoyed the confidence of the proprietors, and until he felt that he could no longer preside over their affairs to the advantage of the Company, nothing on earth should induce him to leave the Company."

Before the meeting concluded, Mr. Hudson made reference to the death of Mr. George Stephenson, who hitherto had almost always been present to witness their proceedings. "History," he said, "would record his name as that of a great and distinguished man."

The next ordinary meeting of the proprietors was held on the 7th of September, 1848, in one of the large engine houses attached to the Derby station. It was announced that there had been an increase from goods' traffic during the half-year of £47,300; but that in passengers there had been an abstraction of traffic in consequence of the opening of part of the main and loop lines of the Great Northern, and the Manchester, Sheffield, and Lincolnshire Railways; but as the falling off had been general over the system, it was hoped that it might be attributed to general causes which improved trade would rectify.

Various negotiations were now completed for improving the relations of the Midland with neighbouring companies. The directors agreed to find the plant and to work the Ambergate, Matlock, and Buxton line, between Ambergate and Rowsley. The North Staffordshire Company entered into treaty for the use of the Midland stations at Derby and Burton-on-Trent. It was arranged that Midland trains should run over the South Yorkshire line between Swinton and Doncaster. An agreement was entered into with the Little North Western Company for the use of the Midland station at Skipton; and traffic arrangements were also made between the Midland and London and North Western Companies, which it was believed would be mutually advantageous. It was announced that for the future their management would be conducted by sub-committees of the directors, which would watch over the several departments of traffic, locomotion, permanent way and works, and finance.

We are now gradually approaching a new era in the history of the Midland Company. Its career since the first amalgamation had been marked by almost steadily increasing prosperity: times of anxiety were now drawing on. The first mutterings of the storm were heard from the North, when, on the 28th October, 1848, at a meeting of Liverpool proprietors, the conduct of the directors was severely criticised. A full explanation of affairs had, however, been promised by the board, and under these circumstances, they must await its publication.

At the February meeting, 1849, however, complaints were made of a want of fulness in the published accounts; and eventually the Chairman consented that the item of £36,000 for parliamentary expenses charged against capital should, if the proprietors wished it, be placed against revenue. A shareholder alleged that the coal business of the company was carried on at very insufficient profit; but to this it was replied by Mr. Ellis, that it was even more profitable than the passenger traffic. Mr. Hudson, with some warmth, defended the course he had pursued; stated that he held from £16,000 to £17,000 worth of stock in the line, which was about as much as when first he joined it; and concluded by asking what motive but to serve the proprietary could he have in "leaving his home, filled with friends, to travel all night in order to wait upon them that day?" His remarks were heartily received by his audience, and a vote of confidence in the directors was carried amid "tumultuous applause."

But two months afterwards, on the 19th of April, 1849, an extraordinary general meeting was held at Derby, to decide as to the nomination of a committee of inquiry. The room was densely crowded. Mr. John Ellis, M.P., presided, and read a letter from Mr. Hudson. It stated, that, during his chairmanship of the Midland Company, he had been identified with the York and North Midland, and the York, Newcastle and Berwick Companies, all of which hitherto had had a common interest; but that now that the Great Northern Railway had been sanctioned, and new relations were arising, and new alliances were contemplated, he thought it would be more satisfactory to the shareholders of the Midland Company that he should resign his office. Mr. Ellis added that this was also a resignation by Mr. Hudson of his position on the direction.

When they met last in that room, on the 15th of February, Mr. Ellis continued, some gentlemen from Liverpool proposed the appointment of a committee of inquiry into the administration and accounts of the Company. The directors then thought it right to oppose that resolution, and they were supported by the proprietors. A very few days, however, had passed, when circumstances came to their knowledge which led the board to see that it would be advisable for the shareholders to look for themselves into the position of affairs. They could not but be seriously affected when the Great Northern Railway was completed. For his own part, he considered that the best way to recoup any losses they might thus sustain, was by a more intimate alliance with the London and North Western Company; and as he was on the North Western direction, he was, he thought, in the best position for coming to a conclusion on that subject. "I can see no way," he said, "in which the two Companies can injure, and many ways in which they can serve each other; and I do not hesitate to give my opinion that the London and North Western is the natural ally of the Midland."

Mr. Wylie, of Liverpool, then rose to move a resolution appointing a committee of investigation to examine into the management and affairs of the Company, "with full powers to call for all books, papers, accounts, and documents, and to take such other steps as they may deem advisable," and to report to the shareholders at an adjourned meeting. After stating some of the circumstances that had led to this proposal, he added, "Yesterday we had an interview with the directors; and I am happy to say they met us as frankly as we went to them, and the committee we propose has the perfect confidence of the board."

The report of the committee of investigation is dated August 15th, 1849. Professional accountants had examined the books of the Company. They stated that "the accounts published and laid before the proprietors from time to time, although not sufficiently comprehensive, yet, in respect of the matter they did contain, are in due accordance with the authentic books of the Company." Proper attention, however, had not always been paid to the vital question, not at that time clearly understood, of the distinctions to be maintained between revenue and capital. For instance, since the amalgamation, thirty-six miles of the Midland Counties line, part of the Sheffield and Rotherham, and thirty-five miles of the Birmingham and Gloucester had been relaid at a cost to capital of more that £900,000, which was "strictly chargeable to revenue." The accountants at the same time laid it down as a principle that revenue ought to bear only the "expense incurred in a bare renewal of a worn-out road," and that substantial improvements might be paid for by capital. The committee had requested Mr. W. H. Barlow, the resident engineer, to state precisely what had been done with this £915,997. He reported that in his judgment the appropriation to capital of the whole, or nearly the whole amount was correct. He stated that heavier rails had been substituted, because heavier engines were now run; that the stations had been enlarged; that the main-lines rail had been used for additional sidings and branch lines, where they were as valuable as new rails; that the maintenance of the permanent way would hereafter be less expensive; that 3000 tons of rails had been used in making points and crossings for new works; and that 1000 tons of new rails had been sent to the Leeds and Bradford line. He argued, therefore, that the whole outlay was thus for "the permanent benefit of the line. The shareholders might contend with justice that revenue is not chargeable with more than the working expenses, repairs, and depreciations of the year, and that they were not bound to expend money to give an improved future value to the undertaking." And the committee expressed themselves satisfied with Mr. Barlow's explanation.

The report suggested important changes in the direction; and especially the immediate selection of some new directors "either in addition to, or in substitution of an equal number of the present board." The committee mentioned that several proposals had been made with regard to the constitution of the board by the appointment of a stipendiary chairman, who should give his whole time to the Company; or that there should be a chairman and two or three other directors paid to devote their whole time to the service of the Company; or that the number of the directors should be increased.

In reply to the proposal to appoint a stipendiary chairman it was contended that such an officer "might arrogate to himself more authority than the rest of the board chose to submit to, and thereby create disunion; or it might be, on the other hand, the rest of the board might think him entitled to have much of his own way." Similar criticisms might be offered on a scheme by which two or three of the directors should devote their whole time to the Company. "As to the third plan," said the committee of investigation, "that of increasing the directors to twenty, with the same allowance as at present, there are none of the objections to which the other two are liable. The number being greater would afford the chance of there being in it more men well qualified for the appointment, and the expense would be no greater to the Company. The great object," they added, "is to appoint capable men, whose position and character are a guarantee for their integrity, and who at the same time are willing to appropriate a due portion of their time to the proper and effective management of the affairs of the Company."

In regard to the rolling stock the accountants had stated that a deterioration of the value of the locomotives had taken place to the amount of not less than £100,000, and in carriage and wagon stock of more than £70,000.

Mr. Robert Stephenson, however, who had been requested to report on this subject, rebutted these calculations with great minuteness, and then adds: "The accountants appear to me to treat the value of the railways and stock as if the concern were about to be broken up and sold for what it would fetch. The question appears to me rather to resolve itself into this: Is the productive power of the concern increased or decreased? The permanent way has been made more substantial. The engine stock has been made more efficient and economical, and the stock of carriages has not only been extended, but in some cases improved in value; in a word, from the commencement, the Midland lines and stock have unquestionably, as a producing machine, been improved in value, which leads me to the opinion that the amounts which have been hitherto carried to capital, have been legitimately so placed."

The committee of investigation then report with tedious minuteness upon the arrangements that had been made by the board in regard to the Leeds and Bradford, and the Erewash lines; but into these details we need not follow them. Concerning the Erewash, they justly remarked that, "from the exceeding richness of the valley in minerals, as well as from the extensive ironworks of the Butterley Company being situated on or near the line, your committee think that in a few years it is likely that this line will be remunerative in itself, as well as become a most valuable feeder to the main line."

The adoption of this report was opposed by Mr. Wylie. He declared that "a more incomplete and inconclusive document he had never seen;" that it was "a report of opinion and not of fact, of apology and not of substance." He also demurred to the value set upon the Leeds and Bradford line. An animated discussion followed, and eventually Mr. Wylie admitted that he "approved of the conduct of the committee generally, but complained of the incompleteness of the report." The Chairman gave some additional information, and promised to furnish any returns which might be found in the office; the amendment was withdrawn, and the original resolution carried unanimously. The Chairman added that he must take his fair share of any blame that attached to the adoption by the Midland Company of the Leeds and Bradford line; but he informed the meeting that the Manchester and Leeds had offered as much as or more for the line than the Midland had given.

The half-yearly meeting took place on the 27th of February, 1850, and between 500 and 600 shareholders were present. The proceeding occupied six hours. The total receipts for the half year amounted to more than

£600,000, being, however, a decrease of nearly £20,000 on the corresponding period of 1848. Out of this large sum the balance available for dividend was little more than £100,000, which would justify a dividend of only twenty-five shillings for the half-year upon the open stock. A line from Leicester to join the Swannington at Desford had been opened in the previous August, and one from Kirkby to Mansfield in October, 1849. Various suggestions were made for the reduction of expense, for the promotion of friendly co-operation with other companies, for the diminution of excessive parochial rates, and for the improvement of the dividends of the Company. It was mentioned that the railways of this country traversed 3000 parishes, that the rates levied in these parishes amounted to £800,000, and that of this amount the railways had to pay £250,000, though they never brought a pauper to a parish, or caused a shilling of expense. At this meeting Mr. Wylie, in a speech of nearly two hours' length, stated that he represented 1200 shareholders in and about Liverpool, who held shares to the amount of £1,623,000, but which were now worth only £524,000 in the market. Their leases and guarantees, he said, had shorn them of their strength. He contended for a reconstruction of the board. His motion, however, was defeated.

In the early part of the year 1850 a further portion of the Great Northern line was opened for traffic; the two companies charging equal fares to all places to which both ran. But so serious was the shock to the finances of the Midland that, at the autumnal meeting, August 23rd, 1850, the dividend was only sixteen shillings on the consolidated stock, the value of which had sunk from £100 to £32 and £33. The board consoled their constituency with the announcement that arrangements had been made with the York and North Midland and other companies for a joint use of the Leeds station; that the Oxford, Worcester, and Wolverhampton board had agreed that, when their line was opened, the Midland Company should run over it into Worcester, instead of, as hitherto, landing passengers and goods at Spetchley to be forwarded four miles by omnibuses and wagons; and that it was hoped that little additional capital would be needed. The Midland Company had 500 miles of railway, and all that remained incomplete was a small portion of the Erewash Valley branch, and the "lift" at Birmingham, for which £50,000 had been voted, both of which would be finished in about six weeks. Every yard that they intended to make would then be at work. At this meeting a suggestion was made that, with a view to economy, lighter engines should be used for some of the work of the line; but it was replied that such an arrangement would be inapplicable to the Midland traffic, which was of a heavy mixed description; indeed nineteen of the engines they possessed were not strong enough for the work. It was also mentioned that it was not intended to appoint a general manager, as the existing arrangement was satisfactory; and that an experiment of having low fares for short distances had succeeded so well, on what might be called the "omnibus traffic" of the Rotherham line, that it would be attempted in other places. It was decided that a statement of the salaries of officers who received more than £100 a year should be submitted at each half-yearly meeting; but this regulation was subsequently, on an appeal from the chairman, rescinded.

Before the proceedings closed a debate again arose with regard to the Leeds and Bradford line, whereupon the chairman said he regarded the re-opening of this discussion with solicitude as having "a tendency towards repudiation." He had very little or no personal interest in the matter, never having had but twenty shares in the Leeds and Bradford Company, which he purchased at a high premium, and which he believed he had sold before the lease was entered into. He was a party to the lease at the time it was arranged, when they were all rather too sanguine as to the value of railway property, and he warned the proprietors to be careful how they interfered with an engagement which they had previously sanctioned by a large majority. He had received several letters on the subject, one of which, from Lord Lifford, remarked that "any attempt to disturb the lease would put an end to confidence in railway property, and damage the characters of those who did it as honourable mercantile men."

WORCESTER.

In the autumn of the year 1850 the junction with the London and North Western Company at Birmingham, and also the link between the Mansfield and Erewash Valley lines were completed; and the branch of the Oxford, Worcester, and Wolverhampton Railway from

Abbott's Wood to Worcester was opened. The passenger receipts during the half-year fell off to the amount of nearly £8000, through the competition of the Great Northern Company; but the increase on goods rose to upwards of £32,000, leaving a sum available for dividend of 25*s.* for the half-year.

For some years after the Midland had secured access to Worcester, they continued to run their through trains on their main line, and they used the loop *viâ* Worcester only for the local traffic. Eventually, however, they obtained permission to send the whole of their traffic by the loop, and to do so on very moderate terms; this concession being granted by the Great Western as a sort of sop that the Midland should not oppose the bill for the amalgamation between the Great Western system and the West Midland lines. In this connection a curious circumstance has been mentioned to the author by Mr. Sturge, of Birmingham. It appears that a project for a line to run from Oxford to Worcester and Wolverhampton, to be called the "Grand Connexion," had been bought up by the Birmingham and Gloucester Company. So lightly, however, was this scheme valued, that when the Midland Company subsequently purchased the Birmingham and Gloucester, Mr. Hudson did not care to retain the right that went with it. He even returned the money that had been advanced by the shareholders upon it, and allowed it to go into the hands of what is now the London and North Western Company. But when the latter went to Parliament, the Great Western also appeared in the field to claim it for themselves. The strangeness of the circumstance attracted special attention, and members of the committee repeatedly remarked that the undertaking really belonged to neither of the claimants, but to a third party who did not appear. Mr. Hudson's mistaken policy in this matter was often regretted; especially as eventually the Midland Company had to buy back that which it had given away for nothing —access by this very route into Worcester.

A special meeting of the Midland Company was held on the 4th of June, 1851, chiefly to approve the acquisition "of the estate and interest of the Leeds and Bradford Railway Company." Mr. Ellis stated that the bill had already passed the Commons. It was considered to be a very important measure; and he made an appeal for the withdrawal of the opposition which it was understood some gentlemen intended to make. Mr. Brancker replied that the Leeds and Bradford scheme was a "preposterous undertaking," "concocted in iniquity," and "not calculated to benefit the Company;" and that, therefore, he responded to the appeal of the chairman with "great personal sacrifice." Mr. Wylie accepted the bill as the best course to be pursued under the circumstances; and the resolution was unanimously adopted.

The year 1851 was in some respects both remarkable and disappointing. The opening of the Great Exhibition created the expectation that the receipts by railways would be unusually large. These anticipations, however, were not realized. A multitude of passengers were conveyed to and from the metropolis, but the competition of the Great Northern Company led to the adoption of such low rates that the wonder was that the lines paid at all. From Leeds to London, for 5*s.* was a merely nominal fare; yet it was found that 5*s.* with full trains was remunerative. But the extraordinary flow of passengers to and from London greatly diminished the traffic elsewhere. The Birmingham and Gloucester traffic, for instance, which was untouched by the Great Northern competition, was affected in a remarkable degree. In one week in August the receipts on that line were £400 less than in the corresponding week of 1850, and in another week were £550 less, though on that line there had been no reduction of fares. "The fact is," said the Chairman, "there has been nobody going to Cheltenham this year; scarcely anybody to Scarborough; and the little Matlock line has experienced a decline in its receipts this year amounting to 20 per cent. All this is entirely owing to the Exhibition."

At the autumnal meeting of 1851 a committee was appointed consisting of five shareholders, each of whom held stock to the amount of not less than £2000, to select gentlemen who, on behalf of the shareholders, should examine and report on all the financial matters of the Company. On the same occasion attention was called to the fact that many proprietors who held very small amounts of shares were accustomed to apply for the free passes issued to those who wished to attend the shareholders' meetings, until the privilege had come to be frequently abused. At the previous meeting, for instance, one person who held less than £5 of stock and seven others who held less than £10 worth had obtained passes, five of whom had not attended the meeting; and 233 persons holding less than £100 of stock had obtained tickets, nearly half of whom were not present at the meeting. Under these circumstances a resolution was, after considerable discussion, adopted (which has since been published in the half-yearly reports), that thereafter "no proprietor holding less than £100 in stock, or shares to that amount, is entitled to travel to and from the meeting free of charge."

In the report presented at the half-yearly meeting on February 27th, 1852, the directors stated that the position of the Midland Company in relation to surrounding railways had been the subject of anxious consideration. It appeared to them, they said, to be essential that the

Company should now "be permanently identified with some Company having a line to and terminus in London." Impressed with this conviction the directors had had repeated interviews with the representatives of the London and North Western Company in order if possible to agree upon terms for an amalgamation of the two undertakings. Each board had made a distinct proposition, and they had actually come within 2½ per cent. of an arrangement: but £60 to the £100 was the lowest price that the Midland directors would consent to take (being a dividend of £3 for the Midland to £5 to the London and North Western), while £57 10s. to the £100 was the highest that the London and North Western would offer. Mr. Ellis, the chairman, said that he had been asked why he had been "so foolish" as to refuse 57½ "when his company was paying only 55s." But they were not to deal as if their line was about to be broken up in a year or two; and the directors were satisfied that the proportions on which they had fixed were the lowest that they ought to recommend the shareholders to accept. If the directors could only succeed in making a satisfactory arrangement for their traffic to London, he had no doubt that the best policy of the Midland Company would be to lie by for a while, and their position would improve. They were at present on a friendly footing with the London and North Western Company, whose interest it also was to work amicably with them; and he, therefore, felt as satisfied as if the amalgamation had actually been effected.

An important negotiation was at this time concluded with another North Western Company, commonly called for the purpose or way of distinction, "the Little" North Western, by which the Midland Company would be able to run from Skipton, which was the end of their Bradford line, to Lancaster and the shores of Lancashire at Morecambe Bay, whence communication could be opened with the Lake District, and the north coast of Ireland. The arrangement was to date from May, 1852, for 21 years, and the rent to be paid was one-half of the gross receipts until they should exceed £52,000 a year, when two-thirds of the excess beyond that amount was to be handed over to the North Western.

A special meeting of the Company was held on the 12th of May, 1852, chiefly to consider the propriety of commuting the sum of £90,000, then payable as annual rent to the Leeds and Bradford proprietors, into a permanent stock of £1,800,000 in 18,000 shares of £100 each, and bearing interest after the rate of 4½ per cent. per annum for 5 years, and afterwards of 4 per cent. per annum in perpetuity. The effect of this operation would be a saving of £9000 per annum till the 1st of July, 1857, and after that of £18,000 a year. The arrangement was approved.

The sanction of the shareholders was also given to a negotiation which had been carried on with a very short line with a very long name. It was "the Manchester, Buxton, Matlock, and Midland Junction," which ran from Ambergate to Rowsley, and was part of a scheme incorporated six years before, with the intention of connecting Ambergate with Cheadle station, near Manchester. At that time the Manchester and Birmingham Railway (now part of the London and North Western system) had frequently been in dispute with the lines that stretched southward; and after various attempts to obtain an outlet in other directions, had projected an independent route toward London by the Churnet valley (a line afterwards made by the North Staffordshire Company); and now they gladly joined in an enterprise for making a Buxton and Matlock line, which would furnish access to the Midland system. They accordingly obtained powers to subscribe £190,000 to the new scheme. But in the same year a change came over its policy. The Manchester and Birmingham Railway was itself incorporated into what is now the London and North Western Railway, the old jealousies with the southern lines of course ceased, sympathy with the new project was turned into alienation, and then financial difficulties arose which suspended further railway enterprises of all kinds. In consequence the capital was, in 1848, reduced, and the larger scheme shrank to the modest proportions of a line 11½ miles long, from Ambergate to Rowsley. It was now proposed that the Midland Company should work the line for 19 years, and pay a rent equal to 2½ per cent on £421,300 of called-up capital. The Cromford Canal, which, in order to prevent injurious competition, had previously been purchased by the projectors of the railway, was also to be taken over by the Midland Company, on condition that interest was paid on its capital to an amount not exceeding £110,000. As the Midland Company held more than 14,000 shares in the Rowsley line, it might in this arrangement be said to be dealing to a certain extent with its own property; the London and North Western Company, however, had some 9500 more, and all its susceptibilities had carefully to be regarded.

In August of this year (1852) some wars of words that had been waged between the Midland Company and the Great Northern culminated into a war of deeds. "The Great Northern having attempted," says a chronicler of the time, "to carry out its agreement with the Ambergate, by running engines into the Nottingham station, which is the Midland property, the Midland did neither more nor less than seize the Great Northern engine, which had brought a train down, just as it was about to start with a new load of passengers to London. The course taken was in accordance with the elephantine dimensions of the object seized, and after the fashion of elephant hunters. Thinking the engine might be like a wild elephant, refractory, the Midland sent some of its own kind to hem it in before and behind, and thus bore it off in triumph, while the poor passengers were obliged to sit patiently looking on at the contest and capture of the trespassing engine."

During the autumn of the year (1852) heavy floods damaged various parts of the line, bursting culverts, causing slips in embankments and cuttings, and undermining the foundation of one of the river piers of the Crow Mills Viaduct, near Leicester. It appears that a miller, who lived hard by the viaduct, was the first to see the timbers yielding, and that he took immediate steps to give the alarm up and down the line. The whole structure soon afterwards fell with a tremendous crash into the boiling waters beneath. The miller, we believe, received £100 from the Midland Company as a reward for his opportune services. Very exaggerated reports were circulated as to the injury the lines had received: some estimated it at £100,000, and others at much more; but the actual outlay was about £10,000. It was found that heavier rails than those at first used were required for the permanent way; and that large additions were necessary to the rolling stock. Meanwhile a considerable amount of debentures were, by a fall in the money market, renewed at a saving of £7000 a year; and an improved arrangement with the post office brought in an additional £4000 per annum.

But the most important transaction of this period was the revival of a project for the extension of the Midland system. Five years previously, as the reader will remember, an Act of Parliament had been passed to enable the Midland Company to make a line from near Leicester to Hitchen. The state of the money market, the depression of railway property, and other circumstances had prevented any progress being made with that scheme; and in July, 1850, the powers of the Act expired. The time, however, had now come at which so valuable an undertaking ought no longer to remain in abeyance; and some of the principal landowners in the neighbourhood of Market Harborough, Kettering, and Bedford appointed a deputation to wait upon the Midland board with offers of support in carrying out such an enterprise. Mr. Whitbread, through whose estates the proposed line would run almost continuously for between seven and eight miles—about one eighth of its course—promised to sell all land that the Company might require at £70 an acre, which was its simple agricultural value; and the Duke of Bedford and other landowners signed contracts to the same effect. The discovery of fields of ironstone in Northamptonshire, on the route of the line, was another weighty argument in its favour; and it was obviously important that the Midland Company, with its 500 miles of railway, and £17,000,000 of capital, should no longer be kept more than 80 miles from the metropolis, where, at Rugby, it was delivering to the London and North Western not less than 325,000 tons of coal, besides goods and passengers—an amount constantly and enormously increasing. It was, too, notorious that the pressure of traffic on the line from thence to London was becoming extreme, and would before long require in some way or other to be relieved.

Such were the facts that presented themselves to the minds of the directors, or were urged upon them by the deputation; and it was also significantly stated that in the event of the present overtures being rejected, the parties locally interested would immediately form an independent company, and that the line would be made. The Midland Directors in reply requested that a month might be afforded for the consideration of the matter; and in that interval they arrived at the decision that it was essential to the protection of Midland property that such a railway should form part of the Midland system. "No man," said Mr. Ellis, who had been taught by some costly experiences in the past, "has a greater horror of extensions than I have;" but he stated that he was convinced that such a line as that contemplated ought not to be in the hands of persons who might have interests at variance with those of the Midland Company. It had also been ascertained that such a line could now be made for an amount lower than any former estimate. "I have no hesitation," he added, "in saying that this is the most important line the Midland Company has ever promoted."

Another great question affecting the politics and the future of the Midland Company, and indeed of railway administration in England, now came under the anxious consideration of the Midland board. It will be remembered that in the early part of the year, certain terms had been proposed for an amalgamation between the Midland Company and the London and North Western, but the negotiating powers had been unable to arrive at an agreement. The two companies, however, remained on very friendly relations with each other; the subject of their possible union was not unfrequently referred to in conversation; and after a meeting held of committees of both companies, a letter was, on the 14th of August, 1852, addressed by the secretary of the London and North Western Company to the secretary of the Midland Company, to the effect that he was instructed to state that a "special committee has the authority of the board to meet a similar committee of your board, and discuss the question of a closer union or amalgamation of the two undertakings."

It is not a little remarkable that two days afterwards a similar communication was addressed by the chairman of the Great Northern Company to the chairman of the Midland. "I have frequently said to one of your colleagues," wrote Mr. Edmund Denison, "that in my opinion an earnest attempt ought to be made to unite the Great Northern and the Midland Railways, and the sensible letters which lately passed between Mr. Glyn and Mr. Russel have determined me to propose to my co-directors (and they have this day consented), that I should at once address a letter to you, offering the principle of a complete amalgamation of the Great Northern and Midland. They compete with each other in the south and in the north, and they cross each other at two or three important points. There are double stations at several towns, and duplicate trains run where single ones would serve the public equally well. A very large annual expenditure would therefore be saved, which would improve the dividends and the real value of both properties.

"An amalgamation of these two railways is so natural, from peculiar circumstances, and is so inevitable, that I apprehend no parliamentary objection would be offered, the two capitals united not being larger than the London and North Western alone."

Mr. Denison went on to suggest that the eastern side of the kingdom might thus come to have its terminus at King's Cross, and that the traffic of the western would be quite as large as the Euston Square and Paddington termini could accommodate. "I see no difficulty," he added, "in the manner of settling the terms of amalgamation, but I shall not say a word in detail upon that point until I hear that your board take a favourable view of the object proposed."

In reply to this communication Mr. Ellis expressed his gratification at the frank way in which the subject had been approached. "Our board is," he said, "equally with yourself, alive to the serious evils which are the inevitable result of competition between two lines which approach and intersect each other, and which have double stations at so many places." They wished to put an end to the running of "double trains where single ones would serve the interest of the public equally well," and "to prevent a reckless outlay of capital in the construction of new lines." He added that candour required him to state that a similar communication had been received from the London and North Western Company; but that the whole subject should have the early and most serious attention of the board.

These circumstances were mentioned at the half-yearly meeting of the Midland Company. The Chairman, however, stated that any discussion upon them would at that time be inopportune, and likely to compromise the ability of the board to do justice to the interests they represented. "We ask you, therefore," he said, "to leave the affair in our hands for the present. We shall lay before you the result of any propositions made or any negotiations entered into as early as possible, and I trust the course we recommend will be entirely acquiesced in by the proprietary." This course was heartily assented to; and two shareholders who attempted to address the meeting were immediately hissed down.

The correspondence between the Midland Company and the Great Northern was continued by Mr. Ellis, on the 9th of October, 1852. In a letter addressed to Mr. Edmund Denison, the Midland Chairman said that further reflection "only tended to confirm the opinions he had expressed in his previous letter." "Entertaining these views," he continued, "I am prepared cordially to co-operate with you in the measures best calculated to effect the object which we both seek to obtain; and I have the satisfaction to assure you that there exists on the part of the directors of the Midland and London and North Western Companies, a sincere desire to come to an amicable and satisfactory agreement with your Company. They are willing to do so by means of an extended arrangement, to be settled by referees of high standing, fully empowered to determine the matter upon a consideration of the objects and intentions of the legislature in sanctioning the respective undertakings. Should you, however, deem it better to promote a bill to authorise a more complete and lasting union of interest between the Great Northern and the united London and North Western and Midland Companies, our boards will be prepared to give that view of the question their immediate and favourable consideration." He added that these opinions had the unanimous assent of the Midland and London and North Western boards, and that a joint deputation would be prepared to meet a deputation from the Great Northern board, "fully empowered to discuss and arrange the details of this important question."

These letters were read at a special meeting of the Midland Company held at Derby, on the 3rd of November, 1852. Mr. Ellis, the chairman, spoke at great length on the evils of competition, and the fact that Parliament had sanctioned lines that ought never to have been made; that railway legislation had been a disgrace to the age, and that the question of amalgamation must inevitably engage the early consideration of the legislature. Then, turning to the position of the Midland Company, he said that there were some who thought the Midland Company should stand alone. "It could stand alone, there was no doubt of that," but the greatest benefits would accrue to both Companies by an identity of interest. He concluded by moving the following resolution: "That it is expedient to effect a permanent union of interest between the London and North Western and Midland Railway Companies, and to amalgamate the undertakings on the following terms, viz.: That the relative values of the two undertakings be ascertained and fixed by three referees of high standing." The resolution was carried by a very large majority, and a bill in accordance with this decision was submitted to Parliament. It was, however, eventually withdrawn in consequence of the appointment of a select committee of the House of Commons, which advised the House not to allow any amalgamation during the session, and which also reported against the amalgamation of very large companies.

We may pass lightly over the next few years in the history of the Midland Railway. A period of rest had arrived between the excitements and dangers of the past, and the time when a bolder policy might be initiated. Four years since, and the dividend was only 16*s.*; it was now 35*s.* The competition of the Great Northern had carried off a large amount of the passenger traffic, and it was only by an increasing goods traffic that the Midland Company had been able to hold on its way.

No wonder that for some time to come it "walked softly." The only outlay of importance in the year 1854 was in the construction of a narrow-gauge line alongside the broad gauge from Gloucester to near Stonehouse, and the making of a mixed gauge (instead of broad only) from thence to Bristol. Arrangements also were effected of an economical and mutually beneficial nature, between the Midland and the London and North Western Companies for the interchange of traffic.

In 1855 the abstraction of the Great Northern of Midland passenger traffic continued; but the chairman, Mr. Beale, not unnaturally drew comfort from the fact that the goods and mineral traffic had had a "prodigious increase." With a wise foresight he expressed the belief that that was "a certain and fast growing traffic, which was peculiarly their own."

The years 1856 and 1857 were almost as uneventful as their immediate predecessors. The turning of certain timber bridges into iron and stone; the arrangement of sorting sidings at Toton and Rugby; improvements in the method of keeping the accounts of the company; the reference to Mr. Gladstone of some weighty matters that were in dispute between the Midland and the North Western, Great Northern, and Sheffield Companies; and the opening, on the 8th of May, 1858, of the Leicester

WELLINGBOROUGH VIADUCT.

and Hitchen line—on which the Wellingborough Viaduct is perhaps the most interesting work—were the chief events of the period. It is, however, worthy of note that, so severe had been the injuries inflicted by the Great Northern competition upon the Midland Company, that in 1857, with 500 miles of railway (without the Hitchen extension) their passenger traffic was £30,000 less than it had been ten years previously, with only 377 miles open. In 1847 their earnings for passengers were 5s. 2d. a mile, and in 1857 they were 4s. 0½d. Happily, the development of goods and minerals had partially recouped this loss.

In the report for July, 1858, the directors referred to the resignation of Mr. Ellis and Mr. Beale, the chairman and deputy-chairman of the Company, and also to the election of Mr. G. B. Paget, who, however, had survived his appointment only a brief period. In consequence of this lamentable event, Mr. Ellis had consented for a short time to resume the duties of the chairmanship.

The only circumstance worthy of special notice in the year 1858 was the severe conflict carried on between the Midland and the surrounding and competitive lines. This, however, at length abated, and all parties returned to more remunerative relations one with another.

In 1859 the directors resolved to extend the Erewash Valley line up to Clay Cross near Chesterfield. An Act for the purpose had previously been obtained, but in consequence of the depressed state of the finances of the Company the powers had been allowed to expire. The proposed line could be used as the main line to the north; and it would open out a coal field of the greatest value. The directors also, in conjunction with the Great Western, resolved to dispose of the Gloucester and Cheltenham tramway. That ancient road had become "like a house without a tenant; an expense without an advantage; a load without a profit." A suitable hotel was to be erected at Leeds. The Castle and Falcon, Aldersgate Sreet, London, was obtained for the erection of goods warehouses; and twenty acres of land were purchased, near the Great Northern terminus, for a Midland goods station; £1000 were also set apart for a foot bridge from the Derby passenger station to the locomotive sheds.

On the 25th of May, 1860, the Midland Company was authorised to construct a railway, 15 miles in length, between Rowsley and Buxton, there to be connected with a line about to be made by the London and North Western from Whaley Bridge to Buxton. For many years past various projects of extension had been entertained. As far back as 1845 several competitive schemes were proposed for thus uniting the eastern and midland counties of England with Manchester and Liverpool. The Boston, Nottingham, Ambergate, and Midland Junction for instance proposed to unite with the Manchester, Buxton, Matlock, and Midland Junction, and thus to provide a through route from the Lincolnshire to the Lancashire coast. But great difficulties had to be overcome, on account both of the ownership of the land and the formation of the country. Buxton, for instance, is nearly 1000 feet above the level of the sea, and if a line were made to get up to it, how would it get down again by decent gradients to Manchester. Although eventually the valley of the Derwent was adopted, and Buxton was left out in the cold, other routes had been thought of. One was by Eyam, Chapel-le-Frith, and the Peak; the other by Castleton and Whaley Bridge. In either case the local population and the trade to be served were of the scantiest; and hence one that went by Baslow Moors came, by the commodities which it was thought would form its chief traffic, to be designated the "Bilberry and Besom Line," while the other through the Peak* was known, on account of the innumerable tunnels on its course, as "the Flute Line."

The then Duke of Devonshire gave his consent to a line being made through his park at Chatsworth, on condition that it was by a covered way, and there is no doubt that that route would have supplied the best levels; but the present duke objected to such an invasion of his

* Another, subsequently proposed, was called the "High Pique Line."

ancestral domains; and after much negotiation with the Duke of Rutland, it was decided that the line should be carried along its present course, at the back of Haddon Hall.

A thousand special precautions had, however, to be observed. None of the trees were to be removed or lopped by the contractors or navvies during the progress of the works; agents and keepers were set to watch the property and the game; one duke wanted the principal station to be at Bakewell, and the other required that it should be at Hassop, and both had to be built; and the line through the park of Haddon Hall was

MONSAL DALE.

carried along the hill side by the excavation of portions —half cutting, half tunnel—which were then covered in.

These difficulties being overcome, and the heavy works of Monsal and Miller's Dale being provided for, the mighty limestone crag of Chee Tor barred the way.

CHEE VALE.*

This is the second tunnel to the north of what is now Miller's Dale Station. Many an engineer had carried his imaginary line from Ambergate to Buxton thus far, but had gone no farther; for, in addition to the ordinary work of piercing a hill of solid mountain limestone, there was the fact that the rock rose abruptly 300 feet in one face above the river, that consequently no shafts were possible, that the tunnel must be made wholly and only from the two ends, and that before the southern end could be touched the river must be spanned by a bridge, and the bridge be approached through another tunnel.

The work, however, was done, and the line to-day

* Chee Tor is immediately to the right of the bridge.

carries the traveller through perhaps the most interesting series of railway works to be found in England.

CHEE VALE.*

At the spring meeting, 1861, the chairman had the satisfaction of announcing a dividend at the rate of 7 per cent. per annum. "The revenue accounts," he said, "were most satisfactory. The rate of increase had been greater than on any other line in the year;" and the directors decided upon some extensions of the Midland system. One of these was in Wharfedale, near Leeds, and was to be carried out in conjunction with the North Eastern. Another was from Evesham to Ashchurch, in the valley of the Avon. A third was from Whitacre on the Midland line to Nuneaton, by means of which, in conjunction with the line from Leicester to Hinckley, the

* The northern end of Chee Tor Tunnel is seen in the distance.

Midland Company would have access from Leicester to Birmingham. Further, a few years previously an independent company had made a short line of two or three miles from the Birmingham and Bristol to Dursley. But such a scrap of railway could scarcely be expected to pay if worked by itself, and it was now agreed to transfer it to the Midland Company for some £10,500, that being something like half its cost. Unfortunately, as time passed on, the remarkable increase of traffic which the Midland Company had been enjoying began to wane, in consequence of the general depression of trade. And so the year 1861 drew to a close.

FOOTBRIDGE IN MONSAL DALE.

CHAPTER VII.

The short line with the long name.—London and North Western's Disley line.—A "block" line.—Midland and North Western "most hostile."—Proposed Midland line to Manchester.—Duke of Devonshire's support.—Whaley Bridge and Buxton extension of North Western Company —"The Three Companies' Agreement" to exclude the Midland from Manchester.—"The Triple Agreement."—The Midland shut out.—A chance meeting —Negotiations between Sheffield Company and Midland for access to Manchester *viâ* New Mills.—Evidence in favour of new Midland line. —Town clerk of Manchester.—Manchester Chamber of Commerce.—Mr. Cheetham.—Other witnesses.—Opposition of London and North Western Company.—Offer of "facilities" over North Western line from Buxton to Manchester.—Sir Joseph Paxton's evidence.—Opposition of Great Northern.—Supposed encouragement to a breach of agreement.—Gouty patients.—Death of Mr. John Ellis.—Eminent services of Mr. Ellis.—Proposed Midland line to London.—The "destiny" of the Midland.—Insufficient accommodation of Great Northern *viâ* Hitchen for Midland traffic. —Delays.—Five miles of coal trains blocked at Rugby.—Witnesses from St. Albans.—Great Northern propose to double their line.—Reply to the proposal.—Mr. Allport's evidence.—Other projects in the field. — Camden Square. — Horticultural perplexities.—Bill passed.—Proposed line from Cudworth to Barnsley.—Importance of the line.—Other railway projections and working alliances.

We have already referred to a short railway with a long name that ran from Ambergate as far as Rowsley—a portion of what had originally been intended to form a connecting line between Manchester and the Midland system. In 1852 this fragment was leased to the London and North Western and Midland Companies for 19 years, at 2½ per cent. interest upon the capital, the North Western being glad to retain a legal hold upon the property in order to *prevent* this line, or any extension of it, from ever becoming part of a through route from Manchester to the metropolis. It was under the influence of the same considerations that the North Western, in the following year (1853), also encouraged a project for a new line from their system at Stockport, by way of Disley, to Whaley Bridge. It was, indeed, stated at the time that the scheme originated with independent parties; nevertheless, clauses were inserted in the bill giving power to the London and North Western to work the line; and eventually, out of a capital for the Disley line and Buxton extension of £310,000, the North Western advanced £299,000. "The accounts show," said Mr. Allport, "on the face of them that the line is London and North Western."

To the construction of this Disley line the Midland Company were naturally and necessarily opposed. They were so because they were vitally affected by any measures for completing the links in the chain of communication across Derbyshire to Manchester; because, though the two companies were on terms of amity, and had previously always acted on the matter conjointly, the Midland were now excluded from participation in the contemplated arrangements; and because the Midland Company's board believed that an effort was being made to fill up the country with a line of a designedly inferior character—a line for blocking up the way, and not for opening it. "The proposed railway," said Mr. Allport, "for some reason which does not appear on the face of it," is run along the high country where there is little or no population; and instead of taking the valley with a gradually rising ascent, "it goes up a steep gradient out of Buxton, to fall down again. The line appears to me to have gone up the hill for the sake of going down again." These criticisms on the project seem to have given offence to the London and North Western Company; and they complained to the Midland board that Mr. Allport's evidence was "most hostile." The Midland board, however, replied that they concurred in the statements of their general manager; that he had their sanction in giving evidence against the bill; that they regretted to find that such a course was deemed most hostile; and they "would have been glad if, by previous communication between the two boards, means had been devised for preventing even the appearance of hostile interests."

On the last day of the year 1856 the Midland Company made a proposal to the London and North Western that the idea originally contemplated in the scheme for the Manchester, Buxton, Matlock and Midland Junction Railway—and set forth in the name that the company bore—should be carried into effect, and that a through route should be made. The Midland board stated that they would subscribe £200,000 towards such an object. It was also known that the Duke of Devonshire was willing to contribute £50,000, and that he had even offered a passage for the line through his park at Chatsworth, if it were necessary. The North Western directors, however, replied that though the local traffic ought to be accommodated, and though they were prepared to join with the Sheffield Company in making a line suitable for that purpose, they could not, as Mr. Stewart, the secretary, expressed it, "recommend their proprietors to become parties to so costly a scheme," as that now advocated.

Meanwhile, however, the North Western Company were promoting, at their own expense, and without the co-operation or the knowledge of the Midland Company, an extension of their Disley line to Buxton—an expense nearly equal to the share they had been asked to contribute for the through line. To this project the Midland Company made no parliamentary opposition. They had been refused a hearing on the original Whaley Bridge Railway, on the ground that they had no *locus standi;* and they were advised that they would have no better claim to appear against the extension than against the original line. The Act for the Whaley Bridge and Buxton line was accordingly obtained (1857).

While the London and North Western Company was

thus steadily drawing on towards Buxton, and doing so by works which could never be available as a through line for either Company, other powers were being brought into play which it was hoped would even more effectually shut out the Midland Company from any access to the North. An agreement, which had made the Manchester, Sheffield, and Lincolnshire Company a dependency of the London and North Western, came, in 1857, to an end; in the following year, despite the strenuous opposition of the North Western, the Sheffield Company entered into alliance with the Great Northern, and thereby opened a new route between the Metropolis and Manchester; and now these three companies, having abated their mutual rivalies, joined in a compact with one another to keep away all intruders from their territories.

With this design an agreement called "The Three Companies' Agreement" was made, and application was made to secure for it the sanction of law. It succeeded in passing the Commons; but was rejected in the Lords, on the ground that it ought not to bear prejudicially upon the Midland Company. What followed is worthy of note. In 1860 another application was made to Parliament for its sanction to this agreement. Again it was opposed by the Midland, who urged the adoption of a "Four Companies' Bill," in which their interests were protected. Both bills, however, were thrown out; and then the three companies resolved to act as if, though twice rejected, their bill had passed; and they succeeded by mutual arrangements in excluding the traffic of the Midland from the entire district. The North Western stopped the Midland at Stockport, and the Manchester and Sheffield at Hyde. Subsequently it was ascertained that by adopting a northerly and circuitous route the Midland Company could yet reach a point of the York- shire and Lancashire line, and so find a route for its traffic from London to Manchester; and an agreement was made, February 28th, 1861, with that intent. But the arrangement had not subsisted more than a few months when it was suddenly terminated; and it transpired that an agreement, dated as far back as 1850, and called the "Triple Agreement," had been entered into between the Lancashire and Yorkshire, the Sheffield, and the North Western Companies, by which they undertook to exclude other companies from the traffic which they jointly commanded, and to use every exertion and inducement to confine this traffic to the lines of the said three companies; and they agreed that if any other company attempted to divert any of this traffic the highest tolls should be charged.

The Midland Company was now effectually excluded from access to Lancashire by any existing route; and the only alternatives that remained were, either to abandon all hope of carrying their traffic in that direction, or to construct an extension of their own Buxton line—which was approaching completion—to Manchester. Instructions were therefore issued to their engineer to examine the country with a view to a through Midland route direct from near Buxton to Manchester.

One day, in the autumn of the same year (1861), the Midland chairman, Mr. Beale, the deputy chairman, Mr. Hutchinson, and Mr. Allport were visiting the country "promiscuously," as Mr. Sergeant Wrangham called it, through which such a line would have to pass. They were not surveying; "the country had been surveyed fifty times by various parties." They had plans that had previously been made, and the ordnance maps with various lines marked upon them; and while driving, walking, and asking their way through the country, they unexpectedly, in a bye lane, met a dog-cart, on which Mr. Lees, one of the directors, and two of the officers of the Sheffield Company, were riding. "And what are you doing here?" the latter good-naturedly demanded. "We will show you," was the reply. "You know the country; perhaps you will accompany us." The Midland officers then stated the object they had in view—to endeavour to select a route for a new line to Manchester. The gentlemen of both companies remained together during the day; and in the course of conversation it was suggested by the Sheffield directors that it would be undesirable for an independent line to be made side by side with their own, and that it might be possible for the Midland Company to have the use of the Sheffield Company's line from New Mills to Manchester. It was further proposed that Mr. Allport—who had previously been for nearly four years general-manager of the Sheffield Company, and was intimately acquainted with all its details—should have an interview on these proposals with the chairman of the Sheffield Company. This was done; and the result was that it was agreed that the Midland should run its own trains over the railways of the Sheffield Company "to or from Manchester, and every other place in Manchester, in Lancashire, or Cheshire, or beyond," and that thus the work would be done by "one hand."*

But though these arrangements simplified the course of the Midland Company, and though not a single landowner opposed the project, the bill encountered the determined resistance of the other powerful interests that had enjoyed a monopoly of the carrying trade of the district; and the Midland Company had to gather up their best arguments to prove the necessity of the line.

One of these was found in the fact that existing routes

* Sir Edward Watkin seems never to have forgiven his board that they arranged these terms, so favourable, as he thinks, to the Midland Company, while he was absent in the United States.

were inadequate. Suppose, for instance, a passenger wished to go from Nottingham to Manchester, two routes were available. By the Great Northern, he would be first carried due east twenty-three miles to Grantham; from Grantham he would turn northward as far as Retford; then westward viâ Sheffield to Manchester—a most circuitous course. Or, by the other route, he would proceed by the Midland Railway to Derby, by North Staffordshire to Macclesfield or Crewe, and then by the London and North Western to Manchester,—by three different companies, with three different sets of trains, and all the contingencies involved in their adjustment, or want of it.

Evidence to like effect was given by various competent persons. For instance, on the 7th of March, 1862, the General Purposes Committee, which represents the corporation of Manchester, passed a resolution that they were "decidedly of opinion that increased facilities of communication between this city and Derby, Leicester, Nottingham, and other places in the midland district are now much required;" and they directed that a copy of this resolution be transmitted to the solicitor of the Midland Railway. In cross examination (March, 1862) Mr. Cripps inquired of Mr. Heron, now Sir Joseph Heron, the town clerk of Manchester, whether he had not been "a great advocate for a communication between Manchester and London by means of the Great Northern system." Mr. Heron replied that by desire of the corporation he had given expression to a desire for such increased accommodation, and that undoubtedly it had been secured.

"You have had," asked Mr. Cripps, "increased facilities?"

"Yes; we have had increased facilities; we have an excellent second route to London, and we have the fares reduced from two guineas, at which they previously stood, to £1 13*s.* by express trains, which is a very great public advantage."

"I understand," continued the counsel, "that you have nothing to complain of at present, so far as Manchester and London communications are concerned?"

"I have not come here," replied the witness, "to make any complaint whatever."

"Manchester has a choice of one of two routes to London?"

"They have; and I suppose there would be a choice of three if this line were made."

"Should you come here equally for a communication for a fourth route?"

"That depends; it is quite possible a fourth route might not be objectionable."

The Manchester Chamber of Commerce also expressed its desire for more direct communication with Derby, Leicester, Nottingham, and other Midland towns; and asked that legislative sanction might be given to any measure that might appear best calculated to provide it. Influential manufacturers, too, bore similar testimony. Mr. Cheetham of Staleybridge, for instance, stated that his firm paid some £1500 a year, for carriage of yarn between his works and Nottingham, Derby, and Leicester; yarn which was made into stockings, a large amount of which subsequently returned to Manchester. Serious inconvenience arose to men of business from having to travel by routes so circuitous, and to owners of goods from having to deal with two or three companies in the carriage of freight. He was of opinion that the new route would be "very much the best, the most direct, and the shortest."

Mr. Kenworthy, the mayor of Ashton, another cotton spinner, gave similar testimony, and especially to the importance of having, if possible, one company responsible for any delay or loss that might occur in railway transit. "It is not," he said, "a question of law, but of getting practical redress. We have had great difficulty in fixing the complaint on the different companies. Latterly we have had very great trouble indeed."

The general manager of the firm of S. & J. Watts, stated that they had very large transactions with retail dealers in about fifty towns in Derbyshire, Leicestershire, and Nottinghamshire. Hosiery, lace, and gloves were bought to the amount of £100,000 a year; all sorts of drapery goods were despatched to the same districts, to the value of £50,000 a year, and the delays in the transmission of this costly property was considerable. Buyers, too, found the routes to Manchester so inconvenient that it was necessary to come one day and return the next, a circumstance which greatly tended to hinder trade. "I have been left," said another witness, "dozens of times at the North Staffordshire station at Macclesfield in times past, sometimes as long as two hours, and sometimes with fifteen or sixteen other passengers."

These arguments were eagerly resisted by the London and North Western and Great Northern Companies; and when it was found that direct opposition might be unavailing, the North Western offered that its own route from Buxton to Manchester—the Disley line as it was called—should be used by the Midland Company, instead of the new line it was proposed to make. "Assuming," said Mr. Hope Scott, "that the London and North Western Company are willing to give full facilities, backed, if necessary, by contingent running powers in case of misbehaviour, and are willing to be at extra costs entailed by greater steepness of gradients, why should not the Midland traffic be sufficiently accommodated over the Disley line?"

"I cannot go into those details," replied Sir Joseph

Paxton. "My opinion is that they will not offer such powers."

"But I do offer them," returned Mr. Scott. "I offer you facilities, with contingent running powers in case of abuse. I offer you facilities into Manchester."

"We know," replied Sir Joseph, significantly, "what 'facilities' are." "If," he subsequently added, "we had running powers over the Disley line, direct into Manchester from Stockport, and accommodation was given there for the traffic, then I think it very likely that my board and the other directors might think that sufficient; but I do not think it is. I think it a very poor way of finishing a great communication between London and Manchester, and Manchester and the Midland districts."

His concluding observation was subsequently confirmed by Mr. Beale. "My opinion," he said, "and the opinion of the entire Midland board is, that the proposed facilities would be totally inadequate, and that they would not give the open vent which the immense traffic of the important Midland district requires. I believe this line, if made, will be one of the main arteries of the kingdom for railway traffic. I may tell my lords that in eleven years the gross traffic of the Midland has increased something like ninety per cent., of which probably upwards of sixty per cent. is upon the development of old lines, and not in the slightest degree in connection with additional lines, and I feel personally quite sure that the public cannot have accommodation unless the line is granted."

When, too, the route by the Disley line was thus offered to the Midland Company, an important qualification was introduced into the terms. The North Western Company expressly required that the traffic should be what they called "proper traffic"; and they stated, for instance, that they would not take Birmingham and

Bristol traffic; though, of course, if the Midland had a line of their own, their traffic might flow that way. It is true that the North Western secretary promised that his company would take any traffic that they might fairly be required to convey; but the Midland Company were not satisfied to leave the question of what might be "fairly required" to the decision of another and rival board.

An objection made by the London and North Western Company to the proposed Midland line was, that it would run more or less parallel with the existing Disley route, and that this would imply a needless outlay of capital. But such an arrangement, it was replied, was frequently found advantageous where there was a diversity of interests. Duplicate lines run for six or seven miles north of Peterborough; the one belonging to the Great Northern Company, the other to the Midland; there being merely a fence between them. Between Leeds and Bradford there are also duplicate lines, and between Birmingham and the Staffordshire districts there are three.

The opposition to the Midland scheme made by the Great Northern Company was based on other grounds. They contended that the Sheffield Company had no right to give the Midland Company facilities of access by New Mills to Manchester, inasmuch as by doing so they would violate obligations previously incurred towards themselves. "I charge the Midland Company," said Sergeant Wrangham, "not with the breach of any agreements, but with abetting the Sheffield Company in breaking agreements that they have had with us, the Great Northern." To this it was replied on behalf of the Sheffield Company, that they might not unnaturally say, 'Here is a company that intends to reach Manchester by a line made side by side with ours. Will it not be better that this multiplication of lines should be avoided; that, as they *will* come into the town, we should let them come, and come over our route, and utilize to our advantage, as well as their own, a part of our line?" To enforce their views the Great Northern filed a bill in Chancery.

One of the objections made before the parliamentary committee to the Midland extension, gave rise to an amusing conversation. It was supposed by the opponents of the Midland line that passengers for Buxton would necessarily have to change carriages at the junction at Blackwell.

BLACKWELL MILL JUNCTION.

Mr. Merewether: "Will you assume that a man comes over the great through line to Blackwell Mill?"

Dr. Robertson: "Yes."

Mr. Merewether: "That is the junction for your invalid?"

Dr. Robertson: "Yes."

Mr. Merewether: "My learned friend has referred to gout—gout is a disturber of the temperament?"

Dr. Robertson: "It is."

Mr. Merewether: "Your gouty patient—a gouty merchant from Manchester—is of quite as warm a temperament as most people."

Dr. Robertson: "Hear, hear."

Mr. Merewether: "Will you bring him from Manchester with his gout, and his Manchester temperament? Will you put him out at Blackwell Mill to get into the branch train to go to Buxton?"

Dr. Robertson: "I have been told so. . ."

Mr. Merewether: "Do you put it as a medical view, that going along a gradient of 1 in 60 * would exasperate a gouty patient more than being put out at the station at Blackwell, and being sent round to Buxton?"

Dr. Robertson: "I consider that going along a gradient of 1 in 60 would exasperate any man, gouty or not."

The Act of Parliament by which the line was sanctioned was passed, and the railway was opened for public traffic, on the first of June, 1863, the day named in the contract.

An improvement of great importance was during this year effected in the arrangement of the passenger service by the opening on the 1st of May, 1862, of the Trent station. At this point great and increasing difficulty had been experienced in the safe and expeditious conduct of the traffic. Trains came in from, and went out in, four different directions—east to Nottingham, west to Derby, north to the Erewash, and south to London. At one time it was the practice to take passengers who were going from Nottingham to London round by Derby and back to what is now Trent, an 18 miles' journey for

* The Disley route.

nothing. Subsequently the Nottingham trains were shunted into a siding at Kegworth, and there they waited till the Derby portions arrived. The opening of the Erewash line, too, necessarily created a dangerous level crossing of lines at right angles at a place called Platts's Crossing, about 200 yards north of what is now the Trent Station.

With regard to the spot itself, its lines, curves, cross-

TRENT STATION.

overs, and junctions, Sir Edmund Beckett has offered some playful criticisms in words to the following effect: "You arrive at Trent. Where that is I cannot tell. I suppose it is somewhere near the river Trent; but then the Trent is a very long river. You get out of your train to obtain refreshment, and having taken it, you endeavour to find your train and your carriage. But whether it is on this side or that, and whether it is going north or south, this way or that way, you cannot tell. Bewildered, you frantically rush into your carriage; the train moves off round a curve, and then you are horrified to see some red lights glaring in front of you, and you are in immediate expectation of a collision, when your fellow passenger calms your fears by telling you that they are only the tail lamps of you own train!"

On the 26th of October, 1862, Mr. Ellis, who had for so long a period been connected with the interests of the Midland Company, died. John Ellis came of a goodly stock: his forefathers were honest Yorkshire yeomen. His father, Joseph Ellis, removed into Leicestershire in 1784,

BEAUMONT LEYS.

where he occupied, until his death, in 1810, a farm which required in its management unusual skill and industry to work it successfully. Left at the age of twenty-one with the care of his brothers and a sister, John Ellis succeeded to a small patrimony, and the good name of his father, which he was wont to say was his best inheritance. He followed his father's calling, and in early life, at Beaumont Leys, near Leicester, he could plough and sow, reap and mow, with any man. In the harvest field it is said that he did not know his equal, and even when rising to eminence in his calling he did not abandon these homelier employments. He milked his cows until he went to Parliament.

Meanwhile, through the late Mr. James Cropper, of Liverpool, he had become acquainted with George Stephenson, and hence the circumstances arose that led to the connection of both of them with the Leicester and Swannington Railway. He early identified himself with the policy of Free Trade; and before a parliamentary committee, expressed the opinion that the English farmer should prepare to grow wheat at £2 10s. a quarter; and he added, he can afford to do so; "a bold thing," it has been remarked, "for a farmer to say in those days."

In 1847 he was sent to Parliament for the borough of Leicester. "He entered into his new duties," says a local writer of discrimination, "with characteristic earnestness; his sagacious judgment and practical knowledge on all questions which he pretended to understand, soon gave him a position in the House, and his opinion on such subjects was not unfrequently asked by some of our leading statesmen."

Mr. Ellis was from the first a director of the Leicester and Swannington Railway, and, for some years, of the Midland Counties Railway. On the amalgamation of the latter with the North Midland and Birmingham and Derby Companies, he was placed on the joint board, and appointed deputy chairman. In 1849 he was elected chairman of the Midland Railway. On resigning this office in 1858, the directors gave expression to the "deep pain" which they experienced at the event; "but remembering," they said, "the express conditions upon which he consented to withdraw a previous resignation, they felt precluded from further pressing upon him the duties and responsibilities of the chair." They rightly recalled the fact that Mr. Ellis had undertaken his office, "at a period of unusual difficulty and mistrust, when embarrassment and ruin hung over so many undertakings of a similar kind;" but that he had encountered the perils of the crisis with a determination which rose superior to the danger, with a confidence which cheered his colleagues, and with a practical sagacity which was of immediate and decisive value.

The gratitude of the shareholders was expressed by a vote of 1000 guineas. Part of this sum was expended in a service of plate, and the remainder in a full length portrait by Lucas; in the background of which is a view of the works and tunnel entrance of the Leicester and Swannington Railway. The portrait hangs in the shareholders' room at the Derby station.

"He will be greatly missed," said a local writer, "by his associates in public life and in works of charity We shall miss his well known face and figure in our public meetings and in our streets. We shall miss his wise counsel, and his genial warm-hearted converse. He has won the respect of all who knew him. His name will be a household word amongst us, and there will long be a kind thought and a good word for John Ellis." *

A period had now arrived in the administration of the Midland Company when it was called to confront new and weighty responsibilities. Hitherto its area of operations had been restricted to the midland districts of England; but its vast and increasing traffic southward suggested the inquiry whether it ought not to be placed in direct communication with the metropolis itself. There

* The *Leicester Journal*, Oct. 31st, 1862.

were some who thought, and some who said, that the Midland Railway had no right to widen its field of operation. When the Manchester Extension Bill was before the Lords' committee, Mr. Hope Scott, the counsel for the London and North Western Company, declared that the "destiny" of the Midland Company forbade its further development. "My learned friend," replied Sir W. Alexander, "was rather oblivious when he said that the Midland Company had no natural terminus in London. Not only was my learned friend tempted to indulge in that somewhat hyperbolical phrase, but he said also, that it was not the destiny of the Midland Company to go to London or to Manchester. It was rather a strange term to use. Destiny! was it the destiny of the London and North Western Railway Company, which was originally a line to Birmingham and Liverpool, to join the Caledonian? Was it their destiny to seek a line to West Hartlepool? Was it their destiny to seek, as they were doing a few days ago, a line to Merthyr Tydfil? Yes; that they are doing. Was it their destiny to seek a line to Cambridge, the very head-quarters of the Eastern Counties territory, which they did when they obtained the line from Cambridge to Bedford? I dare say these lines were passed by my learned friend's able advocacy. They have come to Leicester, they have come to Burton —that is upon the notes—and they have purchased land at Derby, adjoining the head-quarters of the Midland system with the view of competing with the Midland system. And they say, forsooth, that the Midland Company, with 700 miles of railway, coming within 25 miles of Manchester, with £260,000 in the course of expenditure upon their London station, are not to be considered, and that it is not their destiny to reach London or Manchester."

On the contrary the Midland Company had advisedly

looked forward to the time when it would require to have a line of its own to the metropolis, and it had expressly avoided any negotiation which might seem to commit it to a narrower policy. When, for instance, in 1858, an agreement between the Great Northern, the Manchester Sheffield and Lancashire, and the Midland Companies, was drawn up by Mr. John Bullar, in which there was what is called the "amity clause," under which the companies were to abstain from aggression into each others' territories: in this agreement it was declared that nothing it contained was "to prevent the Midland Company making a line to London, after notice" had been given.

At length the time drew on when the Midland board had to face the question of how best to deal with its vast and increasing London traffic. "Perhaps," said Mr. Allport, in 1862, "there is hardly another instance of a large system increasing like ours." In five years the amount of goods and minerals had risen from 676,000 tons to 1,111,000, and was steadily augmenting. True, the Great Northern Company was, by agreement, bound to allow the Midland the use of their London goods and coal stations; but it was soon found that these were so inadequate for the requirements of both companies that, in 1860 and '61 the Midland Company had to go to Parliament for powers to acquire a large amount of land adjoining the Great Northern, where it might have a goods station of its own; and the capital authorised for this purpose amounted to some £340,000.

The accommodation provided by the Great Northern for the Midland passenger trains was also insufficient. Experience has proved that there are certain times of the day most convenient to the London public to travel, and five o'clock in the afternoon is one of these times. Accordingly the Great Northern started one of its chief express trains at that hour; this was followed by a large local traffic; and it became undesirable that the Midland express should follow earlier than 5.35, and even then it was often pulled up by signals before it reached Hitchen. It is true that the Midland were entitled by agreement to fix the running of their trains at hours mutually convenient, and that there was an appeal to arbitration; but, as Mr. Allport remarked, "no arbitrator can enable you to perform physical impossibilities." In fact, in 1862, the Exhibition year, there were nearly 1000 Midland passenger trains and nearly 2400 goods trains delayed between Hitchen and King's Cross. "The Midland," said Mr. Allport, "can never tell with anything like certainty at what time their trains will reach King's Cross. They may be in good time at Hitchen, but delays constantly occur between that place and London, especially near the terminus at Holloway, where the trains are kept waiting outside the tunnel till the station is cleared inside, and they can be admitted. Or if the Midland train comes from the north, depending perhaps for its time of starting on other trains still further north,* and is late at Hitchen, they find of course that other trains have already started before them, and they must take their chance—being a stranger company; and having no control over the management they cannot order a slow train to shunt and let a Midland express pass, though on their own lines such a practice would be at once adopted. Constant complaints are made to the Midland Company of these irregularities, and the Great Northern on many occasions have frankly admitted their inability to avoid them."

Nor was it only on the Great Northern line that the Midland Company had to contend with these difficulties and delays. An enormous traffic was also sent from the

* At Normanton the Midland has to wait for trains from Newcastle and Edinburgh, and at Ingleton for trains from Carlisle and Glasgow.

Midland system to London *viâ* Rugby. In fact, in 1862, the Midland Company paid the Great Northern £60,000 for tolls to London, in addition to rents for the use of their London station, and to the London and North Western no less than £193,000 for traffic by Rugby; and such was the crowded state of that company's line, that, though they had laid a third pair of rails for fifty miles for the up trains, from Bletchley to London, they were unable to accommodate the traffic. On one occasion they suddenly gave notice that they could not convey the mineral traffic from the Midland system: and the coal trains accumulated at Rugby till they were *five miles long*, to the infinite annoyance of the sellers at the fields, and of the buyers in London, who were depending on the arrival of the coal for the supply of their customers. The embarrassment of the Midland Company, too, may be imagined when they received such messages as, "Stop all coals from Butterley colliery for Acton, Hammersmith, and Kew, for three days, as Willesden sidings are blocked up." "The North London are blocked with Poplar coals for all the dealers; Camden cannot receive any more for Poplar." "You must stop the whole till London is clear." "Rugby is blocked so as not to be able to shunt any more." "Camden and the North London are blocked with coals."

In addition to the necessity that thus existed for a more adequate accommodation of the through traffic of the Midland Company to the metropolis itself, it was apparent that a new railway up the country that lay between the Great Northern line on the east, and the London and North Western on the west would be locally beneficial. Grave complaints, for instance, had been made of the insufficiency of the communications directly south and north of St. Albans. Proposals had been made with a view to amendment, and one witness stated that his land was surveyed "almost every winter;" but no improvement had been made. "It is almost useless now," said another, "to make up a stock of goods to keep at St. Albans. People who come over there have so little time, and buyers from the north will not come to us at all. Formerly we did a very great business at St. Albans. The communication by coaches used to be very much more convenient to these northern buyers than the railways are now." "If a railway is made," said another witness, "it will multiply our trade at St. Albans double or treble."

At this period (March, 1863) the county of Bedford generally was described by one of the witnesses as "the most unfortunate county in England," as regarded its railway communications "We have nothing," he said, "but the Great Northern running from Hertfordshire to Bedford, across the estate of Mr. Whitbread at the outskirts, and from Bletchley on the Duke of Bedford's estates on the other side; but with respect to the interior part of the county we have no communication at all." By a new line it was declared "the whole district would be immensely benefited."

"I believe," said a witness, "that the Great Northern Company do all they can, but they cannot do justice to the district with a junction line." It was estimated that the proposed line would serve 50,000 people who did not then have the advantage of railway facilities.

Such were some of the data that led the Midland Company's board to resolve to construct a line of their own from Bedford to London, and their intention was approved by their constituency. There "was not a single dissentient voice that I know of," said Mr. Allport, "though one shareholder objected, who usually objects to everything."

Meanwhile, the Great Northern Company, naturally loath to lose such a customer as the Midland, made an offer of fresh facilities and rights over the Hitchen and London line, in fact of running powers in perpetuity. But in return they required that the Midland Company should guarantee a rent of £60,000 a year instead of £20,000. If it were found that the traffic of the two companies could not be carried on by the existing lines, the Great Northern undertook—on the opinion of an arbitrator, if there were difference between the companies—to put down one or two additional lines between Hitchen and London; but in that case the minimum guarantee of the Midland Company was to be increased to 5 per cent. per annum on the money spent by the Great Northern on such additional works.

But when the best answer of the Great Northern Company to the demand by the Midland for adequate facilities for its growing traffic, was an offer to widen the Great Northern line at the expense of the Midland, the rejoinder was easy and complete. If the old line had to be doubled the cost would be altogether disproportionate to the benefits conferred. Besides the earthwork, there were many of the overbridges that would need to be rebuilt, a large viaduct to be widened, nine tunnels to be doubled, stations to be altered, a suitable junction between the Great Northern and Midland to be made at the London end, a new terminus for the Midland to be erected, and a gradient between Hitchen and Bedford to be improved. "I should think," said Mr. Charles Liddell, "that the duplicating the Great Northern would cost at least £900,000," in addition to other large items of expenditure. Under these circumstances, it was obviously better to make a new line, in a new country, to accommodate new districts, to create new traffic, and to secure independence for both companies. "It is impossible," said Mr. Allport, "that you can reconcile the interests of these two great companies," on the same railway. "We are always second best, and whether there are four lines or a dozen lines, the same thing would be true."

Besides all this, it was by no means improbable that the districts which the Midland Company proposed to occupy would, if abandoned by them, be taken up by another company, and employed as a formidable competitor against Midland interests. Such a line had, in fact, been in contemplation. "The year before last," said Mr. Beale to the shareholders, "a project of that kind was brought forward by persons of great talent, who very nearly succeeded in carrying forward a scheme going over the very district which we have proposed to take. If such had been the case, we should have had to buy it back from the projectors. The Midland Company does not want to be dragged into a Trent Valley business, and have to buy a line at an enormous premium; and if they did not make a line from Bedford, the work would be done by others."

Another point that came under the consideration of the parliamentary committee may be cited, as showing the manner in which individuals are sometimes disposed to assert their rights. It arose from the circumstance that the Midland line was to be carried through the Camden Square Gardens in Camden Town, where it was arranged that a cutting, which must first be made, should be arched over, and that then the garden should be restored to its previous condition. With these terms Lord Camden, the proprietor, was satisfied. Not so, however, one of the witnesses. "It is utterly impossible," he said, "that the garden could ever be restored; because the trees were of fifteen years' growth, the lawn was as old, and got finer and finer every year, and the whole appearance of the square had been improving."

"Then you think," asked the counsel, "leaving alone

the trees, and taking the shrubbery and lawn, it could never be restored for a great length of time, if at all, to its present state."

"No. Because this covered way would act as a great drain, and the grass would not grow."

For these and similar reasons, the parties alleged that "the injury to the property was excessive," and that the works "would generally affect the value of the property in the neighbourhood." In cross-examination this momentous matter was again referred to.

Mr. Venables: "Your trees are large trees, and of fifteen years' growth, you say?"

"Yes."

"Have you examined the plans, and seen how many of them would be disturbed?"

"I have not counted the number, but there are several of them that would be disturbed.

"Would there be more than six disturbed?"

"No; I would not say actually."

"If it should turn out that six trees fifteen years old were taken out of 400, would that be an enormous evil?"

"I think it would be a great evil; but I think many more would be disturbed."

"You know that it is not beyond the resources of gardening ingenuity to put in trees fifteen years old—is it?"

"Quite."

"I respectfully differ from you. But at all events, supposing you had half a dozen or a dozen trees disturbed, and young ones put in in their places, do you not think that that might be compensated for by money?"

And all this was about two poplar trees, two laburnums, and two horse-chestnut trees,—such wonderful vegetable productions as are to be found in an average London square!

Eventually, however, the chairman stated that "the committee were of opinion that the preamble of the bill had been proved;" but so considerate were they of the feelings of the owners of the property in Camden Square, that it was ordered that if they wished, they should have "a clause which would enable them to seek for compensation for consequential damage."

In the course of the year the Midland Company applied to Parliament for power to make a line to connect their main line at Cudworth with the town of Barnsley, by a branch about four miles in length. That town was the centre of a district containing some 66,000 persons, and the chief seat of the linen manufacture—the Dundee of England—and produced a fabric worth nearly £500,000 a year, but it had no communication with the Midland system, except by an omnibus over a very rough road, and it was also very inadequately accommodated otherwise. One of the witnesses declared that "there was no town of equal importance in the kingdom, and indeed there were very few villages, which have such execrable railway accommodation as we have." The station, which was the joint property of the Lancashire and Yorkshire and the South Yorkshire, has "one room 20 ft. square, which serves at once for the booking offices of three railways, for a spice stall, and the sale of the daily papers," and also as a waiting room. Another room, "by a very gross abuse of language," called a ladies' waiting-room, was so small that "one lady of modern dimensions would occupy a very considerable portion of it." In fact, the station arrangements violated the most ordinary requirements of decency. The witness stated his conviction that if a railway were made from Barnsley to Cudworth, all the arrangements would be improved, since it "would lower the character of the Midland Company to be associated with such station accommodation as existed."

"One thing we have for our consolation," he added, "that under no combination of circumstances could the accommodation be worse." That the railway facilities of the town were not highly appreciated, may be inferred from the fact, that of a population of 66,000 in and around Barnsley, there went up to London by the Great Northern in the Exhibition year, an average—if we may be excused the form of calculation—of only a passenger and a quarter a day!

The line that the Midland Company proposed to run from Cudworth to Barnsley was four miles and a half in

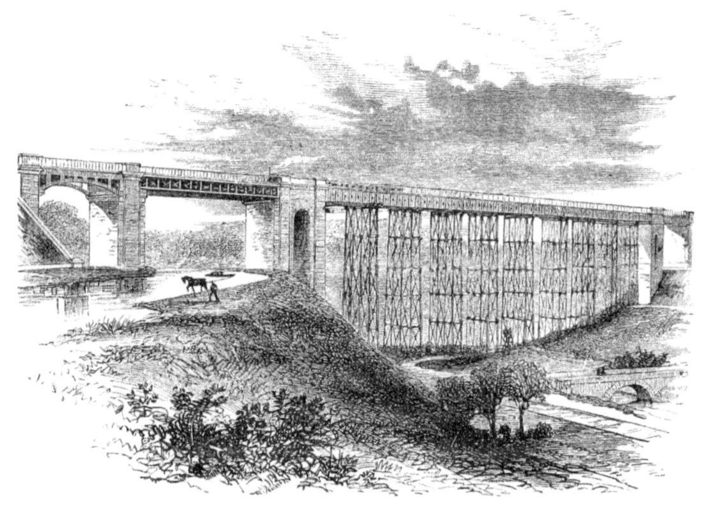

BARNSLEY VIADUCT

length. It was to pass almost close to the large collieries known as the Mount Osborne and the Oaks. From the former some 162,000 tons were raised every year—an amount which could be largely augmented if there were proper communication; and from the Oaks the yield in 1862 was 180,000 tons.

The importance of the proposed line was obvious; but when the bill was before Parliament, it became entangled with a number of competitive projects with which that of the Midland Company had reaily nothing to do. There were the Barnsley Coal Railway, the South Yorkshire, the Manchester, Sheffield and Lincolnshire, the Lancashire and Yorkshire, the Great Northern, and the Leeds and Wakefield, who "had agreements with each other in every possible complication, and all of whom almost accused all the others of having broken those agreements on every possible occasion." Eventually, however, the committee found a way through this labyrinth of perplexities, and the bill was sanctioned.

The directors also decided to recommend the construction of several other extensions; to make a branch from Duffield to Wirksworth and the High Peak Railway; to run a branch from Staveley to the Doe Hill Valley, in order to open up a large and valuable coal field; to double the Ashchurch and Tewkesbury line; to join with the Furness Railway Company in making a railway to be called the Furness and Midland, for the purpose of connecting the coast lines of Cumberland and Westmorland and the Lake District with the Midland Railway at Wennington, on the Little North Western Railway, and with Carnforth. This line is about ten miles in length, and was to cost £150,000, of which the Midland Company was to contribute one-half. Bills were also submitted to Parliament to enable the Midland Company to make working arrangements with the Manchester, Bux ton, Matlock, and Midland Junction; with the Kettering and Thrapstone extension to Huntingdon; the Peterborough and Wisbeach; the Redditch and Evesham; the Nailsworth and Stonehouse; and the Metropolitan.

CHAPTER VIII.

Arrival of a memorable period.—Claims of Sheffield to increased accommodation.—Growth of trade in that town.—Sir John Brown's works.—Town's meeting.—Communication with the Midland board.—Sheffield to be put on the main line of the Midland.—Large outlay.—Terms settled.—Advantages to be conferred.—Remarkable change of opinion in Sheffield.—Rival scheme produced.—The Sheffield, Chesterfield and Staffordshire Company.—Extraordinary pretensions of new company.—Objections to the scheme.—Manchester, Sheffield and Lincolnshire Company's claims.—A small disease and a great remedy.—Astuteness of Midland Company's advisers.—Plan for meeting the difficulty.—The rival scheme defeated in the Commons.—Persistent attempt to defeat the Midland Company in the Lords.—Midland Company's bill passes.—Projected extensions of the Midland system.—Yate and Thornbury line.—Mangotsfield and Bath.—Derby to Melbourne and Breedon-on-the-Hill.—Mr. Beale's resignation as chairman.—Mr. W E. Hutchinson becomes chairman.—Mansfield and Worksop line projected.—Opposition of the dukes.—Difficulties overcome.—Evidence of the necessity of the line.—Vast colliery field.—Rival line proposed by Great Northern.—Proposed line from Barnsley to Kirkburton.—Evidence.—Humorous criticisms of Mr. Mereweather.—Proposal rejected.—Death of Sir Joseph Paxton.—Resignation of Mr. Barwell.—Mr. W. M. Thompson a director.—Bedford and Northampton line.—Evidence before Parliament.—Passing of bill.—Tottenham and Hampstead Junction.—Advantages of the line.—Opposition of Great Northern to the new arrangement.—Cheshire lines.—Proposed new line of the three companies between Liverpool and Manchester.—Access *viâ* Garston inconvenient.—Necessity for additional railway accommodation between Manchester and Liverpool.—Enormous increase of trade of Liverpool.—Evidence.—Complaints of merchants and others.—Cost and probable returns of the projected railway.—New line from Manchester to Stockport.—Omnibus traffic.

The year 1864 was memorable in the history of the Midland Railway. It began with an attempt to meet public claims and to strengthen the position of the Company; but before long the directors were called, with their utmost resources and skill, to repel an attack upon their most vital interests,— an attack which, if successful, would have entailed the most serious consequences on all the future of the Midland Company.

When the route of the North Midland Railway was

selected by George Stephenson, he thought it better to follow the course of the valleys, and to leave the town of Sheffield among the hills on the left, to be afterwards connected with the main line by a branch from Masborough. But with this subordinate position, a population so vast and industries so thriving were not likely to remain permanently satisfied, and the complaints of the Sheffield people would have been entertained by the Midland board at an earlier period, had it not been for financial difficulties of their own. Pressure, however, of all kinds gradually increased. The little passenger station, built some twenty years before, became utterly unsuitable for the traffic; but being jammed in between principal streets of the town, and bounded by numerous vast and costly works, it appeared impossible by any attempt at enlargement to meet the necessities of the case.

Meanwhile the trade of the town increased enormously. During the year 1863, one firm, that of Mr., now Sir John, Brown, consumed nearly 100,000 tons of coal, and 45,000 tons of pig iron. Nearly 30,000 tons of the iron came over the Midland system from Derby, Clay Cross, Hull, from Morecambe, and even from Scotland. "We pay to the Midland alone," said Mr. Brown, "from £35,000 to £40,000 per annum for the conveyance of our minerals and pig iron, out of which £12,000 is paid direct to the Midland Company by us, for what we call 'goods outward,' that is to say, manufactured goods."

At length the Midland board received an intimation that, on the 5th of December, 1863, a town's meeting under the presidency of Mr. Brown, the mayor, would be held to consider the question of railway communication. The chairman of the Midland board shortly afterwards returned an official assurance that his board had resolved, "if assured of the support of the town," to "recommend to their shareholders to apply, in the session of 1864, for an act for a direct line from the Midland Railway near Chesterfield, to Dronfield and Sheffield." This letter was submitted to the town's meeting, the chairman of which spoke in terms of warm appreciation of the intended action of the Midland board. He stated that he had no doubt of the good faith with which the promise had been made; and it was generally admitted at the meeting that the accommodation which the town needed could be best supplied by the Midland Company. It was at the same time suggested that a little pressure from without might be useful to support the Midland directors in commending the project to their shareholders. "The meeting," said Mr. Thomas Smith, a solicitor, should have "faith in the Midland Company, which alone could do for the town that which was really wanted—put it on the main line (cheers). It has been admitted, however, that directors sometimes required a little pressure with their shareholders, to enable them to carry projects of this kind out. With a view to supply the necessary pressure, and put the town in a position to secure a railway to Chesterfield, if they should show any further hesitation, and also in order to support and protect the interests of the town in the matter, he (Mr. Smith) advised the formation of an independent company, which should, by arrangement with the Midland, prepare to give the necessary notices, and deposit plans, the independent company withdrawing on the Midland Company going to Parliament in earnest" (cheers). A committee was appointed to watch over the interests of the town, and to see that the new line and station met their just expectations. After the meeting the mayor sent to the chairman of the Midland Company an account of the proceedings.

Under these circumstances the Midland board took

immediate action. At the general meeting on the 3rd of February following, they obtained the sanction of the shareholders to a bill involving an expenditure of £500,000 for the projected line; and their engineer was instructed to make his survey of the difficult country through which the railway would have to pass. A deputation, also, from the Sheffield committee had an interview with the Midland board, and received a renewal of the pledge given to the mayor; and at the end of the same month, the Sheffield committee forwarded to the directors a resolution which they had just passed, expressive of their satisfaction with the action of the board; taking care, however, to add the following warning against any infringement of the understanding already arrived at: "That this committee, while they rely on these promises, yet desire to impress on the board of directors the peril of any departure from these assurances, as the general public are most anxious on the point, at the earliest period of making the line."

On the 10th of July, 1863, the engineer of the Midland Company met the committee at Sheffield, produced his plans and explained them. It was, however, considered that "the position and approaches of the station appeared too far removed from the business part of the town," and "several departures from the plan in that particular" were suggested, and in these "Mr. Crossley coincided." The Sheffield representative reported that if this plan, as thus amended, "be confirmed by the survey, your deputation thinks that the scheme will, as a whole, be satisfactory to the town."

By these arrangements a very costly and difficult but admirable line was offered by the Midland Company to the town of Sheffield, and the offer was officially accepted by its municipal authorities. Some 1,200,000 yards of cutting, and about an equal amount of embankment, a viaduct 260 yards in length, and tunnels more than 2,000 yards long would be required; the work of which would cost £40 a yard for tunnels, £60 for viaducts, and 1*s.* a cubic yard for earthworks. The whole would involve an outlay of half a million of money. But the benefits conferred would not be disproportionate to the expenditure. Hereafter the principal trains from north to south would run directly through the town; in fact, Sheffield, instead of being approached by a branch from Masborough, would for all the future be on the main line of the Midland system. Passengers from the south, instead of having first to go north to Masborough and then back to Sheffield, would save eight miles; while the distance from Chesterfield to Masborough itself would, over the new route be only slightly increased. Instead of the old Sheffield station—which would be devoted to goods—the new one would be three or four times the area, and would have unlimited facilities for extension; and all the just expectations of a large population and a thriving industry would be more than satisfied.

It was now August. Apparently everything had proceeded fairly and in good faith; when suddenly, to the amazement of the Midland board, it was discovered that some of the very parties with whom these negotiations had been conducted were engaged in prosecuting, not a friendly bill, to be used merely in the event of the Midland's default, but one in the highest degree competitive and hostile; that the mayor himself was to be chairman of the new company; that a large expenditure was to be undertaken; and that it was intended to make a rival line to Bastow, Bakewell, Winster, Ashbourne, and Stafford, with a fork from near Sheffield through Dronfield to Chesterfield, at the heart of the Midland system; and that people of great local influence and wealth had committed themselves to this scheme.

In fact, despite correspondences, conferences, and agreements, the Midland Company and the Midland line were thrown overboard, and for the time being appeared, under the fresh influences that had arisen, to be—nowhere.

The Sheffield corporation, the Cutlers' Company, the Sheffield people, Mr. Fowler the engineer, Mr. John Brown of the Atlas ironworks (both natives of the town), were of one mind and heart in the advocacy of the new enterprise,—an enterprise which would not only have put the new line into the hands of strangers, but would have tapped the traffic blood of the Midland system at its heart. The Midland board could hardly believe their ears; and the only defence which at the moment they seemed able to offer to the assault was—their recognised position, their character as a Company, and the sanctions of good faith. And so the time drew on when Parliament should decide.

When Parliament met, the rival scheme came out in full bloom. It cheerfully proposed that, in lieu of the proposed Midland line, the ground should be occupied by a railway to be called the Sheffield, Chesterfield and Staffordshire Company, which should run in the direction named by its title; that the Midland Company should have the option of using it "on fair terms"; and that the Staffordshire Company should have running powers at arbitration tolls, not only over the whole of the Midland system, but even on to other lines, indeed "to everywhere"; and that the new company should have their own clerks and agents at the Midland stations to which they had running powers. Even for traffic going to the extremities of the Midland system, and beyond, on to points as distant as Bristol or Carlisle, this little bit of a company, with its 12 or 14 miles of railway, if it sent passengers or goods on its own line for a distance of only one, two, or three miles, claimed to receive the rate for the whole distance, and the Midland Company was, as well as it could, to reclaim its share of the amount. "Here is a company," said Mr. Allport, "about which no one knows anything, who come and propose that, at arbitration tolls, they should run over the whole of the Midland system, by merely making 13 or 14 miles, and that in the very midst of our system." "I think it is a most unreasonable thing."

Nor should the fact be overlooked, that, if the Staffordshire line had been made instead of that of the Midland Company, the great want of Sheffield would have remained unsatisfied. Sheffield would still, for all Midland purposes, have remained on the branch from Masborough. "It is idle," said Mr. Allport, "to suppose that we should use and pay tolls upon a link of 13 or 14 miles in the midst of our system, with all our traffic passing through. The number of passengers taken up at Sheffield, as compared with the number we should take through, would be not more than as 1 to 10; and it is not to be expected that we should transfer from our own line the traffic to another and competing company. I have no hesitation," he added, "in saying that the whole of the Midland passenger traffic would go *viâ* Masborough, as at present."

But the proposal of the Midland Company to make a direct line through Sheffield had not only to endure the neglect of its supposed supporters in Sheffield and the preposterous pretensions of the Staffordshire scheme; the Manchester, Sheffield and Lincolnshire Company was scarcely to be outdone in the exorbitancy of its claims. That company is connected with the Midland by a branch at Eckington, a station between Chesterfield and Masborough, by means of which it conveys certain traffic on to Sheffield. But it was contended that if the Midland Company made a line of its own directly through Sheffield, some traffic which had formerly travelled *viâ* Eckington might go by the new and better route. So, for this small disease, the Sheffield Company proposed a sufficiently comprehensive remedy.

They stated that, when the Midland Company had their through line to Sheffield, Chesterfield would become the point of junction between the two systems, and that the Sheffield Company ought to have running powers over the Midland line from Eckington to Chesterfield, and there make its exchange with the Midland. "As the *locus*," they said, "is going to be changed physically, we ask that we should be removed from Eckington to Chesterfield;" and they proposed that a clause should be inserted in the Midland bill that, at the new point of exchange "the said companies shall grant to each other mutual facilities by through booking, through rates, and otherwise, for the convenient transmission of the traffic of their respective systems;" in fact that the Midland Company should be compelled to grant through booking at arbitration rates. In the event of the Midland train arrangements being remodelled, and, for instance, the Midland expresses not stopping at Chesterfield, the Sheffield Company claimed that the exchange of traffic should be made at Trent junction, the Sheffield Company having running powers on to Trent. They would thus, though a line running from east to west, have a position in the heart of the Midland system, with a spur running north to south.

These demands were considered by the Midland Company to be inadmissible. The Midland Company, they said, is going to spend half a million of money to make a better route from Chesterfield to Sheffield; but because in doing so a small quantity of the traffic of another company may be diverted from a route along which it has previously flowed, that company is to be allowed to take up a position, under the guidance or caprice of an unnamed arbitrator, in the midst of a great system of railway which has cost some £23,000,000 of money, and to the construction of which the other company has not paid a penny. Every new line, of course, is made for the more convenient transmission of traffic somewhere; but it was unprecedented that the owners of the less convenient route should have to be compensated, and compensated at such a price as this. When the Midland Company made its extension from Buxton to Manchester it was strenuously opposed by the London and North Western and the Great Northern Companies, because it was seen that some of their traffic would be diverted; but they never asked to be reimbursed for their loss, or for running powers over the new Midland route as a price for their loss. When the Midland Company sought for an act to enable them to construct a new line from Bedford to London, the Great Northern well knew that £60,000 worth of Midland traffic would be diverted from their rails, but Parliament never thought of granting them compensation. The loss, too, actually sustained by the Sheffield Company would be infinitesimal in comparison with the price at which they asked to be reimbursed. The total value of the traffic of all companies exchanged at Eckington was of the gross value of £60,000 a year. Out of that there was a sum of £5000 or £6000 for "terminals" which the Sheffield Company would still enjoy; and deducting this amount out of the £60,000 their share would not exceed £20,000 or £21,000. The Midland Company, however, undertook to provide trains to carry on without delay all the traffic which the Sheffield Company should still bring to the place of exchange at Eckington.

But while enemies were thus exhausting every resource to give effect to these claims, the friends of the

Midland Company were not idle. One day, as he was travelling in a train to London, there glanced across the mind of an astute adviser of the board, this thought: —"We have heard much about this new company,—its vast works, its large cost, and the deposit paid,—but we have heard nothing about shareholders. Who are they? What are they? Are there any? Or is the proposed company, after all, unreal and illegal?" These inquiries were soon answered; answered by the discovery that though the deposit had been paid, yet the three names of the depositors bore the same address; and at once it was suspected that the amount, instead of representing a proportionate payment of a large number of *bonâ fide* shareholders, as Parliament required, had been borrowed *en bloc* for the mere purpose of a deposit, that the standing orders of Parliament had been evaded, and that in fact there were no shareholders.

But how should this suspicion be confirmed, how should the fact itself be proved? The reply was original but conclusive. "Summon the depositors themselves by Speaker's warrants; put them in the box; ascertain from their own lips the exact circumstances of the case; raise the question of the legality of the entire proceedings, and secure, not only a favourable decision, but one which will establish a precedent for the prevention of any similar proceedings hereafter."

The course thus proposed was adopted, and at the commencement of the proceedings before the Commons' committee, March 11, 1864, it was proved by the evidence of the depositors themselves, that the whole amount of the deposit had been obtained as a loan from the *Guardian Insurance Company* on behalf of the promoters of the Sheffield, Chesterfield and Staffordshire Railway Bill. On hearing this announcement and the comments of counsel on either side, the committee stated that they were "of opinion that, as the matter was one of very grave importance, they would require time to consider it." Meanwhile, however, as witnesses on both sides were present, the committee would hear the case on its own merits. The result of this hearing was satisfactory. After a protracted inquiry it was decided in the House of Commons' committee that the Sheffield, Chesterfield and Staffordshire Bill should be rejected; and the Chesterfield and Sheffield line of the Midland Company was approved.

Such, however, was the vitality of the quasi-defunct undertaking, that it followed with its opposition the Midland Company's bill into the House of Lords. It was hoped by its friends that, though their own bill had been rejected, yet, by securing, even for one session, the rejection also of the Midland bill, an opportunity might be secured in a future session of again advancing their own scheme. In this, fortunately for the Midland Company, and, we may add, for the town of Sheffield, they were defeated, and the Midland bill became law.

In the course of this year (1864), projects were announced for the formation of several small but not unimportant lines. One was from Yate, near Bristol, to Thornbury. It was easy of construction, and led to a valuable iron field. Another was from Mangotsfield to Bath, and its formation would connect that city with the narrow-gauge system of the country. A third was from near Derby, past Melbourne, to a junction at Breedon-on-the-Hill, with a tramway that belonged to the Midland Company, and led to Ashby-de-la-Zouch. This line would be six miles in length, and would cost £40,000. Meanwhile satisfactory progress was being made with the numerous works already in hand.

It was matter of sincere regret to his colleagues that in the course of this year Mr. Samuel Beale, M.P., who had been, with much "energy and talent," for many years the chairman of the Midland Company, found it desirable, on account of his health, to relinquish the responsibilities of that office, though he consented to remain a director. It was unanimously resolved by the shareholders, on the motion of Mr. Barrow, M.P., that £1000 should be placed at the disposal of the board to provide some suitable acknowledgment for Mr. Beale's services. The amount was expended in the purchase of plate, which was duly presented; and, in return, Mr. Beale gave to the shareholders his portrait, which was placed in the proprietors' hall at Derby, side by side with that of his old and lamented friend, Mr. Ellis. In the autumn of this year Mr. W. E. Hutchinson, a member of the Society of Friends, who had been connected with the Midland Company from its commencement, was elected to the chairmanship, and Mr. W. P. Price, M.P. for Gloucester, was appointed deputy-chairman.

A vacancy also occurred during this year in the office of auditor, by the death of Mr. Joseph Cripps, of Leicester, who for upwards of twenty years had ably and faithfully discharged the duties of that position. In consequence of this event, the accounts were signed only by the remaining auditor, Mr. Alfred Allott. Major Robert Heane, of Gloucester, a holder of £12,000 worth of Midland stock, was appointed to fill the vacancy.

The years 1865 and 1866 witnessed an important increase to the responsibilities of the Midland Company. Heavy works were in hand, and new ones were in contemplation. During the summer of 1865, the New Mills extension was rapidly advancing; the Dove Holes Tunnel, which governed the rest of the work, was nearly three-fourths through; the tunnel on the Chesterfield and Sheffield line was going forward; the Duffield and Wirksworth branch was commenced; and the contracts of the London and Bedford line north of the Brent were let.

NORTHERN END OF DOVE HOLES TUNNEL.

In addition to these undertakings, further extensions had become necessary in consequence of "numerous hostile schemes" projected by rival companies. "It would have been more consonant with the feelings of the directors," said the chairman, at the February meeting, "if they had been enabled to state that there was not a single bill to be brought before Parliament; but they felt that they could not shut their eyes to what was going on around them, for there were districts that required railway accommodation, and other parties were already at work in the Midland district." "I believe," remarked the chairman, in August, "that this further construction is necessary for the stable and permanent position of the company." The proposed new lines were eighteen, extending for a distance of eighty-one miles, at a cost of £1,684,000; besides a railway from Barnsley to Kirkburton, and an arrangement with the Great Northern and Sheffield Companies for what we shall have to speak of more fully hereafter—the Cheshire lines.

In the course of this year (1865) an important movement was made for the purpose of connecting together the middle and northern districts of Nottinghamshire—the county in which the Midland Company had its birth. The line that ran north of Nottingham ended at Mansfield in a *cul de sac*, or, in expressive railway phraseology, "a dead end"—always a bad thing both for a line and for a district; and so matters had remained for years. Several abortive attempts had been made to diminish the inconvenience that was felt; and when in 1860 a bill was brought before Parliament for a line from Mansfield to Worksop, such serious difference of opinion arose with regard to the subject between the Dukes of Newcastle and Portland, through whose property the intended line would pass, that the project was withdrawn.

At length, in the summer of 1864, it was intimated to the Midland Company that these obstacles were removed, and that both noblemen would lend their support to the projected line. But other difficulties arose; for the Manchester, Sheffield and Lincolnshire Company now appeared with a scheme almost identical with that of the Midland; nor were they appeased until they were promised running powers to Mansfield in return for running powers over their line on to Retford.

A fresh survey was now ordered of the district, and several improvements were made on the scheme of 1859. It had, for instance, been intended that the extension to Worksop should turn off from the Nottingham and Mansfield line, at a point some distance south of Mansfield; that it should bend to the west, and that there should be a second station at Mansfield. It was now determined to carry a new through line across the town, and to build a new station within a few yards of the market place. At its northern end the line would join the Manchester, Sheffield and Lincolnshire to the west of Worksop, near the Shireoaks Colliery. Uninterrupted communication would thus be provided between Mansfield and Worksop on the one hand, and Sheffield on the other.

The benefits to be conferred by the proposed lines were considerable. Mansfield was cooped up in a corner, and its trade had suffered accordingly. Two gentlemen, cotton doublers, who employed some 360 hands, gave evidence of the inconvenience to which they were exposed in carrying on their business with Lancashire. "We may lose more," said one, "by reloading, in the waste that it causes, than the cost of the carriage two or three times over." Mr. William Bradshaw, at whose foundry about 300 persons were employed, and who received some 2000 tons of iron a month from the north of England, complained of the circuitous route by which Mansfield had to be approached. "All I want," said the late Speaker of the House of Commons, in evidence he gave before the committee, "is a better communication from the northern part of the county to the county town."

The district, too, through which the line would pass, deserved better accommodation. At Steetley, between Whitwell and Worksop, are the quarries of valuable stone from which it is believed that Southwell Minster was erected, and which the chairman of the committee remarked was probably "the most famous of all building stones." The quarries at Mansfield are of high quality, but have only a limited though lucrative trade. The proposed railway, with the branch intended to be made to Newark, would open what one witness described as "most magnificent quarries of magnesium stone." The line would also pass in the neighbourhood of the finest timber district in England. The Duke of Newcastle's agent stated that the mere thinnings of 4000 acres of woodland fetched from £6000 to £10,000 a year; and that they were used chiefly for pit and manufacturing purposes. The Shireoaks Colliery, too, which the line would approach, contained several beds of valuable coal; and the engineer and manager expressed a conviction that the entire district which the line would traverse was "a mineral field;" or, as another said, "full of coal." Mr. Heming, the agent for the Duke of Newcastle, also stated his belief that the "entire length" of the line was "full of minerals." These opinions have since been confirmed: and eventually, as the time drew on for the opening of the line, thousands of acres of coal-fields were leased to coal-owners, and it is believed that the Mansfield and Worksop line will rival, if not outvie, the mineral productiveness of the Erewash.

But while the Midland Company was thus contending for the importance of a line between the centre and north of the country, another competitor—in the interest of the Midland's old foe, the Great Northern—came upon the field, and proposed a railway from Mansfield to Retford. On its behalf it was contended that Retford was the second largest cattle market in the kingdom; that the Mansfield limestone quarries would be benefited by the Retford route as well as by the other; that whatever went north-east of Retford, should be carried direct to Retford; though it was admitted that whatever went westward or north-west would go better by Worksop, and that delay in the transit of minerals did not much matter. It was of little consequence—some one humorously suggested—if a load of pig iron was detained; but if a truck of pigs were starved to death in winter weather, or if fish or fruit coming from Hull were delayed *en route* at midsummer, the consequences might be unpleasant to all concerned.

The Midland replied that theirs was the better route, because they passed through a population twice as numerous as on the line to Retford, and because the latter ran through a purely agricultural country without minerals. The decision of Parliament was given in favour of the Midland bill.

Application was also made in the course of this year (1865) for powers to make a line from Barnsley to Kirkburton, there to join a line projected by the London and North Western from Kirkburton to Huddersfield. These two companies agreed that if the Midland bill were sanctioned, a joint station should be made at Kirkburton, and each company should have running powers over the line of the other company. It was urged on behalf of the Midland project that it would be of special value, as the country was "full of mills in the centre, and full of coal at one end." At Huddersfield there were as many as four hundred warehouses for woollen goods, and nearly as many mills. It was also shown in evidence that part of the traffic on the Barnsley and Kirkburton line would consist of leather, bark, and timber. Upon this point Mr. Mereweather thus cheerily criticised the evidence: "I shall not question whether there is some coal in the valley, whether there are some woods in the valley, whether the beasts there have hides, and whether they are ultimately taken off and tanned at another place. Of course there are woods everywhere, and you will not find me contending that round most trees there is not bark, or to deny that that bark is used in tanning. But this gentleman comes and says that this line would be of great advantage to him, because it will help him to the bark. The greatest distance from either end is six miles. The middle of the line is three miles from the end. Your lordships know what is done with bark. It is first of all stacked upon the spot, and must be left to dry, and after being dried, it does not want a bit more locomotion than can be helped. Take the middle part of the line, and assume that there is a wood upon it. The oak does not grow so that when the bark is stripped it can fall into the railway waggon. It has to be put upon a waggon for conveyance to the rail. Do you suppose that the bark will travel three miles to the railway, then be unshipped into the trucks, be taken six miles to Barnsley, and unshipped there. Or is the railway to go and collect the hides of the dead oxen. Hides sold in the Barnsley market are either the produce of the beasts killed by the Barnsley butchers, or the one or two hides which the butcher brings in his cart to sell, having left the carcase in the village. Beasts do not die in heaps. They are killed individually, and to present to your lordships a line picking up hides is absurd. That disposes of the leather business, the bark business, and the timber business."

The bill for this line passed the Commons committee; but in the Lords it was decided that the Midland Company should have access to Huddersfield by running powers in perpetuity on arbitration tolls *viâ* Barnsley or *viâ* Beighton and Sheffield, "local traffic being protected in the usual manner." To these terms the Manchester, Sheffield and Lincolnshire, and the Lancashire and Yorkshire consented, and the bill for the new line was thereupon withdrawn. The Midland Company were also to have accommodation in the Huddersfield station (supposing the London and North Western to consent), of which the Lancashire and Yorkshire and London and North Western are joint owners. Had these terms been conceded at the outset, they would have been willingly accepted; and the Parliamentary costs of £3500 would have been saved. As the bill was not obtained, this outlay, in the usual manner, fell upon revenue.

Two vacancies occurred during the year 1865 in the direction. One, said the chairman, "by the death of our deeply-lamented and highly-valued colleague, Sir Joseph Paxton," who for sixteen years had been a member of the board; and the other by the retirement, through ill-health, of Mr. E. H. Barwell. The seat of the latter was filled by the appointment of Mr. M. W. Thompson, of Bradford. At a special meeting which followed the ordinary autumn meeting, various financial arrangements were sanctioned, and also an agreement for the purchase by the Midland Company of the Redditch station, and for the working and leasing by the Midland Company of the Midland and South Western Junction Railway. During the year an act was obtained for making a line—in which the Midland Company eventually became interested—called the Bedford and Northampton Railway. The affair came about in the following way:—

Three or four years previously, the Midland Company had received notice from the London and North Western that they intended to exercise the old common law right of passing along a public highway, and that they should pass along the "public highway" of the track that ran from Wichnor, on the Birmingham and Derby line, to Burton-on-Trent. To this the Midland did not demur; but they likewise gave notice that they should use similar powers from Wellingborough to Northampton, where they had bought land, and where they opened a temporary station immediately adjoining that of the North Western Company. The two companies also agreed that the tolls from Wichnor and from Wellingborough should be fixed at the same amount.

The junctions* of the Midland with the London and North Western were formed from the east and west sides of the Wellingborough station; but it was soon found

* For several years there was only one junction.

that, however conveniently these might serve as approaches from the north, there should also be access from the south; and this, it was conjectured, might be made at a cost of £4000 or £5000. On examination, however, it was ascertained that it would be a more serious undertaking, since it would have to be carried for at least four or five miles through a very difficult country, at an outlay of £70,000 or £80,000. It was, therefore, abandoned. Meanwhile complaints arose of the inadequacy of the means of communication between Bedford and Northampton; and when a proposal was made by a company called "The Bedford, Northampton and Weedon," to make a line in that direction, it was warmly supported by parties locally interested. The traffic of the district, they declared, had to be carried on by private vehicles or by carriers' carts. "The agricultural interests of that neighbourhood," said Mr. Hurst, of Bedford, "are very extensive. There is a great deal of extremely well-cultivated land, and it would be a great convenience to have this line to convey agricultural produce from one place to the other. Bedford, too, is a very improving, and is becoming a very important town. It has very extensive commercial and grammar schools—I should think an arrangement of schools hardly second to any in the kingdom. These schools are all but free, and the benefits thus conferred might be greatly extended if the facilities of access were increased." "I reckon," said another witness, "that every acre of land properly worked ought to produce something like half a ton of cattle or corn to be exported or imported," and that the freightage thus supplied should, if possible, be accommodated. One gentleman from Northampton, who stated that his firm employed about 1,500 hands, and made more than half a million of boots a year, declared that the rates they paid for the carriage of boots and shoes from Northampton to London were "about as much as they used to pay in the old waggon time." Another witness, who lived at Olney, expressed the great desire of people there engaged in trade to have railway facilities. He mentioned that, as a tanner, he received 500 or more tons of goods in a year, which had to be conveyed by road; and that coals for the town had to be carted from the Midland Company's station at Sharnbrook, a distance of ten miles.

Similar evidence led to Parliamentary sanction being given to the bill, with the omission of the part that extended to Weedon, it being thought to be difficult to make a good junction with the London and North Western main line. The Midland Company did not consent to the terms on which they would adopt this new project until about three weeks before the bill was submitted to Parliament; but eventually they agreed to work the line when completed for seven years, at forty per cent. of the receipts, and at fifty per cent. afterwards.

The Tottenham and Hampstead was another line that arose under somewhat similar circumstances, and that came under the control of the Midland Company under somewhat similar conditions. It starts from Kentish Town; runs up alongside of and then over the Midland main line; crosses over the Great Northern, with which it forms a junction; runs over the Edgware and Highgate Railway; and reaches Tottenham on the Great Eastern line. It has also a connection with the Hampstead and City Junction Railway. It has no independent terminus of its own; but is, by its very nature, a dependency on the stronger systems upon which it abuts. By means of it the Midland Company gains access to the Great Eastern system generally, to the docks at the east end of London, and to the City station of the Great Eastern Company. By using this line, the Great Eastern, which long desired to have a station more westerly than that at Shoreditch, has admission to the St. Pancras terminus, into which it runs certain of its trains, and by means of which passengers to some of the chief Eastern Counties stations can book direct from the Midland terminus.

For the attainment of these objects, the Midland Company agreed to subscribe £183,000, an amount equal to one-third of the capital of the Tottenham and Hampstead Junction Company. The Great Eastern did the same, and the line is now worked by both—each doing its own work. The two companies pay their receipts into a joint fund, making an allowance for working expenses.

To this arrangement, by which the independence of the line was affected, the Great Northern Company objected, on the ground that all control of it would be in the hands of companies which were the rivals of the Great Northern. "Hitherto," said Mr. Seymour Clarke, "it was the interest of this little company that our traffic should come upon its line; but when it is swallowed up by the thousands of miles owned by the Great Eastern and the Midland Companies, it will be their interest to prevent the flow of Great Northern traffic upon it." These objections, however, were overruled.

Several new railway projects were now in contemplation. The directors were invited to join the London and North Western in promoting a line between Huddersfield and Halifax; and agreed with the Great Northern, and Manchester, Sheffield, and Lincolnshire lines in becoming joint-owners of the Stockport and Woodley Junction, the Stockport, Timperley and Altrincham, and the Cheshire lines, the capital of which was £1,850,000, of which the Midland Company was to subscribe a third.

In the course of this year, 1865, a bill was submitted to Parliament, which was destined to place the Midland

Company—along with the Great Northern and Manchester, Sheffield and Lincolnshire—in a commanding position for sharing in the traffic of Liverpool. It is true that, in a sense, the Midland was already there; but it was amid circumstances of great disadvantage to its mighty competitor, the London and North Western Company. In 1861, the three companies already named had obtained power to make a line of their own from Garston to the Brunswick Dock at Liverpool—a terminus where but little passenger traffic was likely to be obtained; but besides this, the access from the east was by a railway "made up," as Mr. John Fowler remarked, "of bits of local lines constructed for other purposes," which chiefly belonged to the London and North Western, and which only "incidentally" came to be available for a route from Manchester to Liverpool. Between Timperley and Garston were several curves, which had to be cautiously passed; and between Manchester and Liverpool there were no fewer than ninety-five level crossings. On the up journey the driver of an engine had to meet sixty-four signals, and on the down journey sixty signals. On the one way he would have to obey a signal on an average of every thirty-six seconds, and on the other every thirty-eight seconds, and he would pass over a level crossing every twenty-four seconds throughout his journey.

Practical difficulties also arose in the working of the railway, from the fact that part of it was under the control of another and a competitive company. Mr. Charles Turner, for instance, gave evidence that though the line ran near his house, and he would have been glad to have availed himself of it, yet he had been detained so often, and, as he thought, so needlessly, that he had determined not to go by it again. "It is perfectly obvious," he said, "that whenever there is a difficulty, instead of running our traffic, which they engaged to do, as their own, they make our traffic subservient to theirs." The difficulties thus to be contended with may be illustrated by the fact that when the three companies* were about to commence running to Liverpool, they sent in to the London and North Western a list of twelve trains which they wished to put on—trains of course fitting their own at Manchester; and the answer received contained an objection to every train on the list. Mr. Cawkwell, no doubt, would have contended that the objections so alleged were good and sufficient; but this only seemed to show more conclusively the necessity of the three companies having a line of their own, and of their ceasing to intrude where they were not wanted.

It is not surprising, therefore, that the three companies were gradually led to the conclusion that it would be necessary for them to have a line of their own—a line which should be connected with their several systems at or near Manchester, which should take a new and independent route, and which should proceed to a central station in the middle of Liverpool. The companies were supported in this decision by the demands that had arisen at Liverpool for more adequate railway accommodation. The vast growth of business in that great seaport necessitated increased means for carrying it. Between the years 1822 and 1863 the timber trade had trebled. The tonnage discharged into Liverpool in 1864 was nearly 5,000,000 tons. It had become, in fact, a sort of axiom among Liverpool men, that the trade doubled every fourteen or fifteen years. In five years the traffic between London and Liverpool increased 40 per cent.; that is to say, in 1859 it was worth £227,000 a year, and in 1864 it had risen to £306,000 a year. If four years more

* The Midland, the Great Northern, and the Manchester, Sheffield, and Lincolnshire Companies.

elapsed (1869) before the new line was opened, it was estimated that the traffic would have increased to nearly double what it was in 1859; yet no really new line, till the opening of that now projected, would have been provided.

Similarly, the railway traffic between Liverpool and Manchester was worth £180,000 a year; and if the amount sent by canal was added, it was estimated that the total would be doubled. Again, if to Manchester were added the towns usually classed with it, the railway traffic between the Manchester district and Liverpool would be worth, it was believed, nearly £400,000 a year.

But the means of carrying on this traffic had by no means increased in similar proportion. It is true, as the counsel for the Lancashire and Yorkshire Company remarked, that the "most enthusiastic hogshead of sugar cannot want to go in less than two hours and a half from Liverpool to Manchester, and the most rapid piece of timber may be satisfied with a journey of three hours." But, on the other hand, it became a serious matter when it could be said that a new line was now asked for "upon very much the same grounds as the late George Stephenson, and those who employed him, proposed the first Manchester and Liverpool Railway. I do not think," said a witness, "I am exaggerating at all in saying that the existing means of communication between Manchester and Liverpool are almost as insufficient for accommodating the present traffic as the two canals, which existed many years before, have become insufficient since that time."

The effects of all this told injuriously in various ways upon the traffic and business of the town. Thus that important trade, the cart owners, complained that the accommodation was so insufficient that they were detained in the streets for their loads for most unreasonable times. One, who carted 150,000 bales of cotton in a year, said that the Lancashire and Yorkshire Company kept his carts standing idle while they loaded their own, and that he had known as many as 57 carts kept waiting for four hours consecutively. Another stated that he had seen 78 carts at a time waiting to go to the Lancashire and Yorkshire line. Merchants also asserted that they suffered serious hindrances in the conduct of their business. Sometimes the timber trade would, in consequence of snow, be delayed for a week or two. In fact, they said, "when an order is received from the country, it is the practice to send down to the wharf to see whether 'the goods' can take it in, and if they cannot, we do not send it until we receive permission. If a man orders 1000 feet of timber, and says it is to go by the Lancashire and Yorkshire line, we have to send to that company to see if they can receive it. We are obliged to know the state of the railway before we can send the goods. If we do send the goods without asking their permission, they very often send it back again." The same remark applied to the canals. "I believe," said a witness, "that they have all the disposition to do whatever they can, but delays occur. Perhaps I might send a few thousand feet of timber to the railway company, and if they have no waggon at the time, the timber is deposited in exactly the same way as those papers are on the floor; the next lot of timber that comes is put upon the first lot, and then it is like goods that we put down the hold of a ship, the first comes out last."

"It is impossible," remarked Mr. Heron, the town clerk of Manchester, "to doubt that the proposed line would be advantageous; and, as it appears to me, it is an absolute necessity that those great systems (the three companies) should have a communication with Liverpool as they have with Manchester, within their own power and under their own control." As an evidence, too, of the inadequacy of the accommodation then provided, it may be mentioned that at that time no passenger train ran on the London and North Western line between the vast populations of Liverpool and Manchester at a later hour in the day than half-past seven o'clock.

That there was a prospect of the capital to be expended on the proposed line receiving an adequate return, was shown by Mr. Denison. "We are going to spend," he said, "upon that line, £750,000. According to the ordinary practice, £75,000 a year will pay 5 per cent. upon that, allowing half to go off in working expenses. If the figures I have given you are right, then that £75,000 a year will be less a great deal than the almost certain increase of traffic in the next three years. So that we can actually pay ourselves 5 per cent. upon our line, without depriving the London and North Western or the Lancashire and Yorkshire Companies of one single penny which they now receive from the carriage of goods and passengers upon the existing line. Again, the £75,000 a year, according to the calculations I have, is less than one sixth of the eastern traffic now coming into Liverpool."

Such were some of the facts submitted for the consideration of Parliament. The result was, that the promoters of the line were successful. In connection with this new line from Manchester to Liverpool, it was also resolved to provide additional communication between Manchester and Stockport. The importance of further facilities of communication between these towns was illustrated by the fact that Mr. Ivie Mackie, of Manchester, had started and maintained a remunerative omnibus traffic on that route. "The little cribs of omnibuses," he quaintly told the parliamentary committee, "such as you have here in London, are not fit for people to ride in. I, being rather above the ordinary size, required increased accommodation, and I thought I would introduce the large Scotch omnibuses simply to show the Manchester people what could be done. I had no idea of establishing it as a business; but finding it a profitable business, I have continued it ever since." "And so," remarked Mr. Mereweather, "I understand you were measured for a seat in the omnibus, and that you started these new ones on that broad basis."

LIVERPOOL, FROM THE MERSEY.

CHAPTER IX.

Important period in Midland Railway politics.—The West Coast route to Glasgow.—The East Coast route to Edinburgh.—Midland Company complains that it is excluded from its share of Scotch traffic.—Difficulty of Midland passenger traffic to Scotland.—Proposals of London and North Western.—Joint ownership and running powers at arbitration rates offered.—Practical difficulties.—Proposed local line from Settle to Hawes.—Overtures of Midland Company to North of England Union.—Proposed Midland line from Settle to Carlisle.—Support of landlords.—Evidence of Lords Wharncliffe and Wensleydale and others.—Hesitating opposition of London and North Western.—Objections to admission of Midland to Citadel Station at Carlisle.—Reply of Midland Company by fact and argument.—Capacity of Citadel Station to receive additional traffic.—Radford and Trowell line.—Opposition of Lord Middleton and others.—A wonderful canal.—Conclusive reply.—Ashby and Nuneaton line.—Rival scheme of London and North Western.—Arrangement for Midland bill to pass with joint ownership by London and North Western and Midland Companies.—Floods.

The year 1866 dated an important epoch in the politics of the Midland Railway extension. While looking forward to the completion of lines that would connect the Midland—by the Furness and Midland—with the Lake District; by the Buxton extension with Manchester; by a connecting link with the South Western system; and by the Bedford line with the Metropolis,—the directors again turned their eyes to the far north, and sought to devise some means by which they might obtain a share of the vast traffic carried on between this country and Scotland.

Nor was this unnatural or unreasonable. Just as the London and North Western Company, when it reached Liverpool, had secured access by way of Preston, Lancaster, Carlisle, and the Caledonian line,—by what is called the West Coast route,—to Scotland; and just as the Great Northern had, by association with the North Eastern and North British Companies, been able to carry a large through traffic between London and Edinburgh

—by what is called the East Coast route; so the Midland Company, having come to occupy an influential position in the midland counties of England, and having stretched its great highway from London to Lancaster, arrived at the conclusion that the time had come when it should form a third and central route from south to north, and should enjoy a fair share of an increasing traffic, worth, even at that period, not less than £1,500,000 per annum.

The precise position which the Midland Company occupied with regard to the Scotch traffic was as follows: By a lease for 999 years of the Little North Western line, it had a line of its own as far as Ingleton. Here the Midland line ended; but it was in connection with another line belonging to another company which ran northward, along the magnificent vale of the Lune, which at Tebay joined the main line of the Lancaster and Carlisle. This Ingleton and Tebay extension originally formed part of the scheme of the Little North Western; but the projectors fell into difficulties, and after spending several thousands of pounds upon the land, and on the partial construction of the works, they were abandoned, and in this state they remained for several years. When times mended, a fresh application was made to Parliament for powers to complete the line, and the Lancaster and Carlisle Company also asked for similar authority; and they, being the more responsible body, were successful. They accordingly completed the works, through a very difficult and mountainous country, and at enormous cost. Subsequently the Lancaster and Carlisle became practically London and North Western, for it is vested in that company according to terms so comprehensive that they are worthy of quotation: the North Western is to have control of the line for 1000 years, "the plant, rolling stock, and moveable property to be used by the lessees during, and to be restored at the end of, the lease"!

Such was the position of affairs down to the year 1866, and the Midland Company was in consequence under the necessity of sending its Scotch traffic over the lines of a company with which it was in competition in almost every large town in England; and the effect of these disadvantages was decisive. Between towns as large as Birmingham and Glasgow the Midland did not carry a passenger, and the goods it conveyed in a year would have filled only a few wheelbarrows; while over the Waverley route the Midland Company sent only about two tons of goods a day, and a passenger once a fortnight. The personal inconveniences also suffered by those who travelled from any part of the Midland system to Scotland were considerable. "It is a very rare thing," said Mr. Allport, "for me to go down to Carlisle without being turned out twice. I have seen twelve or fifteen passengers turned out at Ingleton, and the same number at Tebay. Then, although some of the largest towns in England are upon the Midland system, there is no through carriage to Edinburgh, unless we occasionally have a family going down, and then we make a special arrangement, and apply for a special carriage to go through. We have applied in vain for through carriages for Scotland over and over again. . . . They will not book through from Glasgow to London by us. . . . I have frequently had letters from passengers complaining that they could not get booked through. I have sent letters also to Mr. Johnson from passengers requiring to come to Derby when booking to Glasgow, and they have been told to go by way of Crewe instead of going by Ingleton. I have been in trains myself with passengers who have been booked from Glasgow to Derby by Crewe. It is only recently I had a correspondence with a family who particularly wished to come by the Midland; but they were refused, and were sent by Crewe."

It became, too, a practice of the North Western in the summer months to have their nine o'clock express from London divided at Preston into two, the first portion ran quickly to Carlisle, reaching Edinburgh and Glasgow an hour earlier than before; but the London and North Western Company declined to stop that portion of the train at Tebay, where the Midland passengers might have joined it, and they were taken on by another train which left at ten o'clock. "They say they cannot stop," said Mr. Allport, "although I find in their time-table that that train from London stops at Stafford and at Lancaster—Lancaster for example with 10,000 inhabitants, while Tebay is practically, through the Midland system, in connection with a population exceeding 1,000,000." The consequence was that the Midland could not advantageously compete for express traffic; and thus passengers had to find their way by different and devious routes on to the London and North Western, in order to catch the express trains of the North Western. "I have been by a fast train," said Mr. Allport, "from Derby to Ingleton, and then been attached to a train with six or eight coal-trucks to be carried on to Tebay."

The Midland also complained that at Carlisle it had to encounter a fresh series of difficulties. Needless and invidious hindrances, it was alleged, arose in the forwarding of Midland goods. "I am sure," said the manager of the North British Company, "there has been ill-will. There has been systematic delay."

At length these difficulties in the conduct of the traffic became so serious that the Midland Company opened communications with the London and North Western, in which a better access to Carlisle was insisted upon. The reasonableness of the claim was not denied; and at length the London and North Western mentioned terms upon which the Midland might bring their traffic over the Lancaster and Carlisle. One proposal was that the two companies should share the line, each paying half the rent, and each running over it, without tolls, as if it were their own. But inasmuch as the London and North Western, by its local position, was likely to throw a greater proportion of traffic on the line than the Midland, it was obviously unreasonable that the latter should pay half the cost of the rail and enjoy less than half of the advantage.

Another proposal was that the Midland Company should have running powers over the line at arbitration rates. But arbitration rates would involve constant difficulty. Suppose, for instance, a contractor applied to the manager of the Midland Company for a rate from London to Glasgow, the whole case—with all its particularities—would have to be submitted for the approval of the manager of the London and North Western Company, and if he did not assent the case must go to arbitration. "But," said Mr. Allport, "scarcely a day passes but we are obliged to meet cases by altering our rates at some one or other of our large towns; and if we had to wait, either for the consent of the London and North Western Company to an alteration of those rates, or for arbitration, the time would be gone by, and the traffic would be lost. Parties come to me, and within a very short time three or four of the principal iron-masters have come to me, and said: 'Here is a contract for 20,000 tons, and if you can reduce your rate on the lot to so and so, we can tender, and probably obtain the contract against our competitors.' But the decision had to be made instantly. This very contract I have named was in competition with many iron-masters, and the London and North Western would have had a direct interest in refusing to give their assent."

In the light of such considerations, the Midland

Company claimed the absolute control over their own rates. As to the stations on the Lancaster and Carlisle itself arbitration rates might suffice; but for the through traffic to Carlisle they must be free, for Carlisle meant the Scotch traffic. "Do you insist upon the control of your rates as an indispensable condition?" asked a deputation from the North Western board of a deputation from the Midland board. "Then," said the London and North Western chairman, "the negotiation is over."

The course now pursued by the Midland Company was also affected by some special circumstances. In the session of 1865 a bill had been introduced into Parliament for making a line, to be called the North of England Union Railway, from Settle to Hawes. Originally this railway was projected by gentlemen locally interested, who supported it because it would promote local convenience, and because it would enhance the value of their estates. The chairman of the company was Lord Wharncliffe; and the line would have cost about £500,000.

The Union Company's bill had received the sanction of the Commons, and would doubtless have passed through the Lords had not the Midland Company interposed, and come to an arrangement with its supporters. By this it was agreed that, since the line had been projected chiefly for local purposes, and a gradient had been adopted which would have been unsuitable for a good through line, the bill should be withdrawn; and that it should be reintroduced in the session of 1866, with a better gradient, by the Midland Company. "We gave up the line," said Lord Wharncliffe, in his evidence before the House of Lords, "on the distinct understanding that the Midland Company should apply for the bill this year."

Such were the circumstances under which a bill of the Midland Company came before Parliament for a through line from near their Settle station to Carlisle. It received the cordial support of numerous witnesses. There was not an opposing landowner on its entire length. And the reasons for such support were obvious: the necessity for such a railway was great, the benefits it would confer were numerous, and the injury it would occasion was *nil*. It is true that, on the map, the line looks as if it ran almost close to the London and North Western Railway; but in reality it occupies an entirely different series of valleys, which are separated from those on the North Western line by a range of hills.

Lord Wensleydale gave expression to the anxiety of the people locally interested to be supplied with direct communication, in order that they might send their agricultural produce to the populous manufacturing districts of Lancashire. Such was the satisfaction felt at Appleby when it was announced that the bill had passed the Commons, that the church bells were rung, and the people, as was quaintly remarked, "wrote to the newspapers, and did everything proper under the circumstances." Another witness, Mr. Matthew Thomson, who resided at Kirkby Stephen, and who mentioned that the proposed railway would pass "through about fifteen different estates" which he owned, besides others belonging to his sister,—declared that there was "only one feeling" among the landowners as to the importance of the line, and that it would be of "very great advantage to the occupiers there for the purpose of taking their produce to the consuming districts, as well as for bringing into the district those things which they require." "I have only heard of one dissentient voice in the whole district of Eden Valley," said a farmer, who sent more than 5000 pounds of butter every year to Sheffield, and it came from a gentleman who "had a few trees he was partial to."

The policy of the opponents of the Midland Company's bill was undecided. Mr. Allport had had frequent conversations with the manager of the Caledonian Company; but he "never raised the slightest objection to

CARLISLE STATION.

the Midland Company using the Carlisle station:" on the contrary "always expressed himself most anxious to see them there." Before the case closed, however, it was intimated that Mr. Hope Scott would address the committee on behalf of the London and North Western and Caledonian Companies. "My learned friend, Mr. Hope Scott," said Mr. Mereweather, "is at this moment, I am told, on his legs in another room; but he is rapidly terminating.* We have looked at his notes over his shoulder, and we find that he is getting sufficiently near the end of his speech for us to assure you that he will be here very shortly."

* Legal phraseology, it appears, has its peculiarities.

The London and North Western professed that its objection to the Settle and Carlisle bill was, that the Midland Company intended to use the Citadel Station at Carlisle. "If the Midland Company," said Mr. Cawkwell, "had come for a line to Carlisle without touching our station or interfering with our property, I do not think we should have opposed them now. . . . If they had made their own provision at Carlisle, it would have been a different thing." Even so late as the period at which the bill reached the Lords, and when Earl Amherst, the chairman of the committee, asked Mr. Mereweather if he intended to oppose the line generally, or to confine his opposition to the question of the Citadel Station, the learned counsel hesitated. At that moment, however, a whisper reached them from behind, and he remarked that it was "a ticklish question." On the matter of the Citadel Station a protracted discussion then took place. It should be mentioned that it was originally constructed by the Caledonian and Lancaster and Carlisle Companies. In 1860 it consisted of a single platform for both up and down trains; but, as several other companies sought admission into it, it had been gradually enlarged, till the total cost had amounted to not less than £250,000.

The design of those who opposed the use by the Midland Company of the Citadel Station was, however, not founded upon those facts. It is obvious that if they could have compelled the Midland Company to land its passengers a mile or so east or west of the station to which all other lines from north and south converged, the effect would have been to exclude it from the very traffic it sought to share. If the Midland Company made a new station, "how could they," Mr. Cawkwell was asked, "conduct their Scotch passenger traffic?" "They could form a junction," was the reply, "with the Scotch companies out of Carlisle by which an exchange could be effected."

"Then your suggestion is," it was returned, "that we should not have stopped at Carlisle at all for the purpose of through traffic, but have joined the Scotch companies somewhere to the north of Carlisle?" Mr. Cawkwell's only answer was, "Our suggestion is, that you should not use our property for the purpose of your through traffic." When, therefore, the London and North Western resolved to concentrate their objection on the use by the Midland Company of the Carlisle station, they well knew that if they succeeded in that they succeeded altogether—that without Carlisle station the Settle and Carlisle line would be useless for the objects for which it was intended to be made. To this assertion of exclusive right on the part of existing companies to the Citadel Station the reply was conclusive: for, by the bill of 1866, which authorised the amalgamation of the Caledonian and Scottish North Eastern it was expressly declared that "whereas the railways of the Midland Railway Company form one of the lines of communication between the metropolis and Scotland, it is expedient that nothing should be done which shall impede or obstruct the flow or transit of traffic of every description freely and expeditiously over the lines of the Midland Railway to and from Scotland." And accordingly running powers, and also the use of the Caledonian portion of the Carlisle station, were granted to the Midland Company.

The argument from exclusive right being thus set aside, it was contended that, though there was sufficient accommodation in the Citadel Station for the six companies already there, it would be impossible to admit a seventh. But to this the reply was conclusive, both in fact and in argument. It was conclusive in fact. "In my opinion," said Mr. Rowbotham, the manager of the North British, "the station is not at all crowded." "It is perfectly idle," said Mr. Allport, "to assert that the station cannot accommodate the Midland traffic. I have had the traffic taken out at two or three stations, and in and out of the Carlisle station, both with reference to goods and passengers. There have been 106 trains a day, from the 4th of February to the 3rd of March, going south, from Carlisle: about 37 or 38 passenger trains and 69 goods trains; that is the average for the month. At the north end of the Derby station,—which is a very similar station to the Carlisle,—we have 320 trains out and in, against 106 at Carlisle. At Leeds, again, which is purely a passenger station, we have 255 passenger trains in and out of the Leeds station over a neck of line very like this at Carlisle. I have nc hesitation, too, in saying that the trains in and out of the Newcastle station for passengers are at least ten times more in number than the trains in and out of the Carlisle station. I could find a hundred stations in England with very much larger traffic, varying from double up to ten times the amount, with less accommodation than they have at Carlisle."

Besides the reply from fact, there was also an argument. "How was it," it was asked, "that during the two years in which negotiations were going on for the Midland to run over the Lancaster and Carlisle line it was never suggested that the Citadel Station was insufficient, and that it was never once proposed that it should be enlarged?" "Having pointed out," said Mr. Venables to Mr. William Clarke, the chief assistant engineer to the London and North Western Company, "the impossibility of working the Midland traffic under this system, will you now point out how it was to be worked if they had come by joint ownership over the Lancaster and Carlisle?"

Such were the arguments submitted to the consideration of Parliament; and the bill· passed.

Besides the great and overshadowing project of thus connecting the Midlands of England with Scotland, some other plans of extension were also contemplated. One of these was for a short line from a station called Radford, near Nottingham, to connect the Mansfield line with the Erewash Valley Railway, in order to avoid the circuitous route by Trent, and to diminish the distance by about five and a half miles. It was also intended, by means of a branch from Codnor Park to Ambergate, to have a more direct route to Manchester, instead of that by way of Derby. The bill was opposed by three gentlemen,—a landowner, a clergyman, and a nobleman. The landowner alleged that the line would injure a considerable residential estate and other properties which he possessed, and that some other route might be preferable. To this it was very naturally replied that if an alternative line were proposed the relative merits or demerits of each could be determined; but that it was impossible that "a mere ghost of an imaginary railway should be put in competition with our flesh and blood, or our iron and ballast railway." The rector of Trowell adopted a similar course of objection, and was met by a similar reply.

Lord Middleton's case was more definite. It was alleged on his behalf that injuries would be inflicted on his estate by the projected line. The proposed line would, it was said, sever for two miles the connection of his property with the neighbouring Nottingham and Grantham canal. Undoubtedly it would, was the reply, if no bridges or roads were made over the railway; but then bridges and roads would be made, and must be made, and the company was perfectly willing to make them. "The petitioner had, he said, at great expense, laid out a large extent of land for the purposes of the manufacture of bricks," etc. True; but for any loss on that expenditure he would be paid. The proposed line, it was further declared by the objectors, would "prevent the use of a canal, called Bilborough Cut," which had been "used by the predecessors in estate of your petitioner during many years." True, the canal "*had been*" so used by the said predecessors; but it had been stopped up for 53 years. On a part of the bed of it there was an avenue of trees, 25 to 30 years old; while on other portions corn crops grew, or cattle grazed. A bit of the canal remained open, and on it some kind of boat had a short time since been made to float, and this was the only vessel that had been upon the water there within the memory of man. In addition to all this, it was declared, on behalf of Lord Middleton, that a considerable portion of the estate "contained very large and valuable deposits of minerals." True; but the said deposits were lying beneath old exhausted workings full of water, and it was probable that if any deeper beds were opened they would be flooded also.

Finally, it was contended that Lord Middleton had certain rights over the cut, and that he was required by Act of Parliament to keep it open. To this it was replied that the ownership and the Act were of little avail if part of the canal was actually filled up, and the whole of it disused. "Did you consult your legal advisers," said Mr. Rodwell, "with regard to the terms on which the Bilborough Canal was held?" "No," replied Mr. Crossley; "I consulted the facts."

Eventually, however, the engineer of the Midland Company stated that he had discovered a plan by which the railway could be made, and at the same time "the Bilborough Cut be saved, if it were worth saving." By a slight deviation of the line it could be made to go under the canal. The additional cost to the company would be £1000.

In 1866, the Midland Company projected a line from Ashby-de-la-Zouch in Leicestershire to Nuneaton. It was designed to accommodate the large coal-fields somewhat to the west of the Leicester and Burton Railway, extending between Hinckley on the south and Moira on the north. The cost was estimated at about £300,000. The route selected was prescribed by the nature of the country and the situation of the collieries. But side by side with this proposed line a competing scheme was projected. It was described by a name which gave to it what a critic designated "an entirely illusory aspect of respectability,"—the "London and North Western and Midland Counties Coal Fields Railway;" the fact being that the Midland Railway was entirely opposed to it. The project was brought out in the names of private parties. The chairman of the board of promoters was Sir Cusack Roney, a gentleman who must have had considerable experience in such matters, for it was said that at that time he held office in fifteen different railway companies in England and Ireland. The promoters, however, looked with hopefulness to the London and North Western Company for patronage. "They feel," said Mr. Karslake, "that their little bantling can hardly support itself in a state of existence, unless it have something to which it can cling; and hence we find the extreme anxiety that they have shown in attempting to affiliate their infant upon the London and North Western Company. We do not find that that attempt has succeeded. A sort of faint declaration was put forth that if this line were made, then possibly the London and North Western proprietors might be invited to subscribe for it; but the utmost that we find that is done is this, that if this line should be sanctioned, then the London and North Western will work it. It is just one of those lines which, unless it is assisted by another company, must die a natural death."

At length, however, it was formally announced that the London and North Western Company would subscribe £250,000 towards the share capital of the Coalfields Railway Company, would work and maintain it, and would send over it all their traffic from Burton-on-Trent for Nuneaton, Rugby, or the south. In return the North Western was to be rewarded by direct access to Derby, the head quarters of the Midland system. It is true that they were already at Burton-on-Trent, and could exercise their rights at common law to run over the ten miles thence to Derby; but they preferred an independent route, though it would have involved an outlay of £950,000.

On the other hand the Midland Company contended that their line would cost less than £300,000; and that they ought not to be exposed to competition when they offered ample accommodation to the new comer; but they consented that the North Western should be joint proprietors with themselves in the Ashby and Nuneaton, "either by contributing half the capital or by paying to the Midland a fair interest on the outlay. Consequently," said Mr. Venables, "if there is any public object whatever in taking London and North Western traffic to Derby, we shall take it without the expenditure by anybody of a shilling for that purpose, and we shall not only do that, but we shall give them at Derby a communication with all the other railways that radiate from Derby, whereas they would come to a *cul de sac* at Derby, and would have, at some future time, to obtain some other way of getting on to the other railways. That we offer them instead of spending £700,000 in pure waste." To these terms the London and North Western eventually acceded; the Coal Fields Railway Bill was withdrawn, and the Ashby and Nuneaton was sanctioned.

The autumn of 1866 was marked by floods disastrous to property and life; and in November a singular accident occurred at the viaduct over the Aire at Apperley Bridge, by which the traffic of the Midland to the north-west, to Scotland and Ireland was temporarily arrested. There was also a landslip on the Manchester extension at Bugsworth, by which sixteen acres of land on which the railway stood slipped down the valley, and necessitated the deviation and re-construction of that part of the line. The particulars of these remarkable incidents, and the remedies adopted, will be found in our description of the line.

BUGSWORTH VIADUCT.

CHAPTER X.

Glasgow and South Western Company.—Contemplated alliance with Caledonian Company—Policy of Midland Company.—Door of Scotland shut in their faces.—Proposed amalgamation of Midland with the Glasgow and South Western.—Lateral and longitudinal amalgamation.—Bill before Parliament.—Argument of Mr. Venables.—Humorous reply of Mr. Hope Scott.—Mr. Denison and Mr. Allport.—Rejoinder of Mr. Venables.—Bill rejected.—Heavy liabilities of Midland Company.—Misgivings among shareholders.—Meeting of Proprietors on May 29th, 1867.—Mr. Hutchinson's explanation of Midland policy.—Circular of shareholders.—Meeting at Corn Exchange, Derby.—Proposal to abandon the Settle and Carlisle line.—Efforts to obtain terms from London and North Western.—"Childish" reply received.—Approval of amalgamation bill.—Position of Midland system.—Meeting, August, 1867.—Time of anxiety.—Circular of December 14th.—Alarm.—Rumours.—Criticisms.—Defence of Midland policy.—Special general meeting, January 15th, 1868.—Mr. Hutchinson's explanation.—Reasons for additional outlay.—Committee of Consultation.—Report of committee.—Keighley and Worth line.—Five millions' bill.—Negotiations with London and North Western for access to Scotland *viâ* Lancaster and Carlisle. Terms proposed.—Bill brought before Parliament.—Opposition.—Abandonment.—Bill rejected.—Progress of lines.

The period we are now approaching was marked by events of great interest in the chronicles of the Midland Railway. The earliest of these was in connection with the various efforts made by that Company to obtain a share in the vast and increasing traffic carried on between this country and Scotland. This had been chiefly conducted along two routes, that on the East Coast by the Great Northern, North Eastern, and North British; and that on the West Coast, by the London and North Western and Caledonian: the Midland Board was now of opinion that by virtue of its natural position and growing importance it might justly claim to form a third and Midland route to Scotland. With this object it resolved, as we have seen, to seek Parliamentary power to make a line up the series of valleys which lead from Settle to

Carlisle, where it would reach the door of Scotland, and whence it might, by means of the Glasgow and South Western Railway, find its way onward to the North.

The Glasgow and South Western was originally a line from Glasgow to Ayrshire, and it is still frequently spoken of as the Ayrshire Railway. Subsequently it was extended, *viâ* Dumfries, to Gretna, where it falls into the Caledonian, along which it reaches Carlisle, and by means of which it obtained power to use the Citadel Station. The distance between Carlisle and Glasgow over the South Western is 124 miles; by the Caledonian about 105 miles; but the latter have to suffer the disadvantage of inferior gradients. The special significance of the position of the Glasgow and South Western line was that, whereas the North British was identified with the East Coast route, and the Caledonian with the London and North Western, it provided the only independent course along which a third railway from the South could hope to reach the heart of Scotland.

Scarcely, however, had the Midland Company decided that they ought to make the Settle and Carlisle line and to endeavour to secure an uninterrupted course into Scotland, than it was ascertained that the Glasgow and South Western were on the eve of amalgamation with the Caledonian. In fact, powers had already been obtained which would almost have enabled these companies to amalgamate without further leave or licence; it was reasonable to suppose that they would not allow them to slumber; and on the 17th of August, 1866, the secretary of the Caledonian Company addressed the secretary of the Glasgow and South Western on the subject. "His board," he said, "thought it advisable that the opportunity afforded by the recent powers," obtained by the two companies, "to enter into an agreement for the management and working and apportionment of the revenues of the two undertakings should not be lost sight of; and having no doubt that your board reciprocates the feeling," they had appointed a committee to meet a committee of the Glasgow and South Western board in the hope that an agreement might be come to.

For the Glasgow and South Western to amalgamate with the Caledonian was, however, in effect to amalgamate with the London and North Western; for these two companies were identified in policy and interest. So that, had this further amalgamation been consummated, the effect would have been that the Midland Company would have found that it had made 80 miles of very costly railway from Settle to Carlisle, through a comparatively unproductive country, solely to reach Scotland, but that the door of Scotland was shut by the hands of the several competitors in their faces. Only one course appeared possible to the Midland board: to enter into alliance with the Glasgow and South Western, with a view to the identification of their interests; and negotiations to that end were opened, and terms were arranged for the subsequent amalgamation of the two properties.

Such a union of continuous lines would, it was believed, be in the public interest. Lateral amalgamation, that is, of parallel lines of railway, may repress the fair competition that arises from the working of two independent routes between the same termini; but longitudinal amalgamation, that is, of lines which, not being parallel, can never be competitive, facilitates through traffic by being held in one hand, guided by one policy, and directed to the most efficient conduct of traffic over long distances. Though Mr. Hope Scott humorously remarked that in Mr. Venables' "great longitudinal principle there is about as much latitude as I ever found in describing a longitudinal case," yet we believe that this principle is incontrovertible. "The Glasgow and

South Western Company," continued Mr. Scott, "has been threatened, says my learned friend Mr. Venables, with fraternity or death. It has, however, been able to live, and what is more, it has been able to grow fat. It has reached, says Mr. Johnstone, a dividend which we will call 6½ or 7, whichever you please. It has reached that dividend during the last two years, during which the Caledonian Company has had extra means of oppression over it. It has managed to give a tit-for-tat to the Caledonian Company. It has got to Greenock, which is the best portion of the traffic. It has got running powers and facilities over the Caledonian and over the North British, and has, I say, now a dowry to take with it of 1000 miles of traffic belonging to other companies. Nay, more, it has reached a situation which enables my friend, Mr. Venables, to open it as with a case of amalgamation on equal terms, because the Midland Company and the Glasgow and South Western are in an equal state of prosperity. So that the oppression of the Caledonian Company has not done much harm to the Glasgow and South Western Company; for it has found itself flourishing; its permanent way is in excellent order; its rolling stock is the same, and is abundant and sufficient; so that my learned friend, Mr. Venables, is really obliged to lament that they are not insolvent, because he would then have had a better reason for his bill."

Mr. Hope Scott could not allow, even in the discussion of details, however dry, an opportunity to pass for the play of his wit. In the course of Mr. Venables' speech, that gentleman had said of the Midland Company "they are a prosperous company, and perhaps that is the reason why they have always been a straightforward company." "This," said Mr. Scott, "is an odd view of morality certainly; but of course my learned friend is fully entitled to describe his own clients, the Midland Company, as he likes best. If he had said they had always been a straightforward company, and therefore they had been a prosperous company, one would have understood the moral of it; but the odd thing is, that, having said this of the Midland Company, and having declared elsewhere that the property of the Glasgow and South Western is equal to that of the Midland Company, he has nowhere called the Glasgow and South Western a straightforward Company. Now, sir, I think that was wrong. But in truth he could not do it, for he will not trust them out of his sight, and that is the reason why he asks you to pass this bill. My learned friend found the Glasgow and South Western Company and the Caledonian Company on the eve of amalgamation. What my friend meant was this, if he could be sure of their virtue for the next four years" this bill might have been delayed. Mr. Hope Scott, on the other hand, contended that the amalgamation should be delayed "until the Settle Railway is constructed, and no shorter time has been suggested for its construction than four years. What may arise in that time in the railway world," he asked, "who can say, especially as within that period we shall all be under a new constitution? Perhaps, sir, by the time when this question ought properly to come before parliament, your places may be filled by gentlemen whose seats depend considerably upon the votes of lodging enginemen and discompounded stokers, whose views of railway legislation may be entirely different from your own.

"Now is it fair to snatch from the new parliament the decision which ought to be delayed for four years, and to deal with it by a house for which I have infinite respect, but which evidently does not at present represent properly the people of England? But, sir, the only argument which is alleged for this anticipation—these espousals which are not to become marriage for four years,—is that the lady is fickle; 'fraternity'—not the dagger, not death; 'fraternity,' a something more kindly than fraternity, might influence her, and she might slip through their fingers. Now what does all this depend upon? Why, upon clauses in two Acts of Parliament of last session. Pass this Act in a form simply to repeal those clauses (which, on the part of the Caledonian Company, I freely assent to), and the whole argument for the bill is gone."

Mr. Denison, on behalf of the North British, expressed his belief that the Settle and Carlisle would not be completed, and that therefore any such amalgamation as that now proposed was premature. "We had it," he said, "from Mr. Allport that nothing had been done upon the Settle and Carlisle line. I cross-examined Mr. Allport (as one always does such a witness) with fear and trembling, because sometimes one gets the worst of it, but I do not think I got the worst of it, because what I got from Mr. Allport was, that he was not the man to tell us about it. Now, sir, do you think that if much of that land had been bought, Mr. Allport would not have known of it? Do you think that if the line had been staked out he would not have known of it? Do things go on with the Midland Company which that very able gentleman does not know of? They have placed the shares of the Settle and Carlisle line; the deposit, or the first call, or whatever the word is, has been paid upon them, I dare say; but I should not be very much surprised to hear that the Midland shareholders would not be very much distressed if they were not called upon to pay any more. The agreements with landowners are capable of settlement. Suppose they do, there is a Settle and Carlisle line. Every argument for this bill will be just as good when the Settle and Carlisle is within a few months of completion as it is now."

Mr. Venables replied first to Mr. Hope Scott. "My learned friend," he said, "made an offer at the end of his speech. After speaking entirely on other subjects, he said, 'you made a great point of the possible amalgamation under the clauses of these two agreements; well, we will give up those clauses;' and then he sat down. In what possible manner is he going to give them up? He can represent the Caledonian, and say, knowing perfectly well what is coming of it, that they will give them up. If they could have given them up, they would never have made the offer. But they cannot give them up without the consent of the Glasgow and South Western Company. I am here representing the Midland and the Glasgow and South Western Company. No doubt it would be a great concession to the Midland Company to give up those clauses; but my learned friend says, if the committee will throw out this bill, we, the Caledonian Company, will at some future time consent to repeal those clauses. But if the amalgamation were rejected, what would be the position of the Glasgow and South Western Company? They would be placed in exactly the position in which they were when they made those clauses. On behalf therefore of the Glasgow and South Western, I say, Indeed we will not do anything of the kind. It is perfectly clear that the Caledonian Company, when they made that offer, knew that it could not be allowed, that it was one of those cheap pieces of benevolence for which my learned friend, Mr. Hope Scott, in his professional character, is rather remarkable."

In answer to Mr. Denison's remark, that the amalgamation would be premature, because the Settle and Carlisle was not made, Mr. Venables said: "As to the question of how much money has been laid out, how many stakes have been placed, how many surveys have been made, that might have been very important if this had been a poor owner, or a new company incapable of creating the line which they are authorized and required to make. It is very true that the refusal of this amalgamation, shutting the door to the west of Scotland in our faces, would undoubtedly greatly diminish the value of the Settle and Carlisle line. But I think it is not an argument likely to weigh with the Committee against the bill, that it will utilize and employ for the benefit of the public parliamentary powers which have already been given after full inquiry. The passing of this amalgamation bill will involve the completion of the Settle and Carlisle undoubtedly, as an indispensable condition. To say, therefore, that it is an argument against this amalgamation that we have not made, and perhaps have not begun, and perhaps may not make the Settle and Carlisle line, is an inconsistent argument. There is no doubt that the fear of the opponents is not that it will not be made, but that it will be made, and that by its being made this amalgamation will be efficient. Can there be any better proof that we shall make the Settle and Carlisle line? Moreover, what harm will this amalgamation do to anybody if we cannot use it?" In this view of the matter the Committee of the House of Commons appear to have concurred; and on the 23rd of May, 1867, they declared the preamble to be proved.

In subsequently urging the measure upon the sanction of the Lords' Committee, among the advantages likely to accrue from the amalgamation of the Midland with the Glasgow and South Western, it was shown that a healthy competition would be secured. Although no fresh capital would be expended, and no fresh lines be constructed, the independence and power of free competition on three great routes between England and Scotland would be perpetuated. There would be no necessity for passengers or goods to travel by any particular company. Three direct routes would be open, and open more effectually after amalgamation than before.

"We come, my lords," said Mr. Venables, "not to rob anybody, but to accommodate the public, and to get a fair share of profit in accommodating the public; and if we can give a share of the accommodation to the amount of one-third of all the possible Scotch traffic, we shall probably get a third of the traffic. Of that the London and North Western will lose something, the East Coast companies will lose something; but all three companies together, by improved accommodation and increased competition, will develop the traffic in such a way that in a short time probably the proportion of each company will, notwithstanding what may have been lost to the Midland, be quite as great as at present."

In concluding his speech Mr. Venables said: "We say, my lords, it is a great advantage in this kind of scheme that we do not expend one shilling of capital, that we merely utilize the expenditure of capital which Parliament has already sanctioned. We say that we are entitled, not so much in our own right, as in the public interest, to have an independent route to Carlisle. We say that, for reasons we have suggested to your lordships, the North British Company, which no doubt is entitled to great consideration, will not be injured by this line; and we say that if the amalgamation pure and simple were to be injurious to the North British line, nevertheless, as they themselves now say, they are ready, if the case arises, to suggest protection against possible damage; and I say, my lords, none of the modes of protection which have been suggested are injurious or unjust to the Caledonian Company. I think, my lords, there probably never was a case in which so great an advantage could be gained with so little loss. There has hardly been an attempt to dispute the preponderance of advantage to the public; and I think the evidence results in showing that there would be no hardship whatever to the railway companies."

The committee-room was cleared. After a time the counsel and parties were called in. The chairman then announced that "the Committee had given the most serious consideration to the case, and they were of opinion that it was not expedient to proceed further with the bill."

While the Amalgamation Bill was thus occupying the attention of Parliament, an event of much interest was occurring among the directors and shareholders of the Midland Company itself. Doubt had long been cherished by some of the proprietors as to whether it was wise to prosecute this amalgamation; and their misgivings at length took the shape of overt and organized opposition. An opportunity for expressing these opinions occurred at a meeting of the proprietors held in Derby on the 29th of May, 1867, to consider the propriety of formally considering several bills then before Parliament. Before it took place rumours were rife as to the hostility with which the policy of the directors was in some quarters regarded. More than 1000 shareholders were present, the attendance being so large that the meeting had to be adjourned to the Corn Exchange. Mr. Hutchinson, as usual, presided, and with much self-mastery proceeded to address himself to the business of the day.

After some preliminary remarks, he stated that the great business on which the decision of the proprietors was to be obtained, was the bill for the amalgamation of the Midland and Glasgow and South Western Companies. When the Settle and Carlisle line was projected, Carlisle was regarded as the ultimate resting-place of the Midland Company northwards. But, the chairman stated, when he and his colleagues met the directors of the Glasgow and South Western Company in Scotland in the previous September, they were surprised to find that in a recent session of Parliament the Caledonian and the Glasgow and South Western Companies had obtained clauses which, if exercised, would have amounted practically to an amalgamation. Had these powers been put into effect, the Midland, when they reached Carlisle, would have found the road to Glasgow practically in the hands of one company, and that company the most close and intimate ally of the London and North Western Company, which competed with the Midland in every great town into which the Midland ran. Under these circumstances the directors came to the conclusion to recommend the shareholders to apply for a bill to amalgamate the two companies. Deputations from the Midland directors visited the line and works of the Glasgow and South Western; similar deputations came over the Midland; the accountants of both companies had several times examined the accounts, and their report was favourable; and the amalgamation would secure for the Midland Company a direct route from London, through the heart of England, to Glasgow; and a share of a traffic between the two countries which was estimated at £1,500,000 per annum, and which was every year increasing.

An animated discussion followed, in which strong opinions were strongly expressed on both sides of the subject. Another meeting was held on the following Tuesday, in the Shareholders' Room, when the subject was still further debated, and the decision was reserved till the 13th of June.

These discussions, however, had accomplished important ends. They had cleared the air; they had prepared the way for action when the final vote was to be given.

Meanwhile a number of influential shareholders availed themselves of the interval to submit by circular some considerations which they thought might be useful to fellow proprietors who had not been present at the meeting.

They stated that several of themselves had at one time entertained "a strong objection to the bill; but further reflection, and the full discussion which the subject had undergone, had changed their opinion, and they were now unanimous in regarding the adoption of the bill, which contained no power to create new capital, as of vital importance to the interests of the Midland Company. A similar change of opinion, they believed, had taken place to a large extent among the general body of shareholders." They urged all the shareholders to attend the adjourned meeting on the 13th, and to judge for themselves.

The meeting, which had been formally adjourned to the Corn Exchange, was very large and excited, though in excellent temper. A new element was now introduced into the debate. Since the last meeting the Midland Committee of the Railway Shareholders' Association had opened negotiations with the London and North Western Company with a view to ascertain on what terms the North Western would give the Midland access to Carlisle over the Lancaster and Carlisle line. It seems to have been thought by this deputation that hitherto the Midland Company had been entirely in the wrong, and that the London and North Western directors were ready, if rightly approached, to make the most liberal concessions. Mr. William Sale, a Manchester solicitor, who acted as the secretary of the association, was one of a deputation who had waited upon Mr. Moon and other directors at Euston Square. Subsequently he called upon Mr. Carter, the solicitor of the Midland Company, stated that he had acted as the official organ of the Midland Committee, that he had obtained a statement of the terms which the North Western authorities were prepared to concede, and that these terms he now officially communicated to the solicitor of the Midland Company. It subsequently transpired that though Mr. Sale was the official medium of conveying these terms, yet that neither he nor the association had any responsibility as regards their approval. At this our readers will not be surprised; for it appears that the latest and best terms which the friends of conciliation could obtain from the North Western Company were as follows:—"That it be referred to the President of the Board of Trade to inquire and ascertain what the point of difference was between the Midland and North Western Companies in the recent negotiations respecting the Lancaster and Carlisle line, to determine which company was right, and what should be done as to such point of difference in the event of the Midland Company abandoning the Settle and Carlisle line."

When these negotiations and their results were described by the Chairman of the Midland Company to the meeting, they were received with derisive laughter, and a warm response was given to his announcement that "he had placed that document before his colleagues for their consideration, and he might tell the meeting that the board considered that the discussion of such terms would be idle. The first thing the London and North Western proposed, was to refer to the President of the Board of Trade as to what was the point of difference, and which party was right and which was wrong with regard to the offers which had been made. That question had already been referred to and had been decided by a higher tribunal, namely, a committee of the House of Lords. The case of the London and North Western Company was argued before that committee by the most able and accomplished advocates of the parliamentary bar. Witnesses were examined on both sides; the voluminous correspondence which had taken place between the companies on the subject of the Lancaster and Carlisle Railway was put in evidence; and with what result? Why, after all, that the House of Lords declared the preamble of the Midland Company's bill to be proved, and they passed the Act for making the Settle and Carlisle railway, which they would not have done had they considered that fair terms had been offered to the Midland Company for the use of the Lancaster and Carlisle railway, and that free access had been offered by the London and North Western to Carlisle. What the London and North Western Company proposed was something like this:—Two parties have a suit —a law suit if you choose; the verdict has been given in favour of one of these parties, upon which the other party turns round and says, "We will now submit this matter to arbitration." Mr. Hutchinson added that such an offer and such conduct could only be described as childish.

An animated, and at one time somewhat angry discussion followed, after which a show of hands was taken on the resolution, for which there was an immense majority. A poll was demanded; the voting occupied two hours, and then the chairman moved an adjournment of the meeting till the following Friday, to receive the reports of the scrutineers. The result was as follows:—

Approving the Bill.	Capital Stock. £
Present, 572 persons, holding	1,505,503
Proxies, 1008 "	3,375,112
Total	£4,880,615
Not approving the Bill.	
Present, 34 persons, holding	83,703
Proxies, 994 "	1,367,111
Total	£1,450,814

The position at this period occupied by the Midland Company was one of satisfaction not untinged with solicitude. Having the weight of many and heavy responsibilities, they were looking forward to a time of relief. They were paying interest on a large amount of capital which, as it was expended on works still incomplete, was earning nothing. When those works are finished, "we shall have a system of railway," said a writer of the time, "which plants one foot in London and another in Bristol, whose trunk lies upon the best portions of the midland counties of England, and covers Manchester, Liverpool, and Sheffield; whose head rests on Carlisle, and whose arms, extending east and west, grasp with one, by way of the North British, the traffic of Edinburgh, and with the other, by the Glasgow and South Western, the trade and commerce of Glasgow."

APPERLEY VIADUCT.

In August, 1867, the directors reported that their working expenses had increased in consequence of the payment out of the revenue for the reconstruction of the Apperley Viaduct, of a bridge at Tamworth, and other works injured by floods in the previous year; there had also been a loss of revenue from having to work traffic over the lines of other companies. The amount of unproductive capital had increased to £5,000,000. The loss of the Glasgow and South Western Amalgamation Bill, and the withdrawal of some others, had made it necessary to charge the cost of promoting them to revenue instead of capital, because there would now be no capital accounts under those bills against which they could be charged.

At this meeting an arrangement with the Metropolitan Company was sanctioned. The Midland Company was to have the use of the Metropolitan from King's Cross Junction to Moorgate Street; the former fixing the number and times of their own trains. The Midland was to pay a mileage proportion of gross receipts from traffic, a minimum being fixed for the first year of £4000, of £5000 for the second, of £6000 for the third, and of £7000 for the fourth and each succeeding year. They were also charged £500 a year for the first three years for the use of the intermediate stations, and from £4000 to £6000 a year for station accommodation at Moorgate. The Midland Company also undertook to pay 6*d.* a ton for goods, and 4*d.* for coals, up to 50,000 tons, and 3*d.* for every ton above that quantity. The total fixed minimum charges under the agreement were to amount to from £14,000, to £15,000 a year.

The latter part of the year 1867 was a period of great anxiety to all the monied interests of the country; the conspicuous break down of some of the principal railway companies brought discredit on railway property and on railway administration generally; and though the proprietors of the Midland Company were confident of the substantial soundness of their property, many had misgivings on account of the undefined magnitude of their own financial liabilities, concerning which the chairman had publicly remarked that they "would far outstrip the estimates made four or five years ago."

Affairs, however, were moving quietly on, when, on the morning of the 17th December, a "circular" was received by the proprietors from the directors, an unusual document for them to send. It stated that "under ordinary circumstances the directors would not have deemed it necessary to issue reports of their proceedings except at the general meetings of the Company; but as they are about to deposit a bill in Parliament proposing a large increase of capital, they felt it due to the shareholders to submit to them, without delay, an explanation of the causes which rendered this application necessary."

The introduction was ominous. The circular proceeded:—"At the last half-yearly meeting the Chairman announced to the proprietors that the cost of the extension into London, and of the stations there, would largely exceed the parliamentary estimates. It has, in fact, been found that the value of the property required and the amount of compensations have been enormously in excess of what was anticipated, and it would seem that the cost of carrying the works of a railway into London is such as to defy all previous calculation;" and additional capital for the London line alone would be required to the amount of about £2,150,000.

Further, it had been ascertained, in constructing the Sheffield and Chesterfield and other lines, that there would also be "a large increase of expenditure beyond the parliamentary estimate" to the extent of £1,350,000.

"It has also been found necessary to provide new engines and additional plant and rolling stock, to meet the requirements of the increased traffic of the Company. For this purpose the sum of £960,000 has been expended out of the sums voted by the proprietors at various half-yearly meetings, but the necessary powers to raise the capital have not as yet been obtained. It is now therefore proposed to include this expenditure in the present bill, with power to raise a further sum of £540,000 to meet future requirements.

"The total addition to the capital of the Company will thus be £5,000,000, of which it will be proposed to raise £3,750,000 by shares, and £1,250,000 by borrowing powers."

This circular fell like a thunderbolt through a sensitive atmosphere. Not that it said very much more than had been previously known; but the statements so recently made, that "all previous calculations" had been exceeded, that capital had been spent for which "the necessary powers had not" as yet been obtained; and the demand for a round sum of £5,000,000 additional capital, seemed sufficiently alarming.

The wildest rumours were afloat. It was confidently declared that the company "had been bought up, as the Americans phrase it, 'short,' by a banker or money lender, for this £960,000, or some other sum of money; and that in dire necessity they asked for all these millions, in order to get the trifle that they wanted."

The severest criticisms were offered. It was declared that Mr. Hutchinson and his colleagues had spoken "with a frankness which almost amounts to recklessness." The directors were "upon the horn of a dilemma, for either they and their chief officers are flagrantly ignorant of matters which, if fit for their posts, they ought to understand, or there had been a deliberate concealment of the facts from the proprietors." A pamphlet asserted that the Midland property had been gradually depreciating, and, mile for mile, was not worth as much as in 1865. "The Midland Railway Company," said the *Economist*, "has this week created a panic such as only a great and respected railway can create." "Is upwards of £30,000,000 sterling," demanded the *Bullionist*, "to be imperilled for the sake of an idea?"

Other writers, however, drew other lessons. The Midland proprietors, said one, "must discriminate between the *bonâ fide* objurgations of their fellow-shareholders and the coarse bellowings of speculators, whether dating from Liverpool, Manchester, or elsewhere." "Though unexpectedly large," said the *Observer*, "as the new London lines and stations may be, the company will ultimately get a fair return for their outlay." "Laying a bill before Parliament to ask for a very large sum," said the *Economist*, "is a step so sure to provoke inquiry, that that of itself is presumably honest."

The present writer thus expressed himself, in the columns of the *Daily News*, with regard to the entire position of the Midland Company, and endeavoured to soothe the alarms of the shareholders. It has, he remarked, become the fashion in certain quarters to assert that this company has become "ambitious and aggressive, consumed with a greed of power that has led it to encroach upon the just rights of innocent and injured neighbours. From whom do these complaints arise? They come, in part at least, from friends of the Great Northern, a company expressly intended to flank the whole Midland system from south to north; a company so directly competitive that immediately the Great Northern was opened the Midland's receipts fell thousands of pounds a week, and Midland shares drooped to the lowest point they ever reached. They came from friends of the London and North Western, a company which, beginning with a simple route from London to Liverpool and Manchester, spread east and west and north from Leeds to Merthyr Tydvil, and from Peterborough to Holyhead, which occupied the head quarters of the Great Eastern at Cambridge, which competes with the Midland in every important town it has, and which has recently announced that it has obtained access to one of the most westerly points of the Great Western system at Swansea.

"On the other hand, who can deny that the Midland extensions have been legitimate in themselves, and likely to be remunerative to the company and beneficial to the public? When, in 1862, the Midland had become, next to the North Eastern, the greatest coal-carrying railway in England, when, besides rent charge for stations, it was paying the Great Northern £60,000 a year for tolls on traffic between Hitchin and London (though forbidden to take up or set down for its own benefit any local traffic whatever), and yet could receive no adequate accommodation either on the rails or at the terminus; and when the Great Northern Board had to admit that it was unable to provide for the increasing traffic except by laying down four lines of rails instead of two; when, in addition to all this, the Midland Company was sending traffic *viâ* Rugby to London of the value to the London and North Western Company of £193,000 a year, and yet at one time five miles of laden coal trucks had to wait at Rugby, unable to proceed, causing infinite chagrin to the sellers in the coal fields and to the buyers in London, surely the time had come at which the Midland Company might be permitted the privilege of wishing to provide accommodation for itself. When the Midland system was within thirty miles of Manchester, and could reach it by a link with the Manchester, Sheffield, and Lincolnshire line, only a few miles long, was it not reasonable that the staple trades and vast coal-fields of Leicestershire, Notts, and Derbyshire, should desire some better access to Manchester, than on the one hand by Grantham and Retford, or on the other by Derby and Macclesfield, over the lines of three several companies, whose trains never ran through? And was it not right that the shortest route that exists between London and Manchester should now be opened up? When the 200,000 inhabitants of Sheffield were demanding to be put upon the main line of the Midland, when they were applying every possible pressure to the company, and when the ubiquitous North Western was pushing in with a competitive scheme, by which they tried to obtain compulsory powers over the heart of the Midland system, would it have been expedient that the directors should have still insisted upon landing all their Sheffield passengers at the miserable station at Masborough, and then sending them by a branch to the more miserable station at Sheffield, into which,—as a *British Quarterly Reviewer* has said,—the train now runs 'like a rat into a dust bin'? And when the London and North Western were repudiating to the Midland Company at Carlisle the identical terms which the North Western chairman characterized as only a 'friendly arrangement,' a 'policy of mutual concessions,' when obtained from the Manchester, Sheffield, and Lincolnshire Company at Sheffield, surely it was no unreasonable conclusion, that, if the Midland Company required the means of conducting a fair proportion of the traffic to Scotland, they must provide it for themselves—a conclusion which Parliament approved.

"It was this deprecated policy of 'extension' that has given the Midland Company the measure of prosperity it enjoys. Before its extensions it was a mere dependency of the London and North Western, and that board tried hard to buy it up at £57 10*s*. for each £100 share. And from the time when those negotiations failed that powerful company has laboured, by open attack and by secret treaties, to sap the resources of the Midland and to draw around it a cincture which should cripple it in every limb. It was 'extension' that alone emancipated it from bondage; it was 'extension' that raised its shares from about £30 to the £140 at which they have recently stood, and at which before very long they will stand again. 'I believe,' said Mr. Hutchinson at a Midland meeting, 'there is no railway in this kingdom whose original traffic has been so fiercely attacked as ours.'

"With one prediction I conclude:—Six months ago, through the efforts of astute opponents and of misinformed and timid friends, there was a general outcry against the policy of the Midland Board. Large meetings were held, protracted discussions took place, and the result was—what? Candid statement and good sense prevailed, opposition was conciliated, misunderstandings were explained, and the course of the directors received the warm commendation of their constituency. So it will be again. The free passes so wisely provided for Midland proprietors (other Boards prefer their shareholders at a distance) will facilitate a large gathering; we shall see with our own eyes and hear with our own ears; the reasons for past action will be explained; a wise and conciliatory policy for the future will, I doubt not, be submitted; and after a few safety-valves have blown off their superfluous and dangerous steam, and the thunder of a little Irish invective has rolled harmlessly away, and some estimable gentlemen, holding microscopic proportions of Midland property, have solemnly warned the wealthy shareholders of the certain bankruptcy to which the whole concern is hastening, we shall recover our sober senses and have the candour to admit, as we did last summer, that the directors deserve the confidence of even the most panic-stricken of the constituents whom they honestly and ably serve."

A special general meeting was held on Wednesday, Jan. 15th, 1868, and it was anticipated with much interest and excitement. The large hall was crowded, and in order to give increased space, we cannot say "accommodation," a number of the benches had been removed, and many hundreds of proprietors had to stand. But whatever the world outside might have thought, and whatever the misgivings of individual shareholders might have suggested, the applause with which the directors were welcomed when they entered the room, showed that the confidence of the constituents was undiminished. "There'll be no fighting to-day," said a gentleman standing near us. "That cheer shows it."

The chairman stated that the meeting had been summoned in anticipation of the usual half-yearly meeting, in order to give an explanation of the circular of Dec. 14th, and to point out the provisions of the money bill which had been deposited. It had, he said, been suggested, that a committee of large and influential proprietors shall be appointed for the purpose of consulting with the directors on various matters which are involved in the bill, and he was sure that the Board would very gladly avail themselves of the assistance of such a committee. After explaining some minor provisions of the bill, he proceeded to explain the causes of the increased outlay on the line to London. He showed that the cost of the works originally contemplated had not so much been augmented as that the works themselves had been enlarged. "Undoubtedly," he said, "the value of the property, especially in London and the neighbourhood, rose very considerably between 1862, when the plans were deposited for this railway; but we also found that the traffic to and from London was so rapidly increasing, that if the line had been carried out in only its original proportions, by the time it was opened for traffic the accommodation would have been wholly inadequate."

After illustrating this statement by figures which

showed the enormous development of the London traffic, he said: "I will now call your attention to the increase which has taken place in the capacity of the railway and works, as compared with the original intentions. The railway has been constructed with four lines of rails instead of two, and with steel rails instead of iron for nearly seven miles north of London. The land has been bought and the overbridges have been constructed for four lines of rails. Over the remainder of distance to Bedford only two lines of rails have at present been laid down, and the directors will not lay down the additional rails until the requirements of the traffic shall render it necessary. Having found upon some of our other lines that inferior gradients caused a great deal of inconvenience as well as a great deal of expense, we decided to improve the gradients upon this line, from 1 in 176 to 1 in 200, and from 1 in 129 to 1 in 176 in the tunnel."

Complaints, he said, were made of the enormous increase in the cost of the London line, but this had arisen mainly because of the increased capacity and cost of the accommodation provided. Originally about two acres of land had been secured for the passenger station; afterwards it was found that four acres would be necessary. Originally it had been intended to raise the flooring of the station to the required height by filling it up with earth; afterwards it was decided to excavate it for cellarage, and fifty shops were to be built into the walls that faced the roads. Originally it was arranged to approach the London station by embankment; afterwards it was found that if some 3¼ acres of land were arched over for coal drops, at least 250,000 tons of coals could be disposed of, and a rent for cellarage be secured. "It being evident," said the engineer, "that the productiveness of the line and its beneficial influence on the Midland system would be limited only by the capabilities of the London terminus to receive and despatch traffic, it was decided to utilize as far as practicable every yard of ground which was available for traffic purposes. Additional works had also been required by Parliament during the passing of the Act. They include a covered way through Camden Square, an expensive iron viaduct and other onerous conditions regarding the passage through the Saint Pancras burial-ground, the providing of bridges for two additional lines of rails for all the railways crossed within the metropolis, and clauses for drainage, involving considerable extra expense, introduced by the Metropolitan Board of

BRENT VIADUCT.

Works. There is also the construction of the Brent Viaduct of nineteen arches, required by the Grand Junction Canal Company, instead of an ordinary bridge, and this viaduct is built for four lines of rails."

It thus appeared that after apportioning the expenditure which had arisen for additional works "there remains," said the engineer, "a sum of about £200,000, which represents the excess of expenditure over estimates, the greater part of which is attributable to the large increase in the price of labour and materials which has taken place since 1863, when the estimates were made. The principal extra which arose on engineering works occurred in passing through Hampstead Hill, where the tunnel had to be strengthened and lined. The effects of the increase of prices compelled three of the contractors to abandon their contracts, and the works had to be transferred to other contractors at higher prices, in addition to considerable loss arising from the transfer of working plant, etc."

It is remarkable that the magnificent roof of the station, which might be regarded as the costliest work of all, fell considerably within the estimate. It was originally intended to build it with a span of two arches, and the parliamentary estimate was £5 per square yard for roof and platform. Subsequently it was ascertained that it might be erected with only one span at a cost of about £4 a yard.

On the line itself additional works had also been provided. It was at first decided to lay down only two lines of railway from London to Bedford. Land had now to be bought for four, the overbridges had to be built for four, for several miles rails had to be laid for four; and the cost of four lines of such railway for the first few miles out of London could not be less than £500,000. Originally it was proposed that iron rails should here as elsewhere be used; now steel ones were to be adopted; but iron cost some £6 a ton, steel cost £13, and hundreds of tons are wanted for every mile. Yet was not this increased expenditure a true economy? "We are finding," said the chairman of the London and North Western, "steel rails wearing actually as long as ten pairs of iron ones;" and at the Chalk Farm station a steel rail might then be seen in good order, which had outlasted no fewer than twenty-five iron rails successively placed next to it on the same line. Instead of 209 acres of land near London, 470 acres had been bought; and instead of 368 acres for the rest of the line to Bedford, 710 had been obtained. This increase of cost, indeed, must have been large; but how much larger would it be a few years hence, when every yard of the company's property will be hemmed in by the masses of houses which close around the precincts of every new London line—houses which are often built expressly with the expectation that their sites will be wanted, and that large profits will be realized.

Such were the facts to which with great clearness—without haste and without rest—Mr. Hutchinson called attention. He dealt in a similar manner with the increased outlay which had been made in other parts of the line; and after a lengthened, minute, and exhaustive, not to say exhausting, speech, concluded by announcing the future policy of the Board: "It is—suspension of all works which will not involve too great a sacrifice; postponement of all new lines not yet commenced, or upon which a small outlay has been made; application to Parliament for an extension of time to complete them; the most rigid economy in the expenditure of all moneys, whether capital or revenue, the utmost exertion made to increase the receipts, and the cultivation of the most friendly relations with all the neighbouring companies."

He concluded amid the "loud applause" of the meeting.

Mr. Edward Baines, M.P., then rose, by request of the chairman, to propose the appointment of a Committee of Consultation to confer with the directors especially as to the extent to which the projected lines and works could be relinquished or postponed, and to report to the half-yearly meeting to be held in February. The names were, —Messrs. Edward Baines, M.P., W. Orme Foster, M.P.,

J. Garnett, Robert Leader, W. Overend, Q.C., Charles Paget, A. J. Stanton, Edward Warner, and Joseph Whitworth.

Mr. Baines and other gentlemen supported the resolution with much ability, and the chairman having stated that all information which might be required would be furnished with the greatest pleasure, to facilitate the inquiries of the committee, the resolution was heartily and unanimously adopted.

The committee thus appointed set to work immediately. They had many meetings. They received minute explanations from the directors and officers of the company, and they passed over the whole line from Bedford to London, and carefully examined the works at St. Pancras.

The report of the Committee of Consultation was formally presented to the shareholders on the 19th of February, though it had previously been printed and circulated. It expressed its divergence from some part of the policy of the Board of Directors; but bore abundant testimony to the integrity and ability with which their administration had been conducted. "It is the duty of the committee to report," they said, "that they have received convincing proof of the integrity with which the affairs of the Midland Company have been conducted," of "the trustworthiness of its published accounts," of "the diligence and zeal of the Board and its officials in the performance of their duties," and "the great vigilance and ability" that have been "displayed in watching the interests of the company throughout the wide field over which its lines and works are spread, in developing its mineral and other resources, and facilitating the traffic of the country. The attention of your committee has also been directed to the principles upon which the expenditure of the company has been classed under the respective heads of capital and revenue, which seem to them to be such as effectually to guard against the frequent error of augmenting the apparent available profit, by charging to capital that which should be borne by revenue. Your committee find that all charges relating to the renewal, strengthening, and improvement of the permanent way, works, stations, bridges, and rolling stock, are paid out of revenue; and in addition to this, nearly the entire cost of the carting stock and wagon covers, amounting to about £90,000, which by most other companies is entirely provided out of capital, has been paid out of revenue during the last few years. Interest upon the very large amount of unproductive capital, now amounting to about £5,000,000, is all borne by revenue."

They expressed regret that the company had been led to undertake engagements "beyond what could be properly undertaken at any one time," involving "an amount of liability which cannot be met without great inconvenience to the shareholders." But they added that it was true that these works had been "undertaken when commercial confidence was unlimited, and when the spirit of competition among the great railway companies was beyond control." They were sorry that there should have been delay in the application to Parliament for the creation of additional capital until so large an amount had become indispensable; and also that the sums of money originally estimated for the different works should have been so largely exceeded. On the other hand they wished to make every allowance for wise alterations and improvements that had been made on the original plans. "Increased cost of land, buildings, and severance,—increased cost of all materials,—increased wages of labour, —the doubling of the width of the line, and the laying down of four lines of rails for six or seven miles from

London,—the adoption of steel rails, instead of iron (doubling the cost), for that distance,—the purchase of land for four lines all the way to Bedford, and the erection of bridges to provide for them,—the purchase of a large quantity of land at Hendon for the convenience of mineral and goods trains,—the connection of the Midland with the Metropolitan Line, by a subterranean branch, so as to give access to the heart of London and to railways south of the Thames,—the erection of ale and corn stores,—the providing of larger accommodation for goods and mineral traffic than had been thought needful,—the making of numerous shops and a great amount of cellarage,—and the contemplated erection of a large and splendid hotel and offices at the St. Pancras Station;—all these things no doubt account for the cost of the independent access to the metropolis being likely to reach several millions beyond the original estimate. It is proper to mention that there is every probability of a large passenger traffic in the suburbs of London; and that the extent of mineral and goods traffic which may be had there is declared by experienced persons to be only limited by the extent of the accommodation that can be provided for it. It is an important fact, that the greater part of the mineral traffic which has been brought into London by the North Western and Great Northern Railways, comes from collieries in Derbyshire, Leicestershire, and other counties on the line of the Midland Railway, and it is reasonable to suppose that a very large amount of that traffic will go by the direct and shortest route."

The committee expressed their regret that they were unable to advise any reduction in the amount for which application should be made to Parliament. The money bill for £5,000,000 must be passed in its integrity, after obtaining which it would be competent and advisable to make other applications for the postponement of some of the undertakings. They had also felt it their duty to communicate with the chairman of the London and North Western Company, with a view to such an arrangement of terms with that company, for such a use by the Midland of the Lancaster and Carlisle as should justify the abandonment of the Settle and Carlisle. They were gratified to state that they had been received by the London and North Western officers with frankness and friendship, but that before any further action could be taken in that direction the Midland Company's money bill must be obtained. It would be impossible for the Midland Company to go before Parliament to ask for money for lines for the abandonment of which they were actually negotiating.

The meeting of shareholders at which this report was presented was the ordinary half-yearly meeting of the proprietors. It was stated that the increase of traffic had been large, amounting to an average of £4700 a week. The expenditure in carrying the traffic had also increased.

On the 13th of April, 1868, the Keighley and Worth Valley line was handed over to the Midland Company. It had previously been maintained by the contractors of the Valley Company, though worked by the Midland Company.

Towards the close of the year 1868, terms of agreement were drawn up between the Midland and the London and North Western Companies by which the former was to have free and full access to Scotland over the Lancaster and Carlisle, and by which the Settle and Carlisle was to be abandoned. It was arranged that the Midland Company should have equal rights with the London and North Western "of user and control" between Ingleton and Carlisle, "with joint management by a joint committee, with a standing arbitrator, and with full power to the Midland Company to fix their own rates and fares." The Midland Company was to be "allowed to carry local passenger traffic between Low Gill and Carlisle, and from the receipts of the traffic so carried to be allowed 15 per cent. for working expenses" the balance to be paid to the London and North Western Company. The Midland Company was to pay "a mileage proportion" of rates and fares, the annual minimum being £40,000 a year for the use of the line. The London and North Western was to provide accommodation at intermediate stations for passenger and goods traffic; the Midland Company having power to place their own servants there if desired; for whom accommodation should be provided at a rate to be settled by arbitration. The agreement was to be for 50 years. Both companies were to unite in applying to Parliament for the abandonment of the Settle and Carlisle line.

In the report of the spring meeting of 1869, it was announced that the directors had continued the negotiations with the London and North Western for the use of certain parts of the Lancaster and Carlisle line "as a substitute for the Settle and Carlisle line, which many of the shareholders wished to abandon;" and that eventually terms had been agreed upon. Mr. Edward Baines, M.P., and others expressed their satisfaction at this settlement of the matter, as it was supposed to be. "The Consultation Committee," he said, "were of opinion, as they had been throughout, that it would be a very great misfortune to lay out more than £2,000,000 in constructing a line which for 80 miles would run side by side with another railway, the use of which could now be obtained on fair terms. If the directors could have obtained those terms from the beginning, they would never have dreamed of promoting the Settle and Carlisle line."

The attempts thus made to secure an abandonment of the Settle and Carlisle line were, however, unsuccessful.

After a conflict of six days, the Commons' Committee decided that the evidence given by the Midland and the London and North Western did not justify any such arrangement. To this conclusion they were, we believe, chiefly led by the opposition of the Lancashire and Yorkshire, and North British Companies, the former of whom declared that it was their desire to avail themselves of the Midland's Settle and Carlisle line if it were made, and that they wanted a route to the North independently of the London and North Western. It is curious to observe how, in the ebb and flow of railway politics, when the Lancashire and Yorkshire a very few years later were endeavouring to amalgamate with the North Western, it then came to find that the making of the Settle and Carlisle was an argument for the rejection of the amalgamation; or at any rate a reason why certain special concessions should be made to the Midland Company on the withdrawal of their opposition to the amalgamation.

In referring to this subject, Mr. Hutchinson stated to the meeting, that though the rejection of the abandonment bill "had been a disappointment to many shareholders," no alternative was now left to the directors but "to acquiesce in the decision of Parliament, and to proceed with the construction of the line." He, however, comforted the proprietors by stating, that though hitherto they "had been unable from certain causes to obtain any exact estimate of the Scotch traffic," it was proved in "the discussion on the abandonment bill that the amount of traffic passing *viâ* Carlisle alone, between places in England and places in Scotland, was between £1,300,000 and £1,400,000;" so that, the amount passing by way of Berwick, the east coast route, being some £500,000, the total might be set down at nearly £2,000,000.

During the year an extension of time was obtained for the construction of the Mansfield and Worksop, Mansfield and Southwell, and some other lines; powers were taken by which the Midland Company obtained the Evesham and Redditch line, and also the Tottenham line, by which the Midland obtained access to the Victoria Docks. "A very extraordinary increase" said the chairman, "has taken place in the traffic during the seven weeks of the current half-year, amounting to more than £8000 per week, a sum that far surpassed their most sanguine expectations."

The dividend, which had increased in the spring, was in the autumn further augmented by half per cent. It was announced that the receipts had increased £8400 a week, and that the unproductive capital of £5,000,000 had been reduced to half that amount; £1,000,000 of which was on the new Sheffield line. The Cudworth and Barnsley line was opened for local goods on the 28th of June, 1869; the Bath and Mangotsfield for passenger traffic on the 4th of August; the Melbourne and Sawley line, running *viâ* Castle Donington to Trent, was ready; and all the engineering works of the London and Bedford

RETAINING WALLS, HAVERSTOCK HILL STATION.

were completed, except a small part of the roof of St. Pancras Station. It was ordered that the hotel should be carried to the necessary height and finished in a permanent manner, and that those portions that were originally intended for the company's offices be added to the hotel. It was announced that the bills for a joint use by the Midland, Great Northern, and Great Eastern of certain lines, for a new station at Lynn, in Norfolk, and for giving certain powers to the Midland, in conjunction with the Manchester, Sheffield and Lincolnshire Company, over the Marple, New Mills, and Hayfield Junctions had been granted.

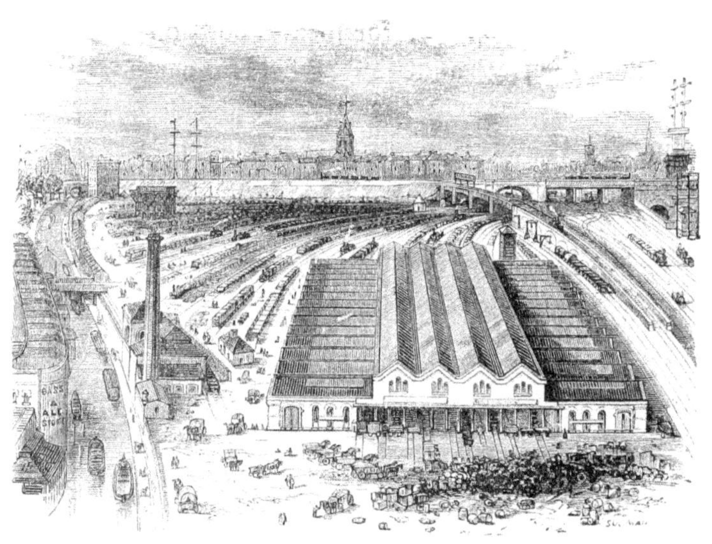

ST. PANCRAS GOODS STATION.

CHAPTER XI.

Opening of New Line to Sheffield.—Unstone Viaduct.—Expiration of Lease of Ambergate and Rowsley Line, and Amalgamation with the Midland Company.—Terms.—State Purchase of Telegraphs.—Stupendous Misuse of Public Money.—Resignation of Mr. W. E. Hutchinson as Chairman of the Company.—Appointment of Mr. W. P. Price, M.P., as Chairman, and Mr. E. S. Ellis, Vice-Chairman.—Amusing Incidents.—Mr. McTurk and Mr. Hadley.—Amalgamation of the Midland and the Little North Western.—Opening of Sawley and Weston and Tibshelf and Tiversall Coal Lines.—Complimentary Dinner to Mr. Hutchinson.—Speeches of Mr. Hutchinson and Mr. Allport.—Progress of the Company.—Battle of the Coal Rates between Midland and Great Northern.—The Agreement.—The Arbitration.—The Award.—The Rupture of the Agreement.—Resumption of former Rates.—Advantages of Preference Stocks.—Line from Birmingham to King's Norton.—Rumours of Fresh Conflicts between the Great Northern and Midland. Attack on the Heart of the Midland System.—Midland and Sheffield Companies' new Projects.—Arrangement between Midland and Sheffield Companies' Chairmen.—Great Northern Company's Derbyshire Lines.—Objections of Midland Company.—Objections of Derbyshire Coal Owners.—Defects of the New Line.—Great Northern Bill for Line from Newark to Leicester passed.—Midland Company carries Third Class Passengers by all Trains.—Wolverhampton, Walsall, and Midland Junction Line.—Bedford and Northampton Line Opened.—Slip at Dove Holes Tunnel.

THE commencement of the year 1870 was signalized by the opening of the new line from Chesterfield to Sheffield. "Direct" communication, such as it was, between the two towns had for some time been carried on by means of an extraordinary vehicle, not unlike an old-fashioned French diligence, which, as we write, may still be seen, apparently turned out to grass and rottenness, in a field at Dronfield. The people residing in that district may well have been surprised at the improvement between the old means and the new, when, on the 2nd of February, 1870, they found they could now accomplish the journey in a few minutes at almost any hour of the day, and with perfect comfort and convenience. The line, however, was opened without any official recognition on the part of the company. It is true that some enterprising country people at Dronfield left their beds at an undesirable hour in a February morning in order that they might be able to say that they saw the up Leeds express pass at 4.7; but the first down train entered Sheffield station, says an eye-witness, "just as if it had been accustomed to do so any time for the last ten years. Spruce collectors

UNSTONE VIADUCT.

asked for your tickets, and slammed the doors, and went their way, and left you to go yours; the whole affair being so business-like and formal and matter-of-course that the operatives, who at twelve o'clock came down in considerable numbers to see what was to be seen, must have returned to their homes considerably disappointed. We have witnessed far more fuss and ceremony over the opening of a drinking fountain or the 'inauguration' of a new parish fire-escape."

An important arrangement was about this period concluded. Our readers will remember the little railway with the long name (the Manchester, Buxton, Matlock, and Midland Junction) that ran between Ambergate and Rowsley, and that had already occupied a prominent place in the world of railwaypolitics. This line formed a portion of the Midland main route to Manchester, but was partly owned by the London and North Western Company, and was held by the Midland on a lease which would expire at Midsummer, 1871. In anticipation of this contingency, and knowing that it was possible that for its renewal terms that were too exacting might, under the peculiar circumstances of the case, be claimed from the Midland Company, an excellent alternative line had already been made from Duffield, a station a little south of Ambergate, up to Wirksworth,—a line which could, if necessary, be continued to Rowsley, and there, joining the Midland main line to Manchester, form an admirable substitute for the existing one. This stroke of policy on the part of the Midland Company saved it at the critical moment from serious embarrassment. As it was, the negotiations came so nearly to a dead lock that the Midland Company's board ordered surveys to be prepared for the completion of the alternative line; and it would have been carried by a tunnel under the Heights of Abraham at Matlock, up the left side of Darley Dale to Rowsley. At the last moment, however, the matter was adjusted, and the directors were able to announce in the report (February, 1870), that they had "negotiated the heads of an agreement with the Matlock directors for vesting the undertaking in the Midland Company alone," who would now take the railway, and also the Ambergate Canal, "with all liability and obligations thereon, and pay the shareholders of the Matlock Company at par in a 5 per cent. stock, with the option of converting it into Midland ordinary stock at any time within twelve months from the expiration of the lease."

This year was memorable for the supposed transfer to

the Government of the telegraphs of the country, including those belonging to the railways. We say the supposed transfer; for, as our readers are by this time aware, the whole affair was one of the most stupendous blunders, to use no harsher term, ever transacted even by an English Government department. It is true that money was paid by John Bull enough to buy all the telegraphs; the only mistake was, that it was paid to the wrong parties: it was not paid to those who had the telegraphs to sell. In a word, it was just as if the reader employed a land-agent to buy the freehold of an estate, and the cash was given him, but he handed it all over to a lessee who had only a short expiring lease; and the purchaser soon afterwards discovered that he had to buy the estate over again from the freeholder.

At the present moment the telegraphs on the principal railways are still the property of those railways; and they will have to be purchased and paid for before they can become the property of the Government. On this subject Mr. Allport said at a meeting of the Statistical Society: "What did the Government do in the case of the telegraphs? They gave thirty years' purchase on the enhanced price of a property which the sellers had not in their possession. In the case of the Midland Company, for instance, the greater part of the wires and instruments belonged to the company, which had an agreement with the Electric Telegraph Company expiring about the end of 1873 or the beginning of 1874. The Government gave the Telegraph Company thirty years' purchase; but the Government has yet to buy what belongs to the Midland Company, and an arbitration as to the amount to be paid is now pending."*

* "Ought the State to Buy the Railways? A Question for Everybody." By a Midland Shareholder. Price One Shilling. London: Longmans, Green & Co.

At the spring meeting of shareholders (1870), Mr. W. E. Hutchinson announced his intention to relinquish his chairmanship of the company. "Although," he said, he "estimated highly the honour of being chairman of that great company, and although he valued very dearly the confidence which the shareholders and his colleagues had reposed in him, he felt that the duties devolving upon him were too arduous. He had arrived at a period of life when some relaxation from business was desirable and necessary; and as he had devoted nearly a third of a century to the service of the company, he thought the time had arrived when he might retire from the chair." Very cordial acknowledgments were made of the services of the chairman. Mr. Edward Baines, M.P., proposed that the sum of £1000 should be placed by the shareholders at the disposal of the Board, partly to be expended in procuring a portrait to be placed on the walls of the Board Room, and the remainder at the disposal of Mr. Hutchinson, for some memorial to be presented to him. Mr. Bass, M.P., desired, through Mr. Baines, to express his opinion that Mr. Hutchinson had been "a most zealous, most upright, and most able servant of the company."

At a special meeting held in May, the new chairman, Mr. W. P. Price, M.P., presided. The contrast between the gravity with which the previous chairman uniformly conducted the proceedings, and the livelier fashion of his successor, struck many. An illustration of the humour in which Mr. Price sometimes indulged may be mentioned. On one occasion, as on several others, Mr. McTurk, of Sheffield, complained that certain injuries had been inflicted upon the Sheffield and Rotherham shareholders, who, he declared, "had had their locks shorn like Samson." The chairman in reply expressed his deep regret that Mr. McTurk "should find himself in the position of Samson, with his locks shorn, but must certainly congratulate him that he had fallen into the hands of so skilful an operator," a remark which, as Mr. McTurk is rather regardless of appearances, elicited roars of laughter.

On another occasion the chairman thus bantered Mr. Hadley. That gentleman had, with lugubrious accents and manner, deplored (he appears always to be deploring something) the slow progress made on the Settle and Carlisle line, the works on which had been retarded by the weather. Mr. Price assured Mr. Hadley that he deeply regretted that the directors could not control the climate; but added, "I have no doubt if we had Mr. Hadley among us we should be blessed with perpetual sunshine." Mr. Hadley further professed to have discovered some discrepancy in the accounts of the passenger receipts per train mile. "Mr. Hadley," said the chairman, "tells you that the passenger receipts are only 3*s.* 6*d.* per train mile, whereas, in fact, they are 4*s.* 1*d.* It is quite true that he drew this distinction: he said men, women, and children, by which I suppose he meant to exclude mails and parcels." "I beg your pardon," interrupted Mr. Hadley; "I gave you the two items. I gave you the men, women, and children, and then I included the other items afterwards; and then I said it was 3*s.* 11¾*d.*"

Mr. Price: "Well you have dropped a few halfpence on the road."

Mr. Hadley: "I think it is no more—say what you will."

Mr. Price: "I have no doubt you are right; but I must leave you to settle the matter with the accountant. The accountant tells me that it is 4*s.* 1*d.*, and I believe him."

In the course of this year the Little North Western

came under the permanent control of the Midland Company. A lease which had been running since February, 1860, at a rental equal to 3½ per cent. had hitherto involved the Midland Company in loss; but calculating on a future improvement in the traffic it was agreed to give "a progressive dividend at 3¾ per cent., in and for the year 1871; increasing by a ¼ per cent. in each of the years 1872, 1873, and 1874, and reaching in 1875 its final and maximum limit of 5 per cent." The Sawley and Weston, and the Tibshelf and Tiversall (coal) lines were during this year opened for traffic.

SAWLEY BRIDGE.

On the 20th of December, 1870, a complimentary dinner was given at Derby to Mr. Hutchinson, at which the testimonial was presented that had been voted at the general meeting of the 16th of February, at which, as Mr. Price said, they desired "to record their appreciation of the eminent services their late chairman had rendered to the company, and to crown with their grateful approval the services of a long and faithful career." In the course of the proceedings Mr. Hutchinson remarked that his connection with the company dated from 1837, now 33 years ago; and, he added, "it sometimes makes me sad when I remember that very few of my colleagues of that period are now left. At this table, my brother-in-law, Mr. Burgess, and Mr. Barlow, our consulting engineer, with myself, alone remain; and with the exception of two or three other gentlemen who have long ceased to be connected with railways, are all that are now left of the old Midland Counties Railway Board, with whom I began my railway life as a director. It unfortunately happened that the Midland Counties Railway and the Derby and Birmingham Railway had each of them routes from Derby to London, in one case by way of Rugby, and in the other by way of Hampton; and the consequence was that a very severe competition soon ensued for the traffic, and I found myself in fierce opposition to my worthy and excellent friend and predecessor in the chair, Mr. Beale, to our excellent legal adviser Mr. Carter, and to the present able and efficient officers of this Company, Messrs. Allport and Kirtley. We contended together for a considerable length of time; but at last our Derby opponents called in the aid of their 'big brother,' the North Midland, and the consequence was that negotiations commenced, and peace was ultimately made between us on the basis of an amalgamation of the three companies. Since that period we have laboured earnestly, zealously, and harmoniously together, in order to promote the prosperity of the amalgamated companies, the mileage of which then became 181 miles in length.

"I have seen," he continued, "many fluctuations in the fortunes of the company. I have seen £100 shares quoted at more than £190, and I have seen them quoted as low as £32 or £33. I have seen our dividends at £7 7*s.* 6*d.* per cent. per annum, and I have seen them as low as £2 1*s.* per cent. Our highest rate of dividend was achieved during the chairmanship of my excellent friend Mr. Beale, in, I think, 1864."

In referring to the career of the Midland Company, Mr. Allport subsequently remarked:—"I say it advisedly, that the Midland now stands in a position second to none in this kingdom. There is one fact which I think shows the position of the Midland Company perhaps as well as anything else that could be named. You will remember that it was proposed in the year 1867 to give a third member to each of seven of the largest towns in this country. It is a singular fact that the Midland Company, in its own right, goes to every one of those seven towns, and is the only railway that does. It is true that to each place there are two or more railways; but no other railway goes to the seven towns except the Midland. I will mention them:—Bristol, Birmingham, Sheffield, Leeds, Bradford, Liverpool, and Manchester. A short time ago I had taken out the population of the country which the Midland Railway accommodates. I think by the census of 1861 the population of England, Wales, and Scotland was about twenty-two to twenty-three millions. The Midland Railway runs to upwards of ten millions of that population."

The remarkable progress of the general traffic that had of late years been made on the Midland system will be indicated by the following summary:—

	1851.	1861.	1870.
Capital Expended... ...	£15,802,614	£21,101,133	£36,851,000
Miles of Line	496	620	826
Average Weekly Return...	£22,814	£40,476	£70,000

So that, as a writer remarked, "while the increase of capital is about two and a third, and the number of miles is much less than doubled (or nearly doubled, if we add the 122 miles of joint line), the gross traffic is more than threefold. The £70,000 a week gross traffic represents much more than three times the work done for the public, who paid £22,814 in 1851. From year to year the Midland has gone on increasing and cheapening the national service that it performs. It has been on an enormous scale a public benefactor. By facilitating trade, and stimulating manufacturing industry; rendering marketable mines of mineral wealth which were formerly almost locked up for want of means of transit,—the Midland lines have promoted almost incalculably the public welfare. We might venture to say that for every shilling the Midland shareholders have had in return for their outlay, the country at large must have gained several shillings."

The year 1871 was signalized by the protracted conflict between the Midland and Great Northern Companies on the subject of coal-rates. "The shareholders are doubtless aware," said the report at the quarterly meeting, "that after many years of negotiation between the two companies, having for its object the freest interchange of coal traffic between their respective systems, and the opening of the Midland coal fields to the Great Northern Company," the rates at which they should thereafter carry the produce of these coalfields to market were adjusted so as to be "fair one with the other" The circumstances that followed were then described by the present writer in a letter in *The Times*, which may be quoted almost *in extenso* :—

"The Agreement.—Before the year 1863 a severe competition had been carried on between the Midland and the Great Northern Companies for the coal traffic, especially to London. The consequence was, that there was such uncertainty as to the rates, that coalowners refused to undertake new contracts or to sink new pits; and this vast industry, which requires safe data on which to calculate, and ground of confidence in the future, was in confusion. As the trade suffered, the railways suffered; and eventually the two companies resolved to end the strife and to seek relief from several embarrassments in the future by what is known as 'the agreement of 1863.'

"This agreement provided that the rates for coal from the Yorkshire, Derbyshire, Notts, and Leicestershire collieries should 'be equitably adjusted to each other.' Accordingly a list of such adjusted rates was prepared and adopted; these rates being by the express terms of the agreement based on 'the shortest existing route by the Midland and Great Northern, or by such other routes and lines as may from time to time be agreed upon by the parties hereunto.' It was also provided that, in the event of any difference hereafter arising as to these rates, arbitrators should have full power to settle what is fair The two companies also declared that they would in all respects' carry on the traffic faithfully the one towards the other, and according to the spirit and intent of this memorandum, and that they would not, by any 'means or inducements whatsoever, prevent such traffic from being carried, or the revenues therefrom divided and apportioned in accordance with the *bonâ fide* intent and meaning of the terms of this memorandum.

"The spirit and aim of this agreement were thus as plain as words could make them; but an additional safeguard was provided. In the mineral districts occupied by the Great Northern and Midland there were two other companies—the Manchester, Sheffield, and Lincolnshire, and the South Yorkshire (the latter now merged into the former), and they were the owners of part of the through route. These companies were accordingly invited to furnish a list of rates at which they would deliver their coals on to the Midland and Great Northern respectively, and they did so. Inasmuch, however, as it was possible that at some future period these rates might be modified, and that thereby the fixed through rates already agreed upon by the Great Northern and Midland Companies might be affected, the contingency was provided against; for, by a minute adopted at a meeting on the 12th of February, 1863, the Midland and Great Northern finally approved their list of rates, 'subject to such alterations as may be rendered necessary by any subsequent action of either the Manchester, Sheffield, and Lincolnshire Company or the South Yorkshire Company.' By these arrangements, both in spirit and in letter, every security was taken that the integrity of the through rates of the two contracting companies should be preserved; an adjusting machinery also was provided for rectifying any irregularity that might arise 'by any subsequent action' of other parties; and in case of difficulty arbitrators were invested with 'full power to settle what is fair.'

"The Arbitration.—The rates agreed upon remained in operation without objection till 1868, when the Great Northern Company desired that an alteration should be made in the rates from the South Yorkshire collieries. The Midland Company contended that the rates were only what was fair, and in 1869 the matter went to arbitration. Sir John Karslake was appointed sole arbitrator, and the two companies agreed that he should have 'full power to determine' the rates for coals carried 'by either or both of the companies' to the 'places mentioned in the said agreement,' so as 'to secure to the companies the full benefit intended by the said agreement.'

"The Award.—The arbitration occupied sixteen months. Evidence was taken that fills a folio volume; the subject was dealt with under all it aspects; and the decision of the arbitrator may be summed up in his concluding words :—'I award that no alteration be made in the rates for coal in the said agreement or submission to arbitration mentioned and referred to.'

"The Rupture of the Agreement.—Scarcely was the award pronounced when the representatives of the Sheffield Company were invited by the Great Northern to King's Cross;* and as the result, the Sheffield Company decided no longer to deliver their South Yorkshire coals direct to the Great Northern at Doncaster as heretofore, but to send it by a circuitous route and at a considerably reduced rate to the more southern point of Retford, the Retford rate on to London (which was originally fixed for the convenience of the collieries situated on the Sheffield Railway, and for which Retford and Beighton are the legitimate routes) being also less than from Doncaster. The effect of this diversion of traffic was to create just that disturbance of the through rate for the correction of which machinery had been provided by the minute of February 12th; and it there fore became the duty of the Midland Company to claim that the adjustment should be made. But with this claim the Great Northern Company refuses to comply.

"The consequence was, that the through rate from South Yorkshire to London was reduced by 11*d.*, and the Midland Company was compelled to make a similar reduction in its rates from Derbyshire; and other reductions have since been made by the Great Northern, which the Midland Company has been obliged to follow, until they now involve a loss to the shareholders of the

* On a subsequent occasion, Mr. Denison, the counsel for the Great Northern, described in the following remarkable words the action of his company :—"The award was in August of 1870. . . . We began to look at the agreement, and see whether we could drive a coach and six through it." Evidence, Great Northern Railway (No. 2) Bill, May 2nd, 1872, p. 9.

two companies to the amount of several thousand pounds a week.

"Such is the end for the time being of one of the most explicit engagements ever entered into. And as I read the words that pledge the companies 'faithfully the one towards the other, and according to the spirit and intent of this memorandum,' and the minute that expressly provides that no disturbing influences from without shall compromise the purport or letter of the agreement, and also the 'full power' given to the arbitrators to determine any point of difference, I am amazed that any responsible body of public men should venture to set such obligations at nought. The terms employed in these documents have, and can have, but one meaning, and I challenge them to put any other reasonable construction upon them. True, the Great Northern directors say that they are willing to refer a case which for sixteen months has been under arbitration. But if one arrangement can be repudiated, what evidence is there that another would be binding? The question really narrows itself to this,—Are treaties between public bodies in this country to be obligatory? And this is a question which concerns not only railway directors and shareholders, but every one who would maintain the honour and the interests of commercial life among us."

The conflict continued for many months, the Midland Company lowering their rates as the Great Northern lowered theirs. At the August Midland meeting it was stated that although the directors were "not able to re port a final settlement of the matter in dispute, the dis astrous competition from the London coal traffic had been abated. Various meetings of the managers and deputations of the Midland and Great Northern Boards had taken place; but at the last of these it appeared that the Great Northern Company were not in a condition to deal absolutely with their own rates, and that any arrangement between the two companies would virtually have left the rates of both subject to the control of others. This, in the opinion of the directors, rendered any agreement impracticable; and it was therefore determined that the Midland Company should pursue its independent course, and an increase had been effected in the rates to London, to date from the 1st of May." But though the severity of the conflict was apparently relaxed, it was in appearance only: the storm which for a time had lulled broke out again, though under different conditions.

At one of the ordinary meetings held during the year 1871, a question arose which is worthy of passing consideration. A proprietor complained that by means of certain preference shares which it was proposed to issue, a priority of right would be given to outsiders over the ordinary shareholders. "For my part," he said, "I do not like preferential capital. I object to a mortgage of 55 per cent. upon my railway stock, before I receive a single penny." He accordingly urged that the new proprietors should have only original or ordinary shares, and then, he said, "they would share fairly among themselves the entire earnings of the company." The reply of Mr Price, M.P., the chairman, was, of course, conclusive He reminded the proprietor, that the debenture debt of the company had been created at a charge of only 4½ per cent., and their preference stock at less than 5; but that inasmuch as their ordinary dividend might be taken at 6½ per cent., it was obvious that there was a clear gain on every £100 they borrowed at these lower rates of one half or three-quarters per cent., all of which went to swell the dividend of the ordinary shareholder. The same principle holds good under all similar circumstances.

A bill was passed during this year (1871), which authorised certain parties in Birmingham to construct a railway from the commercial centre of the town to King's Norton in Worcestershire, but to be worked by the Midland Company. "The line," said Mr. Price, "was much desired by the neighbourhood. It would give to the Midland Company an admirable goods station in the commercial centre of Birmingham, and there was a prospect of a good suburban traffic. It was one of those lines which, if the Midland Company did not desire to work it, which they did, they could not possibly allow to pass into other hands." An arrangement was also made for the Midland Company to share with some other companies in the lease of a line near London, called the South Western Junction. It turns off from the Midland Company's line near Cricklewood, and running southward, joins, as its name indicates, the South Western Railway. The line had been earning 5½ to 6 per cent. the lessees undertook among them to guarantee 7 per cent.

In the autumn of 1871, the railway world was filled with rumours that the conflicts which had raged between the Great Northern Company and the Midland were about to be renewed. From the first hour of its existence the Great Northern had lived and thriven as a vast parasite, drawing its daily life from the trunk and branches of what had been the Midland system. Now it was about, if possible, to fasten itself upon, and to draw the traffic-blood from the heart of, that system. When the parliamentary notices appeared, these reports were found to be true. The attack was to be, not with rates, but with rails. The Derbyshire and Nottinghamshire coalfields of the Midland Company were to be entered in all directions by a series of lines connected with the Grantham and Nottingham branch of the Great

Northern, and,—in association with the London and North Western,—were to be continued through the Erewash Valley to Derby and Burton and to the North Staffordshire lines. The same company had further resolved to construct lines from Newark to Melton Mowbray, Leicester, and Market Harborough.

Other railway projects in these districts were also in contemplation. The Manchester, Sheffield, and Lincolnshire Company, were the promoters of a line from Doncaster to Worksop, and from Worksop to join the London and North Western at Market Harborough. The Midland Company proposed to construct railways from Doncaster, to join their Worksop and Mansfield line at Shireoaks, and to give them a better connection with the North Eastern; and also from Dore, just south of Sheffield, to Hassop on the Manchester line, which would have placed Sheffield and Manchester in direct communi cation Relief lines southward were proposed from Nottingham to Saxby and from Manton to Rushton.

Such was the conflict of contesting claims. As, however, the parliamentary session drew on, it was suggested that there should be some adjustment of affairs before war actually broke out. "I had occasion," said Mr. W. P. Price, M.P., the chairman of the Midland Company, in subsequently recounting the circumstances, "to meet Sir Edward Watkin on other business. After having disposed of that business, the conversation naturally turned upon the lines which either had been deposited at that time or which were going to be deposited; and Sir Edward Watkin, taking the map which he had on his table, and a pencil, sketched out what the known and deposited lines of all the companies were. It was suggested by one or other of us, I do not remember which, that it would be a very good thing if the lines promoted by the three companies could be abandoned for the session, in order to await the issue of the proposal then made to amalgamate the London and North Western and the Lancashire and Yorkshire Companies. I told him, that, so far as we were concerned, we were in some little difficulty about one portion of our scheme, namely, the line from Nottingham to Saxby, because we were feeling very much oppressed by the increasing traffic upon the mineral portions of our line and we were extremely anxious to get an alternative route for some of it: but I offered at once to abandon the Doncaster line, and the Hassop and Dore line, and the line from Manton to Rushton; and he agreed to abandon his Doncaster line, his Market Harborough line, and another. Eventually these concessions were definitely arranged; and the proposed competitive lines of the Midland and the Manchester Sheffield and Lincolnshire Companies were withdrawn. Proposals to the like effect were made to the Great Northern, but, for reasons that will soon appear, were declined.

The Derbyshire bill of the Great Northern was brought before the Commons' committee, May 2nd, 1872. It may be thought that it would have been better that this particular measure should have been promoted simply on its own merits, and that it should have been separated from recent incidents in the annals of the Great Northern Company; but Mr. Denison, wisely or otherwise, distinctly indicated the influence under which the project had been conceived. He referred at some length to what he called "the disputes of last year, which," he said, "instead of being settled, have gone on and got worse instead of better, until it has become necessary to settle them by the promotion of this line." No wonder that Mr. Venables, on behalf of the Midland Company, complained. "We were mulcted," he declared, "in many thousands, by a deliberate breach of faith on the part of the Great Northern, and not content with that, and not content with having triumphed by repudiating their honourable debt, they now came to inflict upon us another and more serious and more permanent injury."

Although the bill of the Great Northern was eventually passed, there are two or three points connected with the opposition of the Midland Company which may be noticed. The first is the remarkable fact that, if the proposed line was supposed to be for the good of the coal owners of the Erewash and Mansfield Valleys, none of those gentlemen, with two unimportant exceptions, could be prevailed upon to give evidence on behalf of the new project. Indeed they felt that a company like the Great Northern, that was so deeply interested in the South Yorkshire coalfields, and which had lately shown such hostility to the Derbyshire coal owners, could now have no favourable intentions towards them. "I think,' says Mr. Robert Harrison, of Eastwood, the manager for Messrs. Barber, Walker and Co., who mentioned that their total output was nearly 750,000 tons for the year, "I think the Great Northern have always fought against the Derbyshire collieries in aid of the South Yorkshire coalpits." The London and North Western too, "has always," said Mr. Venables, "discouraged Derbyshire coal for the protection of Lancashire, and," added the learned counsel, "I say it will be an unprecedented thing to make a line for the purpose of discouraging and checking the competition of the district through which that line passes." "Here are the Great Northern coming, tainted with bad faith; here are the London and North Western coming, with scarcely concealed hostility to Derbyshire and its coalfields." "I think it would be ungrateful," said Mr. Sanders, the mineral agent for the Shipley Colliery Company, "if I did not come here to speak for the Midland Company. And I may say also that nineteen-twentieths of the coal masters in the Erewash Valley are of the same opinion. I have been connected," he added, "with the Coalowners' Association for the last 20 years nearly, and I never saw them so united on any one subject as the question of the Great Northern being introduced into the Erewash Valley." "We cannot," he said, "be better served than we are now. The power of the Midland to carry coal is in excess of the power of production."

Criticisms were also offered with regard to the construction of the new railway. "The Midland Company's line," said Mr. Crossley, "all the way from Codnor Park to the Trent, with one exception of a few yards, is on a descending gradient and in favour of the load; on the other hand the Great Northern line is on a gradient rising for more than two miles in sections of 1 in 100 against the load" The Midland Railway had been laid out by Mr. Jessop so as to follow the natural valley; and "the lines and tramways fall naturally into it;" whereas the Great Northern would in some parts have to be carried on an embankment to the height of 51 feet above and across the Midland. "Therefore I say," remarked Mr. Crossley, "that coals can be conveyed on the Midland Railway at a profit at a much lower rate than they can be conveyed on the Great Northern at a profit."

The half yearly report presented to the proprietors in August, 1872, stated that the Great Northern Company's bills for lines into Derbyshire and also from Newark through Melton to Leicester, both of which the Midland had opposed, had met with the approval of Parliament. The bill for the fusion of the Midland and the Glasgow and South Western Railway Companies, which had again been sanctioned without a dissentient at the spring meeting of shareholders, had been suspended on account of the appointment of a Joint Committee of the two Houses to consider the general question of railway amalgamation.

With reference to these events, Mr. Price, the chairman, said, that in his judgment the invasion of the Derbyshire coalfield was "inconsistent with good faith towards ourselves, and with the integrity of treaties. We believe the lines were uncalled for in the public interests; and they were not even supported by those local interests which they were supposed to be especially designed to serve. We believe that the lines of the Midland Company were fully competent to the traffic, no insufficiency having either been alleged or proved. But since Parliament in its wisdom has thought fit to sanction the invasion, we have no alternative but to submit; and as the subject is a very painful one, and as any discussion would be fruitless, we think that silence is the more dignified and discreet."

Other circumstances of interest occurred during this year in connection with the Midland Railway. One of the most important of these was with regard to third-class passengers. On the last day of March, 1872, we remarked to a friend: "To-morrow morning the Midland will be the most popular railway in England." Nor did we incur much risk by our prediction. For on that day the Board at Derby had decided that on and after the 1st of April they would run third-class carriages by all trains; the wires had flashed the tidings to the newspapers; the bills were in the hands of the printers, and on the following morning the directors woke to find themselves famous, not perhaps in the estimation of railway competitors, but in the opinions of millions of their fellow-countrymen who felt that a mighty boon had been conferred upon the poor of the land. This step had, we believe, long been in contemplation, and in deciding to adopt it the board had had to prepare for what some expected would be a serious sacrifice of revenue; but reasons of high policy won the day, and tens of millions of passengers who have since been borne swiftly and comfortably over the land have been grateful that instead of the narrowness and greed so commonly and often so unjustly attributed to railway administration, a statesmanlike and philanthropic temper has prevailed and triumphed.

Great pressure was subsequently put upon the Midland Company to consent to the withdrawal of these benefits; and it must be admitted that the folly and injustice of the Government in inflicting a fine upon the railways for their liberality, would have amply justified such a course. Several of the companies have somewhat increased the fares for those who travelled by fast third-class trains; happily for the public the Midland Company has remained firm to its original purpose. "If there is one part of my public life," recently said Mr. Allport to the writer, "on which I look back with more satisfaction than on anything else, it is with reference to the boon we conferred on third-class travellers. When the rich man travels, or if he lies in bed all day, his capital remains undiminished and perhaps his income flows in all the same. But when a poor man travels he has not only to pay his fare but to sink his capital, for his time is his capital; and if he now consumes only five hours instead of ten in making a journey, he has saved five hours of time for useful labour—useful to himself, his family, and to society. And," Mr. Allport added, "I think with even more pleasure of the comfort in travelling we have been able to confer upon women and children." We venture to repeat that it is a happy circumstance when the hard realities of railway administration are thus tempered by a spirit and a policy so humanitarian and elevated.

In the course of the year the sanction of the Midland

shareholders was given to a bill promoted for "the construction of railways between Walsall, in Staffordshire, and the Midland Railway in Warwickshire, to be called the Wolverhampton, Walsall, and Midland Junction," and containing permissive power for the company to enter into agreement with the Midland Company for its working and maintenance. The Bedford and Northampton Railway was opened in June, 1872. The line starts about two miles and a half north of Bedford, in the parish of Bromham, and runs chiefly through cuttings to Northampton. Some of the gradients are heavy—one is one in eighty-four. The intermediate stations are Turvey, Olney, and Horton.

During a tremendous storm of thunder, lightning, and rain, on the 19th of June, 1872, which deluged the country far and wide, a slip took place at the northern entrance of the Dove Holes Tunnel on the Manchester line, crushing in part of the covered way that extended beyond the tunnel, and laying an arrest upon the traffic for several weeks. Goods trains, however, were able to run on the 28th of July. The repairs cost £10,000, irrespective of the loss and the diversion of the traffic. "The inconvenience to the public," Mr. Price remarked to the Midland shareholders, "was very much decreased by the assistance rendered by the London and North Western Railway Company; and I am happy to take the opportunity of publicly expressing our grateful recognition of their aid."

CHAPTER XII.

Negotiations between Sheffield and Midland Companies —Proposed joint through line from Rushton to Askerne.—Forty days' battle in the Commons.—The chief portions of the bill rejected.—"Flirtations" of the Sheffield Company.—Bill for Amalgamation of Midland and Glasgow and South Western.—Mr. Price resigns the chairmanship to accept the position of a Railway Commissioner.—Rise of the price of coal.—Rise of the price of everything connected with railways.—500,000 tons of coal a year consumed by Midland Company.—Improved communication between Midland and North Eastern system.—Origin of the Swinton and Knottingley line.—Congestion of traffic at Normanton.—Necessity for improvement.—Passenger traffic to the West.—Opposition line sanctioned by Great Northern and Sheffield.—Sir Edmund Beckett and the Aquabus.—Rival designs.—Mr. Leeman, M.P. and Sir Edmund Beckett.—Evidence of Mr. Harrison and Mr. Bass, M.P.—The "amenities" of Ackworth.—Extraordinary decision of the committee.—The decision reconsidered.—The bill passed.—Running powers under the bill.—Proposed Midland line through Huddersfield and Halifax.—Proposed line from Hammersmith to Acton.—Bills rejected.—Manton and Rushton line sanctioned.—Cheshire Lines Committee Bill for extension to North Docks at Liverpool.—Advantages of the line.—Objections.—Bill approved.—Additional facilities to Birkenhead.—New line to Wigan.—Speech of Sir E. Beckett.—Vast coalfields.—Evidence of Mr. Allport and others.—Bill sanctioned.—Midland Company's access to South Wales.—Existing through routes.—A third through route proposed.—Mr. Noble's evidence.—Mr. Venables' speech.—Hereford, Hay, and Brecon.—History of the line.—Proposed amalgamation with the Midland.—Three years' litigation.—Accommodation at Hereford.—Ironworks and coalfields.—Through traffic.—Swansea Vale line.—History of the line.—Evidence.—Midland proposal to lease the Swansea Vale.—Terms.—Brecon and Neath Railway.—Circumstances of line.—Terms proposed.—Objections.—Evidence.—Reasons influencing the Brecon and Neath.—Mr. Noble's evidence.—Bill passed.—Testimonial to Mr. Price.—Abolition of Second Class.—Opposition of other Companies.—Retaliation Threatened.—"Railway Revolutions."—Lord Redesdale.—Settle and Carlisle line opened for good.—Re-adjustment of Capital Account.—Chairman's retrospect.—Private Waggons.—Lease of Somerset and Dorset.—Floods.

THE great political work of the Midland Company during the parliamentary session of 1873 arose out of events to which reference has already been made. The negotiations that had taken place in the previous year between the Midland and the Sheffield Companies, and which led to the temporary abandonment of their competing schemes, were followed by an agreement to promote a joint line direct from north to south from Askerne, near Doncaster, to the Midland line at Rushton. On this scheme the Midland were not unwilling to enter, as the loss they had sustained by the intrusion of the Great Northern into the Derbyshire coalfields had led them to consider whether they could not claim or reclaim a share of that North Eastern traffic which they had originally enjoyed, but of which the Great Northern had largely deprived them; and the Sheffield Company was glad of a free access to London and of an independence it had long coveted from the "jealous and somewhat hostile neighbours," as Mr. Venables described them, with which it was surrounded. The contemplated outlay was £2,600,000 or £2,700,000, or about £23,000 a mile, on a mileage of 115 miles. It was anticipated that coal would be found upon more than half of the entire route. "The line is to be constructed," said the Company's report, "at joint and equal cost, and with equal rights of user, with running powers to the Midland Company on to the South Yorkshire Districts, and to Grimsby and New Holland; and to the Sheffield Company over the Midland Railway from Rushton to London. It is also proposed, as part of the scheme, to open out, by a line between Conisborough and Shireoaks, an important coalfield at present without access to the markets, and from which a valuable traffic will be secured to the joint lines."

After a forty days' conflict of great severity, the Commons' Committee granted to the Midland and Sheffield Companies the Rushton and Melton portion of the line, also the part from Conisborough to Shireoaks, but took out the great intermediate links of the scheme, and all the running powers to be interchanged between the Midland

and the Sheffield Companies, and thus left the Midland "to find a body for their head and tail by means of the existing lines, a practicable but somewhat circuitous route." In this mutilated condition the bill went up to the Lords, who still further "amended" it by striking out the Rushton and Melton portion, leaving only the Shireoaks—a mere fragment of the original scheme; and the Midland, having duly considered the altered condition of affairs, decided to withdraw what remained of the bill.

In subsequently referring to the various efforts made by the Sheffield Company—of which this was the latest—to enter into alliance with one or another of the surrounding companies, Sir Mordaunt Wells playfully remarked: "What have the Sheffield done? They have flirted with the North Western since 1856; they then flirted with the Great Northern; they then flirted with the Midland; then they flirted with the Eastern Counties and the coal-owners. Then, in 1872, they flirted again with their old love, the London and North Western; and now in 1873, there is a mild flirtation between Sir Edward Watkin and Mr. Allport; and, like all flirts, mark my words, the Sheffield will be left without an alliance with any of them, and will entertain that feeling which all flirts entertain towards all mankind when they have been left completely in the lurch, and she will move about society on her own hook, catching who she can. This is not the less true because it creates a little mirth."

In the course of the year there was a renewal of the application for the amalgamation of the Midland and the Glasgow and South Western. "You are aware," said Mr. Price, "that a bill for that purpose was approved by you in 1869, and another last year; the former of these having passed through the Commons, being rejected by the House of Lords, on account of, as we are informed, the insufficient security for the completion of the Settle and Carlisle line; and the latter bill having been postponed last year to await the report of the Joint Committee of both Houses on the great question of railway amalgamation." This Joint Committee rejected the amalgamation bill, for reasons which nobody knows. It is said that the practice adopted by parliamentary committees, of pronouncing decisions without giving any explanations, is calculated to inspire public confidence in the wisdom of such tribunals, or at any rate to shelter them from imputations of a contrary kind. Our own opinion is (though for reasons different from those commonly suggested) there is much to be said in favour of concealment.

At the conclusion of the proceedings at the spring meeting of proprietors, Mr. Price asked permission to inform the shareholders that that was the last occasion on which he should have the honour of addressing them from that chair. "It is, no doubt," he said, "a matter of sufficiently public notoriety that I have accepted office as one of the three Commissioners to be appointed under the Railways and Canal Traffic Act." He spoke of the great pain with which he severed himself from "a company and from colleagues with which he had been intimately associated for nearly one-and-twenty years. I cannot claim to be one of the fathers of the undertaking, but I may at least say with truth that I have stood by its cradle, and watched and aided others in fostering its growth. From this time henceforth the Midland Company to me must be as one of the great commonwealth of railway enterprise."

The attention of railway managers and shareholders was during this year greatly exercised upon a new subject, but one of urgent practical moment: the enormous rise in the value of labour, coals, minerals, and in fact of all the articles consumed by railways. The outlay of the Midland Company alone for stores, which amounted in the previous year to no less than £1,414,000, gradually increased up to the proportion of in some instances as much as 150 per cent. This was the case with coal, and the magnitude of the additional cost may be inferred from the fact that the Midland Company consumes about 500,000 tons per annum. Similar burdens had to be borne by other lines, so that "though an extraordinary impetus had been given to the trade and industry of the country in the past two years, it had conferred less real benefits upon the railway shareholders as a body than upon any other class of the people, whether capitalist, manufacturer, or labourer." On twenty-three of the leading railways of the kingdom, every 20*s.* of increased traffic which had been brought upon the lines in the previous half year had resulted in a net additional profit of only 4*d.* to the railway proprietors, the balance being absorbed in the increased charges on capital account and augmented working expenses.

During this year the Midland Company lost by death the services of one who is not undeserving of special notice, Mr. Matthew Kirtley, their locomotive superintendent. His father a colliery owner, himself, at the age of thirteen or fourteen, employed on that cradle of the railway system, the Stockton and Darlington line, and afterwards on the London and Birmingham, he was early and through his life identified with railway interests. He drove the first locomotive that entered London, in 1839. When the Derby and Birmingham was opened, he was selected by the Stephensons as locomotive superintendent; on the union of the three lines which formed the Midland Company he retained the same position; and here his responsibilities steadily increased until some 7000 men were directly under his control, including 2000 at Derby. "He was a man of clear sagacity and well-balanced judgment, and possessed a power of organization and arrangement which enabled him to exercise an effective control over the whole of the extensive concern for which he was responsible. In nothing was he more distinguished than in his command of men. Simple in his manners, easily approachable, able to sympathise with the workmen's position and difficulties, and strictly candid, he was singularly happy in dealing with complaints. While sympathising and conciliating, he was also firm and decisive, and, like all strong men, employed few words to convey his resolves." Mr. Kirtley died May 24th, 1873.

The year 1874 witnessed some quiet but important developments of the Midland system, both in the area of its operations and in the policy by which it was administered. In its earlier months much time and labour were devoted to securing the passing of important bills for new lines. One of these was for a railway to improve the communication between the Midland and the North Eastern systems. It appears that after the great fight of the previous session for the bill by which the Midland and Sheffield Companies were jointly to reach the North Eastern at Askerne, Mr. Harrison, the engineer in chief of that company, "formed a very strong opinion" that such a line would not have been advantageous to the parties concerned; but "from the ordnance surveys and contour lines, and some sections" which he obtained, he considered that the right direction in which to run such a line was between Swinton and Knottingley; and "I then suggested it," he said, "to Mr. Allport, and also to the officials of the North Eastern Company." "That," said Mr. Harrison to Mr. Allport, "in my judgment, is your course northward. It will give you almost an unobstructed road, as there is no traffic scarcely upon the line from Knottingley to York; the Great Northern having removed the whole of their through traffic on the new line from Askerne to York, you will have as good access to York as the Great Northern." "I was very much impressed with that," Mr. Allport subsequently remarked; "and after discussing it with Mr. Harrison, and ascertaining from the North Eastern that they were quite willing to exchange running powers, so that York might be the common point of exchange both with the Great Northern and ourselves, I submitted the plan to the Midland Directors, and it resulted in this bill."

The main object contemplated by this line, as we have remarked, was to improve the communication between the Midland and the North-Eastern systems; "and that," said Mr. Venables, "is not a small object." The Midland Company includes more than 1200 miles of railway, and the North Eastern some 1450 miles; "both of them have a very large traffic, and from their geographical position and their peculiar resources of traffic there is a very large exchange, which we propose to improve and facilitate." The intended line would shorten the distance from the North Eastern to Sheffield by seven miles, and would in a still greater degree facilitate the interchange of traffic. The present point of exchange is Normanton, and the approach of the North Eastern to that station is from a place called Burton Salmon, one of the most crowded parts of the system; while at Normanton the weight of traffic exchanged in 1872 was more than 1,500,000 tons, and the passengers 680,000; the proportion of the Midland being about half the tonnage and some 278,000 passengers, taking no account of the Midland main traffic north and south. The position of the Normanton station, with a heavy embankment at the north and a deep cutting at the south, rendered it difficult to extend the area of the station so as to avoid an increasing congestion of traffic. "We have acquired," said Mr. Allport, "about as much land as we can; we have spent within the last few years a large sum of money, but we cannot keep pace with the requirements." In the previous month of November the delays amounted to nearly 1000 hours; which, calculating an engine to work ten hours a day—an outside estimate—would mean that the services of four engines were entirely wasted at that station; and as all railway companies consider that an engine costs from £1000 to £1500 a year, a loss of £4000 to £6000 a year on engine power alone was thus incurred, besides all other inconvenience and loss contingent thereon. "Any one, in fact," said Mr. Harrison, the North Eastern engineer-in-chief, "who has travelled from Normanton to York, must be perfectly aware of the absolute necessity for doing something to get rid of the stoppage which takes place there."

Another of the practical difficulties created by this defective communication between the two systems was mentioned by Mr. Tennant. "We have," he said, "an express train starting from Newcastle at 10 o'clock in the morning, taking passengers that have come in by local trains from Tynemouth, Shields, Wrexham, Morpeth, Alnwick, and as far as Berwick. We cannot start it earlier than 10 o'clock without seriously interfering with a large number of local passengers. The train arrives at York quite in time for a train to go on to London; but we have not been able to make it fit in at Normanton with an important train of the Midland Company which goes through to Bristol and the West of England. We tried it for some time, and we failed; we had not time. Of course our suggestion to the Midland Company was that they should start their train later; but they are tied up at Bristol, and various other places on the line, with other companies' trains, and they could not start it later; and we could not start ours earlier. Although a passenger can start from Newcastle at 10 o'clock and go right through to London, he must start at half-past eight o'clock to catch a corresponding Midland train to the West of England, and from the local towns somewhat earlier.

This important project of the Midland and North Eastern Companies was not, however, allowed to be brought forward without resistance. Another line was advocated by the Great Northern and Manchester, Sheffield, and Lincolnshire Companies, which, starting from Swinton or Mexborough, would run to Knottingley. Mr. Denison, who had now become Sir Edmund Beckett, and who appeared on its behalf, thus referred to Mexborough: "I am old enough to remember when Mexborough was a very small place upon the banks of the Don; when we used to travel from Swinton by a vehicle which should have its name perpetuated. It was called by an ingenious gentleman 'the Aquabus,' meaning a vehicle which went by water through the river Don. He evidently thought it necessary to keep the word ''bus.' But since that time Mexborough has become a sort of Castleford, or almost a sort of Middlesborough; it has iron works and glass works, and it builds boats; though, I am afraid, no more aquabuses."

The main difference, remarked Sir Edmund Beckett, between the proposed railway of the Midland and North Eastern and that which he advocated "is, that our line has more junctions, and goes to more places" than the rival line, and is to a certain extent a more "local line," "but, at the bottom, the two lines are so very identical" that there is little in many respects to choose between them. It appears also that the promoters and the Sheffield Company offered not only that the Great Northern but the Midland and North Eastern should share in it; but the proposal was by the latter companies declined.

"Therefore," remarked Sir Edmund, "it cannot be said that the Sheffield Company are desirous to make this line with the object of shutting everybody else out of it. On the contrary, they desire to get everybody into it. The object has been to make a line that should be an open route or highway to everybody who was inclined to use it upon fair terms."

The proposal for a joint use of the line was objected to by the representatives of the Midland and North Eastern, on the ground that it was undesirable that any part of the control of the railway should be in the hands of those whose interest it would be to thwart the design of those who projected it. "It is said," remarked Mr. Venables, "that the four companies could get on remarkably well together. But we know that if the four companies were upon the line, in some way or other their conflicting interests must be adjusted, occasionally to the injury of one, occasionally to the injury of another, always to the inconvenience of those who are to be postponed. Upon a railway, as upon any other kind of horse, if two men ride, one must ride behind; and if four men ride, three must ride behind. We naturally decline to subject this traffic, which is wholly independent of any rival companies, to their control. They would be only too happy to put a block there which would deprive us of any opportunity of improving the communication in our own hands. They would be glad to take in a dozen companies, and would be ready to take the chance of any inconvenience which might arise. The present route, by which the Midland Company and North Eastern connect, is absolutely in their own hands. They meet at Normanton, with nobody between them,—with no partner north, with no partner south; they have the control in their own hands. It is now proposed, that because they ask to be allowed to create a great public benefit, by shortening the line and improving the service, they are not to do it unless they let in two other companies. What do we take away from them? What wrong do we do them? We take nothing away from them whatever except this,—that whereas we have now a comparatively circuitous route to the North, we propose to make a direct one."

The demand of the competing companies was well expressed by Mr. Leeman, M.P., the chairman of the North Eastern, in reply to Sir Edmund Beckett.

"Do you not think it fair," said the latter, "inasmuch as the Great Northern and Sheffield Companies have been trying to get this line of their own under the circumstances I have described, that they should have running powers in some way, so as to make a little profit out of them, and not the ordinary running powers, which leave no profit to the party possessing them?"

"I do not think so," Mr. Leeman replied; "and I might illustrate the position myself, if I were to ask you the question, would you like to give half your fees to one of your juniors?"

"That is quite a different sort of thing."

"That," returned Mr. Leeman, "is exactly the state of things. The Midland and the North Eastern find nine tenths of the traffic, and you coolly and modestly ask that we should give you one half the profit."

"If the four companies were joint owners it would be," said Mr. Allport, "that the other two companies would be receiving the profit of the traffic which the Midland and North Eastern provided."

A similar opinion was expressed by Mr. Harrison. "If there were four companies interested in it, two of those companies having nine tenths of the traffic, and the most important part of the traffic—the through traffic, and the other companies having merely what they could pick up, it would be no regular system of traffic. . . . The management ought to be in the hands of the company who have infinitely the preponderating weight of traffic to carry. I do not know any case in which there are four companies jointly owners, except Punch's Line, near London." If there were such arrangement, "I have not the slightest hesitation in saying there would become such a block to the traffic that it would defeat the great object for which the lines have been proposed."

Mr. M. T. Bass, M.P., after giving evidence in favour of the bill, was thus cross-examined by Sir Edmund Beckett :—

"But supposing four companies wanted to run through a district, some of them must 'own' and some must 'run,' or else they must have a joint arrangement?"

"Yes; but if those who had an interest in the line were to be masters of the whole, and the others subsidiary, I should prefer——"

"So should I if I were you. You are on the Midland line, and therefore you want the Midland line extended as far as you can?"

"Yes. Besides, the Great Northern people have never done anything for us; and this new line which you are going to carry out (a most wasteful expenditure, according to my notions), goes about ten miles round for every twenty—I mean the line from Burton to Derby and Nottingham."

"The Midland is your railway, in short?"

"Well, it is not more than the North Western and several other railways?"

"But of the two the Midland is a little more yours than even the North Western?"

"We do more business with the Midland; and perhaps I may say to the committee that it is far more convenient that all our traffic should be done by the Midland, because they have lines into all our premises, absolutely into our storerooms."

"That is what I meant by your connection with the Midland being a little closer. You do not complain of that?"

"Not the least."

"You have this excellent connection with the Midland; they do your business, and you naturally want to see their line extended as far as you can."

"Yes."

"And if you had it with the North Western you would equally want to see that extended?"

"Yes."

"So should I if I were you."

In drawing his address to a conclusion, Mr. Venables referred playfully to one or two local objections to the line. One was by the vicar of Ferry Bridge, "who evidently thought he ought to have been told that the Midland and North Eastern Companies would have a station" at his village. If he had only known that there will be one, "I suppose he would not have come here. But as they will have a station, he and his parishioners will be as happy as the day is long, and will be always travelling backwards and forwards along our line." Another series of petitioners declared that in their opinion, "the railway proposed by the Midland Company would seriously interfere with the amenities of Ackworth and the district;" and on a witness being asked whether he thought the said "amenities" would be compromised, he emphatically replied, "most undoubtedly;" though what he or the district meant by the phrase, we must leave to the imagination of our reader.

On the whole case for both parties being completed (June 10th, 1874), the committee room was cleared, and the members remained in consultation for upwards of an hour. When the parties to the bill were readmitted, and the counsel were seated at the table, and silence was restored, the chairman announced that "the preamble of the Midland and North Eastern Bill was not proved, and also that the preamble of the Leeds, Pontefract, and Sheffield Junction Bill was not proved." So extraordinary a decision was regarded as in the nature of a practical joke; it called forth a roar of laughter, in which, we are informed, the members of the committee heartily joined.* A few days afterwards, however, the Midland and North Eastern Bill was re-committed and passed. The estimated cost of the line is £480,000; and the distance is fifteen miles.

Another line proposed this session (1874) by the Midland Company, was for the purpose of improving its direct course to the North of England. In addition to the existing route by Leeds to Skipton, it was intended to make another, sixteen miles in length, from Huddersfield, through Halifax, to Bradford, and to join the present Midland Railway there. Those towns would thus have been placed on the main line, and in direct communication with Edinburgh and Glasgow. The bill, however, was opposed and lost.

The Midland Company also sought for parliamentary powers to construct a line from Acton to Hammersmith. By means of the North and South Western Junction, which turns off from the Midland at Brent, Acton was reached, and from thence it was desired to pass on to Hammersmith, and along the Hammersmith Extension to the Metropolitan District.

This line was objected to by the Great Western Company, on the ground that it was an infringement of an agreement made between that Company and the

* *Railway News*, June 13th, 1874.

Midland in 1863, by which they agreed not to interfere with each others' "district." To this it was replied that London could not be called "a district" for any such purpose. Such an interpretation, it was contended, would have prevented the Great Western reaching the docks at the East of London, because the Midland was there before them; would have even shut the Midland out of London; and was contrary to public policy. "According to such an interpretation, the Midland Company could never," said Mr. Allport, "except subject to the veto of the Great Western, give any additional accommodation in London; and, conversely, the Great Western could never, except subject to the veto of the Midland Company, do the same. I cannot conceive anything more anti-public than a restriction of that kind in the hands of three great companies; and I am quite sure that it never crossed the mind of any Midland director or officer that that clause had the slightest bearing on operations in London." On July 1, 1874, the Lords Committee decided that "it was not expedient to proceed with this bill."

Another Midland project of this year was for a railway of fifteen miles from Manton, on the Syston and Peterborough, to Rushton. Its design was, in conjunction with the Nottingham and Melton line already sanctioned, —and a link of the Syston and Peterborough Railway,— to supply an alternative route from the great central coal-field of Nottinghamshire and Derbyshire to Rushton and the south. Two years previously (1872) a similar bill had been applied for, but had been withdrawn. In 1873 matters had been suspended by reason of the endeavour of the Midland and Sheffield Companies to carry their joint line; but that having been rejected by Parliament, this was revived, and eventually it was approved.

The Cheshire Lines Committee (who, as our readers are

aware, represent the Midland, Great Northern, and Sheffield Companies) this year (1874) applied to Parliament for some important extensions of the area of their operations. The railways of this committee commence at a place a little east of Stockport (at Godley Junction) and run through Stockport, Altrincham, and Warrington, to Liverpool; down also to Knutsford, Northwich, and Chester, with branches to Winsford and other places. A line also is in course of construction which will run to a central station in Manchester, within two or three minutes' walk of the Exchange. The committee now desired to obtain communication with the north end of Liverpool. The three lines owned some 2000 miles of railway; had spent, in their joint operations, about £6,000,000 in money; and had access to the Brunswick Docks, commonly called the South-End Dock System at Liverpool, where they secured a traffic inwards and outwards in 1873 of 300,000 tons; but they had no connection with the docks that stretched six miles in length to the north of the town, and which were steadily extending northward, except by means of tramways alongside the docks, which are constantly occupied by other companies, and by omnibuses carrying local traffic. On those docks it was said that the London and North Western and Lancashire and Yorkshire Companies had no fewer than twenty stations; and the Cheshire Companies claimed some share in the advantages of direct access to such important sources of traffic. The proposed line, too, would free the streets of Liverpool from an enormous amount of cartage.

In the previous year (1873) the Cheshire Companies had, under their several powers, bought twenty-three acres of land for station purposes; but at present they had no access to it. The only ways of reaching it were either by making an underground or deep cut line through Liverpool (and such a scheme had been contemplated in the previous year, at a cost, it was currently reported, of something like a million and a half of money, or by a line skirting Liverpool on its eastern side. The latter course was preferred. The line would, including branches, be thirteen miles long, and would cost £600,000.

The proposed railway would also render another important service. The Midland Company has access from the North over its own line from Skipton to Colne; and it has running powers southwards from Colne to Preston, Manchester, and Liverpool: these privileges having been conceded when the Lancashire and Yorkshire were in Parliament to amalgamate with the East Lancashire, as the price of the withdrawal of Midland opposition. The line now proposed to the north of Liverpool would join the Lancashire and Yorkshire near Aintree, and would thus give direct communication between the Cheshire Companies' Liverpool terminus and the Midland route to Colne, Skipton, Settle, and Carlisle.

Objections to the new scheme were made by the companies already in possession of the district. They said of the proposals of the Cheshire Committee, "that they were entitled to complain" of them. "Yes," replied Sir Edmund Beckett, in his critical, bantering way, "I dare say they will complain. They cannot be prevented from complaining. They were displeased at our getting access to Manchester; they were displeased at our getting access to Liverpool; and they are displeased at everything we have done." It was objected that certain junctions proposed on the line were badly designed. "I never knew," returned the counsel, "a junction that was not badly designed, when it was designed by another company." Mr. John Heywood considered that the line would injure his valuable residential estate; but it was replied that there was already a great road between the railway and the house, and that any real injury would be paid for. "Then," said the counsel. "there is Miss Catherine Horne's petition. I am afraid Miss Catherine Horne will have to be destroyed altogether. I mean to say she has a small property there, and we could not with any decency cut through it. She would not like it if we did, and I am afraid we must buy the whole of it."

This line secured the sanction of Parliament.

The Cheshire Lines Committee also sought, under their additional powers act, for further facilities at Birkenhead. It appears that, under the act of 1861, which amalgamated the Birkenhead line with the London and North Western and Great Western, "facilities" were allowed to the Cheshire Lines Committee. Yet these facilities operated in so ineffectual a way, that the Cheshire Companies felt compelled to seek for powers to run their trains from their own system at Helsby, over the main line, and through the station of the two companies, in order to reach the docks at Birkenhead, and there to conduct their own traffic. "We do not ask," said Mr. Allport, "for any powers over their station or goods warehouses, or the sidings in their stations, but simply to pass over their main lines to enable us to get to the Dock Board Lines." The main contention on the part of the Cheshire Companies was admitted by Parliament; and the preamble of the bill was proved (April 30th, 1874); but instead of running powers being granted, it was thought better that the two companies should be "bound to give all possible facilities to the Cheshire Lines Committee from their stations to all parts of the Birkenhead docks; otherwise it would be in the right of that Committee on a future occasion to apply to Parliament for compulsory running powers."

A third proposal, in this instance of the Midland and Sheffield members of the Cheshire Committee, was to obtain power to connect the railways of the three companies by a line eleven and a half miles long, and at a cost of £300,000, with the Wigan coalfield. Wigan was on the North Western and Lancashire and Yorkshire lines, "hitherto a kind of preserve of those two companies." The line was to start from Glazebrook, on the new Manchester and Liverpool line. This Wigan coalfield covers about half the proposed line.

In submitting the claims of the new line, the chairman of the committee took occasion to remark that "the whole matter appeared to the committee to lie in a nutshell. Of course we must have the engineer before us to prove the workability of the line. But the whole thing turns on the question whether or not you can make out a case of a sufficient amount of traffic to warrant a new line. The committee want to know about the whole district, such as what is the probable amount of coal that there is; how many millions of tons would be likely to be obtained;" and he intimated that they would prefer the evidence of some colliery surveyor who knew the whole of the country. As to delays, the chairman added, "we know it stands to reason that there must be delays where there is a large amount of traffic. I know the Lancashire and Yorkshire system, and I know that delays are enormous."

This demand it was not difficult to meet. The mineral wealth of the district was enormous. There were several places raising quantities of coal of which the unit is 100,000 tons a year. "There is one works alone where it is 1,800,000 tons; there are others which are raising 200,000, 300,000, and 400,000 tons. In fact the figures are so large that they give one hardly any more definite ideas than the miles' distance of the planets and stars, which one says by heart without receiving any clear impressions from them. But I may state that the London and North Western Company alone carry 3,000,000 tons of Wigan coal southward in a year. The Lancashire and Yorkshire also take a very large quantity."

The managing director of one of the colliery companies, near Wigan, stated that they raised 200,000 tons of coal a year; that the thickness of the seams of the district was rather over fifty feet; and that the unexhausted product of their own collieries was 20,000,000 tons. Five other collieries would also be benefited by the proposed new line. The manager of the Hindley Green Collieries mentioned that his company raised 200,000 tons a year; that their railway accommodation was inadequate, and that delays were serious.

It was also shown that, so far as the Midland and Great Northern were concerned, this was a sealed district. The amounts were as follows:—

RAILWAY DISTRIBUTION FOR LANCASHIRE.

	TONS.
By London and North Western	5,698,258
,, Lancashire and Yorkshire	2,874,637
By Midland only	22,617
,, Great Northern	6,668

Mr. Allport stated that such a line would, in his judgment, be a valuable piece of railway construction, and more valuable to the Midland than to either of the other Cheshire Companies. The London and North Western had entered the Derbyshire coalfields, "competition seemed to be the order of the day," and he "did not see any reason why the Midland should not get into the Lancashire coalfields;" and "the difference between Wigan and London by the Midland lines now in construction, would only be about three miles more than by the London and North Western." There would thus practically be between Wigan and London "an alternative route, almost identical in distance with the North Western main route. Then again, in London we serve different districts. We have now four depôts in London: one at St. Pancras, which is at least a mile from Camden Town; we have two on the south side of the Thames; one at Walworth Road, and another at Battersea; and we provide coal depôts in various parts of the city. We have also been frequently asked to get Wigan coal into Nottingham and Leicester, and told that, although they are both close to coalfields, they want the cannel coal of Wigan for gas manufacture." "I know," he added, "several of the large coal and iron masters of the district, and for many years they have asked me why we did not get a line into that country."

The bill was granted, subject to some engineering modifications, to avoid unnecessary interference with the London and North Western line.

A successful effort was also made during this session (1874) of Parliament to improve the position of the Midland Company in the Principality. The condition of railway affairs in South Wales was as follows:—The three great railway systems that approach the West of England, viz., the Midland, the North Western, and the Great Western, had access, by something like parallel lines, to Swansea. The London and North Western had two routes to South Wales. These converged at Shrewsbury, a station the joint property of that company and of the Great Western, and from thence the line proceeded *viâ* Hereford and Abergavenny to the mineral lines in the mineral valleys running generally north and south, with a terminus at Dowlais. They had also another route *viâ* Llandovery, and the Vale of Towy

Railway to Swansea. The Great Western had the coast line, formerly known as the South Wales, reaching to Milford; and also the system of lines once called the West Midland, which conducted them to Worcester, Hereford, and by the Vale of Neath to Swansea.

The third route was the Midland. "In this part of the world," said Mr. Venables, "as in most other parts of the world, the Midland Company form a competing system with the London and North Western Company and the Great Western Company." They came by their own line to Stoke Works, near Worcester, and from thence had running powers by the Great Western to Swansea. These had been granted as part of the condition that the Midland Company should not oppose the union of the Great Western and West Midland systems. But such powers are practically useless unless local traffic can be obtained; "because," as Mr. John Noble, the assistant general manager of the Midland said, "in running over another company's line, the running company makes no profit upon that running; the running company is merely allowed the bare cost of working its trains over the railway; and the whole of the profit of the transaction goes to the owning company. We therefore should have to run over more than 100 miles, if we ran all the way to Swansea, for nothing more than the bare cost of working the trains, and perhaps it might not even cover that." The Midland were, therefore, desirous of obtaining access to South Wales by some other route less encumbered by these "local traffic" difficulties; and the Hereford, Hay, and Brecon and Swansea Vale lines (already constructed) supplied the want.

"I think," said Mr. Venables, "it will appear upon the face of the map that it is desirable that all these great companies who approach this district (all of which approach it by more or less inconvenient ways), shall have each the most convenient way of approaching it. The North Western have that advantage, and the Great Western have that advantage, and these two companies, either of which would willingly exclude the other, are now, not unnaturally, combined to exclude the Midland." "The North Western has nothing to say against us except what it can say with perfect truth, viz., that the amalgamation of this line will enable the Midland Company to compete with the London and North Western for traffic to South Wales, and it is for the sake of establishing that competition that we ask for these powers." "The sole question is whether we, taking a traffic to South Wales, shall take it conveniently and cheaply by utilizing lines which Parliament has already sanctioned, because we do not propose to make a single additional mile; and it appears to me that when Parliament has sanctioned a line it requires a very strong argument to establish the proposition that a line should remain a block and be absolutely useless; but that has been from first to last the policy of the Great Western with reference to the Hereford, Hay and Brecon."

It appears that this line (the Hereford, Hay and Brecon) was authorised in the year 1859, having been promoted by a nominal company, but really by a contractor, Mr. Savin, who also was the originator and maker of the Brecon and Merthyr line. Financial delays and difficulties arose in the construction of the lines; but they were completed, and remained in his hands till 1864. In 1865 the circumstances of many lines in this district, and of the Hereford line among them, were very unfavourable: "1866 was the collapse of many railways." The Hereford line had been amalgamated with the Brecon and Merthyr; but in 1868 was released from that connection. Its condition at this period was deplorable "While the Brecon and Merthyr had it, they allowed the interest upon the debentures to get into arrears, and had contracted other debts for which the Hereford was liable; and therefore, when the railway came back again, they had neither engines nor carriages nor wagons; they had no money, they had the line in bad order, they owed a great deal of money, and some of their debentures were overdue."

Eventually, however, the Hereford Company made overtures to the Midland Company to take the working of the line, and these were favourably received; and though the Great Western had hitherto not concerned itself about the Hereford Company, yet "having," said Mr. Venables, "a very strong rivalry with the Midland Company, it now opposed every obstacle which could be devised by human ingenuity to the traffic" of the Hereford line. Complicated and costly legal battles were fought; and though, at length, the Great Western were defeated by the Hereford Company, yet resistance was still offered to the Midland in the agreement they had with the Hereford to use the line; its validity was challenged, and the right of the Midland to use the connecting line giving access to the railway was disputed. At length, to bring matters to an issue, a formal demand was made for the admission of a Midland train to the junction line. The line, however, was blocked, not only by signals, but with an engine and half a dozen wagons; and the Great Western authorities admitted that this was done by their orders, and they declared that they would obstruct the line by force if necessary. To avoid an actual collision the Midland Company simply protested against such proceedings, and then appealed to the law; and the result was, that during three years' litigation passengers coming from the West by the Hereford Railway had to get out at the Moorfields station of that line, and to go by omnibus to the Great Western station, which the Midland Company had the right to use. The traffic was "very nearly killed," as Mr. Noble expressed it, "by the block;" for "passengers were not very likely to choose being carried in an omnibus through the streets of Hereford when they could get by a through line." Meanwhile the matter was before the Master of the Rolls, Lord Romilly, and the Midland Company was defeated; an appeal was then made to the Lords Justices James and Mellish, who did not even call upon the Midland Company to reply, but set aside the previous decision, and declared that the Midland Company had "a lawful right to come to and from the Great Western line" as "one continuous line of railway." "Being of opinion," said Lord Justice Mellish, "that the agreement itself is legal, and being of opinion that the Midland are entitled to use the Great Western line by virtue of the agreement with the Great Western, I am of opinion that the decree that has been made must be reversed."

The Midland Company in their bill now urged upon Parliament, that as the London and North Western and the Great Western Companies had been authorised to amalgamate various lines that gave access to this South Wales system, similar advantages should be conferred upon themselves. They expressed themselves prepared to join other companies in providing additional station accommodation at Hereford, which was urgently needed; whereas to such a purpose the Hereford Company alone was unable to contribute "anything, because they had no funds." "I may say," remarked Mr. Noble, "on the part of the Midland Company, that we are quite ready to consider with the other two companies the most desirable way of giving that accommodation to the city of Hereford which they desire to have."

With regard to the district served by the Hereford line, Mr. Charles Anthony, six times mayor of Hereford, stated that that city was looked upon as the capital of the district. "There are," he said, "an enormous number of cattle bred in Radnorshire; and on the west side of the city we have some of the finest timber for general purposes, and pit timber particularly, which should find its way to Birmingham, Derbyshire, and Staffordshire. The citizens generally attribute its enormous increase in the markets to the opening up of the country by the Midland Railway. The markets have enormously increased. The inhabitants generally think that the competition would be most wholesome and beneficial to the trade of the city as well as to the county."

"For the sake of the traffic on the Hereford, Hay and Brecon itself," said Mr. Noble, "it would not be worth our while to work it. It only becomes valuable to us as affording the means of access to places beyond Brecon. To those places the London and North Western and Great Western have got their own independent routes. Now the largest places beyond Brecon to which this line takes us for the purposes of this bill are Merthyr and Dowlais, which are two very large and populous places, containing together 100,000 people. There are also some of the largest ironworks in Wales here;" and both the other great companies have, or will shortly have, a route of their own to both places, so that neither of them are likely to use the Hereford line, "because it would simply be abstracting traffic from their own railway." The Midland Company has, however, every reason for encouraging traffic by this route. "There is now a very large traffic from the ironstone fields of Northamptonshire to those very large ironworks at Dowlais. We are now," continued Mr. Noble, "sending fifty or sixty thousand tons of ironstone every year into those works. Then there is also a very large cattle traffic which comes out of this district to the grazing districts of Leicestershire and Northamptonshire;" and there is the anthracite coal which goes largely into the midland and eastern districts.

For the sake of the local line it seemed imperative that something should be done. "The Great Western Railway," said Mr. Noble, "are trying to starve that poor little Hereford Railway; they have nearly killed it, and want to finish it." "If the bill was not sanctioned," said Mr. Venables, "the Hereford line would in all probability be shut up; and there would be a very well laid-out line going through one of the most remarkable and pleasant and beautiful countries, and affording a means of communication with the North and the country inland to the whole of South Wales, absolutely useless." "I do not think," he said in conclusion, "it will be contended that the public advantage is not exclusively upon our side, or that any possible material advantage can be gained by the rejection of our bill. It will be contended by the London and North Western that they will lose some traffic, which perhaps they will. It will be contended by the Great Western that they will lose some traffic, and that they ought to be protected in their two claims,—one of which is to place a truck across the junction at Hereford, and the other is to force us either to use these impossible running powers, or not to get into South Wales at all. They will support these two contentions to the best of their ability—probably with great ability; but the greater the ability they show in proving that they are for this purpose the enemies of the human race, the better for me."

When the claims of this bill were submitted to the committee of the Lords they "decided (July 3, 1874) to reserve their decision until they had heard the evidence on the next bill." On the following day they resolved to give their sanction to both measures.

The other line was the Swansea Vale, which it was proposed also to add by amalgamation to the Midland. We have already seen that the Hereford line brought the Midland Company as far as Brecon. From Brecon its traffic could go south to Merthyr, Tredegar, the Taff Vale, and Cardiff by other lines; but the Midland wished to go south-west to Swansea by a line in effect its own. Between Brecon and Swansea lay two railways; first the Brecon and Neath, and then the Swansea Vale. To the latter we will now refer.

The Swansea Vale Railway was originally promoted as a private line, the property of some colliery owners and others, who wished to send the produce of their pits and works down to the harbour and docks of Swansea. The collieries, steel, tin, copper works, and foundries upon this line are so numerous that, as the manager declared, "they extend nearly every four or five hundred yards from one end of the line to the other." Meanwhile the demands of the district were increasing, and an unopposed bill was, in that session (1874), before Parliament for a large increase of the dock accommodation of Swansea, at a cost of £400,000 or £500,000. To go back, however, to the year 1846, we find that an attempt was then made to obtain the sanction of Parliament to the little railway company, but that it failed in consequence of some incidental circumstances. Still, the construction of the line went on, and eight miles were completed.

At length, in 1855, the Company succeeded in obtaining their Act of incorporation, and, by subsequent legislation, in extending the railway up to a place called Yniscedwyn, and westward to Brynammon, where it joins the Llanelly line.

Difficulties, however, were numerous. "We are a small

company," said Mr. Starling Benson, the chairman, "and have had to work expensively; we have also had to borrow money at a high rate of interest. For some years we paid no dividend, then two or three per cent., and gradually we got up to six per cent." And its later prosperity had arisen, he declared, "simply upon the prospect of our becoming Midland." Having, too, been originally intended only for local purposes, it was constructed, except at the stations, with a single line; its stations were little better than waiting sheds; its siding accommodation was scanty; and at Swansea, though there was a wooden passenger station, there was no goods station of any kind. "I have been over the line a great many times," said Mr. Noble, the assistant general manager of the Midland; "and it is quite evident that they are completely overpowered by their present traffic." Their rolling stock, too, was insufficient. "We have had to lend them an engine or two already," said Mr. Noble. To put the line into a proper condition for the public service, it was necessary that a large sum of money should be expended. "It must," said Mr. Noble, "be something very large"—"a very large sum, no doubt." The doubling of the line, which was indispensable for the proper development of a through route, would "certainly cost more," declared Mr. Venables, "than £100,000." But all this the little company was not prepared to undertake. "Although," as Mr. Venables observed, "a local company may be earning a good income on its line, it cannot afford to lay out large sums of capital." A great company can afford to make improvements whenever they are required, because the amount is only a fraction of the whole capital; but if a small company were to spend 50 or 100 per cent. on its capital in improvements, it would for a time seriously cripple its position. The consequence practically is, that, so long as a company like the Swansea Vale can get a moderate dividend on its capital, it will be slow to make improvements. At the same time, a larger company would not lay out its money on a foreign line—a line which it did not practically own.

Another disadvantage of the Swansea Vale Company, experienced by all small companies under similar circumstances, was, that they could not find enough trucks to carry on a business over large and distant lines. "If they come back empty," said the chairman, "the loss of time is so great that they are not used; but if they belonged to one of the large companies, they find traffic to load them with near the spot, and they deliver the loads, and there is something else to send back again." "We find as a small company that we cannot afford the proper accommodation which the colliery trade requires. We cannot find the trucks and those things which a large company can do." "We are also at a disadvantage through the smallness of our line, that in case of accident or temporary stoppage of our traffic we cannot average our losses. A large accident or a lock-out would take away all our dividends."

This line (the Swansea Vale) the Midland Company proposed to make their own by a perpetual lease, and by guaranteeing a dividend of 6 per cent. per annum on a capital of about £145,000. All this was provisionally arranged. But the difficulties of the case had not yet been overcome; for between Brecon (the most westerly point of the Midland) and the most easterly point of the Swansea Vale lay the property of a third company, the Brecon and Neath Railway. How was their concurrence so to be secured as to provide a through and uninterrupted communication between the Midland system and Swansea? The solution of this question was to be found in the fact that at a previous period it had been arranged between the Brecon and Neath and the Swansea Vale Railways that they should interchange certain running powers over each other's lines, "so as to establish a direct route between Swansea and the North of England." The words were, that the Swansea Vale were "to have the right, if they think fit, to run over and use with their engines, etc., the Brecon and Neath Railway." A through route northward was thus secured, of which the Swansea Vale was the first stage, the Neath and Brecon the second, and (what had now become) the Midland the third; there being "through invoicing and through booking," and all "in the fullest and most unreserved manner."

It so happened, that up to the period when the Midland was contemplating these amalgamations, this Brecon and Neath had been by no means in a prosperous condition. The great highways of the London and North Western and Great Western had carried the traffic by other routes, and this line had been reduced to a state of starvation. "At this moment," said Mr. Noble, "its working expenses are, I think, 93 per cent. of its entire receipts." Mr. Denison, who appeared on its behalf, admitted before the Commons Committee, that "it had gone through great calamities—it had never earned a penny for itself—it had been in a most miserable condition—it had passed through all the stages of poverty because it had not been in a proper physical condition."

Under such circumstances the proposal of the Midland Company seemed highly advantageous. It was, that the Midland Company should take over, with the Swansea Vale line, the running powers it had over the Brecon and Neath, and use them as the Swansea Vale could have used them; in payment for which the Neath and Brecon would receive their mileage proportion of the through rate. This was the largest amount which the Midland Company professed to be able to give; for if they charged the same as their competitors for a through service, and yet allowed the Brecon and Neath a greater share than their mileage proportion, it is plain that the rest of the line would have to receive less than its mileage proportion, which it could not afford to take. "It would," said Mr. Noble, "be a bar toll;" and the practical result would be that the whole line, Brecon and Neath included, would lose the through traffic altogether. Mr. Noble, however, stated that his company was prepared to allow the Brecon and Neath, if they believed that a mileage proportion was "an insufficient remuneration for the traffic carried in Midland trains over their railway, to have the right to go to an arbitrator, and ask him how much more, if any, they should receive out of the through rate." "There is," he said, "a precedent for this, in the terms on which the Midland Company obtained running powers over the South Staffordshire, by the Act of 1867."

But against these proposals the Brecon and Neath entered its protest; and urged Parliament to refuse its sanction to the amalgamation. Piqued at the less favourable terms offered to itself, or backed up by other influences, it declared that it did not want the Midland to come over it at all, and did not want to be made a through route. This may seem very unnatural and strange; but the underlying motive came out in the remarks of their counsel. It simply meant that more money was wanted from the Midland Company,—of course a very natural design considered in itself. "We say," remarked Mr. Pember, "here are two companies who are properly bought up, and naturally we think that you ought to buy us up properly too. If not, we say, let us alone." To this, of course, the Midland

Company could reply: "If we did as you wished, and bought you up, and paid the market value for you, we should pay you next to nothing. If we buy you at any price you might put upon yourselves we should pay you too much. We will therefore adopt the middle course; and as the Swansea Vale are prepared to sell us their right to running powers over your line, we will buy that and pay you a mileage proportion of all the large traffic we shall be able to bring over your half-starved and almost moribund system."

The advantage of making these little fragments of railways into an efficient through line, was obvious to the men of business in the Swansea Vale. Mr. Pascoe Grenfell, for instance, of the firm of Pascoe Grenfell and Sons, copper and iron smelters, of Swansea, cordially supported the amalgamation of these lines. He mentioned that his firm carried on business with the London and Liverpool and the Midland and Northern districts; that the price of copper averaged about £100 a ton; but that in the process of manufacture it rose to nearly twice that amount; that under recent arrangements their goods were delivered *viâ* the Midland Company remarkably well; that goods sent away on the afternoon of one day were delivered at Birmingham on the next morning, and at Hull a few hours afterwards (about as quickly as a letter); and that this was of the greatest service to their business. "Our trade," he said, "has changed very much of late years, since the introduction of railways and telegraphs. Our customers and consumers do not keep, as they used to do, stocks of copper, but they now depend entirely upon us; and sometimes we have a telegram in the middle of the day to send something off the very next day. Then often we have to make shipments, perhaps, of copper of a highly manufactured nature—say at Hull. We have a telegram two or three days before, to say that this copper is going to the Baltic, or Russia, or somewhere else; that the copper must be there at a certain time, as the ship will sail at a certain date."

Similarly a large coal-owner spoke with regard to his anthracite coal. "It cannot be found elsewhere," he said; "it is perfectly smokeless, and is the best fuel for making iron that is known, except charcoal. In Burton-on-Trent, too, they use nothing else for malting but anthracite coal." Another coal-owner and tin-plate manufacturer expressed his desire to see adequate accommodation and a through route provided. The provision on ten or twelve miles of the Swansea Vale line was totally insufficient. "I should like to have a double line made, because we are very often choked up, and our trucks are left for weeks without being able to get at them for want of local facilities." "Of all companies," said another, "the Midland Company do their work the quickest. A truck-load of block-tin would be worth £1000; and if I wanted the quickest despatch, the Midland Company manages, somehow or another, to deliver quickly, and I can get it down on the third day; whereas on the other companies' lines I have not got it till perhaps four, five, six, seven, or eight days. These little delays from which I suffer," he added, "are not less to me than £1000 a year."

It was further contended on behalf of the Midland Company, that, if the demand of the Brecon and Neath were conceded, and Parliament were to consent to exclude the Midland, and to make this "a block line" to shut the traffic out, and practically, to a large extent, to shut up the line, it would assuredly not be to the public interest—that interest which was certainly considered when powers were given by Parliament for the construction of the line. "In the hands of the Midland Company," said Mr. Venables, "it means a line for facilitating the traffic; whereas, in the hands of the other companies, it would be a line for local traffic, but a block-line for through traffic."

"If," said Mr. Noble, "these two bills,—the Hereford, Hay and Brecon and the Swansea Vale,—should pass, I reckon that we shall put life into about 150 miles of the worst railway property in the kingdom. There is the Hereford line earning nothing; there are eight miles of the Mid Wales, and sixty miles of the Brecon and Merthyr, which we feed. The Brecon and Merthyr has nobody else to look to; and here are altogether about 150 miles of railway, which, if our traffic is allowed to run over this line, will have life put into them. The capital expended on these lines has been some millions."

Such was the view taken by Parliament; and the bill passed, July 4th, 1874.

In the month of June the testimonial awarded in the previous August was presented to the late chairman, Mr. Price, who had, as the present chairman, Mr. Ellis, expressed it, devoted no fewer than twenty years of the best portion of his life to the service of the Midland Railway Company.

In the autumn of this year (1874), the Midland Company announced their intention of adopting a new line of policy with regard to their passenger traffic—a policy destined to produce important effects on the railway travelling of this country. The course which had already been taken of allowing third-class passengers to travel by all trains, had entailed consequences which perhaps few had originally anticipated. By the suppression of some of the old third-class trains the distance run on the Midland line was found to be reduced some 500,000 miles a year, and thus a saving was effected of £37,000; yet the number of additional passengers conveyed on that line during the year was 4,000,000, bringing additional benefit to the Company of £220,000 a year. The marvellous productiveness of third-class traffic was also illustrated by the fact that, out of an increased number of passengers during the years 1870 to 1873 on our railways generally, of 113,000,000, no fewer than 111,000,000 of these were third-class passengers. On the Midland system the returns in 1873 were as follows:

First-class	passengers,	1,136,405,	who paid	£228,739
Second	„	2,487,590	„	208,395
Third	„	18,370,053	„	961,312
	Total	21,994,048		£1,398,446

It thus began clearly to appear that the public at large—looking at the nature of the accommodation provided, the price charged, and their own resources—preferred the third class; that less than 15 per cent. of passengers travelled second class; and that the trains must be carrying a large and increasing proportion of dead weight in the form of empty second-class carriages. Of course railways do not exist to run trains, but to carry passengers and goods; and hence the subject pressed on the attention of the Midland board, whether it would not be better to abolish the second-class carriage altogether. This might be done without injury to the public, if second-class passengers could be carried at second-class fares in first-class carriages; and hence the question arose, whether the sacrifice of revenue involved could be fairly borne by the shareholders? On inquiry it was found that already first-class passengers were travelling between, for instance, such towns as Nottingham and Derby, and Bradford and Leeds, at second-class fares; and that—even if the liberality of the Company to the public led to no increase of receipts (an improbable circumstance)—the total loss incurred by the Company by charging only three-halfpence a mile for all (except third-class passengers), and allowing all such to travel in first-class carriages, would amount to only £25,000 a year. Such an arrangement would also secure some economical advantages to the Company. By avoiding the necessity for new rolling stock for new lines about to be opened; by the saving of coal through the reduced weight of the trains; by diminishing the wear and tear of empty carriages and of the permanent way; by lessening labour in the ticket and audit department by having only two classes to deal with instead of three; and by more compact trains under more complete control of the engine, and ensuring the greater punctuality, not only of passenger trains, but of goods and mineral trains:—all these were sources of economy, which the Directors believed would be highly remunerative to the Company. Taking these and other facts into consideration, the Directors startled the railway world and the public generally by the announcement that, on and after the 1st of January, 1875, the second-class passenger would be abolished, and that all the benefits hitherto exclusively enjoyed by the first-class passenger would be bestowed henceforth also upon the second-class.

The response made to this announcement by the other railway companies was unequivocal. They scarcely attempted to conceal their fears and chagrin at the loss that might accrue to them from the sacrifice of part of their first-class receipts. Ruinous competition and retaliation against the Midland Company were threatened. "If you put your hand into our bread-basket," said a director of another company to a Midland director, "we will put our hands into your coal scuttle. Repeated conferences were held at Euston Square—"the Percy and the Douglas both together"—and minatory voices came through the closed doors. "The proposal," said the *Railway News*, "to readjust the rates for the carriage of minerals has, we know, been entertained at Euston; and this, if carried out, must very seriously affect the Midland. We believe we may say that the representatives of the two great competing companies are now taking counsel as to how, without injury to themselves, they may most efficiently retaliate upon the Midland;" and the threat succeeded in depressing the market value of railway securities to the amount of several millions sterling. Midland shareholders, if holders of other railway stocks, became alarmed. They held "indignation meetings," at one of which a director of the Lancashire and Yorkshire went so far as to indulge in a coarse personal attack upon Mr. Allport. Influential proprietors, representing a large amount of capital, sent from Liverpool and Manchester a formal document to the Derby Board, in which they said: "We protest against your proposal to do away with second-class carriages, and to reduce the fares on first-class traffic."

Meanwhile some of the leading organs of the press, instead of estimating the enormous value of the boon about to be conferred on the public, were critical, irresolute, or adverse. It was declared that the announcement of the Midland Board was "a bolt out of a blue sky." An esteemed ex-member of Parliament complained that the new policy of the Midland had been "decided upon in such profound secrecy, and sprung upon the world without any public demand." Another writer, whether complimentarily or otherwise, affirmed that Mr. Allport was "the Bismarck of railway politics." "This is not railway reform," remarked a fourth, "but revolution." "It is really and literally a revolution," observed a London daily paper, "in railway economy."

"The change," said an influential weekly journal, "is, in our opinion, most revolutionary. We feel bound to condemn the hasty step which the Midland Company has taken. . . . We should recommend railway shareholders to take the matter into their own hands." "We see no reason for ecstasies," remarked another, "over the latest move of the Midland Railway Company. . . . It will inflict great annoyance on every lady, and some annoyance on every man with a black coat, who travels by that system of lines." "A democratic and social revolution," observed another, "seems to be looming in the railway future. If the second class is to be definitively abolished," it will amount, in fact, "so long as we are upon a journey, substantially to the excision of the great middle class from English society." "The press and the public," remarked a West of England journal, in an article on the "Revolutions in the Railway World," "are against the turn-the-world-upside-down policy of the Midland." "Of all the changes," said a country journal, "possible in our railway arrangements, that which has been announced by the Midland would have been the last that would have been asked for." A legal luminary thought that the powers of the Railway Commissioners might be invoked to resist the abolition of the second class, on the ground that every railway company is bound to afford "all reasonable facilities for the receiving, forwarding, and delivering of traffic." "An era of fresh discomfort and fresh inconvenience in travelling," another authority declared, "is being prepared for us."

It would have been no wonder if, in the face of such criticism,—amid the misgivings of friends and threats of railway rivals,—the Midland Board had yielded, and had revoked their decision. Surely they might have expected a different response to the announcement of a policy so high-minded and statesmanlike. Happily they stood firm while the storm blew; and after awhile it abated. As discussion proceeded, light began to spread. The travelling public, who, as *The Times* remarked, had not at first appeared "in the least grateful for the boon," began to express themselves in its favour. *The Daily Telegraph*, referring to the complaints that the first-class passengers would henceforward have less of the luxury of exclusiveness, playfully remarked: "The real sufferers are those poor fellows the rich;" but it thought that even such might be brought to contentment with the new arrangements, if the Company would "woo these tassel-gentles back again" by the Pullman carriage, and by generally, for their behoof, "gilding the refined gold." "The highest practicable fares for the least possible accommodation," said another writer, "is henceforth to be a policy of the past;" and it began generally to be admitted that the new plan should be tried.

The Midland Board stood firm. A circular, issued by Mr. Ellis, the chairman, explained the policy of the Directors, and conciliated the confidence of the shareholders; and at a special meeting of the proprietors summoned to decide upon the matter,—though mournful warnings were uttered, and portents or pictures were painted of the Midland Company deserted by its friends, and hemmed in by its foes,—the views of the Directors were sanctioned by an overwhelming majority of votes, by proxies ten to one, and by capital represented by the proxies to the amount of six to one. As the year drew to a close, and the arrangements for the working out of the new policy came to be seen, it was found that the improvement made in the third-class carriages—with cushioned seats, and separate compartments, and wider space, and footwarmers for winter—would be so great, that the net result would be that the third-class carriage was abolished; that second and first-class carriages only were retained, with the third and second-class fares. Subsequently Lord Redesdale brought in a bill into the House of Lords, which may be described as, "An act to compel railway companies to charge first-class passengers higher fares than the companies are content to take, and to compel second-class passengers to travel in less comfortable carriages than the companies are willing to provide;" but "the wisdom of Parliament" did not encourage legislation so retrograde. Millions of passengers are now travelling with incomparably more comfort, millions are paying far lower fares than ever before, and the railway system of the country was never so popular, and so deservedly popular, as it is to-day.

In the course of the spring half-year several new lines were opened,—the Radford and Trowell; the Mansfield and Worksop, on the 1st June; the Ambergate and Codnor Park, six and a half miles long; the Clifton Extension, a mile and three quarters; and some smaller branches about a mile in length.

In July (1875) the Midland Company commenced running their own trains over the London, Chatham, and Dover line into Victoria Station, and the Chatham and Dover service was continued to Child's Hill and Hendon. An unbroken and convenient means of communication was thus established between the northern and southern suburbs.

On Monday, the 2nd of August (1875), the Settle and Carlisle Railway was opened for goods traffic. It was wisely resolved to postpone the use of the line for passengers until all the works were completed and consolidated. "We desire," the chairman publicly remarked, "whenever the passenger traffic is passed over the line, that it shall be in a perfectly satisfactory condition."

At the autumnal meeting, held August 17th, 1875, it was stated that the capital account of the Company stood at £58,560,548. It had been increased during the six months by the large sum of more than £5,600,000. Nearly half of this amount was due to the Midland and North Eastern Bill, which authorised the raising of £66,000; to the Additional Powers Act, £2,400,000; and to the Sheffield and Midland Act, £133,000, making £2,599,000. The remaining cost had been incurred by the extinction of several small companies in intimate alliance with the Midland Company, and the absorption of their capital; by a nominal addition to the capital of the Company through the consolidation of stocks as authorised by Parliament and approved by the shareholders, and by other similar financial arrangements. Among these the Birmingham and Derby capital, which had from the original amalgamation remained separate, was commuted by the granting of ordinary stock at £80 for each £100. The result of these large financial arrangements was, that, instead of the Midland capital being separated into twenty-three stocks, there are now only nine, and it is hoped that these will be reduced to five.

Mr. Ellis also announced that the traffic receipts per mile from passengers were greater than they had been for any half-year during the past twenty-five years. With regard to the large outlay of capital on additional works, the chairman mentioned that it was indispensable, "in order to keep pace with the traffic that pours in upon us," and at the same time it was necessary that railway proprietors should realize the fact that railway construction is much more costly than it was a few years ago. "Lines," said Mr. Ellis, "which then could be constructed at a cost of £30,000 a mile will certainly now cost £45,000 to £50,000 a mile. I am satisfied that I am within the mark when I say that you must add at least 50 per cent. to the cost of construction of all new lines of railway at the present time, as compared with what they would have cost six years ago."

Mr. Ellis also referred to increased cost upon almost every article or appliance used by railways. "You will see by the report," he said, "that we possess 2500 horses. I find that we are paying for them 50 per cent. more than we were paying five or six years ago. A horse suitable for our purposes, which then cost £40, we now pay £60 for. We have also to pay more for provender, much more for the labour of the men attending upon our horses; and I think you may assume that the extra cost of each horse that you possess, including wear and tear, renewals, extra keep, and wages, is not less than £20 per horse per annum. If you multiply 2500 by £20 it will give you £50,000 as the increased cost of our horses per annum; and since it costs you more than 50 per cent. of your earnings in expenses, you must double that amount, and you have to earn at least £2000 a week, or £100,000 a year, in order to pay the mere increased cost on horses. I mention this as one instance in which the expenses of this Company, and of all companies, have risen, in spite of the efforts of the Directors to keep them down."

In the course of his address Mr. Ellis gave the following interesting retrospect of railway events that had fallen within his own observation:—

"It is forty-seven years on the 17th of July last, since I attended the opening of the oldest portion of what eventually came to be the Midland system, I think with my friend Mr. Hutchinson, and perhaps one or two other shareholders now in this meeting. Then was started in England the first locomotive to convey passengers that ever ran south of Manchester. Mr. Crossley, lately our chief engineer, was present on that occasion, and there was also a gentleman, whose name I can never recollect without veneration, and that is George Stephenson. Let me say, now I mention his name, that I think we ought to have a portrait of that eminent man hung in this room. Many of the gentlemen who took part in the early progress of our railway system have left us. But we still have at this board three directors who have taken part in some of those earlier proceedings of the Midland Railway. First, there is my friend Mr. Hutchinson, who, I believe, has given many of the best years of his life to the service of the Company.* Next, there is Sir Isaac Morley, who has been chairman of one of your most important committees for upwards of twenty years. And third, there is my old friend Mr. Mercer, who has attended here almost weekly for a very great number of years. Mr. Hutchinson is the only remaining member of the Board who came on at the amalgamation of 1844. Now, if the Midland shareholders have derived some benefits from the development of the great railway system, it is very gratifying to feel that the community amidst which we live have derived equal or greater benefits."

The chairman referred to a proposal which had been made that the private ownership of wagons on the Midland system should be gradually extinguished. "I believe," he said, "there are at present something like 40,000 wagons, principally coal wagons, running about our system, these wagons being owned by 300 different proprietors. The cost and inconvenience of having to

* Mr. Hutchinson was for several years the superintendent of the Midland Counties line. He resigned this office in July, 1840. The Board requested his acceptance of £500 in acknowledgment of the special services he had rendered "in the very difficult circumstances connected with the opening of a new line," and they recommended his appointment as a director.

assort these wagons when they are mixed up together, so as to deliver them at the different collieries to which they belong, is very great; besides which, we have not the proper control of the construction of these wagons, and we think that it is very desirable that the Company should control in some way their construction. We have therefore arrived at the conclusion, after very careful and anxious consideration, that it is the duty of the Company gradually, and by consent, not by compulsion, to purchase these 40,000 wagons. To do so will, of course, require a large amount of capital, and we propose in the next session of Parliament to apply for powers to raise £1,000,000 on account of these purchases."

In the autumn (1875) it was announced that another important addition was to be made to the Midland system, by the union with it and with the London and South-Western Companies jointly of the lines known as the Somerset and Dorset railway. The lines grouped under that name were originally formed under different auspices. On the 17th of June, 1852, an act was passed authorising the construction of a railway from the harbour at Highbridge on the Bristol Channel, across the Bristol and Exeter line, with which it had a junction, to Glastonbury. Highbridge is situated on the north side of the river Brue, which is navigable to this point for vessels of 80 tons burden; and Glastonbury, about 13 miles distant, is a place of great antiquity and some modern interest. Three years later extensions were authorised to Wells and Burnham, with a pier at the latter; and the year following powers were obtained to construct another line from Glastonbury to Bruton, a distance of 12 miles. The company is also interested in the tidal harbour at Burnham. These railways constituted the Somerset Central.

The Dorset Central had a later origin. It was not till

1856 that the act was passed authorising the construction of a line from Wimborne, on the Dorchester extension of the London and South Western, to Blandford, a distance of about 10 miles. In the following year it was resolved to continue this line along the Vale of Blackmore, a distance of 24 miles, to the Somerset Central at Bruton. The capital to be expended was £400,000.

On the 1st of September, 1862, the two companies were amalgamated as the Somerset and Dorset on equal terms, the lines thus united being 66 miles in extent; and as, by an arrangement with the South-Western, they obtained access to the port at Poole, they formed a through communication between the English and the Bristol Channels.

Some nine years of an uneventful and unsatisfactory history passed away, when it was thought that some extension of the company's lines, which would secure access to the new line of the Midland at Bath, would give the company a better chance of success. Accordingly, in August, 1871, powers were obtained to construct a branch from the line at Evercreech to a junction with the Midland at Bath, and with a branch to the Bristol and North Somerset at Radstock.

The progress of the company, however, has not been encouraging; and, though the Midland brought traffic on to the line, and opened through communication over the line to Bournemouth, the Somerset and Dorset endured the sorrows of a poverty-stricken company; its engine-power was inadequate, and its arrangements defective; and though it probably did its best, the public suffered in those ways in which the public always will suffer unless a railway is fairly prosperous—a truism on which persons both in Parliament and out might reflect with profit.

This state of things continued till a few months since,

when the Midland Company, having by various leases reached Swansea, the policy of amalgamation by lease came to be the order of the day. The Great Western by these means obtained exclusive possession of most of the

SWANSEA.

large area of coal-fields covered by the Monmouthshire lines; and then, it is understood, opened negotiations with the Somerest and Dorset with the view to a similar appropriation, hoping thereby to occupy the whole territory stretching between its Bristol and Exeter extension and the South Western Company's district, and thus to secure an almost undisturbed monopoly of the West. Fortunately for the public, the Midland and South Western interposed, and concluded arrangements with the Somerset and Dorset, by which they are jointly to lease and to use it, guaranteeing the latter a certain minimum traffic receipt per mile—the amount to be gradually increased as years pass and as the resources of the district are developed. It is stated that these terms came into practical operation on the 1st of November, 1875; but, of course, the sanction of Parliament will have to be obtained in the usual way.

The Midland Company also purchased from the new Manchester South District Railway Company their rights in a projected line from Manchester, by way of Chorlton-cum-Hardy and Northenden, to Alderley.

The autumn of 1875 was marked by deluges of rain and by floods, which spread over wide districts of the country, and were injurious, and in some instances destructive, to the railway communication. The midland counties had their full share of these troubles. The river Trent rose seven yards; Burton-on-Trent was flooded, and its artesian and other wells were deluged with surface water and town sewage, and had to be emptied before they could again be used, and on one day 10,000 loaves had to be sent into the town and distributed gratuitously, to save the people from famine. The lines, towns, and villages, along the course of the river suffered seriously. Trent station became almost an island. The lower part of Nottingham was like a sea—yards in depth; till the flood had partially subsided, the traffic could not be resumed, engines and trains even then having to pass through about two feet of water; while, near Newark, the line was carried away, and a temporary bridge had to be erected before the communication could be restored. The scenes thus presented were in the highest degree remarkable, and will live long in the painful recollections of many.

CHAPTER XIII.

Who was Saint Pancras?—Historical Associations.—"An Abomination of Desolation."—Chaos and Cosmos.—The Fleet Sewer.——Level of the station.—Four acres of stowage.—A new Unit of Construction.—The roofing.—One span or two?—Construction of the roof.—Erection of the roof.—The travelling scaffold.—Moving the scaffold.—Size and strength of the roof.—Three floors of railway.—Magnitude of the work.—Cost of the work.—Colouring of the roof.—General appearance of the Station.—Mr. G. G. Scott.—Midland Grand Hotel.—Entrance hall.—Grand staircase.—Drawing and reading room.—Private and bed rooms.—Clock tower.—Basement.—"Potatoes for one!"—Refectory, laundry, etc.—The Manager.—Old St. Pancras Churchyard.—Junction with the Metropolitan.—Kentish Town.—Tottenham and Hampstead.—Belsize Tunnel.—London clay.—The tunnel under construction.—Brent Junction.—South Western Junction.—Mill Hill School.—Woodcock Hill Tunnel.—Herts.—Elstree.—Radlett.—Gorhambury and its associations.—Sopwell Nunnery.—St. Albans.—The Abbey.—Historical incidents.—Water-cresses.—Harpenden.—Beds.—The Chiltern Hills.—"The gulfy Lea."—Luton Hoo.—Luton.—Lord Wenlock.—Dallow Farm.—Geology of the district.—Harlington.—Flitwick.—Ampthill and park.—Houghton.—Geology.—Elstow.—Bedford.—Bedford and Leicester line.—Gradients.—Cost of the line.—"Which Brassey?"—The Ouse.—Sharnbrook Viaduct.—Northamptonshire.—Ironstone.—Wellingborough Viaduct.—Locomotive establishment.—Cuttings.—The Ise.—The Pytchley Hunt.—Kettering.—The Baptist Mission House.—Rushton.—The Triangular Lodge.—Leicestershire.—Market Harborough.—The Mortuary Chapel.—Glen.—"Wigston Two Steeples."—Leicester.—Historical Associations.—Humorous description by Sir. E. Beckett.—Leicester Station.—Syston.—Legends.—Barrow Line works.—Mount Sorrel works.—The Castle.—Soar Bridge.—Charnwood.—Loughborough.—The second Soar Bridge.—Doubling of the line.—Trent Bridge.—Amusing dispute.—Trent Station.—Asphalting.—Borrowash.—Elvaston Castle.—Derby.—Introduction of the silk manufacture.—Duffield Church.—Interest of scenery.—Belper.—Crich Hill.—Remarkable geological formation.—Lea Hurst.—High Peak Railway.—Willersley Castle.—The Arkwrights.—"The cradle of the cotton manufacture."—Matlock.—Darley Dale.—Seat of Sir Joseph Whitworth.—The "Peacock" at Rowsley.—Haddo Hall.—Chatsworth.—Bakewell.—Monsal Dale.—Miller's Dale and viaduct. Chee Vale and the Wye.—Beauty of the scenery.—Blackwell Dale.—Buxton.—Blackwell Junction.—The Manchester Extension.—Difficulties of the country.—Dove Holes Tunnel.—"Swallow Holes."—Difficulties discovered.—Engineering operations.—Perforation of the mountain.—Construction of the line.—English and Irish navvies.—Chapel-le-Frith Viaduct.—Bugsworth slip.—Sixteen acres of land run away.—"A wonderful slip."—Energetic measures. — Timber viaduct built. — Line reconstructed. —Traffic resumed.—New Mills.—Hayfield. — Marple. —Manchester Joint Station.—Midland Goods Station.—New Central Station. —Main line to Liverpool.—Risley Moss.—Railway Works.—Warrington.—Garston.—Central Station at Liverpool.

"AND *who* was Saint Pancras?" we inquired of a friend who was sauntering with us on the departure platform of the Midland Company's London terminus, and who eloquently expatiated on the wonders of the place. "Who?" he replied, stroking his beard and looking as wise as could be expected under the circumstances, "Why, of course, Saint Pancras was—yes—he was—that is, she was—ahem—well, to tell the truth, I haven't the faintest idea!" So we may as well mention that Saint Pancras was a Christian martyr; and that the seal of the vestry of the London parish named in his honour represents him with a sword uplifted in one hand and an olive branch in the other.*

This spot has also other interesting historic associations. Here, formerly, a principal Roman station and encampment stood; and hard by is Battle Bridge, where a great battle was fought between the Roman legions and the Britons under Boadicea. In later days the neighbourhood was devoted to pastoral pursuits; and in the time of Queen Elizabeth, Nash could send his greetings to Kemp the actor in the words: "As many alhailes to thy person as there be haicocks in Iuly at Pancredge." Afterwards the ever-encroaching metropolis drew near, and then covered the once pleasant fields with an interminable wilderness of bricks and mortar, of dwelling places and shops, of factories and "works."

* St. Pancras was the son of Cledonius, a Phrygian nobleman. At fourteen years of age he was taken to Rome by his uncle Dionysius; after whose death, being apprehended as a Christian, and persisting in that doctrine before the Emperor Diocletian, he was beheaded, A.D. 286. —Dr. Hughson's *London*.

Last of all the Midland came; and when it came wrought a mighty revolution. For its passenger station alone it swept away seven streets of three thousand houses, and a church; Old St. Pancras Churchyard was invaded; and Agar Town was almost demolished. Yet those who knew that district at that time have no regret at the change. Time was when here the wealthy owner of a large estate had lived in his mansion; but after his departure the place became a very "abomination of desolation." In its centre was what was named La Belle Isle, a dreary and unsavoury locality, abandoned to mountains of refuse from the Metropolitan dust-bins, strewn with decaying vegetables and foul-smelling fragments of what had once been fish, or occupied by knackers' yards and manure-making, bone-boiling, and soap manufacturing works, and smoke-belching potteries and brick-kilns. At the broken windows and doors of mutilated houses canaries still sang and dogs still lay sleeping in the sun, to remind one of the vast colonies of bird and dog-fanciers who formerly made Agar Town their abode; and from these dwellings wretched creatures came, in rags and dirt, and searched amid the far-extending refuse for the filthy treasure by the aid of which they eked out a miserable livelihood; while over the neighbourhood the gasworks poured their mephitic vapours, and the canal gave forth its rheumatic dampness, extracting in return some of the more poisonous ingredients from the atmosphere, and spreading them upon the surface of the water in a thick scum of various and ominous hues. Such was Agar Town before the Midland came.

But it was some time after the Midland Company resolved to occupy the ground before Cosmos arose out of Chaos. The ground was "cleared," so to speak, of its former dwellings and population; but it long presented a scene more confused and desolate than it is possible to describe. On every hand were huge mounds of earth; heaps of burning clay; the fragments of streets; and labourers digging in holes and passages thirty or forty feet below the level of the earth, apparently intent on something; but what that something was, no one could divine. Parallel with the Euston Road a mighty trench

DOUBLING OF METROPOLITAN RAILWAY.*

was made, in which eventually a tunnel was laid for the use of the Metropolitan Company, when it needs to double its present railway. Further back, another mighty cutting came sweeping round, along which the Midland Company's underground junction with the Metropolitan was to be made. So vast indeed were these subterranean operations, that the St. Pancras Station is, in fact, as a writer has remarked, "like an iceberg, the greater portion below the surface;" and, remarkable as is the engineering skill displayed in the mighty building which

* This engraving represents the scene as it appeared under what is now the *front* of the hotel. The hoarding on the left cut off the Euston Road from the works.

towers so majestically above all its neighbours, "it is as nothing compared with that, not indeed 'displayed,' but cancealed below." For right underneath the monster railway station are two other railways, one above another, and none the less wonderful because they will never see the light of day, but are "irrevocably doomed to 'waste their sweetness' on even less than desert air. These

THE FLEET SEWER.

works are the Underground Railway and the Fleet Sewer;" while the branch of the Metropolitan that joins the Midland, "not only crosses it 'slantendicularly' at the southern extremity, but thence runs up under the western side of the station, only to recross at its northern end to the eastern side, where it gradually rises to its junction about a mile down the line."

The Fleet Sewer was a very difficult work. The Underground Railway operations were "comparatively simple—the mere driving of a tunnel in a somewhat eccentric direction and through rather delicate ground. The Fleet Sewer affair involved the 'taking up' a main artery of metropolitan drainage, the diversion of a miniature—indeed scarcely a miniature—Styx, whose black and fœtid torrent had to be transferred from its bed of half-rotten bricks to an iron tunnel running in an entirely different direction, and that, too, without the spilling of 'one drop of Christian' sewage. To what signal grief came the Metropolitan Company, in its dealings with this identical difficulty, will be remembered. It is no little to the credit of the engineers of the present undertaking that, profiting, no doubt, by the experience then so dearly purchased, they have succeeded in their delicate task without an accident or a hitch."

In designing the St. Pancras Station, it was found that, in order to cross the Regent's Canal at a suitable height, and to secure good gradients and proper levels for stations at Camden Town, Kentish Town, and Haverstock Hill, it would be necessary to raise the level of the terminus from twelve to seventeen feet above the Euston Road, which passes in front; and originally it was intended to obtain this elevation by making a solid embankment of earth. Second thoughts, however, were best; for the station being bounded on three sides by roads, and the difference of elevation being such as to admit of the construction of a lower floor with direct access to these streets, it was resolved that the whole area should be preserved for traffic purposes, and that communication with the rails should be secured by means of a hydraulic lift opposite the centre of the station, at the north entrance. It was also determined that iron columns and girders, instead of brick piers and arches should be used; and, as the area was to be devoted to the accommodation of Burton beer traffic, the distances between the supports were arranged at such intervals as to allow of the largest number of barrels of beer being placed between them. These distances were found to be twenty-nine feet four inches. As the great outlines of the superstructure had necessarily to be adjusted to the position of the supports below, the unit of the entire fabric came to be founded on the length of *a barrel of beer*.

The changes thus contemplated were so important

ST. PANCRAS CELLARS.

that they led to a reconsideration of the question of roofing the station. "It became obvious," said Mr. Barlow, the consulting engineer of the Midland Company, "that if *intermediate* columns were employed, they must be carried down through the lower floor, be about sixty feet in length, and of much larger diameter than the rest of the columns under the station. Moreover, these columns must have carried large areas of roofing in addition to the flooring, involving a greatly increased weight on its foundations, which must have been enlarged accordingly; and as some of them would necessarily have been placed on the tunnel of the St. Pancras branch, special means and increased expense would have been required to carry the imposed weight at these places."

On the other hand, if an arched roof were used that spanned the station, then its floor girders would make a ready-made tie; all the usual arrangements of roller ties required in ordinary roofs to provide for the effects of variations of temperature, would be avoided; the cost of the columns and their foundations, and of a longitudinal girder to connect them, and of a valley drain between the roofs, would be saved; and the whole area would be available for station purposes. When, therefore, it is considered, says Mr. Barlow, "that the Company obtained their station in the metropolis at such great cost for land and works; that its total area, in reference to the extent of railway, is less than that of any of the other important metropolitan termini; and that the Midland system is not yet in communication with all its expected sources of traffic, —the sacrifice of a width of five or six feet, for the entire length of the most valuable part of the working space of the station, could hardly have been justified, even if the saving had been greater than is estimated. As the station has been built, the whole working area is free from obstruction of any kind; and the Company may make any alterations in the arrangements of the lines and platforms which may from time to time best suit their large and growing traffic. The roof is of great strength; it is not more costly than other roofs previously erected; and in regard to its general effect and appearance, it will probably not be deemed unsuitable for the London terminus of so great and important a system of railways as that of the Midland Company."

But we must now go down into the foundations and see how the work of construction is being carried on. In what seems to be the confusion of earthworks worse confounded, the men are laying vast quantities of concrete one-and-twenty feet down in the London clay, and fifty-four feet below the surface of the ground; on these they will build massive brick piers; the piers will carry the columns that support the floor, and each brick pier will have to stand a pressure of five-and-fifty tons. Gradually order appears. The work of 100 steam lifts, 1000 horses, and 6000 men, tell their tale. The colossal brick walls and arches which form the underground tunnels are built deep down in the cuttings prepared to receive them; 720 cast-iron columns, each thirteen inches in diameter, are set with stone bases on the piers; across the station are forty-nine main wrought-iron girders; fifteen similar ones are placed longitudinally; 2000 intermediate girders and innumerable "buckle" plates are riveted together; and thus arise four acres and a half of what will serve at once as the roof of the cellars and the floor of the future passenger station. Its strength is everywhere sufficient to carry the enormous weight of locomotives. The cost of the ironwork was £3 a square yard.

Such being the construction of the cellar and floor of the station, we may now look at the superstructure. Under ordinary circumstances, an erection of this kind would consist of two side walls with a roof resting upon them, but in this instance it may be described as all roof. The girders of the walls and roof spring directly from the undermost foundation, and the iron floor of the station takes the place of ties which hold the whole together. These roof girders, too, are of remarkable construction, resembling in their appearance a lobster's claw, from which the shorter nipper has been broken off; and instead of being set, so to speak, horizontally, they are fixed vertically in pairs, the two pointed extremities meeting, and forming a Gothic arch overhead.

In the arrangement of these girders a special contingency had to be guarded against. It was not enough, by means of massive concrete and brick foundations, to resist the pressure *downwards*, it was necessary also to provide ample resistance against all pressure *upwards*. "A building 100 feet in height by 700 in length offers, as may well be imagined, a considerable object for the attack of a gale of wind; and, being too tightly bolted together to run any risk of being blown down, like an ordinary structure of wood and brick, exchanges this danger for that of being blown bodily over, like a ship thrown on her beam ends by a squall of wind, or carried up, like an unruly umbrella, straight into the sky. To provide against these contingencies, the same piers which prevent it from sinking into the ground are also utilized to prevent its being lifted from it. Through each pier, at a distance of twenty-one feet below the surface, is run an "anchor plate" of great strength, and to the extremities of these each girder is made fast, by means of strong iron rods three inches in diameter. Each girder, therefore, if it lifts, must not only lift with it the enormous additional weight of a solid brick pier twenty-one feet in depth, but must drag this mass, like a stupendous double tooth, from the solid earth in which it is embedded."

Having provided against these two dangers, there is yet a third. Besides the weight to be supported and the lifting tendency to be restrained, there is also what is termed the lateral "thrust." In a building of ordinary construction this is partly borne by the walls on which it rests, and these are strengthened by buttresses, erected where the pressure comes. In this roof the "thrust" is resisted by the solid ground itself, in which the lower end of each girder is, as we have seen, embedded, while the iron floor of the station supplies the place of ties, and binds the whole structure together. For all structural purposes, therefore, the building was complete before any of the walls were commenced; and they are in fact mere screens or partitions, contributing in no way towards the solidity of the edifice. "In result we have an arch, not only of extraordinàry lightness and beauty, but of equally extraordinary strength; whilst in point of economy the difference in the walls and the dispensing with the ties give it obviously an almost equal advantage." The weight of each of the principal arches is fifty tons. We may add that when the roof of the station was originally designed by Mr. Barlow, it was his intention that it should at the south end "terminate against the walls, in the same way as the roofs of the Cannon Street and the Charing Cross stations. But the acceptance of Mr. Gilbert Scott's design for the station offices and hotel led to this arrangement being departed from. In the original design the hotel was carried over the upper portion of the southern range of station offices; but as it was feared the steam and smoke of the engines would find entrance into the hotel windows, Mr. Scott planned a second gable and screen for the southern end, so as to separate the passenger station from the hotel buildings."

The method by which this stupendous structure was reared was not a little remarkable. In order to provide an elevation from which the men could work to raise the girders and form the roof, a new plan was adopted. A gigantic travelling scaffold was designed by the Butterley Company, Mr. (now Sir) G. J. N. Alleyne being the manager. It consisted of two parts, each made in three divisions, so that each part of either stage could be moved separately; and eight miles in length of massive timber, 1000 tons weight, and containing about 25,000 cubic feet of timber and eighty tons of ironwork, were used in their formation. Besides these, there were more than 200 tons of timber employed in fixing them together; and 100 tons of stone and iron were usually in actual use upon them, making a total of 1300 tons; the whole of which had to be carried upon an area of the station not exceeding 90 feet in length and 200 in width; or, in other words, by not more than 96 of the iron columns planted below.

Here then was an enormous scaffolding of 1300 tons weight; but it was even more startling to discover that it stood upon wheels, that the wheels rested on rails, that the rails extended from one end of the station to the other, and that thus the same scaffolding availed for every part. The process by which the movement was accomplished was very simple. A workman was stationed at each wheel, who placed a crowbar in such a position that it could be brought to bear against the wheel. When all were ready, a signal man stood with a loose iron plate and a hammer, which were to serve as a gong, and the moment he struck it each workman pressed his crowbar lever-like against the wheel. The whole mass at once moved a distance of about an inch and a half, and this with very little exertion on the part of the men. The signal was again sounded, the movement was repeated, and any required distance was reached in a few minutes. We may add, that when the scaffolding was done with, it was bought by the Company at the rate of about 9*d.* a foot, instead of its full value of about 15*d.*, and that half of it was cut up, with which to form the wooden block pavement of the station.

No other roof of so vast a span has been attempted. It is double the width of the Agricultural Hall at Islington.

It is ten yards wider than the two arches of the Great Northern terminus, each of which is only 105 feet. We say "only"; yet it is but the other day when those arches were considered to be a triumph of modern engineering. There is in fact in the world nothing of the kind that will bear comparison with it. Yet, gigantic as "is its span,—for it measures 240 feet across, and rises to a height of 100 feet above the rail level,—and constructed as it has been of hundreds of tons of iron framing, it looks so light and pretty from below, that the first impression is that it cannot possibly bear even the glass and slate with which it has been covered. It is only when the pieces of framework are examined separately before being lifted into their places, and the elaborate system of interlacing is seen, under which each section is made to bind the other until the whole is girdered and 'tied' together in almost indissoluble bonds, that all fears vanish, and any sceptic has the ground fairly taken from beneath him."

The strength of this vast structure is, indeed, enormous, and even surprised so experienced an engineer as Mr. Barlow. One day, shortly after the roof was finished, when visiting the works, he found a party of men engaged in raising some of the iron girders which form the screen that hangs across the northern end of the roof. These men had fastened a block, not to one of the principals, but one of the cross pieces, and not at the crown of the arch, but at the side of the arch; through this block they had passed a rope, and with it they were raising masses of iron weighing up to as much as seven tons each. Mr. Barlow at once interposed; but he was assured by an experienced subordinate in charge of the details of the work, that they had lifted even heavier weights by the same means with perfect safety on the day before; and an assistant, who was directed to ascertain the deflection produced by the strain, found that it amounted to only three sixteenths of an inch, and that the moment the weight was removed the iron recovered its position.

The rapidity with which the work of erecting the station was carried on was remarkable. The last fourteen principals of the roof were placed in their position in seventeen weeks, each being 29 feet 4 inches from the other; and the slating and glazing followed at the same speed. There are two acres and a half of glass in the roof. "In consequence," says Mr. Barlow, "of a delay in obtaining face-bricks for the side walls, a considerable number of ribs were erected, boarded, slated, and glazed before the side walls were built; and in that state the roof endured several gales of wind, one of which was unusually heavy, without the slightest visible movement."

As now completed there are now three levels of railway, one above another, at this station: the lowest is the St. Pancras branch down to the Metropolitan; it crosses on a curve obliquely from the western to the eastern side. Above this are the rails of the lower floor which communicates with the street; and above this again are the rails and platforms of the passenger station. There is also the portion of the second line of the Metropolitan Railway, which passes under the end of the hotel and under the southern approaches of the station. Of the magnitude of the work generally, some idea may be gathered from the fact that in the station and its approaches some 60,000,000 of bricks, 9000 tons of iron, and 80,000 cubic feet of fourteen different kinds of dressed stone have been employed.

It may be interesting to add that the twenty-four main ribs, with bolts, ornamental spandrils, etc., cost something more than £1000 apiece. It is estimated that a roof with two spans instead of one would have cost only about £6000 less. With reference to the colouring of the roof of the station, an important improvement has lately been made. When originally completed, it was of a dark-brown hue, and looked heavy and dull. "Its colour," said Mr. Allport, in a discussion on the subject of the St. Pancras Terminus, which took place before the Institution of Civil Engineers, "in his opinion marred, to some extent, the grand appearance which the station would otherwise have exhibited. He thought the colouring of a roof ought, as much as possible, to be made to represent nature; and he certainly never saw a sky the colour of that roof—not even when it was cloudy. He had discussed this matter with Mr. Barlow and Mr. Gilbert Scott on several occasions, and he believed the latter had come round to the opinion, that the colouring ought to be different from what it was. Nature, it had been said, never erred; and in colouring walls nature should be imitated as closely as possible. When the sky was cloudy, it was a light white colour, or pale grey; ordinarily it was a beautiful blue, sometimes tinged with tints of vermilion and gold." Mr. Allport's arguments have, happily, prevailed; and the roof of St. Pancras station has recently been repainted and decorated with a blue sky-like appearance.*

Of the general appearance of the St. Pancras terminus the reader can judge for himself. Occupying a site in the Euston Road, between the Great Northern and London and North Western stations, it is incomparably more complete and ornate than either of them. The design of the station offices and hotel is from the pencil of Mr. G. Scott; it was selected from a number sent in

* Objection has been made by observers to the disfigurement of the station by the advertisements upon some of the walls. The only argument to be advanced in their favour is, that they bring into the pockets of the Midland shareholders something like £1000 a year.

for competition; and is in the ornate Pointed Gothic style. The total frontage is about 600 feet. It is not too much to say that "it is one of the chief architectural ornaments of the metropolis,"—that it is "a veritable railway palace." As another authority has declared, it is "the most perfect in every possible respect in the world."

Before we take our place in the train, and journey over the Midland system, there is one part of the station which deserves special notice. It is the Grand Hotel, which, when completed in a few weeks, will be unsurpassed and probably unequalled for combined comfort and magnificence in Europe. The other day we had the pleasure, in company with the manager, of seeing over it from the laundries and kitchens to the summit of the clock tower, and it may be interesting to our readers to know in detail what the final arrangements will be.

The entrance into the hotel for foot passengers and carriages will be direct from the Euston Road into the western curved wing. Alighting under a magnificent porch, the guest will find himself in a large hall. Immediately to the right are the offices of the manager, for "information," and of the bedroom clerk; and on the left is one for hall porters, and for letters and parcels. Passing along the corridor, there is a small sitting or waiting room on the left; then a gentlemen's lavatory; and above, up a mezzenin, or half-flight of stairs, a ladies' lavatory. Further on is the passenger lift, and in a recess to our left the luggage lift, both of which ascend to the fifth story, and are worked by hydraulic power. Immediately to our right we enter the general coffee room, which sweeps along the whole curved wing of the building, 100 feet long by 30, and 24 feet high, and ventilated with shafts. Close by are the waiters' pantry and the still-room, whence dinners and tea and coffee are served.

Turning through a door at our left, we find ourselves at the foot and in front of the grand staircase. It rises to the third floor, is lighted by three two-light windows which continue up to the roof, a height of 80 feet, and are divided by four transom windows; the whole being crowned by a groined ceiling, with stone ribs and carved bosses at the intersections, filled in with Portland concrete a foot thick, the face being finished with Parian cement, which some day will be coloured and decorated. The groined ribs spring from stone corbels, and are supported by green Irish polished marble columns.

Ascending the first floor of this staircase, on turning to the right we again pass the lifts and lavatories, and reach the general drawing and reading room, a spacious and beautifully decorated and furnished apartment. The five front windows look into Euston Road, over a terrace, which will be adorned with flowers and plants, and covered with an awning in summer. Three side windows look westward down Euston Road, and three others eastward along the whole frontage of the building. From hence we enter the music room, another splendidly furnished apartment; and immediately adjoining there will be "the private coffee room," for the use of which it is intended to make a somewhat higher charge, in order to keep it more select. We are now near the west end of the corridor, which runs from one end of the building to the other, a total distance of some 600 feet, and conducting to the noble suites of bedrooms and sitting-rooms with which present visitors to the hotel are familiar.

We pass along the deep-piled silent Axminster carpet. On our right are suites of rooms, with a balcony in front, looking out upon the wide space in front of the hotel and on to the Euston Road. The spacious and lofty apartments, the handsome furniture, the Brussels carpets, the massive silken or woollen curtains, and the pinoleum blinds; the wardrobes, chests of drawers, clocks, writing tables, sofas, arm-chairs, with which they are supplied, leave nothing to be desired by the wealthiest and the most refined. On the north side of the corridor are apartments equally well appointed, side by side with others less spacious; while on the floors above there are from three to four hundred other bedrooms, of various sizes, but all finished and furnished with completeness. Yet all are to be enjoyed with such moderation of cost that it is obvious that the design of the Company has not been how to make the largest amount of profit out of the hotel, but to give the largest amount of comfort to their passengers.

Continuing our ascent of the grand staircase, we reach the second floor. This is wholly occupied by private apartments and single bedrooms. The western wing can easily be extended so as to give, on four floors, fifty additional bedrooms.

From the eastern end of the fifth floor we enter a room which leads into the clock tower. Here we climb a series of iron ladders, and at length find ourselves out on the open, 130 feet above the ground. Above are the four faces of the clock. They are of iron and glass; they are thirteen feet in diameter; and they are illuminated at night. The hour hands are three feet seven inches, and the minute hands six feet in length. This clock, as well as that over the platform, was constructed by Mr. John Walker, of Cornhill, London.* From our lofty elevation outside the clock tower we look around and beneath. Far below is the mighty roof of the station itself, with

* The platform clock dial is of slate. It is eighteen feet in diameter. The length of the hour hand is four feet five, and that of the minute hand seven feet three. It is the largest clock at any railway station in England.

its ribs and ridges of glass and iron. There are also the Great Northern Station and Hotel, both seeming dwarfed in their proportions by the contrast with the Midland. The dome of St. Paul's and the column of the Monument are beneath the level on which we stand; while for miles in all directions stretch interminable lines of streets, the roofs of countless thousands of houses, the spires of churches, and the vast black swollen receivers of gas-works; while just beneath us, adorning a lofty pinnacle of the hotel, a giant figure of Britannia looks benignly over to the east, with her trident in her hand, but, sad to say, with an electric rod thrust into the crown of her head! The clock tower itself is 240 feet in height.

We descend into the basement of the hotel, where, however, there are more departments of interest than we can stay to describe. We walk over the sawdust-strewn floors to the bottling room, where the bottler is at work; cellar after cellar is unlocked for us, where perhaps £10,000 worth of wine is treasured up in thirty-six gallon casks piled one upon another, or stored away in stacks of bottles arranged with geometrical precision in open wooden bins. Here is the plate room, where the elegant handiwork of Messrs. Elkington is cleaned and placed ready for use. Now we stand in the kitchen, before a fireplace with a vast iron screen full of iron cupboards that keep plates, dishes, and covers hot for use; and turning back the screen, we see the huge fire, in front of which a couple of dozen joints could be cooked at once. "Potatoes for one," says a voice behind us, for an order to that effect has come on a ticket down the lift; "potatoes for one," repeats a subordinate, who with a little gum sticks a ticket on the handle of the cover under which the said potatoes are immediately deposited; a warning bell rings, and the lift carries ticket and potatoes swiftly away to their destination. And as with the potatoes so with ten thousand other commodities and comestibles every day.

We linger for a moment in the refectory, where the chief pastrycook and his assistants are at work. A wedding party is at breakfast upstairs, and we watch the cunning skill with which the wondrous piles of viands of magic mould and brilliant hue and wondrous delicacy have been reared, the builder striving to deceive even the connoisseur as to the composition of the dish before him, and to make him feel, as he thrusts his spoon into the mystic mass, that he is solving a cònundrum. Here is a mighty salmon girt around the ribs with a gorgeous wrapping, and with a parsley crown about his neck,—a victim adorned for sacrifice; while there, in one fell pile, the breasts of a whole covey of partridges lie in a rounded glistering tomb of jelly.

We pause for moment to cool ourselves before the bed of ice covered with canvas, on which rest fowls, game, and fish, oysters in their shells and shell-less. We notice in the next apartment that the vegetables are cooked by steam, in iron steam-chests (fortunately guarded with safety valves); and then we are in the boiler room, with two boilers of 16 horses each, which alternately supply steam and steam-power for the whole establishment.

Hard by is the laundry. Here the washing machine, six feet in diameter, boils by steam and washes to a snowy hue from 2500 to 3000 pieces of linen a day of average size; in twenty minutes the centrifugal wringing machine will extract all the water; and after having passed through the drying closets, the heated rollers of the two steam mangling machines will bring them a stage nearer fitness for use; and finally the airing room will, we dare say, finish them off. But of that we know nothing except that from the fervent heat of its threshold we made a precipitate retreat. The linen of visitors staying at the hotel is got up in a department by itself. Whichever of these subterranean abodes we visited, order, cleanliness, and method seemed to reign supreme.

Among the minor arrangements we may mention that the ventilation of the kitchens is conducted up the "service" staircase and shaft, being completely separated from the establishment generally; that a dust shaft runs from the top floor to the bottom, provided with a closed mouth on each for the reception of dust, and terminating in a fireproof cistern; that apparatus for the prevention and extinction of fires is provided in all parts of the hotel; that electric bells and speaking tubes run in all necessary directions, giving the maximum of accommodation with the minimum of noise; and that an office for the receipt of letters is found on every floor, a leaden weight coming down from the top to the bottom each time the letters are despatched, in order to prevent any one of them being by chance lodged in the tube in its descent.

We may add that the manager, Mr. Etzensberger, has for many years had charge of the Victoria Hotel, in Venice, and also for several years the commissariat of the Nile steamers as far as the first cataract; and we have no doubt that the hotel will fulfil the prediction of Augustus Sala, that it is "destined to be one of the most prosperous, as it is certainly the most sumptuous and the best conducted hotel in the empire."

But our train is alongside the departure platform, ready to start; so we must away, asking our kind reader to accompany us in our journey, and we will endeavour to beguile the way by telling some facts of interest with regard to the Midland line over which we travel, and by pointing out some objects worthy of special notice in the scenes among which we pass.

The train has scarcely left the platform of the station, when we find that we are crossing over the graveyard that belongs to Old St. Pancras Church. The difficulty of carrying the line here without any avoidable disturbance of the graves of the dead was extreme; and, although every precaution was adopted, it is said that a serio-comic incident occurred. "The company had purchased a new piece of ground in which to re-inter the human remains discovered in the part they required. Amongst them was the corpse of a high dignitary of the French Romish Church. Orders were received for the transhipment of the remains to his native land, and the delicate work of exhuming the corpse was entrusted to some clever grave-diggers. On opening the ground they were surprised to find, not bones of one man, but of several. Three skulls and three sets of bones were yielded by the soil in which they had lain mouldering. The difficulty was, how to identify the bones of a French ecclesiastic amid so many. After much discussion, the shrewdest gravedigger suggested that, being a foreigner, the darkest coloured skull must be his. Acting upon this idea, the blackest bones were sorted and put together, until the requisite number of rights and lefts were obtained. These were reverently screwed up in a new coffin, conveyed to France, and buried with all the pomp and circumstance of the Roman Catholic Church."

After passing the churchyard, we cross over the Regent's Canal. Here during the construction of the works was a scene of the busiest activity. "Engines," said a writer at the time, "are flitting to and fro, dragging trains loaded with bricks to the station, and returning laden with clay. Employed in the manufacture of the bricks are two machines that turn out 20,000 each per day, and two others that manufacture 10,000 each per day. These are dried and burnt by a new mode, which is the invention of a German, and while the bricks are being burnt, the clay mould is drying. The building in which this is done is circular, divided into 24 cells, each capable of receiving 15,000 bricks. A chimney passage goes from the interior of each cell to a centre shaft, and the roof of the cells forms the drying ground for the clay. Over the whole is a light tile roof. By this arrangement the most important processes in brickmaking are carried on independently of the weather."

The line now passes under the North London Railway by a bridge of three arches; and their construction was a matter of no ordinary difficulty, on account of the ceaseless traffic on the lines above; it was, however, accomplished without the interruption of an hour. The Midland main line is here joined on the right by the branch which comes up from the Metropolitan. The lines actually converge near the Camden covered way; but the point for the transfer of passengers is at Kentish Town station, where every arrangement is provided for the interchange of communication between the Midland, the Metropolitan, and the London, Chatham and Dover systems.

Immediately north of Kentish Town is a locomotive establishment, with sheds for 48 engines. Here, too, the Tottenham and Hampstead branch line diverges to the left, and, rising by a steep gradient, passes over the main line, and bears away to the right. By its means access is obtained to several suburbs of interest in the north of London; and also, *viâ* Stratford, to the Victoria Docks, and to the Great Eastern system generally. It is a matter of great convenience to residents in the west of the metropolis, that they can travel to many of the chief towns on the Great Eastern, *viâ* St. Pancras, instead of having to go as far east as Broad Street. This is the route usually taken by the Prince of Wales when he goes down to Sandringham.

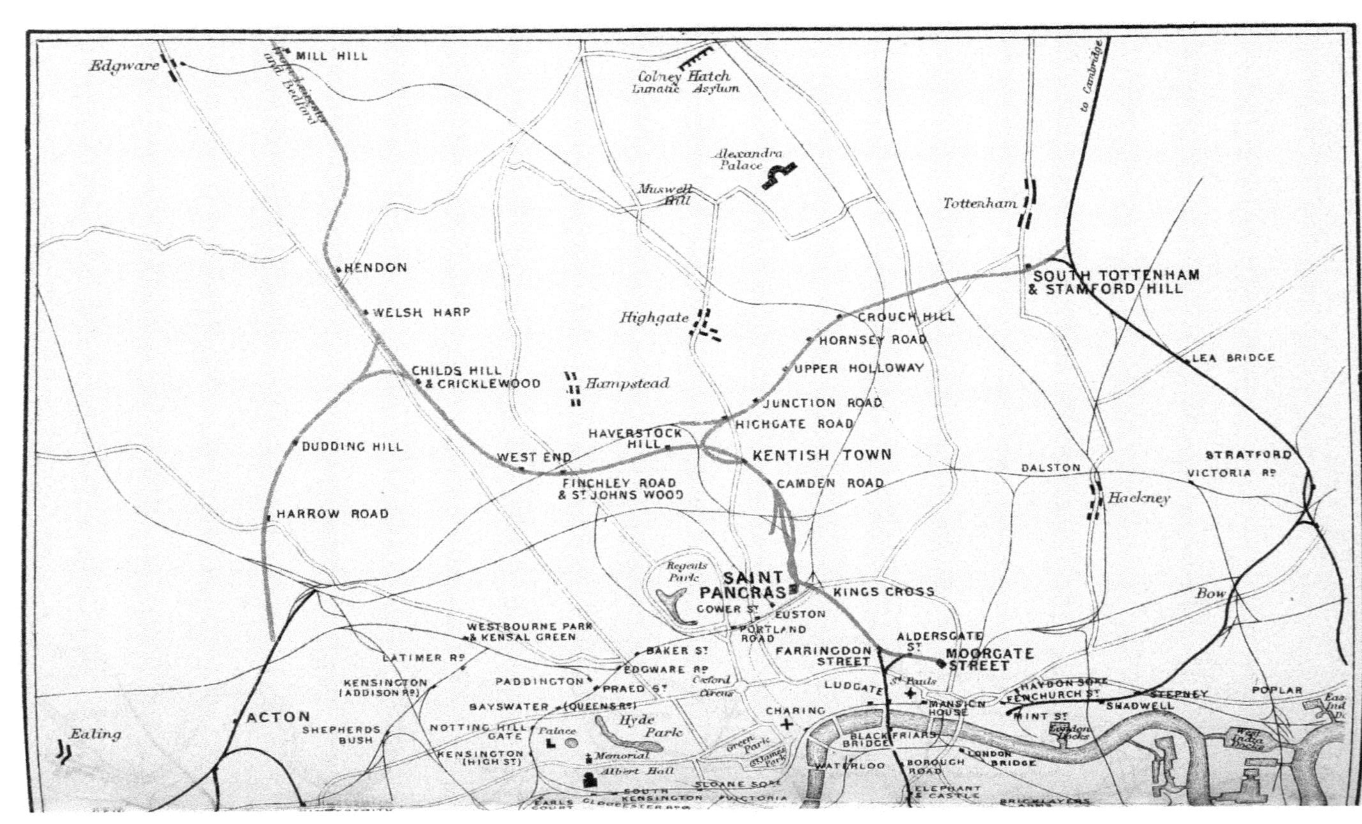

Edgware
MILL HILL
from Leicester and Bedford
Colney Hatch Lunatic Asylum
to Cambridge
Alexandra Palace
Muswell Hill
Tottenham
HENDON
WELSH HARP
Highgate
SOUTH TOTTENHAM & STAMFORD HILL
CROUCH HILL
HORNSEY ROAD
UPPER HOLLOWAY
LEA BRIDGE
CHILDS HILL & CRICKLEWOOD
Hampstead
JUNCTION ROAD
HIGHGATE ROAD
HAVERSTOCK HILL
KENTISH TOWN
DUDDING HILL
WEST END
FINCHLEY ROAD & ST JOHNS WOOD
CAMDEN ROAD
DALSTON
STRATFORD
VICTORIA RD
Hackney
HARROW ROAD
Regents Park
SAINT PANCRAS
KINGS CROSS
Bow
GOWER ST
EUSTON
PORTLAND ROAD
WESTBOURNE PARK & KENSAL GREEN
BAKER ST
FARRINGDON STREET
ALDERSGATE ST
MOORGATE STREET
LATIMER RD
EDGWARE RD
KENSINGTON (ADDISON RD)
PADDINGTON
PRAED ST
Oxford Circus
LUDGATE
St Pauls
HAYDON SQRE
FENCHURCH ST
STEPNEY
POPLAR
BAYSWATER
(QUEENS RD)
CHARING
MANSION HOUSE
MINT ST
SHADWELL
ACTON
Ealing
SHEPHERDS BUSH
NOTTING HILL GATE
Palace
Hyde Park
Green Park
St James Park
BLACKFRIARS BRIDGE
London Docks
West India Docks
KENSINGTON (HIGH ST)
Memorial
Albert Hall
WATERLOO
BOROUGH ROAD
LONDON BRIDGE
SOUTH KENSINGTON
SLOANE SQRE
ELEPHANT & CASTLE
VICTORIA

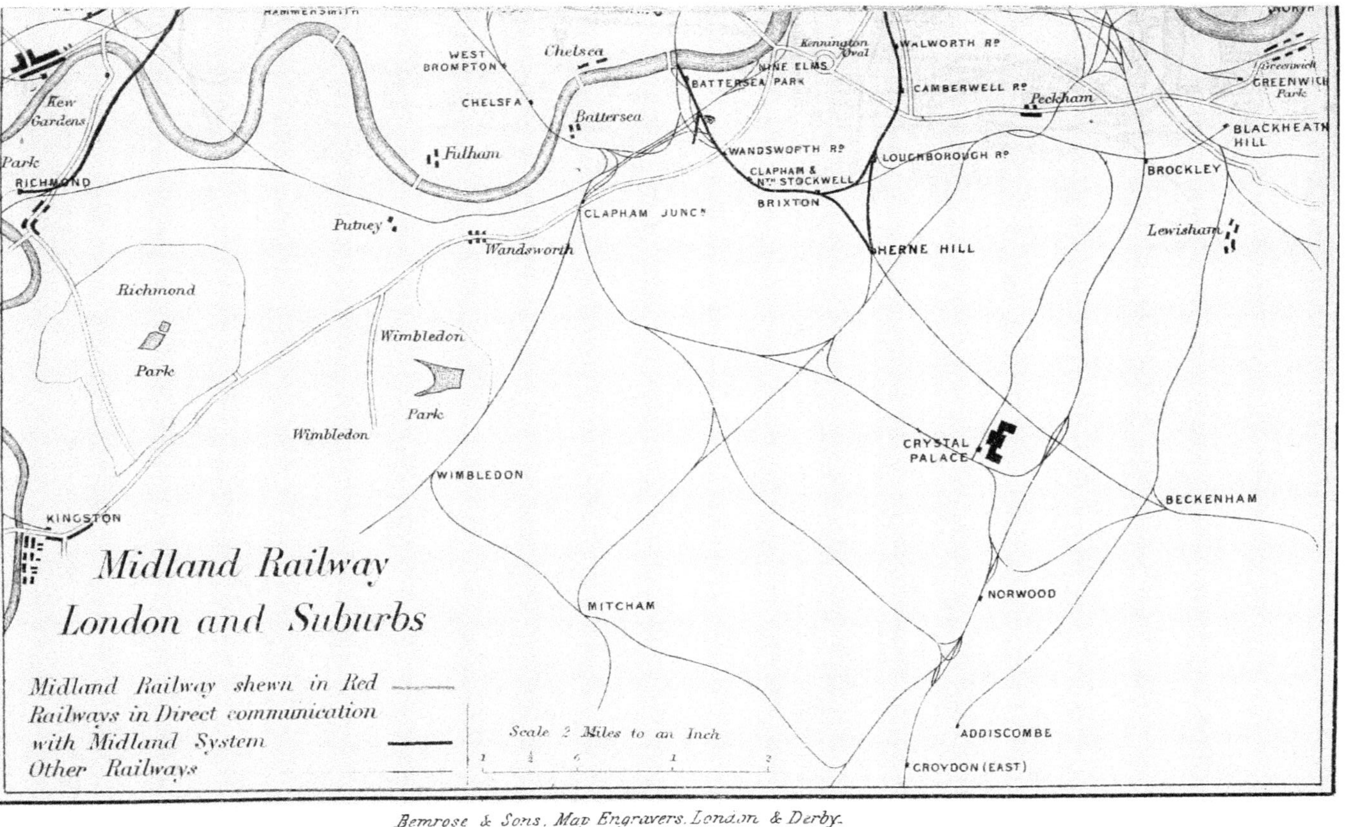

Bemrose & Sons, Map Engravers, London & Derby.

A little north of Kentish Town we pass Haverstock Hill Station. Here in the cutting we observe that, in addition to the massive retaining walls erected on either hand, iron girders stretch across the line from wall to wall to help to resist the inordinate pressure of the London clay. At the entrance to Belsize Tunnel it was found necessary even to erect a series of arches or bridges over

BELSIZE TUNNEL, SOUTH ENTRANCE.

the line, the lights and shadows of which, as the traveller passes under them, have a surprising effect.

This London clay, though troublesome to the engineer, has however its merits. Of it London is built. It fills up what was an ancient gulf of the ocean, and varies from 300 to 600 feet in thickness. Its dark tough soil is occasionally intermixed with green and ferruginous sand and variegated clays, and it contains enormous quantities of organic remains. The fossils of this deposit,—crabs, lobsters, and other crustacea, and leaves, fruits, stems of plants, and trunks of trees,—are innumerable. And it may not make a railway journey through these clay cuttings less interesting when we know that we are riding where crocodiles and turtles have formerly walked, and where nautili have spread their sails to the wind.

We have now entered Belsize Tunnel. The ceremony of laying the first brick of this important work took place on the 27th of January, 1865, at Barham Park, and was in the midst of a driving snowstorm, and of a foot deep of half melted snow. A score or thirty gentlemen assembled to support Mr. Price, then the deputy chairman of the Midland Company, who was to officiate on the occasion; and the brick, bearing his initials, was laid some five feet below the surface of the ground in a circular cutting that would eventually form the shaft; "the said brick being destined, by the gradual undermining of the earth beneath, to take its place at the bottom of the shaft, where it joins the top of the tunnel." A short and lively address from Mr. Price released the shivering group from their duty, and they adjourned to a large timber shed, where the contractor had provided luncheon; where, as the deputy chairman remarked, each sought to "manifest an honourable rivalry to excel;" and where "an amount of energy and cheerful industry" were witnessed which had only to be imitated by other labourers on the field, and eventually all material obstructions to their great enterprise would pass away.

During the subsequent progress of this work the scene presented was one of much interest, though perhaps to many it could scarcely be called attractive. "We obtain access to the tunnel," says a writer, whose vivid description we are happy to quote, "through the contractor's yard, quite a little town in itself, with its offices, dwellings, workshops, stables, etc. About 150 men are employed in or near the yard, and it is the home of above 100 horses. Mr. Firbank has about 1300 men employed upon his length, and many portions of the work are prosecuted night and day without intermission. The tunnel is about a mile and a quarter in length, and in many parts above 100 feet deep. The stuff, or 'muck,' as our guide seemed accustomed to call it, is uniformly clay, but not uniform in its density. In some cases it has been met with so hard as to require to be blasted by gunpowder. We have heard of many stories that have been considered apocryphal, of live toads being found in blocks of stone and coal; but it is a true story, we believe, that in this tunnel a live frog has been found, imbedded in the stiff clay, at a depth of 80 feet from the surface.

"There are five shafts to the tunnel, two of which are to be permanent. We did not splash through the clay,—it was too tough for splashing; but getting to the shaft mouth,—and dodging the two gin horses that are employed to raise and lower the workmen, to haul up the clay, and to lower the timber, bricks, mortar, and other materials,—we sprawled the best way we could into one of the clay wagons, and were swung off and let down to the bottom. On our way we asked our guide (who answered any question put to him very cheerfully, but was by no means a speechmaker) 'What is that pipe for? and that? and that?' And the answers were, 'for air, water, and gas.' And so, sure enough, we found, when we got bumped out at the bottom, and hastened, to the serious damage of our shins, from under the dripping wet and very heavy pellets which kept descending the shaft, that the tunnel is actually lit with gas, and supplied with water and air from the upper regions. We had no occasion to make a note that the expenditure of gas was on a profligate scale.

"The lights, however, were only where the workers needed them, and we gladly accepted a tallow candle, with an improvised clay socket, to light us on our way in this Plutonian region. About eighty yards on each side of the bottom of the shaft there is a species of illumination, and strange sounds proceed from both quarters. Passing along in one direction we reach the lights, and find about a dozen men at work, half a dozen with pick-axes tearing away at the tough clay, and accompanying every stroke with a stentorian noise, half grunt, half groan, which may be a help, but which we thought a waste of lung power; other men were constantly employed in filling the loosened clay into the railway trucks, which run on a gauge 1 foot 7½ inches, and other two in pushing the filled trucks to, and the empty ones back from, the shaft bottom. The miners are protected by immensely strong shorings, which are shifted from time to time as need requires. Leaving the navvies at the end, we floundered to the other end of the tunnel, and there found half a dozen bricksetters casing the 12 feet length which had been cleared for them by the navvies. We may here remark that this is the uniform practice in each of the five shafts. Navvies having cleared a length of 12 feet, the centres are put up, and the bricklayers take their place, the miners proceeding to another end. Both of these classes work night and day continuously by relays. Some of the labourers in the tunnel work for two days and the intervening night without cessation. The finished tunnel is about 25 feet wide, and about 26 feet from the crown of the arch to the bottom of the invert. The brickwork is 3 feet 6 inches thick all round. There are 33 cubic yards of brickwork in each lineal yard of tunnel, and every 12 feet length consumes 50,000 bricks.

"Returning up the shaft, we observe that it has bands

of elm, which we learn are about ten inches by six, placed at distances of six feet. These were used, we believe, for the travelling downwards of the brickwork, which was commenced near the surface, and let down by gradual excavation—a method common in the construction of colliery shafts. The walls of the two permanent shafts, one of which is twelve feet and the other fifteen feet in diameter, have to be lined with blue Staffordshire bricks, which are almost as hard as iron, and impervious to moisture. The walls of the shaft will then be about eighteen inches thick.

"There is nothing very wonderful about boring a hill right on from one side, and coming through at the other, within a few yards to the right or left, higher or lower, than was intended; but we confess to regard it as a great triumph of science and of engineering skill, that ten sets of men should be let down one hundred feet below the surface of the earth, and that two other sets should be set to work on the sides of the hill, and that all the twelve parties should meet, not in a zig-zag hole, but with an opening, even in roof, sides, and bottom, of a massive and costly tunnel."

We may add that the tunnel runs askew under the well-known grove of trees on the hill of Belsize Park, the line being 120 feet beneath them. On emerging from the tunnel we pass under a railway, which is carried by a bridge over our heads. It is the Hampstead Junction of the London and North Western Company, running from Camden Town to Willesden.

We now approach a place of some importance in the administration of the London goods and mineral traffic of the Midland Company—the Brent Junction. Here more than 150 acres of land have been obtained for the use of the locomotive department, and especially for the marshalling of trains for the various lines in the neighbourhood of London to which the Midland has access, or for their being re-marshalled as empties for the down traffic of the Midland Company. Here also the South Western Junction bears away to the left, commu-

BRIDGE UNDER HAMPSTEAD JUNCTION.

nicating with the South Western system; and over it through Midland trains run direct to Richmond and other places to the south of the Thames. Access is also obtained from hence to Clapham Junction, which, Mr. Venables remarked, "is the road to everywhere."

Leaving Hendon, the line runs in a direct course for many miles; and to the left of it, and almost parallel with it, is the old Roman road to St. Albans. A little more than a mile from Hendon, and nine miles from St. Pancras, a railway passes under the Midland. It is a branch of the Great Northern, and runs from that Company's main line, by Highgate and Finchley, to Edgware, which is about a mile and a half left of the Mill Hill Station of the Midland Railway. Here, upon the wooded hills to the right, may be seen the stately façade of Mill Hill School, under the able and successful presidency of Dr. Wearmouth. Its religious teaching is unsectarian.

We are now passing through a district singularly rich and pleasant, which will doubtless become a favourite suburb of the metropolis; and soon we reach the northern confines of the county. When we enter Woodcock Hill by Elstree tunnel, 1060 yards long, we are still in Middlesex; before we have emerged at the northern end we are in Herts. The boundary, unless we can see through the carriage roof and the tunnel top, is invisible, for it is along the summit of the hill. On emerging from the tunnel, we have passed the village on our left. It stands on elevated ground, near the site of the Roman station of Sullonicæ, one of the three principal Roman stations connected with this county of which any traces remain. The manor was granted by Offa to St. Alban's Abbey. The village, though ancient and small, stands in four parishes.

The county of Herts which we are now crossing has many features of interest. "There is scarce one county in England," wrote Camden, that "can show more footsteps of antiquity;" and in the earliest times, he tells us, its hills gave shelter, its woods fuel and timber, and its rich valleys and winding rivers furnished pasturage and food. "Its sweet, clean, and very beautiful air," says a later writer, "led many of our kings to build palaces in the county for their own residence, as well as for the training of their children." Nobles and gentlemen followed the example, so that the county became subdivided into a large number of comparatively small estates; and the competition for land became so keen that it was a common saying, that "He who buys land in Hertfordshire, pays two years' purchase for the air."

At one time silk and cotton were largely manufactured in this county. Turnips were first introduced here in the time of Cromwell, who gave £100 to the farmer as a reward for his enterprise; and wheat, at Wheathempsted, on the Lea, is so fine, that it has given its name to the district.

Geologically, the county forms part of the London chalk basin. There are some 47,000 acres of chalk in Herts, and we shall see much of it. Three miles from Elstree we reach Radlett station, which at one time it was proposed to name Aldenham, after another village in the neighbourhood. Soon after leaving Radlett, we cross over the little stream of the river Colne, and immediately afterwards pass on the left what some will consider to be the most picturesque residence on the Midland line; while the cedars of Lebanon that adorn the park give dignity to the scene. It is Parkbury Lodge, formerly occupied by the Marquis of Blandford.

We now run in an almost straight line till we come in sight of the town and abbey of St. Albans, to the left of which we see the wooded hills of Gorhambury, where Lord Bacon had his country residence. This place derived its name from one De Gorham, who, in the twelfth century, built a mansion, which being called Gorham-Bury, gave its name to the estate. Two hundred years afterwards it was re-annexed to the abbey, to which it had previously belonged; some 200 years later Henry VIII. gave it away; and subsequently Gorhambury was sold to Nicholas Bacon, Lord Keeper of the Great Seal of Queen Elizabeth.

At a short distance westward of the old mansion, Sir Nicholas erected a new one. Here he was frequently visited by the queen, who dated many state papers from Gorhambury. It is recorded that one day, when Sir Nicholas was "under the hands of his barber, and the weather being sultry, he ordered a window before him to be thrown open." Being corpulent he fell asleep, and on awaking found himself in a cool draught, and "distempered all over." "Why," he demanded of the servant, "did you suffer me to sleep thus exposed?" The man replied, that it was because he durst not awake his master. "Then," said the Lord Keeper, "by your civility I lose my life;" and in a few days afterwards he died.

But while we have been telling this story of Gorhambury, and long before we have finished it, we have passed another spot of interest, Sopwell Nunnery, and reached St. Albans. Sopwell Nunnery was founded in 1140, on, it is said, the site of a humble dwelling constructed of branches of trees by two women, who lived here in abstinence and seclusion. Tradition gives us an unlikely derivation from the fact that these women were wont to sop their crusts in a neighbouring well, and thus gave the name to the place. There were thirteen sisters, for whose support sundry estates were left. In 1541, Henry VIII. gave the site and buildings to Sir Richard Lee, who enlarged the premises as a dwelling, and the surrounding grounds he enclosed as a park with a wall.

"The ruins," says Brayley, "are mostly huge fragments of wall of flint and brick; the windows in what appear to have been the chief apartments are square and large, with stone frames; some of them have been neatly ornamented." The gardens, he remarks, are now orchards; and in a wall over the door leading into the principal one is a square tablet of stone, sculptured with a figure holding a broken sword. In an angle in this garden is a strongly arched brick building, with recesses and niches in the walls. "One of the outbuildings is yet standing at a little distance, and is used as a barn."

Verulam was an important British city, and, according to the Roman historians, more ancient than London. British coins, said to have been struck here, bore the name of Ver. Under the Romans the town attained the dignity and privileges of a free city; but this honour was dearly purchased by bringing upon it the vengeance of the hosts of Boadicea. Subsequently, however, it rose to its former lustre as a Roman city. During the persecution of the Christians under Diocletian, Albanus or Alban was here martyred; and in order to inspire terror in others of his faith, the story of his death was inscribed on marble and built into the prison walls. Yet within a few years after the cessation of that persecution, a church was founded in honour of his memory, on the spot where the abbey church of St. Albans now stands; and the marble that told the tale of his shame was removed, and memorials of his fidelity were erected, both there and over the city gates.

The massiveness of the ruined walls, twelve feet in thickness, built of flint and Roman tiles; their wide extent; the immense embankments, called the Verulam hills, and the deep ditches against them; the traces of temples; the innumerable coins and other antiquities,—not to mention what Camden tells about marble pillars and cornices, and statues of silver and gold,—afford abundant testimony of the magnificence of this ancient city.

Many a remarkable story, too, is told in the annals of yonder abbey. How it was enriched with costly garments and vessels, and with the relics of the saint, one of which, we are assured, was restored by monks from Nuremberg, who said that Canute had brought it to them. How the abbey was relieved from all ecclesiastical jurisdiction except that of the Pope himself. How Henry II. withstood the Pope, and kept the abbacy vacant for months; and how, when afterwards it was filled up, and the then Bishop of Lincoln wished to reassume jurisdiction, the king demanded: "What is it, my lord of Lincoln, that you would attempt? Do you think these things were done in secret? I, myself, and the most chosen men of the realm, were present; and what was then done is ratified by writings the most incontestible, and confirmed by the testimony of the nobles. The determination stands good; and whoever sets himself to combat this abbot and monastery, combats me. What seek you? to touch the apple of mine eye?" How it is recorded, many a year afterwards, that the abbey was furnished with the modern device of chimneys, probably the first occasion on which such an event is recorded. How within sound of its walls the battle of

ST. ALBANS.

St. Albans was fought in 1455, the king, Henry VI., being present; and a second battle a few years afterwards. How in the reign of "bloody Mary," "a little heap of ashes and a blackened circle on the grass" on the Abbey Green told that another martyr had fallen at St. Albans for the truth of God; and how eventually the monastery was dissolved, and its lands divided:—all these are chronicles of undying interest and pathos, but over which we may not longer linger.

To turn to conventional railway matters, we may mention that the staple trade of the town is gentlemen's straw hats; ladies' hats being made at Luton. St. Albans is also a great place for watercresses. "When they are in season, and it is warm weather," remarked the station master, "we send away perhaps two tons or more a night, for months together. They go chiefly to London and Manchester, and are packed in hampers containing half a hundredweight each. The watercress beds extend for five or six miles over this district. They are regularly planted: a stone is placed on a bit of the stem, and in due time the whole becomes a mass of green."

Leaving St. Albans we pass among beautiful hills and dales, woods and meadows, farms and farmsteads, till we see on the left an open common, running over the hillsides, and we soon reach the pretty village of Harpenden, nestling down along the side of the valley to the left of the line, and almost embosomed in wood. This place, familiarly called Harden, belonged in the reign of Edward I. to a family named De Hoo. The church appears to have been erected in Norman times. It is built in the form of a cross, with a tower at the west end.

A mile north of Harpenden we run through Westfield Wood, soon after through Ashfield Wood; and we think of the time when these Chiltern Hills were covered with dense forests, the haunts of wild bulls and stags, of bears and wolves, and the hiding-places of outlaws and robbers. We now see a river and a railway approaching us from the right. The former is the Lea, which gives its name to Luton and Leagreave,—"the gulfy Lea with sedgy tresses," as Pope said; "the wanton Lea, that oft doth lose its way," as Spenser declared. The railway is the Luton and Dunstable branch of the Great Northern. It diverges from the main line between Hatfield and Welwyn, and, bending to the west, here passes under the Midland line, and proceeds with a devious course on through Luton to Dunstable. Immediately after we have passed over it we cross the Lea, and are in Bedfordshire. From hence on to Luton the view is very beautiful. We look down from the embankment upon the rich masses of beech and birch woods that encircle the waters, the park, and the mansion of Luton Hoo, one of the noblest residences in this county. It was reconstructed and improved by John Earl of Bute. The river Lea, which meanders through the park, has been formed into a lake nearly a quarter of a mile in width, with islands and plantations, at the foot of the eminence on which the house is seated, and the grounds have had every improvement that could enrich a situation naturally picturesque and beautiful. The whole is the property of Mr. John Shaw Leigh, who has, we believe, the right to stop any passenger train passing on the Midland line when required for the accommodation of his family.

In passing through the chalk cutting near Luton Hoo Park, the geologist may observe a remarkable seam, separating the upper from the lower bed of chalk rock. Though it does not average more than a foot or eighteen inches in thickness, it is very extensive, and is useful "as a line of demarcation between the upper and lower beds of the cretaceous series." Though not uniformly compact, it is excessively hard, and when struck with a hammer has a metallic ring. It abounds in green-coated nodules. It is easily recognised in the cutting, for it was found impracticable to "face" it to the same plane as the softer strata of chalk immediately above and beneath. It does not occur in uniform continuity, but is broken in several places; and sometimes, for a few yards, two beds lie parallel with one another.

The town of Luton is pleasantly situated in a valley between two extended series of hills. Before reaching the station we see the church on our left, the handsome embattled tower of which is chequered with flint and freestone. At the corners are hexagonal turrets. On the north side of the choir are a vestry-room and a chapel founded by Lord Wenlock. He lived in the reign of Henry VI., and Brayley tells us that he rendered services to the crown, and received rewards; was severely wounded in defence of the king at the battle of St. Albans, but afterwards joined the Duke of York. He fought on Towton field, and was advanced to rank and

LUTON.

favour; and then, changing sides, engaged in schemes with the Earl of Warwick to restore the deposed Henry. He raised forces; and was appointed by the Earl of Somerset to high command before the battle of Tewkesbury. The earl, finding himself unsupported in his attack, returned to discover the cause. He found Lord Wenlock, with his troops, standing in the market place; and, enraged at such conduct, with one blow of his battleaxe cleaved the head of Wenlock. The Wenlock arms are in several parts of the walls of Luton church. The lofty spire and handsome building in the middle of the town is the Congregational church.

Luton is the second town in the county. At the time the Midland line was contemplated the population amounted to some 18,000, and it has since largely increased. It is the centre of the straw plait trade; the plait being made in almost all the villages of the county. Mr. James Howard, of Bedford, several years ago estimated the value of the trade at £1,000,000 a year, 75 per cent. of which was paid in wages. This large proportion arises from the fact that the raw material is of little value except so far "as labour is mixed up with it": a product worth 10*s.* consuming a material not worth more than 1*s.* The consumption of coal in this town is between 20,000 and 30,000 tons a year; and the opening of the line caused a saving in that commodity alone to the amount of £5000 or £6000 a year, enough to pay all the poor's rates of the parish.

Concerning the trade of this town, it has been quaintly said:—

> "Some ladies' heads appear like stubble fields:
> Who now of threatened famine dare complain,
> When every female forehead teems with grain?
> See how the wheatsheaves nod amid the plumes!
> Our barns are now transferred to drawing-rooms;
> And husbands who indulge in active lives,
> To fill their granaries, may thresh their wives.
> Nor wives alone prolific, notice draw:
> Old maids and young ones—all are in the straw."

The neighbourhood of Luton is full of historic associations. One of the most interesting spots is Dallow Farm. As the train runs along the embankment to the north of the station, the traveller may see, about half a mile to the left, just under a wood that crowns the height (exactly as depicted by our artist), the gables of an old farmhouse nestling in the valley. This is Dallow

Farm. It was one of the five manses given by King Offa to the abbey of St. Albans in 795. On the dissolution of the abbey, the house, like others, was sold or given away, and became henceforth private property. "In the persecuting times of Charles II., says the Rev. J. Hiles Hitchens, "the Nonconformists met here, secluded from general observation, for divine worship; and in the roof of the house is the trap door by which some of the persecuted Nonconformists escaped from their pursuers. It is said that John Bunyan was concealed for several days in this house. When liberty of conscience was granted by James II., the worshippers in the Dallow Farm removed to Luton, and formed themselves into a Christian community."

DALLOW FARM.

Before reaching Leagrave station, the traveller may notice a bed of chalk like that previously observed. It is so hard that blasting was necessary to excavate it. It divides into thin laminæ, and the natural cleavages have a greenish tinge. It contains numerous fossils.

At Leagrave is an excavation in the drift formation that exhibits a series of sands, gravels with water-worn flints, and clays, through which are interspersed rolled fragments of fossils from the secondary strata. The strata in the ballast pit adjoining the station, show the

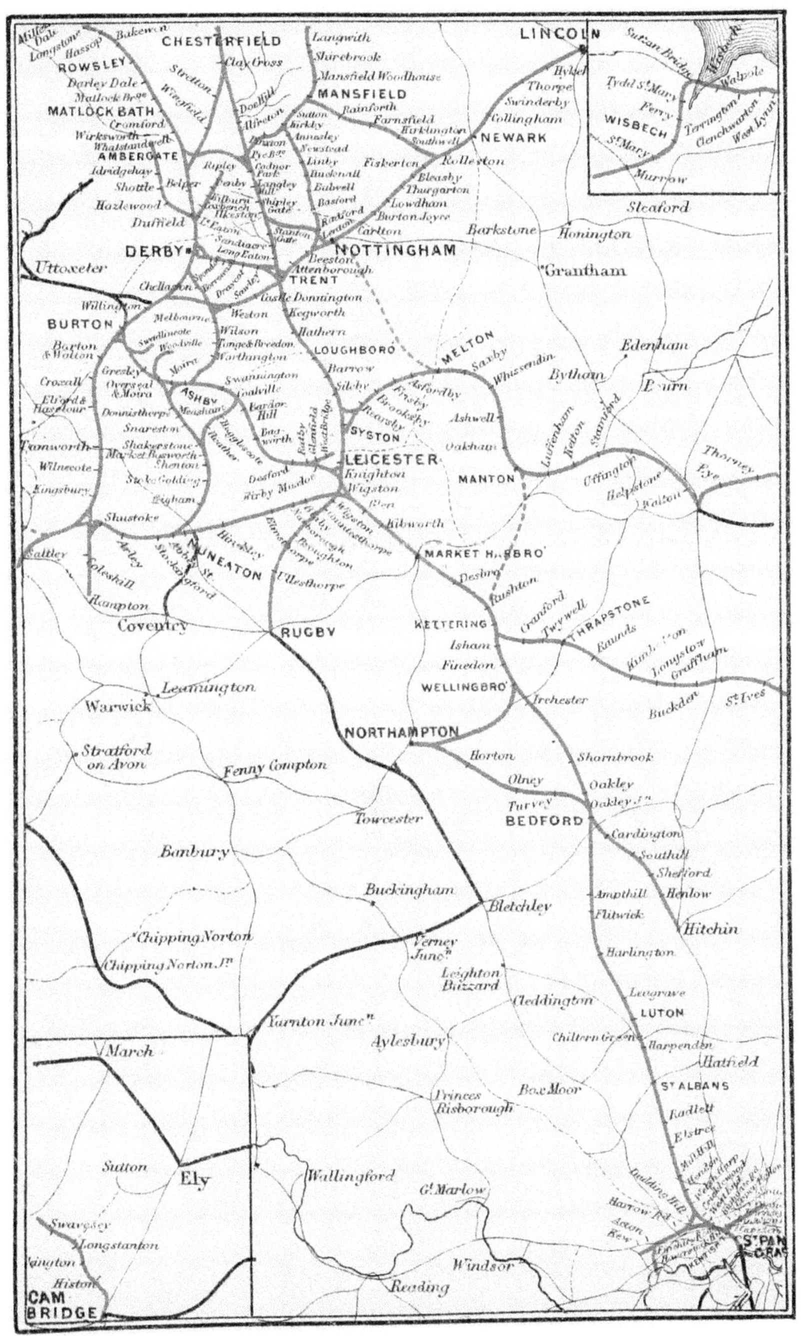

Bemrose & Sons Map Engravers. London & Derby

subaqueous origin of the beds; the lines of stratification by the water being as distinct as though formed yesterday.* The village of Leagrave is on the left of the line. The Lea, which gives it its name, rises at Leagrave Marsh.

About a mile south of Harlington is an excavation known as the Charlton Cutting, "upwards of a mile in length, through the range of hills that constitute the watershed of the district, the springs on the north-west side flowing towards the Ouse, those on the south-east forming the source of the Lea. The Chiltern Hills also form the north-west chalk escarpment, and the scenery from them at various points is very picturesque.

"The deepest part of the excavation at Charlton, where it is about 60 feet deep, exposes the lower chalk, without flints; and beneath this is a bed of dark chalk, almost like clay, containing many pyrites, locally termed crow-gold. The cutting has proved peculiarly rich in organic remains, and has furnished at least one species† new to the geology of England;" and also a portion of jaw, and several teeth of a huge crocodile, besides ammonites from an inch to upwards of a foot in diameter, and a species of nautilus of nearly equal size.

The hill now observed upon our right is known by the Saxon name of "Wanluds Bank." Its naturally rounded sides have been scarped in a remarkable manner; but when or by whom we are unable to ascertain. A short distance before we reach Harlington Station, and between the two hills on the left, is the rising ground of Conger Hill. Behind it is the village of Toddington; and its old park is close on our left. Harlington is prettily situated to the right of the station.

* Mr. J. Saunders, of Luton, has favoured us with some interesting "Notes on the Geology of South Beds," which, he remarks, has been "beautifully illustrated by the extension of the Midland Railway" through the county.

† A Crustacean. See *Geo. Mag.*, Nov., 1870.

"The cutting at Harlington at the north-east side of the hill, where it faces the Oxford clay and greensand strata, exposes a thick bed of heavy dark clay, containing a profusion of selenite crystals. It is succeeded by other beds of a lighter colour, containing a larger proportion of rolled chalk and flints; until, at the south-east side of the hill, or that facing the chalk formation, the beds are composed almost entirely of sand and water-worn fragments from the cretaceous beds."

On the left, as we leave Harlington station, is Harlington Wood End, then Westoning Wood End, and then Westoning. "The cutting," says Mr. Saunders, "south-east from Westoning exposes a dark heavy clay, which, upon a very close examination, furnishes not the least trace of rolled fragments of chalk or flints, or any other substance so frequent in the tertiary clays of this neighbourhood, which would lead to the inference that it had been deposited subsequently to the cretaceous era. It contains, however, what would strongly indicate that it is coeval with the upper greensand, namely, a continuous band of coprolitic nodules,"—an extension of that worked at places farther east for manure on account of the large amount of phosphate of lime that they contain. The fossils are marine, and include teeth of sharks and bones of huge crocodilian reptilia.

Flitwick station is nearly three miles north of Harlington. Near it are two cuttings in what is called the lower greensand, consisting of white and yellow sands with bands of ironstone. These strata extend for considerable distances across the county; and may be observed at Sandy on the Great Northern, and at Leighton on the London and North Western, Railways.

Less than two miles forward we reach Ampthill, pleasantly situated on two hills near the centre of the county. In the church is a mural monument to the memory of Richard Nicholls, who fell in battle, and the ball with which he was slain (a five or six pounder), is preserved. An inscription tells that it was "the instrument of death and immortality."

Leaving Ampthill station, we soon afterwards enter a heavy cutting, and a tunnel through Ampthill Park. Another cutting at the northern end of the tunnel shows a series of beds of clay, brown at the top and merging into dark blue below, with intermediate bands of hard grey limestone, from a foot to eighteen inches in thickness. In the sides of the cutting, at the entrance of the tunnel, the limestone beds show the rise and fall of the strata very clearly. The upper beds of brown clay contain many small crystals of selenite, or spar, as it is often called, very similar to that found in the caverns at Matlock Bath. In the lower beds the crystals are comparatively rare, but are much larger and more beautiful. Among the fossils found were bones of a huge reptile, one vertebra of which weighed upwards of ten pounds.

Passing northward out of the cutting, we observe upon our right the stately mansion called Ampthill House. It was built by Lord Ashburnham in the time of Charles II. In late years it has been occupied by Lord and Lady Holland, by Lord Wensleydale, and subsequently by his widow. Formerly a castle stood on the higher ground behind the house. This was built, Leland says, by Lord Fanhope, in the reign of Henry VI., "with the spoils he won in the wars in France." It formed the retreat of Cat! mine of Aragon while the business of the divorce was being heard at Dunstable. A cross has been erected on the site of the castle.

Ampthill Park is remarkable for its ancient and stately oaks. Houghton Park is now united with it. Houghton House was built by the Countess of Pembroke, sister of Sir Philip Sydney. With the exception of some ornamental portions, which form a picturesque ruin, it has been pulled down. Fine views may from hence be enjoyed over the northern parts of the county. At the town entrance to the park was a lodge, " and a pear-tree, on which Sir Philip is reported to have written part of his Arcadia." The entire neighbourhood is very beautiful, and a favourite resort for pleasure parties.

A mile north of Ampthill we are running almost parallel with the London and North Western Railway from Bletchley to Bedford, but the lines are at some distance from each other. The Ampthill station of the London and North Western is, by road, some three and a half miles from the town; and the benefits conferred by having a railway station close at hand, may be imagined by a traveller who, like the writer, once landed on a winter night at what he thought was Ampthill, but found he had to walk either by a circuitous route along the road, or, as it happened, to avail himself of the proffered and pressing services of an entire stranger to guide him along muddy and invisible paths over hill and dale, grass lands and fallow, and occasionally by some deep wood, where the idea pleasantly occurred that it was a convenient time and place to be murdered in.

About three miles north of Ampthill is a cutting in Oxford clay, the upper portion of which is dark brown merging into dark blue beneath. " It abounds in fossil wood in various stages of carbonisation, the colour of which ranges from brown to a jet black, and is so abundant in places, that some of the navvies thought they were coming upon a coal mine. Running through the mass of clay is an abundance of roots and fibres in inextricable confusion, of the extinct plants that flourished during the deposition of the bed. Associated with these are found belemnites and ammonites; but the latter are so hopelessly compressed and fragile as to render it impossible to extricate them entire, save in the smallest specimens."

As we approach Bedford, the excavations are slight, and exhibit only the drift sands and gravels of the rich valley of the Ouse, in which have been discovered "indubitable evidence that herds of elephants and other similar creatures roamed the primeval hills and forests of Bedfordshire."

We are now in sight of a spot of interest to every Englishman, the birthplace of John Bunyan. He was

ELSTOW.

born at Elstow, in 1628, and was one of the ringers in the church seen among the trees on our right. The tower is detached.

After passing on our right the new middle class "County School" of Bedfordshire, and crossing the Ouse, we notice the extensive and well-known agricultural implement establishment of Messrs. Howard. We are now at the pleasant town of Bedford, having reached it by a line which has cost several millions of money; but which, says Mr. Allport, "have been very well expended, in the interest both of the public and of the Midland Company."

It is thought that the name Bedford is the Bedicanford of the Saxon Chronicle, the word signifying "a fortress on a river." Mention is made of a stronghold on the south side of the Ouse; and subsequently Rufus erected a castle with an entrenchment, and with thick and lofty walls. "While this castle stood," says Camden, "there was no storm of civil war that did not burst upon it." He speaks of its ruins, in his time, overhanging the river on the east side of the town. Not many years ago its site might be traced at the back of the Swan Inn, where there is now a bowling green. Within the walls of the old gaol on Bedford Bridge, the immortal allegorist wrote his "Pilgrim's Progress." For seventeen years he was a Baptist minister in Bedford.

We now enter on the Bedford and Leicester portion of the Midland line. This, as our readers are aware, was intended and was used for several years to give the Midland a nearer approach, *viâ* Hitchin, to London, than had previously been possessed by way of Rugby. The opening of the direct through Bedford and London line has, however, thrown the Bedford and Hitchen portion into the position of a subordinate branch.

In travelling from Bedford to Leicester, the trains have to ascend to and descend from five summit levels, two of them of considerable length and severity. The principal are the Irchester and the Desborough "banks," each of which rise some fifty feet a mile for four miles, or 200 feet in all, and then fall for a similar distance. The cuttings are fifty or sixty feet deep, and the embankments are fifty or sixty feet high, as deep and as high as they could with safety be carried. "But if you could not alter your banks and cuttings," we inquired, "might you not have got over the difficulty, or at any rate diminished it, by tunnelling?" "Yes," replied the engineer; "by putting tunnels at your summit levels, and viaducts at the lowest part of your embankments the proportion of earthwork would have remained the same, and the levels might have been immensely improved. But there was one objection to that: we hadn't the money to do it with. It was just at the time of the Russian war; money and men were very difficult to get, and the shareholders could not be induced to raise more than a million, with which to construct a line sixty-three miles long. "Now, Charles Liddell and John Crossley," said old John Ellis, "there are £900,000 to make your line with. If it can't be done for that, it can't be done at all. So you must put all your fine notions into your pockets, and go and do it for £15,000 a mile. And then there is the rolling stock to find." "And it took," said Mr. Crossley, "a great deal of 'scraping,' to get it done. Mr. Brassey was the contractor for the work, and Mr. Horn was his agent." "Which Brassey?" we asked. "Thomas Brassey," was the reply. "There was only one Brassey. There are Brasseys who are members of Parliament, and that sort of thing, but there was only one Brassey—that was Thomas."

About a mile north of Bedford, we cross the Ouse for the second time. Within a distance of seven miles, we pass over it no fewer than seven times; and the river has so winding a course through this county, that though, as the bird flies, the whole distance would be less than seventeen miles, the water flows not fewer than forty-five.

A little more than three miles brings us to Oakley station. Before reaching it we see the village on our left, and behind it the park, through which the Ouse winds its way. Oakley House is a seat of the Duke of

Bedford. We now ascend the long incline called Sharnbrook Bank. A little south of Sharnbrook we cross over the Ouse by a viaduct. It is the most important viaduct on the line between Bedford and Leicester, and, remarked the engineer, "it was a very troublesome one to make. The water was twenty-five feet deep, and the foundations had to be carried twenty-five feet down through the soft clay at the bottom before a foundation could be found."

About a mile south of Irchester Station we enter Northamptonshire, "the midmost of the midlands." It is so far from the sea, and fish are supposed to be such a rarity, that a proverb declares that "the mayor of Northampton opens oysters with his dagger." The county is three times as long as it is broad, and stretches from the highlands of Edgehill to the fens beyond Peterborough. It is singular that it has no rivers but those to which it gives birth; and its own waters flow both east and west, to the Wash and the Severn. Once it was a land of "great herds of swyne," of charcoal burners, and woad growers and woodlanders. At a later period it was declared by Norden that "the fertilitie, salutarie ayre, pleasant prospects, and convenience of this shire in all things to a generous and noble mynd" early "allured nobilitie to plant themselves within the same;" and, he adds, even "the baser sorte of men here prove wealthie, and wade through the world with good countenance to their calling." It is now a land of "spires and squires," of rich pastures,—the worst of which, Drayton averred, "are equal to the best elsewhere;" of ever-recurring ridge and furrow; of hedgerows and of ash-trees innumerable,—the favourite tree of the Anglo-Saxon.

After passing, on our left, the village and church, we run under a road, immediately north of which is the ancient Roman station of Irchester, on the verge of which very extensive fields of ironstone have, of late years, been opened. Mr. W. Butlin smelted the first piece of ore from this county, and he is regarded as the father of its iron trade. It is remarkable that so lately as in 1836 a shaft was sunk at Kingsthorpe, near Northampton, for coal, while all the while iron was lying unheeded on the surface. Domesday Book had spoken about the "Ferraria" in this district of Edward the Confessor; slags were found in all the old forest lands; royal furnaces existed at Geddington in the reign of Henry II.; but the impression seemed to be that the iron had been brought from elsewhere to be smelted here. Morton refers to the red lands of Rothwell and the neighbourhood, and adds: "There is no iron ore to be met with in this county." The existence of ironstone appears to have first been noticed by a railway traveller, who happened to see blocks of it brought to mend a road near a station. "Thus," says an observant writer, "the iron road led and paved the way to its own resources."

At the present time the Midland line runs for sixteen miles through beds of Northamptonshire ironstone which are many miles in breadth. It is found on the surface, from fourteen to sixteen feet thick; the railway cuttings have laid the beds open; and the town and station of Wellingborough stand upon it. The ore is rich, containing from 35 to 50 per cent. of metal, besides, in some of the beds, 15 per cent. of lime; and it is easily fusible. More recently it has been found near the Twywell station of the Kettering and Huntingdon line, and the ore is of remarkably good quality and thickness. In six years the amount raised here increased 500 per cent.; in 1866 the output amounting to nearly 500,000 tons; and it has since been enormously augmented. Several new furnaces have been constructed, and the district between Kettering and Wellingborough promises to become another Middlesborough. Vast fields of wealth lie here almost untouched, every ton of which will yield traffic and profit to the Midland Company.

A mile north of Irchester the line reaches the verge of a wide valley, along which the Nene flows (and in winter often overflows), and down which the London and North Western Railway from Blisworth to Peterborough runs. The Midland crosses the river and the rail at right angles by a long and lofty embankment, by a viaduct and a bridge. The viaduct is represented in our sketch.* The erection of it was a difficult matter; for, after they were built, all the abutments and the wings slid forwards, without, wonderful to say, displacing a single brick. It was necessary, however, that the side arches should be taken down and rebuilt. "This was a very singular instance," remarked Mr. Crossley, "of how solid masonry may shift without injuring itself. The accident was caused by the pressure of the bank behind the brickwork."

Almost immediately south of Wellingborough Station there is a timber bridge over the Ise; and from near the station itself two branch lines, right and left, communicate with the North Western. That to the left gives the Midland Company access to Northampton.

Wellingborough is situated on an eminence to the west of the station. It was rebuilt, in 1738, after a fearful fire. The town is said to have derived its name from its wells or springs, one of which, "the Red Well," a chalybeate, was formerly in high repute. Charles I. and his queen resided here under canvas for nine days, to have the benefit of the waters.

The requirements of the Midland system and the development of the iron trade in this district have greatly altered the character of the town and its neigh-

* See page 145.

bourhood. Instead of being a quiet station in the midst of a purely agricultural district, it has been made the first great mineral and goods station on the Midland line out of London. Its distance is about sixty-five miles from the metropolis, making a journey to and from Wellingborough a convenient day's work for a goods engine, and accordingly large locomotive establishments

LOCOMOTIVE ESTABLISHMENT, WELLINGBOROUGH.

have been created. Some fifty engines are usually stationed here, and extensive sidings are provided for the marshalling of the trains both up and down. The bird's-eye view we have sketched is taken from the roof of a large provision store established to supply all the horses of the Midland Railway with provender on the district between London and Normanton. There is another district between Bristol and Birmingham, and Nottingham takes the remainder. During the winter season, when this department is most busy (more horses being required for shunting purposes, when cold freezes up the wheels and axles), no fewer than 1400 horses are fed from hence. The corn and hay are bought through the stores, and are here cut, ground, and mixed, and hence forwarded in bags ready for use. Two hundredweight of hay and corn are required each week for each horse, or 140 tons a week for the district.

On the hill on the right of our sketch may be seen the lodging-house for the drivers and firemen who happen to be here for the night. Every provision is made for their comfort.

In various cuttings north of Wellingborough the clay is very heavy, and the banks, after they were made, slipped repeatedly. "These oolitic clays," remarked the engineer to us, "are very soapy; and the ironstone, a ferruginous oolite, presses heavily upon them. After wet weather the clay becomes a mass of grease, and then the stone slides off into the cutting. These slips just north of Wellingborough Station were so frequent that at length they exposed the abutments of a three-arched bridge. It is now a bridge of five arches," as seen in the engraving.

Beside the line to the north of Wellingborough, we observe a river winding its way in so devious a fashion that it is sometimes of a horse-shoe shape. This is the Ise. It rises north-east of Kettering, receives a tributary from the north-west, then flows almost close to the railway down to Wellingborough. It is twenty-four miles long.

After passing some large ironworks on the right, we reach the next station, Finedon; and then comes Isham, with its large mill, known as "The Woollen Mill." The embankment curving towards us from the right is the commencement of the Kettering and Huntingdon branch, at the junction of which we are abreast of a spot on our left of great interest to many. It is the village of Pytchley, the home of the Pytchley hunt.

Here, says a writer in the *Quarterly Review*, not on a clear and beautiful day, for such a "gaudy thing" they do not value, but on some soft ground, with dull weather, an easterly wind and a cloudy sky, "see how quietly along every high road, bye road, and footpath, horses and riders, of various sizes and sorts, walking, jogging, or gently trotting, are converging towards a central point. Schoolboys are coming to see the start on ponies; farmers on clever nags; others on young horses of great price; neatly dressed grooms, some heavy and some light, are riding, or riding and leading horses magnificent in shape and breeding, in the most beautiful condition, all as clean and well appointed as if they had been prepared to do miserable penance in Rotten Row." There, too, are the Pytchley hounds, on their way to a cover that has the advantage of being surrounded by large grass fields, and "enlivened in every direction by the severest fences in Northamptonshire."

THE BAPTIST MISSION HOUSE, KETTERING.

The next station is Kettering, the houses of which climb up the hillside on our right; and above all is the noble spire of the church. Towards the north end of the town, in the direction of the windmill, the passenger may see a large white building, with three dormer windows in the roof. It is known as the "Baptist

Mission House," for in one of the parlours, on the 2nd of October, 1792, Dr. Carey, Andrew Fuller, and others, founded missions to the heathen, and a collection was made of £13 2*s.* 6d., the firstfruits of a harvest of millions sterling devoted to the highest well-being of man. Fifty years afterwards some 10,000 persons assembled here to celebrate the jubilee.

Leaving Kettering, we rise up a heavy incline; pass through some almost perpendicular cuttings, that tell of the presence of iron ore, and soon we are in the neighbourhood of the Glendon iron pits.

Running over an embankment across the valley, we reach the pretty village of Rushton. Within 100

RUSHTON TRIANGULAR LODGE.

yards of the station, on our left, is the singular Triangular Lodge, built by Sir Thomas Tresham. It was the rendezvous of the conspirators of the Gunpowder Plot; and "it would certainly be no unfavourable place; for its form and isolation deny ears to its walls. The trinary symbolism which exists in the name and arms of

Tresham (three trefoils) is here shown forth in every conceivable architectural form and device."

From the Treshams, the estate at Rushton passed into the family of the Lords Cullen. It is said of the second viscount, that "he had been betrothed, at the age of sixteen, to Elizabeth Trentham, a great heiress, but had, while travelling abroad, formed an attachment to an Italian lady of rank, whom he afterwards deserted for his first betrothed. While the wedding-party were feasting in the great hall at Rushton, a strange carriage, drawn by six horses, drew up, and forth stepped a dark lady, who, entering the hall, and seizing a goblet, 'to punish his falsehood and pride,' drank perdition to the bridegroom, and having uttered a curse upon the bride, in stronger language than we care to chronicle, to the effect that she should live in wretchedness, and die in want, disappeared. The curse was in great measure fulfilled."

The clean little village next seen on the left, close to the line, is Desborough. Just beyond the station we reach the summit of the incline, and we now begin a descent which extends for between three and four miles, at the rate of 1 in 132, nearly to Harborough. This is called the Desborough Bank.

Crossing the Welland, we enter Leicestershire, and are at Market Harborough, formerly spelt Haverburgh. The fine church is said to have been founded by John of Gaunt, as a penance for one of his crimes. The town has no lands belonging to it; hence a threat sometimes used to children, "I'll throw you into Harborough field."

Immediately to the left of the station is a burial-ground, and in it a mortuary chapel. It occupies the site of an ancient edifice, of which the porch and the circular doorhead are, we believe, the only remains.

It was originally the pàrish church, and was named St. Mary-in-Arden, or "the church in the wood." It achieved an evil reputation for the celebration of clandestine marriages; the curates were "ignorant and disorderly," and at length the privilege of matrimonial and other services was transferred to the church in the town. Subsequently the steeple fell upon the church, and for thirty years it lay in ruins. The parish of St. Mary is in two different townships, manors, counties, and dioceses. Market Harborough gave shelter to Charles I. on the night before the battle of Naseby, and from hence Cromwell dated his despatches to Parliament, announcing the victory. At Harborough vehicles may be obtained by which the field of Naseby, seven miles distant, may be visited.

Market Harborough Station, and the line for a mile forward, are the property of the London and North Western Company.

Running through the fat pastures of Leicestershire we reach the two Kibworths, one on either side the line. Kibworth Beauchamp, on our left, was the birthplace of Dr. Aikin, the father of Mrs. Barbauld. On the right are the prettily situated church and rectory of Kibworth Harcourt. A little to the south of Kibworth is Tur Langton, where King Charles watered his horse on his flight from Naseby. Almost immediately north of Kibworth is a summit level of the line.

The next station is at Glen Magna, the village of which was once declared to be "great for nothing, except for containing more dogs than honest men." On our left is the Union Canal. When originally proposed, this undertaking shared the opposition cherished against all innovations. It was urged that no canal should be allowed to come within four miles of a populous town; employment, it was said, would thereby be secured to carriers in conveying the various cargoes to and from the wharves.

There are two stations at Wigston,—one on the main line, the other on what was formerly the main line, but is now only a branch, from Rugby to Leicester. The village used sometimes to be called Wigston Two Steeples, on account of having two churches. There is now direct communication from hence, *viâ* Whitacre, to Birmingham, and trains run between that town and London in successful competition with the London and North Western.

LEICESTER.

As we approach Leicester, we see at Knighton Junction the line from Burton-on-Trent and Ashby curving in on our left; we pass through a tunnel, or covered way, 100 yards long, under the "Freeman's Piece" of land; we skirt the new cattle-market on our left, and the cemetery on our right. Looking down on the cemetery is the County Lunatic Asylum, and beyond is the racecourse; while, on our left, across the open green, a baronial looking pile, with flanking towers and turrets, is the County Gaol. It has more than three acres of land within its precincts.

The town of Leicester is full of historic associations. It makes, says an old chronicler, "an evident fair show of great antiquity." Here a British temple stood, and sacrifices were offered. Here the Romans held an important military position. Here the Saxons erected walls of "amazing thickness and strength," "like great rocks," to defend themselves against the desolating incursions of the Danes. Here in Norman times was a city "well frequented and peopled." From this spot, in 1485, Richard went to fight the battle of Bosworth Field; and hither his dead body was brought "without so much as a clout to cover it, trussed behind a pursuivant at arms, like a calf—his head and arms hanging on one side the horse, and his legs on the other, all besprinkled with mire and blood;" a spectacle, says Hutton, which "humanity and decency ought not to have suffered." In the Civil War the town was successfully besieged by the king; and the house where the Parliamentary committee had sat was, we are told, destroyed, "every soul therein was put to the sword," and the kennels ran down with blood. A few weeks later the battle of Naseby was fought, and the town was now surrendered to Fairfax without a shadow of resistance.

With regard to the trades now carried on in this town, Sir Edmund Beckett, on a recent occasion, thus playfully commented: "First of all there is the shoe trade, and 20,000 people are employed in it, and they get leather from everywhere. Leeds is a great place for making leather, and there is a great trade between Leeds and Leicester for leather, besides machinery and wool, and I may add cotton. Another peculiar trade is the making of elastic webbing; and though I read in a scientific paper the other day that it sometimes makes people's toe-nails come off, this was contradicted immediately afterwards, and therefore I don't know which is true; but in spite of the alarm which some people have about their toenails, elastic webbing is made very largely in Leicester. There is also a large cigar trade, and although I do not know that it is very bulky, it is very valuable. There is also the manufacture of articles for the use of the town; and you will be surprised when you hear that one firm uses not less than 5000 tons of wood a year in making bobbins,—reels on which thread is wound, which, however, have a tendency to get bulkier in the stomach and to carry less thread. That wood comes from the agricultural districts. Building-stone also is required here. There is also the pork-pie trade from Melton Mowbray, and I am sorry to hear that the gentleman is dead who had that trade. I remember remarking that the gentleman's pork-pies did not seem to agree with him, either from eating too much or eating too little of them; and I am sorry to say that I was right."

When it was decided to bring the Midland Counties railway into Leicester, the station was to have been in the lower part of the town, near St. George's Church. The present site was, however, eventually selected; the amount of land secured being about nine acres: "an extent," said some local authority, "manifestly absurd," but which has since been found to be totally insufficient. When first erected, the station was pronounced a "magnificent building." It contained offices connected with the general administration of the new company: these have long since been transferred to Derby. The board room opened on to a balcony, from which a view of the line could be obtained. The platform was on only one side of the line, and was sheltered by a projecting shed.

Leaving Leicester for the north, we pass on the left the vast buildings and sidings provided for the goods and mineral traffic. Clearing this busy scene, we have on our right the new Borough Asylum; beyond which, among the trees, is the village of Humberstone, where a coarse kind of alabaster is quarried. On the opposite side of the line is Belgrave, from whence the eldest son of the Marquis of Westminster takes his title. A little farther on, on the same side, the spire of Thurmaston Church appears.

Four miles from Leicester we reach Syston, passing on our way through a cutting in which some splendid blocks of gypsum have been laid bare. The old station stood on the right of the line, but a new one has recently been erected. Immediately beyond is the South Junction with the Syston and Peterborough branch of the Midland Railway. Syston village is to the right. Soon afterwards we see the rivers Soar and Wreke winding their several ways.

There are three spots in the district through which we have been passing, where, according to tradition, a remarkable event occurred. A giant, we are assured, once took three mighty leaps, and cleared the whole distance from Mount Sorrel to Belgrave. His first leap was to Wanlip; his second to Birstall, where he burst himself and his horse; his third, for he managed to take another, to Belgrave, where he was buried. Hence the saying: "He leaps like the bell-giant of Mount Sorrel."

Three miles from Syston we reach Sileby, the railway embankment cutting the village in two; but access between the two parts is obtained by a lofty railway bridge of two arches of considerable height. The Soar winds its way below, crossed by a little bridge.

We shall not have travelled far before we see on our left the celebrated limestone pits and kilns of Barrow-on-Soar, the white smoke from which so drifts through the train, whenever the wind is westerly, that the passenger can recognise the spot by night as well as day. These works supply some of the finest, if not the finest, hydraulic lime in England. It comes from the blue lias, which stretches over a large district, but the quality here is specially excellent. Usually limestone is worked from a hill-side; here it is dug from a quarry, or "delph," some thirty to fifty feet beneath the surface. The thickest bed is about thirteen inches, and there are six or eight beds. The spot is interesting also to the geologist and the antiquary. The geologist has found here specimens of saurians—icthyo- and plesio- saurians; and the antiquary has been gratified by the discovery of some perfect specimens of Roman glass vases, the mouths of which had been closed with lead, and within which are the calcined bones of the dead. A large amphora has also been obtained. All have been presented by Mr. E. S. Ellis to the museum at Leicester.

A little beyond Barrow limeworks we see upon our left a spot well worthy of a visit,—the Mount Sorrel granite quarries. As we walk over the little branch line, about a mile long, that conducts to the Soar and the hill of the Soar, we think of the time when on the height before us, still called the Castle Hill, there was built, towards the close of the Conqueror's reign, a stately castle; a castle which, in King John's reign became, as Camden tells us, "a nest of the devil, a cave of robbers;" a castle which stood here till Henry III. gave command to the forces of Nottingham to invest and destroy it.

The huge granite rock, Mount Sorrel, is described by Professor Sedgwick as an "outlying boulder." How precipitous are its sides is shown by the fact that when a well was sunk for the use of the works to a depth of 100 feet within a distance of 100 yards from where the granite begins, no trace of granite was found,—all was clay.

Before us, as we approach, stand the perpendicular and broken faces of the hill, the windmill (it is said 100 years old) on the summit, and the town and river at the foot. Crossing over the iron bridge, and performing a strategic movement to avoid a diminutive but energetic little locomotive, one of two which perform some of the manifold duties of the Mount Sorrel Company, we are at the quarry.

Here from 500 to 600 men and boys are at work. Some are pecking and blasting the masses of rock from the face of the cliff; some are drawing it away to the sheds, where it is to be broken into the required shapes; its fine grain and splendid cleavage enabling the workmen, by a few blows of their massive hammers, to split it anywhere and almost anyhow they like, so as to be ready for pavings, or crossings, or straight or curved curbstones, or anything else for which granite can be used. These smaller portions again are broken to the size required for macadamizing roads, partly by hand and partly by machinery which, with its iron jaws, first crunches the lumps down like so many enormous nuts, to their proper proportions, and then riddles them out, and pours the macadam stone into one truck and the smaller stone into another, waiting below to receive them. These, when filled, are drawn one at a time on to a weighing machine, which tells how much stone they contain, and they are ready to be despatched down the branch to the sidings, from which the Midland Company will in due course remove them to their destination.

Immediately past the next station (Barrow-on-Soar) on our left is Quorndon, which for a hundred years has been the metropolis of fox-hunting; and a mile forward the line crosses the Soar, just after it has divided into two, the two portions running for some miles on either side of the railway. The bridge is on the skew, and rests on two series—each of ten iron pillars—which go down into the bed of the river. The traveller may perhaps here observe with surprise, that after the river has been divided it seems the wider and deeper for the division.

SOAR BRIDGE, NEAR BARROW-ON-SOAR.

The reason is, that the waters on the right of the line are dammed up for the convenience of two mills.

The railway bridge that here passes over the Soar has recently been reconstructed and enlarged. The new portion was first built. Screw piles were driven into the bed of the river, and then the superstructure was built of wrought-iron girders. After the portion necessary for the widening of the line was completed, the main-line traffic was diverted on to the new portion, and then the old main-line bridge was taken down, and constructed on the new method.

In the recent doubling of the width of the line a difficulty arose here in consequence of the embankment, when tipped, slipping forwards into the river Soar. To stop this "I got," said Mr. Crossley, "several old Trent barges, good for nothing but to be broken up, for about £4 a piece, loaded them with ironstone slag, which is very heavy, and practically insoluble to water, and put them to form the 'toe,' as our men call it,—the 'foot,' as you would call it,—of the embankment. We thus obtained a firm foundation at the bottom of the river; and it held up the stuff afterwards put upon it. As, however, we had taken a slice off one side of the Soar, we had to restore the area of the water-way by widening the river on the other side."

For some miles along this part of the line we have the noble range of Charnwood Hills on our left. "These rocks," said Professor Sedgwick when visiting them, "are of igneous origin, and are entitled to be called mountains." "Yes," replied Professor Whewell, "and here are all the accompaniments of a mountain chain: coal measures on the west, carboniferous limestone on the north, sienite on the east and south, an anticlinal line traversing the centre, accounting for the dislocation of the strata, and referring the origin of the rocks to igneous agency."

On approaching Loughborough we see on our left the mill and warehouse of Messrs. Cartwright & Warners, the largest firm in the town, and, we believe, the largest manufacturers of merino and angola underwear in the world. This firm were the original patentees of the article, A.D. 1794; and they are also spinners of the material of which the articles are made. Directly and indirectly the welfare of several thousands of the population of Loughborough and neighbourhood is dependent upon them. Extensive additions to the establishment have recently been made.

Loughborough, said Leland, is "yn largeness and good building next to Leyrcester of all the markette tounes yn the shire, and hath in it 4 faire strates, or mo, well paved." Leaving the station for the North, we pass along an embankment over Loughborough Moors, famous for their pasturage and hay. A mile to our left is Dishley Grange, with a ruined church in the middle of a farm-yard, where Robert Bakewell, of sheep-breeding renown, was buried. We now recross the Soar, and enter Nottinghamshire by a bridge recently constructed in a manner similar to that adopted with the Soar bridge near Barrow; only, instead of screw piles, cast-iron cylinders were used. These were forced down into the bed of the river on to a foundation of red marl, were emptied, and built in from bottom to top with solid brickwork. The superstructure was then erected.

The next station is Hathern, formerly spelt Hawthorn, said to have derived its name from the hawthorn trees which grow with unusual luxuriance in the parish. From the embankment to the north of the next station (Kegworth) we see on our left the village and the fine spire of the church; and soon, on our right, we observe two mansions, the larger one being Kingston Hall, the residence of Lord Belper.

We now approach a ridge of hills running from east to west, known by the name Red Hill. To this point the line from Leicester has been doubled, giving two up and two down roads; one chiefly for passengers, the other for goods. The congestion of traffic at this part of the Midland system rendered this duplication necessary. The estimate of cost for the addition of a single pair of rails was £9000. The actual doubling cost £20,000 a mile, or, for twenty miles, £400,000. One item in the enhanced price is the fact that wages had risen from 2*s*. 10*d*. or 3*s*. to 4*s*. 6*d*. a day.

Trent Bridge consists of three arches, each of 100 feet span. The piers and abutments are of stone. At the north end are two land arches of 25 feet span, under which the Trent often pours its swollen volume of water. The bridge was commenced in June, 1838, the ironwork being supplied by the Butterley Company.

The northern end of the Red Hill Tunnel is of castellated architecture, the arch being flanked by towers and battlements of stone, contrasting well with the wood-clad hill behind. The tunnel is 170 yards long. The material through which it was made was of so hard a texture that much of it had to be blasted away with gunpowder.*

Scarcely have we emerged from the tunnel, than we are passing over the beautiful Trent, the waters of which spread out widely on either hand.

When the proposed amalgamation of the three companies that originally formed the Midland Railway was under discussion, an amusing controversy with regard to the works connected with this bridge took place at one of the meetings. A North Midland shareholder inquired how it was that the Midland Counties' Company had not performed a work which he thought would entail a very great expense on the united companies—he meant the weir over the river Trent.

Mr. Ellis said that it was made, and nearly all paid for.

Mr. Sutton replied that he had been at the place that morning.

Mr. Ellis added that he had been there also.

Mr. Sutton: "And does Mr. Ellis mean to say that the weir is made and paid for?"

Mr. Ellis answered with emphasis: "I mean to say it is" (applause).

* See page 15.

Mr. Sutton looked incredulous.

Mr. Ellis continued: "The Trent Navigation Company (with which it was whispered Mr. Sutton was connected) has moved for another injunction, but the works are finished and the superintendent has gone. The banks on each side are completed; and," continued Mr. Ellis, in a full tone, "I say it is done, with the exception of clearing away" (applause).

Mr. Jeremiah Strutt stated that the superintendent had gone away, after having executed the work perfectly. Whereupon Mr. Sutton again marvelled. The chairman now repeated to the honourable proprietor Mr. Ellis's assertion that the weir was complete; and added that, even supposing it was contracted for, but not done, it could make no essential difference.

Mr. Ellis said that he had looked at it in the morning, and the water was as low below the new weir as it could be. Not a ripple could be seen where the old weir was, and the company had contracted for the old weir being taken away.

Mr. Sutton (deliberately): "It is not done (laughter). I came here purposely to make the statement that the work is not completed."

Mr. Ellis once more emphatically repeated that it wâs; and Mr. Sutton once more added, "I say it is not."

Here the skirmish closed. The chairman called Mr. Sutton to order, and brought back the attention of the meeting to the business of the day.

Immediately after passing over the Trent Bridge, we cross the "Cranfleet Cut," as it is called, a short canal, the locks of which are under the railway, through which vessels may pass in order to avoid the weir. Less than a mile forward we are at Trent Station.

The Trent Station was opened on the 1st of May, 1862, though it was not completed in some details till some time afterwards. It has greatly facilitated the interchange of passenger traffic from north and south, east and west. It is possible, however, that it has now reached its palmiest days; and that before long, by means of the new lines in course of construction from Melton Mowbray to Nottingham, and that already opened from Radford to Trowell, Nottingham itself may be placed on the direct main line north and south of the Midland system; Derby and the West being served by a service of trains starting from Leicester. At any rate, such an arrangement would be worthy of consideration.

At the Nottingham end of Trent Station, are sidings set apart for the use of men who have charge of the asphalting of station platforms between Lincoln and Derby, Trent, Syston, and Peterborough. The materials consist of engine cinders and gas tar, riddled out into three sorts, and then mixed together hot, the heat being produced by the burning of a little coal. Some small white stone, obtained from Trent river-ballast, is sprinkled over the work when it is nearly finished. The coarsest and second kinds of material are used for what is called "bottoming," and the best for "topping."

Leaving Trent Station for Derby, we pass the "Sheet Stores," and the noble building of Trent College, for the education of middle class boys, and are soon at Sawley. This station was formerly named Breaston, after a village half a mile to the right of the line; it is now called Sawley, after the name of a village a mile to the left. The change was made to avoid the confusion that might arise from the similarity between the sounds of Beeston and Breaston. Sawley was formerly Salle or Sallowe; and at one time it had a charter to hold markets and fairs, and also a market-house. These privileges have lapsed through disuse.

Passing Breaston, the spire of which seems to have crushed down the tower, a large square mansion embosomed in trees is seen on the summit of a hill. It is Hopwell Hall. At the time of the Norman survey, we are told there were in Sawley, Hopwell, and Draycott, "a priest and two churches, a mill, one fishery, and thirty acres of meadow."

The old station at Borrowash was on the bank of a cutting twenty-five feet high; a new one has been erected a little further west. On the right of the line the strong stone wall is the retaining wall of the Derby Canal, which runs alongside the line and above the level of the railway for more than 130 yards. With the canal on the right and the Derwent on the left there is only just room for the line of railway to pass. A little further forward the canal had to be diverted from its course for a distance of half a mile.* In carrying on this work some interesting discoveries were made. On an elevated spot, and about two feet below the surface, the soil had a black tinge; bones that had evidently been burnt were found; and then some seventy or eighty human skeletons were exhumed, some of them being of gigantic stature, and lying due east and west. In one of the skulls was the head of an arrow. A curious box, lined with gold, and containing amulets and jewels, some ornaments, and a small vase, with the bones of a bird, were also discovered, besides the burnt bones of oxen, sheep, and boars. It is believed that there was here a British tumulus, or barrow, and that the place derived its name from "the ashes of the Barrow," Barrow-ash.

Spondon (locally pronounced Spoondon) is the last station before we reach Derby. The manor is in Domesday Book named Spondune; and at that time it had a priest, a church, and a mill. From this point may be

* See page 26.

seen, to our left, the distant Gothic towers of Elvaston Castle, the seat of the Earl of Harrington. In 1643, the Parliamentary forces, under Sir John Gell, attacked and took Elvaston. To complete his conquest over his enemies, according to one historian, Sir John first mutilated the effigy of Lord Stanhope in the church; "nor did his revenge stop here, for he married the Lady Stanhope." The grounds are entered by gates which formerly belonged to the palace of Madrid.

The inhabitants of this neighbourhood were formerly required to "brew four ales, and every ale of one quarter of malt," the profits of the sale of which were to go to the support of the church. "And all the inhabitants of Ockbrook shall carry all manner of tymber, being in the dale-wood now felled that the said priest of the said town shall occupy to the use of the said church."

After leaving Spondon station the line divides into two routes. The left is what is called the Spondon Curve. It was made in order to give additional facilities of access to Derby Station, so that trains, instead of having to "back" either in or out, can now run through.

Derby, the central station of the Midland Railway system and the seat of its administration, formerly had its chief distinction as the first place where a silk mill was erected in England. This was in 1718. "In the early part of the 18th century the Italians exclusively possessed the art of spinning, or, as it is technically called, 'throwing,' silk; and the British weaver had to import thrown silk at an exorbitant price. In 1702, a Mr. Crochet erected a small silk mill; but his capital and machinery were insufficient, and he failed. In 1717, Mr. John Lombe, who had in disguise and by bribing the workmen obtained access to the machinery of the silk throwsters of Piedmont, agreed with the corporation of Derby to rent, on a long lease, for £8 a year, an island or swamp in the river Derwent, 500 feet long and 52 wide. Here he erected, at a cost of £30,000, an immense silk mill. The foundation was formed with oaken piles 16 to 20 feet long, and over this mass of timber was laid a foundation of stone on which were turned stone arches that support the walls. In 1718 Lombe took out a patent, and was proceeding successfully in his business till he died, cut off, as it was thought, by poison, through the agency of an Italian woman employed by the Italian manufacturers whose business he had drawn away to himself." Many throwing mills have since been erected in Derby, and thus this branch of industry became the staple of the town.

Soon after leaving Derby, and running up the noble valley of the Derwent, we pass on our right the Little Eaton Junction; and then we are close to the church on the right of the line, and the village of Duffield is on our left. The church contains a monument to the memory of Anthony Bradshaw. There are the figures of himself, his two wives, and twenty children, whom he perhaps naturally, but prematurely, considered would include his whole family; but three other children being subsequently born, who could not be similarly immortalized, their names and configurations have, sad to say, been invidiously consigned to oblivion! Immediately to the north of the station is the site of what was once the strong fortress of "Duffield Castle." No traces of it survive, except the name it has given to the "Castle Orchards."

At Duffield Station the branch to Wirksworth commences. In looking at the map it seems at first sight strange that a long and excellent line should be made through so quiet a country for the accommodation of so small a town as Wirksworth, especially as it is only three or four miles from Cromford or Matlock stations on the main line to Manchester. But the wisdom of the policy that led to its construction has already been shown.

Leaving Duffield, the interest of the scenery increases. We are now passing from the quieter valleys around the banks of the Trent, and the southern district of the county, and are approaching "the southern outliers" of the mountain range known as the backbone of England, some of the mighty articulations of which occupy the northern parts of Derbyshire, and are popularly known as the Peak. The wide valley of the Derwent contracts; the rounded hills grow steep and rugged; and all around are woods which hang over the rocks, and shelter the ferns and undergrowth beneath. We have already crossed and recrossed the Derwent, and tunnelled under the hills. We now pass another tunnel and another bridge, and are at Belper.

The present station is, we believe, to be superseded by another somewhat farther to the north, and nearer to the centre of the town. Belper is well situated; but little of it is seen by reason of the line running through a cutting about a mile in length, and under some bridges on the way. The traveller will, however, have the consolation, such as it is, of knowing that he is passing very near to mills that employ about 2000 hands; and if he is sitting with his *back* to the engine, and looks sharply out of the window at his right hand, he may obtain a glimpse of the mills of Messrs. Strutt, and of the Derwent, which here, held back by a weir, gathers up its waters to supply the "power." On the west side of the Derwent rises Bridge Hill, the residence of Mr. G. H. Strutt.

Emerging from the Belper cuttings and from another hillside, on the ledges of which the ferns have planted their roots, and from which they hang their foliage over the cold stones in graceful forms, we cross the Derwent.

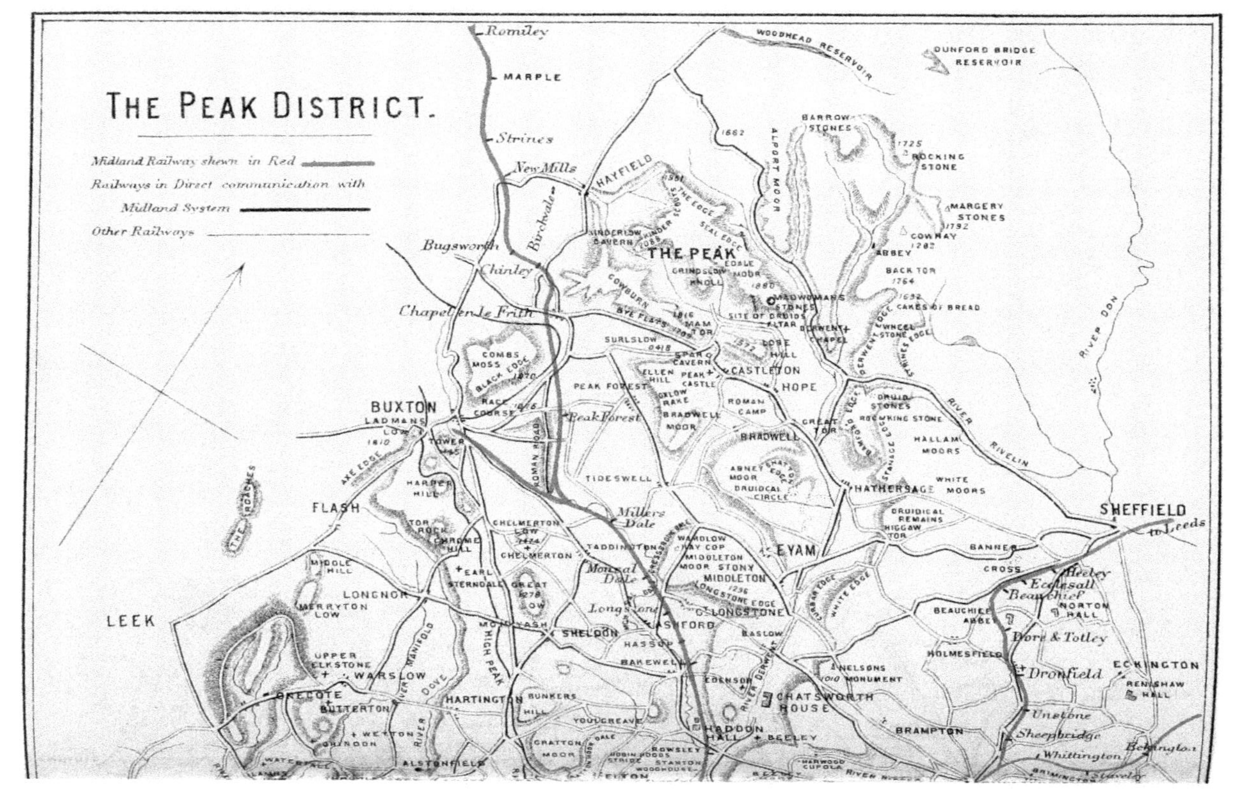
THE PEAK DISTRICT.
Midland Railway shewn in Red
Railways in Direct communication with Midland System
Other Railways
Romiley
MARPLE
Strines
New Mills
Birchvale
HAYFIELD
Bugsworth
Chinley
Chapel en le Frith
BUXTON
LADMANS LOW
FLASH
LEEK
LONGNOR
WARSLOW
HARTINGTON
HIGH PEAK
SHELDON
ASHFORD
BAKEWELL
HASSOP
LONGSTONE
Longstone
Monsal Dale
Millers Dale
TIDESWELL
TADDINGTON
CHELMERTON
Peak Forest
PEAK FOREST
THE PEAK
KINDER SCOUT
EDALE MOOR
MAM TOR
CASTLETON
HOPE
BRADWELL
EYAM
HATHERSAGE
SHEFFIELD
to Leeds
RIVER DON
RIVER RIVELIN
WOODHEAD RESERVOIR
DUNFORD BRIDGE RESERVOIR
ALPORT MOOR
BARROW STONES
ROCKING STONE
MARGERY STONES
BACK TOR
CAKES OF BREAD
DERWENT CHAPEL
HALLAM MOORS
WHITE MOORS
STANAGE EDGE
BAMFORD EDGE
ROMAN CAMP
ROMAN ROAD
BASLOW
CHATSWORTH HOUSE
HADDON HALL
BEELEY
EDENSOR
ROWSLEY
YOULGREAVE
BUNKERS HILL
GRATTON MOOR
ALSTONFIELD
BUTTERTON
ELKSTONE
MIDDLE HILL
MERRYTON LOW
AXE EDGE
THE ROACHES
COMBS MOSS
BLACK EDGE
RACE COURSE
TOWER
HARPER HILL
TOR ROCK
CHROME HILL
EARL STERNDALE
MONYASH
HOLMESFIELD
BEAUCHIEF ABBEY
Beauchief
Ecclesall
Heeley
NORTON HALL
Dore & Totley
Dronfield
ECKINGTON
RENISHAW HALL
Unstone
Sheepbridge
Whittington
BRAMPTON
NELSONS MONUMENT
WHITE EDGE
CURBAR EDGE
DRUIDICAL REMAINS
HIGGAW TOR
BANNER CROSS
STONY MIDDLETON
LONGSTONE EDGE
ABNEY MOOR
DRUIDICAL CIRCLE
GREAT TOR
SURLSLOW
SPAR CAVERN
PEAK CASTLE
ELLEN HILL
COWBURN
SEAL EDGE
THE EDGE
KINDERLOW CAVERN
GRINDSLOW KNOLL
MADWOMANS STONES
SITE OF DRUIDS ALTAR
LOSE HILL
DRUID STONES
WHEEL STONE EDGE
DERWENT EDGE
STRINES EDGE
ABBEY
COWHAY

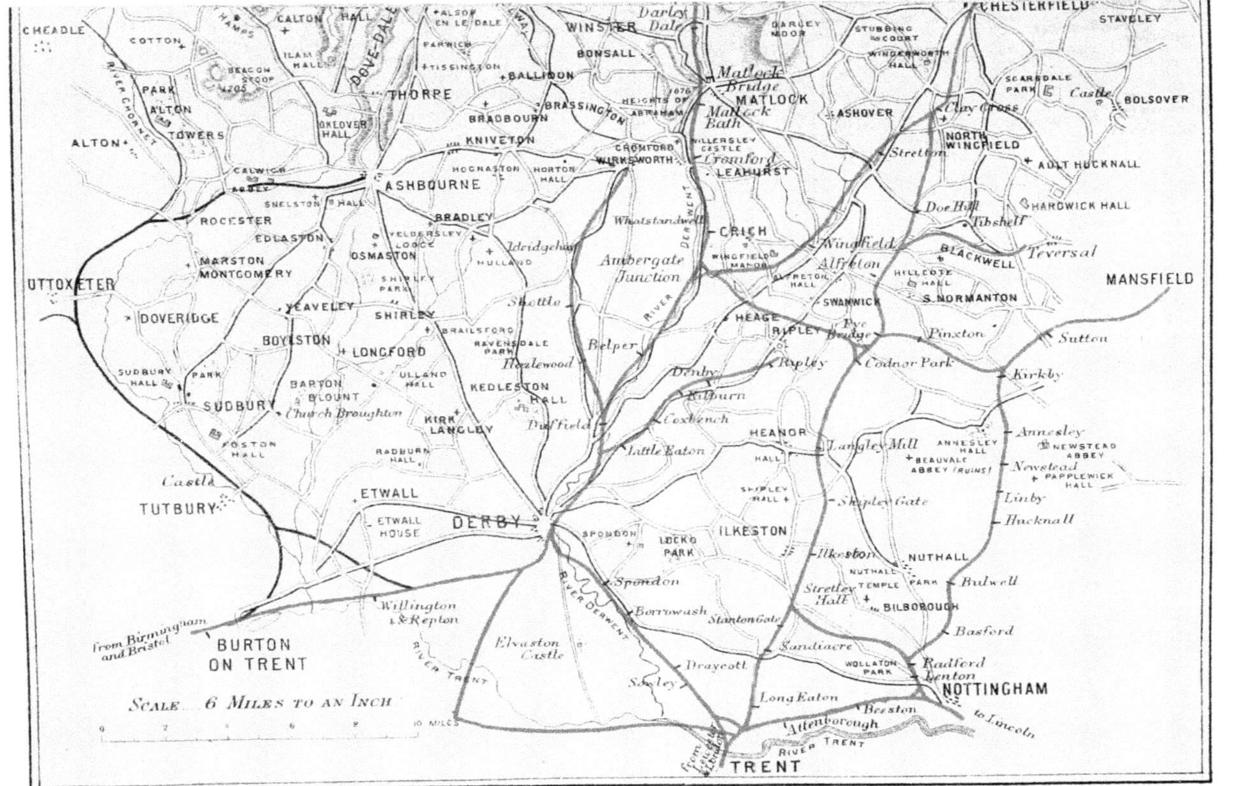

Bemrose & Sons. Map Engravers. London & Derby

A fine valley opens right and left, and we are at Ambergate.

Hitherto the line has been running north, but here its direct course is stayed. In front of us rises the hill of Crich, which compels the main line to turn away to the right and the Manchester line to the left. The name Ambergate is derived from the river Amber and the word *gate*, a passage. Here three beautiful valleys meet, from the north, the west, and the south. The Derwent, overhung with wooded hills, sweeping from the west, and then curving away to the south; the bright, meandering Amber pouring its waters into the Derwent; the "halfpenny bridge," with its three arches, spanning the river; the cattle in the meadows; the uprising crags and cliffs, almost hidden by the birches and beeches that bend over them; and the distant hills filling up the background,—form a scene of singular interest and beauty.

Crich Hill, which rises loftily above us, is itself deserving of a special visit. "There is one spot," says Dr. Mantell, "which perhaps is not equalled in England for the lesson it teaches of some of the ancient revolutions of the globe. It is called Crich Hill." The country around consists of horizontal strata of millstone grit; but Crich Hill, a mass of limestone, has been thrust through once superincumbent strata, the layers of limestone being broken and bent by the dome-like position into which they have been forced. But what could have forced this vast mass of matter to an elevation nearly 1000 feet above the sea? A geologist might suggest that it was the result of volcanic action. And he would be right; for a shaft has been sunk through the limestone hill by miners who were in pursuit of lead, and the ancient melted lava has been found lying beneath. "Such is Crich Hill—a stupendous monument of one of the past revolutions of the globe, with its arches of rifted rock, teeming with mineral veins, and resting on a central mound of molten rock, now cooled down."

Leaving Ambergate, the line sweeps away to the left; then, skirting the slopes of Crich Chase, we see beneath us the valley of the Derwent, and beyond are the hills, covered with woods, that form part of Alderwasley Park (pronounced Arrowslea), "famous for its oak timber."

At Whatstandwell Station, locally abbreviated into Watsall, there is a considerable trade and traffic in the fine stone of the district. From this point also a view may be obtained of Lea Hurst. If the traveller will crane his neck out of the window, and look right ahead in the direction in which the engine is pointing, he will see, about a mile and a half away, a hill top crowned with trees, and the gable of a house peering from among them. The house, though almost covered by ivy, is a comparatively modern erection. Its quaint mullioned windows and high gables, and its oriel, crowned by an open balustrade, projecting from the south end, look down the valley of the Derwent, while all is sheltered from the east by the woods and hills of Lea and Holloway. It is the home of one of England's most honoured daughters—Florence Nightingale. On our left we see the steep inclined plane of the High Peak Railway. It runs from the Cromford Canal to the Peak Forest Canal at Whaley Bridge, in Cheshire. It cost nearly £200,000, but did not pay, and eventually it was leased to the London and North-Western Railway Company in perpetuity.

As we approach Cromford station we observe, across the meadows to our left, standing on a platform on the hill side, the mansion of the Arkwrights,—Willersley Castle. It was built in 1788. It is quadrangular and castellated; it has embattled parapets and a tower gateway in the centre. Thick waving woods and the rocks of Wild Cat Tor fill up the background. Richard Arkwright, the founder of the family, was the thirteenth child of a working man at Preston. He was apprenticed to a barber, and carried on his trade at Wirksworth. He patented his spinning jenny in 1769. Near the line on the left is Cromford Church, founded by Sir Richard Arkwright. It contains a monument by Chantrey. Cromford was "the cradle of the cotton manufacture." Im-

WILLERSLEY CUTTING. A WINTER SKETCH

mediately past Cromford station is a tunnel, and then, a cutting through the rock. Our engraving exactly represents the beautiful appearance presented by this cutting in a recent winter, with its walls of ice. Our illustration is copied from a photograph taken at the time.

Less than a mile from Cromford we are at Matlock Bath. The Heights of Abraham, which are to our left, is a name given on account of their supposed resemblance to those at Quebec. We pass from this beautiful spot by a tunnel under the High Tor, which rises, a mass of limestone, nearly perpendicularly from the water's edge, to a height of nearly 400 feet, its base being hidden with tangled underwood, its slopes covered with elms, ashes, and sycamores, mingled with the light forms of the birch;

HIGH TOR, MATLOCK BATH.

while the Derwent winds rapidly at its base, murmuring over a rocky bed.

Passing Matlock Bridge, which is situated at the "convergence of two valleys which descend from Tansley Moor to join the widening vale of Derwent," and noticing the town which of late years has risen up on its slopes, we are running up the pleasant valley of Darley

Dale. Hard by is the cold and naked slope of Oker Hill, a singular insulated eminence, probably of volcanic origin, rising abruptly from the plain. It is stated to be the site of an entrenched fort erected by the Romans to overawe the disaffected Britons, whom they had driven from the neighbouring lead mines. To this military station "the Romans gave the name Occursus, or the hill of conflict," of which Oker Hill is a corruption. Near the southern verge of the hill are two sycamore trees, said to have been planted by two brothers, who resolved here to part

HADDON HALL.

for ever. Wordsworth commemorates their sorrow and their separation.

Up the wide glen on our right is Stancliffe Hall, the residence of Sir Joseph Whitworth, of engineering renown. The site is one of extreme interest and beauty. In his grounds are quarries of fine stone, from one small corner of which St. George's Hall, Liverpool, was built. These quarries form natural rockeries of vast size. In the churchyard of Darley Dale is a yew-tree, said to be 2300 years old. Its girth is 10 yards.

Continuing our way up this beautiful valley, we approach Rowsley station. Just before reaching it we see the confluence of the Derwent, which comes down from the right, with the Wye, which has flowed down from Buxton. To the right of the station is what was formerly the terminus of the Ambergate and Rowsley line. It is now the Midland goods station. On the left of the passenger station is the well-known "Peacock," with its gables and mullions of the 16th or 17th century, and its good fishing quarters.

CHATSWORTH.

We are now in the neighbourhood of two spots of the deepest interest to tourists,—Haddon Hall and Chatsworth. The former is situated about half way between Rowsley and Bakewell, and is an admirable specimen of the baronial mansions of the 15th and 16th centuries, and is in perfect preservation. Chatsworth is some three miles to the right of the line, and is accessible by any of three or four routes :—by road from Rowsley; by a charming footpath walk among the woods, and over the fields direct from Haddon Hall; and by road either from

Bakewell or Hassop. It is a magnificent residence of an owner distinguished for the highest culture, taste, and wealth. Haddon should first be visited. Its modest proportions, quaint style, and towers and battlements, nestling among the woods, will not unfit the mind for the appreciation of "the Palace of the Peak," with its superb appointments, its picture and sculpture galleries, its orangery and arboretum, its conservatories, and its aqueduct, and the boundless beauty within and around.

About a mile from Rowsley we enter the tunnel or covered way behind Haddon Hall, to which reference has already been made,* and on emerging from it we skirt the sides of a range of hills beneath which the Wye meanders in endless turns along the meadows, and soon the spire and town of Bakewell come into view. This is the principal market town of North Derbyshire. Here, in 924, Edward the Elder planted an entrenched fortress and military station to overawe the disaffected Mercians. The remains of these works may still be traced. On the summit of the Castle Hill is a square plot with a tumulus upon it, hollow at the top; and around are fields known as the Warden Field, the Castle Field, and the Courtyard. In Domesday Book we learn that Bakewell was "a burrough." The waters were held in high repute before the Conquest. The church occupies a commanding position: it is Saxon and Norman, and also contains work of later periods.

A mile north of Bakewell we are at Hassop station; a mile to the right of which is Hassop Hall, the seat of Colonel Leslie. It was garrisoned for Charles I. by Colonel Eyre, in 1643.

Passing the little station of Longstone, where it is said that Henry VII. had a hunting seat, we run between the rocky walls of a cutting into a tunnel through a

* Page 148.

ridge of limestone, called Blackstone Edge. Emerging into the light, we enter on the remarkable scenery of Monsal Dale. We would, however, recommend that if practicable it should be approached by road from Longstone. In doing so the tourist suddenly finds himself at the edge of a cliff from which he can see the vale lying before him; the river, with the "lepping" stones and bridge, the undulating eminences sloping steeply down, the rustic homes of the scanty population, and, not least, the line itself skirting the hills to the left, its viaducts,

NEAR CRESSBROOK.

cuttings, and station; and in the far distance, the tiny hole in the mountain through which runs the iron path from these solitudes on to the busy cities of the north.*

The scenery through which we have now to pass, and the engineering works by which the journey is accomplished, must be seen to be appreciated—they cannot be described at length. The rivers, the valleys, and the railways, seem at certain points to be almost confused together; spot after spot of beauty flashes upon the

* Page 148.

eye of the traveller, and then is gone. A little beyond Cressbrook, at the northern end of Monsal Dale, is a charming view of very unusual beauty, where the line is carried round the bed of the river, between the two tunnels, by a retaining wall of masonry ninety feet high. Again the line burrows into the limestone hills. On emerging into the light, it skirts, at a great elevation, the valley; and, just before reaching Miller's Dale Station, is

MONSAL DALE.

carried over the river by a viaduct, the three centre arches of which are of 90 feet span, and nearly 100 high. The contrast presented between the heavy and abrupt masses of the rocks, and the light and graceful outline of the iron bridge which obliquely overleaps them, is very striking.

Leaving Miller's Dale Station, the railway crosses the valley of the Wye, and then passes into a tunnel. It has not run far when it emerges into daylight, and again crosses the Wye and Chee Vale by a single arch of masonry, the abutments of which rest on the perpendicular rocks on either side.* The momentary glimpse of the scenery right or left has, however, been wonderfully beautiful, for the traveller has crossed Chee Vale at its best part. We now pass along the side of the Vale, and have fine glimpses of some of its interesting peculiarities. It is, however, better enjoyed by the tourist who wanders up its bending course. Now he finds himself closed

MILLER'S DALE VIADUCT.

in on either side with rocks and hills; then naked limestone walls are tinted with lichens and mosses; and anon the ledges and slopes are covered with vegetation, and overhung with mountain ashes, birches, and elms, which intertwine their branches, and hang in a thousand lines and curves of beauty over the swift flowing waters. Now he is climbing steeply up a path a few inches wide, almost concealed by wood; then with bending form he

* Page 149.

creeps under the overhanging walls which the river has worn away; now he is crossing the Wye by a rustic and perilous bridge, and again he is out in the green meadow-lands which fringe the river, where he can watch the May-fly and the trout. And all this wealth of loveliness is on the right and left of the traveller as he flashes over the bridge between the two tunnels, half a mile or so north of the station at Miller's Dale.

TOPLEY PIKE.

The train is now running on a lofty terrace, formed on the hill side, which looks down on the foaming torrent of the Wye. So tortuous is the course of the river, that in the last three miles the railway has crossed it five times. Four of these bridges, though of iron, are of light and even elegant appearance, and at the same time of vast strength.

We are now in the long ravine, called Blackwell Dale.

Here the vegetation thins off, and the country soon grows more open and barren. But the river is with us, first on the right, and then on the left, till we come to the junction of the Buxton and Manchester lines. Here we turn to the left to Buxton, and pursue our way by a course full of interest and beauty. The lofty crags are covered with masses of ivy, and on every ledge, round every base, are tangled woods of ash, and oak, and

PIG TOR.

birch; and every spot is the home of rooks and daws and starlings innumerable. Near Topley Pike, which we see on the left, we enter a tunnel. It is the back of Pig Tor, a "savage-looking headland;" and on emerging from the gloom, we enter Ashwell Dale, and immediately pass the ivy-shrouded toll-house in the valley below, where the line crosses the road by a lofty viaduct. Presently we come to the Lover's Leap. It is a rock on our left close by the road, crested with fir-trees, and forming the entrance to Sherbrook Dell, a quiet glen, at the further end of which is a waterfall.

Here we may pause to quote the words of one well competent to speak of the beauties of this district. "He who would know Derbyshire," says James Croston, "must follow the sweet meanderings of the mountain streams, winding hither and thither through shady

ASHWELL DALE BRIDGE.

nooks and fairy glens, all fringed and festooned with greenery; where the tributary rills come trickling down from the mossy heights, gladdening the ear with their tiny melodies. He must loiter in her bye-lanes, between banks rife with ferns, foxgloves, and blooming hare-bells; where the thick hedgerows and the nodding trees mingle, and form a bower overhead, and the bright sunbeams, playing through the leaves, dapple the green sward with their restless and ever changing shadows." Here in abundance is the trailing "lichen, that clings so fondly to the weatherbeaten rock; the green moss that wreathes itself round the decayed and rotten-looking stump of some old, withered, and blasted tree; the green, dustlike confervæ,—all these, with a host of others, unfold their beauteous forms."

We are now at Buxton, where the stations of the Midland Company and of the London and North Western join one another. Concerning the past history of this town, we are told by a writer, "that in the seventeenth century the gentry of Derbyshire and of the neighbouring counties, repaired to Buxton, where they were crowded into low wooden sheds, and regaled with oatcake, and with a viand which the hosts called mutton, but which the guests strongly suspected to be dog."

At a later period Buxton seems not to have been unduly interesting; for some years ago a writer thus spoke of the pursuits of the visitors: "They hobble up that wearisome treadmill, the Hallbank, and toddle down it again; sit on the benches observing the new arrivals, and admiring the well graduated courtesy with which mine host of St. Ann's, in his white waistcoat, pays his graceful devoirs to each handsome turnout that turns into his hospitable doors. They drink the water, plunge into the water, talk, read, and dream of the water, and wonder how it does not relieve them of their spasms and aches all at once." But those times have passed away, and while the medicinal springs of Buxton have powerful attractions to the invalid, the charms of the place and neighbourhood are numerous and abiding to all.

But we must return to Blackwell Mill, where we left the main line in order to pay a visit to Buxton. And here we may remark that, when it was resolved to make an extension of this Buxton line towards Manchester, serious difficulties had to be encountered. "The thing was," as a practical engineer remarked to the writer, "having got up the hill, how we were to get down again by workable gradients." This problem, however, was eventually solved by the ability and experience of the engineer in chief, Mr. Barlow, assisted by Messrs. Campbell, Campion, and Langley. As early as 1860, Mr. Barlow had begun to study the country with a view to the selection of the best route; and eventually he fixed upon that along which the line now runs. It passes with a gradient of 1 in 90 up a remarkable valley, without water, known as the Great Rocks Dale, following for the first two miles of its course the tortuous course of the valley, with heavy cuttings and embankments, till it reaches Dove Holes, where the summit level is attained, and from whence there is a descent through a very heavy rock cutting to the Dove Holes tunnel. The hill penetrated by this tunnel, forms the northern side of the range known as Cow Low; * and though it stands high and bleak, it is the lowest pass through the hills, which, commencing in Derbyshire and extending northwards through Yorkshire, form what is termed the Backbone of England. The gradient is 1 in 90, "the best that could be obtained without going underground altogether;" and the Midland line is no less than 183 feet below the level of the London and North Western, which passes overhead.

In the Dove Holes hill, through which the Midland line passes, says Mr. Barlow in some particulars with which he has favoured us, "the mountain limestone ceases. The beds dip rapidly to the west, and the old red sandstone and shales then commence and continue onwards for many miles. The tunnel is 2860 yards in

* "Low," in Derbyshire, always means something high.

length, about a third of it being in limestone, and the remainder in sandstone and shale.

"Near the south end of the Dove Holes tunnel, and closely adjoining the turnpike road that leads from Chapel-en-le-Frith to Buxton, is a well-known spot called 'the Swallow Hole.' It is so named because a considerable brook, which rises some miles distant in the direction of Buxton, ran to this hole and there disappeared." This brook attracted the attention of the engineer when laying out the course of the line; but one or two other circumstances subsequently occurred which he did not anticipate. "Between what is now the south end of the tunnel and the turnpike road, there are some limestone quarries in the direct course of the railway, in the rocks of which are many natural fissures which form caverns of various depths. Shortly before commencing the works it was found that a considerable body of water was running through one of these fissures, the flow being distinctly audible in the quarry. Ladders, ropes, and lights were procured; the fissure was explored; and at a depth of thirty feet a very considerable stream of water was seen to be flowing underground from the direction of the Swallow Hole. The effect of this discovery led to such an impression of the peculiarity of the district, and the costly and speculative character of all works carried on in it, that contractors declined to undertake the responsibility except on terms which were considered excessively high. This was an unexpected difficulty to the Company; but, after much deliberation, it was decided to make the tunnel without a contractor, and Mr. James Campbell was appointed to carry out the work, under the superintendence of Mr. Barlow.

"One of the first operations now to be undertaken was to divert this underground river; or, by attacking it above ground, to prevent it flowing underneath until it was out of harm's way. Accordingly a channel was cut near the Swallow Hole, in the direction of the Great Rocks Dale, and the water was turned along it. But now another remarkable circumstance occurred. The river ran along its new course to a point about half a mile south of the tunnel; but here it found another fissure, into which it fell, and disappeared. So matters continued for some six months, when, it seems, the brook filled up this underground cistern; and it then resumed its course along the diverted watercourse which had been provided for it. Finally it found another fissure not far from the present Peak Forest Station, into which it has been running ever since, and from which it is believed there is an underground outlet down the Great Rocks Dale." The course cut for the brook is a total length of nearly two miles through land over which the company had no legal power; and so great was the difficulty, even under the special circumstances, of acquiring this right, that eventually parliamentary authority had to be secured to take possession of the land under one of the "additional powers" acts.

"The body of the underground waters," Mr. Barlow continues, "being thus diverted from the tunnel, the operations of sinking the shafts and driving the heading from the lower end were commenced. These operations were of great difficulty from the extreme hardness of the beds of sandstone and the quantity of water contained in the hill. Nevertheless, by great patience and perseverance, and the excellent arrangements of Mr. Campbell, the work proceeded, and the tunnel, as completed, is one of the finest and most substantial works in the country.

"At the north end of the tunnel there is a considerable cutting formed in the beds of sandstone and shale. The beds rise rapidly towards the north-east, and here a slip occurred, suddenly bringing down an extensive mass of shale which filled up the cutting, and crushed up teen waggons before they could be got out. This of the line was then reformed by a massive covered in masonry."

The perforation of this mountain occupied more than three years. So numerous were the watersprings that were tapped in the progress of the tunnelling, that as many as six engines of from twenty to fifty horse power were employed at a time in pumping. The gangs of navvies had, in this lonely wilderness, to extemporise habitations for themselves, by the erection of conical mud huts, or cave-houses of two or three rooms each, cut in the solid rock, or by cottages built of stone. Many difficulties arose with the men, especially in consequence of the feuds that existed between the English and the Irish navvies; and eventually the latter were driven off the field, and were afraid to return unless they were specially protected at night by the police. The engineer promised that they should be taken care of; and he arranged with the authorities that three policemen should be placed at his disposal. These he directed to appear at certain points of the works, and in certain attitudes and positions, at certain times; and, taking an Irishman under cover of the night to these points at the right moments, he showed one after another of what seemed to be a little army of constables. The three policemen grew into a multitude; the Irishmen were satisfied of the abundant sufficiency of the protection afforded, and they returned to their work.

After leaving the tunnel and covered way at the northern end of the Dove Holes, "the line," says Mr. Barlow, "emerges upon a table land forming the watershed between the Black Brook on the east side and the brooks which rise on the west side and run towards Whalley Bridge. Following the apex of this table land, the line passes close to Chapel-en-le-Frith, where there is a commodious station;" after which it crosses the Black Brook and a tramway of the Sheffield Company, at Chapel Milton, by a stone viaduct of fifteen arches, one hundred feet high. The line then, by a falling gradient, skirts the hill-side still it runs *along* a timber viaduct and *by* a stone one at Bugsworth, where for a moment we must pause.

Here, towards the close of 1866, a remarkable incident occurred. It had been a very wet autumn. England had been drenched with rain; every brook had become a river, every river had overflowed its bed, and the lowlands had been drowned. Railroads generally had suffered; the permanent ways of the old lines had been soddened, and the works of new ones had been carried on with extreme difficulty and with many delays. The new line to Manchester had, however, been completed; goods trains had run for months, and it was intended that in a short time the passenger traffic should commence, when it appeared that there were symptoms of an inclination in some parts of the works near Bugsworth to give way horizontally. The first movement was in the bridge just north of the viaduct, a bridge that crosses the public road; but the fracture was comparatively slight. Then it was found that the five-arched viaduct was going; and that, though it had been built in the form of a curve, it had, by the pressure of the slip, become straight. Two cracks opened in the arches of the viaduct large enough to have held the body of a man; the road bridge was swept away; three large ash trees that had grown on the north side of the high road were carried to such a distance that the road, when reconstructed, instead of being to the south of them, is now to the north; and no fewer than *sixteen acres of land* went down towards the river at the foot of the hill. Here the bed of the "Black Brook," a tributary of the Goyt, was raised several feet, so that it became dry; and the stream had to find a new course for itself in an adjoining field in the next county, Cheshire, instead of Derbyshire; but eventually, as an observer remarked, it "fought its way" backward to its old bed.

"And did you know about this slip?" we inquired of a respectable looking countryman who had come to fetch his milk-cans from the station.

"Yes," he replied. "It was a wonderful slip; but we were not altogether surprised. The road had been partly on the move before. The hill is mostly clay and shale, and it slipped off something harder, I expect. However, it went at last, and no mistake. A goods train ran over the viaduct, if I recollect right, that morning; but it was the last. That day and the day after this road was all of a move. The walls were crackling down; the fences were going; the whole hillside seemed," as he repeated, "of a move. The regular road was stopped; the walls tumbled down, stone after stone, and piece by piece; the road went, and they had to make a new one. The station windows cracked. Yon house was all agait agoin'. It was moving day by day before it went. The owner had a little farm," he added, "and he stayed till he durst not stay any longer."

"You see," said the tenant of the ruined house, as we looked down on some heaps of stones that once formed his premises, "you see, when the paving stones of the cottage floor began to stand up on end, I told my missus it was time we were moving."

"Had you lived there long?"

"Yes, we'd been there a matter of several years," he replied. "Yon was the house, where the big heap is, and that was the 'shippen' at this end of the garden, where I kept my cows. There we stayed, missus, and big dog, and cows and all, till we dursn't stay any longer. Then we flitted."

"And were any of you hurt?"

"No. We got ourselves out, and part of the furniture out; but some of it—chests of drawers and such like—was jammed in, and we had to leave it. A carpenter came from the railway to try to fasten up the roof of the shippen; but I told him it wasn't no use: and it wasn't. So we let the pigs out of the sty and the cows out into the field, and they weren't hurt. But you see those two dead ash trees. They were killed by the slip. They were moved and twisted underground; and when their roots were breaking they cracked like thunder. So when I knew it was no use and I couldn't do anything, I came and stood up here on the bank and watched the house go. It fell at three times, the middle first."

The means adopted by the railway company to restore the line were as effective as the disaster was great. For about ten weeks more than four hundred men were employed night and day—as many as could find elbow room to work. The line itself was first diverted on to solid ground. The bottom of the landslip, which had its seat in the shale, was drained by underground headings of great depth, having lateral headings in every direction in which water could be detected. Meanwhile a new viaduct of great strength, containing about 50,000 feet of Baltic timber; two skew bridges of 30 feet span, with wrought-iron girders; a connecting embankment at one end, and a deep rock cutting at the other, were completed. "The total length of the deviation is about 300 yards. The viaduct has 60 openings of about 20 feet between the centres of the uprights, the greatest depth being about 56 feet." Every difficulty was at length effectually overcome, and the line was opened for passenger traffic in February, 1867.*

* See page 223.

The next station to Bugsworth is New Mills, where we are upon the line of the Manchester, Sheffield, and Lincolnshire Company; now, however, with the little branch on the right to Hayfield, the use of it is shared by the Midland Company. Three miles and a half farther on we arrive at Marple, a station likely to be of growing importance, as the point where the trains respectively to Manchester and Liverpool are finally arranged, and the station and its accommodation have with that design lately been greatly improved. The trains destined for the West shortly afterwards bear away to the left, while those for Manchester, instead of making, as lately, a detour to the right, pursue their way by a new and direct line to that city.

The present Manchester terminus of the Midland Company is the London Road Station. This, a few years since, was rebuilt. Owing to the immense traffic that was going on, and the vast number of trains which had to be received and despatched every day while the works were proceeding, great care and skill were needed, both on the part of those who designed and those who executed the works. No fewer than 450 trains arrived and departed daily; and during one hour of each day some 60 trains were due at the station, equal to one a minute.

The covered roof of this station is 800 feet in length, a distinct platform being provided for both the arrival and departure of each of the two companies, the London and North Western, and the Manchester, Sheffield, and Lincolnshire, so that there are eight lines of rails, 800 feet long, under cover for passenger traffic. The whole length is divided by a road for cabs to pass up and down.

The Midland Company have made special provision at Manchester for their goods traffic. After the trains have run over the Sheffield Company's line as far as Ashbury's Station, the Midland have a separate line to Ancoats, where at an early period they secured a fine old hall, called Ancoats Hall, with its gardens and grounds. There they pulled down houses and pulled up streets, and made their goods depôt on an area of probably some 70 acres of land.

This station was opened on the 2nd of May, 1870. It was about two years in course of construction, and was furnished with every modern convenience and appliance for the easy and rapid despatch of traffic. A shed 300 feet by 328 is provided with arrival and departure platforms, fitted with crane work and hydraulic power. The entire area below is cellared for storage, and above is a room for warehousing goods, fitted with hydraulic cranes for lifting goods from beneath. Hydraulic power is obtained by a 40 horse engine, pumping the water into two upright cylinders, fitted with solid plungers, or, as they are called, "accumulators." These plungers, or pistons, are acted upon by two circular vessels loaded with a weight of 70 tons each, a pressure thus being obtained of 700 pounds on the square inch. The operation is so simple that a boy may work any crane without the slightest difficulty. A piece of ground, about 20 acres in extent, has been laid out for a stone, mineral, and station to station traffic. The cost up to the time of the opening was nearly £500,000.

In addition to this station the Midland Company, in conjunction with the two other Cheshire Companies, are about to erect a new Central Station in the rear of the Exchange at Manchester. This will be a most commodious and convenient terminus, especially for the Manchester and Liverpool traffic. The outlay necessary to secure the accommodation required will be very considerable. "The Central Station at Manchester," says Mr. W. G. Scott, in a communication with which he has favoured us, "will, when completed and opened for traffic, form the main line Midland terminus in Manchester, and being placed in the heart of that great city, adjoining the magnificent Albert Square, the new Town Hall, and the Exchange, must become the favourite point of arrival or departure for all parts of the United Kingdom.

"Leaving this station the line traverses the western suburbs of Manchester, crossing the River Irwell by an iron bridge of large span, and passing for several miles though the property of the De Trafford family, *viâ* Urmston, Flixton, and Glazebrook stations. At this last point the eastern portion of the Cheshire lines diverges in the direction of the city of Chester, and, *viâ* Stockport, Marple, and Ambergate, to London. Proceeding from Glazebrook the line is carried over what is termed Risley Moss; which, in reality, forms a part of that extensive 'bog' well known as Chat Moss, where the elder Stephenson, in the construction of the first Manchester and Liverpool line, had to contend with such enormous difficulties, and which at this point is about twenty-five feet deep. In the case of the Cheshire lines, the whole length of about two miles that passes over the morass was first drained on each side of the course of this railway; temporary cuttings, resembling canals, were provided, and the water was drained from the moss for upwards of eighteen months before the contractors were able to proceed with the excavations down to 'formation level.' These difficulties were eventually overcome, and the line has remained stable ever since.

"Leaving Risley Moss, Padgate Station is passed, and at about sixteen miles from Manchester the ancient town of Warrington is reached. Very important engineering works were required at this place, as the Committee's new Central Station had to be erected near the centre of the town. Extensive cotton mills, workshops, and other valuable property were removed to enable the engineers to construct the viaduct, which carries the line across the town, at a height varying from twenty to twenty-five feet above the street level. A handsome and commodious station, with platforms protected by glass and iron roofing, was here erected, and owing to this station being adjacent to the business portion of the town, the line has been found of immense service for local traffic between Liverpool and Manchester. Continuing westward, the line is carried by a viaduct about sixty yards in length across the Sankey Brook Valley and St. Helen's Canal, and passing through Farnworth, Ditton, and Halewood, reaches Garston, a place which within the last twenty years has risen from a small village to an important and flourishing seaport town.

"The remaining six miles of the journey to the Central Station is constructed through rock cuttings and a number of short tunnels, the terminal station in Liverpool being at the junction of Ranelagh and Bold Streets, the most frequented and central point in the town of Liverpool. The engineering works on the last six miles of railway were extremely heavy and costly. This is admitted to be, both as regards accommodation and completeness, one of the finest termini in the kingdom."

VIADUCT, CHAPEL-EN-LE-FRITH.

CHAPTER XIV.

Trent.—The Erewash Valley.—Long Eaton.—Erewash Canal.—Stanton Gate.—Ilkeston.—The Shipley Collieries.—Heanor and Eastwood.—Codnor Castle and Park.—Pinxton Tramway.—Kirkby Castle.—Coats Park Tunnel.—Alfreton.—Clay Cross.—Return to Ambergate.—Crich Hill.—Limeworks.—Bull Bridge-box.—Wingfield Manor House.—Clay Cross Collieries.—George Stephenson.—Amusing incidents.—Coals and railways.—Wingerworth Hall.—Chesterfield.—Tapton House.—"Old George," his rabbits and bees.—"Revolution House."—Dronfield.—Bradway Tunnel.—Beauchief Abbey and Hall.—Yorkshire.—Sheffield.—Difficult works.—Sheffield and Rotherham line.—Wincobank.—Masborough.—Old main line from Chesterfield.—Staveley.—Treeton.—Rawmarsh.—Wath.—Cudworth.—"Bleak" and "Black Barnsley."—Royston.—Chevet Park and Hall.—Walton Hall.—Wakefield.—Heath Hall and its ghost.—Normanton.—Hunslet.—Leeds.—The Brigg-shot.—Kirkstall Abbey.—Airedale as it was, and is.—Otley and Ilkley Branch.—Wharfedale.—Ben Rhydding.—Dr. Macleod.—Apperley Gap.—Thackley Tunnel.—Guiseley Branch.—Bradford.—Saltaire.—Bingley.—The Worth Valley.—Haworth.—Charlotte Brontë.—The people of the valley.—Keighley.—Kildwick.—Skipton.—Colne Branch.—Yorkshire dales.—Gordale and Malham.—Settle.—Clapham.—Ingleborough.—Lancashire.—Hornby Castle.—Lancaster.—Morecambe.—Carnforth.—Engineering difficulties and successes.—The Lake Side Station.—Barrow-in-Furness and Piel Pier.

Trent Station, for passenger traffic purposes, is a central ganglion of the Midland system; and here we now take our departure along the great trunk line, up the Erewash Valley, for the North. Time was, and not far distant, when both the vale and the line were in different financial circumstances from those of to-day; and amusing stories are told of how the original projectors of the railway had to hawk their shares about, and how they considered it a triumph of diplomacy when they had disposed of one or two. Now the line is loaded with the mineral wealth of the valley; and yet it leaves enormous stores behind. In fact, a map of the valley marked with the spots that indicate the coalpits, presents an appearance as if the district were suffering from a malignant attack of black small-pox.

The Erewash Valley is called after the name of the river, which first issues from a grassy bank near Kirkby, and is represented in the initial letter on the first page of this volume. The river itself is said to derive its own title of Erewash, Erwash, or Errewash, from the Cambro-British word Erwyn, the river of heroes. It separates Derbyshire and Notts; and, as the line crosses and recrosses the water, the traveller is now in the one county and now in the other. The valley and the line descend from within three or four miles of Clay Cross to the Trent Station, and thus form a specially convenient incline for the loaded trains of minerals bound for the south; while, from the slopes on either hand, many tributary branch lines feed the trunk. In addition to the mining population with which the valley teems, there are numerous villages occupied by small manufacturers of hosiery and lace, who take their products to the county town, and bring back supplies of food and clothing for themselves.

One of the first of these is the large and increasing village of Long Eaton, conspicuous in which are the extensive waggon works of Mr. J. S. Claye, and the new lace factory of the Messrs. Fletcher. Extending to the northward, are the numerous and commodious cottages occupied by servants of the Midland Company; and then we see the large engine stables and sidings of Toton. This is a place of almost as much importance in the working of the mineral traffic of this district as Trent Station is for the passenger traffic. Here the loaded trains for the North and the empty ones from the South are marshalled for their next journey to their respective destinations; and for this service some five and twenty miles of sidings have been laid down.

The Erewash Canal now comes into view. This work was begun in the year 1777, by the coalowners, in order to secure a watery way from Langley Mill to the Trent, opposite the Soar. The railway and canal run nearly parallel with each other for many miles. The general direction of the canal is nearly north for eleven miles and a quarter; it falls 108 feet by means of fourteen locks. So great was the traffic that at one time the shares sold for three times their original value.

On a hill-top upon our left, the village and church with a large chancel, of Sandiacre now appear. It was formerly called Saint Diacre. Stapleford is on the right, and on the high ground behind is Bramcote. At Stapleford is the handsome residence and grounds of Colonel Wright. We soon observe, about a half a mile to our left, the smoking chimneys of the vast ironworks of Stanton Gate. The river Erewash meanders on our right, and the Erewash Canal runs parallel to us on our left. We now pass a tall chimney, near the top of which, at a height of perhaps 200 feet from the ground, is a narrow cornice, some six feet in width: when it was finished one workman wheeled another round it in a barrow. The village of Trowell is now near the line on the east; and, just as we pass over the river, and are for a moment in Nottinghamshire, the branch line from Radford to Trowell joins us. We have not remained in Notts for half a mile when, crossing the Erewash, we are again in Derbyshire; then another minute, and we recross the river. The hills on our left are occupied by the town and church of Ilkeston. For many years this town was approached by an inclined plane of the railway, worked by horses. With this arrangement the people became dissatisfied; they called a town meeting, and invited Mr. Allport to attend. "I went over," he said, "and attended the meeting; heard all that was to be said; and the proposition was this: The station at present was at the north end of the town. They proposed that we should make a better station, that we should go to parliament to buy land, make a road, and build two bridges, one across the river, and the other across the canal, and they would form the road and repay us for the land. An engagement was entered into, and eighteen persons signed the agreement. We went to parliament, obtained powers, constructed our portion, and paid for the land; and to this day we have never even been refunded the money we paid for the land, and the whole cost of land and road has fallen upon us." *

Of the development of the coalfields of this valley, an illustration may be furnished by the example of the Shipley collieries which are now near at hand.

"When first I recollect the Shipley collieries," said Mr. Sanders, the agent, in evidence before parliament, "the output was not more than forty to fifty tons per annum. At the present time (1872) it is nearly 400,000 tons per annum."

We now reach Langley Mill. On our left are the hills, crowned with the village and church of Heanor,—a spot visited by many an English lad with interest as the scene of the early life and sports of William Howitt, whose "Boy's Country Book" has been as interesting to many as "Robinson Crusoe." It was by the river Erewash that the incident occurred, so graphically described, of the tailor's theft of the bathers' clothes. On the hills on the right are the church and hall of Eastwood, and in the centre of the village is the Sun Inn, where the Midland Company had its birthplace.† We are now in the heart of the collieries of the Erewash Valley, the most extensive of which is, we believe, that known by the name of Messrs. Barber and Walker, at the head of which is Mr. Robert Harrison.

We now pass through an undulating but uninteresting

* Evidence: May 30th, 1872. † See page 8.

country, thinly wooded, with pits at work every here and there, or worked out, until on the hill about three-quarters of a mile on the left of the line may be seen, by good eyes, the remains of Codnor Castle. Here, six hundred years ago, on an eminence in the undisturbed seclusion of the park, was a castle, deeply moated, approached from the east by an avenue of trees, which looked far down the valley of the Erewash. On its western side was a spacious courtyard, well fortified; the massive round towers were battlemented, and had cruciform loopholes for the bowmen. Within these defences was the main building, portions of which remain, consisting of outer and inner

CODNOR CASTLE.

walls, and containing several windows and doorways, part of a turret, and a chimney. Near the ruins is the dovecote, a circular stone building of considerable height, covered by a tiled roof, from which a square wooden turret rises. The immensely massive walls are honeycombed within for hundreds of bedchambers. Near is a spacious pond, which, though on the summit of a high hill, is said never to be dry, a circumstance which has given rise to a local distich:—

"When Codenour's pond runs dry,
Its lordes may say good-bye."

But "good-bye" they have said long ago; and now the

district is known only for its ironworks. These are connected with those at Butterley by a private railway. In every direction on the hill-side are pouring forth the red gleaming fires of the blast and puddling furnaces, and the smoke of the huge chimneys; while all around are tramways, canals, engines, and trucks, bearing their costly burdens hither and thither. The new lines of the Great Northern may here be seen upon the right.

On reaching the next station, Pye Bridge, we observe on our left the extensive ironworks of Messrs. Oates, of Riddings.

Just beyond Pye Bridge, the Midland line divides, and curves right and left. To the right it runs on to the well-known collieries and district of Pinxton, and in the course of a few miles joins the direct line from Nottingham to Mansfield. The old Pinxton tramway ran in the same direction, the curves of which had to be altered before they were suitable for a railway. It had wound right and left around the bases of the little hills on either hand. This was no disadvantage with a horse road; for, in proceeding up hill, the windings were only like those which a good waggoner makes in going up hill; and, in descending, the flange of the wheel pressing against the rail would ease the load downwards. The four deviations that had to be made for the railway may be noticed if we pass from Pye Bridge to Kirkby. We may add that over the hill on his right he will pass Kirkby Castle; but all that is left is some thirty yards of thick rubble wall, five or six feet thick. From the heights on which the castle stood might be seen the hills and dales far away to the south,—a fine expanse both then and now.

Returning to the main line at the north of Pye Bridge, we enter on what is known as the Erewash Valley Extension, a much more modern affair than the Erewash

Valley line. The act was obtained in 1859, and the construction was begun in 1860. The line is short, but there are some heavy works upon it. One of these is a cutting through sandstone and "bind;" and another is the Coats' Park Tunnel, some 1200 yards in length, which runs through the upper coal measures. It touches some "smut" at the lower end of the tunnel.

Almost immediately north of the tunnel is Alfreton, the Alfredingtune of the Saxons, said to have been built by Alfred the Great, and where, it is stated, he had a palace. Here on a fine day is a beautiful view of some of the Derbyshire Hills, Crich Stand being conspicuous upon the summit of the more southern of them.

The town of Alfreton is about a mile to the left of the station. The line, which has been rising from Codnor Park to this point, now begins to fall away to the north. It rises again at Doe Hill, and then inclines downwards as far as Clay Cross.

Several important coal lines run off at our right,—to the Blackwell, Tibshelf and Teversall, and Pilsley collieries; and before long we find ourselves near, and almost under, the church of North Wingfield, which stands boldly on the crest of the hill. We are soon at Clay Cross itself; and here we join the direct line from Derby, and then run into the station.

At this point we must ask our reader to pause in his journey, and then to take a flight more easy to accomplish in fancy than in fact. On our first trip from London to Manchester and Liverpool, we turned off the old North Midland line at Ambergate, and swept away to the left. We will now return to Ambergate, and come down the line from thence to Clay Cross.

The station at Ambergate stands near the southern entrance of a tunnel, to which we have already referred.*

* Page 49.

On emerging into daylight, we see on our left the Crich Limeworks, erected by George Stephenson at a cost of £20,000, for the purpose of profitably disposing of the small coal produced from the Clay Cross pits. There are twenty kilns; and these would burn, if required, 1000 tons of limestone a week, and would in that case consume some 500 tons of coal. The limestone is brought to the kilns by an inclined plane, down what appears to be a perpendicular hillside. The loaded trucks in their descent draw the empty ones up. When these works were first established, lime was largely used by farmers for their turnip lands. A few years afterwards, however, Liebig published a book to show that when lime and manure were mixed, the lime absorbed the ammonia, and did more harm than good. The trade fell off, and this lime is now used by farmers only when preparing their land. for wheat. Large quantities of Crich lime are also consumed in fluxing, in the manufacture of gas, and for kindred purposes.

Leaving the limeworks, we cross the Amber several times in a short distance, we pass over a road, and then under what seems to be an ordinary bridge, but it is the aqueduct of the Cromford Canal, and heavily laden barges are perhaps being towed over our heads while we are running beneath. This is Bull Bridge, the interesting peculiarities of which we have already described.*

On the left of the line are some limeworks of the Butterley Company. Here is the "Bull Bridge Box," wherein we found a one-armed guardian of the sidings, and a very respectable guardian too. On his hut wall was fastened a "Stirling" tract, admonitory of the perils of the public-house.

"Well," we asked, looking at his armless sleeve, "and how did this happen?" And he told us how it was

* Page 50.

caused years ago in the shunting of some tip waggons at the making of the Leicester and Hitchin line.

"And so the Company have found you a berth?" we inquired.

"Yes, sir," he answered cheerily; "and they will let me keep it as long as I behave myself."

A mile or so farther on the line enters a cutting, and approaches the Wingfield Tunnel. The redness of the soil on the slope is caused by the quantity of clay that was burnt here for ballasting the line. The tunnel is short, but a fine view may be enjoyed from the top of the hill through which it passes. Crich Hill is south-west, and north and south is the valley of the Amber, closed in by copses, farms, and wood-covered hills, while the river winds through the meadows beneath. Half a mile from

WINGFIELD MANOR HOUSE.

the north end of the tunnel we pass a mill on the right, still known as "the wire mill," though now it grinds flour; and on our left, on the summit of a hill, partly hidden in summer time by trees that climb up its slopes, are what appear to be the towers of a castle, a spot that grows more and more beautiful as it is approached by the visitor. It is the ancient manor house of Wingfield.

"And which is the road to the manor house?" we inquired of a little girl whom we met on the road.

"Eh," she replied, as if in a sentence she would exhaust all possible information on the subject; "eh, and you must go along the road, and turn up by my grandmother's!"

Bless the child! she thought all the world knew her grandmother, for she was all the world to her. It was almost cruel to say a word that might help to dispel so beautiful an illusion, but we were obliged to reply,—

"And where, my dear, is your grandmother's?" And then she pointed out the pretty winding ways over hill and dale along which she had come, and which would surely lead us safely to her grandmother's and to our destination.

Passing down the beautiful glen that separates the rectory of Mr. Hulton on the right from the manor house hill on the left, we stood in front of this fair historic pile. It is "one of the most charming ruins in the kingdom," and "a goodly specimen of domestic architecture of the later part of the fifteenth century." "The great hall is more than seventy feet long." Wingfield was built by Lord Cromwell. Mary Queen of Scots was detained in confinement here for nine years, under the custody of the Earl of Shrewsbury, who was husband of "Bess of Hardwick." During the Civil War Wingfield was taken from the Royalists by Sir John Gell, and the castle dismantled.

Three quarters of a mile north of Wingfield we pass a coal branch. It turns off to the right, somewhat abruptly disappears into a tunnel in the side of a hill, and after a run of about a mile, reaches the Shirland Colliery.

A short distance north of Stretton Station, and

just before we enter the Clay Cross Tunnel, is another summit level of the line, and from hence it continues to fall down as far north as Kilnhurst. From the red sides of the heavy cutting a tincture of iron seems to flow on our left, and the black wall on the right appears to be made of coal. The Clay Cross Tunnel is ventilated by nine shafts. It passes under a cold and dreary hill, on which is built the mining town of Clay Cross, and over which runs the ancient Rykneld Street.* Coal has been worked in this neighbourhood for a hundred years. As pumping machinery was little understood, water soon accumulated, and coal could be drawn out only along levels run into the hill-sides from the outcrop; and as there were no means of carrying it to any distance from the pits, it was disposed of only by "landsale" for local purposes.

When the North Midland line was in course of construction, the question arose how the locomotives were to be supplied with coke, no coal at that time being allowed to be used; and George Stephenson, the engineer, —as a friend of his remarked to us,—"tried to get to the bottom of this subject, as he tried to get to the bottom of any and every difficulty, greater or less, that presented itself to his mind. He learned that coke was made near Dronfield for some steel melters; he traced the bed of coal that supplied this coke as far as Staveley, where the Midland would pass; and he entered into communication with the Duke of Devonshire's agent for the lease of the Staveley property. But before concluding any arrangement, Stephenson sent by the Chesterfield Canal and by sea to London, and to the coke ovens of the London and Birmingham Company at Camden Town, samples of the deep soft coal of Staveley, and of the black shale coal at Dronfield, that it might be determined which of

* The course of this ancient way can be traced at frequent intervals across this county. In one place it is known as "Straight Lane."

the two would yield the better fuel for locomotive purposes. The report was so strongly in favour of the Dronfield coal that the negotiations for the lease of Staveley (which did not then yield the black shale coal) were relinquished. The outcrop of the Dronfield coal was traced to the neighbourhood of Clay Cross, and it was found in the cutting at the south end of the tunnel. Overtures were now made for the Wingerworth estate, where it was intended to sink pits and work the coal for railway purposes; but these negotiations also came to an end. Stephenson then bought and leased some small properties in the immediate neighbourhood of Clay Cross, sank a pit, built a number of coke ovens at a cost of £3000, and on the day of the opening of the North Midland line, not only supplied all the engines with coke, but sent a train of coal from Clay Cross to Derby."

For thirteen years after the Clay Cross collieries were opened they had to contend with difficulties. Other pits had been sunk, the yield of coal in the district had greatly augmented, and yet the area of consumption had enlarged but little. In addition to this, a strong prejudice existed against the coal itself. Its bituminous character made it resemble the seaborne coal of the north, so familiar to and valued by Londoners; and the metropolis would then, as now, have welcomed it; but it was considered impossible that it should be carried so far by railway, and sold at a remunerative price, in competition with the north country coal brought by the coasting colliers. But in the midland counties the bright swift coal of the district was cheap, and the people preferred it. Nottingham, Derby, Birmingham, Leicester, Burton, would have none but it. This new coal, they said, "was not their kind of coal."

Everywhere the agents returned unsatisfactory reports, and amusing stories were told of the objections of customers. A woman at Duffield, for instance, had been assured that if she wanted to keep the fire in, she had only to put a little "small" on the top, and leave it; and she tried the experiment. On her return, however, she found, as she thought, that the fire was out; and, disgusted, she took up the tongs to carry the black mass away into her back yard; but she had only got half across her room when the lump fell into two, burst into a blaze, and nearly set fire to the woman and her house. At Birmingham the agent was sent for by a man who was confined to his room by gout. His indignation was extreme. "Why," he said, "it spits, and fumes, and squirts, and squeaks by day and by night; I can neither eat, nor drink, nor sleep, for the noise it makes." Only one man in the town of Nottingham could be prevailed upon to be a customer: the landlord of an inn; but he affirmed that it was the most sociable coal he had ever seen in his life. "If me and my wife," he said, "go out for a walk, it goes out too; and when we come back, and I put the poker into it, it comes back as well." In addition to these arguments and prejudices, come the fact that the coke made from these pits was not of the quality expected; and, as soon as a line was opened from York to Darlington, the superior quality of the Durham coke drove that from Clay Cross out of the market.

In connection with these circumstances an incident occurred that ought to be mentioned. Shortly after the death of George Stephenson, when his son Robert was in Egypt, examining the then proposed Suez Canal, an agreement was made between the proprietors of the Clay Cross collieries and the London and North Western Railway, to convey 60,000 tons of coal to the metropolis, at the rate of a halfpenny per ton per mile. Robert Stephenson, however, after his father's death, was the largest proprietor in the company, and accordingly the arrangement was not concluded till on his return his sanction could be obtained. This he refused to give, on the ground that such a rate of carriage would be injurious to the railway company; and he would not, he said, consent to sacrifice the interests of the company, of which he was the consulting engineer,—and, as he considered it, his own honour,—for his private interest as a Clay Cross proprietor. Once more the company was placed in difficulties; and one result of the withdrawment of this contract was, that a change took place in the partnership of the company, and the concern passed, with the exception of one original shareholder, into the hands of Mr. (now Sir) William Jackson, Sir Morton Peto, and Sir Joshua Walmsley, who immediately carried out the arrangement with the North Western Company on the terms previously proposed.

In the year 1847, ironworks were established at Clay Cross, principally for the purpose of using the coals that were not saleable at a profit in the markets. The native ores were a long time smelted without much success; but for many years ores have now been brought from Northamptonshire, which, when mixed with those of Clay Cross, have been proved of excellent quality for all foundry purposes.

Two miles to the north of Clay Cross, Wingerworth Hall stands boldly out on the slope of the hills on our left. It was purchased by Nicholas Hunloke, in the reign of Henry VIII. "His grandson, while attending on James I. in his progress through Derbyshire, fell dead at the king's feet." The Hall was held by the Parliamentary forces in 1643. "The grounds extend for a considerable distance up the slopes of the hills."

On either hand a river may now be observed following the course of the line. It is the Rother, which when first seen, is a little stream; but as it attends the line, and is crossed and recrossed, the brook eventually becomes of sufficient importance to give its name to Rotherham.

Four miles north of Clay Cross is Chesterfield. It derives its name from the Castle Hill, at Tapton, a little to the north of the town, of which "castle" or "chester" it was "the field." It stood on the Roman road that ran from Derby to York. The neighbourhood has been the scene of many vicissitudes in English story. The town itself has little to attract; though its remarkable rather than beautiful spire is a conspicuous object. It is twisted out of its original position, both to the south and west, probably by the heat of the sun acting through the lead with which the wooden spire is covered.

Immediately beyond the station, the hill-side on the right is seen to have been broken and blackened by the *débris* from some coalpits. These were "wallow pits," that is worked by hand, or "ginney pits," that is worked by horses. Some of them appear to have been managed on the scale on which it is said coal-mining was formerly carried on: the miner began in the morning, sank his pit by noon; and before night had obtained coal enough to reimburse him for his capital and his labour.

Just beyond this hill is another on which Tapton House is situated. This was the residence of George Stephenson; and his friend, Mr. Charles Binns, the manager of the Clay Cross works, has recounted to the writer many interesting incidents of the habits of the eminent engineer. "He was a man," said Mr. Binns, "of very large ideas. He was large in all his ideas. He was large in his religious ideas. If you put anything new before him in science or nature, he kept it in mind till he had worked it out as far as possible to its ultimate results. If it were a peculiarity in an animal, 'Why,' he would inquire, 'was it so?' If there was some difference of form in an object, how did it become so? He would tell how that his father had an engine in a wood; and how when George was a little lad he used to go and watch the birds, their nests and their ways! He was tenderly attached to all animals. He kept rabbits at Tapton, and he loved to notice their habits, and to sport with them. He had a tiny dog; and he would put it among the rabbits to see them play together. They would stamp their feet at it, and gambol and run races with it; and Old George would look on to see that on no consideration the dog should hurt the rabbits or the rabbits the dog. He was also very fond of bees. He did not understand them scientifically; but he would go with his wife "Betty," as he called her, and watch their ways, and would poke his finger into the hive till they clustered on his finger. They never stung him, except once; and then he got some carbonate of soda and cured the wound. He was as pleasant a man as you ever could find when he was in a good humour; but if he took a dislike to any one, it was very difficult to get him rid of his prejudice against the offender." Trinity Churchyard, on the opposite hill, to the north of Chesterfield, contains the grave of George Stephenson.

About a mile forward, the line, which from Clay Cross has been double, divides: two of the four lines of railway bearing away to the left, and carrying the traveller along the new main line towards Sheffield. A heavy embankment leads past the Sheepbridge Station and the extensive works of the Sheepbridge Iron Company; and soon afterwards we see to the north the village of Whittington. Here formerly was an inn called "Revolution House," because in 1688 a meeting of "Friends to Liberty and the Protestant Religion" adjourned here after they had assembled on the moor. In 1788 the centenary of the event was celebrated by many persons of influence and eminence.

Passing over Unstone Viaduct, to which we have already referred,* we see to our right a mineral line curving away to the east. From this point the Midland Company are about to make a loop of their own, which, touching several collieries and works, will join the main line at the south end of Dronfield Station. From Unstone we climb up an incline of 1 in 90 to Dronfield, on the Drone, a place of increasing importance in connection with the coal and iron industries. Here, so far back as 1794, Messrs. S. & J. Lucas took out a patent for making small castings, comprising fancy and useful articles of various descriptions, by melting ordinary pig in crucibles until it becomes as fluid as water, and then running it into delicately formed moulds. The whole district from Sheepbridge to Dronfield is rich in ironstone and coal, and before long will probably form an unbroken series of works.

A mile north of Dronfield we enter the great Bradway Tunnel. It is a mile and a half long, through millstone grit, and it pierces the hills that so long separated Sheffield from direct communication with the South. In sinking the shafts of this tunnel the influx of water was so great that it is estimated some 16,000 gallons flowed in every hour, and it had to be pumped out by means of seven or eight engines erected for this purpose, and working day and night. As soon, however, as the "heading" was driven through,—a sort of little pioneer tunnel,—"we got rid," remarked Mr. Crossley the other day, "of the water; and this is an illustration of the advantages of having a heading in such works. This water, coming from the millstone grit, was of unusual

* Page 260.

purity, was carried down to Sheffield, and there furnishes an unfailing supply for all station purposes."

On emerging from the tunnel we are in a deep cutting through shale and sandstone, along the foot of which we see the once underground river which the tunnelling set free. On coming out into the open we have on our left the river Sheaf,—after which Sheffield takes its name, —and which alone separates us from Yorkshire.

Beauchieff Station is near a spot of much interest, Beauchieff Abbey. Five minutes' walk on the right of the

BEAUCHIEFF ABBEY.

line, would bring us within sight of the short thick tower of the chapel, and a lane leads to the gates of the Beauchieff estate, immediately within which is the chapel. On the left of the abbey a long ridge rises, covered with dark green woods. Service is held in the chapel every Sunday. A bend in the road which winds up the hill beyond the abbey is the way to Beauchieff Hall, a mansion built in the reign of Charles II. The village of Norton lies about a mile further back. Here an obelisk of Cheesewring granite stands on the village green to the memory of Chantrey, who was born here in 1781, and who was buried here. The house, "which has been modernised and spoilt," is at Jordansthorpe, to the left of the village from which Chantrey in his early days used daily to carry milk on the back of a donkey to Sheffield. Adjoining the village is Norton Hall, the residence of Mr. Charles Cammell.

Returning to Beauchieff Station, and renewing our journey, we see the Sheaf still upon our left. We flash over it for a moment into the next county, and back again into Derbyshire; and at Heeley we again enter, and shall for many a mile remain in, Yorkshire. Of this county it has been said: "It is not only that a vast extent of landscape studded with church and tower and minster, with crumbling walls of castle and abbey, and rich with the site of many a famous battlefield, stretches away till it is lost among the grey masses of the opposite hills; but that the whole wide scene, so beautiful and so interesting from its host of associations, is looked upon from a rough foreground, purpled with heather, and broken into deep scars of rock; or from a lofty hill of wood, with a foam-whitened stream dashing onward from below, and then winding out from the hills to glance like a thread of silver across the wide green landscape." There is, we may add, "no part of England of equal extent which is so rich in historical sites, or which has maintained so decided a political importance from the very dawn of history to the present day."

Sheffield is approached through a tunnel under the grounds of the Duke of Norfolk, who has a seat hard by. The station is built in the valley of the Sheaf. This site was chosen simply because almost insurmountable engineering difficulties prevented the selection of a more central position. It was not an easy work to build a railway station over a river like the Sheaf. Yet it was done; and three arches of fifteen feet span, and of great length cover in the river and carry the line. The station buildings stand on the solid; the rails and roof are over the water. "The roof is of iron and glass, and is supported by forty-two iron columns. There are one and three quarter miles of wrought-iron girders, and about 90,000 bolts and rivets in the roof; and 37,500 feet of glass. The footbridge is 105 feet long. The clear span is ninety feet, and the weight about thirty tons. The total weight of the wrought and cast iron is 630 tons. The building is of rock-faced wallstone, tool-dressed, and the style of architecture is Grecian, with Gothic headings. The platforms are 700 feet long, and 30 feet wide." At the north end are two docks; at the south end there is one. Four lines of railway run through the station; a spacious area opens in front of it, and it has all the appliances suited for the administration of the executive and the accommodation of the public."

Leaving the station for the north, we pass through heavy and difficult works, in what is called "The Park." This is a high hill of sandstone overlying coal measures and clay; but the stone had been quarried, and nothing but *débris* left in its place; and the coal had been "got," so that, as Mr. Crossley remarked, "We dared not tunnel. The only course left was to make an open cutting for about half a mile, with an immense number of bridges, till we came out into the valley of the Don. We cross over the river and the turnpike road with a bridge, and then we have a long viaduct through the low part of Sheffield."

At Attercliffe there is a station, and a large iron bridge over the road; and soon afterwards we see on our left the former station imbedded in a mass of ironworks, whose contiguity rendered its extension impossible. We now pass on to the old Sheffield and Rotherham line, upon which we shall run nearly as far as Masborough. This railway, when originally contemplated, like all the earlier lines, encountered much opposition. "A hundred and twenty inhabitants of Rotherham," we are told, "headed by their vicar, had petitioned against the bill, because they thought the canal and the turnpike furnished sufficient accommodation between the two towns, and because they dreaded an incursion of the idle, drunken, and dissolute portion of the Sheffield people as a consequence of increasing the facilities of transit."* These and similar objections had weight, and the Lords' Committee rejected the Bill in 1835. But the promoters were resolute; in the following year they were successful; and on the 31st of October, 1838, the line was opened. A pilot engine was sent first, and then followed the train itself, with its "very elegant" carriages painted yellow, carrying Earl Fitzwilliam, the directors, and other influential persons, who were delighted with the "wonderful velocity" with which they "shot along; and who wondered still more when on the return journey they passed the pilot engine."

The region through which we pass from Sheffield to Masborough would be a desolation were it not full of the grimy life which does its dark and necessary work; and, in doing it, tears open the bowels of the earth, flings vast masses of *débris* in every direction, and fills the air with inky smoke and endless din. Behind Attercliffe are the wooded hills of Tinsley Park, rent and seamed with collieries, quarries, and works.

Brightside is on the Don. Its name is scarcely so appropriate to the district as that of Grimesthorpe, through which we have just passed. The next station is Wincobank, on the hill of which is a "large camp, nearly circular, with a deep ditch and vallum," from which extends north-east what is called the Roman Ridge. It is a bank partly natural, formed by a fault in the coal for-

* *Sheffield and Rotherham Independent.*

mation, and partly artificial. On its south side is a deep ditch. This ridge has been traced from Sheffield as far as Masborough. "It is probable," says Murray, "that these lines formed the main defences of the Brigantes on this side of their territory."

In this district the Midland Company have recently been making extensive additions to their line. In order to prevent the possibility of a block during the coming season of heavy traffic, three and three quarter miles of additional sidings have been laid on the down side of the line at Wincobank, and two and a half miles of sidings on the up line at Grimesthorpe. A third line of rails has been laid down between Wincobank and the Holmes station, in order to relieve the main line traffic; and an engine shed is being erected in the neighbourhood capable of accommodating forty-eight engines. The Company have also just erected at Sheffield a bonded warehouse at a cost of £30,000. It is 150 feet high, and is divided into four compartments. The two upper floors are to be devoted to the storage of corn, and their capacity will be equal to 25,000 sacks, or about 3000 tons weight.

Masborough is the next station. The ironworks here, founded by Samuel Walker in the middle of the last century, were probably at one time the largest in Europe. Southwark Bridge, over the Thames, was made at Masborough.

Rotherham, standing to the east of Masborough, is at the confluence of the Rother and the Don. The noble proportions, lofty spire, and crocketted pinnacles of the church of All Saints may be discerned, even though, as Rickman remarks, there are the "tall black cones of the Masborough forges for a foreground."

Having arrived at Masborough by what is now the direct main line of the Midland Company, we may glance at the other route, which for some years formed an integral part of the original North Midland Railway, and served as the only available line from the South to Sheffield. The point of divergence was, as we have seen, a little north of Chesterfield, where both lines cross Whittington Moor. Bearing a little to the eastward, we soon reach Staveley, a place of historic interest as formerly the residence of the Lords of Frescheville, a family of renown in the 17th century; but now better known for its vast and famous ironworks. How greatly the largest anticipations of mineral wealth of this district have fallen short of the actual result may be illustrated at Staveley. When the North Midland line was being made the Staveley Company asked that sidings might be provided for their use. To this request the railway authorities demurred; but eventually it was arranged that the sidings should be put in; but that the Staveley Company should pay interest on the outlay until the traffic sent on to the railway should amount to 20,000 tons a year, after which they should be free. At the present time the Staveley Company places on the railway that amount of traffic many times told.

Passing over a viaduct of five arches, we approach Eckington, on the wood-encircled hill on the left of which is Renishaw Hall, the seat of Sir G. Sitwell. The handsome church and village of Eckington are seen about a mile to the west after we have left the station, though partially shut in by woods and hills. It is a busy little place, with some foundries for making scythes and sickles. The Renishaw furnaces are close to the station.

Three miles from Eckington we pass the Beighton Junction of the Manchester, Sheffield, and Lincolnshire Railway. The Midland Company has no passenger station here, though the line is useful for the interchange of goods traffic. Half a mile forward we cross the Rother, and enter Yorkshire. We now pass under a bridge which carries the Sheffield line over our heads, and a fine viaduct belonging to that company is seen on our left. Another mile brings us to Woodhouse Mill Station; and two miles farther on we have before us, on our right, the village of Treeton, in which it is said that Bradshaw, "the regicide," was buried; but from whence his body was subsequently removed, and hanged at Tyburn. When actually passing Treeton we cannot see it, for we are in a cutting; but it is visible either on approaching or on leaving it.

Half a mile from Treeton we cross, for the fourth time, the Rother, which with many curves pursues its way at the foot of the Canklow woods, which cover the hills on our right, and over which peeps the tower of Boston Castle. For some distance the train now runs on an embankment, from which extensive views may be obtained on either hand till we arrive at Masborough.

Leaving Masborough through a cutting, the line bends away for three or four miles to the right, along the valley of the Don, till we reach Rawmarsh. Here are the Rockingham China Works, "where porcelain four-post beds have been made." On the right, over the Don, is Thrybergh Park. For three centuries it belonged to the Reresbys; but in 1689 it was gambled away by Sir William Reresby, who became "a tapster in the King's Bench prison."

Wath Station is on an embankment. This village is called Wath-upon-Dearne, to distinguish it from another Wath. The Midland line crosses the Dearne just north of the station, and the river with various windings accompanies the line on the left nearly till we pass through a tunnel, 149 yards long, and reach Darfield. The village and church stand on an elevation, from whence a wide range of country may be seen. The traveller may observe from the railway the monument erected in the churchyard over the remains of the 189 men and boys who were killed by an explosion in the Lundhill Colliery in 1857.

The line now winds away to the left; crosses the Dearne four times: the third and fourth times near some richly wooded hills, beneath which the river winds away to the west to Barnsley. We next reach Cudworth, whence there is a branch to Barnsley. This line commences about three quarters of a mile north of the Cudworth station, and soon carries us over one of the most imposing works on the Midland system—the Barnsley Viaduct.* It is more than 1000 feet in length; has three stone piers, on which massive girders rest; and the space from one abutment to another is supported by fourteen very lofty iron piers. These are bolted together, and though light in appearance, form a very safe and substantial structure.

Barnsley is situated on two eminences, and used to be called "bleak Barnsley." The "bleak" is now changed to "black." It is estimated that the value of goods manufactured here is not less than £1,000,000 annually. There are some fifty collieries in the neighbourhood.

Resuming our journey from Cudworth to the north, we observe, on our left, the square tower of the church of Royston. We have now reached another summit level of the line, having been ascending, though by excellent gradients, almost the whole distance from Kilnhurst; the line now continues to fall away as far north as Methley. Near Royston is the Chevet viaduct of thirteen arches; and on our left, about half a mile distant, are Chevet Park and Hall, a house of the time of Henry VIII., and the residence of Sir Lionel Pilkington, Bart. On our right, after passing the fine woods of Haw Park, a view may be obtained of Walton Park, a spot to every

* Page 178.

naturalist of romantic interest. About two miles north of Royston is the Chevet Tunnel, 688 yards in length, passing through which we reach Sandal and Walton Station; and then are on a lofty embankment, from which views are obtained east and west over a wide sweep of country. On a hill crowned with trees are the scanty remains of Sandal Castle, where the Duke of York rested the night before the Battle of Wakefield. From a great distance on the right a line is seen approaching, which at length passes under the Midland. It is the Great Northern from Doncaster to Wakefield. And less than half a mile farther on we are running over another line that comes from east to west: it is the Lancashire and Yorkshire, from Pontefract to Wakefield. On the summit of the hill to the east is the square tower of Crofton Church, beyond which, about three miles distant, are Nostel Park and Priory, but they are hidden from our view by Crofton Hill. From this embankment, too, Walton Park can be seen to the south-east. When the observer is passing over the second of the two railways, he will notice that the canal winds its way in a serpentine form like a gigantic letter S. Over the top of the S, and on the summit of the hill, is a wood, with a dip of open land immediately on its left: that wood is in Walton Park. The Hall itself stands low over the hill,—is, in fact, almost surrounded by the water of the lake. The Midland has access to the Kirkgate and Westgate Stations at Wakefield, both of which are points of junction with other lines.

Resuming our journey on the main line, we next pass Oakenshaw, and are soon in a heavy cutting where little is to be seen,—the greater the pity. For on our left are the village of Heath, the fine common of Heath, and the old hall of Heath, once owned, it is said, by Witham Witham, who was bewitched by a certain Mary Paunall who was executed at York for the offence. To add interest to the spot, we are also assured that the ghost of one Lady Bolles, "a baronettess," the only one ever made, and made one by Charles I., haunts the house. What more could be desired to lend attractiveness to the spot? A mile north of Oakenshaw, we pass under a Roman road; and a little farther on a branch of the Lancashire and Yorkshire is seen approaching on our left from Wakefield; it joins the Midland at Goose Hill Green. Another mile brings us to Normanton, a centre towards which lines converge from different districts, and where the readjustment of trains renders it necessary for both passengers and railway servants to be somewhat specially careful to know that they are "right."

Of Normanton itself we see little, though it lies immediately to our right. But on leaving the station we run for some distance on embankments of considerable elevation, from whence extensive views may be enjoyed over a wide range of country to the east and west of the line. A mile from Normanton Station the North Eastern line passes off to our right, and soon afterwards we cross the canal, the locks of which are conspicuous, that has come hither from Wakefield, and now falls into the Calder; then we cross the Calder River itself. The woods on our left are in Methley Park, the seat of the Earl of Mexborough. Methley is a place of antiquity, and is mentioned in Domesday Book.

The line now pursues its course on an elevation along the valley of the Aire, the flat meadows of which are formed by deposits from fresh water inundations laid on the rugged basis of an old arm of the sea. The river and its canal are conspicuous on our right. Passing Oulton on the left, in the neighbourhood of which the last wolf in Yorkshire is said to have been killed by John of Gaunt, we reach Woodlesford Station, and see the fine woods of Swillington on the hills on the right. Beneath them are extensive coalfields. Here also is the well wooded deer park of Temple Newsam, perhaps the Templestowe described in Ivanhoe. The next station is Hunslet, from which we soon reach the Wellington Terminus, jointly used by the Midland and the London and North Western Companies.

Of Leeds it were easy to say much, and difficult to say

LEEDS.

little. It must suffice to observe that here Romans smelted iron; that after their departure Leeds became an independent kingdom; that subsequently to the Conquest the place is described in Domesday as "Wasta;" that a great castle was erected here, no trace of which remained when Leland came, and said of the place, that it was "a praty market toune, as large as Bradeford, but not so quick as it." In 1642 it was taken by the Royalists, and retaken by Fairfax.

"It stands in a fertile country, intersected with rivers,

and possessing rich beds of coal. It communicates with the Humber and the German Ocean by means of the Aire and Calder Navigation, which allows vessels of 120 tons to come up to the town," and with the Mersey and Liverpool by the Leeds and Liverpool Canal. Its rise, however, to its present state of importance and prosperity is of comparatively recent date. It probably was a seat of the cloth trade from an early period, perhaps as far back as the time of Edward III.; and its cloths were called "narrow," says De Foe, when compared with the broad cloths of the West of England. The cloth market was first held on the bridge over the Aire, and the refreshment "given the clothiers by the innkeepers being a pot of ale, a noggin of porrage, and a trencher of boiled or roast beef, is called the *brigg-shot* to this day." Leeds is now the greatest cloth market in the world.

On leaving the grimy manufacturing suburbs of Leeds, near which the Wellington Station stands, we are charmed to find suddenly that our train is pursuing its way up the beautiful valley of the Aire, with its water courses and water power, its quarries and woollen manufactories, its wooded hills and stately mansions innumerable.

The first object of special interest that we pass is the abbey of Kirkstall. It is on our right; and in no other part of England are "the centuries brought into such close strange contact" as in a spot like this, in which "many a manor and grey village church, rich in memorials of ancient days, rises with a strange and almost pathetic contrast" alongside of the enormous factories and towns of modern civilization.

The abbey was founded by Henry de Lacy, in 1152, in fulfilment of a vow; and here a colony of Cistercian monks were invited to settle from Fountains Abbey. They throve, got into debt, got out again, and were finally "dissolved" in 1540, the site being granted by Henry VIII. in exchange to Thomas Cranmer, and eventually it came into possession of the Earls of Cardigan.

KIRKSTALL ABBEY.

The church is in the form of a cross, with a square tower at the intersection; but in 1779 a large part of the tower fell. The east window is pointed; the west is Norman. Noble remains survive of the nave and aisles, of cloister, court, and chapterhouse, of refectory and infirmary. "It is to the neglect of two centuries and a half," says Whitaker, "the unregarded growth of ivy, and the maturity of vast elms and other forest trees, which have been suffered to spring up among the walls, that Kirkstall is become, as a single object, the most picturesque and beautiful ruin in the kingdom. Add to all the mellow hand of time,—the first of all landscape painters."

"Since the day," says Professor Phillips, "when Henry de Lacy brought the Cistercians to this sweet retreat (1152), how changed are the scenes which the river looks upon! Then from the high rocks of Malham, and the pastures of Craven, to Loidis in Elmete, the deer, wild boar, and white bull were wandering in unfrequented woods, or wading in untainted waters, or roaming over boundless heaths. Now hundreds of thousands of men of many races have extirpated the wood, dyed the waters with tints derived from other lands, turned the heaths into fertile fields, and filled the valley with mills and looms, waterwheels and engine chimneys. Yet is not all the beauty of Airedale lost; nor should the thoughtful mind, which now regards the busy stream of the Aire, lament the change. The quiet spinner is happier than the rude and violent hunter; the spirit of true religion fills these populous villages, as well as it once filled those cloistered walls. The woods are gone, and in their place the iron road; but that road conducts the intelligent lover of beauty to other hills and dales, where art has had no contest with nature, and by enabling him to compare one region with another, corrects his judgment, heightens his enjoyment, and deepens his sympathy with man."

On reaching Apperley, a line is seen rising by a rapid gradient upon our right. It is the Otley and Ilkley branch, and was opened August 1st, 1865. The line runs through the magnificent scenery of the valley of the Aire, towards the upland which separates it from the valley of the Wharfe. The principal station is Guiseley, which crowns the ridge, and up to which the line rises nearly all the way by a gradient of about 1 in 60; but as it sweeps on through the magnificent dale of the Wharfe, it descends at first by a gentle fall and then by a heavy gradient. Menston Junction, the next point on the line, is situated at one angle of the triangle by means of which the two railway systems communicate. Another angle is occupied by the next station, Burley, and the third is at Milnerwood

Junction. The lines between Menstone and these last two points are the exclusive property of the Midland Company. Between Milnerwood and Burley, however, is the central portion of the joint line from Otley to Ilkley, over which the two companies run in common, and which is one of the most beautiful portions of the whole route. The length of the North Eastern line from Arthington to Ilkley is about nine miles; but that of the new portion from Otley is only six. From Ilkley to Burley the line is a steep ascent. The only cuttings are near Burley, and they are not of great depth. The deepest

BEN RHYDDING.

met with on this part of the line is between Milnerwood and Otley. It is, however, through a sandy formation, whereas a deep cutting in the neighbourhood of Guiseley is through rock. The remainder of the line to Otley lies at the base of Otley Chevin.

This valley of the Wharfe has, however, special interest to many beyond that created by the beauty of the scenery. Around its breezy hills and flowing waters cluster memories of health restored and of life prolonged. Ben Rhydding and Ilkley have thus become centres of attraction to growing numbers. Thirty-one years ago, where there are now the vast and stately mansion and the thriving village, were then only the wide ranges of the heathery hillsides and the game and sheep pastures extending away for many a mile on every hand. Mr. Stansfeld,

BEN RHYDDING, NORTH WING AND TOWER.

a relative of the present member of parliament, had, however, been to Graeffenberg, under Preissnitz, and had derived so much benefit from the medical treatment he received, that he resolved to form a company, and to plant a similar establishment here; his motives in this undertaking being both philanthropic and financial. Accordingly he erected what is now the central part of this noble building, in the Scottish baronial style of architecture, and Ben Rhydding came into being. The work was successful. In 1847 Dr. Macleod came as the physician in charge; eventually he became the proprietor, and won for himself wide and deserved esteem for his skill, kindness, and enterprise. Important additions were from time to time made by him to the building. The north and then the south wings were added, and other improvements effected, until standing on the slopes of the moorland hills, 500 feet above the sea, enclosed with wood, and adorned with gardens, flowers, and a thousand objects of interest, Ben Rhydding has become one of the

ILKLEY.

most beautiful and attractive spots in England. More than seventy acres of land are connected with the mansion; accommodation is provided for 150 patients; and everything is supplied that is calculated to ensure the health and comfort of the inmates. Ilkley is the next station.

Returning to Apperley, and pursuing our way westward, we cross the valley and river of the Aire by means of a viaduct. Here, in the month of November, 1866, an incident of special interest occurred. There had been for some time such a downfall of rain as had been unknown in the recollection of "the oldest inhabitant" of the district. The river Aire had been fed by tributary rills that flow down the slopes of the valley as far away to the north-west as Malham and Clapham,—rills that had swollen into torrents; and on the night of the 16th the river near Apperley had overflowed its banks to a breadth of half a mile, until all communication by road had been arrested. A platelayer was returning along the line from his work, when, on passing over the viaduct, he suddenly discovered a rent in the masonry of the stone arch he was crossing,—so suddenly, indeed, that he nearly fell into the abyss, and only by a leap reached the other side in safety. He hastened forward with the tidings; the station-master at Apperley immediately made arrangements to stop the down trains; and then, knowing that an up goods' was nearly due, went forward to meet it. Hurrying along the line lantern in hand, and followed by the platelayer and station-porter, he had not reached the viaduct when he saw the goods' emerge from the tunnel. The red lights were waved; the driver saw them, and shut off the steam, the fireman applied the brakes, and then both men leaped off and escaped. Had they stayed to reverse the engine, it, too, might have been saved; but with the momentum it had acquired it came onward, fell into the hole, struck the already broken arch with a fearful crash, and in a few minutes the viaduct went down like a pack of cards, carrying with it engine, tender, guard's brake, and a train full of dead meat intended for the London market. "We had just time," said the station-master, "to get back to the station, where the signals had stopped the Otley train full of passengers coming from Otley statutes, when we heard the crash of the falling viaduct. All was broken to pieces except the engine; and all the fragments were washed away except the heavy oak frameworks and the wheels and springs. A gang of thirty men from the locomotive staff came down from Derby; put rails into the river under the engine-wheels; drew her inch by inch by windlasses out on to the meadow, and up an incline on to the line. Then they did the tender the same. But they were three days and three nights before they could make a start with the engine." The most energetic measures, also, were at once adopted for the reconstruction of the road: the piers were rebuilt; sixty new iron girders were cast, brought, and fixed in their places; and *in five weeks* from the time the viaduct fell, "Apperley Gap" was closed, and the traffic was resumed. It had been estimated by competent judges that the work would have required six months to complete.

Soon after leaving the viaduct we enter the tunnel that pierces Thackley Hill. Here, also, a singular combination of circumstances occurred. The rain had been falling long and furiously, and the London express had just passed the hill, when a flash of lightning struck the southern entrance of the tunnel, and flung the heavy coping stones down upon the line as if they had been pebbles. Meanwhile, beyond the western end of the tunnel, alarm had been felt lest a reservoir connected with a mill should burst its banks; and the owner, to prevent its contents flowing upon his property, had had the bank cut, so as to turn all the water upon the railway. The water accordingly swept its way two or three feet deep into the tunnel, carrying with it bales of wool and barrels of oil, against which the express ran, and by which (fortunately without injury) it was arrested. To be sealed up in a tunnel by lightning at one end, and to be met by a deluge at the other, was a remarkable combination of misfortunes.

Emerging from the tunnel we have a range of wooded hills upon our left, and the Aire on our right. Across it, approaching from the north, is a new branch railway from Guiseley to Shipley, which is intended to place Ilkley and Bradford in immediate communication. Though the line is short, the works are heavy. The

AIREDALE VIADUCT, ON GUISELEY LINE.

engraving represents one of the viaducts,—not the largest. It carries the line over the valley of the Aire.

At Shipley the branch line turns away, and runs up a wide valley down which the Beck flows from Bradford to the Aire at Shipley. The town is said to have derived its name from being a "broad ford" over a marsh. It "has little ancient history preserved, though it must have been a seat of ironworks in the Roman period, a number of Roman coins having been discovered in the midst of a mass of scoriæ, the refuse of an ancient foundry in the neighbourhood of the town. The supply of ore is still abundant; but the works, though considerable, are not so extensive as perhaps might have been anticipated. The great supply of coal in the neighbourhood has, as in the case of Leeds, been one of the main causes of the growth of the prosperity of the place. In the Civil Wars of the reign of Charles I. Bradford stood for the Parliament, and twice repulsed attacks from the Cavalier garrison of Leeds before it was taken by Newcastle, Lord Fairfax cutting his way through the besiegers to Leeds; but his wife being made prisoner before she

BRADFORD.

could (on horseback) reach the brow of the hill, Newcastle sent her to her husband in his own carriage. Bradford is now the great centre of the worsted trade; Norwich, which was the cradle of the trade, being now supplied from Bradford 'with finer yarns than she can herself make, and at a far lower price.' The earliest manufacture of Bradford, however, was that of woollen cloths."

Less than a mile from Shipley is Saltaire—named after

its founder, Sir Titus Salt, Bart. Of the processes carried on in the factory, which covers twelve acres, and where eighteen miles of cloth a day can be made, we can say nothing; but of the town, the chapels, the baths, the almshouses, the infirmaries, the schools, the club and institute, and the Saltaire Park, it has been well remarked that the whole is the realization of a great idea, and shows "what can be done towards breaking down the barrier that has existed between the sympathies of the labourer

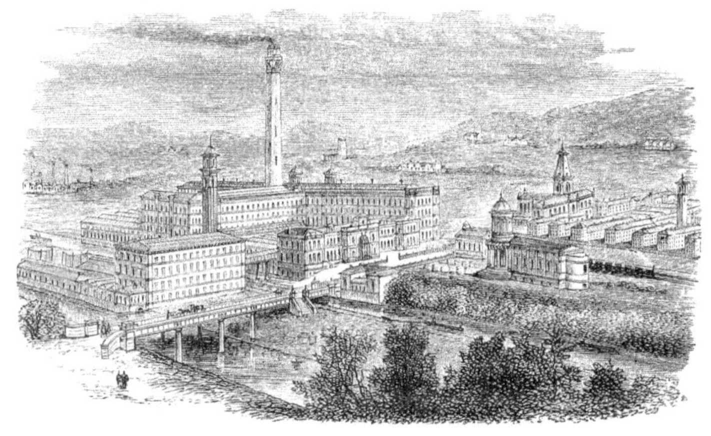

SALTAIRE.

and the employer. No finer picture could be imagined by the dreamer who could think of a probable future of progress for mankind, than that of a city where education is open to every child,—where labour is respected,—where intemperance is banished,—where the graces of life and the higher intellectual pleasures are open to the enjoyment of all,—and where misfortunes are tempered by forethought and kindness. Such is Saltaire."

Rising behind Saltaire to a height of nearly 1000 feet is a hill, the summit of which is known as Baildon Common. The train now runs through Hirst Wood; and then the country opens suddenly and beautifully on

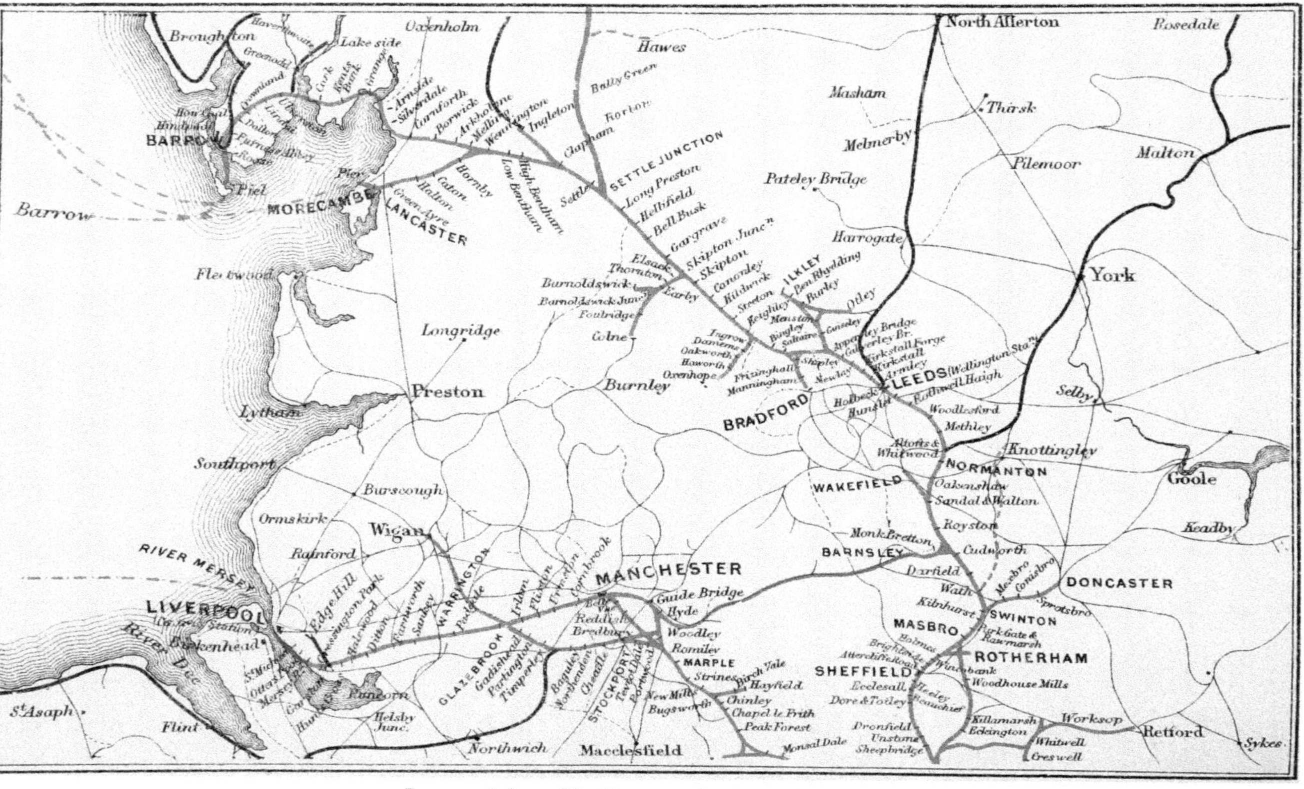

Bemrose & Sons. Map Engravers. London & Derby.

either hand, the hills on the right looming largely and finely to the north; and, passing through a tunnel 150 yards long, under part of the town, we reach the pleasantly situated worsted-making Bingley.

The lordship of this place was bestowed by William the Conqueror on one of his followers. There was also, some 250 years ago, a castle; but no traces of it remain. On the moist banks at Bellbank once grew the rare fern *Trichomanes radicans*. It was discovered by Dr. Richardson. It is possible that a diligent hunter may find specimens of it in the neighbourhood.

Near Bingley are, what were somewhat glowingly described at the time as, "the noblest works of the kind perhaps to be found in the universe, namely, a fivefold, a threefold, a twofold, and a single lock, making together a fall of 120 feet; a large aqueduct bridge of seven arches over the river Aire, and an aqueduct on a large embankment over Shipley Valley." On the day of the opening "five boats of burden passed the grand lock, the first of which descended through a fall of sixty-six feet in less than twenty-nine minutes." At Skipton the canal is 272 feet above the Aire at Leeds; and farther west it rises as much as 500 feet above the level of the sea at low water. This undertaking was forty-six years in progress: it was completed in 1816. It connects the vast manufacturing district of the valley of the Aire,—Leeds, Bradford, Keighley, and other towns,—with Lancashire and Liverpool.

About a mile from Bingley, on the summit of the steep hill on our left, are some large square rocks projecting over the precipice, and easily recognised. They are known as the Druid's Altar; and behind them is the wide expanse of Harden Moor. Beyond the rugged heights on the opposite side of the valley is the far wider expanse of Rumbold's Moor, behind which, to the north, at a distance from Bingley, as the bird flies, of five or six miles, is Ilkley.

As the line runs on an embankment from which we have fine views on either hand, we notice that the hills on the left gradually decline; and, as we skirt round the outlying flank of some of them, we find a valley opening to the south, at the entrance to which Keighley is situated, down which comes the river Worth, and up which runs the Worth Valley branch of the Midland Company. It rises about 500 feet in less than five miles. Here is one spot of special interest: the village of Haworth,—the home of Charlotte Brontë. The church, with its grey tower, stands above the village, and behind it rise the moors. It is doubtless such a church that Miss Brontë had in her mind when she wrote, "This is an autumn evening, wet and wild;" the wind "hurries sobbing over hills of sullen outline, colourless with twilight and mist. Rain has beat all day on that church tower; it rises dark from the stormy enclosure of its graveyard; the nettles, the long grass, and the tombs, all drip with wet." The parsonage is a plain house a little higher up the hill than the church, and looks out on the graveyard and the moors: "a wilderness, featureless, solitary, saddening," but with "the blue tints, the pale mists, the waves and shadows of the horizon," and the line of "sinuous wave-like hills, the scoops into which they fall only revealing other hills beyond of similar colour and shape, crowned with wild bleak moors."

Of the scenery of the neighbourhood generally she wrote: "It is not grand; it is not romantic; it is scarcely striking. Long low moors, dark with heath, shut in little valleys, where a stream waters here and there a fringe of stunted copse. Mills and scattered cottages chase romance from these valleys; it is only higher up, deep in amongst the ridges of the moors, that imagination can find rest for the sole of her foot, and even if she finds it there, she must be a solitude-loving raven—no gentle dove."

The people of the valley of Haworth, Mrs. Gaskell declares, have "little display of any of the amenities of life. Their accost is curt; their accent and tone of speech blunt and harsh. Something of this may probably be attributed to the freedom of mountain air and of isolated hillside life; something be derived from their rough Norse ancestry. They have a quick perception of character, and a keen sense of humour; the dwellers among them must be prepared for certain uncomplimentary, though most likely true, observations, pithily expressed."

Hard by Keighley Station are the works of Messrs. J. and J. Craven, the mansion of the partners, and the ornamental chimney-stack. The chimney is double, and up one of the two shafts is a spiral staircase which conducts to an observatory near the top, from which far-reaching views may be obtained. The town is one of the busiest and wealthiest in Yorkshire. "They mean," said one who knows them, "money; money is what they want; money they will get, and when they get it they keep it." The chief trade is the manufacture of machinery—of woollen spinning machines for export, and of sewing, washing, and wringing machines. No cotton is worked here. Coals come chiefly from near Leeds. A fine walk may be enjoyed from Keighley along the hilltops, by the Druid's Altar to Bingley.

The line continues its course to the north-west,—the noble range of hills of Rumbold's Moor on our right,—passing spots the names of which are suggestive to the antiquary. We now cross over the highway which leads from Steeton, under the hills on the left, to Silsden, on our right, and up a hill of three miles long to Silsden Moor and Addingham. On these hills is a reservoir for the supply of the Leeds and Liverpool Canal. On Rumbold's Moor itself nothing can live but heather—"ling" as it is called. The tourist will "lose sight of land," and see nothing but sky and ling, the latter in autumn in beautiful bloom.

We now approach the hills on the right, on which rise the village, church, and hall, of Kildwick, the latter furnishing, says Murray, "a very good example of a Craven 'hall,'" of the seventeenth century. Passing Cononley Station, we run over the Bradley "Ings," or meadows; and, keeping the Leeds and Liverpool Canal on our right, we soon reach Skipton, the so-called "capital" of Craven. It is spoken of in Domesday as Scepeton, from *scep*, a sheep. It is still surrounded by vast sheep walks. A castle, which has survived from the times of the Conquest, stands on ground so elevated that from its battlements we have looked down into the rooks' nests, built on the topmost branches of the lofty elms, and watched the parents feed their callow young.

From Skipton the Midland has a line to Colne, and from thence has running powers southward. This branch was originally constructed in order to make a connection with the East Lancashire, then an independent company; and the Midland subsequently obtained the running powers to Liverpool and Manchester as the price of their consenting not further to oppose the amalgamation act of the Lancashire and Yorkshire Company, whose bill the Midland had once thrown out. These powers were held in reserve in the event of the new company behaving unfairly to the Midland, but hitherto they have been in abeyance. The opening of the Settle and Carlisle has, however, lately led to arrangements between the Midland Company and the Lancashire and Yorkshire, which will probably cause a considerable amount of the enormous traffic between Lancashire and Scotland to be sent by this route.

The course of the Midland now bears away to the north-west among the western dales of Yorkshire, shut in by rugged hills and wide-stretching moors covered with heather—scenes which are little trodden by pedestrians, but abound with scenes of extreme beauty and grandeur.

At Bell Bank Station we are at the nearest point from Malham, three and a half miles distant, close to which are Gordale and Malham Coves.* "Gordale chasm is probably unrivalled in England (and even in the Scottish highlands we should not easily find a scene that would surpass it) in its almost terrific sublimity."

> "Gordale chasm, terrific as the lair
> Where the young lions couch."—WORDSWORTH.

At Malham the Aire takes its rise. It "has a very singular origin. On the limestone hills above Malham is a large piece of water, once larger than at present, fed from an immense area of dry rocks which absorb the rain and yield a part of their stores to this elevated lake." Malham Water is on the line of the North Craven fault, overlooked on the north by the limestone ranges of Hardflask and Fountains Fell. The natural exit of the water is to the south, as a superficial channel distinctly shows; but instead of following this channel, and falling in a mighty cascade over the tremendous precipice of Malham Cove, "the water sinks into an open jointed limestone rock, and bursts forth in a full and perpetual stream at its foot. This is the Aire; it is speedily augmented by a stream from the cleft rocks of Gordale and other small branches, and flows south through an undulating country till its valley opens into the broader and more level regions of Craven."

At Hellifield there is a new line to Clitheroe. It will place the Lancashire and Yorkshire Company in more

* The landlord of the Buck, at Malham, will, if written to, send a trap for travellers to Bell Busk Station.

direct communication with the Midland, and, *viâ* the Settle and Carlisle, with the north, and aid the interchange of traffic between both companies.

The next station we pass is Long Preston, and soon afterwards the junction of the Settle and Carlisle line is seen on our right. *Setl* is the Anglo-Saxon for a seat. Five miles and a half forward we pass over a remarkable timber viaduct, and are at Clapham, where the trains for

CLAPHAM STATION AND VIADUCT, AND INGLEBOROUGH.

Scotland have been wont to turn off to the right, and run for four or five miles to the station at Ingleton, where they come under the control of the London and North Western Company. Clapham is a place of much interest, being one of the most accessible points for those who intend to visit Ingleborough Mountain,—that "huge creature of God," as Gray calls it,—or the wondrous limestone caves of Clapham, that stretch half a mile into the earth; and it is not improbable that further researches may open up chambers leading yet farther into the recesses of the mountain. Stalactites and stalagmites may here be seen in every stage of their formation, from a drop to a pillar. One stalagmite is ten feet in circumference at the base and two in height, it is estimated that it is the growth of 260 years. One part of the cave is called the "Gothic Archway." A stream of water flows through the cave. Excellent accommodation is to be had at the inn close by the Clapham Station.

The summit of Ingleborough is the site of an ancient British camp. It is of an irregular quadrangular form

AQUEDUCT NEAR LANCASTER.

400 yards on its longer side, and 220 on its shorter. The area enclosed is some fifteen acres, within which are the horse-shoe foundations of nineteen ancient huts, about thirty feet in diameter, all of them opening to the south. Ingleborough is 2361 feet high. Here beacon fires used to be burnt, to give warning of a threatened incursion of the Scots.

Between Bentham and Wennington we enter Lancashire, where we find the junction of the Midland and Furness Railway, and then pursue our way by Hornby. The castle stands on a conical hill washed by the river,—a site formerly occupied by a Roman villa. It is a place full of histories of sieges and struggles "from the time of the notorious Colonel Charteris down to the period when the poet Gray received inspiration from its battlements." Anon we proceed down the beautiful valley of

LANCASTER.

"the stony Lune," as Spenser calls it, to the Green Ayre Station of the Midland Company at Lancaster. The Castle Station of the London and North Western Company is a short distance farther forward. Some of the Midland trains run into it.

From Lancaster the Midland Company has immediate access to Morecambe. We pass over the iron bridge across the Lune depicted in our sketch, and leaving on our left another and older bridge which conducts to the

Castle Station, we run under the lofty embankment of the Lancaster and Carlisle line, and are soon out in the fields on our way to Morecambe. A few years ago the very name, except as that of a beautiful and dangerous bay, was scarcely known; and in the present time, in all legal documents the old name of Poulton, an obscure fishing village which stood upon this spot, is retained. Within the last twenty years, however, a large and increasing town has arisen: the promenade has been completed; by the aid of the Midland Company, the sea-wall has been extended; the new pier has been built, improvements and enlarge-

MORECAMBE.

ments have been made in all directions; and visitors and residents have become so numerous that the place is known among many as "Little Bradford." The handsome and commodious railway station, the pleasant seaside views, the interest of the neighbourhood, the wide-spread bay, the cheering coastline of hill, and to the north and west the mountains of the Lake District, have made Morecambe one of the most attractive spots on the English coast.

Returning to Wennington Junction, and curving to the right, we are on the Midland and Furness line, and soon passing Melling, we run over a viaduct of thirteen arches that crosses the Lune. Here a fine view of the river may be enjoyed, with Hornby Castle in the distance. Emerging from a tunnel under Melling Moor, we observe various country seats, pleasantly situated on the hill-sides; and on our left, at Arkholme, across the valley, is the noble residence known as Storr's Hall; and, in a few minutes, we cross over the London and North Western main line, immediately north of Carnforth Station, and reach the Carnforth Station of the Furness Company. Here, strictly speaking, we should pause, and leave the rest of our journey westward to the historian of the Furness lines. But that company has a special intimacy with the Midland, and there are two points which they may be considered to hold almost in common: access to the Lake District by the Lake Side Station, at Windermere, and to the Isle of Man and Ireland, *viâ* Piel Pier, near Barrow-in-Furness. We may, therefore, briefly refer to these two places.

Leaving Carnforth for the West, we pass along the line of coast that encloses Morecambe Bay on the north. Many hairbreadth escapes are recorded of those who used to try to cross these sands even on foot. "The registers of the parish of Cartmell show that not fewer than one hundred persons have been buried in its churchyard who were drowned in attempting to pass over the sands. This is independent of the similar burials in other churchyards in adjacent parishes on both sides of the bay. The principal danger arose from the treacherous nature of the sands, and their constant shifting during the freshes which occurred in the rivers flowing into the head of the bay."

It is not surprising that great difficulties were encountered by the railway engineer in crossing the estuary of the Leven. The borings told of nothing but sand for a depth of thirty feet. "In one case the boring was carried seventy feet down, and still there was nothing but sand. It was necessary, in the first place, to confine the channel of the river to a fixed bed, which was accomplished by means of weirs formed of 'quarry rid.' No small difficulty was experienced in getting these weirs run out in the right line, in consequence of the eddies produced by the tide at its flux and reflux washing deep holes in the sand on either side. When the current had at length been fixed, a viaduct of fifty spans of thirty feet each was thrown over the channel, and in the viaduct was placed a drawbridge to permit the passage of sailing vessels. To protect the foundations of the piers of this viaduct, as well as the railway embankment, weirs were also formed parallel with the current of the stream, which had the further effect of retaining the silt inland, and thus enabling large tracts of valuable land to be reclaimed.

"The crossing of the Kent estuary was accomplished in a similar manner, by means of weirs and embankments, over ground where the borings showed the sand to be of the depth of from fourteen to twenty-one feet; a viaduct of similar dimensions to that across the Leven providing for the outfall of the river. The land reclaimed behind the embankments at this point is now under cultivation, where only a short time since fishing boats were accustomed to ply their trade." Eventually by the use of iron piles the engineer overcame these difficulties, and found a solid foundation amidst the shifting sands for the piers of the extensive viaducts that he stretched across the mouths of the rivers.

At Ulverston we pause, and take the branch line that leads in a north-easterly direction up the beautiful valley of the Leven to the southern verge of the lovely lake of Windermere. Here the traveller, instead of finding himself, as at the Windermere station of the London and North Western Company, a mile away from the lake, and several miles from Ambleside, has simply to walk from the platform of the station on to the deck of the boat, and he is in the midst of scenery which grows more and more delightful, until he reaches the northern shore of Windermere, within a mile of Ambleside. This is incomparably the more pleasing route by which to visit the Lake District.

LAKE SIDE STATION, WINDERMERE.

For passengers to the north of Ireland, the route to be taken is past Ulverston, in a westerly direction, till the wondrous pile of Furness Abbey is reached. Here the train usually divides: travellers going to Barrow traveling in one portion, those to the steamer in another. The former soon reach the remarkable town of Barrow, which for centuries was a mere dull fishing village, and which even a few years since consisted of a few fishers' and sailors' cottages; it now includes a population of some 25,000 souls. Iron has done it all. The train with the voyagers turns away to the left along a pier that takes them far out to sea to Piel Pier, where the steamer is lying alongside, ready for them to embark. Boats to the Isle of Man run also through the summer months; the

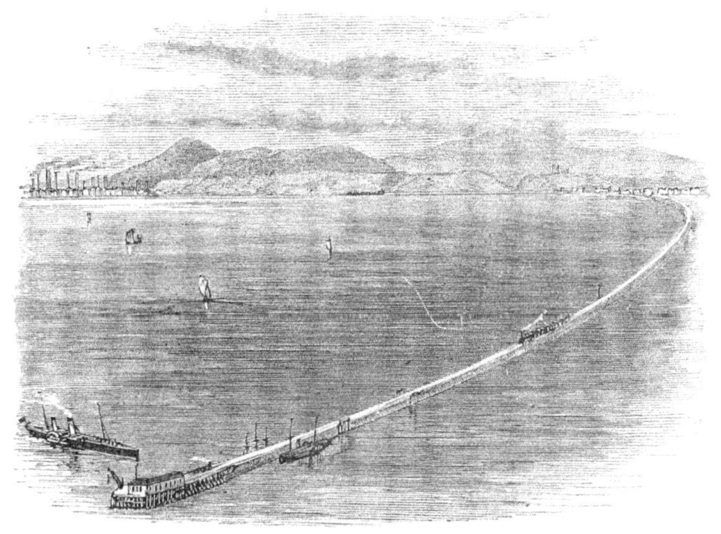

PIEL PIER, NEAR BARROW-IN-FURNESS.

Belfast steamships ply all the year round, and are, we believe, in all respects admirably built, found, and managed. The agents are Messrs. James Little & Co., of Barrow-in-Furness.

CHAPTER XV.

The newspaper express.—The Settle and Carlisle projected.—Extraordinary difficulties of the country.—The Pennine Chain.—Mr. Sharland.—Settle Station.—The dinner hour.—"Machines" and bogs.—Settle. — Craven limeworks. — Stainforth. — "Bridges, ancient and modern."—An old tarn.—Helwith.—The boulder clay. —Geologists and engineers.—"Slurry."—Selside.—A pot hole.—Blea Moor.—"Batty Wife."—A moorland town.—Batty Moss Viaduct.—Storms.—"A forlorn party"—The contractor's hotel. —"A mile a week."—Blea Moor Tunnel.—Shafts.—Railway cuttings and marble mantelpieces.—A journey through a tunnel.—Hoisting a boiler up a mountain.—Tunnel work.—Dynamite and potted lobster.—The Dent Valley.—Ribble Head.—Dent Head.—Constructing a viaduct.—Arten Gill.—Cow Gill.—Views of the country.—Rise Hill Tunnel.—Inside a tunnel.—Strange sights and sounds.—Garsdale.—"The Moorcock."—The Hawes branch.—An extraordinary embankment.—Dandry Mire Viaduct.—Remarkable geological formation.—Railways at the glacial period.—Lunds Viaduct.—Ais Gill Moor.—Westmorland.—The old manor houses.—Bad company.—The Forest of Mallerstang.—Ais Gill Viaduct.—Deep Gill.—Pendragon Castle.—The Morvilles.—The Countess of Pembroke.—Intake Bank.—Birkett Tunnel.—The Pennine fault.—Rock drilling machine.—Geological formation.—Wharton Hall.—Kirkby Stephen.—The waterfalls.—Smardale Viaduct.—"The last stone."—Alarming incident.—Enormous works.—Drilling and blasting.—Boulders.—Crosby Garrett.—Gallansey Cutting.—Griseburn Viaduct.—Crow Hill Cutting.—Helm Tunnel.—Orm and Ormside.—Ormside Viaduct.—The Eden.—Appleby.—Historic associations.—The border wars.—Cromwell's declaration.—The Restoration.—Water wanted.—Battle Brow Bank.—A skew bridge.—Trout Beck.—Newbiggin Hall.—Amusing incident.—Crowdundle Beck and Viaduct.—Westmorland.—Visit to the works.—Culgaith.—Waste Banks.—The Eamont and the Eden.—Eden Hall and its "luck."—Longwathby.—Robberby Beck.—Eden Lacy Viaduct.—A cofferdam.—Long Meg and her Daughters.—Lazonby.—Kirkoswald.—Barren Wood.—Samson's Cave.—The Nunnery and its history.—Armathwaite.—Drybeck Viaduct.—A landslip.—Eden Brow.—Heavy works.—Carlisle.

If a long day's work or pleasure is wanted, commend us to one of the newspaper expresses. We do not mean to say that to leave St. Pancras at 5.15 a.m. would not tax the fortitude of the most inveterate early riser, unless he had spent the night at the Midland Grand; but the ordinary specimens of our sleep-loving race might manage to catch the train in its downward course, say at Bedford, Leicester, or Trent. At any rate, whoever does not go, the newspaper express train goes, with eager speed and exact punctuality; and the traveller on the Midland finds himself careering along the magnificent valleys of the High Peak country at a time when common mortals are eating their breakfasts; that he has reached Manchester at ten o'clock; and that he is on 'Change before the Manchester manufacturers.

Our errand, however, was in a somewhat different direction. We had heard, as everybody had heard, a great deal about a certain new railway in the North, which is to bring England and Scotland more closely together. "The Settle and Carlisle" is a line which (as dear Tom Hood says of Miss Kilmansegg's leg) was "in everybody's mouth, to use a poetical figure." Some millions of money had been spent upon it; Midland shareholders had long eagerly awaited its completion; and the great east and west coast lines had been preparing, with whatever fortitude they could summon, to share a traffic worth, it is said, two millions a year, with their great and growing Midland rival. It was generally understood that the line was approaching completion; that some twenty goods trains a day would soon be hastening up and down those then silent valleys, and that the passenger traffic would commence so soon as the stations were finished and the road was consolidated. So we resolved to go and see that part of the world for ourselves.

It was well known, when the Midland Company decided to secure a route of their own to the gates of Scotland, that no common difficulties would have to be overcome. Years before, Mr. Locke, the eminent engineer, had been daunted by the obstacles he met, and had

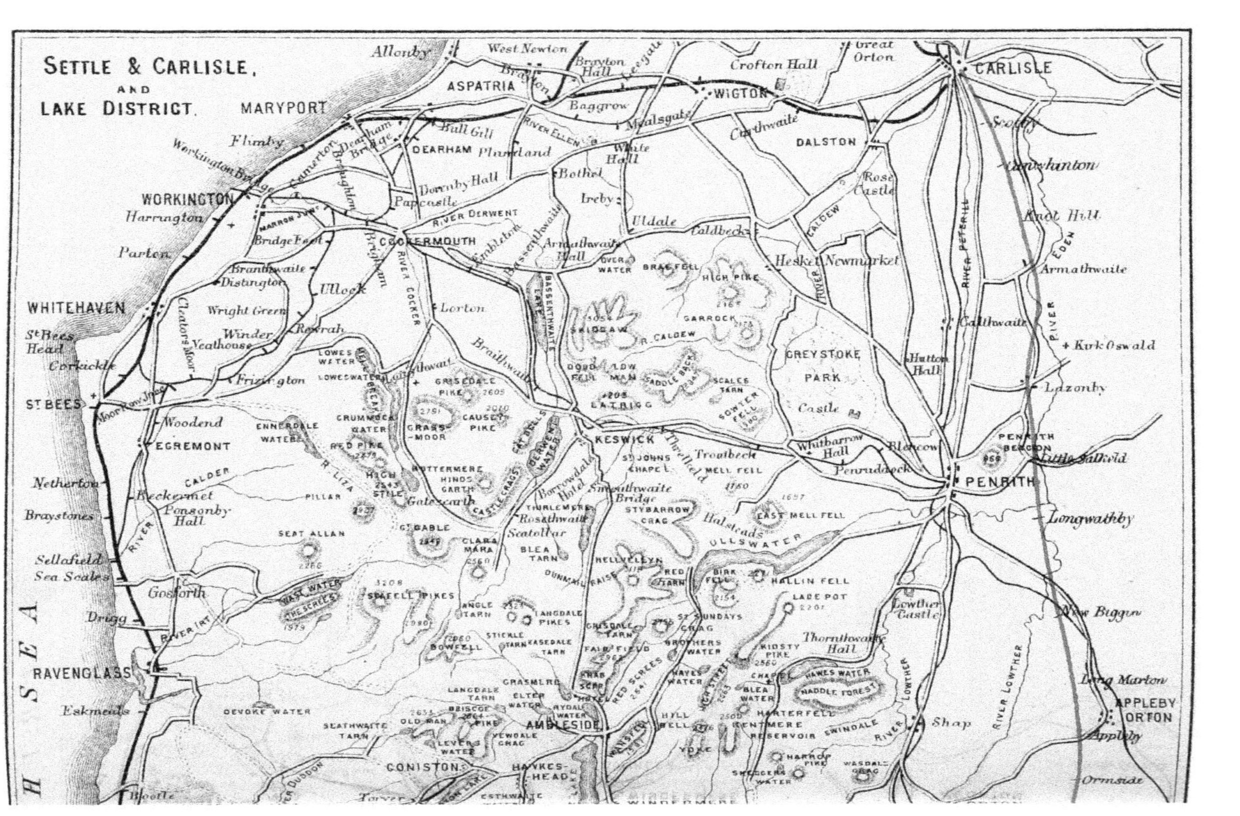
SETTLE & CARLISLE,
AND
LAKE DISTRICT.
CARLISLE
WIGTON
ASPATRIA
MARYPORT
WORKINGTON
WHITEHAVEN
ST BEES
EGREMONT
RAVENGLASS
COCKERMOUTH
KESWICK
PENRITH
AMBLESIDE
CONISTON
APPLEBY
ORTON
DALSTON
GREYSTOKE
PARK
ULLSWATER
BASSENTHWAITE LAKE
DERWENT WATER
HAWES WATER
SEA

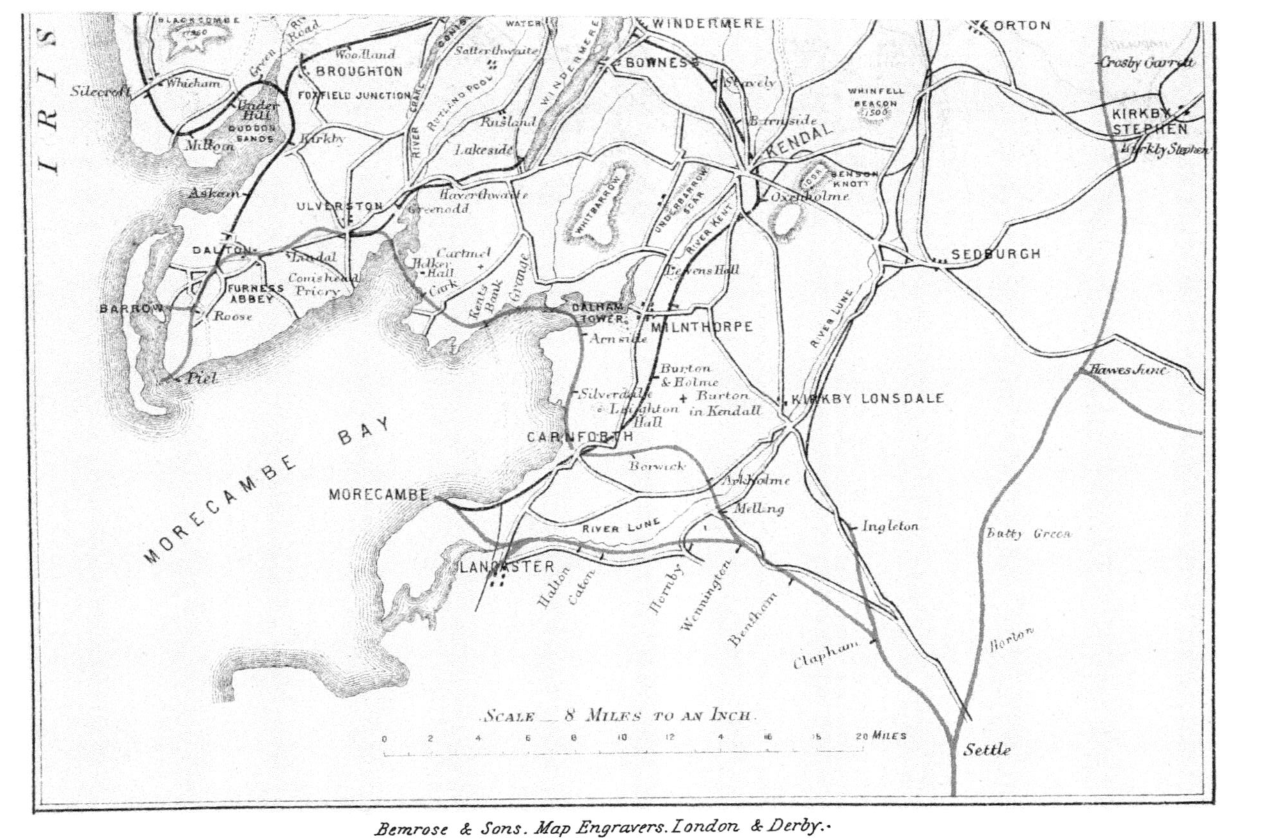

Bemrose & Sons. Map Engravers. London & Derby.

of ground big enough to build a house upon all the way between Settle and Carlisle." A railway for merely local purposes might indeed have been made by running up and down steep gradients, and twisting and twirling right and left with rapid curves, so as to avoid cuttings or embankments; but such a line would have been useless for the very purposes for which the Settle and Carlisle was to be constructed. An ascent would also have to be made over the country to a height of more than 1000 feet above the sea, by an incline that should be easy enough for the swiftest passenger expresses and for the heaviest mineral trains to pass securely and punctually up and down, not only in the bright dry days of summer, but in the darkest and greasiest December nights. Knowing all this, the engineers set to work. However great the obstacle that lay in their path, they had simply one of four courses to take—to go over it, or to go under it, or to go round it, or to go through it: *go* they must. Hence the marvellous variety of work, the endless resources of ingenuity, and the immense demands of labour and capital which characterise this remarkable railway.

After the visit of the general manager and engineer, the first pioneer sent into this remarkable country on behalf of the Midland Company was a young engineer named Sharland. A Tasmanian by birth, he had been for some time professionally engaged on the Maryport and Carlisle Railway, and had become familiar with this entire district. Immediately on his appointment he started off to find the best route for the proposed line, and in ten days walked the whole distance from Carlisle to Settle, taking flying surveys and levels, and determining on what he considered the best course for the railway to take. Unhappily, a very few years afterwards, though he was apparently strong, and unusually commanding in figure and appearance, the toils of his work and the severity of the climate to which he was exposed suddenly developed lurking seeds of disease, and he died at Torquay, regretted by all who knew him.

The first sod of the new line was cut near Anley, in November, 1869; and, by the time of our visit, skill, energy, and money had brought the work nearly to its completion. As our train began to slacken speed for Settle Station, and we saw the new line curving away to the north, we were at the base of a rugged but beautiful valley, down which the roaring Ribble runs. Near the southernmost end of this valley, the town of Settle ("quite," says an admirer, "a metropolitan town") stands among wooded hills, overhung, as one writer says, "in an awful manner," by a lofty limestone rock called Castleber; while far beyond, on the left and right, rise above the sea of mountains the mighty outlines of Whernside and Pennegent, often hid in the dark clouds of trailing mists. Up this valley the new line runs, pursuing its way among perhaps the loneliest dales, the wildest mountain wastes, and the scantiest population of any part of England; yet destined to become one of the world's highways, along which the busiest merchants, the costliest produce, and the ponderous mineral wealth of England and Scotland will hie their way.

Settle presented, when we first saw it, a strange and confused appearance. The pretty passenger station, built of freestone and in Gothic style, was nearly finished; the walls of the spacious goods shed were almost ready to receive the roof, and the commodious cottages hard by for the Company's servants would soon be completed; but around were whitewashed wooden sheds, the temporary offices or homes of the Company's staff, and innumerable piles of contractors' materials no longer required, but ready marked off in lots for a great clearance sale.

It is the dinner hour, and a strange silence prevails throughout the works. Navvies are taking their siesta on the great piled-up baulks of timber, in various and grotesque attitudes; apparently sleeping as composedly, and certainly snoring as satisfactorily, as any alderman could hope to do on his feather bed; while ever and anon some foreman or mason comes to his wooden cottage door, and wistfully gazes at the strangers, wondering what their

THE AMBULANCE.

errand may be. Two vehicles (if so they could be called) standing in the yard, deserve special notice. One, the ambulance, a covered-in homely-looking four-wheeled conveyance, has completed for a time its humane but melancholy work, and is marked with chalk as a "Lot" for sale.

THE BOG CART.

"And what is this for?" we inquired, as we stood in front of the other vehicle, one which our Scotch friends might well call "a machine," that consisted of a huge barrel, over which was a light cart-body and shafts, so arranged that as the horse pulled, the barrel would turn round underneath like a gigantic garden roller.

"You'd be a long while before you guessed," was the reply; and our attempts were in vain. "We used to fill it," said our informant, "with victuals, or clothes, or bricks, to send to the men at work on the line, across bogs where no wheels could go. I've often seen," he added, "three horses in a row pulling at that concern over the moss till they sank up to their middle, and had to be drawn out one at a time by their necks to save their lives." And another Midland engineer subsequently remarked that he had watched four horses dragging one telegraph pole over the boggy ground, and the exertion was so great that one of the horses tore a hoof off.

But the dinner-hour is over. A busy tribe of masons are chip, chip, chipping the rough stones into shape; the carpenters are fitting their timbers together; the cattle are driven into the truck for the dinners of the colony of "Batty Wife's Hole" up the line; the locomotive that is to convey us has drawn, with full steam up, alongside the platform; and Mr. E. O. Ferguson, the company's engineer, is ready to start. We are ready also, and in a minute our engine is puffing and snorting its way up the incline of 1 in 100 that runs fourteen miles and more to the summit level, near the entrance of the great Blea Moor tunnel.

Leaving behind us the stone-built and cleanly houses and streets of Settle, we rise up a heavy embankment containing a quarter of a million cubic yards of earth, and then enter a blue limestone cutting, where spar lodes of copper have been found, and a likely place, it was thought, for lead. We now pass the works of the Craven Lime Company, which, by favour of the Midland authorities, had for some time past been sending off large quantities of lime and limestone by the then unopened railway. The great kiln is formed by one continuous chamber, built in an oval, and communicating with the flue, so that the fire is never allowed to go out, but keeps travelling round. The workmen stack the coal and lime in front of the fire, and when the lime is burnt and has become cold, it is unloaded, and the kiln is restacked. The lime is said to be of admirable quality for fluxing, bleaching, and agricultural purposes, as it is nearly perfectly pure.

SHERIFF BROW BRIDGE.

Three miles from Settle we reach Stainforth. Here, about half a mile on the left of the line, the Ribble has a fall down a rock twenty feet in height. This is Stainforth Force; and though the cascade is not itself visible from the train, we can see the spot where the fall must be. Just beyond the Force we observe what we learn is the site of a Roman camp; a large column of rough stones indicates the centre, and is thought to be part of the remains of the camp itself. A mile beyond Stainforth we for the first time pass over the wide rocky bed of the Ribble by a three-arched bridge. Here the engineers had great difficulty in selecting the best route to be taken; the alternatives being, whether to cross and re-cross the river, or by two very heavy cuttings, and perhaps tunnels, to take the line farther to the east. The bridge is built at an angle of 34 degrees, and the long wing walls that sustain the embankment are of ingenious construction, though they were not liked by the builders on account of the number of "quoins" or corners they required.

We now recross the river, and enter a cutting seventy feet in depth, the clay slate strata of which have the remarkable peculiarity of standing perpendicular to the level of the line; they are also rippled like the sands on the sea shore. Here a county road has for many years been carried over the Ribble by a little bridge; but the county authorities refused the railway company permission to make a level crossing, so the public road had to be diverted and conducted over the river and the railway by a viaduct of considerable length, which, standing beside its little old predecessor, furnished, our engineer remarked, a contrast between "bridges, ancient and modern." Near this spot the line passes along what was once the bed of the river, which had to be diverted along a new course blasted out for it; and by the side of the river a long wall has been erected to protect the embankment from floods. The people at Helwith are chiefly engaged in working the slaty kind of stone we passed in the cutting. It comes out in bedded slabs, perhaps 15 feet wide and 18 feet long, varying from six inches to two feet in thickness, according to the natural beds. It is used for tanks, pavings, landings, troughs, and tombstones.

We now run for nearly half a mile on the only bit o

level line between Settle and Blea Moor. It is on the bed of an old tarn, through which the engineers had to sink for the foundations of the bridge; and in doing this they found they were at the bottom of what had been a lake. To our right lies the quaint old village of Horton in Ribblesdale, behind which are the great heights of Pennegent, rising, as one has said, from the deep vale, with his rounded back like a monstrous whale. "Where is Pennegent near?" we inquire of Mr. Ferguson, our engineer. "Near nowhere," he replies. "Everything is near Pennegent." We now stop at a wooden tank to give our engine water, for it is the best water on this part of the line; and then we enter a cutting. It is of a material we have noticed before, and the fame of which has spread far and wide among engineers,—the boulder-clay. Geologists will take us back to what they call the glacial period, and tell us how, when much of this fair England was lying under the wild waste of waters, the boulder-clay lay as the soft mud beneath; and how the melting icebergs dropped their freights of boulder stones, scratched, grooved, and striated by mighty glaciers, into the clayey bed beneath.* But the engineer views the subject from a different standpoint. He will narrate how it resists almost all his efforts to cut through it; how it is to-day so hard that it must be drilled with holes, and blasted with gunpowder; and how to-morrow, because some rain has fallen, it will turn into a thick gluey clay, so adhesive and tough that when the navvy sticks his pickaxe into it he can hardly get it out again; or if he does, will not have loosened so much as a small teacupful of stuff. Even when it has come out as dry rock and been put into the tip-wagon,

* One geologist was so charmed with some of these boulders, that a mighty specimen was sent to him at Gloucester, where it adorns his garden.

a shower of rain, or even the jolting of a ride of a mile to the tip end, will perhaps shake the whole into a nearly semi-fluid mass of "slurry," which settles down like glue to the bottom of the wagon, and when run to the "tip head" will drag the wagon over to the bottom of the embankment. "I have seen," said our engineer, "sixteen tip-wagons lying at one time at the bottom of the tip; and they would all have gone if we had not put on what we call a bulling-chain between the tip-rails, which, the moment the wagon tipped its load, pulled up the wagon, and prevented it from following."

"I have known the men," remarked Mr. Crossley to us the other day, "blast the boulder-clay like rock, and within a few hours, have to ladle out the same stuff from the same spot like soup in buckets. Or a man strikes a blow with his pick at what he thinks is clay, but there is a great boulder underneath almost as hard as iron, and the man's wrists, arms, and body are so shaken by the shock, that, disgusted, he flings down his tools, asks for his money, and is off."

Two miles from Horton, and nine miles from the junction south of Settle, is the village of Selside. Half a mile from the line is a remarkable chasm in the limestone called a "pot hole," and named after one Allan Pot. Explorers from Settle have descended it by means of rope ladders to a depth of 300 feet. These pot holes seem to be fathomless; for they will carry off any amount of water poured into them, and save all trouble of surface drainage. There is an underground stream into this pot hole, and there is a waterfall from it. The engineers also found a similar hole sixty feet deep near the line, and to prevent the possibility of any slip of the works in that direction, they filled it up. In doing this, an old tip-wagon fell to the bottom; and it being more trouble to recover it than it was worth, it was left there.

Four miles from Selside we cross the turnpike that runs from Ingleton to Hawes; and now the heaviest part of the works begins. The changes here made by the construction of the railway have been stupendous. A few years since, not a vestige of a habitation could be seen. The grouse, and here and there a black-faced mountain sheep, half buried among the ling, were the only visible life. Beyond the valley lay the great hill of Blea Moor, an outlying flank of the mighty mountain Whernside, covering 2000 acres of land, where sundry farmers feed their sheep according to the number of "sheep gaits" they possess. A few months afterwards, dwellings had been erected for the 2,000 navvies who were to work at the viaduct and tunnel, and £20,000 worth of plant had been put upon the ground before the works could be commenced. We may add that the principal owner of the moor required the Company to bury their telegraph wires, in order to prevent injury to his grouse when on the wing.

This is the moorland town, if by such a title it can be dignified, of Batty Green. Tradition offers two explanations of the origin of the name—a name which, till recently, was local and obscure, but which henceforth will be identified with some of the most important and difficult railway works in the land. Once upon a time, we are told, a person named Batty wooed and won a fair damsel who lived in Ingleton Fells; but after a while he fell into evil ways, and went on from bad to worse, until his wife sought refuge from her miseries in a watery grave in what is locally called a "hole" of fathomless depth. The other tradition, scarcely so affecting, is, that the aforesaid Mrs. Batty, pursuing the even tenour of her conjugal and domestic duties, was simply wont to supply her washtub with water from a "hole" which has thus had fame thrust upon it. We leave our readers to make their choice which tradition they prefer.

The town of Batty Wife had, when we visited it, a remarkable appearance. It resembled the gold diggers' villages in the colonies. Potters' carts, drapers' carts, milk carts, greengrocers' carts, butchers' and bakers' carts, brewers' drays, and traps and horses for hire, might all be found, besides numerous hawkers who plied their trade from hut to hut. The Company's offices, yards, stables, storeroom, and shops occupied a large space of ground. There were also the shops of various tradespeople, the inevitable public-houses, a neat-looking hospital, with a covered walk for convalescents, a post-office, a public library, a mission house, and day and Sunday schools. But, despite all these conventionalities, the spot was frequently most desolate and bleak. Though many of the men had been engaged in railway making in rough and foreign countries, they seemed to agree that they were in "one of the wildest, windiest, coldest, and dearest localities" in the world. The wind in the Ingleton Valley in the winter was so violent and piercing that for days together the bricklayers on the viaduct were unable to work, simply from fear of being blown off. At the present time, though the viaduct is wide and well protected by substantial parapets, such is the fury with which the western winds blow up the hollow between Whernside and Ingleborough that it is averred that it would be at the risk of one's life for a person in such weather to walk over alone. Yet here five great railway works follow one another in succession—the viaduct, the embankment, the cutting, the tunnel, and then another viaduct.

The labour of commencing and carrying to a completion so remarkable a series of works in such a district was necessarily increased by the local difficulties. In former times, when coaches* ran between Lancaster and Rich-

* Mail coaches first went from London to Glasgow by Kendal and Shap roads 100 years ago.

mond, the journey across these elevated wilds was allowed to be most harassing. It was no unusual thing for rain to come down upon the travellers "in torrents; for snow to fall in darkened flakes or driving showers of powdered ice; for winds to howl and blow with hurricane force, bewildering to man and beast; for frost to bite and benumb both hands and face till feeling was almost gone; and for hail and sleet to blind the traveller's eyes, and to make his face smart as if beaten with a myriad slender cords." And now all these hardships had to be borne by the workmen on the line. "The wet heather, the sinking peat, the miry and uneven pathways, the little rills draining the hills and winding and leaping on the edge of the huts, dark clouds dissolving in showers and drenching everything permeable to water, the wind moaning in the brown heath in sympathy with the people and the place, were sights and things to be remembered in a ramble over the moors."

Even Mr. Sharland, at the commencement of engineering operations in this district, was destined to learn a lesson of the severity of the climate. When he was engaged in staking out the centre line of the then intended Settle and Carlisle, and had taken up his quarters at a little inn on Blea Moor (a bare and bleak hill 1250 feet above the level of the sea, and miles away from any village), he was literally snowed up. For three weeks it snowed continuously. The tops of the walls round the house were hidden. The snow lay eighteen inches above the lintel of the front door,—a door six feet high. Of course all communication with the surrounding country was suspended. The engineer and his half-dozen men, and the landlord and his family, had to live on the eggs and bacon in the house; in another week their stock would have been exhausted; and it was only by making a tunnel, engineer-like, through the snow to the road that they got water from the horse-trough to drink.

Such were the scenes among which, in the first week of December, 1869, a "forlorn" party, as military men might well call it, commenced the gigantic undertaking of making the Settle and Carlisle Railway. It was known that at this point the heaviest work would have to be done; and here, therefore, according to the practice of railway people, the task was begun. Half a dozen men might be seen wending their way across the moors, and carrying with them a levelling staff. The first thing to be accomplished was to ascertain the best means by which to open communication between the Ingleton road and the mountain-side through which the tunnel was to be made. Picking their way among the peat bogs and the heather, sinking in every now and then, perhaps up to their knees, they at length reached the hillside of Blea Moor, and surveyed the prospect spread out around them. For miles and miles away stretched the bare and rugged hills and the rolling mountains and moors; not a vestige was to be traced of a human habitation, or even of any sort of shelter for man or beast. As they looked southward, the vast and gloomy outline of Whernside lowered over them on the right; Ingleborough was before them; and Pennegent and the great hills of Western Yorkshire were to their left.

But they did not stay long in contemplation, and it was decided that a tramway should be laid across the moors from the Ingleton road up to the mountain. But here, at the outset, difficulties arose: the landowners were hostile to any practical operations being taken, and a bill for the abandonment of the line was, by the influence of sundry Midland shareholders, being pressed upon Parliament; so, although arrangements could be made, no definite action could be taken till the following June. By that time it was thought that perhaps the abandonment bill would be rejected; possession could be obtained of the land, and work be commenced.

On so desolate a field of operations, it was of course necessary that accommodation should be secured for the workmen. The Midland Company are renowned for their hotels—of which they have three, in London, Derby, and Leeds; their contractors now provided a fourth, of which we are happy to give an engraving. It was what one of Mr. Charles Dickens's friends would call "a wan"; what the reader, with more decorum, would

THE CONTRACTORS' HOTEL, BLEA MOOR.

perhaps designate a "caravan," on four wheels, resembling those vehicles in which certain peripatetic pot and brush sellers take up their residence, and from which they dispense their wares to a confiding public. Here ten contractors' men lived for many months hard by the Ingleton road; and from thence they sallied forth day by day to their work.

In addition to the spacious and cheerful accommodation thus provided, some tents were erected on the hill-side of the future tunnel, the materials for which were carried on donkeys' backs. These preliminaries completed, and possession of the land being legally secured, the work of construction commenced by the formation of the tramway across the moors, from the road to the foot of the hill. This was a distance of two miles and a half. As Mr. Ashwell remarked to us, "We worked like Yankees, and laid nearly a mile a week. A month after we began, we had a locomotive running over it. We used it till within a month of the opening of the line and some of it was there the other day. It would scarcely, however, have done for a main thoroughfare, for there were gradients of 1 in 25, and of 1 in 16; and there were curves of two and a half and three chains radius;* but up and down and in and out we went till we reached our destination."

Meanwhile arrangements had to be made for getting stone suitable for the works. A quarry had to be found. "Ordinarily," said Mr. Ashwell, "you can get the help of the people of the district, who tell you of the brooks, or the stone-pits, or where you are most likely to find anything you want; but the only inhabitants here were the grouse. Search had therefore to be made, and trial holes to be sunk in various directions; and eventually, in the bed of a mountain beck, about half a mile from what is now the tunnel mouth, stone was traced; and from it, eventually, upwards of 30,000 cubic yards were taken."

The first work at the tunnel itself was the sinking of the shafts. This was done by the aid of a "jack roll," which is like the windlass over a common well, until horse gins could be got into position; and these in their turn were superseded by four winding engines, placed at the four principal shafts, with which the work involved in making the shaft and lifting out the *débris* was accomplished.

"But how in the world did you ever manage to get that lumbering, ponderous engine up here?" we inquired of our friend, Mr. Ashwell. "Pulled it up with a crab," he replied. "A crab!" we asked, "what's that?" "Well, a windlass perhaps you call it. We fixed the windlass in its place; laid a two-foot gauge road up the

* A chain is 66 feet; a curve of one chain radius is therefore a circle of 132 feet diameter. A three chain radius would mean a circle the diameter of which is 132 *yards*.

hill-side in places sometimes as steep as one foot perpendicular rise in two and a half feet length, and then dragged it up 1300 feet above the sea. By having crabs placed one above another, we pulled up first the boiler, which weighed two tons and a half, and then the engine, the lot weighing very likely six tons. The riveters put it together. It was a strange thing to hear the 'tap, tap' of the riveters' hammers up there in that howling wilderness. When one engine was set to work, we used it for drawing up some of the others."

"And did you get them all up that way?" "Well, no; we had to get another up the flatter side of the hill; and that was more difficult still, because of the bogs. We managed that on a drug,—a four-wheeled timber wagon sort of thing. It was an uncommonly strong one, you may be sure. We brought it along the Ingleton road; and then, for two miles and a half, we pulled it by means of two ropes working round the boiler; as one rope was drawn off the other was rolled on. And so, stage by stage, we dragged it over the rugged and boggy ground, and up to the top of the mountain on which it stands." And there for four years and more those engines did their almost ceaseless work, the two at either end winding materials or men up the inclined planes from near the tunnel mouths, while the others were lowering bricks and mortar in "skeps" down the shafts, or raising the excavated rock or the water that found its way into the workings, and threatened, ever and anon, to drown them out.

From the tunnel ends, and from the bottoms of the shafts "headings" were run till they met. "You see," said Mr. Ferguson, the engineer, "there is room for only four men to work at one time and one place in making a tunnel; and if we had not had shafts from the top, the tunnel would really have had to be bored by eight men, and I am afraid the patience of the Midland shareholders would have been exhausted before the Blea Moor tunnel was finished. But every shaft we sank gave us two more faces to work at, and two more gangs could be put on. By such an arrangement, seven shafts and two tunnel entrances would give sixteen tunnel faces; sixteen gangs of men, day and night, could work; and thus the tunnel could be completed in four years, instead of thirty-two, a period which would have landed us in 1903." Besides, four at least of these shafts are permanently required for the proper ventilation of the tunnel.

"When we had made our shafts," continued our engineer, "we began to run headings north and south, till, at last, they met. The strata through which we had to pass were limestone, gritstone, and shale; but in making the heading we chiefly followed the shale, because it was the easiest, though this sometimes brought us to the level of the rails, and sometimes to the top of the arch. We now started what we termed a 'break up'; that is, we enlarged a certain portion of the tunnel sufficiently to enable us to put in the arch in brick, filling in the space behind the brickwork with *débris*, which, being interpreted, means any loose rock we could get hold of. We then excavated the tunnel down to the floor, till the level of the future rails was reached."

So the work went on, from Sunday night at ten till Saturday night at ten; relays of men relieving one another at six in the morning and six at night. The rock was broken up by hand-drilling, the holes being filled with dynamite, guncotton, or gunpowder, and fired by means of a time fusee. "What is dynamite?" Dynamite looks very much like potted lobster. It will not explode unless heated to 420 deg. Fahrenheit. If a match is placed against it, it burns like grease. It can be carried about in one's pocket; and is even carried about in the men's trousers' pockets to warm it for use. At the same time it has such terribly explosive powers that railway companies dare not convey it; and every ounce used on this line had to be carted from either Carlisle or Newcastle, and cost about £200 a ton, or more than five times as much as gunpowder. We may add that the temperature of the headings, before they were joined, was 80 degrees; but, when the passage was made through, the heat fell 23 degrees, and the thermometer stood at 57. Black damp was met with in the headings, and also an explosive stone; yet, although the strata through which the tunnel passed were of so hard a nature as to require blasting throughout, the compressed air in the hill forced the stone outwards where excavations had been made; and the atmosphere had such an effect on the rock, that the tunnel had to be arched from end to end. It was anticipated that the cost of the tunnel could not be less than £45 for every yard formed, and we have no doubt these expectations have been more than realized.

Meanwhile the task of erecting the viaduct at Batty Moss was laboriously carried on. It stands on the watershed of the Ribble and on Little Dale Beck, and is the largest work on the line, consisting of 24 arches, the height of the loftiest from the bottom of the foundation to the level of the rails being no less than 165 feet. The arches are each of 45 feet span, and they are nearly semicircular in shape. The foundations have been carried 25 feet down through the peat-washing and clay, and they all rest upon the rock. The arches are of brick; and in constructing them, an arch was finished in fine weather every week, the first five of them being completed in five weeks. It is estimated that a million and a half of bricks were used in these arches. The work is of the most solid and durable character, and the stones are of very large dimensions, some of them

K K

weighing seven or eight tons, and many courses being from three to four feet in thickness. Every sixth pier is made of enormous strength, so that if, from any unlooked-for contingency, any one arch should ever fall, only six arches could follow. The lime used for mortar is hydraulic lime from Barrow-on-Soar. The first stone of this vast structure was laid by Mr. William Ashwell, October 12th, 1870; and the last arch was turned in October, 1874. Our engraving represents the Batty Moss Viaduct in course of construction. As many

BATTY MOSS VIADUCT.

viaducts embellish these pages, it was thought it would be more agreeable to the reader to have some of them depicted in some intermediate stage of their erection.

But we now move forward from the viaduct on to the great embankment that succeeds it; and as we do so, we notice right athwart our path the mighty range of Whernside, nearly 2500 feet in height; so, to avoid it, the line bends to the right, and before long we enter the cutting that leads to Blea Moor Tunnel. We first run through a short tunnel and under a mountain stream called Force Gill. This gill was the source of much trouble to the engineers, for it carried away their temporary bridges and drowned their quarries; but it now runs peacefully above our heads along a large stone trough that has been set with hot asphalte to insure its being watertight.

The cutting itself is through strata principally of millstone grit and black marble, both of which cropped out on the surface before the work was begun, and some 400,000 cubic yards of which had to be removed before the tunnel entrance was reached. How many hypothetical marble mantel-pieces were destroyed in the process we have not been informed.

We can now see through the "spectacles" of the powerful little engine which is drawing us, that we are approaching the mouth of what may perhaps be more strictly called the "covered way" that leads to the famous Blea Moor Tunnel. It was intended to make the entrance some distance farther north; but eventually it was thought safer (in order to avoid any slipping of earth down the mountain or down the sides of the cutting, which would have been nearly 100 feet deep) to cover in the cutting, and, in effect, to commence the tunnel 400 yards farther south.

We are now in the tunnel. Nothing is to be seen but the lamp, which our engineer has just lit, dangling from the roof, and throwing its bull's-eye light on the tunnel wall. Nothing is to be heard but the roar of our puffing snorting little engine, and the hollow reverberation of the mighty cavern. Onward we go, beneath a mountain, which rises yet 500 feet above our heads; when suddenly some sharp shrill whistles are sounded, the speed is slackened, and we find ourselves slowly moving among groups of scores of men with flickering lights and candles stuck on end on the projecting crags of the rocky tunnel sides. For a moment we pause. "What's up?" shouts a deep voice; and some answer, inarticulate to us, is returned.

The steam is turned on; again we move forward into the thick black night; other whistles follow; other lights glimmer and gleam; another group of workmen is passed, looking, by the red light of their fire, a picture

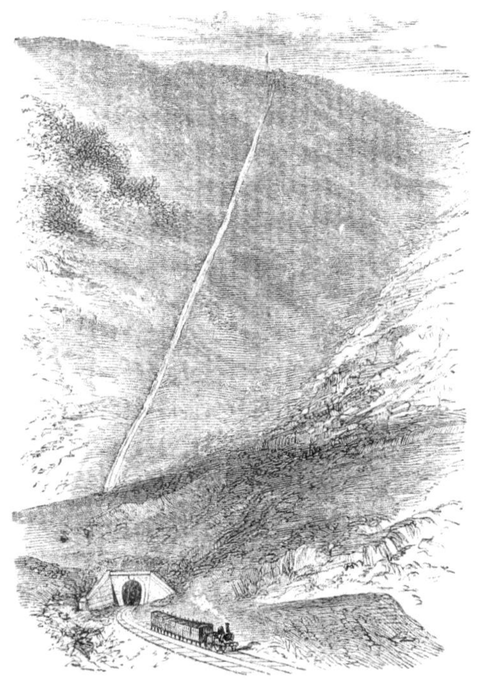

BLEA MOOR TUNNEL—NORTH END.

fit for Rembrandt; and at last, not unwilling, we emerge into the sweet bright light of heaven.

Four hundred yards from the southern entrance of the tunnel we were at the summit level of contract No. 1; some 1150 feet above the sea, a greater elevation than that attained by any other railway in England except the Tebay and Darlington branch of the North Eastern, which at Stainmoor is 1320 feet above the sea. The line now begins its descent towards Carlisle: the tunnel itself inclines downwards, and its drainage runs north.

Alighting from our engine, we stroll forward to look at the next viaduct: it is in the magnificent Dent Valley, the town of Dent being, however, some eight miles to our left. This viaduct is 200 yards long, of ten semicircular arches, rising 100 feet above the public road, and also over a little mountain torrent that falls into the Dee, which runs hard by on our left. The line continues

DENT HEAD VIADUCT.

up the valley of the Dent, which is richly cultivated at its base, but is enclosed right and left by hills that soon become too steep to retain the soil, much of which is carried downwards into the meadows, or is washed away by the waters of the river Dee, which rushes and roars over a bed wonderfully paved, as though by hand, with black marble; the line itself skirting along the hill-side at an elevation of some 300 feet above the stream, and not more than 200 yards from it.

But it was time for us to return to Settle. We had been

drawn up, as we have said, by an engine; but "No. 568" had gone, and our carriage was to run down the incline of 14 miles by itself. In the morning, when ascending, we noticed that only the up line of the permanent way was in use, and we asked whether there was any possibility of meeting a train coming down. "Oh no," said our engineer; "there are only two other small engines on the road, and they always cut out of the way when they see us coming." So having been drawn back through the tunnel by one of the aforesaid little engines, and started off at the other end on our descent, we trusted to the law of gravitation, the strength of our brake, and the skill of our engineer. "We can drop you down in 20 minutes," he remarked; and all we need add is, "drop us down," he did.

Resuming with the company of our reader our journey northward, we ought, however, to pause and visit a spot of much interest,—the spring at Ribble Head. "The source of this important river is at a short distance from the Hawes road, between Batty Green, and Gearstone Inn, on the right hand side. The water issues from the springs in the limestone rock with a grassy mound in the centre; and then, after purling over a bed of pebbles for about twenty yards, it drops with a jingling sound through various openings, and continues its course for some distance underground." It is pleasing to look upon this "insignificant stream, murmuring its sweet mountain music, and its clear water sparkling in the morning sunshine, and then to compare it with its full-grown self at Lytham."

Starting northward from the Dent Viaduct, and creeping up the side of the hill, we reach, at about 17 miles from the commencement, the end of the first contract, and enter on "No. 2." This was about 17 miles in length; was placed in the hands of Messrs. Benton and Woodiwiss in September, 1869, and was commenced early in the following year. It includes some of the most difficult work between Settle and Carlisle.

Dent Head (where the Dee takes its rise, and from whence it flows into the Lune) is at the beginning of this contract, and is one of the wildest and loneliest parts of Yorkshire. All around is wild moorland, closed in by vast hills. A few minutes' walk along the heavy cutting brings us to what is now known sa

ARTEN GILL VIADUCT.

the Arten Gill Viaduct. The gill is deep; the banks on each side are steep; and before the viaduct was commenced there was a waterfall of 60 feet descent. The stream is spanned by a viaduct 660 feet long, of eleven arches, each of 45 feet span, and the rails are 117 feet above the water. The viaduct is built of the same sort of stone as that which, when cut and polished at Mr. Nixon's marble quarries close by, is known by the name of black or Dent marble. Great difficulty was experienced in obtaining a firm foundation for several of the piers, and then they had to be sunk in some cases as much as 55 feet. "It would be impossible," said the resident engineer, "to build piers to such a depth in loose ground like this, and to keep the sides from falling in; we therefore use strong and numerous supports; and to look down some of these foundations ready for putting in the masonry, it seems like one confused mass of timber and strutting." The foundations were, however, eventually laid on the rock, and then the lofty superstructure was reared.

The method by which the erection of such works is carried on in the case of these high viaducts, is indicated by our engraving. A light timber stage, called a "gantry," is constructed on each side of the work, sufficiently wide to allow of the piers and abutments being built between. A jenny, or crane, is then placed on a movable platform extending from one stage to the other. The materials are wound up either by hand or steam power, and are then moved slowly along till they can be lowered to the exact position they are to occupy. As soon as the masonry is built up to the height of the gantry, a fresh lift of timber is put on, the crane is raised to the new height, and so the work is continued to another stage. By these means stones of great size can be used: one in this viaduct measures fourteen feet by six feet, is a foot thick, and weighs more than eight tons; and the total amount for this work alone was upwards of 50,000 tons.

Dent Dale is about ten miles in length. "It is," said a writer fifty years ago, "entirely surrounded with high mountains, and of difficult access to carriages, having few openings where they can enter with safety. In this secluded spot landed property is greatly divided; the estates are very small, and for the most part occupied by the owners." Yet in this "secluded spot," the engineer has come, and where "carriages could scarcely find a safe entry," he has laid down his paths of iron, and run his mighty trains.

Soon after leaving Arten Gill we come to an occupation bridge, which perhaps will not have so much as a passing thought of interest from the ordinary traveller; yet in order to obtain a firm foundation, it was necessary that a shaft should be made some 30 feet deep, and then that piles should be driven five-and-twenty feet lower down into the earth. "We now pass through a cutting containing 95,000 cubic yards, and for the next mile the work is comparatively light. A large culvert over Keld Beck is, however, well worth going down the bank to see. Owing to the very sidelong ground, it was found necessary to build this culvert in steps, and the water pouring over them forms a cascade of 20 or 30 breaks, and has a very pretty effect."

In the neighbourhood of this part of the line the scenery, says our engineer, is "beautiful. A bird's-eye view is obtained of the vale of Dent. Nearly 500 feet below, now sparkling in the sunlight, and now losing itself among some clusters of trees, winds the river Dee, while, first on one side, then the other, is the road that leads to Sedbergh. No busy smoky town is to be seen close by or in the distance; nothing but the greenest of green fields, speckled over with lazy herds of cattle, while here and there lie the homesteads whose inhabitants have that simplicity of life which rural solitudes alone can give. The valley, however, is not always a scene of peace and quietness. In July, 1870, there swept along it one of the most terrific storms that had occurred for many years. A thunderstorm caused the river to swell so suddenly that a wave of several feet in height came rushing, not only along the bed of the river, but also along the road, with resistless force, carrying everything before it."

We next find ourselves running along a cutting from which 150,000 cubic yards have been removed, across the middle of which runs the only accessible road between the valleys of Garsdale and Dent,—a steep and rugged one, rising to the height of nearly 2000 feet above the level of the sea. Emerging from the cutting we are upon an embankment which crosses Cow Gill at a sharp angle, and at a height of 80 feet above the stream. A culvert wide enough for a horse and cart to be driven through, has been built in the bottom, and is of the unusual length of 540 feet; 14,000 tons of stone were used in its construction. The arch is pointed, or Gothic, on account of the unusual weight it has to carry.

A short distance from the northern end of Cow Gill is Black Moss or Rise Hill Tunnel, one of the largest works on the line. Let us visit it as it appeared when in course of construction. We toil up the steep side of the Cow Gill ravine, and come to a small opening in the side of the hill which serves as the temporary heading into the tunnel. But there is not much to be seen here, so we mount to the top, go as far as the first shaft, and taking our place in the iron "skep," at a given signal are rapidly lowered into the depths below. "To one unaccustomed to such travelling, the sudden falling through space produces a giddy sensation, and involuntarily we clutch the chain by which we are suspended. We soon arrive at the bottom, where for some minutes we can see nothing owing to the sudden change from light to almost perfect darkness. Candles, however, are given to each of us, and following our leader we carefully pick our way to that part where the men are working. When one's eyes get more accustomed to the light, what a wonderful place it seems! Solid rock above, below, and on each side; what an enormous amount of labour must have been expended in forming this subterranean passage, 26 feet wide, and 20 feet high, at such a depth below the ground!

"After a long walk, we arrive at the face, where we see some 30 or 40 miners hard at work, whose occupation consists of drilling holes in the rock, which are afterwards charged with gunpowder and exploded. These men work in couples; one holds the drill, or jumper, and slightly alters the position of its cutting edge after every stroke, and the other, by repeated blows of a hammer, forces it into the rock. Great stalwart men are these miners, who seem to wield their heavy hammers with ease, and bring them down on the drill with tremendous force, the sharp click of each blow betraying to even an inexperienced ear the hardness of the material which is being worked. Contrary to our expectation, the air seemed to be very good, but that we were told has only been the case since an opening has been made into the other shaft, through which a constant current of fresh air is passing."

To a stranger, it has been truly said by one who visited this tunnel, there is something unearthly in the sounds and sights of these mining operations. "Dimly burning candles, uncouth looking waggons standing on the rails or moving to and fro, men at the facings, some above and some below, with their numerous lights like twinkling stars in a hazy night, the noise of the twirling drills beneath the terrible force of big hammers wielded by stalwart men, and the hac, hac, or half sepulchral grunt at each stroke, the murky vapour, the chilling damp, and the thick breathing, make a novice to such scenes feel a thrill of more than ordinary pleasure when he ascends to breathe the unpolluted mountain air, and finds that all dread of being engulfed in the rocks (140 feet below the surface of the earth) has fled. As we are leaving, we are alarmed at hearing heavy explosions and feeling the ground shake beneath our feet; but it is only the miners firing the charges in the pit below. It is strange that though the tunnel is cut through the solid rock, it has had to be lined with masonry for three-fourths of its length for fear of any pieces becoming detached and falling on the permanent way."

In the course of the erection of this tunnel a temporary village had to be built, with huts, sheds, and store-rooms, for 350 persons on the hill-top, at an elevation of 1300 feet above the sea level. From here there was a tramway down a steep incline to the road in Garsdale, 600 yards in length, up which all the railway material for this portion of the line had to be drawn by a rope worked by steam power.

In this tunnel there are two permanent shafts. Nearly all the material removed in the boring of the tunnel had to be lifted by steam power to the top of the hill; but it is curious that, owing to the scarcity of ballast, much of it had to be brought down again, and deposited in the permanent way.

On leaving the tunnel, the line emerges into Garsdale. Here a different view from that with which we have become familiar appears; and instead of a wild and dreary waste, we have a kindlier clime and brighter scenes. Some 400 feet below us the stream may be observed winding over its rocky bed at the foot of the steep-sided valley, in the direction of Sedbergh; while to the west the country opens out in extensive views. Soon we see, upon our right, a roadside inn, called "The Moorcock," notable in the district as standing at the junction of three roads. This inn is at the head of three valleys: the Wensleydale, winding eastward down to Hawes, along which the Midland has a branch line in course of construction; the Garsdale Valley, going westerly towards Sedbergh; and the Mallerstang, leading northwards towards Kirkby Stephen.

These valleys and their roads all meet; and travellers innumerable have been wont to dismount their mountain ponies at "The Moorcock" to refresh themselves with mountain dew, perhaps the more willingly from the thought that it has been many a mile since they had such an opportunity before, and that it will be many another before they will have one again.

As an indication of the inaccessibility of this spot, we may mention that every tip waggon here used by the contractor had to be brought by road up from Sedbergh, and that the carriage of them cost a guinea each. At this point 100 were required.

The line to Hawes will, at its termination, form a junction with the Melmerby branch of the North Eastern. The changes in the policy of the Midland Company curiously affected the destiny of these branches. When the Midland Company resolved on making its Settle and Carlisle railway, powers were obtained for making the Melmerby branch to unite with it. But when the Midland Company decided to apply to Parliament in 1869, to abandon the Settle and Carlisle, it was thought that the Melmerby and Hawes extension was unnecessary, and powers for its abandonment were also sought; and, unfortunately for its promoters, were only too successful. Meanwhile the Midland bill abandonment was rejected; the Settle and Carlisle had to be made; so, once again, for the third time, the North Eastern in 1870 had to ask that the deceased powers of the Melmerby line might be revived; and their request was granted.

An embankment was here required to carry the line, and tipping went on for two years. But the peat yielded to the weight placed upon it, and rose on each side in a bank, in some places fifteen feet high. After more than 250,000 cubic yards had been tipped, it was decided that a viaduct of twelve arches over the deepest part of the works must be made. The work thus erected is some fifty feet high, and for nearly the whole length it had to be sunk an additional fifteen feet through the peat before a firm foundation could be obtained.

These difficulties are doubtless to be accounted for by the geological formation of the country. The strata belong to what is called the carboniferous period. "But they are overrun," remarks Mr. Story, the resident engineer, in some notes with which he has favoured us, "by the glacial drift, which at times exceeds a depth of

DANDRY MIRE VIADUCT.

eighty feet, and is composed of a stiff blue clay, filled with boulders of every size up to fifty tons weight. These boulders are the fragments of the stratified rocks of the district, some grit and some limestone; and an examination of them shows that they have been transported in some way or other for many miles from the place where they were originally deposited. The surface of them is marked in a very peculiar way with deep indentations, which show they must have met with some rough treatment on their journey, no doubt caused by their passage over the rocks of the district, the surfaces of which are marked in a similar manner."

In carrying on these works a curious circumstance occurred. A gullet (a sort of preliminary cutting, with steep sides, and big enough for a few tip waggons to be pushed in) had been made, and the rails laid in it. But in the night the rain fell; the walls of the gullet slipped in; the road was buried several yards deep in slurry and mud; and there it was left. Two years passed away. Another and deeper gullet was made onward from the cutting; and to their surprise, the men, as they were digging out the boulder clay, found the remains of a former tram-road. "A splendid discovery," said one concerned in the work, "for a geological fellow. He could prove lots from this. 'Here is a railway in the glacial drift,—in the glacial period; rails, sleepers, and all. Then the world must have been inhabited then; and they had railways then; and very likely a Settle and Carlisle railway into the bargain.' 'There is nothing new under the sun.' "

"A short distance farther on," says Mr. Story, "is Lunds Viaduct, of five arches, and in the bottom is the quarry from which a great number of the viaducts and bridges were built. Another short tunnel, and a mile or two farther the line crosses over Ais Gill Moor, and attains its highest altitude of 1167 feet above the sea, from whence it falls almost uninterruptedly down to Carlisle, 1 in 100 being the ruling gradient. The country here is very wild and rugged. Stone walls mark the division of the properties, and scarcely any house can be seen to remind one that the country is inhabited. On the west rises Wild Boar Fell, with its grandly impressive outline, which after sunset looms dark and terrible, and seems to frown on all around. On the east is Mallerstang Edge, which rises to an altitude of 2328 feet above the sea, five feet higher than the Wild Boar opposite. A very narrow constricted valley runs between, along which in winter the wind sweeps with bitter blasts."

Three miles from the Moorcock, and in a cutting, we have entered the county of Westmorland. The boundary is marked by a stone wall; but as there are scores of stone walls in the immediate neighbourhood exactly like it, we must leave to the sagacity of our reader to determine for himself which is the particular one in question.

The county, however, when one gets into it, is full of interest, and many objects around us are suggestive of the history of the past. "All the old manor houses," for instance, "and other edifices were built for defence against the incursions of the Scotch. The larger houses had areas or yards, strongly walled about, and garnished with turrets and battlements. Within these enclosures they shut up their cattle during the night, and thence they gave notice of an enemy by the firing of beacons and other modes of alarm. Even the farmhouses were secured by strong doors and gates, and had small windows, crossed with strong bars of iron; and many of them had a cowhouse and stable in their lower story."

This was at the time (and the time lasted long) when danger was rife in these border lands; and when on many a mountain-top beacons blazed, startling the night:—

> "A score of fires
> From height and hill and cliff were seen;
> Each with warlike tidings fraught;
> Each from each the signal caught;
> Each from each they glanced to sight
> As stars arise upon the night."

Times happily have changed. We are not now saddened by the sight in these dales of the women carrying manure into the fields in wicker panniers on their shoulders, "while the men lay in groups on a sunny bank, employed in knitting;" or, as Pringle describes, the "beautiful servant maids of this county, toiling in the severe labours of the field, driving the barrows or the ploughs, or sweating at the dung-cart." Manners have mended, too, since it would have been said of any idle fellow: "He keeps vara bad company, t' parson and sich."

We are now passing down what all old maps designate "the forest of Mallerstang,"—renowned for its deep woods and its hunting parties,—though few traces of the forest can be found. Skirting along the hill on the left of the valley, in order to avoid too rapid a descent, we cross over numerous culverts, through which the mountain torrents flow down from the limestone hills toward the river Eden, covering it with rich soil. "Mallerstang," says an interesting writer, "with its high mountain ranges on the east and west of the line, with the farmsteads and fields on the slopes and in the hollows of the hills, will often call forth the admiration of railway travellers. Baugh Fell, Wild Boar Fell" (with its great cape-like head, on the summit of which the shepherds were wont to hold their horse races), "Lunds Fell, and High Seat, with their compeers, will always, when free from mists, form an exquisite mountain landscape. At one time Mallerstang, with its crowding forest trees, was the haunt of wild animals and of every variety of game; and here the lordly owners of the manor, with their retainers and serfs, were wont to make both woods and hills echo with their shouts of glee over the slain of the chase. Though the upper part of the Eden Valley is now occupied by a few industrious and peaceful farmers and shepherds, there was a time in the past when the slogan of border chiefs and their clansmen sent a terror through Mallerstang, and when fire and sword did terrible work to man and beast. The desolation in Mallerstang and other portions of Westmorland was so complete that the county, with those of Durham and Northumberland, was considered by William the Conqueror not worth surveying."

Soon after leaving Ais Gill Moor, the line passes over Ais Gill Viaduct of four arches, and attains a considerable elevation above the road that runs by the river Eden, here still a stream.

One spot of great interest must not be unnoticed here: it is the bridge, depicted in our engraving, over a ravine called Deep Gill. It is half bridge, half culvert, and is a

DEEP GILL.

fine piece of engineering work. Above it is the Wild Boar Fell, where tradition says the last wild boar was killed by one of the Musgrave family, and from this incident it takes its name.

On the east of the line, in a narrow dale overlooked by mountains, and washed by the Eden, is Pendragon Castle. Tradition tells us that it was erected by Uter Pendragon, and that he wished to make the river surround the castle, but failed; and hence an adage that "Eden will run where Eden ran." Its founder, it is said, was slain, with one hundred of his courtiers, by poison put into his "favourite spring," near the castle. Here Sir Hugh Morville, of a Norman house, lord of Westmorland, one of the knights implicated in the murder of à Becket, held his brief but lordly tenure; and his sword was long preserved in Kirkoswald Castle as a memento of the assassination. In the year 1341 this ancient forest seat of the Morvilles was burnt by the Scots under King David; and though rebuilt, it was again destroyed 200 years afterwards (1541). After being deserted for more than a century, the famous Anne, Countess of Pembroke, who, dressed in "a petticoat and waistcoat of black serge," built castles and churches, founded hospitals, spent £40,000 on her "manor mills," fought great law-suits, and married two husbands, with whom she had "crosses and contradictions," took the restoration of the castle in hand. It is said that she could "discourse of all things, from predestination to slea-silk;" and that when an objectionable candidate was forced on one of her boroughs, she wrote, "I have been bullied by an usurper; I have been neglected by a court; but I will not be dictated to by a subject. Your man shall not stand." In 1685, however, Pendragon Castle once more fell; enormous quantities of stone have of late years been removed for making fences, and all that remains of the former grandeur of the once stout strong-hold, are the crumbling ruins of a square tower.

After passing through a heavy cutting, the line is carried along the Intake Bank, about 100 feet high. At this point an extraordinary circumstance occurred: the tipping proceeded *for twelve months without the embankment advancing a yard*. The tip rails, during that whole period, were unmoved, while the masses of slurry, as indicated in the engraving, rolled over one another in mighty con-volutions, persisting in going anywhere and everywhere, except where they were wanted.

Another heavy rock cutting, and the line enters Birkett Tunnel, which has been made through what is called the Great Pennine Fault. Here we pass through shale, mountain limestone, magnesian limestone, grit, slate, iron, coal, and lead ore in thin bands, all within a hundred yards. "The most curious combination," remarked Mr. Crossley, "I have ever seen." In the same side of the hill the strata rise up from a horizontal position till they are perpendicular. Geologists had said that lead would be

INTAKE EMBANKMENT.

met with in the tunnel, and their predictions were verified; but it was not obtained in sufficient quantity to be of practical value. Part of the tunnelling was done by Burleigh's rock drilling machine, driven by compressed air. "We timed it carefully," says a writer in a local journal,* "and saw a hole a foot deep driven in five minutes. Two men drilling by hand would take forty minutes to do the same work." "This tunnel is also

* *The Appleby and Kirkby Stephen Herald.*

partly lined," says Mr. Story, "as beds of shale were interspersed with the rock. It is 428 yards long. Soon after coming out of the tunnel a fine view is obtained of the valley of the Eden, with the Cross Fell range beyond, and the peculiar pyramidal shaped hills of Dufton, Knock, and Murton, to the north. Far below are the winding river, and the woods and the grassy slopes that border it."

Of the geological formation of this district, Phillips* remarks that "the whole escarpment of the Pennine chain from Brampton to Kirkby Stephen has been caused by an immense disruption coincident with the elevation of a ridge of partially exposed slate rocks. The effect of this disruption is the relative displacement of the strata on the two sides of it (in one part to the extent of 1000 yards at least) for a length of 55 miles. Perhaps the whole world does not offer a spectacle more impressive to the eye of the geologist than that afforded by the contrast between the mighty wall of mountain limestone rocks, soaring to the height of 2500 feet above the vale of the Eden and the plain of Carlisle, and the level beds of the red sandstone deposited in later times at the foot of the ancient escarpment, upon the relatively depressed portion of the same mountain limestone series."

About a mile before we reach Kirkby Stephen the line passes through the Wharton Park estates, and about half a mile on our right is Wharton Hall, the seat of the now extinct Dukes of Wharton. It was left to fall into ruins till, of late years, it was repaired and re-opened. In the kitchen and hall are vast fireplaces, memorials of the hospitality of other days. What was formerly the chapel has been converted into a dairy. Once a noble park surrounded the Hall. Of the first Duke of Wharton, it

* "Geology of Yorkshire."

is related that his father spent £80,000 on elections; and of his son that he allied himself with the Pretender, made peace with the Government, ruined himself by his prodigality, and at 32, entered a convent, where he died.

The market-town of Kirkby Stephen lies nearly two miles to the east of the station, and is 300 feet below the level of the line. It is the second largest town in Westmorland, and contains about 2000 inhabitants. Near the town are two objects of special interest,—the Ewbank Scar and Stenkrith Falls. At Ewbank Scar the water leaps over a ridge of rock, a distance of 60 feet; and at Stenkrith, which is near the station, the waters "rush, and bound, and spout, and spread, and contract, over or through the creviced rocks, with roaring and hissing;" and after a storm they may be seen "dashing, bounding, and whirling with maddened speed; and then rebounding from the other side, in heaps of water and spray, rumbling, rolling, and seething, with a noise of thunder."

From Kirkby Stephen the works of the railway are comparatively light till we arrive at Smardale Viaduct. This is, we believe, the highest viaduct on the Midland system, being 130 feet from stream to rails; and its length is 710 feet. In sinking the foundations of this viaduct an unexpected difficulty appeared. The river seemed to be running clear immediately over the solid rock, which appeared to supply an excellent foundation. "We began to sink," said the engineer, "but not a bit of rock was to be found. The limestone rock and the 'brockram' were gone; and we had to go down 45 feet through the clay till we came to the red shale, and upon it we built."

The viaduct is a noble work. It is erected of a grey limestone obtained from a quarry about a mile higher up the stream. No better material could have been found. "Self-bedded as it was, not much labour was required to bring it to the proper shape; and the immense blocks in which it could be worked, rendered it well adapted for the construction of such narrow piers." As no sand, or anything like sand could be obtained on this contract the material used was clay burnt hard, and ground with lime in mortar mills. This proved an admirable substitute. The parapets and arch quoins are of mill-

SMARDALE VIADUCT IN COURSE OF CONSTRUCTION.

stone grit. More than 60,000 tons of stone were used in the construction of this viaduct. It crosses over Scandal Beck and also over the South Durham Railway; and a siding at some little distance from this point, running into the South Durham, enabled the Midland contractors to bring 1000 tons of material a week for several months on to the works of the new line. From this viaduct we can see on the right "the Nine Standards," as they are called, on the hills to the right of Kirkby

Stephen; to the north-east is the Pennine range; on the south-east the mountains of Ravenstonedale, while beneath us are the rich lands and woods of the valley, and the fine slopes of Scandal Beck.

The work of constructing Smardale Viaduct was commenced in the autumn of 1870, and occupied four years and a half. As its completion was regarded with special interest, the contractors invited the wife of the engineer-in-chief to lay the last stone. Accordingly this massive block, six feet in length, was, with fitting ceremony, lowered into the bed prepared for it, and it will long bear the inscription: "This last stone was laid by Agnes Crossley, June 8th, 1875."

In connection with the prosecution of these works in this district an alarming incident occurred. A party engaged on the line were one evening returning from their duties, and, having a rough road to walk upon, and a good incline, it occurred to them (engineer-like) that they could ride down the hill in a tip waggon. Accordingly they placed a plank as a seat across a waggon, and having armed themselves with a piece of timber called "a sprag," to be used if required as a brake, they set off. Merrily they went along, and the excellence of the pace, which increased every moment, was unquestionable. At length, as they were approaching their journey's end, and as the line some distance forward was blocked with loaded trucks, it was thought wise that the speed should be reduced; and accordingly the brakesman leant over the side, and applied his sprag. A sudden blow, however, knocked it out of his hand; he jumped off to pick it up, but could not overtake the waggon. "And there we were," said an engineer, who was one of the party, "running down an incline of 1 in 100 at 20 or 30 miles an hour, with a 'dead end' before us, blocked up, and going faster every minute."

Mr. Woodiwiss, the contractor, seized the plank on which the passengers had been sitting, and tried to sprag the wheel with it; but could not get it to act, till, at last, by standing on the buffer behind, putting the plank between the frame of the waggon and the side of the wheel, and pressing it sidewise, he managed to pull up the runaway truck just in time to prevent a perhaps fatal collision.

Contract "No. 2" now ends. Before leaving it we may remind our reader that, in the carrying on of works like these, much obviously depends upon the administration of the affairs over a wide area of operations, and in every detail. "Unlike the construction of a building or a ship, where, by reason of its compactness, the master can have the men working as it were beneath his eyes, the various gangs of men were here distributed over a length of three-and-twenty miles;" and it was necessary to ensure that they were doing their work, and doing it well, not only while the engineer was with them, but when he was unavoidably elsewhere. Mr. J. Somes Story was the resident engineer, and on our visit to his contract he courteously supplied us, as did all his brethren, with every assistance for the preparation of this narrative.

The work actually accomplished on this contract alone was enormous. Forty-seven cuttings, five viaducts half a mile in length, four tunnels, altogether a mile long, 68 road bridges, and 100 culverts, besides fencing, draining, and a thousand other things form an extraordinary accumulation of work. Added to this was the fact that owing to the high level to which the line was carried (nearly 1200 feet above the sea), it was found that the fall of rain was greatest where the line was highest; and that instead of some 25 inches average, as at London, the amount in 1872 at Kirkby Stephen was

60 inches, and at Dent Head 92 inches. The effect was injurious in three ways: the number of working days per week was reduced from six to three or two; the men left for parts of the country where the weather and the work were more settled; and the cuttings and embankments were soddened and damaged. The wildness as well as the wetness of the country, the scarcity of population and of accommodation made it impossible to induce the men, unless they were allowed to work short time and at excessively high wages, to remain. A hundred and sixteen huts were erected for them; reading rooms, schools, and chapels were provided; but with only partial success. As soon as a gang was properly organized, it was broken up by several of the men leaving. Works that were "in full swing" one day were almost deserted the next; and though 1700 or 2000 men were the greatest number at work at one time, more than 33,000 came into and went from the service of the contractors on this one portion of the line. And apart from the severity of the work or of the weather, "they are a class of men," remarked the engineer, "very fond of change."

A quarter of a mile from Smardale Beck the line enters a tunnel through limestone rock mixed with flint; and thence we pass along an open cutting 740 yards in length, and nearly 50 feet deep, forming an immense gorge in the rocks, from which 70,000 yards have been excavated.

The peculiar nature of this material occasioned special difficulty. The silica ran into the limestone in such a way that part was of one material, and part of the other; the workman did not know which he was coming to, and he sometimes blunted half a dozen steel drills to make a hole a foot deep.

"Now just explain," we inquired of our engineering friend on this section (Mr. Drage), "exactly how this drilling is done."

"Well," he said, "the direction in which the hole is to be made is usually pointed out by the ganger, and the hole is then bored either by a drill or a jumper. A drill is a short steel bar, and when pointed in the right spot, is hit on the head with a heavy hammer; the jumper is longer, and is jumped up and down in the hole by the man who holds it, until he has got to a sufficient depth. The jumper is seldom used in tunnelling, there being less room for the workmen."

"And at what rate do they carry on such work?"

"They will get a foot down through limestone in half an hour or so; and the men who jump will earn 10*s*. a day at the rate of about 5*d*. a foot, in eight or ten hours a day."

"When the hole is made, what next?"

"The safety fuse is put in, which is like a long string, and is composed of some explosive material covered with canvas. It is very tough, and when lighted burns gradually. The hole is then charged with gunpowder,—about a pint—or two 'tots,' as they are called, being usually enough, but sometimes four 'tots' are used in a shot. The fuse is put in first, then comes the powder, and lastly the 'tamping,' as it is called, which is the material that is rammed in to fill up the hole. When the hole is drilled, a stone is put upon it until other holes are ready. Then the men retreat, sometimes 100 yards away, and the shots are fired by a man appointed for that service. It was he who also put the powder in."

"Your drills must wear out rapidly in such work?"

"Yes; but there is always a smith's shop near at hand, and he sharpens the drills by heating and then hammering them out to an edge."

Sometimes in breaking up the boulders that lay, tons weight, in the way, dynamite was used. A bit of it, as big as half a candle, which in shape it somewhat resembles, is laid on a rock, the fusee is attached to it, a lump of clay as big as two fists is squeezed on to it, and when fired it will split the boulder through and through into any number of pieces—a boulder as big as a horse. It seems to act downwards as if a multitude of wedges were driven down into it.

Leaving the cutting, we are on Crosby Garrett Viaduct. It crosses the village at a height of 55 feet, and has six arches. It is principally built of the limestone from the cutting we have just left. "At Crosby Garrett," Mr. Crossley remarked, "we found the same red shale bed that we had at Smardale; and this revealed the interesting fact that the mighty limestone hill which we had to pierce in making Crosby Garrett Tunnel was superimposed upon the shale, and must be newer a great deal than the shale."

On the summit of a steep hill at the northern end of the village stands the ancient church, with its low square tower. The views from the churchyard are very commanding, the situation for such an edifice being unequalled along the line. The station platforms are in a cutting 55 feet deep.

From Crosby Garrett the line goes along an embankment to Gallansey Cutting, where the strata present a remarkable appearance, being coloured, before the grass grew over them, with masses of purple, yellow, and blue, and containing clay, sand, marl, limestone, and sandstone intermixed, as though some violent convulsion of nature had destroyed the regularity of the beds. Lumps of limestone and sandstone are still to be seen near the bottom of the slopes.

Two miles from Crosby Garrett, at Griseburn, is another viaduct, of seven arches, 74 feet above the stream. The piers and abutments are built of limestone brought from the cuttings already passed, and the arches are turned with bricks made on the spot.

Not far from this work we enter Crowhill Cutting. It runs to a depth of 40 feet, and for a distance of half a mile, through boulder clay. In forming the gullet through some parts of the cutting, masses of granite were found, some weighing as much as four tons each, and so numerous were the boulders that, as the engineer expressed it, " there was as much boulder as clay." The granite was like that seen over the hills at Shap, ten miles away; and the amount of gunpowder consumed in blasting was enormous, sometimes as much as a ton a week.* The work occupied more than five years and a half, and huts for 100 men had to be built.

From hence we pass along an embankment nearly half a mile in length, and in some places 60 feet deep, till we reach Helm Tunnel, in the neighbourhood of which the " Helm wind " blows in terrific blasts from the west; and we soon reach the station and then the viaduct of Great Ormside. The work up to this point was very heavy. After the temporary roads had been laid for tipping the banks, the ground in some places slipped away so that the metals had to be lifted and packed up with stones to enable the contractor's engines to pass up and down. This doing the work over and over again, here and elsewhere along this line, not only caused extraordinary delays, but swallowed up large sums of money.

Orm, after whom this village and this viaduct are named, was governor of Appleby Castle in 1174. Near Penrith there is a large cairn called Ormstead. The church has, in its north aisle, a burying place belonging to Ormstead Hall. This Hall was built as a place of defence as well as residence, being turretted and

* There are also " ice-borne rocking stones on the high moors above Settle."—*Quarterly Review.*

embattled. Near it, two hundred years ago, on the banks of the Eden, several brazen vessels were found, some of which apparently had been gilt.

The Ormside Viaduct has a noble appearance from the point at which we had the pleasure of sketching it. The lofty piers, the wide expanse of the work, the green and wooded slopes down to the broad and rushing Eden, which the line now crosses for the first time, and the view between the arches, of the winding river, and of the background of woods, hills, and mountains, present a

ORMSIDE VIADUCT.

scene full of interest and beauty. The viaduct is of 10 arches, 90 feet high. The sight from the viaduct itself is equally fine. Here the Eden bends away beneath the deep woods on the west; close at hand stands an immense rock, looking like the lower basement of an ancient castle; while almost immediately opposite is a remarkable projection of laminated red sandstone wondrously waterworn, called Clint Scar. From Ormside a beautiful walk to Appleby by the river side may be enjoyed. In the construction of this viaduct it was found necessary that one of the piers should stand in the river. When a pier has to be laid in deep water, a cofferdam has ordinarily to be made; but as in this instance there were only about two feet of water, it was merely diverted from the spot where the pier was erected. The engineer accordingly made some rectangular boxes of inch board, which were held together by braces; the bed of the river formed the bottom of the box; clay puddle was pressed

APPLEBY.

in; and thus a watertight breakwater was made round the space for the workmen to carry on their operations. The water was now pumped out; the rock excavated in the usual manner, by means of picks, hammers, and wedges, till the proper depth was reached; and then the foundation was laid, and the pier carried up to its proper height.

The next place we reach is Appleby, $42\frac{1}{2}$ miles from Settle. The view of the town as seen from the line, and depicted in our engraving, is very pleasing. The station is on a considerable elevation, and is 525 feet above the sea, although there has been a fall of 212 feet since we left Crosby Garrett. Directly in front of us is the church, with its square tower, nave, chancel, and aisles, built in the 14th century on the site of another church of far more ancient date, which was burnt down by the Scots. It contains fine altar tombs of the renowned Countess of Pembroke and of her mother. It is dedicated to St. Lawrence; and the seal of the borough represents on one side the arms of the town, and on the other the figure of the saint lying naked on a gridiron in the midst of burning coals. In the middle of the view before us is the town, almost encircled by the beautiful river; and the left is closed in by the hill, covered with fine trees, among which stands "Appleby Castle," the residence of Admiral Elliott; while in front of it, near the lodge gates, is the grand keep of Cæsar's Tower, 80 feet high, and covered with ivy, said to have been the Aballaba of the Romans.

Many an interesting and many a tragic story might be told of the annals of Appleby. Though it is the county town, it has now only some 1500 inhabitants; but the time was when the population is believed to have exceeded 11,000. The fire, sword, and plunder of Scottish invaders again and again laid it low. During the reigns of Henry VIII. and William and Mary it was in ruins. In the year 1598 a plague broke out with such violence that the town was almost deserted, and the markets were held five or six miles away; and in the Civil War, the blood-red waves of battle again rolled over the scene. When Cromwell's proclamation against Charles II. was made, no one, we are told, in the "loyal" town of Appleby could be induced to appear in "so horrid a villany;" so "the soldiers had recourse to a fellow in the market, an unclean bird, hatched at Kirkby Stephen, the nest of all traitors, who proclaimed it aloud, while the people stopped their ears and hearts."

In Leland's time Appleby was but "a poor village, having a ruinous castle, wherein the prisoners were kept." This castle, the Countess of Pembroke records, had been "of note ever since William the Conqueror's time, and long before." "I continued," she remarks, in 1651, "to lie in Appleby Castle a whole year, and spent much time in repairing it." She also, she says, "helped to lay the foundation stone of the middle wall of the great tower of Appleby Castle, called Cæsar's Tower, to the end that it might be repaired again and made habitable, if it pleased God, after it had stood without a roof or a covering, or one chamber habitable in it, since about 1567."

At last, it was believed, times of peace had come in with the Restoration, and the outbreak of loyalty at Appleby was unbounded. There were as many bonfires in the town as houses; a scaffold was erected, hung with cloth of arras and gold, to which a procession, after divine service, repaired, carrying amid the music of trumpets a crown of gold; and the people drank to the health of the king upon their knees.

As an illustration of the smaller matters that have to be regarded in laying out a new railway, we may mention that it was found necessary that some 50,000 gallons of water daily should be provided at Appleby for the supply of passing engines; but though the engineers searched far and wide over the neighbouring fells, the nearest mountain streams were some three miles distant. Eventually it was resolved to erect a pumping engine and establishment close by the river, and the water is raised from thence into a tank at the station, a height of 140 feet. There is electric communication between the station and the pumping-room.

Leaving Appleby for the north, there is a heavy

embankment called Battle Barrow Bank, some 40 feet high, and containing a quarter of a million cubic yards of material. Hard by this spot, in 1281, a white friary was established, near which once stood a home for lepers. A farmhouse now occupies the site. Along this bank we cross over a skew bridge. Some idea of the serious nature of railway work may be conveyed by the fact that this bridge, small as it seems, contains about 5000 cubic yards of masonry, and that in building it 10,000 loads of stone were required. These were fetched from the Dufton quarries, two miles away, and involved no fewer than 10,000 journeys, each of four miles out and home, a distance of say 40,000 miles, which is nearly twice the distance round the world.

Three quarters of a mile from Appleby Station, and near the old Roman road, the line crosses the Eden Valley line of the North Eastern, with which it has communication by a branch, and then enters a cutting, 50 feet deep, of boulder clay, with here and there a bed of sand. "Going northward," says Mr. Drage, "we reach Long Marton, where we get a splendid view of the mountain pikes which lie on the east of the line, three miles away, called Murton, Dufton, and Knock, and rise respectively 1950, 1570, and 1306 feet above the level of the sea. Along the sides of the fells near these pikes are several lead mines in operation, which return a fair profit to the proprietors. Trout Beck, at Long Marton, is crossed by a viaduct of five arches, 60 feet high. It is built of red sandstone from the excellent quarries in Dufton Gill, about two miles east of the line. At Stamp Hill, a mile farther on, some gypsum quarries near to the line are being worked, and the produce is sent away by the Eden Valley line from Kirkby Thore. The cutting here, and also the one at Blackleases, about a mile farther on, is through boulder clay of somewhat lighter description than that found in cuttings at the south end of the contract. Each of the two former cuttings is about a quarter of a mile long, and they are 25 and 40 feet deep.

"The village of Kirkby Thore lies a mile to the south-west, and is the reputed birthplace of the renowned Hogarth. The scenery around this district, embracing Lowther, Shap, and the intervening villages, is very grand; the country gently rises towards the Lake District. Saddleback and Skiddaw are seen standing out among the distant mountains. A little farther on is Newbiggin, a village near Crowdundle Beck. The line here passes through the estate of W. Crackenthorpe, Esq., of Newbiggin Hall; and the fine old oak trees, and the wood on the banks of the Beck, present a lovely appearance. The line is now 100 feet lower than at Appleby."

Newbiggin Hall stands at the northern end of the village. Over the front door is an inscription:—

> "Christopher Crackenthorpe men did me call,
> Who in my tyme did builde this Hall,
> And framèd it as you may see,
> One thousand five hundred thirty and three."

The church at Newbiggin tells of the merits of one Richard Crackenthorpe, a clergyman, "who brought reputation to this family;" and of whom "King James I. used to say he ought to have been a bishop; but," the inscription significantly adds, "he never made him one."

Six miles from Appleby we are at Newbiggin Station, near which is the village. In this neighbourhood, in the early days of the Settle and Carlisle line, the engineer, Mr. Sharland, and his staff had been one day busily engaged in making their surveys not far from this wood, when an elderly gentleman, with frill shirt very carefully got up, and the rest of his dress to match, came up to the little party.

"May I inquire," he asked in a somewhat decided tone, "in what you are engaged on my property here?"

"We are surveying for a new line," was the reply.

"A new line!" he exclaimed; "where to and from?"

"From Settle to Carlisle."

"And which way is it to go in this direction?"

"Our present plan," replied the engineer, "is to go through that wood."

"What! through my wood, my old oak wood, that no one has touched a bough of for years and years!" and the proprietor became as indignant and excited as a benignant old gentleman with a frilled shirt front could be expected to be. Mr. Sharland, however, did his best to explain the matter and to pacify the proprietor, and they parted.

Subsequently Mr. Allport and Mr. Crossley being in the neighbourhood, called on Mr. Crackenthorpe, the Druid-like reverer of his ancient oaks, and placed such arguments before him that he was somewhat placated; and afterwards, meeting Mr. Sharland in the midst of the oak wood, their discussion of the matter was renewed with a calmer equanimity.

"Well," said Mr. Crackenthorpe, "there is only one condition I have now to make."

"You have only to name it, sir, and it shall be attended to," was the reply.

"It is that you spare me the largest and finest oak in my wood."

"Certainly."

"Do you know what I want it for?" continued the proprietor.

"No, sir; but whatever you want it for, it shall be saved."

"Well," said Mr. Crackenthorpe, good naturedly, "it's to hang you and all the engineers of the Midland Railway upon it, for daring to come here at all!"

Near the village of Newbiggin is Crowdundle Beck, which derives its name from the fact that the dale receives the united streams from Croix Fell, and Dun Fell. Here is the Written Crag, as it is called, because of the inscriptions in Latin found upon it. "At Crowdundale-wath," said Camden, "are to be seen ditches, ramparts,

CROWDUNDLE VALE AND VIADUCT.

and hills thrown up." They are about half a mile south-east of the Written Rock, and cover about twenty acres of ground. Crowdundle is a place of some interest. The valley or dell itself is deep and narrow. The viaduct, some 55 feet high and 100 yards long, crosses about half of it, and the railway embankment the other half. The water of the beck flows at the foot of the wood-covered hills on our left, over a gravelly bed some 20 or 30 feet wide, and then passes away under one of the northern arches of the viaduct. The hill and tunnel to the left in our engraving are to the north of the line, and in the direction of Carlisle. The scene presented during the progress of the works has been well described by one who visited them. "In the deeply wooded glen at Crowdundle Beck," he says, "where the previous night nothing was to be seen but sombre looking trees, deserted masonry and earth excavations, and where a deathlike silence reigned, now all was life and work and noise. The rattling of steam cranes, the puffing of engines, the clang of masons' and carpenters' tools, and the din of tongues, and the singing of birds, were like life from the dead. The stillness of ages appeared to be ruthlessly broken, and the wooded banks of the once secluded glen" will now become more and more familiar with the rolling trains and the intrusion of civilization. Where the workmen who were so busy all came from, and at that early hour, seemed wonderful, for human habitations were not to be seen.

"On reaching the almost perpendicular bank on the Cumberland side of the viaduct, I was richly paid for the toilsome ascent, for the views of mountains and woods, all robed in their summer hues, were grand beyond description. Light coloured clouds hung like beautiful drapery on the mountain ranges in the Eden Valley and Mallerstang, and the misty gauze, flushed with sunshine, draped Murton Pike with rare beauty. On the west and north the country was thickly wooded, and on the east was a partial glimpse of Cross Fell, and the neighbouring mountains. On the south-west the country was more open, and green meadows and pastures and graceful trees formed a picture of such a charming character, that the image of beauty can never fade from one's mind. To brighten the enchanting scene there was the little stream far down, chanting its ceaseless song, and with its silvery wavelets forming a well-defined boundary of Westmorland and Cumberland." *

The next railway work of interest is at Culgaith, locally called Coolgarth, and formerly written Calfgarth. It is a tunnel 660 yards long, through hard red marl; and then there is, as one has described it to us, "a nasty piece of sidelong ground running down to the Eden. The narrowness of the space along which the line had to pass, brings the foot of the slope close to the river, so that an encroachment was actually made upon the water, which caused an alteration of the county boundary." This spot is called Waste Banks. Then comes a short tunnel, which it was originally intended should be a cutting.

About a mile beyond Waste Banks, a beautiful view opens out to the west, and we see below us the confluence of two rivers: the one on our left is the Eamont, locally called Yammon, which has come down from Ulleswater, and now falls at right angles into the Eden. Many streams, indeed, find their way northward to the Eden. A local couplet says:

> "There's Loother, and Yammont, and lile Vennet Beck;
> Eden comes, and clicks 'em 'a by the neck."

Looking up the Eamont we see finely timbered slopes running ruggedly down to the sides of the rapid river, where the salmon are sporting, and where the fishing, we are assured, is "something wonderful." It is interesting to notice that the salmon seldom go further up the Eden than this point: they prefer the Eamont on

* There appears to be a general (and particular) haziness in the English mind as to the confines of these two counties, and even official documents are sometimes at fault. The War Office not long since described the "Keswick Volunteers" as the second "Westmorland Rifles." Is the name, we may ask, of Westmorland really West-mere-land, the land of the western *meres;* or West-moor-land, the land of the western *moors?*

account of its gravelly bed. Here, as we pause abreast of the junction of the two rivers, and look in a north-westerly direction, we have a view of Eden Hall, the residence of Sir Richard Musgrave, Bart., the chief of the famous border clan of that name. The estate is beautifully wooded, and abounds in every kind of game. There is also a vast rookery among the woods towards the Hall, where interesting scenes of rook life may be witnessed on an autumn evening; while to the water's edge the deer come strolling down to drink. The railway runs through about four miles of Sir R. Musgrave's grounds, and takes some 55 acres of his land. At the outset the baronet was strenuously opposed to such an intrusion upon his property; but, eventually, he was one of the most energetic enemies of its abandonment. It has been remarked by a competent judge that if a house were erected on the high ground to the right of the line, and made to look over in the direction of the Eamont towards Penrith and the Lake District, with that wonderful fore and middle ground of meadow, field, woodland, hill, and dale, and Eden Hall estates, it would occupy the finest site between Carlisle and the metropolis. An old drinking glass called the Luck of Eden Hall is preserved. It is enamelled with colours, and the letters I H S on the top indicate the sacred uses to which it has been devoted; but the legend is that a company of fairies were sporting near a spring in the garden, and that after a short struggle it was snatched from them; whereupon they vanished into thin air, exclaiming:—

> "If that glass either break or fall,
> Farewell the luck of Eden Hall."

The village of Longwathby, or Long-waldeof-by, as the name was formerly spelled (Langanby, as it is locally pronounced), is now upon our right, and near it is a fine old bridge of three arches. A mile forward is a viaduct of seven arches over a stream called Briggle Beck; and another half-mile brings us to Robberby Beck (a suggestive name) crossed by a Gothic arch of considerable size. The Eden has been on our left since we passed Waste Banks, but near Little Salkeld station it takes a fine bend to the right, and we cross it by a viaduct of seven arches. Here some difficulty was experienced by the engineers in getting a foundation down on the red sandstone, in consequence of the gravel that had accumulated in the bed of the river; and it became necessary to make a cofferdam. Accordingly a double row of piles was driven into the bed of the river so as to form an oval; "puddling" was put between the two series of piles, to keep the water from running in; the water inside the oval was then pumped out by engines, and the foundation excavated and cleared. The river, however, is subject to heavy floods. The autumn of 1872, when this undertaking was being carried on, was extremely wet; the piles were flooded over, and some of the temporary work was carried away; but, at last, all difficulties were overcome, the workmen laid their masonry on the rock, and raised thereon the piers which to-day carry the arches and the trains. This is the Eden Lacy viaduct. We may add that on crossing the Eden we are on the red sandstone; hitherto from Settle nearly all has been limestone.

On the summit of a hill now upon our right we may find the remains of a Druids' temple, known by the name of "Long Meg and her Daughters." "Long Meg" is an upright unhewn square stone, 15 feet in girth, and 18 in height, the corners of which point to the four points of the compass. Long Meg's numerous progeny, it has been playfully said, "of 66 strapping daughters, form a circle of about 350 paces, and there, in an erect attitude, await the commands of their grandmother. Some of these juveniles measure from 12 to 15 feet in girth, and 16 feet in height. In that part of the circle nearest Long Meg, four of her daughters form a square figure, and towards the east, west, and north two of her more bulky daughters are placed in the circle at a greater distance from each other than any of the rest. No doubt this arrangement was made that the elder daughters might keep watch and ward over the younger ones."

About a quarter of a mile from this interesting spot the line goes through the grounds of Colonel Sanderson, whose house is seen on the right; and the bridge, which it was necessary to erect, is the most ornamental work on the line. After passing over a long embankment, we run through an egg-shaped tunnel, from which we emerge near Lazonby. It was intended that this should have been an open cutting; but the material being sand, and the line going almost close to the vicarage, a "covered way" was preferred. This village is in the midst of interesting historic associations. A Roman road passes; there are cairns on the waste lands hard by; at Castle Rigg there are ruins, encircled by a moat; about a mile away is the ancient village of Kirkoswald, sloping down from the north towards the river bank, and named after the renowned "king and martyr" of Northumberland; and near the "kirk" are the crumbling remains of an old castle,—"one of the fairest fabrics that ever eyes looked upon." From this point onwards for miles the scenery is full of loveliness. The railway works, too, have a very characteristic appearance because of the intense contrast of their colour with the rich greenness of meadow, field, and foliage around: this is on account of their passing through the "new red," and very red, "sandstone." It varies in quality and character, being of coarser and harder grit at this point than in the direction of Carlisle; but it is the same geologically.

On leaving the covered way we see Lazonby Hall upon our left; and then we pass into a heavy cutting, 50 feet in depth and a third of a mile long, of this red sandstone; from which, after the work itself was cleared, splendid blocks were cut and carried away for building purposes. We now enter and run for some three miles through an ancient and extensive forest, called Baron or Barren Wood, in some places thickly timbered with oak and ash, fir and beech; and in others covered with brushwood and bracken. A heavy cutting runs through the wood for a distance of nearly a mile; and at one point the line is so near the river, that on the one side it has the appearance of being in a deep cutting, and on the other upon a precipice that slopes 150 feet sheer down to the water's edge. The scenery at this point is such that the traveller will often wish he were able to stop the train every few minutes to enjoy it. Here, among beautiful views, are the remarkable rocks that raise, for perhaps 100 feet, their "shattered and fretted summits, and form the entrance to what is known as Samson's Cave. The water washes the base of these huge rocks; but some pieces of iron and wood have been driven in as hand-holds, and footsteps have been cut in the rock for the convenience of the curious." So, says a visitor, moving cautiously round the jutting crag, he passed under these "overhanging rocks, worn by age, rain, sunshine, and storm into such fantastic shapes," and, with some sense of relief, reached a point of safety at the entrance to the cave. In doing so he disturbed a colony of jackdaws; and a hawk flew from its eyrie, on a ledge among some stunted shrubs, just where a honeysuckle was coming into flower, strewn with down and feathers.

On the other side of the river is some of the most

beautiful sylvan scenery in Cumberland; and the "Nunnery" walks are of great repute on account of their ancient date and their present loveliness. They abound with "shady paths beneath archways of living green, leading down to the margin of the Eden." The river banks sometimes appear like beetling precipices, and anon are softened down with shrubs and trees; while farther on a wall of rock rises on either side the torrent, the glen becomes narrower and more gloomy. Two successive cataracts roar down the rocky slope; the second, "after its desperate leap, being nearly involved in midnight darkness by the mass of wood which overhangs its abyss," while the "over-arching cliffs and solemn shades reverberate the roar."

The Nunnery is so named from the religious house established here by William Rufus, who "trembled, like other profligates, amidst his impiety, and was willing enough to secure a chance of heaven, provided it could be obtained by any other means than virtuous practice." At the dissolution its inmates consisted of a prioress and three nuns, whose revenues from 300 acres of land and other property were said to be only eighteen guineas,—the smallness of the amount being attributed to the border conflicts.

Returning to the line, we pass along a sandstone cutting; then through a hill of sand; two tunnels quickly follow, beyond which is a rock cutting; there is a third tunnel; and, once more, a cutting 60 feet deep. All along our course the Eden winds beneath us with majestic curves and wonderful beauty, until, at Armathwaite, with its ancient quaint old square castle; its picturesque viaduct of nine arches 80 feet high; its road bridge of freestone; its cataract, where the water "pours in sonorous violence over a bed of immovable crags, which whirl the stream into eddies;" and its elm, said to be the finest in Cumberland,—we are surrounded by objects of interest and beauty which (to employ an expression never used before) it is more easy to imagine than to describe.

Soon after leaving Armathwaite we pass over one of the heaviest embankments on the line. It stretches from the station to a little beyond Drybeck viaduct, and contains nearly 400,000 cubic yards of material. As two and a half or three such yards of "stuff" would quite fill a tip waggon, it is plain that at least 133,000 separate journeys had to be taken, and 133,000 such loads had to be filled and emptied, before even this one work could be completed. This viaduct has seven arches, and is 80 feet high above the surface.

About a mile forward, and before reaching High Stand Gill, we pass a point where the river Eden curves so closely under the sloping hillside that serious difficulty arose in carrying on the work. "Shortly after we began to tip," remarked the resident to us, "a landslip took place, and the whole ground (some five acres) began to move. The ground between the line and the river 'blew up,' on account of being unable to resist the pressure of the embankment; and the whole thing slid down towards the water." It had been known at the outset that this spot would be troublesome; and it had even been confidently predicted that no railway could ever be carried here. A proposal had been made that the line should be carried further to the left, by piercing the hill with a tunnel; but the hill itself was on an inclined bed, and, enormous as it was, might, if tunnelled, move. The engineer-in-chief, Mr. Crossley, finally resolved to carry the line across the slope; and though the incline of the bank was 200 feet from top to bottom, and though the bank slipped, and carried with it trees forty or fifty years old for a distance of 150 feet, driving the river sideways actually into the next parish, the difficulty was eventually overcome by similar means to those which were employed at the Soar Bridge, in Leicestershire. The hill-side was also cleared of water by means of vertical shafts driven into the ground, and deep drains carried from one to another; and these holes were filled in with rock, which also served as a friction bed to stay the movement of the slip. The whole of the contents of the previous heavy cutting, containing upwards of 160,000 yards, were tipped here before a safe foundation could be provided. On the left-hand side of the line, just beyond this point, is Eden Brow, the residence of Mr. Thomas Horrocks. Before reaching High Stand Gill Station is a viaduct 60 feet high, with four arches; and on the left of the station are considerable gypsum quarries. Immediately forward we pass over a long and heavy embankment, containing about 190,000 yards of earthwork and several bridges; and the line then passes under the public road by a handsome skew three-arched bridge.

From hence to the end of our journey the country and the railway works become more quiet and less interesting. Cumwhinton Cutting, however, is 1100 yards long and 40 feet deep. A mile farther on is Scotby, a small village with two stations, one belonging to the Midland Company and the other to the North Eastern; and soon afterwards we pass through the property of Mr. Sutton and others into the large goods station of the Midland Company, which here occupies an area of some 40 acres. The contractor for the whole of these works, from Crowdundle Beck northward, was Mr. John Bayliss; the engineer of the last contract was Mr. Paine, of Carlisle The passenger trains will run about a mile forward into the Citadel Station of Carlisle, and then join the other companies that so numerously congregate there.

In the prosecution of the works of this line the chairman took a very special interest. His visits and counsel in every stage of its operation, when the district was most difficult of access, when the works were rude and incomplete, and when the weather was in the last degree inclement, were most helpful to those who were struggling with the extraordinary difficulties of the undertaking. "The successful opening," writes an engineer, "and, I may almost say, the success of the whole undertaking, is due to the untiring energy and attention shown by our present chairman, Mr. Ellis; and, personally, I have felt that with his assistance I could pull through anything when I had his confidence and countenance." We should not be doing justice to those of our readers who are Midland shareholders if we omitted to draw their especial consideration to this fact.

DERBY CURVE BRIDGE.

CHAPTER XVI.

Derby to Birmingham.—Little Chester.—Findern.—Repton.—Foremark Hall.—The Dove.—Burton-on-Trent.—Messrs. Bass: their trade and traffic.—Drakelow Park.—Barton.—The Forest of Needwood.—Tamworth.—Fazeley Canal.—Whitacre Junction.—Lawley Street.—A useless viaduct.—View of Birmingham.—King's Norton.—Worcester and Birmingham Canal.—Weoly Castle.—Hawksley Hall. — Cofton Hall. — Lickey Hills. — The Lickey Incline.—Working the incline. — Bromsgrove.—Stoke Works.—Brine springs.—Droitwich.—Legends and facts.— Westwood Park.—Salwarp and Richard Beauchamp.—Hinlip Hall: conspiracies and concealments.—Opposition to canals.—Worcester.—Historical events.—The Severn.—Crookbarrow Hill.—"O. W. and W."—Croome Court and Park. — Defford Viaduct. — Bredon Hill.—Gloucestershire.—Ashchurch Junction.—Cleeve Cloud.—Cheltenham. — The Zoons Farm. — Ermine Street. — Gloucester. — Hill range.—Gloucester and Berkeley Canal.—Priory of Llanthony.—Hempstead. — Broad Barrow Green. — Stonehouse. — Nailsworth branch. — Stroudwater Canal.—Opposition to it.—Woodchester Park.—Dursley. — Berkeley Castle.—The murder of a king.—Stinchcombe Hill.—Stancombe Park.—Nibléy.—William Tyndale.—Wotton-under-Edge. — Tortworth.—Wickwar. —Yate. — Thornbury Castle and town.—Coalpit Heath line. — Mangotsfield.—Bridges or tunnels?—Tramway —Bitton Cutting. — Pockets of iron. — The Golden Valley. — Weston. — Bath.— Kingswood.—Bristol.

WE must now ask our reader to return with us to Derby, and to start on a visit over the Midland Railway to the West. In our journey we shall travel, in the first instance, over one of the oldest portions of the Midland system,—the Birmingham and Derby line, as it was called. And we may add, that the construction of it was easy; that the works are light; and that there is no tunnel.

Leaving the Derby Station we pass under the Manchester and London road, and soon the village of Little Chester is seen on our left. It was formerly a Roman castra. Emerging from a cutting, we are in a fine open country,—the verdant valley of the Dove; and we now cross, by an iron bridge, the Trent and Mersey Canal, which runs for a considerable distance on our right. This watery highway, sometimes called the Grand Trunk Canal, is between 90 and 100 miles in length; and at one time was so prosperous that its £50 shares were worth from £600 to £700 each.

On the right is the village of Findern, formerly owned by the powerful family of the Fyndernes. There is a tradition that "Fyndern's flowers" never died. There

DERBY.

was once a Nonconformist college here. On the left, among the trees, is the lofty spire of Repton Church. This village is full of historic interest. It was once a Roman colony; it was long the capital of the Saxon kingdom of Mercia, and the burial place of kings; on several occasions it was a battlefield; it was the site of a rich priory; and its church was twice destroyed. No wonder that it is a favourite haunt of the antiquary, and that it well rewards the researches of the English student of history. But long before these facts can be stated we have reached Willington Station, standing on an embankment. Three miles distant is Foremark Hall, built on the banks of the Trent more than 100 years ago. Less than a mile west of Willington we pass under a bridge, and then immediately over a tributary of the Dove; while to the right the Dove itself, crossed by two bridges, may be observed. The nearer bridge carries the road to Derby; the farther one carries the canal over the Dove by a bridge of nine arches. We now cross the Dove. The village of Egginton is on the right; and on the left the topmost battlements of Newton Castle rise among the trees on the summit of a hill.

We are now at Burton-on-Trent, so called to distinguish it from the fifty or sixty other Burtons in the land. There are few small towns, it has been remarked, so rich in historical associations as this. "More than one pitched battle has been fought near it; and the Trent, in its vicinity, has often been disputed inch by inch, and blood has flowed like water." But "bitter" as may be some of the memories of the past, bitterness* has been the chief source of the material prosperity of this town, and the traffic thus yielded to the Midland Company has been large. As long ago as 1866 the manager of the one firm of Messrs. Bass gave evidence that during that season they had brewed about 190,000 quarters of malt; and that the weight they had sent out from their yard during their previous season was more than 100,000 tons, in 36,656 waggons; equal to 1000 trains of 36 trucks each. The inwards weight was 72,000 tons, and came in 29,702 waggons. The following year the amount had risen 20 per cent., and has since largely increased.

* It was remarked on one occasion by some humorous member of parliament in the house, that Mr. Bass had "bitterly" complained about something or other.

"The whole trade of Burton," said the manager, "has trebled in 10 years." "We have paid the Midland Company," said Mr. Bass, M.P., in 1866, "nearly £17,000 for a single month's traffic. But that is not the average. Ours is a season trade; we do very little in the summer compared with what we do in the winter. Last year, I think we paid the Midland Company £100,000, beside what we paid to the other companies. The traffic of Burton," he added, "is very nearly £400,000 a year;" and the traffic here and elsewhere so rapidly increased that it was scarcely possible for the railway companies to provide sufficient trucks to carry it. So great became the demand that the waggon builders were unable to build waggons fast enough. "We ordered 1000 trucks," said Mr. Allport, in May, 1866, "which would cost about £75,000; and instead of having them delivered in about six months, as we expected, I do not think they are all delivered even now, and it is nearly eighteen months ago. There is the same demand everywhere."

Leaving Burton, a branch bears away on our left to Ashby-de-la-Zouch and Leicester. We also see Drakelow Park, situated on the Derbyshire side of the Trent, and "rendered famous from being the point where King Henry II., with his army, forded the stream in pursuit of his disaffected barons." The line now passes close to the village of Branston, and then we reach the station of Barton and Walton-on-Trent. The church at Barton was built by "Dr. Taylor, one of three sons of a peasant in whose cottage Henry VIII. was entertained by the forester when he lost his way in hunting."

The Forest of Needwood now opens on the right, where of yore kings hunted deer and wild boars. It is of about 6000 acres; but at one time was far more extensive. "Beneath its woods to the left, three rivers, the Trent, the Tame, and the Mease," mingle their waters. The Trent and the Tame are now crossed by a viaduct which cost £14,000; and we enter Warwickshire at Tamworth. The Midland passes over the Trent Valley line of the London and North Western by an embankment of considerable elevation. The stations of the two companies are connected. Extensive views may here be enjoyed of the country; of the town of Tamworth, once the site of a Mercian fortification, and the home of several Mercian kings; of Tamworth Castle, built, it is said, by the daughter of Alfred the Great; and of Drayton Manor, backed by the Sutton Coldfield hills, the seat of

HAMPTON STATION.

Sir Robert Peel. "No one," remarked the late baronet, "who looks on this district; no one who sees the extent of its woodlands, the delightful rivers that water it, enriching the spacious meadows that border them; who sees also the extensive champaign country, affording the opportunity of arable cultivation for pleasure and profit,—can be surprised to find that, in the earliest times, it was the chosen seat of those who were the conquerors of the country." In the plain brick church is the grave of Sir Robert. He declined a tomb in Westminster Abbey.

We now pass over the Anker Viaduct.* The next

* See page 66.

embankment crosses the Fazeley Canal, which connects Birmingham with the Coventry and Trent and Mersey Canals. At the village of Fazeley, part of which may be seen on the right, in 1785, Mr. Peel established his cotton mills, and there are still extensive cotton works and other manufactories here, belonging to the family. Passing Kingsbury Station we soon reach Whitacre Junction, now an important point in this part of the Midland system, as it affords connection with Leicester on the east, Hampton on the south, Birmingham on the south-west, and Derby on the north. It is by the Wigston and Whitacre Junctions that the Midland Company now has direct communication between London and Birmingham.

A run of 10 miles over a level line, and through fat meadow lands, brings us to the confines of Birmingham, one of the most enterprising and influential towns in the kingdom, but

LAWLEY STREET GOODS STATION, BIRMINGHAM.

of which our space forbids us to say anything. Here we see upon our right the very extensive goods and mineral station of the Midland Company, at

Lawley Street, formerly also the passenger terminus of the Birmingham and Derby line.

Upon our left we may notice a long brick viaduct, now unused. When it was built the Grand Junction line (which afterwards formed part of the London and North Western) was on terms of intimacy with the Great Western Company; and this viaduct was intended to connect those lines together, the Oxford and Birmingham scheme having been originated as "a scourge to the London and Birmingham Railway." The project for the union of those lines was defeated; but the viaduct was built in the hope that some day the union would be effected. "It cost," as a competent critic remarked the other day, "no end;" but it is not likely ever to be worth anything to anybody. Near this point the Midland Company unites with the London and North Western, and finds access to the New Street Station, Birmingham.

It may be well for passengers to the West to observe that the quick through trains do not, as a rule, enter the New Street Station at Birmingham, but are taken direct from Saltley, on the Birmingham and Derby line, to Camp Hill, on the Birmingham and Bristol. From near Moseley Station, a mile forward, after crossing the canal, "a view is obtained of the enormous town of Birmingham, with its numerous spires, towers, and chimneys rising above the haze and smoke in which its ordinary buildings are commonly invested." At King's Norton, seven miles forward, "paper and rolling mills, india-rubber works, gun-barrel and bayonet manufactories flourish. The hamlet of Lifford, hard by, confers the title of viscount on the noble family of Hewitt." The church has a remarkably fine crocketed spire. A "curious vocal pedigree" records that the ancestors of a parish clerk here held their office for upwards of two hundred years. The Worcester and Birmingham Canal on our left passes through a tunnel nearly two miles long; and it is so straight that it can be seen through from end to end. We shall shortly observe on our left, down in the valley, the fine open sheet of water which forms the reservoir.

Nearly two miles from King's Norton we pass close by Northfield on our right, where there are the ruins of an ancient fortress, called Weoly Castle. It must at one time, with its defences, have occupied nearly two acres of ground, and it was surrounded by a large deep moat, filled with water from a brook. The parish church has, on the north side, an ancient doorway, with a round Saxon arch, which is thought to have been part of a Saxon building. The country around is well timbered.

We now pass Hawksley Hall, at the foot of the Lickey Hills. "The old mansion was fortified and garrisoned for the parliament; but, in 1645, the soldiers refused to defend it when they saw it attacked by the king in person, and it was demolished." The fine range of the Lickey Hills is now seen on our right. On their summit is a monument in memory of the sixth Earl of Plymouth. We now enter Groveley Tunnel, 400 yards in length; and then pass through the Cofton estate. The Hall is an interesting timber mansion of the sixteenth century. As we pass along the embankment, we observe another picturesque half-timbered house, with numerous gables; it is Barnt Green House. At Barnt Green Junction the Midland line to Redditch, Evesham, and Ashchurch turns off on our left.

The Lickey Hills consist chiefly of new red sandstone, the summits and sides of which are, says Murchison, "covered with a vast quantity of the pebbles of the disintegrated conglomerate of that formation; but their northern end, called the Lickey Beacon, is a trap rock.

A lower ridge of quartz is composed of the older rock, extending for a distance of three miles, having all the appearance of a mountain chain, being covered with heath; while the higher Lickey, which attains an elevation of 1000 feet above the Severn, is verdant to the summit, a distinction which is well explained by the difference in their lithological structure."

At Blackwell we arrive at the verge of the most interesting railway work on this line,—the Lickey Incline. Our readers are aware of the circumstances that originally led to the selection of this route for the railway,* and that it rendered unavoidable the passing down this incline. It is interesting, however, to recount the difficulties which were involved in the arrangement, and to observe the way in which they were overcome. The serious question was, how so steep an incline as 1 in 37 for two miles, from a point 400 feet above Cheltenham, could be worked safely. At an early meeting of the Birmingham and Gloucester Company, we find the chairman referring to the subject. He stated that "increased economy had been practised in the locomotive department;" and, as an illustration, "on the Lickey Incline they had done away with tenders, and had substituted tank engines, in which the waste steam was turned into the boiler, the water of which was kept at a great heat. They had, he said, solved the problem whether the inclined plane should be worked by locomotive engines, as at present, or whether it would be better to have fixed engines, or the pneumatic railway. It had been ascertained that a fixed engine could not be worked at less than £1200 a year, and they all knew the inconvenience which attended the use of ropes. Indeed, he believed there was no question as to the superiority of locomotives, the only question was as to the expense.

* Page 73, and onwards.

That expense had now been brought to somewhat about £1200 a year; and, if so, all the other circumstances decide in favour of the use of locomotive engines. But the locomotive engines which they now employed were only probably of half the power of those that might be employed in working the Lickey. By-and-by the engines must be entirely different, but it would be arrant folly to throw away what had cost £40,000, and lay out now another £60,000 in replacing them. By degrees these engines must be replaced."

At the present time the trains passing up the Lickey Incline have to be assisted with tank engines, three being required for this service. The expense of the maintenance and working of each is not less than £1200 a year; in addition to which there is the cost of workshops and machinery, amounting to £800 per engine per annum; and there is the interest on the £3000 which a locomotive is worth. The annual expense of working the incline as compared with a level or a good gradient is thus over £4000 a year, or nearly £2000 a mile. Every precaution is adopted to prevent the possibility of accident. Nothing is allowed to stand on the down rails at Bromsgrove Station while another train is descending the incline, lest by any possibility there should be any deficiency in the brake power or in the bite of the wheels, and it should overrun the distance intended. The result of these precautions has been that this portion of the line is worked with complete success, and with perfect immunity from accident.

About half way down the incline, on the left of the line, is a reservoir, the water of which is carried in pipes laid under the six-foot down to Bromsgrove, for the engines and station. Formerly the Company had to pay £50 a year for the water they here required.

"The town of Bromsgrove," said Leland, "is all in a

manner of one street, very large, standinge in a plain ground. The town standeth something by clothinge," a trade for which that of needles, nails, fishhooks, buttons, and coarse linen has been substituted. "The heart of the town," he adds, "is meetly well paved. I rode from the Wyche to Bromsgrove, a four miles, by enclosed ground, meetly wooded, and well pastured; and in this waye I passed over two or three bridges over the water that cometh from the Wyche." The tower and spire of the church are nearly 200 feet in height, and stand up boldly from the vale. They are not to be surpassed, said an old writer, "for antique elegance by any others in the county." Some of the more ancient houses in this town are "framed of wood, and curiously decorated with black stripes and cross pieces, scollops, flowers, leaves, and other ornaments." In the neighbourhood are some remarkable echoes.

Two miles and a half beyond Bromsgrove is the Stoke Works Station, a seat of the salt manufacture, at the head of which is John Corbett, Esq., M.P. The Romans required the Britons to pay tribute of salt (salarium) as "salary." This word salarium is said to have originated the term "salt" as used at Eton Rock salt at Stoke was discovered in 1828. At Droitwich the brine flows on the surface. Here the ordinary springs are pure; but a "brine smeller" from Cheshire, after examination of the geological formation of the locality, expressed his belief that mines might here be opened, and his predictions were verified. "The salt," says Murray, "is in beds of immense thickness, and the proprietors excavated the solid material; but subsequently they preferred to pump up the beautifully transparent brine from a depth 160 feet lower than is reached at Droitwich."

We now leave the Midland proper (unless travelling

by a "special" or a through goods train), and run to Worcester and on to Norton Junction, by the Oxford, Worcester, and Wolverhampton division of the Great Western.* The distance between the two pairs of rails (popularly called the six-foot) is here wider than usual. It is accounted for by the fact that formerly there was the mixed gauge for both broad and narrow gauge trains; but the outer rail has been removed. This portion of the line is now under the administration of a joint committee of the two companies.

On approaching Droitwich, the line turns to westward across the Salwarp River; and running along the north side of the town, again bends southward, and reaches the station. The Salwarp took its rise in the Lickey range; and passing through Bromsgrove, Stoke Prior, and Droitwich (where it formerly received the overflowings of the salt springs), runs by Westwood House towards the Severn.

Droitwich is supposed to have been the Salinæ of the Romans, and is said to have been populous as far back as the Conqueror's time. The salt works are more than 1000 years old. Tradition tells that the salt springs at one time failed; but that they were miraculously reopened through the intercessions of Richard de Burford, chancellor to Thomas à Becket. Whereupon Fuller remarks that this "unsavoury lie hath not a grain of probability to season it; it appearing by ancient authors that salt water flowed there time out of mind, before sweet milk was given by either mother or nurse to this saint Richard." At the Domesday survey the springs were annexed to estates around, in proportion to the wood those estates could supply. The principal pits belonged to the crown, and there were

* The Midland through goods continue on the old main Midland line route *viâ* Droitwich Road, Dunhampstead, and Spetchley.

great restrictions on their use; till, about the close of the seventeenth century, Mr. Steynor sank pits in his own ground, and vindicated at law his right to do so. In 1725, Sir Richard Lane bored through a stratum of gypsum, which had formed the floor of the springs; and immediately a stream of brine rushed up with such force as to drown the workmen at the bottom of the pit. Such was his success at the trade, that other proprietors followed his example.

Immediately to the right of Droitwich Station is Westwood Park, the seat of Sir John Pakington, now Lord

WESTWOOD PARK.

Hampton. It has 200 acres laid out "in rays of planting," around the mansion. The fine old mansion stands on an eminence, and forms a square, from each corner of which is a wing. There is a lake of some 60 acres. The house was the retreat of divers Royalists and High Church divines during the Civil War, who, "repaid the hospitality of Dorothy Lady Pakington, by aiding her in the composition of her celebrated work, 'The whole Duty of Man.'" She also had "The Decay of Christian Piety" attributed to her!

Immediately south of Westwood Park is Salwarp, a

village renowned as the birthplace, in 1381, of the famous Richard Beauchamp, Earl of Warwick, of whom it is recorded that, when twenty-one, at the coronation of Henry IV.'s queen, he jousted all comers; that subsequently he defeated Owen Glendower and the two Percies; that he overthrew and would have slain an Italian knight at Verona; that he was "eminently successful in all the glorious battles of Henry V. in France;" that he was designated by the Emperor Sigismund as "the Father of Courtesie;" and that he performed innumerable other deeds as well in valour and chivalry.

A mile and a half from Salwarp, on our left hand, is the village of Martin Husingtree; immediately passing which, we cross over Atterburn Brook, and see Hinlip Hall before us on our left. This has been a place of unusual interest. It was built in Tudor times, and was provided with all the special safeguards suitable for a period of insecurity. "In fact," says one who visited it, "whoever has wandered with the writers of modern romance through towers, turrets, winding passages, creaking staircases, and dark closets, would here find themselves at home; there is scarcely an apartment that has not secret ways of going in or going out; some have back staircases concealed in the walls; others have places of retreat in their chimneys; some have trapdoors; and all present a picture of gloom, insecurity, and suspicion." The builder has contrived, as Gray says,—

> "To raise the ceiling's fretted height,
> Each pannel in atchievements cloathing;
> Rich windows that exclude the light,
> And passages that lead to nothing."

Such *was* Hinlip Hall; and from so suitable a spot, the sister of Lord Monteagle wrote to him the secret letter which led to the disclosure of the Gunpowder Plot; but four of the conspirators were so effectually concealed, that though it was known they were here, it occupied eight days to find two of them. Two surrendered after three days, having had only one apple to live upon; the others had been fed by "a quill, or reed, through a small hole in a chimney that backed another chimney into a gentlewoman's chamber; and by that passage caudle, broths, and warm drinks, had been conveyed to them." How disappointing, after all these romantic incidents, to find that the present Hinlip Hall is only a modern mansion, erected in the Italian style on the site of its renowned predecessor, and that it is the residence of Mr. Henry Allsopp, who, it is to be feared, has not even a drop of conspirator's blood in his veins.

Having passed Hinlip, we cross the Worcester and Birmingham Canal. To this project great opposition was made. It was solemnly affirmed that, by increasing through such means the outlet for coal, the collieries would be exhausted, and the manufacturers depending upon them be ruined. It is amusing to notice that a later writer, severely criticising these statements, adds, that they were advanced by the very people who had been anxious to supply the metropolis with coal from the midland districts, "to the certain destruction," says the writer, "of the Newcastle trade." These arguments, however, had such weight, that parliament ordered a survey to be taken of the coal country; and it was not till after a favourable report had been received, and the projectors of the canal had undertaken to relinquish all claim to the millstreams, and to provide themselves otherwise with water, that with an expenditure of £15,000 the act was obtained. The fall from the summit level near Birmingham, to the Severn is 450 feet.

Worcester is said to have derived its name from Wyre-Cester, the camp or castle of Wyre; a forest of that name still existing. Many traces of Roman occupation have been found in the town and county. During the Heptarchy Worcester was the principal Mercian see. After the Conquest, Earls of Worcester were created, and the civil power was entrusted to them. Here Henry I., Henry II., and John kept Christmas; hither Elizabeth came and granted many privileges; and here James II. "touched," for the king's evil, in the cathedral. Worcester was the first city that openly espoused the cause of Charles I., and in 1651 it became for the third time the scene of civil war, and witnessed the very last struggles of the Royalist party. "Twice," says a sound Royalist, "the desperate valour of the cavaliers made a stand in the main thoroughfare, and thus by their gallantry stayed the foe, and gave the young king time to escape. This was the memorable 'Worcester fight'; and for her services on this and the preceding occasions, the city bears upon her scroll, '*Civitas fidelis*.'" *

Leaving Worcester in a south-easterly direction, we see the broad flood of the Severn flowing southward. Dyer tells us of the "copsy bank," and

> "Mountain woods,
> And winding valleys, with the various notes,
> Of pipe, sheep, kine, and birds, and limpid brooks,"

that are found where "the wide majestic wave of Severn slowly rolls," and upbears "the trading bark." It rises in Plynlimmon, in Montgomeryshire. Salmon were formerly so plentiful in its waters, that Dr. Nash says, it was found necessary to insert a clause in indentures that apprentices should not be fed upon it more than twice a week. The Severn is a free navigation, and at one time it was common to "track" vessels up the stream by manual power, ten or twelve men dragging at a barge.

Two miles and a half from Worcester, we see Crookbarrow Hill on our left. It was formerly a Roman and

* See page 131.

perhaps also a British station. The name means a "hill of burial." In later days there was here a manor house surrounded by a moat. We now have the village of Norton on our right close to the line; and the range of hills we have had upon our left crosses our path, and winds its way more directly south. Emerging from them, the Oxford, Worcester, and Wolverhampton line (commonly called "the O. W. and W.") takes its course eastward; and we join the old main line of the Midland.

Three miles south of Abbott's Wood Station, we pass through a wood, full of game, and observe upon our right the fine park of Croome Court, the seat of the Earl

CROOME COURT.

of Coventry. Here, on what was formerly little more than a barren heath, a former earl "planted the slopes, drained the morasses, drew his belts of plantation round lands rendered fertile by his skill and laudable perseverance," and filled the scene with quiet beauty.

The next station is Defford, just south of which is the remarkable viaduct over the Avon depicted in the engraving. It is iron throughout, from the lattice floor of the permanent way, through which we look down upon the river flowing beneath us, to the covering of the massive buttresses upon which the iron columns and their tables stand. The entire structure rests upon piles driven into

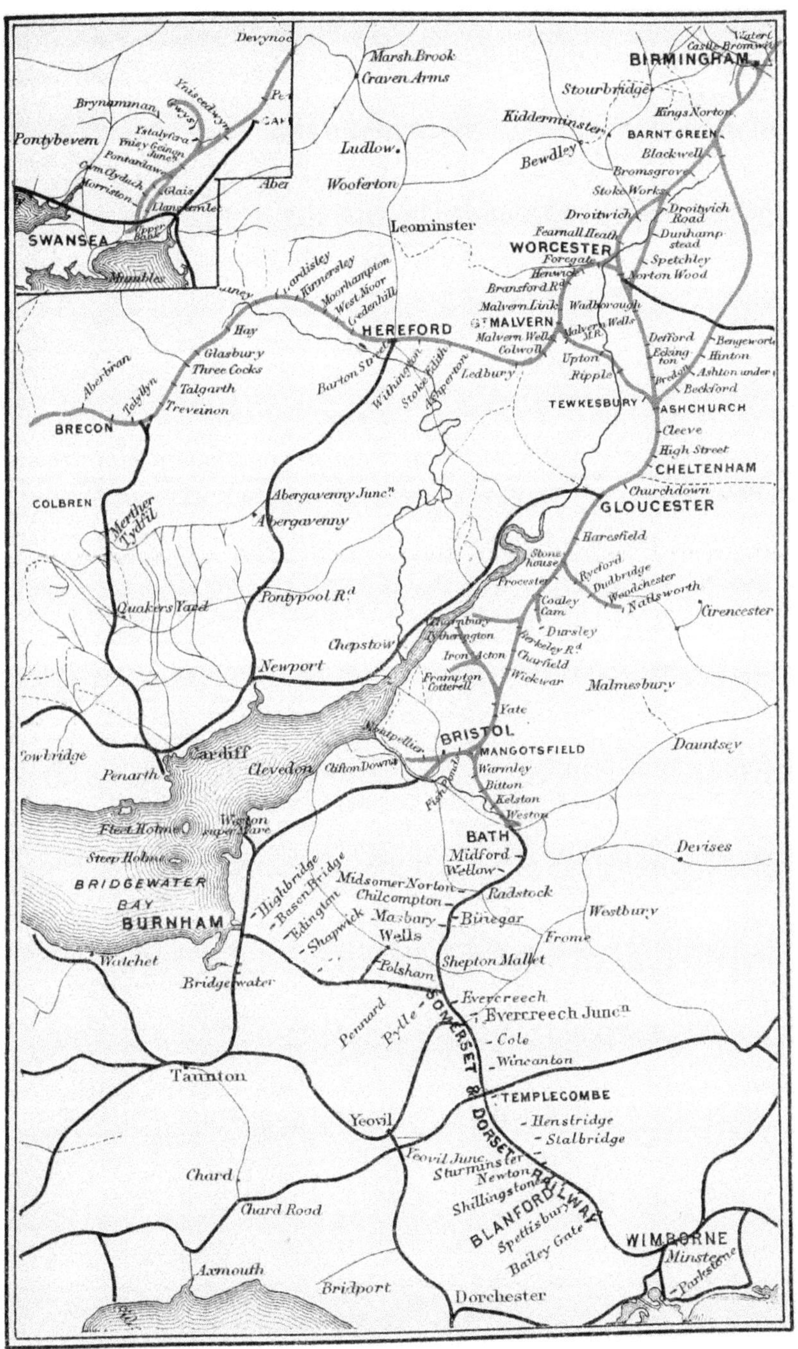

Bemrose & Sons Map Engravers, London & Derby.

the bed of the river. Some years ago, in order to ascertain whether these were sound, they were examined by divers. An engineer, too, being of an adventurous turn of mind, resolved to make a personal investigation, equipped himself in the diver's costume, and went down into the river. But, while moving about in semi-darkness, his inquiries were abruptly terminated by his falling over a heap of stones; his inverted position interfered with the proper action of the diving apparatus; the water rushed

DEFFORD BRIDGE.

in; and he was within an ace of being drowned. Fortunately, his friends came to the rescue, and he was jerked up out of the river, as one of them expressed it, "like a great fish at the end of a line."

The fine mountainous mass of Bredon Hill that now stretches on our left rises to the height of nearly 1000 feet, and divides the Vale of Evesham from the Cotswold district. On the summit is a tower, from which widespread views may be enjoyed. In its quarries lias fossils are abundant; and here Roman coins have been found among the works of a doubly entrenched Roman camp.

Many rare plants will reward the researches of the botanist.

About a mile south of Bredon Station we again cross the Avon, and are in Gloucestershire. Another mile or so brings us to the important junction of Ashchurch, where the line from Barnt Green, Redditch, and Evesham, joins us from the east; and the line to Tewkesbury and Malvern goes away to the west. Four miles from Ashchurch, having passed a spot named "Starve-all Farm" on our left, we reach Cleeve Station; about a mile to the left of which is Bishop's Cleeve; and behind which Bushcomb Wood climbs upon the heights of Nottingham Hill,—the first bold projection of the range that now accompanies us. Bishop's Cleeve was originally the residence of a small fraternity of monks. The church, a spacious and curious edifice, contains examples of the architecture of different periods, from Saxon times to the last century. The tower, which rises from the centre of the church, was built in lieu of a spire which, in 1696, fell upon the chancel. The rectory, standing in front of the village, was originally a residence of the Bishops of Worcester. On the hills continuing to the south, and called Cleeve Cloud, are many traces of Roman military positions; and the end of the ridge is fortified with a deep vallation, 350 yards long, in the form of a crescent, inaccessible on every side except the front. We now pass Prestbury, cross over the Chelt, and are at Cheltenham.

In the time of Edward the Confessor, the manor of Cheltenham belonged to the crown, to which it contributed annually a few pounds, and also 3000 loaves for the king's dogs. It subsequently rose in value, and, according to Domesday Book, paid 20 cows, 20 hogs, and £20 tribute, besides 16*s.* in lieu of the bread. The situation of the town is pleasant; it is sheltered on the north-east by the fine amphitheatre of the Cotswold Hills, and opens to the Vale of Gloucester on the south and west.

Leaving Cheltenham, the railway, which has been running nearly south, bears away to the south-west, towards Gloucester. The line is worked on both broad and narrow gauge, and is used by both the Midland and the Great Western. Their stations at Cheltenham, however, are in different parts of the town. On our left the range of hills to which we have already referred continues. Leckhampton Hills are nearly 1000 feet high, and include some of the boldest of the Cotswolds. "They are broken more precipitously, and exhibit a greater extent of bare rock of granulated stone than any other." One of these scars, from its craggy and gigantic form, is called the Devil's Chimney. The rare frog orchis is here found.

Two miles from Cheltenham, and we are abreast, on our left, of Badgworth, a pretty village embosomed in trees; and a mile farther is Churchdown, with Churchdown Hill rising behind it to the height of some 850 feet. The circumference of the base is about four miles. From the summit extensive views may be enjoyed down the vale, and also of the fine amphitheatre of the Cotswolds behind Cheltenham. Hard by is "The Zoons Farm," a name which may interest our philological readers. We now cross the celebrated Ermine Street. It has come from near Wallingford, through Cirencester, down the Birdlip Hill, six miles to our left, and continues in a straight line to Gloucester.

Gloucester is pleasantly situated on a gentle eminence by the Severn, "about a mile above the confluence of the two channels into which that river is divided by the island of Alney, and about 40 miles above its junction with the Bristol Channel." The origin of the city is believed to be British. It was then called Caer Gloew, which, according to Camden, means "the city of the pure stream;" others think that Gloew was the name of the founder. So much for fame! The Romans here established a colony, called Colonia Glevum, as a check to the Silures,—the inhabitants of South Wales. After the departure of the Romans the city surrendered to the West Saxons, by whom it was named Gleau-Cester, whence its present designation is immediately derived. The noble Gothic tower of the cathedral, surmounted by four pinnacles, is plainly seen from the line, as we leave the station for the south.

The county is naturally divided into three distinct districts,—the hill, the vale, and the forest. The hills run through the county from north-east to south and south-west, nearly parallel with the Severn and Avon. Between Cheltenham and Dursley they fall to a level of only about 250 feet; near Wotton-under-Edge they rise to 800. "Between Dursley and Wotton-under-Edge this high ground spreads out, and a tract of lower elevation branches from it in a south-west direction. The extensive vale that lies between the hills and the Severn is divided into the upper and lower, or the vales of Gloucester and Berkeley."

As we leave Gloucester, we observe, within 500 yards of us, the Gloucester and Berkeley Canal. It is 16½ miles long, and was made to unite the city with the Bristol Channel. The port is the most inland in the kingdom; and the masts look as if the ships had drifted out among the meadows.

We have scarcely cleared the suburbs of Gloucester than, about half a mile on our right, and near the deep southern bend of the river, there are the remains of the priory of Llanthony. It was founded, in 1187, by monks who had been driven from an older priory of the same name in Monmouthshire. Originally this was intended only as an adjunct to the elder; but Edward IV. united both, and made this the principal. After the dissolution the buildings were used as farm offices. The principal entrance (on which are the arms of the Earls of Hereford), the walls of the great abbey barn, and some of the domestic buildings, remain. In digging the canal the foundations of the old church are said to have been reached, some bodies disturbed, and some ancient coins found.

A mile after passing Haresfield, on our left is a range of hills, called Broad Ridge or Broad Barrow Green, more than 700 feet high, on which is the site of a remarkable camp. There is an entrenchment 15 feet high, and 600 yards long, stretching from one side of the hill to the other. The bold promontory, called Beacon Hill, is "enclosed by a transverse vallation, 50 feet deep, and containing 15 acres;" it is connected with the former. Here it is thought was a British station, subsequently occupied by the Romans. A spot resembling a prætorium may be traced; and on this a beacon, which would be seen from afar, was afterwards placed, and hence the name of the hill.

We now reach the junction. The Great Western, alongside of which we have been running, rises and bears away to the left, while the Midland bends slightly to the right. At Stonehouse each of the two companies has a station. Whitefield was at one time curate of Stonehouse, and commenced his out-door preaching in the churchyard, "the church being too strait for the people."

At Stonehouse we observe a line bearing away to our left; it is the Nailsworth branch of the Midland. It crosses the Stroudwater Canal, follows the course of the Great Western for a couple of miles, and then turns southward. Nailsworth is a populous village, with "woollen cloth, flock, and pin manufactories." Almost immediately past the junction, we cross over the Stroudwater Canal. It forms a part of the Thames and Severn Canal. As early as 1730, it was proposed to render the Stroudwater navigable; but repeated attempts to open up any kind of navigation in this direction were obstinately and successfully resisted. It was not till nearly half a century later that an act was obtained to make a canal from the town of Stroud to the Severn; but when it was opened, it was found to be of infinite service to the clothing towns of Gloucestershire and the country generally. In length it is only about eight miles, it has a fall of 802 feet. From the commencement of the Stroudwater Navigation to its completion there had been, as far back as 50 years ago, 39 lawsuits.

The range of hills that now sweeps along on our left, clothed with fine beeches, forms part of Woodchester Park, a place of great beauty, and of special interest for the Roman antiquities that have here been discovered. "Perhaps," says Lysons, "so many Roman remains have scarcely been found in an equal space in any part of England." The magnitude of the ruins indicates that this must have been "the residence of at least the governor of this part of the province, and occasionally, perhaps, of the emperor himself." The size and richness of the tesselated pavements here are superior to any found in Britain, and equalled by few elsewhere.

Three miles from Stonehouse, and twelve from Gloucester, we are at the junction of the line that runs to the old town of Dursley. Leland speaks of it as "a praty clothinge towne." Dr. Edward Fox was born here. Fuller calls him "the principal pillar of the Reformation, as to the managery of the politic and prudential part thereof." He was afterwards Bishop of

Hereford. Some springs, Rudge tells us, issue from the churchyard "like boiling water" in so copious a manner that, at about one hundred yards' distance below, they drive a fulling mill, and they are never known to diminish in quantity. "As they rise they cover a fine level gravelly bottom for about fifteen feet square, with nearly two feet of water, wherefore the inhabitants call it Broadwell;" and further back it was called Ewelme. "This is a Saxon word, signifying the head of a spring; and it is conjectured that this remarkable water gave name to the town; as in British dwr is water and ley" is a common appellation for pasture ground. The town stands at the foot of a steep hill covered with woods of beech.

We are now at Berkeley Road Station, and about two miles to our right, behind the rising ground, in this beautiful vale of Berkeley, are the town and castle. The manor was granted by the Conqueror to a retainer, and Berkeley Castle was founded soon afterwards. It is nearly a circle in form, the buildings standing in an irregular court, with a moat. The lofty and massive keep is the most ancient part; it is flanked by towers. During more than seven centuries it has stood, and has witnessed many memorable transactions. Here Edward II. was murdered, it is recorded, with a plumber's iron "intense ignito."

> "Mark the year, and mark the night,
> When Severn shall re-echo with affright,
> The shrieks of death through Berkeley's roofs that ring,—
> Shrieks of an agonising king."

"His crie," says Holingshed, "did move many within the castell and town of Birckelei to compassion, when they understode by his crie what the matter ment." The dungeon room, leading to the keep, is said to have been the scene of this tragedy.

During the Civil War Berkeley Castle was held for the king, but was captured. Dr. Jenner was born at Berkeley.

Half a mile south of Berkeley Road Station we are abreast of Stinchcombe, beyond which is Stinchcombe Hill, rising 725 feet above the sea, and behind it is Dursley. The hill is a favourite resort of visitors, for from its summit ten counties can be descried. South of Stinchcombe Hill is Stancombe Park, near which is the site of a Roman villa. It extended over six acres, and is thought to be the only specimen that has been uncovered of a large Roman villa, with the foundations of its summer and winter apartments completely visible. South of Stancombe is Nibley. This, in 1471, was the scene of a fierce encounter between Viscount Lisle and Lord Berkeley. They had been engaged in a great lawsuit for the possession of the manor of Nibley, and being impatient at the delay, challenged one another to combat, and met with their retainers at Nibley Green, a little to the south-west of North Nibley, and nearer the line. Lord Lisle and 150 men fell in battle, and the victorious Lord Berkeley rifled his opponent's house. The challenge and its acceptance are both extant.

On Nibley Knoll is a column 111 feet high, erected in memory of William Tyndale. The hill that extends southwards from thence is occupied by Westridge Wood, in which is a Roman encampment. Under the southern end of the hill is Wotton-under-Edge, which derives its name from its situation, immediately under an "edge" of the Cotswold Hills. The town was destroyed by fire in the reign of King John; the ancient site retains the name of the "Brands." It is a borough by prescription.

When abreast of Wotton-under-Edge, we have Tortworth Court and Park on our right, the manor house and rectory being near the station. The word "tort" means twisted, and it well describes the upheaved strata of the earth in this neighbourhood; for "perhaps no district of similar extent in Great Britain presents so many different geological formations as the picturesque tract round Tortworth. Taking its church as a centre, this district is made up of nearly every sedimentary deposit, from the inferior oolite to the lower silurian rocks."

The name of Wickwar is believed to have been derived from "wick," a turn in a stream, and "War"; the manor having belonged to the family of De la Warre. It is well watered by two streams which run through the town. Yate village is to the left of the station. At Yate is a gatehouse of the time of Edward I., the lower part of which is in excellent preservation, and has a fire-place and mantelpiece. The road through Yate conducts to Chipping Sodbury. Beyond is Little Sodbury, in the manor house of which Tyndale translated the Bible. Near it, on the summit of the hill, are the lines of a strong Roman camp, 200 yards by 300 in size, intended to protect this bank of the Severn from the inroads of the Silures. Hence the name "bury," a camp; and "sod," the south.

At Yate Station a line branches off to Frampton Cotterell, and also to Thornbury. In reaching the former we twice cross the Frome,—once on leaving the main line, and again within a short distance of Frampton. The ancient town of Thornbury is beautifully situated on the bank of the Severn. Its castle, magnificent in its incompleteness and ruin, was begun in 1511, by the Duke of Buckingham. His execution for high treason interrupted the work; it has never been restored, and much has gone to ruin. Some portions, however, present an admirable specimen of the architecture of the early part of the 16th century. The building, had it been finished, would have formed a quadrangle, enclosing an area of two acres and a half. The town consists principally of three streets, in the form of the letter Y, "having," says Leland, "first one longe strete, and two hornes goyne out of it."

Leaving Yate Station we cross Yate Common, and in less than a couple of miles reach Westerleigh, the church of which has been destroyed by fire; but some portions, including the tower, remain. Half a mile farther on, a branch line is seen running out on our right. It is the Coalpit Heath mineral line, and it continues for a distance of about a mile and a quarter From the Laurence Hill Junction to Fishponds on the main line was originally a part of the Coalpit Heath tramway.

The old Mangotsfield Station was closed for passenger traffic, when the new line to Bath was opened; and a new station, more suitable for the purposes of a junction, was formed half a mile farther south. Special arrangements also are made here that any delays in the through communication between Bath, Bristol, and the North shall not interfere with the local traffic between those towns.

Leaving the Bristol train to pursue its course by an almost westerly route, the Bath train runs nearly south. In a short distance a third line is seen on our left, approaching from the old Mangotsfield station,—the three forming one of those irregular triangles which are so convenient for the interchange of traffic and of routes, an arrangement somewhat common on the Midland system. Kingswood is now on our right; indeed we have been rounding it since we left the junction. Passing through a rather deep cutting, we reach Warmley.

In designing this line (much of which runs through a valley closed in by hills, and crossed and re-crossed by a river) the alternatives necessarily were—tunnels or bridges? It must either be carried along the slopes of the Avon Valley, and pass over the river six times, or else it must be brought farther to the north through the Golden Valley, and enter Bath at a different point, and by a higher level. Fortunately bridges won the day,—lattice iron bridges, as strong as they are beautiful.

We are now running parallel with the old Avon and Gloucestershire tramway, along which coals used to be brought from Coalpit Heath, to be shipped at a wharf near Keynsham. The tramway is connected with the Kennett and Avon Navigation of the Great Western Railway Company, and it was proposed that some three miles of it should be purchased by the Midland Company, and utilised in the construction of their new line; but the negotiations fell through.

Leaving Oldlands Common, where a considerable trade is carried on in hat-making, the Midland line crosses by a cutting over the tramway tunnel. The tunnel when made was not lined; but it had to be lined by the Midland Company for a distance of some 90 feet, to enable it to carry the weight.

"We now go through a heavy cutting, called Bitton cutting," said Mr. Howard Allport, the resident engineer, in some remarks with which he favoured us, "part of which is Pennant rock, as it is locally named; from whence we obtained a fine building stone for the greater part of our bridges. Nearly 250,000 cubic yards of material had to be excavated. The stone attracts the attention of the traveller by reason of its intense redness; but this colouring arises, not from the stone itself, which is, when freshly broken, a sort of grey, but on account of the filtration over its surface of water from a thin vein of a fine hæmatite iron ore which lies in the crevices of the rock. This vein is in places a few inches in thickness, running off to nothing; though it may be that not far off there are considerable amounts. It lies especially in fissures, or, as the miners call them, 'pockets,' in the rock. It has doubtless been carried here by the percolation of water; and in the course of ages the pockets gradually became filled till they formed a solid mass. Now the water filtering through them stains with a rich hue the rocks beneath.

"At the south end of the cutting we reach Bitton Station, which accommodates Bitton, Swinford, and the neighbourhood. At the top of the hill on the left of the

BITTON BRIDGE OVER THE AVON.

station are some mounds which indicate the former site of a Roman encampment. A tumulus may be seen within 50 yards of the line on the left of the station. A beautiful elm grows on its summit."

The village of Bitton is on our left. The river Boyd has come down the so-called Golden Valley (golden, however, only to those who can change its coal into cash), and now runs through the village. From Bitton southward we are on a heavy embankment, a mile and a quarter long, containing nearly 400,000 yards of earth. We now cross the Boyd by a stone bridge of three arches, after which Boyd-town, or Bitton, is named; and then over the Avon itself for the first time by an iron lattice bridge. This is the boundary of the counties: we are in Somerset.

About a mile farther we reach the village of Saltford, and cross the Avon for the second time. The Great Western line, which has just emerged from a tunnel, is seen approaching on our right. The hills now draw in on the left, and we are in a deep valley, along which the Avon is wending its way; on the south side of which is the Great Western line, and over which the Midland line crosses and recrosses. The steep hill on our left is

WESTON BRIDGE OVER THE AVON.

occupied by Kelston Park, the trees of which almost overhang the line. At the corner of Kelston Park, and about seven miles from Mangotsfield, we cross the Avon for the third time; then run under the Bristol and Bath turnpike, the road being carried over the line by a girder bridge; then we cross the Avon for the fourth time, and enter the parish of Weston. Here are the hydraulic lias limestone works of Messrs. Shaw. The Weston Station, which comes next, accommodates two important suburbs of Bath; and here the Avon is crossed for the fifth time. We now catch sight of the line of the Somerset and Dorset Company bearing away on our right; then the goods station of the Midland Company; we pass over the Avon for the sixth time, and enter the Bath Station.

This station is conveniently situated in the western part of the town, where four roads meet. It is about half a mile from the Great Western Station. It has this great advantage over its rival that the Midland Station is on the level; and those who have had to climb the steps of the Great Western will know what that means. The Bath Station is a handsome and commodious structure The three spans of the roof are 110 feet in breadth, and the length of the covered way is 250 feet.

From Mangotsfield to Bristol is six miles. The line at first runs due west, the great Kingswood district being to the south. It was here that Whitefield preached to the mighty assemblies of colliers, 20,000 of whom gathered at a time to listen to his words; and when, as he said, the white gutters made by their tears ran down their black faces. We now reach the Fishponds Station, and are soon at "the capital city of the west of England."

Bristol, situated on a tidal river, and near an extensive coalfield, was early distinguished for its commercial prosperity; and for many centuries was the second city in the British dominions. At Bristol the Midland Com pany has three stations: that at Temple Mead, which it shares with the Great Western, a second at St. Philips, and a third at Clifton Down.*

* See page 85.

CHAPTER XVII.

Nottingham, Mansfield, and Worksop line.—A prediction.—The coal-field.—Five hundred millions of tons.—The ironstone-fields.—Hopeful anticipations.—Wollaton Hall.—Newstead.—Mansfield.—Creswell Crags.—Worksop.—Trent, Nottingham, and Lincoln line.—Attenborough.—Ireton.—Beeston.—Nottingham.—Newark.—Lincoln—Rolleston Junction.—Southwell.—Mansfield.—Nottingham and Melton line.—New bridge over Trent.—Bridge building.—Pneumatic process.—The line southward.—Plumtree.—Widmerpool.—Dalby-on-the-Wolds.—Grimstone Tunnel.—Saxelby Tunnel.—Asfordby Tunnel.—Melton.—Kettering and Manton line.—Crossing the Welland Valley.—Wing.—Manton.—Syston and Peterborough line.—Queeniborough.—Melton Mowbray.—Stapleford Hall.—Manton.—Whiston.—Kelton.—Burleigh House—John Clare.—Leicester and Swannington line.—William Stenson—Mr. John Ellis.—Proposals for a railway.—Coalville.—Ashby-de-la-Zouch.—Moira.—Bedford and Hitchin line.—Barnt Green and Ashchurch loop line—Redditch.—Eveham.—Ashchurch.—Worcester and Swansea route.—Malvern.—Hereford.—Credenhill.—Morehampton.—Brecon.—Swansea.—Leicester and Rugby line.—Kettering and Huntingdon.

The large amount of space unavoidably occupied by an attempt to do any justice to the works upon the great main lines of the Midland Company, and to the objects of interest around them, compels us, however regretfully, to make but a brief reference to the subordinate routes of the system.

One of the most important of the branch lines of the Midland Company is that which extends from Nottingham to Mansfield and Worksop. When it was first proposed that a railway should be made in this direction, a certain witness, giving evidence before a Parliamentary committee, was asked whether he was familiar with the country between Mansfield and Nottingham.

"Perfectly," he replied.

"Do you imagine a railroad could be made from Mansfield to Nottingham?"

"I should say," he replied, "it would not pay a farthing per cent."

At that period, however, and for many years afterwards it was not known how vast are the mineral resources of this valley. In 1868, however, Sir Roderick Murchison, who had more than once visited the Newstead and Hucknall district, expressed the opinion: "I believe that in all that country you will certainly find a very good coalfield; but," he added, "these rich proprietors will never hear of having coal-pits sunk near them." A very short time, however, had elapsed before the remunerative character of the coal trade improved; until, by the unprecedented increase of iron production, and the "leaps and bounds" of manufacturing industry, the demand was so stimulated as to occasion the coal fever of 1872 and 1873, and landed proprietors here as elsewhere became anxious to lease their royalties.

It is too soon to hazard conjectures as to the development in this district of the future coal supply. But there is no coalfield the possibilities of which are so large; and it is safe to say that the data furnished each year widen its limits.

The trains running from Nottingham to Worksop pass uninterruptedly over thirty miles of magnesian limestone and new red sandstone. The passenger looking eastward will see one after another costly and well-designed collieries rising, the shafts of which have recently penetrated the top hard coal at 400 yards or more from the surface. The royalties which have been let on the Nottingham and Mansfield line since the year 1870, now opening out, represent at least 500 million tons of coal.

Nor are the geological features of the district without bearing upon the remunerative nature of the traffic

The depth of the best seam of coal being not less than 400 yards, the means by which it is extracted must be entirely different from those of older coal districts, such as Staffordshire, or even the Erewash Valley. It will be more remunerative to bring the coal long distances underground by steam power to capacious shafts up which great quantities are drawn, than to sink many shafts at short distances. The points and sidings connecting each plant with the railway will be fewer in number, but they will receive an enormous tonnage of coal. It will be possible for the Midland Company to collect the traffic with great expedition, and with little or no shunting; and it is obvious that for a locomotive to take a train of empty waggons to a set of sidings, to find there a train of coal in readiness, and to be able to take it away a long distance without break of couplings, is nearly the most remunerative employment she can have.

Further, looking south from the Castle-rock of Nottingham, there is another great mineral, destined to as vast a development as the coal that lies to the north. The Mineral Statistics show no increase of production in ironstone so rapid during the last few years as that in the county of Northampton; and it has been proved to lie in equal richness through Leicestershire and Rutland, as far as the borders of Nottinghamshire. This district the Midland Company are now opening up by their extensions from Nottingham to Melton, and from Manton to Rushton; and when these lines are finished, the coal on the north, which is specially suited for smelting purposes, and the ironstone to the south, will find one another; and all the economy of back carriage, so much insisted on by Mr. Jevons in his work on coal, will be brought into full play. In truth this coal and iron district is only now on the eve of development; and it needs but energy, skill, and prudence to see in the midland counties another and perhaps greater Cleveland. To the Midland Railway Company this district rightfully belongs, and that company must remain its most convenient highway of commerce.

These hopeful anticipations are certainly corroborated by the results already secured. "The Mansfield traffic," said Mr. Allport, in May, 1873, "has been increasing at a rate that is probably unequalled on any other line. Till recently there was very little traffic on it indeed. The first colliery began to sell coal about eight and a half years ago: there are now three collieries on that line, each sending about 300,000 tons,—nearly 1,000,000 of tons" There are also other royalties "coming into operation the Duke of St. Albans, at Bestwood, of between 3000 and 4000 acres," and the Papplewick and Newstead royalties, each of similar area; "and there is a fourth which is almost let. Those four collieries in a few years will be sending almost as much as those in existence, or from 2,000,000 to 3,000,000, down that Mansfield branch."

In the laborious and exhaustive inquiry of the Royal Commission on Coal, appointed in June, 1866, the subject of the extension of the Notts and Yorkshire coalfield eastward came under consideration. The available coal in the British Isles is given in the report as 90,207 millions of tons, with the addition of 56,273 millions existing at a workable depth under strata which overlie the coal measures. Of this possible extension, 23,082 millions, or more than 40 per cent., is credited to Notts and to Yorkshire, as lying under the permian and new red sandstone formations.

Leaving Nottingham for Mansfield, we run for a short distance over the direct line to Trent, and then turn off to the north. We have not gone far before we see upon our left a new branch connecting this line with the Erewash *viâ* Radford, the new and extensive Wollaton Colliery, and Trowell, near Ilkeston. Wollaton Hall also is seen in the park upon the left. It is a noble and picturesque mansion, "a combination of regular columns, with ornaments neither Grecian nor Gothic, and half embroidered with foliage, crammed over frontispieces, façades, and chimneys." It was built about the year 1590, by Sir Francis Willoughby, of stone from Ancaster, "out of ostentation to show his riches," carried

WOLLATON HALL.

on horses' backs in exchange for coal dug on his estate. Passing through busy mining and stocking-making populations, we reach Hucknall Torkard, in the churchyard of which Byron was buried; and soon we are in the neighbourhood of Newstead, so intimately associated with the memory of the poet. The Leen rises in the grounds of the abbey. It is stated that a former owner of the estate received £10,000 special compensation for the injury inflicted upon it by the railway.

The summit level of the line is at Kirkby Forest, where, in the high grounds, known as Robin Hood's Hills, is the anachronism of a tunnel. The uplands hard by "offer pleasant rambles over gorse and ling, and wide and beautiful views in every direction. On a clear day, the towers of Lincoln Cathedral first catch the eye, while the southern horizon is bounded by the rocks of Charnwood. Nearer home are the woods of Newstead and Annesley in one direction, and those of Hardwick in the other, with the spires and villages of Kirkby and Sutton just at our feet."

NEWSTEAD ABBEY.*

Mansfield, near the source of the small river Maum, is of special interest as the point from which Sherwood Forest and the "Dukeries" can best be visited. The town is crossed by a stone viaduct, the arches of which are between 50 and 60 feet high, and we are soon in the neighbourhood of Mansfield Woodhouse. We now pass through a yellow magnesian limestone of a remarkably fine quality, of which there are considerable quarries near at hand.

* This engraving is copied from a photograph in a volume recently published by Messrs. Allen, of Nottingham, beautifully illustrating, by description and by photography, the interior and exterior of the abbey.

Going forwards we soon cross the boundary of the county, and are in Derbyshire; and we continue in our short journey northwards to cross and recross from Notts to Derbyshire. The course of the line was drawn somewhat westerly to avoid infringing on Welbeck Park. It would have been much more convenient to carry the line somewhat farther to the right, through a natural depression in the range of hills known as Creswell Crags, but the engineers were required to divert it, and construct a tunnel some 500 yards long. At Creswell a branch leaves the main line, and runs in a westerly direction to Seymour, near Staveley, where it joins a coal branch which formerly belonged to the Staveley Company, but which has been bought by the Midland Company. Communication will thus be provided between the centre of the Worksop line and the Midland system near Staveley.

The worst gradient on this line is between Whitwell and Worksop, and is 1 in 120 The worst curves are across Mansfield, and at the northern end of the line, about a mile and a half west of Worksop, where the junction is made with the Manchester, Sheffield and Lincolnshire Company, over whose line the Midland proceeds to Worksop itself.

One of the most important of the branches of the Midland system is that which runs from Trent to Nottingham and thence to Lincoln. The first portion was, as our reader is aware, part of the original Midland Counties line, the extension eastward was made at a subsequent period. It is remarkable that this extension was completed in the course of a year, Mr. Hudson considering it a matter of policy to show the advocates of the Great Northern that the old established companies could do the work as well as any new projectors, and could even supply a part of the district to which the

Great Northern was looking while others were thinking about it.

Leaving Trent eastward we cross from Derbyshire over the Erewash into Notts; and soon reach the village of Attenborough, which is seen immediately on our right. It is honoured as the birthplace of one who, in a dissolute age, retained a Puritan simplicity of character and earnestness of purpose, who took a high place in that Civil War which laid deep the foundations of English constitutional freedom; who commanded the left wing of the Parliamentary army at the battle of Naseby—the intrepid, generous, upright Ireton, son-in-law of Oliver Cromwell. "Yet that which is best worthy of love in thy husband," wrote Cromwell to his daughter, Bridgett, "is that of the image of Christ which he bears; look on that, and love it best." But it was the remains of Ireton, that after the Restoration were dragged from their resting place in Westminster Abbey, hung on a gibbet at Tyburn, and the trunkless head fixed on a pole. The house in which Ireton was born, was on the west side of the churchyard.

To the right, on the hill-side, beyond Attenborough, are Clifton Hall and Grove, the former a modern brick mansion, the latter a noble avenue, beneath which flows the broad expanse of the Trent. The beauties of both are immortalized by H. Kirke White. Chilwell and Beeston are three miles from Nottingham. Here is a Nonconformist College; and here also are the gardens of the celebrated florist, Mr. Pearson. Soon we run through the new mineral sidings, some 20 miles in length, provided for the accommodation of the coal traffic of the Mansfield Valley.

Approaching Nottingham, we pass on our left the junctions with the Mansfield Valley lines, and then we see on our left the lofty height of the so-called castle of

Nottingham; it is, however, in fact, only the remains of a large modern mansion, burned out, but not burned down. Yet around that hill cluster a thousand historical associations of events of the deepest interest connected with the annals of England. We now reach the station; with its locomotive establishment, where 50 engines are stationed; and its large coal wharves; the whole occupying some 20 acres of land.

Leaving Nottingham station we pass on our left the Great Northern terminus; we run alongside of the Great Northern line; and afterwards, curving round the wooded hill of Colwich, where we see the new red sandstone interlaced with a stratum of gypsum, we go under the new Derbyshire branch of the Great Northern, and are out in a fine open country. In connection with the construction of this part of the Midland line an illustration may be mentioned of the inordinate charges levied upon railways. After the line was opened, the proprietor of an estate through which it passed sent in an enormous claim for works which it was alleged had not been executed, but which it was said the company had undertaken to do. The engineer declared that the allegations were wholly untenable, and recommended the board to reject the claim. "But, surely," they replied, "we must have made some omissions; and will it not be better to compromise the matter by paying part?" "No," returned the engineer; "we have done all we promised; I would advise that you pay nothing." Eventually it was resolved to submit the matter to the arbitration of the late Speaker of the House of Commons; the representatives of both interests met; the claims were one by one investigated; and every item was disallowed.

We now run through a rich and pleasant country, by Burton Joyce, named after the family of De Georz, where the Trent approaches us from the south; by Lowdham

Fiskerton, and Rolleston where a branch diverges to Southwell and Mansfield; and then crossing the Trent, by the Weir, and running over the fine meadow lands, we pass by Newark Castle and are at Newark Station.

As we leave Newark, we see the spur of line that runs down to the Great Northern Railway; and as we cross the Great Northern itself, we observe on our left the remarkable bridge by which the Great Northern crosses the Trent. The next station is Collingham, about a mile beyond which we leave Notts and enter Lincolnshire. At

NEWARK CASTLE.

Swinderby, which we soon pass, operations have recently been carried on for the discovery of coal. After passing Thorpe we may, from the left window of the carriage, observe before us the hill and minster of Lincoln, which rise as a mighty landmark in the midst of this ordinarily level county. At the same time a range of hills is seen approaching from the left, and it continues stretching away to the right, on which are the well-known "hill villages," and to which the white roads are seen climbing up. This range stretches from the north to Lincoln, and from thence to Grantham.

Returning to Rolleston Junction we may remark that Southwell contains the finest ecclesiastical structure in the county; and this is also believed to have been the site of the Roman station ad Pontem. "Pursuing our way northward, the line goes to Kirklington and Farnsfield, two agricultural villages rich in rural scenery. For the accommodation of the numerous villages the Company has here erected a goods warehouse, and put in a coal siding." Four miles farther bring the passenger to

LINCOLN.

Rainworth. Though about ten miles have now been run the engineering difficulties have been small; but on entering the beautiful region of Sherwood Forest we find that the heaviest part of the work had to be done. From Rainworth the permanent way is on an embankment, which shortly afterwards is succeeded by a cutting 32 feet deep; then another embankment 25 feet deep, and Southwell Road is now crossed by a girder bridge of 66 feet span. Nottingham Road is spanned by an arched bridge; an embankment follows; the river Maun and the lands connected with it are passed by nine arches 50 feet high, and 400 in length, and, taking a curve, we are on the main line that runs into Mansfield Station.

Returning once more to Nottingham we shall learn that operations are there proceeding for carrying a new branch of the Midland system over the river Trent, and away to the South. This is the Nottingham and Melton line. It will, when completed, leave the present station to the east, pass under the bridge that carries the London Road over our heads, cross the canal, and, at the

VIADUCT ACROSS RESERVOIR NEAR MANSFIELD.

distance of half a mile, approach the Trent. The bridge that will here carry the line over the river will be a noble structure. There will be three main openings, each of 100 feet span; and five land arches or "flood openings" at either end, each of 26 feet span. The river openings will be spanned by light wrought iron lattice girders supported by cast iron cylinders which will rest on the bed of the river and be filled in solid with brickwork. The flood openings will be brick arches with stone facings, and their foundations will go an average distance of some 20 feet down, to the rock. There will be, in fact, almost as much work below ground as above, in consequence of the poorness of the upper ground, which is liable to be scoured out or shifted by the heavy floods to which this valley is exposed. The parapet is of cast iron, and of pleasing proportions.

"Well, now," we remarked to Mr. E. Parry, the resident engineer, "tell us more exactly how you go to work in building a bridge like this."

"The first thing we do," he replied, "is to set out the

TRENT BRIDGE, ON NOTTINGHAM AND MELTON LINE.

centre line, and then to fix the position of the main and lesser piers. This done, we take out the foundations of the piers, two or three at a time, and as we go down through—in this case—sand and gravel, the water comes in, and we have to keep pumping night and day with steam pumps driven by portable engines, until the foundations are completed and built up, nearly as far up as the ground level. From this point we begin what is called the 'neat' work; and we carry the piers upwards till we reach the point of the springing of the arches. The centres—arched ribs of timber covered with planks—

are next set up between each pier, and on these the brickwork for the arches is built; the centres are then removed and the brickwork stands of itself. Soon after the arches are keyed in, the triangular portions between the backs of the arches are filled up to the requisite height, and lastly the parapet is fixed in position. Meanwhile we shall be sinking the cylinders in the river, and preparing them to receive the main girders."

"How do you sink your cylinders?"

"The first thing is to drive a number of timber piles down into the bed of the river in such a position that the iron cylinder may afterwards be put within them, and so be guided down to its place. After the timbers are fixed, they are braced by what are called 'walings,' or stout planks fixed across near the top and bottom of the piles so as to keep them securely in position. Several lengths of cylinder are now bolted together, and are lowered down inside the piling to the bed of the river. The water is, if possible, pumped out of these cylinders; or, if this be impracticable, divers are sent down, and the materials round the lower edges of the cylinders are removed. Meanwhile baulks of timber and iron rails or other heavy things that may be at hand are laid across the tops of the cylinders, so that they may be weighted down into the river's bed. The water is sometimes got rid of by the pneumatic process."

"What is that?"

"By the pneumatic process air is pumped into a cylinder till it contains three, four, or five atmospheres; and, instead of the ordinary pressure of 15 pounds to the square inch, there may be 40 or 70 pounds; and the cylinder is cleared of water. In that compressed air the men work. Of course, provision has to be made so that they shall be able to get in and out; and for the stuff to be removed without diminishing the pressure; and this is done by what is called an air-lock. The men first go into a chamber; and, the door of it being closed after them, the air in that chamber is raised, by pumping, to the density of the air in the cylinder below; the door communicating with the cylinder itself is then opened, and the men go in to their work. The pneumatic method is at present in operation in the construction of a railway bridge over the Firth of Tay,—a bridge, I believe, two miles long. The pressure downward of the cylinder, and the clearing away of the material beneath it, is continued till it rests on a firm bed. The cylinder is then filled from bottom to top with brickwork."

"Inside a cylinder is rather an odd place to work in, isn't it?"

"Not so strange as it seems. It's only like working in a well, perhaps eight or nine feet in diameter."

After crossing the Trent Bridge the first object of interest that we come to is a bridge over the Grantham Canal: this is a skew bridge, at a large angle. It has brick abutments and wrought iron plate girders. We now run along a heavy embankment pierced with numerous "flood openings;" we see West Bridgeford on our left; and, before we are off the embankment, which is two miles long, we have passed the village. We next enter a heavy cutting in the red marl. Its greatest depth is 50 feet, the material being used in the formation of the embankment we have just left. At the present time (December, 1875) 100,000 yards have been excavated, or one-third of the whole; and it is being cleared, in fine weather, at the rate of 600 or 700 yards a day; an amount which will fill 320 wagons; so that it will take about 300 such days' work with the present number of men, to finish the cutting.

"But if you put on your full strength at both ends," we inquire, "would you not clear it sooner?"

"Yes; but we can't put our full strength at the south end; because most of the stuff is wanted to the north, so it must be taken out at that end, and tipped on to the embankment. Then, again, we cannot continue our maximum even in fine weather without interruption. When, for instance, the embankment approaches a bridge we have to stop tipping, and the material has to be carefully wheeled up to the back of the brick-work of the bridge, and there well 'punned,' or rammed in, first on one side, and then on the other, till the embankment is well clear of the bridge; and not till then is the tipping resumed; otherwise the bridge would be shaken by the continual vibration caused by the tipping. There are ten such bridges in a mile in this embankment."

Three miles from Nottingham is the pretty village of Edwalton; not unlikely, if the proprietor approve, to be a residential district for Nottingham. The railway station is in a cutting. A quarter of a mile farther forward we emerge from the cutting on to an embankment, and then there is another cutting and embankment and we reach the village of Plumtree, where we cross the road that leads to Keyworth by a very oblique skew bridge.

Plumtree Station is five and a quarter miles from Nottingham. From hence we continue with cuttings and embankments, till we reach a tunnel at Stanton-on-the-Wolds. It runs through boulder clay and lias shale, the former being very much like the boulder clay of the North, but not quite so bad. "We have now (December, 1875)," continues our engineer, "some 200 yards of the tunnel done out of 1100. The greatest height of the hill over head is only about 60 feet. This would, however, have made between 80 and 90 feet of a cutting, which is too deep. There is a heavy cutting at both ends; and, on emerging from that to the south we reach, at eight miles from Nottingham, Widmerpool Station."

The next object of interest is the Roman Fosse Way, which we cross over by a girder bridge. It is said that some enterprising and irreverent engineer suggested that sacrilegious hands should be laid on the work of Roman times, and that the Fosse should be somewhat twisted, to allow the Midland line to pass easily over. Reverence for the past, however, was too strong for innovation, and a long skew bridge has been constructed.

The line continues with ordinary works by the villages of Upper and Nether Broughton, which it leaves on the left; we have Willoughby on our right; and we pass under the road in a cutting 30 feet deep. "Following this cutting," says Mr. J. W. D. Harrison, the resident engineer, on this the second contract, "is a heavy embankment, containing nearly 400,000 cubic yards of earthwork, which crosses the valley east of Old Dalby-on-the-Wolds. The old hall in this village is notable as having been the residence of Judge Jeffreys. The line crosses over the road leading from Old Dalby to Nether Broughton, and shortly after enters Grimstone Tunnel. This is nearly three quarters of a mile long, and is being worked from five shafts, the deepest about 200 feet. The stratum here, and indeed throughout the whole of the contract, is blue lias. In carrying on the work much water was tapped, and in several places very heavy ground was encountered. The bricks for the work are made on the spot, from the material excavated from the tunnel, the southern entrance of which is in Grimstone Gorse, of fox hunting renown. A cutting a mile long, and containing nearly 300,000 cubic yards of excavation follows. It is divided into two parts by a tunnel 100 yards long. The village of Grimstone we pass on our right.

"Emerging from the cutting, a short embankment brings us to the village of Saxelby, prettily situated on the left of the line. Two roads leading to the village are crossed over by a girder and a two-arch bridge respectively. On leaving the village Saxelby Tunnel, 500 yards long, is entered; this is at the present time being worked from each end and from a shaft in the centre; the road from Asfordby to Welby crossing on the summit. Small cuttings and embankments now alternate for a mile and a half, when the valley that lies between Asfordby and Welby is crossed by a heavy embankment, 46 feet deep at the deepest part, and containing 200,000 cubic yards of earthwork. The road from Asfordby to Welby is crossed over, the great depth of the embankment necessitating a heavy bridge. At this point a tramway intended to carry ironstone from Holwell, a village some three miles away, joins the line.

"Asfordby Tunnel, 400 yards long, is now entered, and a short distance beyond the south entrance, the road leading from Asfordby to Melton is carried over the line. The river Eye, a navigable stream, is now crossed by a girder bridge, and four arches to carry the flood water. Ten additional arches, each of sixteen feet span, are also being erected in the adjoining field for the same purpose. The new Great Northern Railway line passes over us at this point, and a branch from the same line runs into the Nottingham and Melton line shortly before its junction with the Syston and Peterborough Railway. The total length of this contract is seven miles. Messrs. John Aird and Sons, of Lambeth, are the contractors. The prevailing gradient is 1 in 200."

The chief difficulties connected with the construction of the latter part of this line have arisen from the fact that,—whereas the old Syston and Peterborough Railway followed the course of the valleys of the Eye and the Welland, and the main line from Leicester northward follows the course of the Soar,—the line from Nottingham to Melton has to be carried at something like right angles directly across the hills and dales of the wolds of Notts and Leicestershire.

As this line is intended, in connection with the Melton and Manton part of the Syston and Peterborough Railway, to join a new line in course of construction from near Kettering to Manton, and so to form a new main route direct from Nottingham to the Midland trunk line at Kettering, we may briefly describe, in the words of "the resident," the course that this latter portion will take. "The Kettering and Manton line," says Mr. Crawford Barlow, "is about fifteen miles and three quarters in length. It has to cross nearly at right angles the valley of the Welland, and from the fact of this valley being bounded by high table land on its southern side, and by a ridge of hills of considerable height to the northward, the works of the line are necessarily of a heavy character.

"Commencing from the southern end, near Rushton, the line first intersects a hill of ironstone, extensively worked by the Glendon Iron Company; thence it crosses the river Ise and the Harpers Brook by two viaducts. On reaching the village of Corby, the line commences a descent towards the Welland Valley, passing first through a considerable cutting, and thence by a tunnel a little more than a mile in length, by which it enters the broad valley of the Welland a considerable height above the river, at a point about a mile south-west of the village of Gretton. The line continues its descent by gradually following down the hill-side, parallel to the river, for a distance of about three miles, past Gretton and Harringworth.

"Between Harringworth and Seaton the line crosses the river Welland itself by a viaduct about 60 feet in height and three quarters of a mile in length; and, after passing over the London and North Western Company's branch line from Rugby to Stamford, continues to intersect the high ridge on the north side of the Welland Valley close to the village of Glaston. This ridge is pierced by a tunnel a mile in length. From thence the line passes on to Manton, crossing a narrow ridge of hills near the village of Wing, through which it passes by a little tunnel of about a quarter of a mile in length.

"The line passes in its course the villages of Great and Little Oakley, Stanion, Weldon, Corby, Gretton, Harringworth, Seaton, Glaston, and Uppingham; and stations will be provided to suit the requirements of the district."

The line has been laid out by Messrs. Barlow Son and Baker, and is being executed under their instructions by Messrs. Lucas and Aird, the contractors.

The Syston and Peterborough branch of the Midland starts from the Syston Junction of the main line, and for some distance follows the course of the Wreake. Soon upon our right is Barkby Hall, and a little farther on the tapering spire of Queeniborough Church. Here Rupert had his head-quarters in 1645. About ten miles from the junction we reach Melton Mowbray, renowned for pork pies and hunters. This town will soon become a centre of railway communication. After passing Saxby Station the line curves to the south, how suddenly may be seen by the views we obtain of Stapleford Hall, the seat of the Countess of Harborough. At the south-eastern angle of the park, we observe the now dry ditch of what was once part of the Oakham Canal. This canal must have greatly contributed to the well-being of the county; for it appears that when it was first used the roads were not very good. Bayley complained that he had seen, on a hill-side, a road covered along the centre with "immense fragments of rugged stone, thicker and harder than even the heads of the surveyors who had directed them to be laid down. Here they were laid, in hopes that coaches, carts, and waggons would gratuitously pulverize them;" but the said vehicles proved to be "like the rich wayfarers in the parable of the good Samaritan,"—they went by on the other side.

Manton, the next station to Oakham, is partly built upon the hill that the railway pierces by a tunnel. It is an ancient village. The church is believed to have been a collegiate church in the reign of Edward III. It is said that at the dissolution, "the houseling people, that is the communicants, numbered 100," yet that "Sir William Smith, one of the brethren of the Chauntry, did the duty of the cure for £3 6*s*. 6*d*., and his diet." At Manton the new line south to Kettering will commence.

Leaving Manton we observe a range of hills (at the foot of which flows the Chater) drawing in from the right, on the summit of which is Wing. Robert de Montford, it seems, in the reign of Henry II., was persuaded by the monks of Thorney Abbey, to give them a moiety of this parish. His brother Thurstan, who succeeded him, withheld the grant; and, says Brewer, "dispossessed these lazy gentry of their share of the church. To a demand for restitution he gave a flat denial, and not only refused to pay the abbot a sum of money, said to have been due by his brother, but also to pay the legacy he had bequeathed." But the Church was too strong for him; and the king, through the Earl of Warwick and Bishop of Lincoln, forced him into compliance; the holy men in return becoming sureties for the health of his soul, "as also of the souls of his wife, sons, brother, and all his ancestors." Having thus "got their fingers into this manor," the monks could not be easy till they had secured the whole of it; on attaining which they guaranteed the health, not only of the former owner's own soul, and that of his family and ancestors, but of his successors also!

About two miles from Manton the village of Lyndon is on our left. This was formerly a royal manor. The church stands behind the Hall, and in its simple burying ground is the grave of Whiston. It is said of him that in 1725 he was accustomed, with other learned men, to attend Queen Caroline one evening a week, to discuss matters of science. One day the queen, complimenting his candour, requested him to mention her faults; and after some persuasion, he stated that her irreverent behaviour at chapel had produced an unfavourable impression. The queen said nothing, but about six weeks afterwards again requested him to tell her of her faults. "Madam," he said, "I have laid it down as a maxim never to tell any person of more than one fault at a time, and never to mention a second until the first is mended."

Passing Luffenham and the junction with the London and North Western line to Rugby, we reach Ketton. This is an ancient village. The tenure of the property is by knights' service; and "it is a curious fact that the sheriffs of the county collect annually a rent of two shillings from the inhabitants, *pro ocreis reginæ*, which can only be translated 'for the queen's boots.' This may perhaps have been sufficient in early times to have supplied a queen with boots for a year," but scarcely so now.

A little more than a mile from Ketton we cross over the Welland, and enter Northamptonshire. After passing Stamford, with its noble churches and its willows by the water-courses, we see upon our right, beyond the trees, "in all its pristine glory, the palatial type of an Elizabethan house, the building of the great Lord Treasurer—

'Burghley House by Stamford town.'

The chimneys are formed of coupled Doric columns, and strangely peep above the trees of the noble park, when no other portion of the house can be seen. Few houses retain as much of their original form, though the trim gardens and formal hedges which must once have surrounded it are wanting to complete its character. The interior is incredibly rich in the accumulated treasures of three centuries,—in Venetian furniture, royal beds, oriental china, Gibbon's carving, and historical heirlooms, from the Lord Treasurer's cup, given him by Elizabeth, to the candelabra of the Duke of Wellington's funeral."

Passing Helpstone, where John Clare, the Northamptonshire poet was born, in 1793, of parents even then receiving parish relief, and who tells us of his literary gifts,—

> "I found the poems in the fields,
> And only wrote them down,"—

we soon reach Peterborough, join the Great Northern Railway, enter its station, and then taking our way down to the Great Eastern, find there the end of our journey.

To the Leicester and Swannington line we have already referred. But while this volume has been passing through the press, we have been favoured with some particulars concerning the early days of the railway, to which we may briefly advert. Mr. Joseph Stenson, of Leeds, informs us that it was his late uncle, Mr. William Stenson, who took the earliest initiative in this matter. He was an engineer. He first undertook the sinking to the deep coal at the Shipley collieries, and also in the Forest of Dean, in Gloucestershire. "He was well known in Derbyshire, where he introduced and erected the first of Boulton & Watts' (so-called) double-power engines, and did sundry surveys for the Derbyshire collieries. He was a native of Coleorton, in Leicestershire; and on the occasion of a visit he came to the conclusion that a coal of high quality could be found in the direction of Whitwick and Swannington. He bought land; made arrangements for sinking pits; and took in as partner the late Mr. Whetstone, a worsted spinner, of Leicester, and the late Mr. Samuel Harris, a relative of his own. Difficulties, however, arose; letters were sent to Mr. Whetstone assuring him there was no coal; burlesques and squibs were posted on the gates and walls representing 'a colliery without coal'; and at this period the affair would have come to a stand, but for the determined perseverance of William Stenson, who, driven

GROBY TUNNEL AND BARDON HILL, LEICESTER AND SWANNINGTON LINE.

almost to his wits' end, continued to sink at *one* pit. Having got to the first coal, he went to Leicester with a sample in a case; and called on Mr. John Ellis, who heartily congratulated him."

Mr. Stenson now proposed a scheme which brought further relief to the undertaking. He called upon Mr. Ellis, and asked that gentleman to aid him in getting up a railway company to make a line from the colliery to Leicester. "We have now been getting," said Mr. Stenson, "the old Coleorton coal for some months; but we want to get the deep coal, which is better. The Derbyshire coalmasters send their coals by canal. *Our carting beats us.*

But I see a way to relief if we can but get up a railway company. I've tried the ground with my theodolite, and find no difficulty in making a railway; though a tunnel will, I think, have to be made through the hill between here and Groby. And mark what I say: Leicester will soon be supplied from our own county." Such were the circumstances which, we are assured, induced Mr. Ellis to take the steps to which we have already referred,* and led on to the formation of the Leicester and Swannington Railway, and all its important commercial and national results. "To the late Mr. Ellis," adds Mr. Stenson, "belongs the honour of getting up, by his great moral and material assistance, the first elements of life in a railway in the town of Leicester."

There are two routes from Leicester to the Leicestershire coalfield: one direct from the West Bridge Station,† through the tunnel; the other *viâ* Knighton Junction on the main line. Coalville,—how incongruous that "ville" sounds in such a connection!—is the centre of this coal district. The people, houses, roads, fields, everything, are grimy. Coal-laden trucks block up the sidings. Coal-laden trains are groaning and grunting hither and thither. Coal lines glide off in various directions, or suddenly turn unexpected corners and surreptitiously disappear; while every here and there, in the bottoms of distant valleys, and on the tops of remote hills, may be seen the tall shafts rising amid the green fields; and the masses of black smoke and white steam proclaim afar that a world of busy life is labouring in the shafts and drifts hundreds of fathoms beneath our feet. A quarter of a mile on either side the line just beyond Coalville are the pits of Snibston on the left, and of Whitwick on the right; while from the sidings may be seen the steep inclined plane leading up to the Swannington pits.

* See page 5. † See page 92.

The only town on this line is Ashby-de-la-Zouch. It received its name from one Alan de Zouch, a baron of Brittany, "who, in the reign of Henry III., married the heiress to the manor." Here, it is said, Mary Queen of Scots was a prisoner; here James I. was hospitably entertained; here the Royalists held their own against King Charles's enemies; and here, in the church, the Countess of Huntingdon was buried, in 1791, "in the white silk dress in which she opened the chapel in Goodman's Fields." A mile west of the town was "an extensive meadow, of the finest and most beautiful green

ASHBY-DE-LA-ZOUCH CASTLE.

turf, surrounded on one side by the forest, and fringed on the other by straggling oak trees, some of which had grown to an immense size," on which Sir Walter Scott describes, in his story of "Ivanhoe," the "gentle passage of arms." It is still called Ashby Field.

The coalfield of Leicestershire has been divided into three parts: Moira, on the west; Ashby, in the centre; and Coleorton, on the east. In the Moira district there are twelve workable seams of coal, altogether not less than 55 feet in thickness; the main coal section being 14 feet. Hull states that in the main coal of Moira, especially in the Bath Colliery, a stream of salt water, beautifully clear, and of nearly the same composition as sea water, trickles down the coal-fissures at a depth of nearly 600 feet. In the deep sinking at Moira Colliery the number of beds of all substances passed through was 400, of which 41 were coal, many of them thin; about 20 were sandstone; and there were some seams of iron-stone. The main coal had a thickness of 14 feet; another was four or five feet; and altogether 46 beds of coal were found, with an aggregate thickness of 100 feet. The salt water that issues here is taken down to Ashby-de-la-Zouch, and is considered to be beneficial for rheumatic and scorbutic affections.

There is also the Bedford and Hitchin branch, forming part of the main line to London. By this route we cross over on a level the London and North Western branch from Bedford and Bletchley, and passing Elstow on the right, and Cardington on our left, enter the Southill Tunnel, the only one on the whole line from Leicester to Hitchin. It is about half a mile in length. It runs through clay, which is very heavy, and required careful and strong timbering before the lining could be put in. The work, however, was in good hands, Mr. John Knowles being the contractor; "and John Knowles," remarked Mr. Crossley to us the other day, "was a good tunneller." A mile to the right of Southill station is a spot with the suggestive name of Dead Men's Cross. Crossing the boundary of the county into Herts, we ere long see upon our left the Great Northern main line approaching; we draw nearer, we rise to its level, and we enter Hitchin.

The Barnt Green, Redditch, Evesham, and Ashchurch loop line of the Birmingham and Bristol, runs near many spots of interest. It crosses the Worcester and Birmingham Canal; has a station at Alvechurch, once a place of importance; passes Bordesley Abbey, which Henry VIII. gave to Lord Windsor instead of Stanwell, near London; Redditch, of needle-making renown; and Alcester, locally pronounced Aulster, where "six hundred and odd" pieces of Roman coin were once found in an urn, and where "urns are occasionally met with in every quarter of this vicinity, though they are usually knocked to pieces by the inadvertence of the rustic labourers." Evesham, the next place of importance, rises from the banks of the Avon, which here bends like a horse shoe, and shows the "ancient architecture of the town itself, back by the venerable tower, the antique churches, and

AT EVESHAM.

the ivied walls of its once flourishing abbey." "The towne of Evesham," said Leland, "is metely large, and well builded with tymbre. The market sted is fayre and large. There be divers praty streets in the towne. The market is very celebrate. In the town is no hospitall, or other famous foundation, but the late abbey."

We now pass Bengeworth, where formerly a castle stood; but the monks and the military did not agree, and it came to ruin; then Hinton-on-the-Green, where there is a manor house of the 16th century; then Beckford, where there is an old mansion restored, in the grounds of which "is a walk 460 feet long, planted on each side with box, which has attained the height of thirty feet," supposed to be 400 years old; and, in a few minutes, we reach Ashchurch.

We have already indicated the series of lines by means of which the Midland Company is able to pursue its course from Worcester to the south-west, as far as Swansea. Ten miles from Worcester we are at Malvern Wells; and 20 miles more bring us to Hereford,

MALVERN STATION AND HOTEL.

where the celebrated dispute * took place with regard to railway rights was put to an issue. We are now on the Hereford and Brecon, which the advent of the Midland Company has redeemed from obscurity, and the district from all the pains and penalties that attended the existence in its midst of a poverty-stricken railway company. Less than five miles brings us to Credenhill, where, on the summit of a hill upon our right, is an encampment of 50 acres, enclosed by a double and precipitous ditch.

* See page 305.

At Morehampton, "Offa's Dyke may be seen in an unaltered state, 20 yards south of the station;" at Eardisley a small portion of an ancient castle remains, and not far away is an oak, with an immense head, which covers a surface of 324 feet in circular extent," and some of the branches of which are two feet in diameter. Near Kinnersley Station is the castle, built in the time of James I. At Whitney the line is carried over the Wye, "considerable difficulties being experienced in its construction in the piling of the arches of the bridge.

HAY AND THE WYE.

Twenty miles from Hereford we are at Hay; and four more bring us to Glasbury, the views all along the line in the neighbourhood, with the Wye in the foreground and the wooded hills below, being extremely beautiful. Ten miles farther we are at the Talyllyn Junction, locally called Tathlyn, of the Brecon and Merthyr; and after passing through a tunnel, and seeing magnificent views of the Breconshire hills, we reach the county town.

From hence we travel over the coy and reluctant Brecon and Neath line, which, since the advent of the

Midland, has been able to make very needful and important improvements. We then proceed through a district, at first pleasant and fertile, and afterwards one of the loneliest and most desolate in the kingdom, until, at last, with some sense of relief, we catch sight of the crowded villages and civilization of the Swansea Vale. From Brecon to Swansea is 41 miles.

Of the remaining branches of the Midland system we

GLASBURY AND THE WYE.

can say little or nothing. There is the Wigston Junction to Rugby, by Countesthorpe, Broughton Astley, and Ullesthorpe; and, passing by Churchover on the left, and Harborough Magna (so called to distinguish it from Market Harborough), we cross over the valley of the Avon by what was at the time declared to be "one of the most beautiful viaducts in the kingdom," and are at Rugby. This station is the joint property of the Midland and of the London and North Western Companies. There is also the Kettering and Huntingdon line, with its ironstone fields rapidly increasing their output; Kimbolton Castle, the seat of the Duke of Manchester; and the mansion of Hinchingbrook, once the residence of the Golden Knight, who here entertained

BRECON CASTLE AND VIADUCT.

Queen Elizabeth; and where Charles I. was taken from Holmby by Cornet Joyce.

But our space is gone, and we must turn away from the thousand scenes of beauty and interest through which the Midland passes, to observe some of the methods by which so vast and varied an administration is conducted.

CHAPTER XVIII.

Twenty thousand shareholders.—Shareholders' meetings.—The Company's seal.—Chairman's address.—Scenes dull, and scenes animated.—The Board.—Directors' Committees.—The Secretary of the Company.—The General Manager.—The Superintendent.—Appointments. — Superintendent-inspectors. — Guards. — Inspector-guards.—Pointsmen.—Clerks.—Tickets.—The Detective Department.—Amusing incidents.—The Goods Department.—A visit to St. Pancras Goods Station at night.—The Locomotive Department. — The new locomotive establishment at Derby. — Visit to the works.—The erecting shops.—The lower turnery. —The wheel turnery—The boiler shop.—"The buzzer."—The express.—Riding on an engine.—Awkward accidents.—"A bird with one wing."—"Pinching" an engine.—Engine drivers and their ways.—The night mail.—Unpleasant contingencies.—Night work.—The mail.—The post-office van.—The running shed.—The last new engines.—Statistics of engines.—Twice round the world every day.—The new carriage and waggon works.—New carriages.—Civil engineers.—Services of engineers.—Growing prosperity of railways.—Conclusion.

THE ultimate source of all power of origination or administration in a railway company is the proprietary, present—personally, or by proxy—at their legally convened meetings. These are usually held half-yearly, in February and August; and at them the report for the half-year, a copy of which has previously been sent to every shareholder, is submitted for adoption, the dividend is declared, the policy of the board is explained, and other business relevant to the occasion is transacted. The present number of the Midland shareholders is upwards of 20,000.

The meetings of the Midland proprietors are held in the shareholders' room at the Derby Station; though, in times of special interest or excitement, they have been adjourned to the Derby Corn Exchange. The scene presented on such occasions is interesting and sometimes animated. The spacious hall is not unworthy of the uses to which it is appropriated. The directors' platform extends across one end, and is decorated with the portraits of several former chairmen of the Company: Mr. John Ellis in the centre, Mr. W. E. Hutchinson on his right, and Mr. Beale and Mr. W. E. Price on his left. Some 500 shareholders, leaving their names with the attendants at the foot of the stairs, and having the free tickets, with which all have been provided, stamped for "return," saunter into the room, and gradually fill the seats. Precisely at half-past one the chairman appears, followed by the other directors, and these by the chief officers of the Company. After a few minutes the chairman calls upon the secretary to read the advertisement legally summoning the meeting: a necessary form, but to which no one pays any particular attention. At its conclusion the chairman directs that the seal of the Company be affixed to the list of shareholders, an act which gives them their final and full qualification to take part in the proceedings. This seal closely resembles the arms of the Company that are painted on the passenger carriages and impressed on the covers of this volume. The deer in a park represent the town or *by* of the deer, —Derby; on the right hand, the castle and ships are the arms of the city of Bristol; and on the left are those of Birmingham. The arms of Lincoln are depicted under the deer, with Leeds on the right and Leicester on the left. On the seal of the Company, Nottingham, however, is represented instead of Bristol. The dolphin is on the left, the salamander on the right, and the wyvern on the top of the shield. At the time of the Saxon Heptarchy, Leicester was the capital of Mercia, and the wyvern was the crest of the Mercian king.

The chairman now proceeds to address the meeting. He explains the principal figures and facts mentioned in the report, and indicates the policy, and reasons for the policy, of the board. These speeches are uniformly received with the hearty good-will of the meeting. "Ours," as Mr. John Ellis used to say, "is a sort of family affair. We know if we put our money into it we can have it out again when we want it"; and this seems to be the kindly spirit in which the shareholders have been long accustomed to regard that which elsewhere is considered only in its hard financial aspects.

It is, however, to be regretted that the dignity and interest of these meetings are sometimes imperilled by the persistent obtrusiveness of one or two old-established bores. A bore which pierces through a resisting substance till it lets in light, may, even if unpleasant, be useful; and a shareholder who could make an effective attack upon any important part of the policy or administration of a public company, or point out a more excellent way in which its business could be conducted, and who could by facts and figures sustain his argument, might be a benefactor. But that 500 men of business should be compelled to waste their time in endeavouring to understand the half-audible, half-coherent gentlemen who *will* explain the exact construction and the minutest details of the last new mare's nest that a lively imagination or a defective arithmetic has provided, is a trial of patience which ought not to be made, and for which an abrupt remedy would be justifiable.

On some occasions the scene presented at the half-yearly meeting has been full of excitement. In the special meeting, January, 1868, probably 1000 shareholders were present; many of the benches ordinarily employed having been removed to make standing room for the throng to crowd more closely together. Nothing, however, destroyed the good humour and the general sense of confidence of the Midland proprietary; and patiently they "stood it out" for about three hours.

Amusing incidents sometimes occur. "I should not

have addressed this assembly," we heard a legal shareholder exclaim, with forensic indignation, "had I not been invidiously pointed out by my learned friend—if he will allow me to call him so—as the gentleman with the blue necktie;" and of course so monstrous an imputation could not but be resented. Or fancy a speaker standing on a window-sill, high above the heads of the seething mass of shareholders, with legs outstretched and arms uplifted with the passion of his elocution, wishing to know, as he had done on a previous occasion, whether certain lines affiliated to the Midland system were remunerative or not; fancy his demanding, at the topmost reach of his voice, "Mis-ter Chair-man, I want to know a-bout our af-fi-li-ations!" The whole audience turned to look at the speaker, and roars of laughter drowned the rest of his inquiry; while a clergyman beneath, surveying through his eyeglass the unabashed orator, remarked to a neighbour: "What a beautiful conception, and what a happy delivery!"

Of recent chairmen perhaps Mr. Price has been the most humorous, though his able expositions of railway policy proved that his forte did not lie in banter alone. A mournful shareholder, in dolorous accents and phrases, had been deploring the slowness of the rate with which the works on the Settle and Carlisle line had been carried on during the previous winter. "Well," said Mr. Price, in a confiding and penitential manner, "I must really confess that the directors of this Company are very deficient in one important qualification for their office: they have no proper control *over the weather*. I can only regret, sir, that you yourself are not upon our board; then I am sure we should be blessed with perpetual sunshine."

We believe, however, that we are only expressing the opinions of the whole proprietary when we say that no one has occupied the position of chairman of the Midland Railway Company with more general satisfaction and success than Mr. E. S. Ellis. Even the fact that he is the son of one who many still affectionately call "old John Ellis" is a presumption in his favour. It places him, so to speak, in "the line of the succession." With the caution and accuracy of Mr. W. E. Hutchinson, with much of the ease and force of speech of Mr. Price, and with perhaps a combination of courtesy and firmness in which he has been excelled by none of his predecessors, he has won the confidence and esteem of the shareholders and of the public. It has been his good fortune, too, to occupy this position at a time when the success of the administration of the Company has been assured, and when there is everything to encourage the hope that the future will be one of growing prosperity.

The directors of the Midland Company are 15 in number. Each must be a holder of not less than £2000 of Midland stock. It is considered desirable that the directors should be resident in, and to a certain extent be representatives of, the chief towns or districts through which the Midland line passes, and from which it draws its resources.

In the appointment of directors they are, in the first instance, nominated by the board; the selection is afterwards confirmed by the proprietors. At various times proposals have been made for what has been called "popularising" the directorate. But the arguments against such a course have been deemed conclusive; and some of the largest public companies that have till lately favoured the other method, are finding it better that their boards should take a more direct initiative, in the selection of gentlemen to fill up any vacancies that may arise.

The ordinary meetings of the board are held on the first Wednesday in the month. The directors are also divided into several committees, which deal with various departments of administration. There is, first, the Way and Works Committee, which has under its control the maintenance of the line and the real estate of the Company, the construction of new sidings, and the alteration or re-arrangement of stations. Secondly, there is the Traffic Committee, which has under its cognizance all applications for private sidings, traffic arrangements with other companies, memorials from the public for increased train or station accommodation, additional waggons required, and compensation; and the appointment of servants for the traffic department have to be sanctioned by this committee. Proposals for new lines are considered by the board. Thirdly, the Locomotive Committee, and Carriage and Waggon Committees, deal with the accommodation required for the conduct of those departments. It gives orders for additional engines, and controls the remuneration paid to servants in these departments. The rolling-stock of the Company is under its control. Fourthly, the Finance Committee deals with financial matters; provides the funds out of which payments are made; sees that the receipts for stocks and shares are properly accounted for, and issues share certificates and coupons.

The next is, fifthly, the Construction Committee. It is divided into two parts: the one takes under its cognizance all questions of construction of lines that arise north and east of Derby; the other of all those to the south of Derby and Lincoln. Sixthly, there is the Parliamentary Committee, which sits when parliamentary business is on, and determines what powers shall be sought in the construction of new or the maintenance of old works. Seventhly, the Stores Committee makes the yearly contracts for the supply of the materials and stores required on all the old lines. Each November certain standard makers are invited to tender for a year for the articles usually required. The committee then exercises its discretion as to which tenders it will accept. Each committee superintends and checks the disbursements connected with its department; the signature of a member of that committee is required to every voucher for a payment; and the voucher is also always certified by the chief officer of the department. Finally, the General Purposes Committee, which consists of the whole board, has submitted to it all questions involving additional expenditure in new works, or alterations of old lines, increase of rolling-stock, etc. These matters are brought forward at one General Purposes Committee for consideration, and, if approved, at another for confirmation.

Passing from the board to its officers, we may notice that the Secretary is the legal representative of the Company. He keeps the minutes of the board and of the various committees. He has charge of the registers of stocks, shares, and loans, and also of the deeds of conveyance of land to the Company. He receives all money, pays all accounts, and distributes the dividends. He negotiates the terms on which the Company exercises its powers to borrow under the various Acts of Parliament. He collects the rents accruing to the Company. He has the adjustment of the parochial assessment of the Company's property, for the purposes of taxation, and pays the rates and taxes. This department includes seven divisions. 1st, the Secretary; 2nd, the Assistant-Secretary; 3rd, the Debenture Stock and Loans Office; 4th, the Transfer Office; 5th, the Cashier; 6th, the Rents; and 7th, the Rates and Taxes. In these offices some forty clerks are employed.

Mr. James Williams took his first railway appointment in 1844; was on the staff of the East Lancashire, and of the Manchester, Sheffield, and Lancashire Companies; and was chief accountant of the West Midland Railway. He also was engaged with a large staff in Ireland, under the direction of the Irish Railways Commission, and aided in the preparation of the report submitted in 1868. Mr. Williams became Secretary of the Midland Company, January 1st, 1869.

We need not say that the General Manager of the Midland Railway is Mr. James Allport. Mr. Allport's railway career commenced in the service of the Birmingham and Derby Railway, of which he became the manager some time prior to the amalgamation. In 1844, the amalgamation of that railway with the North Midland and Midland Counties took place. There was not, of course, room for three staffs of officers; and the new positions were given to those who had been connected with the largest of the three associated companies. The North Midland Company's manager became the manager of the whole; and Mr. Allport went to the North to assume the charge of the Newcastle and Darlington, which grew while he was connected with it into the York, Newcastle, and Berwick. In 1850 he resigned this position to become Manager of the Manchester, Sheffield, and Lincolnshire Railway; and in 1853, he returned to take charge of the Midland. In 1857, Mr. Allport engaged in some important shipbuilding operations in the North, meanwhile occupying the position of a Midland director; and, in 1860, he was again requested to resume the position of General Manager.

In the remarkable development of the Midland system that has taken place during the last few years, Mr. Allport has had his full share of responsibility and toil. His devotion to the interests of the Company has been, in the opinion at least of rivals, only too absorbing; and vehement are the attacks that have, in consequence,

MR. JAMES ALLPORT.

sometimes been made upon him. "The great difficulty that I have had in dealing with this case," exclaimed Sir Vernon Harcourt, "and in considering it, is to wonder what in the world the Midland Company have desired it for. I cannot help thinking that it is one of those things which have their rise in the ambitious hearts of traffic managers. Mr. Allport would make an invasion of this sterile district. I do not see why his ambition should not be satisfied. I do not think he will find much more to reward his labour and his expenditure than Charles XII. did when amongst the snows of Russia."

Yet the heat of controversy has generally been tempered with some admission of the remarkable ability with which the policy of the Midland has been defended. "I admit, and I admit freely," said Mr. Liddell, in a case in which he was opposing the Midland Company, "and I must compliment Mr. Allport on, his great accuracy, and his singular power of answering complaints of this sort. I think it a most remarkable thing, the manner in which he can answer those complaints; and that he has done it in many cases I admit."

Such a life as that of Mr. Allport during the years that have witnessed the development of the Midland system from what it was to what it is, must necessarily have been a life of conflict. To carry on negotiations that affected thousands of shareholders, tens of thousands of travellers, and millions of money; which has retarded or hastened the growth of towns, the progress of commerce, the social and political relations of the nation; to have been concerned in events by which the lines of the Company have increased to 1200 miles in length, by which its capital has been augmented to more than £50,000,000, and by which the income has increased to £5,000,000 a year, could not have been done without a practical sagacity, a mastery of detail, and a persistency of will which ought not to pass by unnoticed. Such services, it is true, are not in themselves conspicuous, however conspicuous may be the results; but it is on that account they should be the more clearly recorded on an occasion like the present. To sit hour after hour, and day after day, giving evidence before a committee of Parliament, explaining the policy of a company, and the justice or expediency of a bill; to be ready with an infinite variety of details, and dates, and names, and negotiations, respecting the history and administration of the Company; to meet the designedly ambiguous or misleading inquiries of opposing counsel; to parry their astutely delivered thrusts; to show how a new treaty may be negotiated without compromising the validity of an old one, and how a new line may be made into the territory of an old ally without a breach of equity,—to do this before critical professional witnesses, while every word is recorded for future reference and use; and to do this till the questions and answers fill *a hundred and fifty pages folio* consecutively: all this demands qualities which it will be allowed are rare and remarkable.

The next department is that of the Superintendent. He has charge of the running of the trains, the safe working of the line, and the signal and other similar arrangements. The Goods Manager has charge of the goods stations, and warehouses, and their contents. When a goods train emerges from a goods department on to the main line it is under the jurisdiction and care of the superintendent, till it again reaches a goods station. The signalling agents of this department are of great importance. When a new line is being completed, or an old one is altered, the superintendent has to prepare a report of the description, the position, the instruments, and the mode of working the signals which he considers should be adopted, and to submit the report to the

General Manager. He has also to select the different ranks of servants that may be required: station-masters, clerks, signal-men, and porters;—omitting only those connected with the goods and the "way and works";—and duly considering the nature of the positions to be occupied, and the character, qualifications, and length of service of the persons to be appointed.

While new berths are thus prepared, candidates are from time to time coming forward. When additional men are required, nomination forms are sent to the directors to ask if they have any eligible persons to name. These lists being returned, and other names being perhaps added, the candidates are sent for and examined, as to their height, health, age, eyesight, hearing, ability to read any kind of writing, and so forth. Very occasionally instances have been known in which the men have satisfied the ordinary requirements of the examination, but have been afflicted by colour-blindness which might have interfered with the accuracy of their reading of night signals. Porters for the passenger department are not accepted if they are less than 5 feet 8 inches high, or for the goods if they are less than 5 feet 7 inches. Their age must not exceed 25. These conditions being satisfied, the name is put down on a list of "approved candidates," from which appointments are made as vacancies arise. Ministers and schoolmasters not unfrequently recommend clever lads, who have grown up in their schools, for positions in the Company's service. If there is *primâ facie* evidence in their favour, they have a free pass sent to them to come to Derby for examination; and, if eligible, and there are vacancies, they are appointed.

Men who have once left the service to enter other companies are never received back again.

"When applications are made by the servants of the

Company for promotion," remarked a gentleman in this department, "we turn to their pedigree, and if their history proves that they are eligible for such an appointment as that which they seek, the circumstance is recorded; when vacancies occur this list is looked through; and the best men are selected. To all these positions we promote from our own ranks; and hardly ever by any chance appoint an adult clerk or a man who has been employed in any other railway company, though we are often asked to do so. When a man is dissatisfied because his application for a certain post is not entertained, we almost always send for him; we hear what he has to say; we produce the record of his service, and scarcely ever fail to convince him that we are acting justly. The numerous extensions of the Midland system have afforded unusual opportunities for giving all reasonable promotion to our staff."

In this department an important service is rendered by what are called "superintendent inspectors." Each of these has a division of the line allotted to him. Any irregularity that occurs in the working of the traffic, the running of the trains, or the conduct of the servants, is reported to the superintendent himself, and copies of these reports are sent to the inspector in whose district the circumstance occurred. Meanwhile, every guard of a train, as he goes along, enters sundry memoranda in a book (from which at the end of the day he makes out a journal on a sheet of paper), of the work of the train, and the times of its arrival at and departure from every station. He also mentions any detaching or coupling of vehicles; states any delay that may have arisen on the way, and accounts for it. If these entries explain themselves, well and good; but if any further inquiry is needed, an extract is made and handed over to the district inspector, who sees the parties concerned, reports upon it, and states his conclusions and the reasons for them.

"The 10.14 was detained three minutes over time here last Monday, and on Tuesday the same train was delayed two minutes by a horsebox," says the inspector to the master of a roadside station; "how was it?"

"Well, on Monday, Lord So-and-So was going to Scarborough with his family; there were six children, three servants, and any quantity of luggage, and they wouldn't be hurried; and on Tuesday, as we were getting a horsebox out of the siding, the coupling broke, and we had to put another on before we could start."

A few more inquiries are made, the inspector endorses his instructions with a memorandum, then perhaps he goes elsewhere on similar errands. If wrong has been done by the Company's servants, further investigation may be necessary; and if the "way and works" or "locomotive" department's servants are implicated, a joint investigation is made by representatives of those departments; and fines are inflicted, or the men are reduced or discharged, according to the gravity of the offence. The final appeal is practically to the general manager, though a reference may be made to the directors. This, however, is seldom done.

Guards are usually appointed from the ranks of porters, and are at first employed as occasional guards with extra trains. The station-masters are asked to give the names of the porters who are most competent for these purposes; the candidates are then searchingly examined by the superintendent in all the rules of the Company as they affect the duties of guards, and especially in all the regulations that are provided to ensure the safety of the men and the protection of passengers in any eventuality that may arise. The men who are approved are then put on as "porter guards;" those porters who prove themselves most efficient in such services, are eventually appointed as full guards. In addition to the ordinary guards, there are a number of what are called inspector guards, one of whom is selected to take charge of each excursion train, a duty involving special responsibilities and care, and all the other guards of that train are under his control.

Pointsmen have very responsible duties. The posts at which they serve are arranged into three classes: 1. There are the most important junctions on the system. 2. The less important junctions, and where the traffic is smaller and the complications fewer. 3. The ordinary sidings and minor posts. The men enter the third class first. Their conduct must be good for a twelvemonth uninterruptedly before they can have an advance. In addition the first class men have a bonus of £5 every Christmas if they have not been guilty of offence against the rules of the Company involving punishment.

Clerks are first taken at the age of 14 to 17, and are gradually trained and promoted in the Company's service. By these arrangements a large number of youths rising up with a knowledge of the Company's methods of doing business is secured, who are qualified to occupy any posts that may be opened.

We may add that the Superintendent of the Midland Railway is Mr. Needham. He was engaged on the Birmingham and Derby line when Mr. Allport, Mr. Kirtley, and Mr. Walklate were connected with it. He has occupied several positions of importance on the Midland system: as station-master at Birmingham, as district superintendent at Leicester, as outdoor superintendent, and now for many years as superintendent.

There are two branches connected with his department on which it may be interesting to our readers to dwell; and, in doing so, the writer may be allowed to repeat some words he has used in *The Hour*,—a newspaper which, he ventures to say, has laid the English public under the deepest obligations for its faithful and fearless exposures of some of the gross financial enormities of the present day.

"There are about a hundred acres of tickets used on the railways of the kingdom every year," we recently remarked to a friend.

"How in the world do you make that out?" he asked.

"Well," we replied, laughing at his scepticism, "in order to make the calculation easy for your intellect by using round numbers, suppose we say that 100 tickets would occupy a square foot."

"Thank you," he replied; "I admit it."

"And as there are nine square feet in a square yard, that would be 900 tickets for a yard; or, in round numbers again, say 1000."

"Granted."

"Well, then, there are 4840, or, for simplicity's sake, let us put it at 5000 square yards in an acre; so that would make 5,000,000 tickets for an acre; and as about 500 millions of passengers travel by railway in a year, we may conclude that they require 100 acres of tickets to satisfy their enormous demands. As gross receipts from passengers amount to about £25,000,000 a year, we may consider that these bits of paper come to be worth about a shilling each on the average."

"Well," he said, "you've an odd way of suiting the laws of arithmetic to your private convenience; but you seem to be right."

We may now notice the measures that are adopted for the production of railway tickets, and the various stages of their brief but significant history. The cardboard of which they are made is usually supplied direct and complete in shape and colour from the manufacturers, in boxes of about 50,000 each, at a cost of about a shilling a thousand. The colours are various, according to the class of carriage for which they are to be used, and the ordinary or special service for which they are wanted. On the Midland line seven plain colours are employed—that is when the ticket is of uniform colour; and besides there are some half white and half yellow, or red and blue, or drab and green. Others have a broad band of one colour crossing a card of perhaps two other colours; and others have five bands alternating; white, red, blue, or green. Certain colours are for "down" line, and certain others for "up" line trains. The exceptional colours are for excursion trains, and for the different classes of excursionists, and are varied as occasion may require. The reason why so much diversity is employed is because it sometimes happens that excursion tickets are issued for two or three succeeding days; and by a different coloured ticket being issued for each day, the collector can tell at a glance that the one handed to him is the right one for that day. There are also, for many stations, market tickets. Picnic tickets are the ordinary day tickets endorsed.

The printing of the tickets is effected by an ingeniously constructed machine. If instructions are put on the back of the tickets, this is by a separate process and with black ink. All being completed, the tickets are placed in a kind of tube or hopper, down which they descend, and from which they are drawn one by one across a printing machine, which performs upon them two operations, the one the printing and the other the more difficult one of giving the consecutive numbering. This little instrument is so ingeniously contrived that if any difficulty arises, and the consecutive numbering does not go forward in perfect order, a spring is released, which rings a bell, the attention of the attendant is arrested, and he at once proceeds to ascertain the cause of the irregularity. On this point the greatest care is taken, as on no account must any tickets with duplicate numbers be permitted to be issued.

The number of tickets usually allowed to a railway station is a six months' supply; but the actual number this may represent varies endlessly. In one instance for a particular ticket a six months' supply may be only 50, in another case it may mean 10,000. The demand at the station for more tickets is sent, in the first instance, to the audit office, with a specification of the station, and route for which they are required, the number, colour, class, and description (that is, whether they are "single" or "return"), and also the last progressive number that was issued, and the last progressive number that is on hand. If this requisition is approved, it is forwarded to the ticket printing department, and executed. Orders for excursion tickets are issued direct from the superintendent's office.

The number of tickets thus produced for the service of a large company is enormous. Each printing machine will, if allowed to proceed, print 5000 or 6000 an hour; but changes have very frequently to be made that arrest its activities. Sometimes only five tickets are required before the type has to be changed; and sometimes the machine runs its course undisturbed till 10,000 are completed. From 15,000,000 to 20,000,000 may be wanted by one company in a year; yet so excellent are the arrangements made, and so respectable are the men employed, that during the thirty years through which this service for the Midland Company has been under the direction of Mr. Mills, of Derby, no instance has occurred of any ticket having been misused by one of his employés.*

After the tickets are printed by the department and received by the station, they come under the care of the booking clerk. This office is of quite modern creation. When railways were first opened for passenger traffic, the precedent of the old coaching days was followed: the traveller had to give his name, and to pay his money, and then his seat was "booked," the written receipt for the money serving as his ticket; and the names of "booking office" and of "booking clerk" survive. Under his custody the tickets have to be arranged in their order and class, and so arranged that they are accessible at a moment's notice in compliance with the imperative demands of paterfamilias, who, arriving at the station at the last moment before the train is due to start, has under his parental care three small children, who cannot be made to stand still, and three trucks of luggage which three several porters seem intent upon wheeling away in three divergent directions, while he is endeavouring at at the very same instant to secure his tickets, to provide the "needful," and to count the change.

In order to meet the hurried demands thus made upon the booking clerk, many ingenious arrangements have been devised within the narrow confines of his office. The walls of the booking office are provided with ticket-boxes or tubes, each of which contains a certain number of tickets, numbered, as we have already remarked, consecutively. These tubes are made of wood with metal rims, and are so constructed that the whole column of tickets in them lies sloping downwards in front, while at the bottom there is a small opening frontway, through

* The general printing of the Midland Company has for many years been very efficiently done in the large and excellent establishment of Messrs. Bemrose, of Derby.

which one ticket, and no more, will slide. As the weight of the column always presses upon the slanting bottom ticket, it will spring forward at the least touch, and thus the booking-clerk is enabled to get what he wants by the mere touch of one of his fingers. Having slipped the ticket from the tube, he pushes it under the stamp which prints the date; he then takes the money, calculates the change, and pays it from small round bowls containing severally gold, silver, and copper; and all in less time than it takes to tell.

On the departure of the train a further duty devolves upon the station clerk. He has to make an entry of the number and classes of tickets he has issued, and the destinations of the travellers. How is this to be done? Easily, through the ingenious arrangements provided. When the clerk takes a ticket from the tube, he contrives, by a dexterous movement of his finger, to draw the next ticket a little forward, so that it shall stick out a little, and serve as a tell-tale. The train having gone, the clerk glances round for the protruding tickets, and can see at once to what stations and for what classes tickets have been issued. He goes to one of them. It is, we will say, a first-class for Manchester, and is numbered 1,019; and, on reference to his book, he learns that the last ticket issued for the last train but one was 1,000. It is accordingly evident that for the train just gone 18 first-class tickets have been sold, the value of which comes to so much money. The consecutive numbers of the tickets and the amount received for them are entered in the columns provided for the purpose.

Attempts to defraud railway companies by means of forged tickets are seldom made, and still more seldom successful. In 1870, a man who lived in a toll-house near Dudley, and who rented a large number of tolls on the different turnpikes, in almost every part of the country, devised a plan for travelling cheaply. He set up a complete fount of type, composing stick, and every requisite for printing tickets, and provided himself with coloured papers, colours and paints to paint them, and plain cards on which to paste them; and he prepared tickets for journeys of great length, and available to and from different stations on the London and North Western, Great Western, and Midland lines. On arriving one day at the ticket platform at Derby, he presented a ticket from "Masbro' to Smethwick." The collector, who had been many years in the service of the Company, thought there was something unusual in the ticket. On examination he found it to be a forgery; and when the train arrived at the platform he gave the passenger into custody. On searching his house upwards of 1000 railway tickets were discovered in a drawer in his bedroom, and the apparatus with which the forgeries were accomplished was also secured. On the prisoner himself was the sum of £199 10*s*., and it appeared that he came to be present at the annual letting of the tolls on the different roads leading out of Derby. The punishment he received was sufficiently condign to serve as a warning to all who might be inclined to emulate such attempts after cheap locomotion.

Amusing incidents sometimes occur in the collection of tickets. A few years ago we were in a train that had stopped at the ticket platform. A hulking boy of about fourteen offered a half ticket. "You're more than twelve," said the inspector. "No, I ain't," returned the lad. "Well, then," he replied, looking him all over, amid the amusement of the passengers and the confusion of the youth, "all I can say is, you're an uncommon fine boy for your age." But a newer excuse has lately been given. "This your boy, ma'am?" inquired a collector of a country woman; "he's too big for a 'alf ticket." "Oh, is he?" replied the mother. "Well, perhaps he is, *now*, Mister; but he wasn't when he started. The train is ever so much behind time,—has been ever so long on the road,—and he's a growing lad!"

The police and the detective department of a great railway is a subject on which we might say much, but on which, obviously, it behoves us to say little. It is unfortunate that such an institution should be necessary; yet necessary it is, not only for the discovery of offences committed by the few dishonest men who may find their way into the Midland Company's army of many thousand men, but also to guard against the eccentricities,—to use a mild term,—of the public themselves. So, having some curiosity to know something about this department of human industry and ingenuity, we had an interview with one who was well qualified to inform us.

"Well, yes," he said; "we've a goodish bit of work to do, of one kind or another. There are the waiting-room loiterers, who walk off with passengers' luggage that doesn't belong to them; and sometimes our own men go wrong, and we have to 'run them in,' or to get a 'creep' (a warrant) to search their houses. There's one fellow now who used to be in the Company's service who is 'wanted.'"

"And so you have a regular staff who do the detective business of your Company?"

"Not a very 'regular' staff," he replied, smiling; "for I'm afraid they are rather irregular in their ways and words, and even appearance. But they do their work all the better for that, you know."

"Perhaps so," we answered. "And your men find themselves in rather odd circumstances sometimes?"

"Why, yes. We have had a man lie under a heap of straw three days and nights, waiting to see who would come and fetch away a roll of cloth that had been hidden there. And we've had another ride on a truck sheeted down all the way from London to Glasgow; and what with the shunting and the shaking, he had rather a baddish time of it before he had done. In fact, he suffered so much that we don't often do that now; but we have had holes bored in the front and back of the covered goods trucks, so that men inside can see for'ard and aft, as the sailors say. At first we had only a few done; and when it was found what they were for, they came to be regarded with suspicion; and a porter, seeing one, would hammer it as he went by, and sing out, 'Who are you inside? How are you, old fellow?' But now we've had so many done that nobody can tell whether they are in use or not for our purposes; and it's more comfortable riding in one of them than lying flat on your face under a tarpaulin. And almost the first time we used a bored truck we made a haul."

"How did you manage that?"

"Well, you know Stretton sidings. It's a lonely place in a cutting just this side of the tunnel. One of our goods trains was robbed. It used to take wine, among other things, to the North; the wine casks were broached. We put two men into a bored truck, to watch the train from end to end, whenever it stopped. It went all right till it reached Stretton sidings, where it had to be shunted for an express to pass. No sooner was the 'goods' safe in the sidings than the driver left his engine, and, helped by the signalman, uncovered a truck that carried wine, drew a lot off into buckets, gave some of it to the signalman and brakesman, and took the rest on to the engine for the stoker and himself. It was a regular plant. My men saw it all, but they knew it was no use to show themselves, for if they had then and there taken the offenders into custody, there was no one to drive the engine. So they were allowed to finish their little game at their leisure; and, after the express had passed, the 'goods' followed, and went right on to Masboro', where plenty of help could be obtained, and where they (driver and stoker) were taken into custody, and the buckets were found wet with the wine."

Perhaps the chief difficulty in the prevention of offences of this kind among railway servants arises from the false code of honour which exists among the men themselves,—a code, unhappily, found also elsewhere,—which hinders them from actively repressing crimes which they would not themselves commit, or even perhaps countenance, but which they will not expose. "You'll do that once too often, mate," they will say to an offender; but beyond a mild remonstrance they will seldom or never go; and should inquiries be made in regard to thefts which they must have seen, their powers of observation will be found to have been singularly circumscribed, and their memories singularly treacherous. The culprits are thus, if not encouraged, yet connived at, and perhaps go on from bad to worse, till they are ruined; their companions are suspected and compromised, and perhaps demoralised; their employers are robbed, and no one is really benefited by acts which, if the honest workman would simply resolve at all costs should not be done, would not be done.

But if the men are at fault in these matters, the public are not blameless. Claims are made by respectable firms for robberies which took place, not when the goods were on the railway, but before they left the warehouse, and the yawning vacuity which the consignees discovered in the hamper at the end of the journey might also have been found by the consignor before it left his premises. But manufacturers always assume the spotless innocence of their own servants and the exceptional depravity of railway people; and the most distant hint to an employer that possibly some mistake was made in packing his goods, will sometimes lead to as explosive a repudiation as if his own honour was assailed.

An illustration of this sort of thing recently occurred. A claim had been sent in to a railway company for two dozen pairs of boots, which, it was alleged, had been stolen while on the journey. "I examined the hamper myself," said a chief of the detective department to the writer, "and I was certain that it could not possibly have held the quantity of boots said to have been packed in it. So I went over to L——, to see the head of the firm. I was shown into a little office, with windows all round, and with a glazed door at the entrance. A bland-looking white-haired venerable gentleman received me. I stated my errand, inquired some particulars, suggested some difficulties, and at length ventured vaguely to hint the inquiry whether it was possible that some error might have been made by his people. In a moment the blandness of the venerable-looking gentleman had gone. 'Do you mean to say, sir,' he exclaimed, as he rose from his oak armchair, 'that my people have robbed me, sir, and robbed you, sir? I know what you're driving at, sir, but I won't have my servants insulted, and I won't be insulted by you, sir. I shall communicate with your directors, sir, and I wish you, sir,' he almost screamed out, as he took hold of the office door, before which I made a rapid retreat as he slammed it vehemently in my face—'I wish you, sir, A VERY GOOD MORNING, SIR!' I expected and hoped that every atom of glass in the door would have been shivered, but I am sorry to say it survived; and I expect," added the detective in a subdued tone, "that the bland-looking gentleman has ever since been sending all his goods by the London and North Western, which is our chief competitor for traffic in that town."

"Yes," he continued, after some other remarks, "we

are always changing our plans. The thief never knows when he is safe—in fact, never is safe. The man whom he thinks so innocent a companion,—a greenhorn, he fancies,—is perhaps the very one who was sent to watch his movements; and the next day as he stands in the dock will be a witness against him." The slice of Melton pork-pie so generously presented to an apparent accomplice was actually given to a detective in disguise. Every detail of the incident was immediately reported to the superintendent, and steps were taken accordingly. The jobber, as he seemed to be, who leaned with folded arms on the pig-sty wall, and congratulated the owner on the fat sides of his pigs, and slyly suggested that they must have had a nice bit of cheap barley, knew as well as the porter who owned them that the barley had not slipped out of the sacks quite accidentally.

Even when thieves have run all the hazards of their craft, and have securely possessed themselves of the property of others, they are seldom really enriched. It is "easy come, easy go" with those who rob railways. They prey upon others; but others prey upon them. Many an illustration might be given, but one will suffice. A certain railway porter had stolen a roll of ribbed trouser cloth, and, fearing to keep it in his possession, resolved to dispose of it to a Jew tailor, who was known not to be unwilling to purchase such articles at a low figure. On entering the shop with his bundle he was cordially received by the clothier, who guessed the nature of his errand. "And vaat can I do for you, my tear?" the man of business tenderly inquired.

"Well, you see—I'm a porter, and I've got a bit of cloth, you know, that I came lucky by" (a technical term).

"Quite right, my tear; and ow mootch have you got? and ow mootch do you want for it?"

"Well, I don't know," replied the porter; "you see I haven't measured it, but I want the most I can get for it."

"All right," said the Jew; and then looking sideways through his shop window down the street, he suddenly exclaimed, "I say, man, koot, koot."

"What do you mean?" urged the surprised vendor.

"Koot your stick," continued the Jew, "through my back door, and run your hardest, the police are coming," and he lifted up the movable lid of his counter to facilitate the escape of the porter, who, leaving his ill-gotten wealth upon the counter, was not slow to avail himself of the advice given, and who felt considerable relief when, having passed through the kitchen and yard of the clothier, he found himself in another street, safe out of harm's way, and no policeman in sight.

Next day, nothing doubting, the porter called again, and after passing and repassing, to make sure the Jew was within, entered the shop.

"Good morning," said the porter.

"Good morning, young man," returned the Jew, with a little reserve of manner. "Vaat can I do for you?"

"Oh, I called about that bit of stuff, you know."

"Bit of vaat?" inquired the Jew.

"The bit of cloth I left here yesterday—you remember."

"Bit of cloth you left here yesterday?" returned the man of business, with an air of what our French friends call "pre-occupation" and reserve. "Vaat do you mean, young man?"

"Why, you know," continued the porter, with emphasis, "I brought a bit of cloth yesterday to sell you—a bit I'd come lucky by."

"Vaat! to my haus—you brought it here! Vy, I never see you before in ma life. Tell me vaat you mean."

So the man repeated in emphatic words, how that he had come the day before with a roll of cloth, how that he was going to sell it, and that they were talking about the price when they were interrupted by a policeman passing along the street, and "you know," he added, "I left the cloth just here, and went out the back way through your house and yard." But so monstrous an imputation upon his reputation the Jew could no longer resist.

"Judith, my tear," he called out at the top of his voice to his daughter,—"Judith, my tear, fetch a policeman; here is a railway porter who has robbed his master, and wants to bring disgrace upon a respectable tradesman." And Judith hied herself out into the street in apparently hot pursuit of a minister of justice. There was no time to be lost. The terrified railway servant performed a strategic movement down the street in the opposite direction, leaving behind him for ever his ill-gotten spoils in the possession of the tender-hearted and scrupulous Israelites.

The position of Manager of the Goods Department of the Midland Company, is occupied by Mr. Newcombe. He was formerly a carrier by road and railway, having conveyances working in connection with Chaplin and Horne, and Carver and Co., between all the chief towns in England and Scotland. In the year 1850, owing to the principal railway companies having determined to become their own carriers, and generally to dispense with the services of agents, Mr. Newcombe accepted the post of goods manager under the York, Newcastle, and Berwick Railway Company, at Newcastle. In 1855 he was appointed general goods and mineral manager of the Great Western, the head quarters of which were at Paddington. Two years afterwards he was appointed to be general manager of the Midland Railway, consequent upon Mr. Allport's retirement to engage in iron shipbuilding, at Yarrow; in 1860, Mr. Allport left the firm with which he had been connected, and Mr. Newcombe was induced to give up the post of general manager to enable Mr. Allport to resume it. The board also arranged for his removal to London, to organize and conduct the Company's carting arrangements, which had been performed by Pickford and Co. This post he held for eight years, when at the death of Mr. Walklate, in 1868, he was appointed general goods and mineral manager.

The duties of the goods manager include the arrangement of trains for all goods and mineral traffic; the fixing and quoting of all rates for goods and general merchandise; the purchase and distribution of horses and all vehicles used in the shunting and cartage operations of the Company; the supervision of the entire goods and mineral staff of the Company; the appointment of agents, clerks, and porters, subject to the approval of the board; attendance at conferences of various companies; and general management, working, and conduct of all matters relating to the goods and mineral traffic of the Midland Company.

On the vast and multitudinous arrangements by which, in the chief towns of England and in hundreds of smaller ones, such a department does its work, we cannot dilate. But it may give some vividness to our understanding of the method of operation, if we visit one principal goods station, say St. Pancras, at 10 o'clock some night, and see what is going forward.

Having secured the assistance of a competent and courteous guide, we pass on amid the glancing of railway lights, the sound of passing trains, and the clatter of ponderous vehicles; to the "inwards" department of the great goods shed. If all is dark without, all is light within. This "inwards" platform, on which we are now standing, runs the length of the shed from north to south,—a distance which, with the additions now being made, will be 1000 feet or so from end to end. On the left of this platform is the "van dock" in which the vans are standing; on the right is the "truck dock," where the train has been placed which is now being loaded. All the morning and afternoon vehicles have been coming in, loaded to enormous heights with the cargoes they have obtained at the London "receiving offices" of the Company, at the Castle and Falcon, Regent's Circus, the Borough, and elsewhere; and now the business is at its height.

The appearance at first presented is one of inextricable confusion. Vehicles are rattling in and out of the yard; innumerable and mighty heaps of bales, barrels, hampers, crates, baskets, and bundles, throng the platform, and seem to become every moment more numerous and more vast; workmen run hither and thither with little trucks loaded with goods of all sorts and sizes; cranes swing round in all directions, and the chaos seems to be complete. But as we grow familiar with the scene, we find that order prevails. We notice that the vans, as they enter the shed, are at once placed under the orders, no longer of the drivers, but of "van shunters," who, with their horses, do nothing else but regulate the movements of the vans, so that no place all along the "van dock" is unfilled, or filled by the wrong vehicle. At the present moment some eighty of them—all backed up to the left-hand edge of the platform—are discharging their contents under the hands of a hundred men, in four-and-twenty gangs, each with its checker, loader, and barrow-men. Besides these there are ten capstan lads and their foremen; the train setters and their foremen; and the superintendent in charge of the whole.

The "outwards" platform is arranged in some twenty

different "berths," as they are called, named after the principal towns to which the Midland runs, and distinguished as such by the names hanging overhead on great wooden labels—Birmingham, Bristol, Liverpool, Leeds, Bradford, etc. The goods intended for these different destinations are brought into these divisions respectively. No sooner is the train marshalled in its dock on the right-hand side the platform than the "truckers" bring forward the goods to be loaded, or the cranes are worked by machinery, and "forthwith a huge bale, or a heavy forging, is seen dangling in the air, and is swung round and deposited in the truck or waggon as tenderly as a mother would place her sleeping child in its cradle." In the trucks themselves, the loaders are at work reducing the incoherent heaps of goods into compact masses of cargo, and so adjusted that they shall not suffer by friction or shaking on their hurried journey.

The first chief down train is the 2.35; it contains fruit, butter, and wool. The fruit is from the South of England, the Channel Islands, and France, and it goes to the midland counties and Manchester. Twenty tons of apples and plums a day throughout the season is not unusual, and sometimes forty tons of oranges in a night; each box, containing from one to two hundredweight, must sweeten a good many mouths. The wool comes from the London wool warehouses, where it has changed hands at the periodical wool sales, which last perhaps a couple of months at a time, and which supply an almost continuous traffic of wool to the North for eight or nine months of the year.

The variety of goods thus despatched is enormous. Grocery and tea from the docks and bonded warehouses; furniture, made in London, but unfinished,—"in the white" it is called,—to receive the last touches of the cabinetmaker's and of the polisher's art when it reaches its destination, and is not in such danger of being scratched or injured by a journey; carriage-builders' work in the same condition, and for the same reasons; drugs from the wholesale houses for country druggists; skins from Bermondsey; mustard from Colman's at Norwich; spirits (especially gin) from the London distillers; and oil, and a thousand commodities besides, are consigned by metropolitan merchants and traders to the care of the railroad for their country customers. The principal work on the "outwards" platform has to be accomplished within a specified period, namely, between about 2 o'clock in the afternoon, and say 4 o'clock the next morning. This pressure is unavoidable. The chief articles sold in London during the day cannot be packed by the owners and obtained by the Company except in the course of that day. The amounts brought in are constantly increasing as the afternoon wears on, and the business from 8 o'clock in the evening till midnight is at its height. From that time it slackens, the last express goods leaving at 2.25 in the morning, and then there are two "clearing up" trains, as they are called, to finish up with. The goods received at 6 o'clock to-night at the railway receiving offices, have to be delivered in Yorkshire by 7 o'clock next morning, as rapidly as the Post Office delivers its letters; and so numerous and weighty are the trains, that each must be despatched to a minute at the time appointed in the working time-tables, failing which there will be on the part of the authorities at Derby—to use the expressive phrase of a subordinate—a "tremendous noise."

We now cross over from the western or "outwards" platform to the eastern or "inwards." It also occupies the whole line from north to south of the goods shed, one side being bounded by the trucks dock, the other by the van dock. The procedure on this side is simply the reverse of that upon the other; instead of goods being received by road from the metropolis, to be sent into the country by rail, goods are received by rail from the country to be sent into the metropolis, chiefly by road. There is, however, on this side an even greater diversity of goods than upon the other. London produces a great multitude of articles which it forwards to the provinces for consumption; but London receives a still greater multitude for its own use—in fact, every conceivable article under the sun. No wonder, then, that upon the "inwards" platform we find cases of hardware from Birmingham, casks of shoes from Leicester, hampers of lace from Nottingham, agricultural implements from Lincoln, crates of earthenware from Staffordshire, skips of lint from Chesterfield for Guy's Hospital, boxes of biscuits from Reading, sacks of seed from Wisbeach, hats from Luton, mangles from Keighley, ale from Burton, castings from Leeds, tins of butter from Liverpool, whisky from Glasgow, trusses of canvas and bales of hides from Leith, and last, but not least, "mild cured Cumberland bacon" direct from the United States!

Let us watch the process of unloading. There are five-and-thirty waggons now alongside the platform. The side of each is let down, and is resting on the edge of the platform, so as to form a bridge across which the little trucks may be run direct into the body of the waggon. The "checker" places himself alongside the waggon with the invoice in hand, which has come from the "sending station," and which shows what were the contents of the truck when it was despatched. Another man, named a "caller-off," assisted by two porters, rolls the goods out of the waggon, or lifts them out with the crane, and the "caller-off" shouts out to the checker the name and address upon the package, or the private mark which is used as the equivalent. The checker examines his invoice, and if he finds a corresponding entry, checks it off. Meanwhile, you must take care of your head, for the crane is at work, and the facile application by hydraulic pressure of Bessemer steel to human skulls would not be pleasing. "Facile" we may truly say, for the motion is as easy and as rapid as can be desired. First the crane picks up a crate of earthenware from Hanley, weighing fourteen or fifteen hundredweight; next a case of hardware from near Wolverhampton; and then the truckers run in, and bring out bags of nails, half a hundredweight each, scythes, a bicycle, a royal prize, and a few dozen other articles which completed the load. The truck is now clear, and as soon as room can be made for the operation it will be run on to the "traverser," and at once drawn sideways on to the next line of rails, or perhaps right across to the "outward" lines, where it will be ready to be re-marshalled and re-loaded as part of the next down train.

We now enter a "lift," and in a few seconds have reached the floor above, and are in a room used as a store for goods that have lost their owners, or that have been damaged, or that await the order of the consignee. From hence we pass into the cheese-room, which is set apart for the convenience of one American cheese merchant, who sometimes has here a stock of 14,000 or 15,000 cheeses, each enclosed in a wooden box, the shape of the cheese, and each weighing about half a hundredweight. They are dated according to their dairies, and each is marked with the distinguishing brand.

The next apartment is a vast general warehouse for goods that are waiting orders, but it might, we think, be called "the bottle room." Here are bottles innumerable, in crates, in cases, or in "mats" only, containing a gross each; bottles for wine and spirits, for salads and sauces, for fruits and pickles, for oils and medicines; bottles for the doctors and (with the broad arrow, "the rogues' mark" as it is called) for the Government, besides glass pestles and mortars, and measuring glasses, by which physic can be administered, if the patient prefers, a quart as a dose. These bottles come chiefly from Castleford, Swinton, and Mexborough, but also from Scotland and elsewhere. We find in one part of this room a Government inspector who has a department here, and who examines one by one the bottles and stoppers which the contractors have sent, before they are packed up for despatch to the India stores in Belvedere Road for transmission to the East. In this room we observe casks nearly filled with sand, ready to be used for the extinction of fire, for which in some instances it is more effective than water.

The scale on which business is done at such a station is enormous. The van that for a moment stops the way as we leave the "inwards" contains a dozen huge coils of paper intended for a London daily journal. We notice upon one the words "5863 yards," weighing "598 net lb.," so that there are three miles of paper in that coil, and thirty miles of it in the van. The amount of meat and fish received at this station is large. Forty or fifty tons of mackerel or of white herrings will be delivered in a day. Dead meat from the midland counties, and even from Scotland and Ireland, comes in regularly, and sometimes 100 trucks of live cattle will arrive for the cattle-market days. The range of buildings hard by, with the name of Messrs. Bass conspicuously painted at the corner, is 300 feet square; each of the three floors is two acres in extent, and each contains 30,000 barrels of 36 gallons of ale; while the minerals received at St. Pancras, including those sent to the other London stations of the Midland Company, amount to some 700,000 tons per annum; enough to fill 100,000 trucks, or 2000 a week;

enough in a year to make a coal train that would stretch nearly 300 miles long, or from London to Newcastle-upon-Tyne.

The locomotive establishment of a great railway company is obviously one of its most important departments. To provide engine power enough, and not too much, for the work to be done; to be prepared for any contingencies that may arise by increase of traffic or otherwise, without being lavish in outlay; to keep every one of the 5416 pieces, of which an engine is composed, in good order; to have 1200 or 1300 such engines and tenders in their proper places, and at the right time; and to have effective command of the 7000 men engaged in the various branches of this one department,—this is to occupy a responsible and influential position.

The arrangements of the locomotive establishment at Derby are at present undergoing considerable alterations and enlargement. In a few months a vast area of new buildings will be finished, and changes will be made which will make the locomotive works as effective, and (for the departments it includes, and proportionately to the rolling stock and length of line) as capacious as any in the kingdom.

The new erecting and fitting shops will be a vast and complete building. It will contain three bays of 50 ft. span each, and alongside, and connected with it by large arches, a fitting shop, with three bays 40 feet span. The whole will be 450 feet long. There are also in course of construction new iron and brass foundries, together with large coppersmiths' shop, boiler-makers' and smiths' shops, all placed in convenient positions, for not only the new additions but also the existing workshops. All these shops are of equally liberal dimensions with the large erecting and fitting shop.

When an engine is brought into this erecting shop, it

will be drawn along the centre road of one of the bays till it arrives at the point where it is wanted. It will then be taken bodily up by a travelling crane, and lifted on to the right or left pit, as one might lift a baby out of one cradle into another alongside of it. When the repairs are completed, the engine will be taken up again, and placed on the centre line of rails, to be drawn out of the shop. Every arrangement will be made here for the simultaneous repair or erection of about 70 engines; this, with the addition of the present erecting shops, gives a repairing capacity of about 120 engines.

We enter the erecting shops, three in number: one set apart for the repair of goods engines, one for passenger, and one for "rebuilds," renewals, and new engines. In the first two of these are engines of various kinds, sizes, and ages, in various stages of reconstruction. In the third we see a mere frame resting on an iron table; the next has its boiler and firebox in position, and men are at work inside the firebox, lighted by gas jets, supplied through flexible india-rubber tubing; others are in the pit beneath the engine, while one is standing high up on the top of the boiler, busily engaged at some part of the dome. Farther on are groups of men fixing together the cylinders, slide-bars, and motion plates, etc., all of which require the most accurate adjustment. Then we find one under the hands of those who are clothing the naked iron loins of the boiler with bands of wood, to keep in the heat of the boiling water; these bands in their turn being kept in their places by strips of iron, while the whole are covered with thin sheet-iron plates. After a few finishing touches from the fitters, the engine is ready to go into the hands of the painter, there to receive the usual coats of stopping up, priming, painting, and varnishing, previous to the introduction to its daily labours.

In other parts of the shop may be seen men adjusting

the tubes, 160 to 225 of which are required for an engine. "We are now using only one type of boiler," remarks our friend, who accompanies us through the works. "Instead of having different sizes, we make them all alike; 30 or 40 sets are put in hand at once, and any one part of a boiler will do for any other boiler, which is an immense boon." "But suppose an engine is too small or too old to receive so large a boiler as your new type," we inquire, "what then?" "We make scrap of it," was the suggestive reply. All the erecting shops are supplied with powerful travelling cranes, traversing from one end of the shop to the other. These are all driven by a small endless cord or band, not more than ¾ inch diameter, yet so arranged that they can lift from 25 to 30 tons as readily as the same number of hundredweights. The shops are also heated in winter with steam, and the pits in these several shops are supplied with gas through flexible pipes.

Leaving the erecting shop, we enter the Lower Turnery. The sight which here presents itself is striking. The whole place, and it is very large, seems alive; wheels, shafts, and bands, above and below, in endless variety of revolution. Planing, slotting, shaping, and drilling machines; axle, cylinder, crank-turning, and screw-cutting lathes, and other machines; and each and all attended with a busy host of white jacketed men standing and moving about in every direction: a combination that in itself presents, with its throng of men, its whirl of straps and wheels, its clatter and hum of machinery, a spectacle remarkable to a visitor, but totally indescribable by a writer.

We descend from our elevation, and mingle in the busy scene. Cylinders are being finished and fitted; some are being planed on several sides at once; others are being bored so as to make them perfectly true; a few are being surfaced up, so as to make them impassable to even such a subtle gas as steam; whilst others are being finished ready to take their important share in the working of the locomotive. Axles are being turned at both ends at once; while in another part may be seen a row of lathes, paring into shape the rough uncultivated form of a crank shaft (rough from the forge) as easily as a thumb nail might peel an orange, only with infinitely greater accuracy. In fact, here everything is turned, turning, or about to be turned; turning being apparently the infallible remedy for every ill, until the part is ready to fit with some other part in the exact place assigned to it in the locomotive.

We next pass through the wheel-turning shops, where there are about 30 lathes or more at work, together with other special tools. In this place we see tires of from five to 15 cwt. being prepared for their duties, cut and shaved, and slices taken out as easily and remorselessly as if the metals (steel not excepted) had ceased to be hard. Now we see a great pair of driving wheels, with the axle in place, having six tools operating on it at once. In the wheel-pressing shop, wheels are pressed on or off the axles by hydraulic presses, as one would slip, though not quite so easily, a glove on or off one's fingers. Here may also be seen large furnaces for expanding the tire before shrinking it on the wheel centre; also fires for again expanding the tire, when by some cause or another it is required to be taken off; also key-grooving, rim-slotting machines, as well as many others necessary for fixing the wheels, tyres, and axles, securely to each other.

We look into the spring shop, where stalwart men are at work, bending, setting, and tempering springs of all sorts and sizes required for the different engines; and where also in one corner may be seen the testing machines, to which each spring is taken, and tried before going out. We next pass into the smiths' shops, a long building all aglow with the flames from 50 or 60 smiths' hearths, each with a complement of men hammering and welding some red-hot piece of iron, or preparing the same for a severer ordeal under one of the several steam hammers that are placed down the centre of this shop.

Then there is the boiler shop, where boilers are dangling uncomfortably in the air, or are seated in every attitude on the ground, and where a multitude of men are driving rivets and hammering plates so as to make such an unconscionable noise that, having some regard left for our auditory nerve, for the loss of which perhaps the Midland Company would not give compensation, we make a precipitate retreat.

Before we conclude our visit, we look into the pattern shop, where in every position and on every wall are patterns, shapes, and models of all the different parts of an engine that require casting in either brass or iron; where pattern-makers are at work readjusting old models or forming new ones. Retracing our steps, we pass back through the top or light turnery and fitting shop. This is as busy a place as the kindred establishment below. Wheels and straps are flying overhead in all directions; machinery of all kinds is in motion; among them are emery wheels for surfacing slide-bars, slotting and drilling, screw cutting machines, slot drills and machines for preparing eccentrics and straps, connecting-rods, valve-spindles, slide-bars, cross-heads for the piston-rods, pumps, injectors, whistles, brass mountings, as well as many other details we have no time to enumerate.

But while everything is in full drive around, there is a strange contrast in the appearance of the men. Unlike all the other departments, there is an air of listlessness and apathy here. Our presence seems to everybody far more interesting than the work on which the men are engaged. "How is it?" we inquire. "It's only a few seconds," replies our guide, "to the dinner-hour, and the men's stomachs know it. There! that's the buzzer." Instantly the men are off; their jackets are put on as they go; and in less than half a minute not one is to be seen. The busy machinery is slowly coming to a stand, and we are the solitary spectators of a silent and deserted scene.

Having now visited the locomotive works we may watch the locomotive itself at its work. And here we may remark that there is nothing (except perhaps a good dividend) of which railway directors and managers are so proud as of their express trains. Commodious stations, easy gradients, costly engineering works, are all very well, but they are only means to an end, and the running of these expresses is, so to speak, that end. Like a mighty shuttle in the vast loom of the national life, the express flies backwards and forwards on its swift and straight career, with half a kingdom for its weft. We are, therefore, not surprised at the pardonable pride with which those more immediately concerned watch its career. One's own admiration of the locomotive never seems to tire (except perhaps when our tire comes off). This mighty and intricate machine, constructed of thousands of pieces, all of which are put together, as George Stephenson used to say, as carefully as a watch; which an hour or so ago had not strength enough to drag its own weight over the floor of the stable in which it stood, is now ready, with ribs of steel, and bowels of brass, and food of fire, and breath of steam, and with the power of perhaps 1000 horses, to draw a mighty train for a 100 miles, if need be, without a pause. So intricate, yet so true, will be its movement, that some of the machinery will, as it runs, divide a second into eight equal parts, and the pistons will be passing backwards and forwards along the cylinders at the speed of about 1000 feet a minute! Yet this stupendous power is under the easiest control, and can be made to run at the rate of a mile a minute or a mile an hour by a single movement of the regulator.

The scene is always one of interest and excitement before the down express starts. The train is ready; the engine is attached; the last passengers are taking their seats; porters bustle about with luggage on their shoulders, or trundle along mountains of baggage in wicker-work trucks, which have the appearance of something cross-bred between a clothes-basket and a cradle. One man endangers the head of the public generally by the manner in which he carries a huge box; another is evidently of opinion that he is perfectly justified in bruising any one's shins, because he has first shouted, in tones which no one can understand, "By y'r leave"; but, as a rule, everything is proceeding as rapidly and as orderly as is practicable. The last moment has come; the last farewells are uttered; the signal is given; the "chay-chay" of the engine, at first heard at perceptible intervals, becomes a continuous sound; and before the last van has cleared the platform, the train is running at rapid speed on its new journey.

The first impression produced by riding on the engine of a fast train is exhilarating. There is a sense of novelty, of swiftness, and of power. But if continued for any length of time, there is a strange feeling in the calves of one's legs,—a sort of cramp,—the effect of the firmness with which one has to stand on the footplate in order to resist the "dither" of the engine. The next feeling is that everything is very hard and very hot. The graceful bounding appearance that an engine seems to a looker-on to have when it is running is appearance only. Everything on a locomotive is as unyielding as iron and steel can make it. Nor is it any wonder that it is hot, for within a few feet of the footplate are three or four hundred gallons of boiling water, and also a firebox that is a seething cauldron of five or ten hundredweight of coals that are, not only burning, but burning like a blast furnace under the highest possible draught, as if fifty blacksmiths' bellows were at full work upon it; while to prevent any lateral escape of any of this volume of heat, its sides are covered in by a non-conducting wooden "clothing" around the boiler. Sometimes, indeed the flame becomes so great as to pour right through the ten feet length of the 200 tubes that run from the firebox along the boiler, and, mounting up the six or seven feet of the chimney, will flow out at the top a foot in length. "I have known," said an engineer to the writer, "when an engine was pulling a very heavy load, the exhaust steam (that is, the steam that has done its work in the cylinders and is passing away by the chimney) cause such a vacuum in the chimney, and draw the air so strongly through the fire and along the tubes, as to make the engine hum like a threshing machine. I have even known a locomotive to be, so to speak, red-hot; that is to say, I have seen the smokebox door at the front end of the engine, under the chimney, red-hot. The draught had been so great that it carried some hot coals through the boiler tubes; the smokebox door did not fit tight; the draught inside sucked in the air from outside, and soon made the smokebox plates red-hot." But this, we ought to say, was some years ago, and was not on the Midland.

Of course the moment the speed of the train is diminished, and especially when the steam is shut off, the intensity of the draught in the engine fire is stopped, and awkward accidents have sometimes occurred in consequence. The mass of heat, flame, and smoke which has tended towards the chimney at once rises up, and endeavours to find egress in some other direction; and if the furnace door happens to be opened, it may pour out at that. If the fire is "green" (that is, if coals have only lately been put on), there is a large volume of a smoke that has all the properties of fire-damp, being full of gas that will explode from the heat of the furnace when it comes in contact with the outside air. "I remember," said an engineer to the writer, "a foreman of locomotive works being on an engine with me, and he was stooping down to examine some fittings near the furnace door, when suddenly the driver shut off the steam. The draught was arrested; the smoke, instead of being burnt as it passed over the fire and through the tubes, instantly accumulated over the fire and at the furnace door, and being highly charged with gas, exploded, and in an instant frizzled off the whiskers and eyebrows of my companion, and, indeed, every hair of his face and head that was not covered by his hat."

It is not always pleasant work to drive, or even ride upon, an engine. Formerly no protection was afforded from the full force of the wind and the severity of the weather, and the driver, as he ran on the keenest winter night on the top of the loftiest embankment, had

> "To bear
> The pelting brunt of the tempestuous night,
> With half-shut eyes, and puckered cheeks, and teeth
> Presented bare against the storm;"

perhaps sometimes feeling, as did the sailor in the gale of wind when it blew so strongly that, as he averred, happening to yawn with his face to windward, he was obliged to turn to leeward before he could close his jaws. Even under ordinary conditions on an engine, in summer you are too hot, except your face, and you are sometimes half blinded by dust; in winter your feet and body are perhaps warm, but your head is so cold that you can't tell whether you have any ears or not. In rain, if you are running fast, every drop that touches your face feels like a pin pricking you. This is how it is that drivers and firemen have such red faces,—it is the effect of the weather. It also affects the throat. A driver of any length of service can hardly ever sing.

Speaking with a driver about his engine and his work, he remarked, in his own homely and effective style, "Yes, it's sharpish, as you say, in cold weather. I once had a fireman,—he'd been a fitter, and been brought up in a warm shop. It was Christmas Eve. When we were getting water at Tamworth he put his hand into the tender to feel if it was getting full, and then he put his wet hand on the hand rail, which was covered with ice, and in a minute his hand was frozen to it. As he tore it away it fetched the skin off his four fingers, just for all the world as if he had put them on a red-hot bar. He was also frostbitten in the chest, and was eight weeks off work. He'd never lost time before, but in cold winters he has suffered ever since."

"We like," he continued, after some other remarks, "we like to keep the same engine while her legs is good. Then we shift to another while she is repaired, and then we go back again. We like to stick to the old 'un same as we do to a house. You see we,—the engine and me,—get used to one another; know where everything is to be found, and what she can do. A good engine-man takes a pride like in his engine, as if, you know, she was his own property, and we know what we can coax out of her; and, what's more, what we can't. What do I mean by coaxing her? Why, you see an engine wants to be managed like, same as a woman does. We have to fire the engine on the lightest part of the road, that is when she's running down banks and such like, and has the least blast on. If we put coal on when the blast is strong up the chimney, the small coal goes into the smokebox and flies up out of the chimney. It would be wasted, and would dirty the carriages, and settle on them. It is the fireman, you know, that watches the fire, and keeps the steam up by the indicator, as the driver requires him; and both driver and fireman have also to keep a sharp look-out ahead.

"I've been a goodish time in the service. I started as a fitter as a boy, mostly in the running shed. I was driving before I was 30, and had been 'firing' before that. How many miles do I run? Why, 76 miles out and 76 miles home—152 miles, or 1000 miles with oddments in six days, or 50,000 miles in a year, if we don't lose time or make 'over.' Time was, when I worked goods, I never saw my children except when they was abed; now the trains are worked more regular and comfortable for the men. No; never had an accident in my life. Have had many narrow escapes. In my opinion more men get injured by jumping off their engines than by staying on."

"Did I ever read 'Mugby Junction'? Yes; I've read it, and don't think much to it. I don't believe any driver ever told Muster Dickens anything of the sort. Why not? Well, sir, if you'd ever run over a poor fellow on the road, and had to pick his poor dead limbs together, as I've had to do, you wouldn't speak cold-blooded like about it, as Muster Dickens said the man did: 'Tain't in human natur'; 'tain't in driver's natur', leastwise. So I don't believe a word about it. But them romancing people never know, sir, when they're telling the truth and when they ain't—that's my opinion."

There are many among us who, like the writer, are fond of looking at trains. It is pleasant to watch them by day, as they run through the silent fields, where the grazing cattle scarcely lift their heads, and the timid sheep lie quietly in the furrows, and the hen partridge crouches with her brood only for a moment in the dry dust of the gravelly cutting, and the loose horse, though he gallops away, and then stops and stares and snorts, is not really frightened, but only pretends that he is.

We like, too, to go down to the roadside station at night, and see the down mail pass. We were there the other night. All was silence and darkness, except the sound of the rain pattering on the roof, and the glancing lamps of two or three porters, one of whom, with a lantern in his left hand, was writing in a small memorandum book, while others, with lamps suspended round their necks, were greasing the axles of some carriages, the forms of which could scarcely be distinguished. We paced the platform up and down for a while till we knew that the "up goods" was nearly due. We could hear it approaching. First a distant rumble through the pitch darkness, and then came slowly forwards the glancing form of a huge and powerful goods engine. The furnace door is opened, and instantly the steam is lit up into what seem to be mighty folds of flame; and then, as the train goes ponderously by, we see a long, low, solid line of trucks, covered in by wet shiny black tarpaulins, which glisten in the light of the station lamps: that train, a vast unconscious thing,—knowing nothing, hearing nothing, caring for nothing, peering forward into the night with its white eyes, and looking backwards on the iron path it has been treading with huge blood-red sightless balls.

"Look up," shouts a voice. "Stand back," bawls another. "The down mail," remarks a porter at our elbow. And scarcely has he said the words than a great flaming eye is seen up the line; the gradual boom of the approaching train grows louder and louder; the red light of the furnace glows beneath the engine wheels; the iron gullet of the monster flings red-hot sparks high up into the air; and then the thundering gleaming mass roars and rushes by at 50 or 60 miles an hour; and, as it rolls away into the darkness at the other end of the station, the train seems to be burning its way through the sable night, with the strength, the straightness, and the fury of a cannon ball. "What a fool a man must be to travel in a thing like that," says an observer who is standing by; and then he adds, "Perhaps, I shall travel in it myself to-morrow."

In running engines even by day a sharp look-out has always to be kept to see that the line is clear a-head; lest, perchance, through a gap in a hedge, or by a gate left ajar, the farmer's stock may have strayed upon the line. Not long ago the driver of an express train, on rounding a curve, observed, to his dismay, a horse and cart standing right before him on the rails. There was not time to stop; but, believing that the more violent the blow with which his engine struck the intruders the less would be the hazard to himself, he turned on the steam to its full, and in a moment afterwards both horse and cart were sent to "smithereens." The train kept on the rails, and indeed scarcely seemed to feel the shock; but it could hardly be pleasant to be riding on the engine while cart wheels and horses' legs were flying in the air.

Other important matters have to be attended to in other parts of the night mail. There, inside the capacious Post-Office van, is a busy scene. The clerks are actively engaged all the way in sorting into pigeon-holes the letters they receive upon the journey, and in sealing up the leather bags they leave on the road. "All of a sudden," says Sir Francis Head, "the flying chamber receives a hard blow, as if a cannon shot had struck it. This noise, however, merely announces that a station-post we were at that moment passing, but which is already far behind us, had just been safely delivered of some leather letter bags, which, on putting our head out of the window, we saw quietly lying in the far end of a large iron-bound sort of landing net or cradle, which the guard a few minutes before had, by a simple movement, lowered on purpose to receive them. But not only had we received four bags, but at the same moment, and apparently by the same blow, we had, as we flew by, dropped at the same station three bags, which a Post Office authority had been waiting there to receive." Meanwhile the guard, whose face, " besides glittering with perspiration, was, from the labour of stooping and hauling at large letter-bags, as red as his scarlet coat, which was hanging before the wall on a little peg; until at last his cheeks appeared as if they were shining at the lamp immediately above them, almost as ruddily as the lamp shone upon them," leaves his bags, pokes his burly head out of a large window behind him into pitch darkness, in order to ascertain the precise moment that the train clears certain stations, and that he may duly chronicle the same in his time-bill.

And so, far and wide over the land, while the nation is slumbering, railway trains are carrying the cargoes of the Post Office, not only along the great lines of communication, but in a hundred divergent directions besides; in a manner, for all the world, as an imaginative writer has declared, to be compared " to the fiery tracks and sparks created by the sudden ignition of a sack-full of fireworks of all descriptions; of rockets, catherine wheels, Roman candles, squibs, stars, crackers, flower-pots,—some flying straight away, while others are revolving, twisting, radiating, bouncing, exploding in every possible direction, and in all ways at once."

When an engine has finished its journey of 150 or

200 miles out and home, it usually undertakes a little trip on its own account. Uncoupled from the train, it runs forward a few yards, backs by a "cross over" road to the next line of rails, and then hies itself away, like a boy just released from school, to the engine stables.

For a good deal has to be done to a locomotive after it returns from one journey before it is ready for another. The intense heat, the rapid motion, and the high pressure to which every part of the intricate and costly machinery has been exposed, renders examination, cleaning, perhaps repairs, indispensable. The engine has become tired, so to speak, with its work, and needs an interval of rest. Its joints have become relaxed, its tubes have become clogged with coke, its grate bars and firebox with clinkers, and though the water and steam are left in the boiler to cool, it will require four-and-twenty hours before the whole engine has recovered its ordinary temperature.

On approaching the running shed, which forms the stable or home of that engine, "she" is brought slowly over an ashpit which is sunk between the rails, where the furnace bars are lifted, so that in a moment the furnace can void the red-hot contents of its stomach, over which cold water is instantly poured. The driver now examines the working parts of his engine, enters in a book a report of what repairs he thinks are necessary, and there is seldom a journey performed but he requires, or thinks he requires, something to be done. He now takes his lamps to the lamphouse to be cleaned and trimmed by the lampmen; and being off duty, he goes, with his satellite fireman, homeward; and then the cleaners come, push their long flexible iron rods along the tubes of the boiler, clean out the firebox, and at intervals the boiler also, for the stomach of a locomotive is so delicate that unless regularly cleared from all incrustation of lime from the water, she will without metaphor, spit it out; in other words, will "prime."

We enter the cleaning shed. Here a motley, merry, shining, and greasy crew are distributed over, under, and around the travel-stained engines, and with cloths and rags and scrapers are speedily but effectually cleaning off the dirt; while others are daubing their engine over with a greasy composition, "just to preserve her complexion," as a bystander remarks.

While we watch these grooming operations, a grave-looking member of the locomotive staff, sometimes called the "house-surgeon," approaches, accompanied by an engine-driver. They enter into conversation, and after closely examining some portion of the engine, "the doctor" looking round at the empty stalls says: "Well, we can't help it; we must send it into the shops;" and we thus learn that bad weather and hard work have a deleterious effect even upon constitutions of iron. Near at hand we see an engine slung upon its haunches, and a little knot of men assisting the "doctor" in his investigations, who at length evidently arrives at the conclusion that some severe surgical operations will be necessary.

We ought here to state that two large messrooms have been built for the accommodation of the men connected with this department. The smaller of them will hold 100 men, and cooking is carried on for nearly 200. Here also, by the wish of the men, an arrangement has been made so that they may be addressed by clergymen of different denominations during the meal times. The larger and more modern one is a spacious well lighted building, the walls cheerfully picked out with bright colours. It will seat about 400, and regularly cooks for 600 or 700 men.

At one end are placed the ovens, boiler, and steaming apparatus, hedged in from the hungry hordes by a strong counter; the remainder is laid out with long tables and forms running parallel to each other, and having a central gangway down the whole length of the building. The greatest martinet of a naval officer could not object to the whiteness of the tables and floor, the blackness of the stoves, the brightness of the brasswork and fittings, or to the extreme cleanliness of the cooking-pans supplied for the men.

We will not recount all the cook told as to the marks by which the private ownership of the various dishes is known. It must be sufficient to state that in this great room, crowded with impatient diners, within five minutes these innumerable men, with their innumerable tins of food, cooked in their own innumerable ways, and carrying their innumerable cans and baskets, may be seen quietly eating their innumerable dinners. There is also a fine three storied building erected especially for drivers' lodgings in the event of the men being unable to get back to their homes the same night. This building is fitted up with a large cooking stove, with a room with fires and steam-pipes for drying wet clothes, and with a lavatory. There are about 22 bedrooms, all comfortably arranged, so that each man has a separate chamber, a clean and comfortable bed. The corridors and landings are all heated by hot water pipes, and hot and cold water can also be obtained in abundance. Downstairs is a small room supplied with newspapers and periodicals for the use of the men.

With regard to the new engines of the Midland Company we may remark that the new standard goods engine has six wheels coupled, 4 feet 10 inches diameter, with cylinders of 17½ inches diameter, and 26 inches stroke. This engine in working order will weigh about

35 tons; and, with the boiler pressure of 140 lbs. per square inch, is capable of drawing on a level, at a speed of 20 miles per hour, a load equal to 850 tons; and on an incline of 1 in 100,* at the above speed, will draw a load of 350 tons. The tender will hold 2320 gallons of water; it has a coal space of four tons; and it weighs, in working order, about 28 tons. The engine and tender when loaded will weigh 63 tons.

The main line passenger engine as used for express traffic, has six wheels, four of which are coupled, and a smaller wheel at the front or leading end. The coupled wheels are 6 feet 8 inches diameter, with cylinders of 17

THE LAST NEW MIDLAND EXPRESS ENGINE.

nches diameter, and 2 feet stroke. It will weigh when in working order 36 tons, and with the boiler pressure of 140 lbs. per square inch, is capable of drawing, on a level, at a speed of 45 miles per hour, a load equal to 240 tons; and on an incline of 1 in 100, at the above speed, will draw a load of 120 tons. The tender will hold 2320 gallons of water; it has a coal space of four tons; and the whole weighs, in working order, about 28 tons. The engine and tender *when loaded weigh not less than 64 tons.*

* The reader will here observe how wonderfully a gradient of any steepness tells against the drawing power of even the best engines.

The following is a list of the principal locomotive stations, with the average number of engines "in steam" at them :—Derby, 94 engines ; Birmingham, 72 engines ; Sheffield, 47 engines ; Leeds, 48 engines ; Toton, 54 engines ; Nottingham, 49 engines ; Leicester, 52 engines; Wellingborough, 49 engines ; London, 69 engines. The distance run by the Midland engines during the last half year was nearly 11,000,000 of miles, equal to about 60,000 miles every day, or to two and a half times round the world every day.

We may add that the Break-down Trains are under the control of the Locomotive Department.

The new Carriage and Waggon Works of the Midland Company at Derby will form by far the largest establishment of the kind in England. The land purchased amounts to no less than fifty acres, and the actual area of the buildings will be twelve acres. They will be approached by a line turning off under the first bridge through which the trains pass as they start from Derby towards Birmingham. The arrangement of the establishment will be simple and complete. There will be two series of buildings, one for wood, the other for iron. At the north end of the wood department will be first the timber-yard, containing wood in logs and planks; then the buildings for the sawing mills, where there will be every variety of the latest and best wood cutting machinery ; thirdly the drying sheds ; fourthly the waggon shop for building and repairing waggons ;

THE BREAK-DOWN TRAIN.

fifthly the carriage building and repairing shop; and lastly, in the series, the carriage painting and finishing shops.

Parallel with these will be the series of shops for the ironwork that is required in carriage and waggon building. First will come the general stores, and the foundries for brass and iron; next the smithy, including the spring-makers', the bolt-makers', and wheel repairing shop; and then the fitting and turning of the ironwork, and for the making up of the wheels. Sidings, and traversing tables will be laid between all these various shops, and also through them, so that there will always be more than one way by which trollies or trains can get in and out.

In the arrangements of these new works every possi-

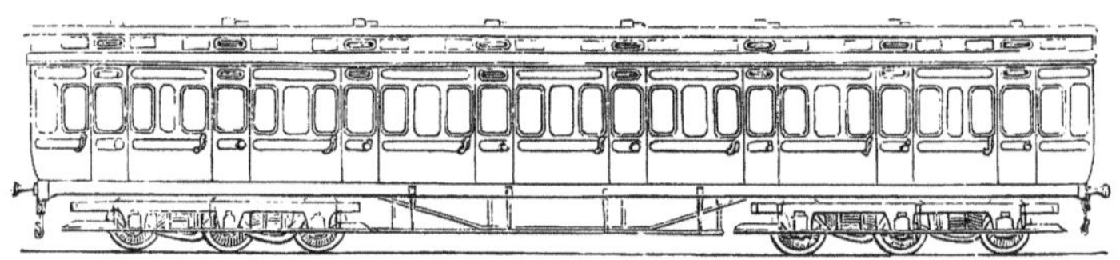

NEW MIDLAND PASSENGER CARRIAGE.

ble appliance will be used for the saving of labour. "Machines," as Mr. Clayton remarked, "will do everything that machines can do economically; and hydraulic power will be used extensively." It is intended that in the department for woodwork there shall not be a fireplace; and, as five lines of railway and 85 feet of space will separate the iron shops from the wood, it is believed that it will be easy to prevent fire in the only department where it can arise from extending to the other. All the shops are at least 70 feet apart. So large and complete will be the resources of the new establishment, that a large number of new carriages and waggons can be built there in addition to keeping the present stock in good working order.

The passenger carriages that have recently been added to the stock of the Company, and which have awakened such general admiration, have cost from £500 to £600 each. About 350 have been ordered, and some 200 have been delivered. In addition to these there are nearly 50 of the new type depicted in the engraving. They are three feet longer than the Pullman; they rest on two six wheeled bogies (or pivots); and each has four first class and four third class compartments, and a luggage box. It is believed that they will ride more easily and steadily than any yet used. We may add that no more carriages of the older type will now be built.

Mr. Samuel W. Johnson succeeded Mr. Kirtley as head of the locomotive department. He had previously held office in several other companies; his last appointment, before coming to the Midland, being that of locomotive superintendent on the Great Eastern for seven years.

Besides the engineers of the locomotive department there are the civil engineers, to the remarkable results of whose labours in all parts of the Midland system these pages have already borne testimony. The position of engineer-in-chief has for many years been occupied by Mr. Crossley, who in the course of a lengthened experience has planned for Parliament some 600 miles of railway, and constructed 300. Having, "in consequence," as the last report observes, "of failing health," retired from the service except as far as concerns the completion of the Settle and Carlisle line, the department has been arranged into two sections: that of "the engineer for lines under construction," at the head of which is Mr. Underwood; and that of "the engineer for lines open for traffic," which is under Mr. A. Johnston.

"It must be very nice to be a railway engineer," remarked a lady to a gentleman of that profession; "and be able to travel about anywhere you want to go to for nothing."

"Yes, madam," was the enigmatical reply; "it would, as you say, be very nice to travel about for nothing *if we were not paid for it.* But you see," he added, "railway engineers are like the cabman's horse. The cabman had a very thin horse. 'Doesn't your horse have enough to eat?' inquired a benevolent lady passenger. 'Oh yes, ma'am,' replied cabby; 'I gives him lots o' victuals to eat, only, you see, he hasn't any time to eat 'em.' So it is with the railway engineer: he has lots of pleasure of all kinds, only he has not any time to take it."

The service rendered by our engineers is worthy of more honour than it receives. True they are "monarchs of all they *survey;*" yet how many persons, says one of them, "rushing through the country at sixty miles an hour in a first class carriage, bestow as much as a passing thought on the labour that was expended on that narrow track of road that they whirl over in even a minute of time! Little do they think how that portion of the line was constructed bit by bit by the combined efforts of thousands of their fellow-creatures, some of whom have required almost a lifetime of study and experience before they could contribute their mite of knowledge to the general undertaking. It may be the genius of one man who directs and sets the whole of the mighty machinery in motion; but he would be powerless unless the orders he issued to the many parts were thoroughly understood in all their many details; and unless every bolt, every little screw, were performing its proper duty, the machine would collapse, and every effort to make it move would but involve the destruction of every part."

The solicitors of the Midland Company are the eminent firm of Messrs. Beale, Marigold & Beale, of Great George Street, London. Mr. Samuel Carter, formerly at the head of this firm, occupied for several years the remarkable position of being solicitor to both the London and North Western and Midland Companies. This was at a time when the latter was regarded almost in the light of a humble dependency of the former.

But our space has gone; and, however reluctantly, we and our readers must part. We have mentioned many facts of interest with regard to the Midland Railway: we have left more untold. We will only add, that in the growing usefulness and prosperity of this Company in particular, and of railways in general, we have perfect confidence. Already 16,000 miles of English railway interlace the land; 12,000 engines, which would of themselves make a train 90 miles long, and are worth nearly £3000 apiece, run a distance every year equal to that from the earth to the sun and back again; 25,000 carriages bear rich and poor by almost every train; waggons, numerous enough to stretch from St. Pancras to the Equator, convey our goods; money equal to the amount of the national debt has been invested, not on useless wars, but for the social, commercial, and moral welfare of the community; and able statesmanlike minds are devising how far all these benefits can be made more complete and far-reaching. The midland counties have become a suburb of the metropolis. The patriotic Welshman can travel from Pontrydfendigaid to Mynydd-yslwyn, and rejoice. The Scot can ride from north to south, as Lord Macaulay finely puts it, "by the light of a winter's day." With the space and resources of an empire, we enjoy the compactness of a city. Our roads are contracted into streets, our hills and dales into parks, and our thousand leagues of coast into the circumference of a castle wall. Nineveh was a city of three days' journey round. Great Britain can be traversed in one. For questions of distance, we are as mere a spot as Malta, as St. Helena, as one of the states of the Ægean. "A hundred opposite ports are blended into one Piræus, and to every point of the compass diverge the oft-traversed walls that unite them with our engirded Acropolis"

RAIL TESTING MACHINE AT ENTRANCE TO BELSIZE TUNNEL.

APPENDIX.

MIDLAND DIVIDENDS.

	June.			December.			Year.		
	£	s.	d.	£	s.	d.	£	s.	d.
1844 N.M.	2	2	0	3	0	0	Say 5	2	0
1844 M.Co.	2	2	6						
1845	3	0	0	3	13	9	6	13	9
1846	3	10	0	3	10	0	7	0	0
1847	3	10	0	3	10	0	7	0	0
1848	3	0	0	2	10	0	5	10	0
1849	1	10	0	1	5	0	2	15	0
1850	0	16	0	1	5	0	2	1	0
1851	1	5	0	1	7	6	2	12	6
1852	1	10	0	1	12	6	3	2	6
1853	1	12	6	1	12	6	3	5	0
1854	1	15	0	1	17	6	3	12	6
1855	1	15	0	1	17	6	3	12	6
1856	2	0	0	2	2	6	4	2	6
1857	2	2	6	2	10	0	4	12	6
1858	2	2	6	2	15	0	4	17	6
1859	2	12	6	3	0	0	5	12	6
1860	3	5	0	3	10	0	6	15	0
1861	3	2	6	3	10	0	6	12	6
1862	2	15	0	3	5	0	6	0	0
1863	2	17	6	3	10	0	6	7	6
1864	3	10	0	3	17	6	7	7	6
1865	3	5	0	3	10	0	6	15	0
1866	3	0	0	3	2	6	6	2	6
1867	2	15	0	2	15	0	5	10	0
1868	2	10	0	2	17	6	5	7	6
1869	2	17	6	3	5	0	6	2	6
1870	3	2	6	3	7	6	6	10	0
1871	3	5	0	3	15	0	7	0	0
1872	3	10	0	3	15	0	7	5	0
1873	3	7	6	3	5	0	6	12	6
1874	2	15	0	3	5	0	6	0	0
1875	3	0	0						
1876									
1877									
1878									
1879									
1880									
1881									
1882									
1883									

THE MIDLAND GRAND HOTEL, ST. PANCRAS.

The Midland Railway Company are the proprietors of four Hotels: the Midland Grand Hotel at St. Pancras, of which a description has been given in this volume (pages 345–350); the Queen's Hotel, adjoining the Wellington Midland Station, Leeds; the Midland Hotel, adjoining the Derby Station; and the North Western Hotel, adjoining the station pier, Morecambe. The three first are under the direct administration of the Midland Company; and all are first class establishments for families and gentlemen. Mr. Etzensberger is the manager of the Midland Grand; Mr. James Allen at Leeds; Mr. W. Towle at Derby; and Mr. W. Hartley is the lessee at Morecambe.

As the magnitude and sumptuousness of "the Grand" may deter some from availing themselves of its accommodation, it may be right to state that the charges are not only moderate for the unusual advantages they secure, but do not exceed those of any first class hotel in the metropolis. An hotel porter attends the trains in London, Derby, and Leeds.

Passengers who are booked through between London and Edin burgh, Glasgow, or stations north of those cities, by the Midland Railway, are allowed to break their journey by remaining one night at Leeds; passengers who are booked through between London and Edinburgh, Glasgow, or stations to the north of those cities, by Midland Railway, may break their journey by remaining a night at Derby; and passengers holding through tickets from Scotland to stations west of Birmingham, or, *vice versâ*, may break the journey by remaining a night at Derby.

With regard to the terms on which the Midland Company undertake to convey passengers or goods, we must refer our readers to the official regulations of the Company; but it may be convenient for us to state, in an unofficial way, some of these arrangements.

Greenwich time is kept at all the stations; and passengers who are as far west as Bristol should be aware that this makes a difference between the geographically local time and the railway time of nearly 12 minutes. Passengers should at all the principal stations be five minutes earlier than the times mentioned on the time tables, and at intermediate stations they should be ten minutes earlier.

With regard to passengers, it should be noticed that children under three years of age travel free; and those above three and under twelve, at half price. A passenger with either a single journey or return ticket, is not permitted to leave any train at an intermediate station (unless it is advertised that the journey may be broken at that station) without giving up his ticket, in which case he will forfeit all further right to it. Passengers in private carriages (not being servants) must take first class tickets, as the carriage rates do not include the privilege of reduced fares, and such passengers may change on the journey into the Company's first class carriages, if they please.

Tickets are issued at intermediate stations, conditionally on there being room in the carriages of the train by which the passenger books. If there be no room, the money will be returned if the ticket is produced at the booking office immediately on the departure of the train for which it has been purchased.

Passengers are requested to examine their tickets and change before leaving the booking office counter, as claims for alleged mistakes cannot be recognised afterwards. Tickets must be shown to the Company's servants, or delivered up to them when demanded; any person failing to produce his ticket is liable to be charged the fare from the most distant station from which the train has started. Parties cannot re-book at an intermediate station by the same train. Single journey tickets (with a few exceptions) are only available on the day of issue.

Passengers who allege that they have lost or mislaid their tickets, and apply for a return of their fares, should be aware that the Company does not hold itself liable for the consequences of any such mistakes.

The exclusive use of a compartment of a first class carriage may be engaged if not fewer than four tickets are taken, and written notice is given to the station-master, at the departure station; not later than two hours before starting, if at a terminal station from whence the train starts; or the previous day if at an intermediate station. If more than four seats are occupied in a reserved compartment, the additional fares must be paid. Saloon carriages are kept at St. Pancras, Derby, Leeds, Bradford, and Gloucester, and, if not previously engaged, may be had for the accommodation of pleasure parties or families, on application at any of those stations on the previous day.

Invalid carriages, each with a couch, upon which an invalid can recline, are kept at London (St. Pancras) and Derby, and can, unless previously engaged, be had upon due notice being given to the station-master at St. Pancras or Derby, and arrangements can be made for these carriages to go through to any part of the kingdom to which there is direct communication. Four first class fares as a minimum will be charged.

Footwarmers are supplied in first and third class carriages on the application of passengers at all the principal stations, for the through trains in the winter months.

There are refreshment rooms at the St. Pancras, Luton, Hitchin, Rugby, Leicester, Trent, Derby, Sheffield, Normanton, Leeds, Bradford, Bath, Gloucester, Ashchurch, Birmingham, Burton, Peterboro', Nottingham, Malvern Wells, and Lincoln stations. Luncheon baskets can be obtained at Derby, Leicester, and Trent. These can be taken by the passenger into the carriage, and delivered up when he has finished his meal.

Lavatory and dressing rooms, for the convenience of passengers travelling on the Midland Railway, are provided, under the management of Mr. Faulkner, at the following stations: St. Pancras, Trent, Nottingham, Derby, Sheffield, Normanton, Leeds, and Bradford.

First and third class return tickets are issued between all stations on the Midland Railway where single journey tickets are issued, available for the return journey for six months, except between the following stations: to and from all stations between Hendon, South Tottenham, Moorgate Street, and St. Pancras, the return ticket is available for seven days; between London and Birmingham, and stations west of Birmingham, including Saltley and Camp Hill, one month; between Bristol and Bath, seven days.

First and third class return tickets are issued between most of the principal stations on the Midland Railway and principal stations on the following railways, for distances above 50 miles, available for a month:—All Scotch lines; Bristol and Exeter; Cheshire Lines Committee; Cockermouth, Keswick, and Penrith; Cornwall; Furness; Great Eastern; Great Northern; Lancashire and Yorkshire; London and North Western; Manchester, Sheffield, and Lincolnshire; North Eastern; North Staffordshire; Somerset and Dorset; and South Devon. Return tickets, available for a month, are issued also between St. Pancras and Dublin, Belfast, Londonderry, and principal stations in the north of Ireland If a passenger with a return ticket travels one journey in a higher class of carriage than that for which the ticket was issued, he will be required to pay the difference between the single journey fares of the two classes respectively for that journey.

First class passengers are allowed 120 lbs. and third class passengers 60 lbs. of personal luggage, not being carried for hire or profit, free of charge. All excess above the weight allowed will be charged for as excess.

The ordinary charge made for excess luggage of passengers for distances not exceeding 30 miles is a farthing a pound; for distances not exceeding 50 miles one halfpenny, and so on with a gradual increase until for a distance exceeding 300 miles the charge is 2*d.* per pound. Commercial travellers' extra luggage is charged, if booked at the commencement of the journey, according to a reduced scale, and they are allowed the privilege of booking their luggage from the station from which they start to the station at which their day's journey is to end, whether it be a return journey or otherwise, although they may have occasion to stop during their day's business at intermediate stations. Passengers' heavy luggage, when conveyed on carriage trucks by passenger trains, is charged 6*d.* per mile per truck. The minimum charge is 7*s.* 6*d.*

Bath chairs, when accompanied by passengers, and conveyed at the owner's risk, are charged, for a distance not exceeding 12 miles, 1*s.*; above 12 miles and not exceeding 25 miles, 1*s.* 6*d.*; and so on with an increasing charge until for 75 miles, and not exceeding 100, the charge is 4*s.*

Perambulators and bicycles are charged half the above rates.

The wide spread diffusion of newspapers and periodical literature has rendered it necessary to make special provision for their cheap and rapid circulation, by railway as well as by post. Accordingly it is provided that single newspapers or several copies of newspapers or periodicals published at intervals not exceeding one month, are conveyed between any two stations on the Midland Railway, irrespective of distance, at the uniform charge of one halfpenny per copy. The charge is in all cases to be prepaid by affixing one of the Company's labels to each packet. The rates do not include collection or delivery. The parcels must be open at both ends. Labels varying in value from one halfpenny to tenpence each, to be used for the conveyance of single newspapers and newspaper parcels not exceeding 12 lbs. in weight, can be obtained in sheets, on application to the General Manager, Derby.

Parcels are conveyed by all trains. They must be delivered at the respective stations of the Company at least 10 minutes before the departure of the train they are intended to be forwarded by.

The Company do not undertake to deliver parcels received by passenger trains at country stations on their line where the distance from such station is more than half a mile. Parties residing at a greater distance are requested to inform the station-masters what arrangements they wish to be made for the delivery of their parcels.

Gentlemen having seats in the country, and residing occasionally in London, may have fruit and vegetables for their own use conveyed from any station in the country by passenger train, and delivered in London at reduced rates, particulars of which may be ascertained on application to the "Superintendent, Midland Railway, Derby."

Packages of a light, frail nature, or such as are bulky in proportion to their weight, such as paper boxes, containing artificial flowers, paper bonnet or hat boxes, straw bonnets, packages of lace, light furniture, etc.; are charged 50 per cent. increase upon the ordinary parcels rate.

Van parcels are conveyed daily (Sundays excepted) to and from London, and stations on the Midland Railway, at one-half the ordinary rates for parcels. The rates for van parcels include delivery within the usual limits, but no less charge is made than the lowest ordinary charge for a parcel exceeding 7 lbs. in weight. The van parcels are conveyed to and from London by the first morning stopping train, and are required to be delivered at the Midland Company's receiving offices or stations before the usual hour of closing the day previous. All packages intended to be forwarded as van parcels at the reduced rate of charge must be legibly marked "VAN PARCELS TRAIN," or they will be charged at the ordinary rates.

Van parcels are also conveyed at greatly reduced rates between London and Luton, and Belfast, and between London, Luton, Bristol, Bath, Gloucester, Cheltenham, Worcester, Birmingham, Burton, and Derby, and Dublin.

Returned empty packages. All returned empty packages, by passenger train, except milk cans, are charged according to the following scale:—Not exceeding 25 miles, 2*d.* each package; above 25 and not exceeding 75 miles, 4*d.* each package; above 75 and not exceeding 150 miles, 6*d.* each package; above 150 and not exceeding 250 miles, 9*d.* each package; any distance above 250 miles, 1*s.* each package. The maximum charge is 1*s.* The weight of returned empties sent by passenger train is limited to ½ cwt. Fish empties in bulk are not conveyed by passenger train, and a charge is made for them when sent by goods train. Returned empty milk cans are conveyed free.

The above rates only apply to packages which have been sent full in the first instance by passenger train, all other empty packages are charged full parcels rates. The charges are required to be prepaid in all cases, and include delivery within the usual limits.

Pianofortes, when conveyed by passenger train on a carriage truck in a road van belonging to the sender, are charged the rate for a private four-wheeled carriage, at owner's risk; when sent without the van, they are charged ordinary parcel rates at owner's risk; minimum charge, 5*s.*

Sewing machines are charged ordinary parcels rates, at owner's risk; an additional charge of 50 per cent. being made when conveyed at Company's risk.

Corpses are charged as follows:—adult, 1*s.* per mile, minimum charge when a vehicle is specially put on the train, 20*s.*; minimum when no special vehicle is used, 10*s.*; child under 12 years of age, 6*d.* per mile; minimum when a vehicle is specially put on the train, 10*s.*; when no special vehicle is used, 5*s.*

First and third class season tickets are issued between St. Pancras, King's Cross (Metropolitan Railway), Farringdon Street, Aldersgate Street, Moorgate Street, Ludgate Hill, and the various stations as far as Bedford, at rates which may be obtained on application to the General Manager, Midland Railway, Derby; Mr. Chas. Mills, St. Pancras Station, London, or through the Station-Masters at any of the Stations mentioned above. These tickets are issued for periods of nine, six, or three months, at proportionate rates. Periodical tickets are issued at half-price to children under 15 years of age; and also to scholars, students, apprentices, and articled clerks learning a trade or profession, and not in receipt of a salary, up to 17 years of age, at half-price, upon production of a certificate from the master of the school, the principal of the college, or their employer, as the case may be. To governesses actually engaged in tuition, upon production of certificate to that effect, first class tickets will be granted at reduced rates. A deposit of 10*s.* for each first class, and 5*s.* for each third class ticket is also required, which will be restored if the ticket is given up immediately on expiration. First class periodical hunting tickets are issued during the hunting season from October to April inclusive. Double journey tickets for horses used in hunting can also be obtained, available for return the same day.

First and third class season tickets are also issued between most of the stations on the Midland Railway, at prices which can be obtained on application at the General Manager's Office, Derby. Periodical tickets are issued at half-price to children under 12 years of age. They are also issued to scholars, students, apprentices, and articled clerks, learning a trade or profession, and not in receipt of a salary, up to 17 years of age, at half-price, upon production of a certificate from the master of the school, the principal of the college, or the employer, as the case may be.

The Midland Railway Company have introduced the celebrated American Pullman Drawing-room and Sleeping Cars upon their system; and trains of these cars are now running regularly between London (St. Pancras) and Leeds and Bradford, and London (St. Pancras) and Manchester and Liverpool. On the opening of the Settle and Carlisle line these cars will be run between London (St. Pancras) and Edinburgh and Glasgow.

INDEX.

LIST OF SUBSCRIBERS.

Midland Directors.

	COPIES
Ellis, E. S., Esq., Chairman of Midland Company, Leicester	10
Thompson, M. W., Esq., Vice-Chairman, Guiseley, Leeds	10
Cropper, J. W., Esq., Dingle Bank, Liverpool	1
Heygate, W. U., Esq., M.P., Roecliffe, Loughborough	1
Hodgkinson, Grosvenor, Esq., Newark	1
Hodgson, H. T., Esq., Harpenden	6
Hutchinson, W. E., Esq., Oadby Hill, Leicester...	3
Jones, C. H., Esq., Huddersfield	2
Kenrick, T., Esq., Edgbaston, Birmingham	2
Lloyd, G. B., Esq., Edgbaston Road, Birmingham	1
Mappin, F. T., Esq., Thornbury, Sheffield	1
Mason, Hugh, Esq., Ashton under Lyne	3
Paget, G. E., Esq., Sutton Bonnington, Loughborough...	1
Thomas, Charles, Woodcote, Stoke Bishop, near Bristol	1

Audit Committee.

Baines, Edward, Esq., Burley, Leeds	2
Leader, Robert, Esq., Sheffield	1

Officers.

Allport, James, Esq., General Manager, Derby	10
Noble, John, Esq., Assistant General Manager, Derby...	2
Speight, Robert, Esq., General Manager's Department	1
Williams, James, Esq., Secretary of Midland Company, Derby ...	1
Needham, E. M., Esq., Superintendent, Derby	2
Pakeman, E. A., Esq., Superintendent's Department, Derby	1
Newcombe, W. L., Esq., Goods Manager, Derby	1
Boylan, A. H., Esq., Goods Department, St. Pancras	1
Millar, C., Esq., Goods Department, St. Pancras	1
Johnson, Samuel W., Esq., Locomotive Superintendent, Derby ...	2
Adams, William Henry, Esq., Locomotive Department, Derby ...	1
Johnston, Andrew, Esq., Engineer, Derby	1
Gratton, J. S., Esq., Engineer's Department, Derby	1
Crossley, John S., Esq., Engineer's Department, Barrow-on-Soar ...	1
Sanders, Jno. H., Esq., Architect's Offices, Derby	1
Story, J. S., Esq., Engineer's Department, Kirkby Stephen	2
Ferguson, E. O., Esq., Engineer's Department, Settle	1

	COPIES
Payton, Anthony, Esq., Engineer's Department, Chesterfield ...	1
Drage, J., Esq., Engineer's Department, Appleby	1
Clayton, T. G., Esq., Carriage and Waggon Superintendent, Derby...	2
Pettifor, Joseph, Esq., Stores Department, Derby	1
Bradley, J., Esq., Accountant's Department, Derby	1
Fisher, J. A., Esq., Accountant's Department, Derby	1
Allott, Alfred, Esq., Auditor, Sheffield	2
Beale, Marigold, & Beale, Messrs., Solicitors, Great George St., S.W.	6
Billington, Robert John, Esq., Locomotive Department, Derby ...	1
Jones, C. H., Esq., jun., Locomotive Department, Derby	1
Underwood, John, Esq., Engineer, Derby	1
Cartledge, John, Esq., Midland Railway, St. Pancras	1
Farmer, Edward, Esq., Midland Railway, Derby	1
Payne, W. Percy, Esq., Midland Railway, Derby	1
Holt, Francis, Esq., Locomotive Department, Derby	1
Tickle, W. H., Esq., Engineer's Department, Derby	1
Ward, E. R., Esq., Superintendent's Department, Derby	1
Barlow, Crawford, Esq., Engineer's Office, Midland Railway, Kettering	1
Harrison, J. W. D., Esq., Engineer's Office, Old Dalby	1
Meredith, W. L., Esq., Engineer's Department, Derby...	1
Whitaker, W., Esq., Goods Manager's Department, Derby	1
Fittall, John Edward, Esq., Goods Department, Derby	1
Halford, Samuel, Esq., Central Station, Liverpool	1
Scott, W. G., Esq., Engineer's Department, Central Station, Liverpool	1
Halford, John, Esq., Goods Department, Derby	1
Potter, G., Esq., Midland Railway, Bedford	1
Bland, Joseph, Esq., Derby	1
Prince, P., Esq., jun., Signal Department, Derby	1
Bloxham, F. Say, Esq., Locomotive Department, Chesterfield ...	1
Wilson, Charles, S., Esq, Engineer's Department	1
Turner, G., Esq., Locomotive Department, Derby	1
Chawner, George, Esq., Goods Department, Derby	1
Paine, S. H., Esq., Engineer's Office, Warwick Road, Carlisle ...	1
Whitaker, Alfred, Esq., Carlisle	1

Peers and Members of Parliament, etc.

Devonshire, His Grace the Duke of, Chatsworth, viâ Chesterfield ...	2
Belper, The Right Hon. Lord, Kingston Hall, Derby	1
Auckland, The Right Hon. Lord, Edenthorpe	1
Bateman, The Right Hon. Lord, Shobdon Court, Herefordshire ...	1
Bright, The Right Hon. John, M.P., Rochdale	1
Adair, Hugh Edward, Esq., M.P., 63, Portland Place, W.	1
Gower, Granville Leveson, Esq., M.P., Titsey Place, Limpsfield, Surrey	1
Hill, T. Rowley, Esq., M.P., Worcester	1
Corbitt, John, Esq., M.P., Droitwich	1
Smith, F. C., Esq., M.P., Bramcote Hall, Nottingham	1

	COPIES
Mundella, A. J., Esq., M.P., 16, Elvaston Place, Queen's Gate, S.W....	1
Lancaster, John, Esq., M.P., Bilton Grange, Rugby	1
Marling, Samuel S., Esq., M.P., Stanley Park, Stroud, Gloucestershire	1
Rothschild, De, Esq., M.P., New Court, St. Swithin's Lane, E.C. ...	1
Macnamara, H. T. J., Esq., Royal Commissioners for Railways, House of Lords	1
Peel, Sir Frederick, Bart., Royal Commissioners for Railways, House of Lords	1
Price, W. P., Esq., Royal Commissioners for Railways, House of Lords	2
Thorp, The Venerable Archdeacon, Kemerton, Tewkesbury	1

SHAREHOLDERS, ETC.

Adcock, William, Esq., North Lodge, Melton Mowbray	1
Addison, John, Esq., C.E., Maryport	1
Adlington, William S., Esq., Kirk Hallam, near Ilkeston	1
A Friend	25
Aldam, William, Esq., Normanton...	1
Aldam, William, Esq., Frichley Hall, near Doncaster	1
Aldous, Alex. James, Esq., " St. Andrews," Southsea	1
Alexander, William Lancaster, Esq., Oak Hill, Lorton, Cockermouth	1
Allard, William, Esq., Camp Hill, Birmingham	1
Allatt, Rev. James, The Manse, Newton-le-Willows	1
Allen, James, Esq., Queen's Hotel, Leeds	1
Allen, Richard, & Son, Messrs., Nottingham	2
Alleyne, Sir John G. N., Bart., Butterley Car, Alfreton	1
Allhusen, C., Esq., Stoke Court, Slough	1
Allport, Howard, Esq., Nottingham	1
Alvey, William, Esq., Hardstaft Heath, Chesterfield	1
Anderson, William, Esq., 132, St. Vincent Street, Glasgow	1
Ansdell, John, Esq., Cowley House, St. Helen's...	1
Arkle, Benj., Esq., King Street, Liverpool	1
Arkwright, Alfred, Esq., Wirksworth, Derbyshire	1
Arkwright, J. C., Esq., Cromford, Derbyshire	1
Armitage, S. S., Esq., 34, Mansfield Road, Nottingham	1
Ash, William, Esq., Holland House, Weston-super-Mare	1
Ashmead, Geo. C., Esq., Land Agent, Bristol	1
Ashwell, Henry, Esq., Mount Street, New Basford	1
Ashwell, J. H., Esq., Engineer to Queensland Government ...	1
Asling, A., Esq., Midland Railway, Ashby-de-la-Zouch	1
Atkinson, Thos., Esq., Regent Square, Doncaster	1
Augarde, J. J., Esq., View Mount, Waterford	1
Auld, William, Esq., 65, St. Vincent Street, Glasgow	1
Ault, John, Esq., Eastwood, Notts	1
Aylwin, C. H., Esq., Sorrento, Bromley	1
B. A.	15
Baggaley, W. B., Esq., Short Hill, Nottingham	1
Baines, George H., Esq., Wolston, Coventry	1
Baines, John, Esq., Tamworth	1

	COPIES
Baird, John, Esq., 11, Kirk Street, Townhead, Glasgow	1
Baker, W., Esq., Avenue Road, Bournemouth	1
Baldwin, Benj., Esq., 7, Market Place, Loughborough...	1
Banks, Morris, Esq., Oaklands, Edgbaston	1
Barber, Samuel J., Esq., Ivy Cottage, Eastwood, Notts	1
Barber, Thos., Esq., Eastwood, Notts	1
Barker, Edward, Esq., Swinton Hall, near Rotherham	1
Barker, John L., Esq., 13, Pall Mall, Manchester	1
Barlow, W. H., Esq., C.E., High Combe, Old Charlton, S.E.	1
Barnes, Thomas, Esq., Chairman of Lancashire and Yorkshire Railway Company, Farnworth, Bolton	1
Barras, John, Esq., Broom Lodge, Rotherham	1
Bartholomew, Charles, Esq., Ealing	2
Barwick, John, Esq., Chellaston, Derbyshire	1
Baskerville, Walter J. M., Esq., Clyro Court, Hay	1
Basley, Thomas Sebastian, Esq., Hatherop Castle, Gloucestershire ...	1
Bassett, Joseph Henry, Esq., Countesthorpe, Rugby	1
Bateman, Rev. J., West Leake Rectory, Loughborough	1
Bayley, J., Esq., Pelham Crescent, Nottingham	1
Bayley, J. C., Esq., 20, Walbrook, London, E.C....	1
Bayliss, John, Esq., Victoria Street, Westminster	1
Bayly & Fox, Messrs., Bristol	1
Bayly & Fox, Messrs., Plymouth	1
Beale, William John, Esq., Bryntirion Bontddu, Dolgelly	1
Beattie, W. G., Esq., London & South Western Railway Company	1
Beaumont, Rev. W., Coleorton Rectory, Ashby-de-la-Zouch	1
Beeson, Henry, Esq., Thrussington, near Leicester	1
Bell, John, Esq., Waverley Street, Nottingham...	1
Bell, William, Esq., Waverley Street, Nottingham	1
Bembridge, James, Esq., Long Eaton, Nottingham	1
Bemrose, Henry Howe, Esq., Lonsdale Place, Derby	1
Bemrose, Wm., Jun., Esq., Lonsdale Place, Derby	1
Bennett, Barwell E., Esq., Marston Trussell Hall, Market Harborough	1
Bentley, Henry, Esq., Eshalt House, Woodlesford	1
Berry, John C., Esq., Wisbeach	1
Bewick, Thos. John, Esq., Haydon Bridge, Northumberland	1
Bingham, Thomas, Esq., Staveley, Chesterfield	1
Binns, Charles, Esq., Clay Cross	3
Birch, W. Singleton, Esq., Upton Street, Manchester	1
Bird, Mr. John, Sheffield	1
Birmingham Patent Tube Company, Smithwick, near Birmingham ...	1
Boam, Henry, Esq., Litchurch Villa, Derby	1
Boddington, W. R., Esq., Borrowash Station	1
Boden, William, Esq., Rowsley, Bakewell...	1
Bolland, William T., Esq., Spring Grove, Hunslet	1
Books, Wm., Esq., Croft House, Hinckley	1
Boomer, John, Esq., Edlington, Rotherham	1
Booth, C. A., Esq., Watford, Herts	1

	COPIES
Booth, D. H., Esq., Pembridge House, Ipswich	1
Booth, Richard, Esq., Glendon Hall, Kettering	1
Booth, William, Esq., Eastwood, Notts	2
Borradaile, Frederick, Esq., East Hawkhurst	1
Boulger, Rev. John, Pennant, Llanrwst, near Conway...	1
Bowers, T. G., Esq., Kelston Station	1
Bowers, William, Esq., Harewood Park, Cheadle	1
Boyer, John, Esq., Quorn House, Leamington...	1
Bradshaw, William, Esq., M.D., Pepper Street, Nottingham	1
Bradshaw, W., Esq., Goods Department, St. Pancras	1
Bray, Henry, Esq., Lincoln Street, Nottingham	1
Brentnall, Charles, Esq., The Grange, Normanton, Derby	1
Briggs, Archibald, Esq., Stanley Hall, Wakefield	1
Briggs, Christopher, Esq., The Lees, Bolton-le-Moors	1
Briggs, John Joseph, Esq., King's Newton, Derby	1
Brocklebank, Ralph, Esq., Chilwall Hall, Liverpool	1
Brocklebank, T., Esq., Springwood, Liverpool	1
Brocklebank, T., Jun., Esq., Huskisson Street, Liverpool	1
Brook, Henry, Esq., North Court Lodge, Blandon	2
Brook, W., Esq., Honley, Huddersfield	1
Brooks, J. H., Major, Flitwick Manor, Ampthill...	1
Brown, Alderman, Daisy Hill, Rawdon, near Leeds	1
Bruxner, Rev. G. E., Thurlaston, Hinckley	1
Bryson, Jameson, & Co., Messrs., Hull	1
Bunton, John, Esq., Hornsey	1
Burke, James St. George, Esq., Q.C., The Auberies, Sudbury ...	1
Burkett, William, Esq., King's Lynn	1
Butler & Tanner, Messrs., Frome	1
Butlin, Thomas, Esq., 25, Camden Square, N.W.	1
Buxton, S., Esq., Belper	1
Caldecott, Charles M., Esq., Holbrook Grange, Rugby	1
Calvert, J. M., Esq., Gargrave, near Leeds	1
Cammell, Charles, Esq., Norton Hall, Derbyshire	1
Carlile, James W., Esq., Thickhollins, Huddersfield	3
Carroll, Geo. F., Esq., Bolton Spa, Tadcaster	1
Cartwright & Warner, Messrs., Loughborough	5
Chadwick, G. & Co., Messrs., Masborough	1
Chamberlain, Thomas, Esq., Windsor	1
Chambers, Jos., Esq., Spondon Station	1
Cheese, Edmund H., Esq., Kington, Herefordshire	1
Claridge, George, Esq., Ampthill	1
Clarkson, W. W., Esq., De Montford Square, Leicester	1
Clatworthy, J. W., Esq., Long Eaton	1
Clatworthy, William, Esq., Long Eaton	1
Claye, Aked, Esq., Long Eaton	1
Claye, S. John, Esq., Manor House Works, Long Eaton	1
Clayton, Nathaniel, Esq. (Messrs. Clayton & Shuttleworth), Lincoln	1
Clouston, Peter, Esq., Park Terrace, Glasgow	1

	COPIES
Cock, Edward, Esq., Dean Street, St. Thomas' Street, S.E.	1
Cooke, Rupert Thomas, Esq., Cecil Road, Dronfield	1
Cooper, James N., Esq., Bromwich Grange, St. John's, Worcester ...	1
Coote, Thomas, Esq., St. Ives, Hunts	1
Corbin, Rev. John, Haringey Park, Hornsey, N.	1
Corbitt, William, Elm Tree Bank, Rotherham	1
Cotton, William, Esq., Midland Railway, Derby...	2
Cox, Charles, Esq., Old Basford, Nottingham	1
Cox, William, Esq., Burton Street, Leicester	2
Craven, John, Esq., Care of Craven, Speeding, Bros., Sunderland ...	1
Cross, Robert, Esq., Bakewell	1
Crumpstone, Thomas B., Esq., Bank Street, Leeds	2
Darbishire, Henry Ashley, Esq., Oakdene, Eden Bridge, Kent ...	1
Darnell, Charles, Esq., Goods Department, Bradford	1
Davenport, James, Esq., Springfield House, Merland, near Rochdale	1
Denison, Lieut. W. E., Carlton Club, London	1
Dickinson, Joseph, Esq., Midland Railway Agent, Melton Mowbray...	1
Dickinson, Joseph, Esq., Egston Terrace, Clay Cross	1
Dinington, James, Esq., Broome House, Didsbury	1
Duckett, Richard, Esq., Wigglesworth, near Settle	1
Eagle, Edward, Esq., Langley Mill	1
Edmondson, John B., Esq., Miltonville, Crumpsall, near Manchester	1
Ellenshaw, John, Esq., Kirkstall, near Leeds	1
Elliott, Admiral, Appleby Castle, Penrith	1
Ellis, Charles, Esq., 21, College Hill, London, E.C.	1
Ellis, George Henry, Esq., Southfield, Leicester	1
Ellis, John Edward, Esq., The Park, Nottingham	4
Ellis, John & Sons, Messrs., Leicester	3
Evans, Captain John, Highfield, Derby	1
Fawcett, D., Esq., Cambridge	2
Fenton, G. W., Esq., Frisby Station	1
Fernie, Captain and Mrs., Chase Lodge, Hendon	1
Filliter, Freeland, Esq., St. Martin's House, Wareham...	1
Finney, Frederick A., Esq., Queen's Chambers, Manchester	1
Firbank, Joseph, Esq., Newport, Monmouthshire	1
Fleming, Dr. Wm., Rowton Grange, near Chester	1
Fletcher, C. E., Esq., Long Eaton	1
Ford, James, Esq., Wraxall Court, Chairman, Bristol and Portishead	1
Foster, W., Esq., Midland Railway, Ashby-de-la-Zouch	1
Fox, James, Esq., Regent Street, Barnsley	1
Fox, James, Esq., Civil Engineer, 32, Albion Street, Leeds	1
Fry, Thos. J., Esq., 12, Lower Kevin Street, Dublin	1
Full, A. R., Esq., Crookham House, Newbury	1
Fullagar, Frank, Esq., Leicester	1
Fullam, John Martinson, Esq., 18, Mellon Street, Hull	1
Gall, James, Esq., The Bank, Eastwood, Notts	1

	COPIES
Galton, Douglas, Esq., 12, Chester Street, Grosvenor Place, S.W. ...	1
Gardner, Samuel, Esq., Bawtry	1
Garlick, William, Esq., 10, Hyde Terrace, Leeds	1
Garside, Joseph, Esq., Carlton House, Worksop	1
Gell, Samuel H., Esq., 6, Clumber Street, Nottingham	1
George, Thomas, Esq., Littleover Hill, Derby	1
Gething, William, Esq., Mansfield, Woodhouse	1
Gibbs & Canning, Messrs., Tamworth	1
Gill, J. Laurence, Esq., Barrow-on-Soar, Loughboro'	1
Gill, William K., Esq., 25, Polygon Street, Pancras, N.W.	2
Gillett, F. C., Esq., The Manor House, Borrowash	1
Gimson, T. F., Esq., 17, Chesham Road, Brighton	1
Glover, John, Esq., Tamworth	1
Godber, John, Esq., Whybourn House, Hucknall-Torkard	1
Goddard, Ebenezer, Esq., Oak Hill, Ipswich	1
Goddard, Joseph, Esq., Stoneygate, Leicester	1
Goldney, Rev. H. N., Southborough, Tunbridge Wells...	1
Goodman, Davenport, Esq., Eccles House, Chapel-en-le-Frith ...	1
Gordon, Alexander, Esq., Ashlendie, Arbroath	1
Gower, J. E. Leveson, Esq., Finchampstead, Wokingham, Berks ...	1
Grafton, Samuel, Esq., Beeley, Bakewell	2
Grant, William, Esq., Weir House, Kibworth Beauchamp, Leicester...	1
Gray, Samuel, Esq., Elmwood House, Calverley, near Leeds	1
Gray, William, Esq., Annesley Colliery, Nottingham	1
Gregory, Henry G., Esq., Fisherton Mills, Salisbury	1
Grimwade, Edward, Esq., Norton House, Ipswich	1
Gripper, Edward, Esq., Mansfield Road, Nottingham	1
Groom, Edward C., Esq., Hoveringham, Notts	1
Grove, William R., M.D., St. Ives, Hunts	1
Grundy, John, Esq., Summerseat, near Manchester	1
Guest & Chimes, Messrs., Brass Works, Rotherham	6
Gutch, John James, Esq., York	1
Gutteridge, Thomas, Esq., 14, Airedale Place, West Street, Leeds	1
Haddon, J. B., Esq., Lubbenham Lodge, Market Harborough ...	1
Hage, William, Esq., Bilsthorpe, Newark-on-Trent	1
Hall, Rev. E. M., Spondon, near Derby	1
Hall, Frederick, Esq., Oak Grove, Collegiate Crescent, Sheffield ...	1
Hall, John Charles, Esq., M.D., Surrey House, Sheffield	1
Hall, Joseph, Esq., Yate Station, near Chipping Sodbury	1
Hamilton, William, Esq., 17, Woodside Crescent, Glasgow	1
Hammond, James, Esq., Antcliffe, Skipton	1
Hanbury, John James, Esq., 11, Coupland Street, Beeston Hill, Leeds	1
Harley, Rev. Robert, F.R.S., Burton Bank, Mill Hill, N.W.	1
Harrison, Henry, Esq., J.P., Sharrow, Sheffield	1
Harrison, William, Esq., (Messrs. Harrison & Co.), Rotherham ...	1
Hartley, James, Esq., Hayfield House, Crosshills, *viâ* Leeds	1
Haskett, William, Esq., Plumpton Hall, near Penrith	1
Hatfield, George, Esq., The Hermitage, Braithwaite, Doncaster ...	1

	COPIES
Hawkes, H., Esq., Coroner, Northfield	1
Hawkins, Nathaniel, Esq., Putloe, near Stonehouse	1
Hay, James, Esq., Kirkby Stephen	1
Hays, J. C., Esq., Railway Station, Clay Cross	1
Heath, D., Esq., Midland Company, Sheffield	1
Heelis, Thomas, Esq., Woodlands, near Skipton, Yorkshire	1
Hemingway, E., Esq., 74, Douglas Street, Litchurch, Derby	1
Henshaw, A., Esq., Brecon	1
Herbert, Thos., Esq., The Park, Nottingham	1
Hewetson, John, Esq., 1, Lansdown Terrace, Hull	1
Heygate, Sir Frederick William, Bart., 43, Eaton Square, London	1
Heymann, Henry, Esq., Stoney Street, Nottingham	2
Higgins, Colonel, Picts Hill, Bedford	1
Hives, Thomas, Esq., Rutland Hotel, Ilkeston	1
Hobson, J. A., Esq., Derby	1
Hobson, Matthew, Esq., Field House, Ilkeston	1
Hodgkinson, E., Esq., Clay Cross	1
Holdsworth, Thomas, Esq., Alma House, Clay Cross, Chesterfield ...	1
Holland, C. B., Esq., Ashcroft, Sheffield	1
Holly, William, Esq., Ockbrook	1
Holmes, Alfred W., Esq., Milford Lodge, Derby	1
Hopes, William, Esq., Brampton Crofts, Appleby	1
Howard, James and Frederick, Messrs., Bedford	1
Howe, John Henry, Esq., 26, Green Lane, Kettering	1
Hubbersty, Philip, Esq., Wirksworth	1
Hudson, Edward, Esq., East Cliff, Sheffield	1
Hudson, James, Esq., St. Andrew's Place, Penrith	1
Hunter, John, Esq., Belper	1
Hurtley, Henry, Esq., Malton	1
Hyatt, Edward, Esq., North View, Castle Donington	2
Ind Coope & Co., Messrs., Brewers, Burton-on-Trent	1
Ismay, Imrie & Co., Messrs., Water Street, Liverpool...	2
Jackson, George, Esq., Mount Pleasant, Greenodd, near Ulverston ...	1
Jackson, J. P., Esq., Stubben Edge, Chesterfield	1
Jarratt, Rev. Robert, Bourton-on-the-Hill Rectory, Moreton-in-Marsh	1
Johnson, Rev. J. L., Malton, Yorkshire	1
Johnson, Joseph, Esq., 16, Napier Street, Leicester	1
Johnson, William, Esq., Rickerscote, Stafford	1
Johnstone, David, Esq., Greenock	1
Joicey, John, Esq., Newton Hall, Stocksfield-on-Tyne	2
Jones, Joseph T., Esq., Dent Head, Sedbergh, Yorkshire	1
Joyce, Francis, Esq., Silsoe, Ampthill, Beds	1
Kind, J., Esq., Thurgarton Station	1
King, Joseph, Esq., 20, Burton Terrace, York	1
Kirby, John, Esq., Humberstone, Leicester	1
Kirkstall, The, Forge Co., Kirkstall Forge, Leeds	2

	COPIES
Kirtley, William, Esq., Locomotive Department, London, Chatham, and Dover Railway	1
Knight, J. P., Esq., General Manager, London, Brighton, and South Coast Railway, London Bridge	2
Lace, F. J., Esq., Stone Gappe, Cross Hills, Leeds	1
Lancaster, John, Jun., Esq., South Bank, Milverton, Leamington ...	1
Leather, J. Towlerton, Esq., Leventhorpe Hall, Leeds	1
Leslie, C. S., Esq., Hassop Hall, Bakewell	1
Lewis, Henry, Esq., Annesley Colliery, Nottingham	1
Lewis, James W., Esq., Radnor House, Arboretum Street, Nottingham	1
Liddell, Charles, Esq., 24, Abingdon Street, Westminster	1
Liddell, Matthew, Esq., Prudhoe Hall, Prudhoe-on-Tyne	1
Lisle, A. P. de, Esq., J.P., Garendon Park, Loughborough	1
Litherland, William, Esq., 25, Bold Street, Liverpool	1
Litler, Henry W., Esq., Wallerscourt, near Leamington	1
Little, Messrs. James & Co., Barrow-in-Furness...	4
Locket, George, Esq., Highwood House, Mill Hill, Hendon, N.W. ...	1
Lowe, E. J., Esq., F.R.S., Highfield House, near Nottingham ...	1
Lowe, Henry, Esq., Norfolk Road, Edgbaston, Birmingham	1
Lowe, J. L., Esq., Engineer's Office, Derby	1
Lowther, Sir Charles, Bart., Swillington House, Leeds	1
Lucas, Edward, Esq., Dronfield, near Sheffield	1
Lumsden, Sir James, Bart., Arden, N.B.	1
Macdonald, L., Esq., The Elms, Draycott, near Derby	1
Macfarlane, W. A. C., Esq., The Hollies, Ellesmere, Shrewsbury ...	1
Mackie, John, Cliff House, Crigglestone, near Wakefield	2
Macleod, Mrs., Ben Rhydding	6
McDonald, J. Allen, Esq., 19, Millstone Lane, Leicester	1
McInnes, John, Esq., Heath Bank, Wallersley, Cheshire	1
McIntosh, James, Esq., Duneevan, Oatlands Park, Weybridge ...	5
McVeagh, Mrs. Mary, 2, Burlington Street, Bath	1
Mainwaring, S. K., Esq., Oteley, Shrewsbury	1
Mann, Thomas Alfred, Darley Hall, Barnsley	1
Manton, H. J., Esq., Northfield	1
March, J. O., Esq., Leeds	1
Mather, Myles Edward, Esq., Glen Druidh, Inverness	1
Matthews, John, Esq,, Burton-on-Trent	1
Maw, Matthew, Esq., Cheaton Hall, Kirton, near Lindsay	1
Mawby, J. Esq., Frizzinghall Station, near Shipley, Yorkshire ...	1
Mawkle, Thomas, Esq., Norwood Cottage, Casterton, Kirkby Lonsdale	1
Maxwell, W. H., Esq., M.D., The Munchies, Dalbeattie, Dumfries ...	1
Meakin, George, Esq., Hanley, Staffordshire	1
Mellor, George, Esq., 2, Grove Terrace, Osmaston Road, Derby ...	1
Mellor, Richard, Esq., Westfield Lodge, Huddersfield	1
Mercer, John, Esq., Kirkby...	1
Middlemore, Mrs., Thorngrove, Worcester (per W. P. Price, Esq.) ...	1
Mills, John Robert, Esq., 11, Bootham, York	1

	COPIES
Millward, Richard, Esq., J.P., Thurgarton Priory, Southwell, Notts...	1
Milne, Samuel, Esq., Burton Joyce	1
Milner, Henry, Esq., Mill Hill Station	1
Minney, Joseph, Esq., Bulwell Station	1
Mitchell, Joseph, Esq., F.R.S.E., 66, Wimpole Street, London ...	1
Mitchell, J. H., Esq., 12, Upper Wimpole Street, W.	1
Mosley, Sir Tonman, Bart., Rolleston Hall, Burton-on-Trent	2
Murgatroyd, Thomas, Esq., Skipton	2
Mylne, J. E., Esq., 27, Oxford Square, Hyde Park, W....	1
Nall, Joseph, Esq., The Grange, Papplewick, Notts.	1
Nash, Charles, Esq., Canons Marsh, Bristol	1
Neilson & Co., Messrs., Hyde Park Locomotive Works, Glasgow ...	2
Neumann, Henry, Esq., Winnington, Northwich	2
New, David, Esq., J.P., Waverley House, Waverley Street, Nottingham	1
Newsum, Henry, Esq., Timber Merchant, Lincoln	1
Newton, G. B., Esq., Secretary, North London Railway, Euston Station	2
Newton, William, Esq., The Square, East Retford	1
Nicholson, Benjamin, Esq., Annan...	1
Nicholson, Joshua, Esq., Leek	1
Nicholson, William & Son, Messrs., Builders, Leeds	1
Nunneley, Joseph, Esq., Market Harborough	1
Oliver, Thomas, Esq., Kimberley, near Nottingham	2
Ollis, F., Esq., Bristol	1
Orchard, C., Esq., Bristol	2
Ord, Mrs. J. E., Langton Hall, Leicestershire	1
Owen, James, Esq., Keddleston Road, Derby	1
Paget, Alfred, Esq., West Street, Leicester	1
Paget, Joseph, Esq., Stuffyn Wood Hall, Mansfield	1
Paley, Edward G., Esq., Lancaster...	1
Palmer, Sir Geoffrey, Bart., Carlton Park, Rockingham, Leicestershire	1
Parker, John, Esq., Finedon, Northamptonshire	1
Parker, Rev. William, Comberton Rectory, Pershore	1
Parkinson, George, Esq., Rye Croft, Crosshills, *viâ* Leeds	1
Pattenson, Rev. R. C., Melmerby Rectory, Penrith	1
Payton, Anthony, Esq., Chesterfield	1
Pearson, Thomas John, Esq., Park Villa, Worksop	1
Peat, Edward, Esq., Beehive Mills, Lenton, Nottingham	1
Peckover, Algernon, Esq., Sibaldsholme, Wisbeach	1
Peel, Thomas, Esq., Hornby Station, Lancaster...	1
Peill, Rev. John Newton, Newton Tone Rectory, near Salisbury ...	1
Penrhyn, Rev. Thomas, Huyton Vicarage, Liverpool	1
Peters, Charles Augustus, Esq., Duffield, near Derby	2
Phillips, H. R., Esq., Albert Gate Yard, Knightsbridge	1
Pochin, Henry D., Esq., Barn Elmes, Barnes	1
Potter, F., Esq., Sawley	1

	COPIES
Potter, Thomas, Esq., Trowell, Nottingham	1
Powell, Samuel, Esq., Craven Lodge, Harrowgate	2
Powell, William F., Esq., Cluniter Dunoon, Argyleshire	1
Purvill, William, Esq., The Laurels, Sunningfield, near Hendon, N.W.	1
Rake, Herbert, Esq., Richmond Villas, Swansea	1
Ramsden, Sir James, Bart., Barrow-in-Furness	1
Ratcliff, Robert, Esq., Scalpcliffe House, Burton-on-Trent	1
Rawdon, Richard T. Williamson, Esq., Leeds	1
Rawlings, John, Esq., The Birches, Saltby, Birmingham	1
Rawson, George, Esq., 5, Lanesfield, Clifton, Bristol	1
Rawson & Best, Messrs., Solicitors, Leeds	1
Rayner, Edward W., Esq., 16, Exchange Buildings, Liverpool ...	1
Read, A., Esq., Rowsley, Bakewell...	1
Reay, Stephen, Esq., Secretary, London and North Western, Euston	1
Rees, Richard J., Esq., Somerset and Dorset Railway, Glastonbury ...	1
Reeves, Robert, Esq., Ashton's Green, Parr, St. Helens	2
Renals, John, Esq., Lenton Works, Nottingham	1
Renshaw, W., Esq., Wellingborough Station	1
Richardson, James P., Esq., Morecambe	1
Rigby, J. & Co., Messrs., Neptune Works, Temple Street, Manchester	1
Rigby, T., Esq., 6, Prince of Wales Road, Hendon, N.W.	1
Roberts, Joshua, Esq., Alfreton	1
Robertson, Samuel, Esq., 9, Portland Square, Bristol	1
Robinson, E. S., Esq., Sneyd Park, Bristol	1
Robinson, Henry Martin, Esq., The Newlands, Leamington	1
Rodger, James, Esq., Clairmont Gardens, Glasgow	1
Rodgers, James, Esq., 64, Wood Street, Ashby-de-la-Zouch	1
Ross, E., Esq., Sec., Manchester, Sheffield, and Lincolnshire Railway	1
Rowntree, John S., Esq., 28, The Pavement, York	1
Rushton, Joseph, Esq., J.P., Monk's Manor, Lincoln	1
Sale, Rev. Richard, St. Lawrence, Ramsgate	1
Salmon, Mr. James, Sheffield	1
Salt, Sir Titus, Bart., Saltaire, Yorkshire	1
Salt, Titus, Esq., Jun., Milner Field, Yorkshire...	1
Saner, James, Esq., Craven Lodge, Nightingale Lane, S.W.	1
Sankey, Richard, Esq., Bulwell Pottery, Nottingham	1
Seal, Stephen, Esq., Coxbench House, Darfield	1
Shackleton, Messrs. James & Sons, Hebden Bridge, near Manchester	1
Shand, Mason & Co., Messrs., 75, Upper Ground Street, Blackfriars	1
Sharpe, R. F., Esq., Haselour Station	1
Shepperd, G., Esq., Bristol	1
Sherbrook, Henry, Esq., J. P., Oxton Hall, near Southwell, Notts ...	1
Shipp, Daniel, Esq., Wisbeach	1
Sidgwick, J., Esq., Skipton	1
Sim, William, Esq., 4, St. Bernard's Crescent, Edinburgh	1
Slaughter, Mihill, Esq., Stock Exchange, E.C.	1
Smedley, Messrs., Bros., Eagle Iron Works, Belper	1

	COPIES
Smilter, William Lionel, Esq., Upperthorpe, Sheffield	1
Smith, Dr. Charles, 10, Surrey Street, Sheffield	1
Smith, Euan, Esq., 120, Shakspeare Street, Nottingham	1
Smith, Francis Nicholas, Esq., Wingfield Park, Derby	1
Smith, George Belk, Esq., 11, Melbourne Place, Bradford	1
Smith, George Fereday, Esq., Grovehurst, Tunbridge Wells	1
Smith, George Walker, Esq., Gordon House, Everton, near Bawtry...	1
Smith, H. Etherington, Esq., Norris Hill, Ashby-de-la-Zouch ...	1
Smith, J. Stores, Esq., J.P., Sheepbridge Works, Chesterfield ...	1
Smith, Messrs. Samuel, & Co., Goswell Road, London	1
Smith, William, Esq., Regent Street, Derby	1
Smith, William, Esq., Westwood House, Broccobark, Sheffield ...	1
Smith, William Seth, Esq., Langley, Guildford	1
Smythies, Rev. E., Hathern Rectory, Loughborough	1
Somerville, William, Esq., jun., Wiltsbridge, Bristol	1
Spokes, Sir Peter, Knight, Reading	1
Sprent, William, Esq., Chester House, Fareham, Hants	1
Spruce, Samuel, Esq., Albert Road, Tamworth	1
Statham, Mrs., Green Bank, Belper	1
Statham, William, Esq., Green Bank, Belper	1
Steel, Thomas, Esq., Bank Buildings, Sunderland	1
Stenson, Joseph, Esq., 16, Coventry Place, Leeds	1
Stephenson, B., Esq., 25, Tavistock Square, London	1
Stock, T., Esq., J.P., The Priory, Northfield, near Birmingham ...	1
Stolly, William, Esq., Ockbrook, Derby	1
Stretton, Clement E., Esq., Glen Magna, Leicester	1
Strickland, Edward, Esq., 2, All Saints' Court, Bristol	1
Strutt, Hon. Arthur, Milford House, Derby	1
Sudbury, William, Esq., Derby Road, Ilkeston	1
Sulman, Thomas, Esq., Essex Street, Strand	1
Sutcliffe, Rev. T., 68, Belmont Street, Southport	1
Swain, Joseph, Esq., De Montford Square, Leicester	1
Symonds, F., Esq., Melton Mowbray	1
Taggart, Robert, Esq., Tarn House, Ilkley	1
Tanner, Harbert, Esq., Seathwaite Cottage, Frome	1
Tarbotton, M. A., Esq., The Park, Nottingham	1
Taylor, H. Dyson, Esq., Greenhead Lane, Huddersfield	1
Taylor, John, Esq., Queen's Road, Nottingham	2
Taylor, John, Esq., Longwood, Bingley, Yorks	1
Taylor, Robert, Esq., Hill Foot House, Harrogate	1
Taylor, William, Esq., Raleigh Street, Nottingham	2
Tennant, Thomas Robert, Esq., The Hall, Kildwick, Leeds	1
The Right Worshipful the Mayor, Nottingham	1
Thomas, Rev. W. Jones, J.P., M.A., Llan Thomas Hay, Hereford ...	1
Thompson, E. Vaughan, Esq., Bedford Row, London	1
Thornley, Robert, Esq., Brooklands, Bromsgrove	1
Todd, Matthew, Esq., 60, Horton Road, Bradford	1

	Copies
Tolme, Thomas, Esq., 15, London Gardens, Bayswater...	1
Tombs, Samuel, Esq., Saint Andrew House, Droitwich	1
Toplis, F. S., Esq., Bristol	1
Town Hall Library, Mansfield, per Isaac Heywood, Esq., Librarian ...	1
Tretheroy, Henry, Esq., Silsoe, Beds	1
Trueman, Henry, Esq., The Lea, Esher, Surrey...	1
Tuckwood, G., Esq., Beaumont Terrace, Lincoln	1
Turner, John, Esq., Cononley, *viâ* Leeds	1
Turner, Messrs. W. & Son, Caledonian Works, Sheffield	2
Tyzack, William, Esq., jun., Abbey Dale House, Sheffield	1
Underwood, T., Esq., Newstead Grove, Nottingham	1
Unwin, George, Esq., 109 A, Cannon Street, E.C.	1
Vaughan, George, Esq., Surbiton Grange, near Leicester	1
Venables, G., Esq., Q.C., Mayfair, W.	10
Vergette, William, Esq., Peterborough	1
Vivian, Messrs. H. H., & Co., George Street, Birmingham	1
Waddington, J. H., Esq., Orsdall, Retford	1
Wainwright, William, Esq., Hoe Place, Woking, Surrey	1
Wainwright, W. J., Esq., Secretary, Glasgow and South Western ...	2
Walker, Frederic, Esq., Oakley House, Abingdon, Berks	1
Walker, Geo. & Son, Headingly, Leeds	1
Walker, J. B., Esq., Park Drive, Nottingham	1
Walker, John, Esq., 68, Cornhill, London, E.C.	2
Walker, William, Esq., Dethick, Cromford, Derby	1
Walker, William, Esq., Lea Wood, Cromford, Derby	1
Walker, William, Esq., Park Valley, Nottingham	1
Wall, George, Esq., Dale Road, Kentish Town, N.W.	2
Wallis, John, Esq., Kettering	1
Ward, W. G., Esq., The Park, Nottingham	1
Wardle, William, Esq., Winsbill, Burton-on-Trent	1
Warren, Frederic, Esq., The Priory, Saint Ives, Hunts	1
Warry, George, Esq., Shapwick House, Shapwick, Bridgwater ...	1
Warwick, J. A., Esq., Ockbrook	1
Watson, John, Esq., The Manor House, Brigstock, Thrapstone ...	1
Weatherburn, Robert, Esq., Carnforth	2
Westinghouse Continuous Break Company, Liverpool...	1
Weston, William, Esq., Eastwood, Notts	1
Weymouth, Dr., Mill Hill, N.W.	1
Wheatley, Richard, Esq., Royds House, Mirfield	1
Whitaker, Rev. E. Wright, Stanton-by-Bride, Derby	1
Whitaker, W., Esq., Honorary Secretary, Midland Railway Literary Institute, Derby	3
White, John, Esq. (of Arddaroch, Dumbartonshire), 53, Princes Gate	1
Whitworth, Sir Joseph, Bart., Stancliffe, Matlock	2
Wickes, John, Esq., Sparkhill, Birmingham	1
Wild, John R., Esq., Annesley Grove, Nottingham	1

	COPIES
Wildgoose, Robert, Esq., Lea Mills, Cromford, Derby	1
Williams, Alfred, Esq., Salisbury	1
Williams, Charles, Esq., Salisbury...	1
Willink, W. W., Esq., 3, Hyde Park Street, London	1
Wilson, George, Esq., Sharrow Mills, Sheffield	1
Wilson, William, Esq., Kirkby Stephen, Westmoreland	1
Winn, William, Esq., 46, London Road, Gloucester	1
Winnington, Major Edward, The Shrubbery, Stanford, Worcester ...	1
Winterbottom, James, Esq., 4, Cotham Vale, Bristol	1
Wombell, John, Esq., Bookseller, Ilkeston	1
Wood, Edmund S. W., Esq., Watlands, Langport, Stafford	1
Wood, G. J., Esq., Secretary of Chesterfield and Boythorpe Colliery	1
Wood, John, Esq., 48, Liversage Street, Derby	1
Wood, Joseph, Esq., Kirkgate, Shipley, near Leeds	1
Wood, William, Esq., 1, Edge Lane, Liverpool	1
Woodiwiss, A., Esq., Derby	1
Woolley, John, Esq., 15, Oxford Road, Dukinfield	1
Worsley-Worswick, R., Esq., Normanton Park, Hinckley	1
Wright, F. Beresford, Esq., Aldercar Hall, Langley Mill, Notts ...	1
Wright, FitzHerbert, Esq., J.P., The Hayes, Swanwick, Alfreton ...	1
Wright, G. A., Esq., Bingley Station	1
Wrigley, N. Richard, Esq., The Mount, Horsford, Leeds	1
Young, Alexander, Esq., Tokenhouse Yard, E.C.	1
Young, A. N., Esq., Lloyd's, London	1